The Poetics of Islamic Legitimacy

THE POETICS OF ISLAMIC LEGITIMACY

Myth, Gender, and Ceremony in the Classical Arabic Ode

Suzanne Pinckney Stetkevych

INDIANA
INDIANA
University Press
Bloomington & Indianapolis

This book is a publication of
Indiana University Press
601 North Morton Street
Bloomington, IN 47404-3797 USA

http://iupress.indiana.edu

Telephone orders 800-842-6796
Fax orders 812-855-7931
Orders by e-mail iuporder@indiana.edu

The paper used in this publication meets the minimum requirements of American National Standard for Information Sciences—Permanence of Paper for Printed Library Materials, ANSI Z39.48-1984.

Library of Congress Cataloging-in-Publication Data

Stetkevych, Suzanne Pinckney.
The poetics of Islamic legitimacy : myth, gender, and ceremony in the classical Arabic ode / Suzanne Pinckney Stetkevych.
p. cm.
Includes bibliographical references and index.
ISBN 0-253-34119-1 — ISBN 0-253-21536-6 (pbk.)
1. Qasidas—History and criticism. 2. Arabic poetry—622–750—History and criticism. 3. Arabic poetry—750–1258—History and criticism.
4. Politics in literature. I. Title.
PJ7542.Q3 S757 2002
892'.7104309—dc21

2001008295

1 2 3 4 5 07 06 05 04 03 02

For Julian, Qays, and Khalid

Contents

Preface

Throughout the classical Arabic literary tradition, from pre-Islamic times down to the first third of the twentieth century, the qasida (ode) held sway over the domain of poetry. Within that tradition the courtly panegyric ode, with its unparalleled genre stability and its vast corpus of contextualizing anecdotal materials, is eminently suited for the study of the relation of poetry and ceremony to political authority and the rhetoric of rulership.

My aim in the present work is, above all, to integrate the classical Arabic poetic tradition into the contemporary humanistic study of Arabo-Islamic culture. The overarching argument is that the classical Arabic panegyric ode (that is, the celebratory poem dedicated to a patron or ruler, the *qaṣīdat al-madḥ*) created, encoded, and promulgated a myth and ideology of legitimate Arabo-Islamic rule. I attempt to demonstrate that the qasida is intimately and integrally bound up in the political and ceremonial aspects of court life and that, far from being merely descriptive, prescriptive, or abjectly sycophantic, as some critics have claimed, it plays an active role in the ritual exchanges, the sensitive negotiations, and the mythopoesis of the Arabo-Islamic court. I have employed current ideas in the humanities and social sciences to explore the tradition of praise poems to Arabo-Islamic rulers in terms of ancient Near Eastern sacral kingship, supplication and negotiation, gender and political power, rituals and ceremonies of allegiance, and imitation and competition for the insignia of religio-political legitimacy.

As a basis for the interpretation of key poetic texts and passages of the literary lore that accompany them in the classical Arabic source materials, I have tried to produce translations that are understandable and aesthetically accessible to readers of English, and then to situate these texts in terms of the cultural, political, and historical environment that generated them. Needless to say, all translations involve some degree of betrayal of the original, and the Arabic texts themselves can be very treacherous going. For the reader of Arabic, the bracketed numbers at the end of the English translations are keyed to an appendix of the Arabic poetic texts. The specialist will need to refer to the Arabic source materials for variants in the texts and to the commentaries for varying interpretations.

Growing out of my earlier work in myth, rite, archetype, and gender in the classical Arabic ode, particularly in *The Mute Immortals Speak: Pre-Islamic Poetry and the Poetics of Ritual* (1993), and my historicist method of contextualized interpretation, most explicitly in *Abū Tammām and the Poetics of the ʿAbbāsid Age* (1991), as well as a number of my articles published over the past decade, the present work focuses on the *qaṣīdat al-madḥ* as the preeminent poetic genre of the classical Arabic tradition. At the same time, I have broadened the historical scope to encompass the pre-Islamic foundations of the Arabic panegyric ode in poems addressed to Arab kings of the sixth century C.E., the Islamicization of the Arabic poetic tradition in the seventh century through praise poetry to the Prophet Muḥammad and, subsequently, to the rulers of Arabo-Islamic dynasties, ranging from the caliphs at Damascus (seventh through eighth centuries) and Baghdad (eighth through ninth centuries) to local rulers of tenth-century Syria and Egypt, and, finally, the Cordovan caliphs of Islamic Spain. This work thus traces the development of the classical Arabic panegyric ode from its inception in sixth-century pre-Islamic times through the end of the Arabic poetic golden age of the tenth century.

The first chapter, "Transgression and Redemption: Cuckolding the King," explores the poetics of transgression and redemption in two renowned odes by the late-sixth-century pre-Islamic court panegyrist al-Nābighah al-Dhubyānī. As literary cultural context for the poet's most celebrated poem, the ode of apology to the Arab king al-Nuʿmān, the chapter first presents the reason for the apology, said to be al-Nābighah's notorious poem in which he describes in shocking detail sexual intercourse with the king's wife. The cuckolding of the king is interpreted metaphorically and politically as emblematic of sedition, of usurpation of royal power and prerogative. Al-Nābighah's "apology" to the king, with its myth-based formulation of ancient Near Eastern kingship and evocation of Solomon and the jinn, is analyzed as a ceremony of submission and allegiance and as a ritual for reaffirming royal dignity and might.

Through a reading of "Suʿād Has Departed," the celebrated poem of conversion to Islam by Kaʿb ibn Zuhayr, seventh-century poet and companion of the Prophet, the second chapter, "Transmission and Submission: Praising the Prophet," examines the co-option of the pre-Islamic panegyric ode of praise and submission to sacral kingship to function as a ritual of submission to the new religion of Islam and a ceremony of allegiance to the Prophet Muḥammad. Thus the ancient Near Eastern myths of sacral kingship become part of the legitimizing myth of Arabo-Islamic rule and the pre-Islamic qasida is converted into an integral part of Arabo-Islamic court ceremonial. The poem, in turn, generates the myth of the Prophet's donation of his mantle to the poet as an emblem of conferring protection and salvation in return for submission (*islām*/Islam).

The third chapter, "Celebration and Restoration: Praising the Caliph," studies the poetics of Islamic political hegemony and hierarchy during the Umayyad caliphate at Damascus (seventh through eighth centuries) through a victory ode by al-Akhṭal, the poet laureate of the Umayyads, that celebrates the caliph ʿAbd al-Malik ibn Marwān's defeat of the Zubayrid challengers to the caliphate. Special emphasis is placed on the negotiating function of the ceremonial qasida in the competition for political status that accompanied the restoration of Umayyad authority.

Another poem by al-Akhṭal forms the subject of the fourth chapter, "Supplication and Negotiation: The Client Outraged," this one composed after the poet's Umayyad liege lords allowed the slaughter of his tribe by a contending faction to go unpunished. Framing his qasida with subtly nuanced traditional imagery of wine and of camels, the poet exploits the ceremonial and ritual aspects of the qasida to move from submission and supplication to challenge and threat as he negotiates for restitution (the blood-price for his slain kinsmen) and for recognition of the status of his tribe within the Umayyad political hierarchy.

The fifth chapter, "Political Dominion as Sexual Domination," picks up the theme of gender and sexual politics that concluded chapter 1 to present a contrast in the use of metaphors of sexual domination in two panegyric poems from the early ʿAbbāsid period (eighth through ninth centuries). The first, an eminently lyrical poem by Abū al-ʿAtāhiyah, plays with the conceit of the poet's desire for the caliph's slave girl, only to have her turn out to be a trope for the caliphate itself. The poem ends with the poet renouncing his sexual desire as a metaphor for the renunciation of political power. The second, a renowned victory ode by Abū Tammām, celebrates the ʿAbbāsid capture of the Byzantine "virgin" city of Amorium. Here, rather than renouncing sexual desire, the Muslim army's rape of the Byzantine city functions as an expression of the Muslims' participation in the divinely appointed caliph's sexual, military, and political domination of the Byzantine infidel.

The sixth chapter, "The Poetics of Political Allegiance," examines the poetics of praise and blame in three odes by al-Mutanabbī, the celebrated tenth-century panegyrist, whose career and oeuvre bear witness to the decline of the ʿAbbāsid caliphate at Baghdad in this period and the concomitant rise of local dynasties. The first poem, to the Arab prince Sayf al-Dawlah of Ḥamdānid Aleppo, is studied in light of the relationship between military victory (against the Byzantine infidel) and Islamic legitimacy, as celebrated on Islamic holidays. The discussion then addresses two poems to Kāfūr, the black eunuch slave ruler of Ikhshīdid Egypt, that exhibit the poetic interplay of constructs of race, class, and gender. The first of these constitutes a ritual of transfer of allegiance from Sayf al-Dawlah at Aleppo to Kāfūr in Egypt. The final poem is one of bitterly derisive invective against Kāfūr, which, it is argued, is essentially a rite of retraction of allegiance.

The final chapter, "The Poetics of Ceremony and the Competition for Legitimacy: Al-Muhannad al-Baghdādī, Muḥammad ibn Shukhayṣ, Ibn Darrāj al-Qasṭallī, and the Andalusian Ode," turns to one of the challengers to the ʿAbbāsid hegemony at Baghdad, the Umayyad caliphate at Cordova in Islamic Spain. Starting with the qasida as part of the ceremonial idiom of the Arabo-Islamic court and as one of the insignia of legitimate rule, the chapter examines two mid-tenth-century poems preserved as part of a historical chronicle that depicts the actual court ceremony for the Feast of Breaking the Fast that took place in a given year. It then shows how masterpieces from the Islamic east are imitated to bolster the prestige of the newly declared Cordovan caliphate. The final poem, by contrast, dates from the period of political chaos that accompanied the disintegration of the Cordovan caliphate (early eleventh century). It demonstrates at once the achievement of a self-confident Andalusian poetry and the breakdown of the ceremonial exchange of poem and prize that, in the Arabic literary tradition, signifies the descent from civilization into barbarity.

In no way do I wish to suggest that my approach in the present study is exclusive or exhaustive. The classical Arabic qasida flourished for about a millennium and a half, datable as far back as the fifth or sixth century C.E. and continuously productive until the first third of the twentieth century—and the future, of course, remains open. It is anticipated that for Arabic readers, this study will be understood as a contribution to a continuing and lively intellectual tradition of creative exploration of the classical literary foundations of Arabo-Islamic culture, a tradition that, with the globalization of literary culture, is carried on by scholars from a variety of cultural and disciplinary backgrounds. The relative dearth of studies of classical Arabic literature in western languages, however, means that any individual study runs the risk of giving a distorted or idiosyncratic picture to the western reader. In that light, let me emphasize that although most of the poems selected for this study are ones that are highly prized by the Arabic literary tradition, and thus representative of that tradition, they nevertheless have been selected from a vast and rich corpus and in light of a particular strain in Arabic court poetry that I have endeavored to expose and explore. Inevitably, this is done at the expense of other aspects and elements of this vast and multifaceted tradition. The western reader can get a sense of the range of literary critical and historical possibilities by considering the present study in light of such works as Jaroslav Stetkevych's *The Zephyrs of Najd: The Poetics of Nostalgia in the Classical Arabic* Nasīb (1993), which explores the intimate and emotive archetypes of autochthonous Arab expressions of loss and yearning in the elegiac opening section of the classical ode; the two-volume collection edited by Stefan Sperl and Christopher Shackle, *Qasida Poetry in Islamic Asia and Africa* (1996), which demonstrates the astounding influence of the Arabic qasida form on virtually all the literatures of the Islamic world; and Roger Allen's *The Arabic Literary Heritage* (1998), which offers both background and overview of the development of the Arabic literary genres and their criticism. As for this study, it is my hope that it will encourage others to undertake further explorations in Arabic literature that will bring it increasingly into the purview of contemporary humanistic studies.

Acknowledgments

This book represents work undertaken over about the past decade, and during that time I have benefited from the kindness and expertise of many friends and colleagues. Deserving of special mention for their steadfastness during good times and bad at Indiana University are Asha Swarup, Consuelo Lopez-Morillas, John Walbridge, Hussein Noor Kadhim, Majd al-Mallah, Ayman el-Haj, Samer Mahdy Ali, Akiko Motoyoshi, Imed Nsiri, and Paul B. Nelson. At various crucial moments, both academic and otherwise, others, too, have provided the encouragement and direction necessary to produce this book; I mention in particular Hassan el-Banna Ezz el-Din, Ezz al-Din Ismail, Muhsin Jassim al-Musawi, James Monroe, Michael A. Sells, Stefan Sperl, and Ross Brann. For their expertise and thoughtfulness I would like to thank the two colleagues who served as readers for Indiana University Press, Roger Allen and Clarissa Burt. A special category of gratitude and affection is reserved for my comrade in arms, Jaroslav Stetkevych. The shortcomings of the book are all my own.

I would like to acknowledge as well the generous institutional support that provided me with the time and resources to undertake the research for this project. Fellowships from the Fulbright Foundation and the American Research Center in Egypt allowed me to spend my sabbatical year 1992–93 in Cairo, Egypt, and support from the Joint Committee on the Middle East of the Social Science Research Council and the American Council of Learned Societies allowed me to return to Cairo in the summer of 1994. A Ruth N. Halls Professorship in the Humanities (NELC) at Indiana University, 1994–99, provided generous funds in support of research. A Fulbright Fellowship to Jordan in the spring of 1997 allowed me to further pursue new avenues of research and to present my ideas to colleagues at the Jordanian University in Amman, as well as to colleagues in Cairo, Egypt, and Kiev, Ukraine. Finally, the Solomon Katz Visiting Professorship in the Humanities at the University of Washington in Seattle in spring 1999 provided a lightened teaching load and a lively camaraderie that allowed me to complete drafts of the remaining chapters and begin to pull the full manuscript together.

My appreciation goes as well to the editors and publishers who have granted permission to reprint previously published articles and chapters that in revised form constitute parts of the present book. In revised form the second part of my "Pre-Islamic Poetry and the Poetics of Redemption: *Mufaḍḍalīyah*

119 of ᶜAlqamah and *Bānat Suᶜād* of Kaᶜb ibn Zuhayr," in Suzanne Pinckney Stetkevych, ed., *Reorientations: Arabic and Persian Poetry* (Bloomington and Indianapolis: Indiana University Press, 1994), pp. 21–57, appears as chapter 2. "Umayyad Panegyric and the Poetics of Islamic Hegemony: al-Akhṭal's *Khaffa al-Qaṭīnu* ('Those That Dwelt with You Have Left in Haste')," *Journal of Arabic Literature* 28, no. 2 (1997): 89–122, forms, with some revision, chapter 3. Parts of my Arabic study "Qaṣīdat al-Madḥ wa-Marāsim al-Ibtihāl: Fāᶜiliyyat al-Naṣṣ al-Adabī ᶜabr al-Tārīkh" (The Panegyric Ode and the Ritual of Supplication: The Efficacy of the Poetic Text throughout History), in ᶜIzz al-Dīn Ismāᶜīl, ed. *Al-Naqd al-Adabī fī Munᶜaṭaf al-Qarn 3: Madākhil li-Taḥlīl al-Naṣṣ al-Adabī,* etc. / *Literary Criticism at the Turn of the Century, Papers Presented to the First International Conference on Literary Criticism (Cairo, October 1997),* 3 vols., 3:175–96, appear in expanded English form in chapter 4. Chapter 8 of my book *Abū Tammām and the Poetics of the ᶜAbbāsid Age* forms the basis for the second part of chapter 5 of the present work. My article "ᶜAbbāsid Panegyric: The Politics and Poetics of Ceremony: Al-Mutanabbī's ᶜĪd-poem to Sayf al-Dawlah," in J. R. Smart, ed., *Tradition and Modernity in Arabic Language and Literature* (Surrey, England: Curzon, 1996), pp. 119–143, and my chapter and translations, "Abbasid Panegyric and the Poetics of Political Allegiance: Two Poems of al-Mutanabbī on Kāfūr," in Stefan Sperl and Christopher Shackle, eds., *Qasida Poetry in Islamic Asia and Africa,* volume 1: *Classical Traditions and Modern Meanings;* volume 2: *Eulogy's Bounty, Meaning's Abundance: An Anthology* (Leiden: E. J. Brill, 1996), 1:35–53; 2:92–105, have been revised and joined together to form chapter 6. Of my chapter "The *Qaṣīdah* and the Poetics of Ceremony: Three ᶜĪd Panegyrics to the Cordoban Caliphate," in Ross Brann, ed., *Languages of Power in Islamic Spain: Occasional Papers of the Department of Near Eastern Studies and Program of Jewish Studies, Cornell University,* no. 3 (Bethesda, Md.: CDI Press, 1997), pp. 1–48, the main part has been revised to form chapter 7, and the section on Abū al-ᶜAtāhiyah forms the basis for the first part of chapter 5.

A Note on Transliteration

For the transliteration of Arabic names, terms, and bibliographical citations I have followed the Library of Congress system with slight modification; for longer passages, such as lines of poetry, proverbs, and Qurʾānic quotations in the text and notes, I have used a more phonetic system, including the elision of unpronounced vowels and the transcription of assimilated consonants (*al-ḥurūf al-shamsiyyah*).

The Poetics of Islamic Legitimacy

One

Transgression and Redemption
Cuckolding the King
Al-Nābighah al-Dhubyānī and the Pre-Islamic Royal Ode

Pre-Islamic Poetry and the Formation of Arabo-Islamic Culture

The Arabo-Islamic panegyric ode has its literary antecedents in the praise poems presented to the petty Arab kings of the pre-Islamic period, the pagan era that came to an end with the advent of Islam, traditionally dated as year 1 of the Hijrah (1 H. = 622 C.E.). Known as the Jāhiliyyah, or "Age of Ignorance," the pre-Islamic era saw the formation of the rich cultural and literary traditions upon which the new religion and civilization of Islam were founded. It was during this period that an autochthonous Arab Semitic culture, rooted in the civilizational bedrock of the ancient Near East and the residues of the Hellenistic age, and subject to Christian and Judaic, Byzantine, and Persian influences, developed as its preeminent form of expression the classical Arabic ode or qasida (*qaṣīdah*).[1]

In the classical Arabic literary compendia these odes are presented in the context of narrative anecdotal materials (*akhbār;* singular *khabar*) concerning the poet and the occasion for the poem. Together, this lore and poetry provide a textual base to investigate the ways in which the originally oral poetry of the pre-Islamic period was transmitted, preserved, selected, and molded by Muslim hands into a literary corpus and a cultural construct that served to advance the interests of an Arabo-Islamic political, religious, and literary-cultural hegemony. This chapter will examine the qasida as the vehicle for the cultural transition from the pagan to the Islamic age and as a form of discourse eminently suited to articulating an ideology of legitimate rule.

The lore and poetry of the pre-Islamic period continued to be orally transmitted until the second–third Islamic centuries (second through third centuries H./eighth through ninth centuries C.E.), when the process of their collection and editing by Muslim scholars began. This was done in some cases to form a linguistic corpus on the basis of which to interpret the sacred text of the Qurʾān; in others, to form a literary corpus to preserve and promote ideas of Arabness (*ʿurūbah*) and manly virtue (*murūʾah*). Given what we know about the process of oral transmission as well as the complex textual history of pre-Islamic poetry during the Islamic period, for the purposes of the present study we will accept the pre-Islamic poetic corpus as an authentic component of the Arabo-Islamic literary tradition, rooted in the pre-Islamic oral tradition, though not historically (i.e., textually) verifiable at that period.[2]

Scholarship in orality theory over the past several decades suggests that the poetic text is, through its rhyme, meter, formulaic construction, and rhetorical devices, essentially mnemonic in nature and thus more stable than the prose anecdote. I will therefore continue to follow the approach established in my earlier work of treating the prose anecdotes as literary lore rather than historical fact.[3] This approach has the advantage of not forcing us to choose between mutually exclusive or contradictory anecdotes, but instead allowing us to read the variants for the interpretations of the poem, and its poet, that they convey. I thus consider classical scholar Gregory Nagy's remarks on the mythicization of the poet in the Panhellenization of Greek poetry equally applicable to the poetic lore of the Arabic tradition:

> [T]he identity of the poet as composer becomes progressively stylized, becoming ever further distanced from the reality of self-identification through performance. . . . Once the factor of performance slips out of the poet's control, even if the performers of his poetry have a tradition of what to say about the poet as a composer, nevertheless, ***the poet becomes a myth; more accurately, the poet becomes part of a myth, and the myth-making structure appropriates his identity.*** [emphasis mine][4]

Above all, in this chapter, we will examine the poems and their accompanying prose anecdotes to elicit from them a myth and paradigm of the relationship between ruler and ruled, that is, of sedition and submission presented in terms of transgression and redemption.

Although much of the pre-Islamic poetic corpus that has come down to us is tribal rather than courtly, and thus most often takes as its culminating theme the poet's boast of himself and of his tribe,[5] there is as well a substantial body of praise poetry presented at the courts of Arab kings or to powerful tribal overlords. Chief among the Arab kingdoms were the Lakhmids, a vassal state of Sāsānid Persia with its capital at al-Ḥīrah in Iraq, who at the period under discussion professed Nestorian Christianity, and the Ghassānids, a Byzantine client state based in Syria and fervent adherents of Monophysite Christianity.[6]

In this chapter we shall investigate within their traditional anecdotal context two renowned odes by al-Nābighah al-Dhubyānī (active 570–600 C.E.), one of the most acclaimed poets of the pre-Islamic age, who composed panegyric at both the Lakhmid and Ghassānid courts.[7] The first is his notorious "Are You Leaving Mayyah's People (Description of al-Mutajarridah)," a poem that combines passages of delicate lyricism with others of shocking sexual explicitness. As we shall see from the anecdotal materials discussed below, the Arabic tradition assigns this poem to the period when al-Nābighah was the poet laureate and companion (*nadīm*) of the Lakhmid king of al-Ḥīrah, al-Nuʿmān ibn al-Mundhir, Abū Qābūs (Nuʿmān III, r. 580–602).[8] Further, this poem is taken to be a description of al-Mutajarridah, al-Nuʿmān's beautiful and promiscuous wife, and thus the occasion for the poet's flight, under a death threat, from the Lakhmid court at al-Ḥīrah and his taking refuge at the rival Ghassānid court of ʿAmr ibn al-Ḥārith at Jābiyah.[9] It was apparently from there that al-Nābighah issued his three celebrated poems of apology (*iʿtidhāriyyāt*)[10] to his erstwhile patron al-Nuʿmān, through which he was eventually reinstated at the Lakhmid court. Of these, the literary tradition has bestowed precedence upon "O Abode of Mayyah," as reflected in its role in the anecdotes concerning the poet's reinstatement at the Lakhmid court, which we will discuss below, and its inclusion in a number of the recensions of the foremost collection of pre-Islamic odes, the *Muʿallaqāt* (Suspended Odes).[11]

The most widely accepted explanation for al-Nābighah's flight from the court of the Lakhmid king al-Nuʿmān ibn al-Mundhir to that of his Ghassānid rivals involves the poet's alleged composition of verses that include an intimate physical description of al-Mutajarridah, a description so explicit, it was claimed, as to suggest—or rather confirm—a sexual relationship between the two. In the *Kitāb al-Aghānī* (Book of Songs), the celebrated literary compendium by Abū al-Faraj al-Iṣbahānī (d. 356 H./967 C.E.), we find several variant versions of this explanation that make for lively reading, among them:

> Al-Nābighah held a high and privileged position in al-Nuʿmān's court and was one of his boon-companions and intimates. One day he caught sight of [al-Nuʿmān's wife], al-Mutajarridah, and came up to her, feigning surprise. Her veil slipped and she covered herself with her hand and fore-arm. So plump was her fore-arm that it almost covered her face. Then he composed his qasida which begins "Are you leaving Mayyah's people." . . . Al-

The Poetics of Islamic Legitimacy

> Nābighah recited this poem to Murrah ibn Saʿd al-Qurayʿī, who in turn recited it to al-Nuʿmān. The king was filled with rage. He threatened and frightened al-Nābighah until he fled to his own tribe, then made his way to the kings of Ghassān in Syria [lit. Shaʾm] and composed panegyric for them. And, it is said, that ʿIṣām ibn Shahbar al-Jarmī, al-Nuʿmān's chamberlain, warned [al-Nābighah] and informed him of what al-Nuʿmān wanted to do [to him], for he was his friend, so [al-Nābighah] fled.[12]

A somewhat livelier version, whose transmitters include illustrious scholars of the canonical poetic tradition, such as Ḥammād [al-Rāwiyah], Ibn Sallām [al-Jumaḥī], Abū ʿAmr ibn al-ʿAlāʾ, and Ibn Qutaybah, runs as follows:

> The reason that al-Nābighah fled from al-Nuʿmān was that once he and [the poet] al-Munakhkhal . . . al-Yashkurī were sitting before [al-Nuʿmān]. Now al-Nuʿmān was misshapen, leprous, and ugly, whereas al-Munakhkhal . . . was one of the most comely of the Arabs, and al-Mutajarridah, al-Nuʿmān's wife, had had her eye on him. The Arabs used to say that al-Nuʿmān's two sons by her were [actually] al-Munakhkhal's. Then al-Nuʿmān said to al-Nābighah: "O Abū Umāmah, describe al-Mutajarridah in your poetry." So he composed his qasida in which he described her: her abdomen, her buttocks, and her private parts. This roused al-Munakhkhal's jealousy, so he said to al-Nuʿmān, "No one could compose such poetry except one who had tried her!" Al-Nuʿmān took this to heart. When news of this reached al-Nābighah, he was afraid and fled to the Ghassānids.[13]

At this point the narrative shifts to al-Munakhkhal and relates that he was the paramour of Hind bint ʿAmr ibn Hind, and when news of this reached her father, he had al-Munakhkhal imprisoned and killed.[14] The *Kitāb al-Aghānī* narrative then returns to the subject of al-Nābighah and relates his residing at the Ghassānid court where he served as panegyrist to ʿAmr ibn al-Ḥārith al-Aṣghar and, after the latter's death, his brother al-Nuʿmān, until the Lakhmid king al-Nuʿmān ibn al-Mundhir called him back to his court at al-Ḥīrah.[15]

The Poem of Transgression: The Description of al-Mutajarridah

A few preliminary remarks are in order before reading al-Nābighah's ode "Are You Leaving Mayyah's People," the poem that the tradition claims is a description of al-Mutajarridah and the cause for the poet's expulsion or flight from the Lakhmid court. As a guide to reading the poem, the reader should note that the entire poem falls thematically into the category of the elegiac prelude (***nasīb*** or ***muqaddimah***), the traditional qasida opening section. Nevertheless, we can observe a progression of theme and mood within the confines of this *nasīb*-contained structure. The poem can be divided, for the purposes of our discussion, into three parts: (1) an elegiac prelude (*nasīb*), lines 1–5, opens the poem with the tradition-honored theme of the separation of the tribes of the poet and his mistress or beloved, here named Mayyah; this leads into (2) an erotic description of the beloved (*tashbīb*) and her effect on the poet, lines 6–29; and finally, (3) the poem concludes with a hardcore sexual description that in Arabic poetic terminology could be construed as either boast (*fakhr*) or invective (*hijāʾ*), lines 30–34. It should be remarked, too, that the only proper names that appear in the poem are Mayyah (line 1) and Mahdad (line 5), both among the conventional poetic names for the poet's beloved, and that the descriptions are also of a conventional nature, so that, except for the suggestive use of the adjective *al-mutajjarad* (see line 13), there is no internal textual evidence for the identification of a specific woman being described.

Al-Nābighah al-Dhubyānī's "Are You Leaving Mayyah's People (The Description of al-Mutajarridah)" (*A-Min Āli Mayyata*)[16]
[meter: *kāmil;* rhyme: *-dī*]

1. Are you leaving Mayyah's people tonight
 or on the morrow?
Hastening with provisions
 or without?

2. The departure was close at hand
 except that our camels
Had not yet departed with our goods, though it was
 as if they had.

3. The cawing crow proclaims
 that our departure is tomorrow,
Thus the black full-feathered crow
 informed us.

4. There will be no greeting for tomorrow,
 no welcome,
If the separation from loved ones
 comes tomorrow.

5. The time for the journey has come
 and you have not bade Mahdad farewell,
[Neither] morning [nor] evening will we ever
 meet again.

6. On the trace of a beautiful girl
who shot at you her arrow
That struck your heart,
but did not kill you.

7. She was content with that,
since your tribe and hers were neighbors,
With sending messages
and with affection.

8. Her love struck his heart
with a piercing arrow
Shot from the back
of a twanging bow.

9. She glanced with the eye
of a tent-reared fawn,
With striped markings, deep eyes,
with a necklace adorned.

10. A string of beads
adorns her throat,
Of gold that gleams
like a blazing meteor.

11. Her skin as soft and pale
as a yellow silken gown,
Her figure perfect, like a supple bough,
exuberant, swaying.

12. Her belly slender,
with delicate soft folds,
Her breasts, firm and high,
rise toward her breastbone.

13. The two sides of her back smooth
as softened leather, not too broad,
Her buttocks full, soft and white
her naked flesh (*al-mutajarradī*).

14. She appeared, standing between
the two halves of the curtain
Like the sun when it rises with
auspicious stars.

15. Or the pearl of a seashell, its diver
so overcome with joy
Whenever he sets eyes on it, he cries, "In God's name"
and prostrates himself in prayer.

Transgression and Redemption

16. Or like a statue carved from marble,
        erected on a pedestal
    Constructed with baked brick,
        plastered with gypsum.

17. Her veil dropped—
        surely by accident!—
    So she grabbed it and veiled herself from us
        with her hand.

18. With a hand hennaed and smooth
        as if its fingers were ʿanam boughs
    So tender and pliant
        you could tie them in knots.

19. She looked at you, desiring to speak,
        but afraid to,
    Like a sick man looking in the faces of his visitors,
        too weak to speak.

20. She reveals through [lips dark and soft]
        like the wingtips of the dove of the aykah-tree
    [Teeth like] hailstones against
        antimony-blackened gums.

21. Like chamomile blooms on the morning
        after a rainfall:
    The top petals dry,
        The lower ones still moist.

22. The king claims her mouth
        is cool,
    Sweet where you kiss it,
        delightful where you sip.

23. The king claims
        (though I have never tasted it)
    It's so sweet that when you taste it
        you cry, "Give me more!"

24. The king claims
        (though I have never tasted it)
    That the [mere] redolence of her saliva
        quenches him who thirsts.

25. Her handmaidens take her necklace
        and string the pearls
    In order, one after another,
        in uninterrupted sequence.

26. Were she to stand before
a gray-haired monk,
Who served God, celibate,
devoted to prayer,

27. He would gaze [in ardor] from
her beauty and her lovely speech,
And think she was the path to righteousness,
though she is not.

28. So alluring her voice
that were the mountain she-goat
Of the sun-scorched hills to hear it,
she would draw near.

OR

If you could speak like that
the mountain she-goat
Of the sun-scorched hills
would draw near to you.

29. Her hair coal-black and curly,
thick and lush,
Like grape clusters weighing down
their propping sticks.

30. When you touch,
you touch a gentle rise,
Overflowing its place,
filling your hand.

31. When you thrust,
you thrust into a rise
That swells when you feel it,
daubed with compound perfume.

32. When you pull out,
you have to pull hard from a tight [place]
Like a strong youth yanking on a strong rope
[to pull a water bucket from a well].

33. And when it bites [you]
its sides squeeze hard,
Like a toothless old man
when he bites.

34. No one who comes to drink [here]
will go back to the place he has left,

9

Transgression and Redemption

And no one who has left after drinking
will move on to a new water-hole. [1]

The Elegiac Prelude (Nasīb): *Lines 1–5.* The prelude captures the poet (the "lyric I" that is the conventional poetic persona of the classical qasida) in a state of dread, denial, and anticipation before the inevitable separation of the tribes. The poem employs repetition and a certain redundancy to convey emotional complexity and ambiguity: the desire to deny the inevitable combined with a sense of being already overtaken by it. Line 1 opens the poem with a question, "Are you leaving?" but we soon realize that it is not a question of whether the poet is departing, but only one of when—tonight or tomorrow?—and how—provisioned or not? The commentary suggests that "provisioned" is intended to mean "farewells," i.e., having had a chance to exchange farewells or not.[17] Line 2 conveys the sense of inevitability—the poet has not actually departed, but, psychologically, the pack camels have already virtually departed, the departure is imminent. In line 3 imminence is compounded with inevitability, the motif of the crow whose cawing signals departure, termed the "crow of separation" (*ghurāb al-bayn*), whose voice is the voice of Fate. The poet makes one more attempt to stave off the inevitable in line 4: to withhold greeting and welcome from a personified tomorrow is to refuse to recognize it, to deny it. Nevertheless, when we reach line 5 the time of departure has now come, its finality and certainty established by the perfect tense of the verb *ḥāna* (the time has come). The poem plays acoustically with the roots *w-d-ᶜ* and *w-ᶜ-d* (a root-play termed *jinās* or paronomasia), respectively, in the words *tuwaddiᶜ* (farewell) and *mawᶜid* (meeting place, rendezvous) to say that it is too late for the poet to bid his beloved farewell and that the two will never meet again.

Looking back, we can see that the repetition and apparent redundancy in the very simple and traditional diction of the first five lines is employed to achieve a subtle movement from the confusion, denial, and uncertainty to the finality of permanent separation. This repetition occurs particularly with two key words or roots. The first is *gh-d-w* (to come or go early in the morning), whence *mughtadī,* "leaving on the morrow," an active participle with imperfect or future force that acquires acoustic and semantic prominence through its placement as the rhyme word of the first hemistich of the qasida's double rhymed opening line; *ghadan,* "tomorrow," appears in the same position in line 3, creating a near rhyme with the end rhyme word *al-aswadū* "black";[18] and the same word occurs twice in line 4: *bi-ghadin,* "for tomorrow," in the first hemistich, and *fī ghadī,* "[on] tomorrow," as the rhyme word for the line. The obsession with "tomorrow" thus intensifies through line 4, only to be overtaken by the passage of time in line 5. A similar obsessive repetition occurs with the second word or root *r-ḥ-l* (to depart, travel), and again the repetition involves a progression: *afida t-taraḥḥuli,* "the departure was close at hand" (line 2), to *riḥlatanā ghadan,* "our departure is tomorrow," its fate sealed by the crow's decisive and incontrovertible cawing (line 3), to the finality in line 5 of *ḥāna r-raḥīlu,* "the time for journey has come"—this is it.

In the Arabic poetic tradition the responses to the situation presented in line 5 are basically two. One, the most common, is to accept the finality of the loss and move on to other things—usually the poet's solitary questlike liminal journey (*raḥīl*) that brings him ultimately to the court of the patron and his praise, or to the poet's rejoining his own tribe as a mature member of the warrior aristocracy. The other one is to reclaim that past through reverie and recollection. Actually, we often find a double movement, where the poet starts with the recollection of the beloved, but then through an act of will or determination, cuts it off (the standard transition [*takhalluṣ*] phrase *da*ᶜ *dhā* [leave off this]; see below). In the present poem, we find that the poet, although having admitted to the physical separation and presumably having departed, never to see his beloved again, has nevertheless not performed that (psychological) act of will and determination. Thus his mind and imagination are not focused on where his journey will take him; instead they turn back to follow the track or trace of recollection. In this respect, the phrase *fī ithri,* "on the trace" or "in the tracks" of the beloved, appears carefully chosen. For although the commentary says it means "after"[19]—after you departed, after your affair with this woman—where the poet really goes in the poem is not on his journey; rather, he follows the memory-trace of the beloved.

The Erotic Description (Tashbīb): *Lines 6–29.* What follows is an erotic description of the beloved, termed *tashbīb.* A lyric-elegiac evocation of the now lost beloved opens with the convention of the arrows of the beloved's glance piercing the poet's heart (lines 6–8) and proceeds to a lyric-erotic description of quite exquisite delicacy of the beloved and her physical charms. The surface beauty of this passage in many ways speaks for itself; nevertheless, on closer examination further richness is revealed. First, although beautifully rendered, the elements of this description are familiar. Some are more broadly conventional, but the overall effect of the passage is to evoke the renowned erotic descriptions of the most illustrious pre-Islamic poet, Imru' al-Qays, in his celebrated *Muʿallaqah* (Suspended Ode), particularly his *bayḍati khidrin* ("egg" or "white one" of the curtained women's quarters) passage. A few lines will suffice to demonstrate the similarities:

> Slender-waisted, white,
>   not flabby,
> Her collarbone shone like
>   a polished mirror.
>
> Now hiding, now baring a cheek
>   long and wide,
> She guards herself with the glance
>   of a wild doe at Wajrah with fawn
>
> And a neck like the neck
>   of a white antelope,
> Not overly long when she raises it,
>   or lacking ornament.
>
> A head of hair, jet-black,
>   adorns her back,
> Luxuriant as a bunch of dates
>   on a cluster-laden palm.[20] [2]

The effect of what we might now term this intertextual link is not only a poetic resonance between the two texts, but an association of al-Nābighah with the notorious sexual exploits of his profligate predecessor. The explicit, if stylized, description in lines 12–13 of the beloved's abdomen, breasts, back, buttocks, and naked flesh would be sufficient to indict the poet for fornication. In other words, to the Arab audience, a passage such as this is explicitly sexual and unquestionably illicit. It does not help exculpate the poet that the rhyme word used for stripped or naked flesh, *mutajarrad,* cannot help but evoke the name, or sobriquet, of al-Nuʿmān's wife, al-Mutajarridah. The term *mutajarrid* or *mutajarrad* denotes one who strips herself, or is stripped, naked, but also as an epithet "a woman . . . fine-skinned and plump, in respect of the denuded or unclad . . . parts of her body . . . or when divested of her clothing."[21] In the case of al-Nuʿmān's wife it hardly conjures up visions of chastity or conjugal fidelity. Indeed, the very idea of stripping and exposure is directly opposed to the ethos of female virtue as it applied to the *ḥurrah,* that is, a free woman of the upper classes of the Jāhilī minor monarchies or tribal warrior aristocracies, as opposed to the captive or slave girl/servant. The beloved of the classical Arabic qasida convention is quite explicitly a *ḥurrah,* whose status is reflected in chastity and inaccessibility expressed in terms of veiling, curtaining, and confinement.

The illicit relationship between the poet and the beloved is thus expressed in terms of his attainment of this forbidden and carefully guarded prize.[22]

In keeping with the social and poetic status of the *ḥurrah*, the description of the beloved is not merely of natural physical beauty, but of luxury, indulgence, and wealth. The beloved is constantly associated with luxury items. Hence we find necklaces, gold beads, the luxury garment of the yellow silk gown, the pearl, the statue. She has the pale, soft, plump body of a protected, veiled, and confined woman of the upper classes, whitened teeth, antimony-darkened gums, soft, uncallused hands dyed with henna; she is adorned with gold and pearls. She is served by handmaidens who help in her adornment and string the pearls for her necklaces. The accouterments of luxury and adornment are woven into the poetic texture in various ways. Some are introduced with metonymic intent as actual attributes of the beloved: she is adorned with a string of gold beads (line 10); has smooth hennaed hands (line 18), white teeth and antimony-darkened gums (line 20), handmaidens, and pearl necklaces (line 25). Others are brought in via simile: her skin is like a yellow silken gown (*siyarā'*) (line 11), her back smooth as fine leather (line 13); she is like a pearl (line 15), a marble statue (line 16).

In addition to characteristics of aristocratic luxury and adornment—cultural elements—there is also a discernible category of natural elements of description and simile. From the animal world, we find her eyes like a gazelle fawn (line 9), her voice so lovely that it lures down the timid mountain she-goat (line 28), her dark soft lips like the wingtips of a dove (line 20). From the vegetable world, elements of freshness and fertility are invoked through simile that indicate youthful (and sexual) prime: her figure swaying like a supple bough (line 11), her fingers soft and pliant like ʿanam boughs (line 18); her teeth like chamomile blooms after rainfall (line 21); her lush head of hair like heavy clusters of ripe grapes (line 29). From the mineral, including astral, world, her gold necklace is like a blazing meteor (line 10), her appearance like the sun rising under auspicious stars (line 14), her teeth like hailstones (line 20). Although these are apparently drawn from the natural world, we should keep in mind that the physical attributes they describe are those associated with a life of ease and cosmetic adornment available exclusively to the women of the tribal elite.

Finally, there is the category of human images that take the form of *tamthīl* (allegory). These occur in line 19, where the urgency and inhibition of the beloved to speak is compared with a sick man desiring to speak to his visitors trying to convey with his eyes what his mouth is too weak to speak. Line 26 is again evocative of Imru' al-Qays's *Muʿallaqah:*

At one like her the staid man
gazes with ardor,
When she stands in her full stature
between woman's gown and maiden's shift.[23] [3]

So lovely is the girl that even the monk, devout and celibate, finds himself gazing with ardor. Again, the beloved's modesty and beauty ultimately derive from, and are intended in the poem to convey, her elevated status.

There is as well a sort of subdued series of actions which seem to serve merely as pegs or pretexts on which to hang the descriptions—line 14, "She appeared . . . "; line 17, "Her veil dropped . . . "; line 19, "She looked at you . . . "—but which could also be foregrounded a bit in the reading to describe a seduction scene. As they stand, they are perhaps more suggestive than narrative. Line 17, "Her veil dropped . . . " also serves as a tie-in with the anecdotes (*akhbār*) associated with this poem, but within the poem it fits so seamlessly that we might guess that it generated the anecdotes.

Not so seamless is the passage from lines 22–24, which stands out from the rest of the descriptive section, flagged, as it were, by the anaphora, "The king claims . . . " It is tempting to read it as an interpolation inspired by some of the anecdotes. Whatever the case, it clearly constitutes a break in the lyric-elegiac mood of the passage, taking on a tone that is declamatory, defensive—or mockingly ironic ("though I have never tasted it!"). There is a further contrast: whereas the rest of the descriptive passage is predominantly visual, this section deals explicitly with kissing. Indeed, through the use of kissing, tasting, and thirst-quenching, there is a description of a sexual act (though not explicitly *the* sexual act). This three-line section also stands out texturally from the rest of the descriptive passage in its rich alliterativeness, particularly in the chiastically (*abba* pattern) and antithetically structured line 23, where the sounds/letters *z*, ʿ, *m*, *dh*, and *q* run riot:

zaʿama l-humāmu wa-lam adhuqhū annahū
ʿadhbun idhā mā dhuqta qulta zdadī

It is important for our reading to be informed by a full semantic sense for the word *dhāqa/yadhūqu/dhawqan*. Essentially it means to taste (as with the tongue), or test, but extends to mean to perceive, to experience. Although its figurative use moves, on the one hand, toward the conceptual, to mean intellectual discernment or relish (like the English: to have good taste in art or music, etc.), on the other hand it is used to enhance the sensory and physical aspects of experience. Hence the Qurʾānic "*dhūqū ʿadh-*

āba l-ḥarīqi" (Taste the torment of hellfire!) (Qur'ān 3:177) and expressions such as *dhāqa r-rajulu ʿusaylata l-mar'ati wa-dhāqat ʿusaylatahu* (the man tasted or experienced the sweetness of the carnal enjoyment of the woman and she his) (Lane, *dh-w-q*). (*ʿUsaylah,* diminutive of *ʿasal,* honey, means male and female sexual fluids, or deliciousness or sweetness; the dual denotes the male and female genital organs, because they are the means of experiencing delight [Lane, *ʿ-s-l*].) Thus, too, the intensive participial form *dhawwāq* means a voluptuary, a man who marries often, repeatedly. Thus the rhetorical insistence on *dh-w-q* in line 23 introduces a sensory physicality and intensity, indeed carnality, into the otherwise more visual and aesthetic description that precedes and follows it. And surely that sweetness to which only her husband can testify refers to more than just kisses. However provocative, the tone is immediate without being coarse, and the conceit of citing the authority of her husband on the sweetness of her kisses, while disclaiming any firsthand experience, adds an air of wistfulness and charm.

The Invective (Hijā'): *Lines 30–34.* The same cannot be said for the concluding section of the poem. At line 30 the lyric-erotic tone of the preceding description of the beloved's body gives way to a bold declarative tone that we would ordinarily associate with the heroic boast (*fakhr*), which is one of the standard options for the "goal" (*gharaḍ;* plural *aghrāḍ*), the third or concluding section of the classical qasida form. Within the context in which the classical Arabic literary tradition has placed this poem, however, this passage functions as invective (*hijā'*), another of the classical *aghrāḍ*, directed against al-Nuʿmān. For inasmuch as the honor of the warrior aristocracy is expressed in terms of the chastity (i.e., the protection and confinement) of their womenfolk, as opposed to female slaves, servants, and captives, dishonor is expressed in the defilement or debauchery of their women. Al-Nābighah's concluding lines present an altogether shocking description of the sexual act with the beloved, but once we have regained our composure it behooves us to examine the rhetorical strategies the poet has employed to achieve this effect.

First of all, there is a change of address from the basically third person description of the preceding lines to a three-line series of second person temporal-conditional sentences (the particle *idhā,* "when" or "if," straddles the border between the temporal and conditional in English). Although this construction implies the poet's firsthand experience, the effect is more powerful than the use of the first person would have been, since it suggests that the subject could be anyone—the impersonal, indeterminate "you." The promiscuity suggested in this invective is thus quite at odds with the erotic description (*tashbīb*) of the poetic seduction scene or rendezvous of lovers in which the poet, at pains to describe the jealously guarded chastity of his beloved, describes the dangers he faces. Again, Imruʾ al-Qays provides an example from his *Muʿallaqah:*

I stole past guards
to get to her, past clansmen
Eager, could they conceal it,
to slay me.[24] [4]

In al-Nābighah's poem the anaphora-like effect of the repeated conditional pattern in lines 30–32 leads quickly and inexorably to the sexual act. What deserves notice is that nowhere in these three lines or the two that follow is there any occurrence of a specifically sexual term, whether action or body part. However seemingly explicit in effect, there is no explicit or obscene diction. The verbs used are *lamasa* (to touch), *ṭaʿana* (to thrust, usually a spear), *nazaʿa* (to yank, esp. a bucket rope; to pull off, esp. a garment) and finally *ʿaḍḍa* (to bite). It is the blunt physicality of these verbs, as opposed to such euphemisms as "threading the needle," that gives the passage its shocking coarseness. Nor is what is being touched, thrust into, and pulled out of and what is biting what explicitly named; rather, we find epithets whose denotants are left for us to fill in: "a gentle rise" (line 30), "a rise that swells" (line 31), "a tight [place]" (line 32). These lines clearly demonstrate the classical Arabic rhetorical proposition that figurative language is more effective than literal (*al-majāzu ablaghu min al-ḥaqīqi*). I would suggest that the effectiveness and obscenity of these lines lies precisely in the poet's use of figurative language, for it forces the listener or reader in supplying the denotant to furnish his/her own graphic picture.[25]

Another aspect of the closing section is the poet's choice of imagery that is, in the end, both striking and conventional. We already saw in lines 22–24 the association of kissing and sexual intercourse with drinking, a metaphorical association whose basis is the idea of satisfying a thirst, a bodily appetite. In lines 31–32 this is developed into the image of getting water from a well. The passage begins by using "plastered" (*muqarmad,* from *qarmad/qirmīd,* a word of Greek derivation meaning baked brick or gypsum; Lane, *q-r-m-d*) to describe the walls of the beloved's vagina as "daubed with . . . perfume," suggesting the gypsum-plastered walls of a well. The image is further developed in line 32 to describe how physically demanding intercourse with the beloved is in terms of a strong youth yanking on the bucket rope to pull a water-laden bucket from a well. Again, the simile is more graphic than mere realistic description could ever be; the same holds true for line 33.

The concluding line shifts almost imperceptibly into a tone and diction that lack the obscene or pornographic bite, if you will, of the four preceding lines. Although the image of drawing water from a well provided by the previous lines leaves no doubt as to the conventional metaphoric intent of line 34, yet the softness of the language and the latticework of wordplay, combining antithesis and chiasmus, yields a closure that is strangely ambivalent in tone. The wordplay centers on the words/roots *warada* (to come to water) and *ṣadara* (to return from water):

lā wāridun minhā yaḥūru li-maṣdarin
ʿanhā wa-lā ṣadirun yaḥūru li-mawridī

(Literally: No one coming to drink water from her changes to a watering-place other than her; and no one leaving after drinking from her ever changes to another place to drink.) As the commentary explains: Whoever wants this woman, wants no one other than her; and whoever has already had her never wants anyone else.[26] Had this line occurred, for example, after line 29 as the closure of the poem, we would read it as a delicate metaphor in line with the preceding section of lyric-erotic description and take it as quite hypothetical, "were any man to desire her . . . " and we would associate it with the water delightful to taste of lines 22–24. However, as closure to the final obscene passage of lines 30–33, we get the sense of a procession of lovers whose appetites she alone can satisfy. In this context, the connotations of sexual purity versus defilement that are associated with the image of the spring or pool of water come to the fore. For in the Arabic symbolic lexicon, a spring or pool of limpid water at which no man or beast has drunk is an expression of chastity, whereas, by contrast, one muddied and befouled by a tribe and its herds constitutes an expression of sexual defilement or debauchery.

How, then, do al-Nābighah's "Are You Leaving Mayyah's People (Description of al-Mutajarridah)" and its accompanying lore relate to the traditional valuation and interpretation of his avowed masterpiece, "O Abode of Mayyah"? To answer this we must understand the economics of the presentation of the panegyric ode, and particularly, with a poem of apology or excuse (*iʿtidhāriyyah*), the idea of redemption. That is, the poem of apology must be of a high enough value to compensate for the poet's transgression. The incident related above in the first al-Mutajarridah anecdote constitutes, by traditional Arab standards, sufficient outrage toward an Arab king, especially when taken together with the poem that is said to allude to al-Mutajarridah, to warrant al-Nuʿmān's wrath and intention to execute al-Nābighah. In this regard it is worth noting that throughout the classical Arabic poetic tradition the composition of erotic poetry or poetry that describes a woman's physical attributes (*tashbīb*) is considered tantamount to carnal knowledge of her. In the second anecdote, however, the dramatic effect is considerably heightened, first by the explicitly stated accusation that al-Nābighah had illicit sexual relations with al-Mutajarridah, and second, by the participation of none other than al-Munakhkhal al-Yashkurī, who serves the Arab reader as a vivid reminder of the usual, and hence anticipated, outcome of such affairs (in both versions of his death). In other words, given this state of affairs, al-Nābighah faces a death threat, so that his poem of apology must, in effect, redeem a human life—his own.

A comparison of these two poems in the rhyme letter *dāl* (*dāliyyah*s) will make it clear that the primary effect of the juxtaposition of the two poems within the narrative sequence of the anecdotes is to heighten the literary and sociopolitical effect of al-Nābighah's poem of apology (*iʿtidhāriyyah*), "O Abode of Mayyah." For in a broader socio-symbolic context, to cuckold the king is the ultimate expression of sedition, the usurpation of the king's authority, and the appropriation of royal prerogative, i.e., insurrection (*fitnah*). For what could be more exclusively the king's prerogative and sacrosanct domain than (visual/sexual access to) the body of his wife, consort, or concubine? On this level cuckolding the king functions as a synecdoche (the part for the whole) for any encroachment on the royal domains or prerogatives. At the same time the body of the king's wife, consort, or concubine serves as a symbol or metaphor for the polity or realm, a symbol that is rooted in the ancient Near Eastern concept of kingship ritualized in the *hieros gamos* (sacred marriage or ritual coitus), which expressed in the ritual intercourse between the king and his consort the fertility of the fields and the prosperity of the realm (further explored in chapter 5). In this respect, then, "Are You Leaving Mayyah's People (The Description of al-Mutajarridah)" represents not merely an affront to royal dignity, but an act of sedition. In its insolence and obscenity, it makes a mockery of the dignity and authority of the king.

The Poem of Redemption: Supplication and Reincorporation

In analyzing al-Nābighah's poetic masterpiece, I will argue that the poet has achieved a union of rhetorical strategy and poetic structure. Given the poet's precarious situation, the performative or purposive aspect of his ode of apology (*iʿtidhāriyyah*)[27]—to reestablish relations between al-Nābighah and al-Nuʿmān and to negotiate the poet's reentry into the Lakhmid court—determines the poet's rhetorical strategy. In this respect the qasida constitutes a ritual of (re)incorporation. This negotiation is initiated by the outsider/poet who performs a ritual that comprises submission, supplication, declaration of allegiance, and presentation of a gift—the qasida itself. Applying Marcel Mauss's formulation of gift exchange to the Arabic courtly exchange of qasida and prize,[28] we can say that the qasida functions as a "token" that represents, embodies, and symbolizes, in its presentation, the enacted ritual of submission and supplication. The successful poet/negotiator virtually entraps his addressee by engaging him in a ritual exchange that obligates him to respond to the poet's proffered gift (of submission, allegiance, praise) with a counter-gift (in this case absolution and reinstatement), or else face opprobrium. This is because the poet's presentation of the qasida constitutes, in effect, a challenge, and the patron loses face if he does not take up this challenge. In the Arabic panegyric qasida (*qaṣīdat al-madḥ*), to take up the challenge is for the patron to live up to, i.e., enact, the virtues that are attributed to him therein. Acceding to the poet's request, granting him his boon, etc., thus signals and symbolizes, as a "counter-token," his acceptance of the poet's offer of allegiance and proffered praise while at the same time enacting and confirming the virtues attributed the patron in the qasida. That is, if the patron wants to accept the gift of praise, he must pay for it with the reward or counter-gift. If he declines to pay, the praise is, ipso facto, retracted. In poetic terms this retraction can take the further form of invective (*hijāʾ*), which has the effect of negating the positive effects of *madḥ* (see chapter 6).

What transpires in the ritual presentation of the qasida, then, is really what we are familiar with from all negotiations. When they break down, the one offering to negotiate—even though this appears as a weakness—gets the upper hand and the positive public relations, while the respondent must either agree to negotiate, and therefore necessarily concede or compromise, or lose face and be accused of hostility and intransigence.

Al-Nābighah executes his rhetorical strategy through his employment of the traditional full three-part structure of the classical Arabic panegyric ode.[29] (1) The poem opens with an elegiac prelude (*nasīb*), lines 1–6, that features a conventional theme of that section, the ruins (*aṭlāl*) of the abandoned encampment of the poet's erstwhile mistress, here named Mayyah, and the poet's reminiscence of its habitation and desertion. (2) There follows the desert journey (*raḥīl*) section, lines 7–20, in which the poet describes the mount that will carry him to his patron, the sturdy and determined she-camel, which, again according to convention, he compares at length to an oryx bull pursued by a hunter and his hounds. (3) The poem concludes with a praise (*madīḥ*) section, lines 21–49, in which the patron, al-Nuʿmān, is compared with Sulaymān (Solomon) (lines 21–26), praised for his generosity and perspicacity (lines 27–36), asked for forgiveness (lines 37–43), and finally compared to the mighty river Euphrates (lines 44–47), before being presented with the poet's closing plea (lines 48–49).

Thus, read as a rite of (re)incorporation, the abandoned abode of the prelude serves admirably to express the poet's despondency over failed previous allegiances, whether al-Nābighah's broken-off relations with al-Nuʿmān or his disappointment with the Ghassānid court, the desert journey section conveys the sense of the poet's resolute yet dangerous return to the Lakhmid fold, and the praise section establishes the king's authority and the poet's submission to it.

Traces of three pre-Islamic myths or legends are found in this qasida: first, that of Lubad, the last of the seven eagles of the longevous pre-Islamic Arab sage Luqmān (line 6); second, the myth of Sulaymān (Solomon), the prototypical ancient Near Eastern magician-monarch, commanding the jinn (lines 22–26); and finally, the Cassandra-like figure of Zarqāʾ al-Yamāmah, who sees the future but is not believed by her tribesmen and who serves as the origin legend for the use of kohl on the eyes (lines 32–36). It is worth noting that these Arabian (and, in the case of Sulaymān/Solomon, Hebrew) origin myths or legends reflect the ancient civilizational wellsprings from which Arabo-Islamic culture drew. Of particular interest with regard to the poetics of the qasida, as we shall see below when these mythic elements are discussed in detail, is the condensed, non-narrative form in which al-Nābighah evokes, rather than retells, these myths and how these brief references or allusions to myth are subordinated to his overall rhetorical strategy.

Two things occur, I will argue, in the transfer of this oral pre-Islamic ode into the Arabo-Islamic literary corpus. First, pre-Islamic mythic concepts of legitimacy as encoded in the panegyric are adopted as part of the legitimizing rhetoric of the Arabo-Islamic praise poem. Second, through the medium of the poetic commentary, the non-narrative allusions to the myth are fleshed out into full narrative "stories." At this point we are able to establish a connection between poetic text and commentary on the one hand, and Qurʾānic text and commentary on the other. Further, we will see the mythic and folkloric elements of both the poetic and scriptural traditions regenerating themselves in the increasing popular genre of stories of the prophets (*qiṣaṣ al-anbiyāʾ*).

With the above points in mind, we will now turn to a detailed analysis of the poetic text itself, after which the relation of the poem to its accompanying anecdotal materials will be further discussed.

Al-Nābighah al-Dhubyānī's "O Abode of Mayyah" (*Yā Dāra Mayyata*)[30]
[meter: *basīṭ;* rhyme: *-dī*]

1. O abode of Mayyah on height and peak!
    It lies abandoned,
  And so long a time
    has passed it by.

2. I stopped there in the evening
    to question it;
  It could not answer, for in the vernal camp
    there was no one.

3. Nothing but tethering pegs
    that I made out only slowly,
  And the tent trench, like a water trough,
    hollowed from the smooth hard ground.

4. Its far edges had been repaired
    and packed down hard
  By a slave girl with a hoe
    in the dew-drenched place.

5. She cleared the way for the channel
    that had been blocked,
  And extended it up to the two tent curtains
    and the piled-up goods.

6. By evening the abode was empty,
    by evening its people had packed up and left;
  It was destroyed by the same fate
    by which Lubad was destroyed.

7. Turn away from what you see,
    for it is irredeemable,
  And raise the saddle-rods on a she-camel
    brisk as an onager, solid.

8. Piled high with compact flesh,
    her teeth squeaking
  Like the creaking of a pulley
    when the rope runs through it.

9. As if my saddle at the end of day
    when we passed by al-Jalīl, where the panic grass grows,

Were mounted on a lone and cautious
oryx bull.

10. One of the oryx of Wajrah,
his trotters painted,
His belly slender, and gleaming
like a sword polisher's unmatched blade.

11. At night a night-traveling rain cloud
from Gemini overtook him,
And over him the north wind
drove freezing hail.

12. The voice of the hunter calling his dogs
so alarmed him
That he stood the night through on his feet,
beset by fear and bitter cold.

13. Then the hunter set
his hounds on him,
And his sharp-hoofed, hard-sinewed feet
kept on kicking.

14. And "Slim," when the hunter
set him on the bull,
Lunged like a warrior thrusting his spear
from a covert.

15. Then the bull pierced him above the shoulder
with his horn,
And drove it through, like a farrier
lancing a camel's abscessed leg.

16. As if his horn protruding
from the dog's side
Were a meat skewer drinkers forgot
on the fire.

17. The dog kept chewing at the protruding tip,
contracted in pain,
Biting at the hard, blood-darkened,
crooked horn.

18. When "Shredder" saw his companion
killed on the spot,
And no way to obtain the bloodwite
or revenge,

19. His soul said to him:
There's nothing to be gained,

Your friend is neither safe
nor standing firm.

20. Such a she-camel
conveys me to Nuʿmān,
Whose beneficence to mankind, both kin and foreigner,
is unsurpassed.

21. I see no one among the people
who resembles him,
And I make no exception
from among the tribes—

22. Except for Sulaymān,
when Allāh said to him:
Take charge of my creatures
and restrain them from sin.

23. And subdue the Jinn,
for I have allowed them
To build Tadmur
with stone slabs and columns.

24. Then whoever obeys you,
reward his obedience
In due measure and guide him
on righteousness' path.

25. And whoever defies you,
chastise him with a chastisement
That will deter the evildoer—
but do not harbor rancor,

26. Except toward him who is your equal
or whom you outstrip
Only as a winning steed outstrips
the runner-up—

27. I see no one more generous
in bestowing a gift
Followed by more gifts and sweeter,
ungrudgingly given:

28. The giver of a hundred
bulky she-camels,
Fattened on the Saʿdān grass of Tūḍiḥ,
with thick and matted fur,

29. And white camels, already broken in,
wide-kneed,

On which fine new Ḥīran saddles
have been strapped,

30. And slave girls kicking up the trains
of long white veils,
Pampered by cool shade in midday heat,
lovely as gazelles,

31. And steeds that gallop briskly
in their reins
Like a flock of birds fleeing
a cloudburst of hail.

32. Judge with perspicacity
like the girl of the tribe:
When she looked at a flock of doves
hastening to drink at a dried-up puddle

33. Two sides of a mountain enclosed them
and she followed them with eyes
Clear as glass, not inflamed
and lined with kohl,

34. She said: Would that these doves
and half again their number
Were ours, together with
our single dove.

35. So they reckoned and found them
as she reckoned
Ninety-nine,
no more, no less.

36. They made up a hundred
including her dove,
And she counted them quickly
up to that number.

37. No, by the life of Him whose Kaᶜbah
I have anointed
And by the blood I have spilled
on stone altars,

38. And by the protector of the birds
who seek the refuge of the sanctuary,
Unmolested by the riders of Mecca
between the spring and the thicket,

39. I never said those evil things
that were reported to you,

If I did, then let my hand be palsied
till I cannot raise my whip!

40. It was nothing but the calumny of enemies
for which I suffered;
Their speech was like a stab
that pierced my liver.

41. I've been told that Abū Qābūs
has threatened me,
And no one can withstand the lion
When it roars.

42. Go easy! May the tribes, all of them,
be your ransom,
And all my increase
both of herds and progeny!

43. Don't fling at me more
than I can withstand,
Even though my foes should rally
to support you.

44. Not even the Euphrates
when the winds blow over it,
Its waves casting up foam
on its two banks,

45. When every wadi rushes into it,
overflowing and tumultuous,
Sweeping down heaps of thorny carob bush
and sticks and boughs,

46. And out of fear the sailor clings fast
to the rudder
After fatigue
and sweat,

47. Is ever more generous than he is
in bestowing gifts,
Nor does a gift today preclude
a gift tomorrow.

48. This is my praise:
if it sounds good to you,
I have alluded—may you disdain all curses—
to no gift.

49. This is an apology: if it has
availed me nothing,

Then its author is indeed
down on his luck. [5]

The Elegiac Prelude (Nasīb): *Lines 1–6(–7).* Al-Nābighah opens his poem with an evocation that is at once intimate and universal. The topos of the desolate ruins of the encampment where the poet's beloved once dwelt (*aṭlāl*) is one so essential to the qasida that it serves in itself as an announcement of the genre. Together with the two-hemistich "key signature" of meter (*al-basīṭ*) and rhyme (*-dī*) (the rhyming of the two hemistichs of the opening line [*maṭlaʿ*]), it declares its generic identity as qasida, as well as its specific identity. The image combines this external enunciatory function with the intimate and individual—the poet's specific formulations of genre-based elements, especially as grounded in his own personal experience, through the proper name of the beloved, Mayyah, and the locus of his loss, "on height and peak." The opening line thus serves to establish a point of contact between the poet and the listener or reader: a literary one, inasmuch as he declares his poetic intentions in terms of genre and form; and an emotional one—the intimate yet universal experience of loss and the remembrance of loss. Gian Biagio Conte's remarks on the openings of Greek and Latin poems are equally pertinent to the Arabic poetic tradition:

> Especially in the archaic period of Greek literature, the "incipit" of poems and even prose (as in Herodotus) had all the importance of a title or heading; its function was that of the author's "signature." . . . The opening of a work boasts a supreme position in composition because it is particularly memorable and *quotable* and is consequently an indispensable guide to interpretation for both reader and philologist. But for the author, poetic memory implicit in the opening verses is redeemed by the way it invests the very substance of the work with a literary identity. It is the quintessential literary act. The opening situates the poetic act and by situating it justifies it. The opening is, first and foremost, a bold signal asserting "This is Poetry," because for our cultural tradition this is the way poetry begins. Once the word has issued from the living voice of the poet's personal invention and has entered the code of poetic tradition, it has the responsibility of imposing the emblematic *quality* of poetry upon its new host discourse. . . . The first line . . . acquires emblematic value and can stand for the work itself. . . . it signals . . . the relation between a specific composition and its literary genre. . . . [31]

Although I have stated above that the experience of loss is universal, each poetic tradition selects its own motifs and images for its expression. In the Arabic tradition the locus of loss, and therefore likewise the ignition point for memory, is the ruined abode. In the "sentimental education" that the qasida tradition entails, that is, the emotional and aesthetic formation it confers, so evocative does the image of the ruined abode become that it generates a virtually Pavlovian response, not only triggering the memory of loss and the identification of one loss with others, but also becoming the psychological focal point in the process of poetic composition itself. Indeed, the image of the ruined abode is the germ or quintessence of the qasida. In this vein, Jaroslav Stetkevych and John Seybold have suggested the "oracular" nature of the abandoned campsite.[32] Certainly it does function within the Arabic poetic tradition as the locus—poetic and psychological—where the poet is able to evoke his poetic voice.

This brings us to the complex relationship between poetry and memory in oral poetic traditions. For not only is poetry mnemonic in form and purpose—as has been amply established and discussed by scholars such as Walter Ong and Eric Havelock,[33] but it is also, as the Arabic tradition so eloquently demonstrates, generated by memory. The qasida is generated by memory, or the realization of oblivion, ephemerality, and is charged with achieving "permanent memorability,"[34] in other words, with guaranteeing the memory of that which would otherwise be overtaken by oblivion.

The Arabic poetic tradition captures with remarkable clarity and efficiency the pivot point between oblivion and memory in the image of the poet stopping at the traces of an old encampment that spark his memory. Given this traditional opening image, it is not surprising that the mood of the first section of the qasida is one of sorrow, of nostalgia, of melancholy. The extraordinarily rich emotional nuances and metaphorical possibilities of the poetics of loss has been extensively explored by Jaroslav Stetkevych in his book *The Zephyrs of Najd,* which bears the subtitle *The Poetics of Nostalgia in the Classical Arabic* Nasīb.[35] An important contribution of that work is J. Stetkevych's emphasis on mood, not merely subject matter, in the qasida, and the sensitivity to the modulation of moods throughout the qasida form. For the present discussion, I would like to emphasize the appropriateness of the abandoned-abode motif for embodying the dialectically opposed concepts of oblivion and memory, that is, the simultaneous absence and presence of that which is gone but remembered.

Having established, then, the poetic efficacy of these traditional elements, let us explore further how al-Nābighah employs them. The opening line captures the complexity of the instant that memory is sparked: it evokes first the exhilaration of the instant of recognition—an effect achieved by both the apostrophizing of the place "abode of Mayyah" and the upward motion its location suggest, "on height and peak!" Deflation is immediate, however: "It lies abandoned. . . . " The mood is one of despair and nostalgia, and the attempt to "reconstruct" the abandoned abode and "reclaim" or "recall" the lost past ensues. There is considerable psychological movement as the poet stops at evening before the traces of the encampment. His first impulse is to question it; the lack of response confirms both its desolation and his (line 2). In line 3 he begins to reconstruct the spring encampment. Slowly and with difficulty he is able to discern and identify the tethering pegs and the traces of the drainage trench that once surrounded the camp. This leads him back in time to when the camp was inhabited, as he sees with his mind's eye the slave girl working to repair the ditch where it had caved in. But no sooner has his memory conducted him to the tent curtains and the piled-up belongings than it brings him too to the memory of departure, the *moment,* as opposed to the *locus,* of loss. We have thus now experienced or traversed a full emotional gamut from an initial exhilaration at the moment of recognition sparking a first joyful memory of the beloved, to recreating the past, only to experience once more, through memory, the loss.[36]

It is worth noting, too, what does not appear in this qasida, that is, any description of the beloved, Mayyah, or of the poet's relationship with her. This is attributable to the power of the genre itself, its well-established conventions and its formative effect on the poetic imagination of both poet and listener or reader—the mere mention of a beloved allows the listener/reader to generate his own vision of Mayyah and the story of the poet's love for her.[37] In other words, the description of the poet's beloved and his experience with her are not explicitly presented in this qasida, but rather evoked in the listener's or reader's mind through an intertextual process that is ultimately metonymic in character.

The agent of oblivion is time, invoked in this elegiac prelude in two phrases that frame the six-line passage: in line 1, "And so long a time has passed it by," and in line 6, "It was destroyed by the same fate / by which Lubad was destroyed." If time/fate (usually denoted by *dahr*) is the great eraser of traces, its ubiquity in the qasida tradition can perhaps be explained by its antithetical role to that of the poet and poetry: oblivion versus memory. The two rhyme words, *al-abadī* (time) in line 1 and *lubadī* (Lubad) in line 6, exhibit a phonetic and semantic (perhaps etymological) near identity that serves as opening and closure to the act of remembrance. *Abad* is a synonym of *dahr* that conveys "time in an absolute sense, . . . a long time that is unlimited . . . time, or duration, or continuance or existence, without end; endless time, . . . eternity"; the verbal form *abada* means "he remained, stayed, abode or dwelt constantly, continually or permanently" (Lane, *a-b-d*). The effect of al-Nābighah's formulation is to express the temporal and psychological distance of the abode, the irretrievability of the past. That is, the permanence and continuity of time serves only to set off the temporary and ephemeral quality of human existence. The poet's attempted reconstruction ultimately fails, as recollection of the inhabited abode leads inexorably and temporally to the recollection of tribal departure and abandonment.

In line 6 the poet expresses his realization and acceptance of the finality of his personal loss by identifying it with the proverbially and mythically embedded common wisdom, i.e., that nothing lasts forever, that time destroys all things. The name Lubad resonates both etymologically and mythically. The verbal form of the root, *labada,* means "he remained, continued, stayed, abode, or dwelt, in the place . . . and clave to it" (Lane, *l-b-d*), its semanticity and phonetic closeness to *abada* suggesting an etymological link (although *l-b-d* has a physical denotation of clinging or sticking that is lacking in the more temporal *a-b-d*). The nominal form *lubad* thus means "one who does not travel, . . . nor quit his abode, . . . or place" (Lane, *l-b-d*), likewise suggesting permanence and continuity, but with an ironical twist it is also the name of the last of Luqmān's seven vultures, so named because Luqmān, whose life span was to coincide with that of the consecutive lives of the seven vultures, thought that Lubad (and hence he himself) would live forever (Lane, *l-b-d*). Luqmān ibn ʿĀd was known to the Arabs of the Jāhiliyyah for his wisdom and longevity and figures a number of times in the pre-Islamic poetry of Imruʾ al-Qays, al-Aʿshā, Labīd, and Ṭarafah, as well as that of al-Nābighah.[38]

The legend alluded to in the present poem is given by the philologist Abū al-Faḍl al-Maydānī (d. 518 H./1124 C.E.) in his *Majmaʿ al-Amthāl* (Collection of Proverbs), citing Abū ʿUbaydah, as follows:

> "Time outlasted Lubad" (*ṭāla l-abad ʿalā lubad*). By "Lubad" they mean the last of the vultures of Luqmān ibn ʿĀd. He had been granted a life span the length of the lives of seven vultures. So, he would take a vulture chick and put it in a hollow in the mountain that he lived at the foot of. Each chick lived five-hundred years, more or less. Each time one died, another took its place, until all of them perished except for the seventh, which he then took and put in the same place and named it "Lubad." It lived longer than all the others, so the Arabs coined the proverb, saying "Time outlasted Lubad."[39]

Another version of the Luqmān legend adds an etymological turn to the ending:

> . . . When only the seventh [vulture] remained, his nephew said to him, "Oh Uncle, is the life span of this one all you have left?" Luqmān replied,

> "This is Lubad (Time [itself])," for Lubad in their tongue meant time (*dahr*). When Lubad's life span was over, Luqmān saw him falling and cried out to him, "Rise, Lubad!" And he tried to rise, but couldn't. Then he fell and died, and Luqmān died with him. Because of this they coined the proverb "Time outlasted Lubad" (*ṭāla l-abad ʿalā lubad* or *atā l-abad ʿalā lubad*).[40]

Just as the proverb encapsulates a narrative legend in a condensed mnemonic form, so too does al-Nābighah's poem. Both feature the mnemonic and rhetorical device of assonance and/or pun between the words *abad* and *lubad,* which function with an ironic twist as both synonyms and antonyms. Through the positioning of the rhyme words al-Nābighah's qasida evokes both the mnemonically condensed aphorism and the narratively extended legend, bringing the "conventional"—that is, commonly accepted—wisdom to bear on his intimate experience of loss.[41]

Of concern in the context of the present argument is the role of the qasida in conveying the myth and legend of the Jāhiliyyah into the Islamic age. The mnemonic form and function of oral poetry renders it stabler than narrative prose forms. As will be argued further below, I would like to propose that, contrary to the claim of narrative failure or incapacity in Jāhilī poetry, the encapsulation of myth and legend in condensed non-narrative allusions served as a guarantor of their preservation into the Islamic era. Al-Nābighah's poem does not attempt to retell the legend of Luqmān and his seven vultures, rather he presents the essential message or moral of that story in the most condensed form—just as the proverb does. On the one hand, this condensed non-narrative form serves as a "hook," to use Mary Carruthers's term,[42] on which to hang the fuller narrative. At the same time, if the less memorable narrative should become lost or confused, the preservation and promulgation of the essential message is assured. Just as the trace of the abandoned encampment can evoke the poet's full memory of his past experiences, the poetic allusion through the mention of the name Lubad to the legend of Luqmān serves to spark the memory and evoke the full narrative legend. Both function as "souvenirs," mementos that both prod and preserve memory.

The transition to the journey section is unequivocally signaled in line 7. The imperative *ʿaddi,* "turn away," that the poet addresses to himself functions semantically, phonetically, and conventionally to signal the end of the elegiac prelude of the qasida and the opening of the journey section. The imperative brusqueness and phonetic harshness of *ʿaddi* likewise jolt us into a new and different mood, serving just as the equally conventional *daʿ* or *daʿ dhā* "leave off," "leave off this" (of which it is phonetically a metathesis) to indicate a dramatic act of will and change of mood and tone. Small and self-evident as these conventional pivot words or signposts, *ʿaddi* and *daʿ*, may at first appear, their importance lies not merely in signaling a surface transition from one thematic section of the qasida to another (what traditional Arabic literary criticism terms *takhalluṣ*),[43] nor even in the change of mood and tone that they effect. Rather, we must emphasize the act of will that they so succinctly encapsulate and the centrality of that act of will in the psychological drama that occurs within the full qasida form. The phrases "turn away!" (*ʿaddi*) and "leave off!" / "leave off this!" (*daʿ / daʿ dhāka*) capture that *crucial* and *decisive* instant of resolve—and I note here that the etymological sense of crossing and cutting of these English terms is precisely what the Arabic terms in this conventionalized usage express.[44]

How essential this instant of resolve is to the progression of mood and structure of the full qasida becomes evident in those formal variants in which this act of will is missing: the *ghazal*—a short monothematic love lyric form that does not extend beyond the theme and mood of the elegiac prelude; and qasidas such as those of the premier Umayyad lyricist, Dhū al-Rummah, whose long poems convey with masterful elegiac lyricism the failed attempt to transcend the nostalgia of the elegiac prelude section. Thus, its absence can signal the absence of that resolve, the failure of that will, without which triumph over adversity cannot be achieved. Just how fundamental to the formal and structural progression of the qasida this psychological instant is can perhaps also explain why in later (ʿAbbāsid) bipartite qasidas we nevertheless so often find what I have termed a "vestigial *raḥīl* (journey)," often of one line only and usually exhibiting the signal *daʿ* ("leave off!"). Thus, even when the journey section is omitted, the crucial instant of psychological transition is often preserved. Essential to this act of resolve is also an instant of realization, that the past can be remembered but not regained. Time moves inexorably forward; it is not circular.

The Desert Journey (Raḥīl): *Lines 7–20.* If the prelude section combines stasis, "I stopped there" (line 2), with a psychological movement into the past that creates a sense of arrested motion, of interruption or even regression, the journey section (*raḥīl*) presents from its onset a dramatic shift to energetic activity, departure, and directionality. The change in tone and mood between these two formal sections is evident when we compare the crepuscular elegiac tribal departure that the poet remembers in line 6, one that expresses a process of desolation, with the brisk vigor and momentum of saddling and journey described in lines 7–9. The poet achieves the latter effect first by the change in verbal mood to the imperative—no longer a passive victim, the poet is "taking charge" of himself, as the imperatives are spoken by him and addressed to him. The poet then compares his mount, the she-camel, first to the onager, the traditional embodiment of irrepressible stamina, and then, in the squeaking of her teeth, to a pulley, whose rope runs continuously through it with mechanical predictability. Finally, in line 9, the poet introduces what will constitute the bulk of the journey section, an extended allegorical simile in which he compares his she-camel to an oryx bull who is first caught in a hailstorm and then attacked by a hunter's hounds.

In his work on the hunt in pre-Islamic poetry Jaroslav Stetkevych has established the function and meaning of the extended allegorical hunt scene as it occurs in the journey section, particularly in contradistinction to the heroic hunt theme that occurs only in the final third section of the qasida. The litterateur al-Jāḥiẓ (d. 255/868–9) had already duly noted in his *Kitāb al-Ḥayawān* (Book of Animals) that when the prey in the *raḥīl* hunt passage is slain by the hunter and hounds, the poem is an elegy (*rithā*ʾ); whereas if the animal successfully fends off the hunter and hounds, the poem is boast (*fakhr*) or panegyric (*madīḥ*). J. Stetkevych points out further that the prey is the protagonist—the figure with which the listener or reader identifies.[45] I, too, have argued elsewhere that the extended animal similes of the journey section are not at all "digressions," as previous scholars have suggested, but rather concise reiterations of the essential message and structure of the qasida, functioning in poems such as the present one as allegories of the poet's own psychological drama.[46]

Thus, the drama presented in lines 9–19 is in the form of a "contest," with the oryx bull at first beset by a hailstorm, bitter cold, and fear. His first reaction is inaction—standing alert and fearful through the cold and rainy night, afraid that if he lies down or sleeps, the hunter's hounds will attack (lines 10–12). Once the hunter actually sets his hounds on him, however, the oryx bull resorts to action, kicking (line 13) and piercing the dog with his horn (line 15). The graphic description of his victims follows, one hound twisting painfully to chew on the bloodied horn that has pierced him (line 17), and finally, the hounds' retreat (lines 18–19), signaling the triumph of the oryx bull. It is, I believe, this poetic enactment of the contest and triumph over adversity that is the crux of the oryx simile and that describes the fortitude and determination of the she-camel, but, also, in a more essential way, the poet's own act of will as first expressed in the *ʿaddi* ("turn away") of line 7. Thus we see that the transition or passage that the journey section effects is not expressed merely in terms of the description of the poet's or she-camel's physical journey and the hardships of the desert crossing, but rather it expresses above all a psychological transition from a passive to active disposition, from victim to victor, that is effected above all by an act of will.

When the poet declares in the transitional line 20, "Such a she-camel / conveys me to Nuᶜmān," we should thus understand that it is the poet's determination and fortitude that are above all intended. The arrival at the patron's court serves as a structural signal, alerting us to the fact that we have now reached the praise section proper (*madīḥ*) of the panegyric ode.

The Praise Section (Madīḥ): *Lines 20–49.* Convenient as the term "praise section" is as a descriptive label and general classificatory term for the final section of the panegyric qasida, it will become immediately clear from our discussion that what transpires here is not merely praise of the patron, but a complex literary and courtly ritual that entails supplication and negotiation, oath and absolution, allegiance and legitimization, and in this poem in particular, apology or excuse (*iᶜtidhār*). Having identified the variety of activities that take place in the praise section, we must recognize that they are expressed in the overt form of praise of the patron. It is therefore imperative that we attempt to determine the function of praise and its relation to the functions that the panegyric ode performs.

An extensive amount of work has been done in the field of Homeric and classical studies generally on the ritual or ceremony of supplication. Most recently, Kevin Crotty's work includes a number of insights that are especially pertinent for the present study. Chief among them is his recognition that supplication is a form of ceremony (in my terms, though not his, it is a form of ritual as well) and of praise; moreover, he adds, "it is praise from the distinctive and troubling perspective of the loser."[47] Further, inasmuch as glory (Greek, *kleos*) in a warrior aristocracy is a commodity, the ceremony of supplication, which entails praise for glorious deeds (or virtues), is looked upon as a commercial transaction; that is, it involves what I would term in light of my applications of Mauss's theories a ritual of exchange.[48] The self-abasement of the supplicant confers upon the supplicated a sense of power that is pleasurable, for supplication is an act of recognition of the power of the supplicated and entails the "pleasurable aspect of pity" that the supplicant elicits in the one supplicated.[49] Citing Agathe Thornton, Crotty states that supplication is a "ceremony that puts a moral constraint on the one supplicated to do as asked, and brings punishment on the one who refuses."[50] To my mind, the self-abasement and the eliciting of pity that are essential to the ceremony or ritual of supplication contribute to our understanding of the essential structural and thematic roles performed by the elegiac prelude (*nasīb*) and the journey section (*raḥīl*) in those functions, such as supplication and negotiation, that are accomplished in the *madīḥ* section. Another classicist, Simon Goldhill, focuses more on the act or institution of supplication

> as a social ritual which articulates the boundaries of power. A suppliant by the act of supplication acknowledges the power of the supplicated figure and attempts from a position of weakness to prevent the figure of power from using his power or to direct it in a particular way. On the battle field, supplication is a matter of life and death where the defeated attempts to control the absolute power of the victor to kill. . . . Supplication is an appeal for limitations to the use of power, for a relation of exchange to bound the relation of dominance. . . . The interplay between the claims of the institution [of supplication] and the acceptance of the institution by the figure of power constitutes supplication as an uneasy instantiation of the control and contestation of power.[51]

Given what we are told about al-Nābighah's predicament and the internal evidence of the poetic text, it is clear that his "apology" or "excuse" (*iʿtidhār*) is above all a form of supplication. Indeed, inasmuch as every Arabic panegyric ode (*qaṣīdat al-madḥ*) is part of a ritual exchange or negotiation in which the poet explicitly or implicitly presents in the qasida a demand for reward or favor (*jāʾizah*), then every panegyric ode constitutes, to some degree, a poem of supplication (for further discussion, see chapters 2 and 4). We can conclude from this, then, that the praise that plays so prominent a role in the Arabic panegyric ode, and thus in the classical Arabic poetic tradition altogether, does not proffer gratuitous flattery or abject sycophancy, but rather performs an explicit and necessary ritual and ceremonial function. Indeed, we will argue throughout this study that it performs, or can perform, a number of such functions.

In the case of al-Nābighah's poem of apology what comes to the fore is the function of the qasida as part of a ritual of submission and self-abasement that forms part of the supplicatory ritual. The poet presents himself as powerless, the king as powerful. The poem at one level thus functions as an expression of this power relation: the poet's recognition of the king's might and submission to it. Inasmuch as the purpose of this poem is to seek absolution or forgiveness it necessarily entails the recognition of the king's moral authority. At the same time, it seeks to persuade. In this respect the "institution of supplication" as embodied in the presentation of the qasida becomes a form of negotiation. Goldhill's remark, cited above, that "[s]upplication is an appeal for limitations to the use of power, for a relation of exchange to bound the relation of dominance" is especially pertinent here. The exchange involved in this case is, first, that of submission for forgiveness. The ritual or ceremonial abasement of the poet-supplicant and exaltation of the patron-ruler serves as a physical enactment or embodiment of the ruler's power—a live demonstration, if you will. Given that power, might, authority, and legitimacy are concepts or abstractions, they require constant demonstration or confirmation; that is, they only exist when they are enacted. This is the preeminent function of court ceremony—it is a physical enactment or embodiment of the ruler's authority and legitimacy; the qasida itself is then the verbal enunciation of that authority and legitimacy.

The virtues for which the patron is praised are those the polity—that is, the ruler and his subjects—regards as requisite for an authoritative and legitimate ruler: notably, in the Arabic tradition, might, justice, and magnanimity. But in presenting the qasida in the form of a ceremonial supplication, the poet does not merely describe the patron's virtues. Rather, the qasida presents a challenge to the patron, one that amounts to a form of entrapment or blackmail. Therein lies the power of the supplicant-poet. In al-Nābighah's poem, for example, the poet praises the king for his justice, generosity, acuity, and might; but the poem at the same time challenges the king to prove or confirm this praise through an immediate action that all present will witness as proof of his authority and legitimacy—his worthiness. We can reduce the qasida ceremony to the simplest case or pattern: a poet comes before a patron offering him a poem praising his generosity and requesting a gift. The patron, if he denies the request, at the same time denies the claim of the poem, that he is generous, and in doing so undermines his own moral authority as a legitimate ruler. To legitimize himself, that is, to confirm the veracity of the virtues enunciated in the panegyric, the patron must accede to the poet's request or demand. In the present, more complex poem, then, the poet challenges the king to prove his justice, generosity, acuity, and might by forgiving or absolving the poet.

A second aspect of the praise poem is again a subject that has received much attention in classical Greek, especially Homeric and Pindaric, scholarship, that is, the concept of *kleos,* fame, immortal renown.[52] In terms of the Arabic tradition, which equally recognizes this principle, we are given to understand that the gift that the poet offers in the form of the poem is that of immortal renown and, further, that it is a coveted commodity for which the patron is prepared to pay dearly.

Let us turn now more closely to the text itself. Line 20 conveys the goal of the journey section: the arrival at the court of the patron and the praise section (*madīḥ*) of the qasida. The previous sections have demonstrated both the poet's abasement—the failure, loss, and passivity of the elegiac prelude (*nasīb*)—and his resolve and determination—the courage and perseverance of the journey section (*raḥīl*). The poet's act of will in the journey section, however, is at the same time an act of trust or faith in the magnanimity of the patron. As we reach line 20 we arrive at the point where the patron can either betray that trust or fulfill it. The challenge is presented: the poet claims that the patron is renowned for his unsurpassed beneficence to kinsman and foreigner (and all that "near" and "far" imply). The term *faḍl* in particular conveys munificence born of superiority, closely akin to our notion of "noblesse oblige" and to the theological sense of "grace," that is, "beneficence or generosity shown by God to man" (*Webster's Third New International Dictionary*). Thus with remarkable precision the diction of line 20 conveys submission to the patron, recognition of his authority, and a challenge to demonstrate his superiority by fulfilling the poet's trust. Clearly, however flattering this line might be to the patron, for us to dismiss it as mere praise or sycophancy is to miss much of what is going on in the poem. Likewise to take such panegyric as merely a prescriptive vision of the ideal ruler is to ignore the complex dynamics of the poet-patron interchange.

In the subsequent lines (21–26) the poet raises the stakes: he further magnifies al-Nuʿmān by his claim that no one can measure up to him; no one, that is, except Sulaymān (Solomon). The introduction of Sulaymān at once condenses a body of ancient lore and myth and brings it to bear on al-Nuʿmān. The comparison with Sulaymān is a guarantee of legitimacy that contains both religious and mythic components. It establishes an identity or "mythic concordance," to use Paul Connerton's term,[53] between al-Nuʿmān and Sulaymān; that is, however, on the condition that al-Nuʿmān behave in accordance with Solomonic virtue as al-Nābighah presents it in lines 22–26, and also with the grand scale of munificence described in lines 28–31. These lines constitute nothing less than a catalogue of precisely those luxury items or precious commodities that are used as "tokens" in the gift exchange ceremonies of the pre-Islamic warrior aristocracy, that is, what is termed in the Greek counterpart *agalmata*:[54] the best bred camels with "name-brand" Ḥīran saddles, delicately-cared-for slave girls (i.e., those intended for courtly pleasures, not for manual labor), steeds sleek and swift. These remained the traditional prestige gifts throughout much of the Islamic period, and, inasmuch as they formed part of the ritual gift exchange of qasida for reward (*jāʾizah*), the qasida can be counted among them.

The passage comprises three component virtues: generosity, justice, and right guidance, subsumed under an overarching concept of cosmic power or divine appointment. It is interesting to see how the poet has achieved the (con)fusion of the identities of Sulaymān and al-Nuʿmān and to note with what extraordinary concision the poet has encapsulated the pre-Islamic / ancient Near Eastern concept of mythic magician-king or ideal ruler. Rhetorically, the identification of al-Nuʿmān with Sulaymān is achieved by what we might term the elative extended simile. The most common form of this structure in pre-Islamic poetry is the formula exemplified later in this poem, comparing al-Nuʿmān to the mighty Euphrates: *fa mā l-furātu . . . yawman bi-ajwada minhu* . . . (lines 44–47). "The Euphrates . . . *is not more generous than he*. . . . " Here we have a variant: "I see *no one*, with the exception of Sulaymān, *more generous than he* in giving gifts. . . . " (lines 21–27). The effect of this structure is that the description, strictly speaking, of Sulaymān, in lines 22–26, comes to describe al-Nuʿmān, while at the same time the description, strictly speaking, of al-Nuʿmān, lines 27–31, applies equally to Sulaymān. On a subtler level, the choice of pronouns plays a similar role: al-Nuʿmān is referred to in the third person as "he" (lines 21, 27–30); but the effect of Allāh's second person address to Sulaymān as "you," particularly in the ceremonial context of the qasida being delivered to the patron, is for the patron-addressee, i.e., al-Nuʿmān, to equally function as the referent of the pronoun "you" as Allāh's words are being uttered by the poet. This is particularly the case for lines 24–26, which offer homiletic advice on kingship. In other words, the string of imperatives of Allah's command to Sulaymān becomes directed by the poet to king al-Nuʿmān: "Take charge . . . restrain . . . subdue . . . reward . . . guide . . . chastise . . . do not harbor rancor" (*qum . . . fa-ḥdud . . . khayyis . . . fa-nfaʿ . . . wa-dlul . . . ʿāqib . . . lā taqʿud ʿalā ḍamadī*) (lines 22–25). On a subtler yet more profound level, the divine appointment of the king is identified with the poet's voice. This concept reverberates, as we shall see in subsequent chapters, throughout the Arabo-Islamic tradition of caliphal panegyric in which the poet's voice affirms Allāh's appointment of the patron as the legitimate leader of the Islamic polity (*ummah*). Of particular pertinence to al-Nābighah's plight is the closing advice of this passage (lines 25–26), that the ideal ruler, whether Sulaymān or al-Nuʿmān, should not harbor rancor against someone who is of lower status than he is. This is the traditional Arab virtue of *ḥilm* (forbearance, clemency), the idea that it is undignified to exhibit wrath or vengefulness to those beneath one's station. A further confusion or conflation of identities ensues later in the poem with the imperative *wa-ḥkum* ("Judge!") that opens line 32. While on the one hand it signals the opening of the poet's direct address to the patron, on the other it echoes the imperatives of God's commands to Sulaymān of lines 23–25.[55]

My intention here is, in part, to demonstrate the rhetorical potency of non-narrative forms. In evaluating al-Nābighah's qasidas, Albert Arazi states, "Moreover, he seems to have been completely lacking in narrative sense; al-Nābigha is incapable of telling a story."[56] What I have attempted to show is that al-Nābighah is not trying to recount the story of Sulaymān and the jinn; rather he is trying to evoke it to play a functional role in a ritual of reconciliation. It is the effectiveness of the ritual, not the cohesion of a plot, by which a qasida was, and should be, measured. Here, the effectiveness of the mythic concordance established between Sulaymān and al-Nuʿmān is achieved by rhetorical, poetic, non-narrative means. Furthermore, we can see in lines 21–31 a declaration of allegiance, or, more precisely in terms of the actual presentation of the poem at court, an offer of allegiance. This is the poet's basic challenge and offer: that if the king treats him in accordance with the Solomonic model he presents, the poet will recognize al-Nuʿmān's "Solomonic" legitimacy and authority. If al-Nuʿmān rejects the offer, the deal is off, the panegyric is retracted, and the king has demonstrated, enacted, his own unworthiness and lack of legitimacy and authority. In other words, for al-Nuʿmān to reject the poem—i.e., to refuse the poet's request—would be to reject this comparison or identification with the prototypical ancient Near Eastern magician-monarch, and thereby to deny his own legitimacy. Through this passage we can also discern how the qasida was able to encode ancient Near Eastern myth in this encapsulated form that then makes the transition into the Islamic world, where it is narratively reconstituted.[57]

The myth and legend of pre-Islamic Arabia are evoked once more in the following section of the poem, lines 32–36. As noted above, the imperative *wa-ḥkum,* "Judge," that opens this passage echoes the imperatives that Allāh addresses to Sulaymān in the preceding passage (lines 22–25), while at the same time it constitutes, strictly speaking, the poet's admonition to the king not to judge rashly, but rather with perspicacity and discernment. The passage invokes a story concerning the fabled pre-Islamic Cassandra-like figure Zarqāʾ al-Yamāmah, or possibly another of the "blue-eyed Arab women" (*zurq al-ʿuyūn*), the female sage (*ḥakīmah*) Bint al-Khuss.[58] The story told here is an eminently folkloric one whose substructure is that of a riddle or puzzle: if you take a flock of doves (or in some versions sand grouse) and add half again as many, then add one more, you get one hundred. How big is the original flock? We would probably state it algebraically as $x + \frac{1}{2}x + 1 = 100$; solve for x (answer: $x = 66$). Of course the poet here is proceeding with a certain amount of indirection. However straightforward his presentation of the riddle, the connection of the story with the verb "judge" is metaphorical, for by the visual acuity of al-Zarqāʾ the poet intends her mental acuity, discernment, and perspicacity, which allow her to see into the future, not just count flocks of doves. Certainly, too, it seems that what the poet really alludes to is the story of Zarqāʾ's ability to see what her tribesmen could not, evoking thereby the concept that a person of great discernment can perceive what the generality of men cannot. For the final phrase of line 33, "eyes / Clear as glass, not inflamed / and lined with kohl," alludes to the etiological myth for the use of kohl on the eyes, the myth of Zarqāʾ al-Yamāmah. Iraqi scholar Maḥmūd Shukrī al-Ālūsī (d. 1342/1924), who likewise argues that al-Nābighah's lines should be taken to refer to Zarqāʾ al-Yamāmah, rather than Bint al-Khuss,[59] relates the story as follows:

> Al-Zamakhsharī said "More perceptive than al-Zarqāʾ" (= "the blue-eyed girl") (*abṣar mina z-zarqāʾ*) is one of the most wide-spread proverbs. She was one of the daughters of Luqmān ibn ʿĀd and was the queen of al-Yamāmah. (Al-Yamāmah was her name and the country, al-Yamāmah, was named for her). . . . She was one of the three "blue-eyed women" and was of the tribe of Jadīs. When Jadīs killed Ṭasm, Ḥassān ibn Tubbaʿ raised an army of the tribe of Ṭasm against al-Yamāmah. When the army was three nights' distance from Jaww, al-Zarqāʾ mounted the fortress known as al-Kalb and gazed at them, but they had camouflaged themselves with trees. So she recited in *rajaz* form:
>
> I swear by Allāh that trees have crawled
> Or donkeys have begun to pull at something. [6]
>
> But her tribesmen didn't believe her, so she said, "By God, I see a man snapping at a shoulder-blade or patching a sandal," but they paid her no heed, until the army attacked them at daybreak. And when Ḥassān conquered her, he asked her, "What food did you eat?" "White flour," she replied, "every day with marrow." Then he said, "With what do you line your eyes?" "With antimony (*ithmid*)," she replied. And he slit open her eye and saw black veins of antimony. She was the first of the Arabs to line her eyes with antimony.[60]

By this subtle indirection the poet alludes to his own case, which he hopes al-Nuʿmān will judge with Zarqāʾ-like clairvoyant discernment. Once again, there is an implicit challenge, for the poet has put a rhetorical spin on his plea for discerning judgment—i.e., only a judgment in the poet's favor will be considered discerning, thereby confirming the comparison of al-Nuʿmān with al-Zarqāʾ and establishing the king's justice and wisdom, his moral and mental capacity to rule.

Lines 37–43 constitute the performative core of the poem. As I have established in earlier work (see also chapters 2 and 4), an observable change in the mode of poetic discourse traditionally occurs at this point in such panegyric odes.[61] That is, there is a change from the usual "thick" or opaque poetic discourse replete with specifically poetic diction and dense with metaphor, to a "thin," transparent, and straightforward (though by no means rhetorically simple), seemingly prosaic discourse. The contrast sets the performative core off from the rest of the qasida and renders it stark and stripped-down, forceful and direct. Lines 37–40 are the poet's oath whereby he intends to establish his innocence. Al-Nābighah does not name Allāh directly, but by epithet and indirection in a manner through which the poet establishes his own credentials as a believer who has performed his obligations of rite and sacrifice and hence is worthy of divine protection. Thus he invokes Allāh as the Lord of the Kaʿbah that he has anointed, of the altars upon which he has made blood sacrifice, and, as though now invoking the reciprocal obligation of deity toward believer, as the protector of those that seek sanctuary, here referring to the sanctuary at Mecca, whose birds were protected. The poet swears an oath that he never said those things his enemies have accused him of saying, i.e., the source of the king's wrath.

Two points are of interest here and, as we shall see, again in chapter 2. First, the poet does not apologize or excuse himself in our sense; rather the poetic ritual of apology (*iʿtidhār*) consists of a denial of the charges and the swearing of an oath. It is hard to know just what to make of this. The anecdotal materials that accompany this poem, and likewise those that accompany the renowned poem of apology of Kaʿb ibn Zuhayr (the subject of chapter 2), present blatant wrongdoing on the part of the poet. So, at least in the classical Arabic tradition, the poet's denial of wrongdoing and placing the blame on his calumniators (*wāshī,* plural *wushāt*) was not given credence—regardless of our estimation of the historicity of these narrative anecdotes. The only way we can explain this is by understanding the poem as a performative ritual that is concerned, therefore, not with veracity, but with efficacy. The denial in this respect becomes not so much a lie as a ritual recantation or abjuration of the alleged misdeed. It is only with this understanding of lines 37–40 that the following lines (41–43), with their plea for mercy, forgiveness, make sense. Second, within the poem the poet does not specify the nature of his wrongdoing, except apparently that it was verbal.[62] The omission of any clear mention of the offense has several functions. First, it avoids the unpleasantness and embarrassment, not to say danger, of reminding the king of his subject's alleged outrage against him; second, it relegates the alleged offenses to textual non-existence, verbal oblivion. Particularly if we are dealing with words spoken against the king, then the omission of them in the (immortal) poetic text amounts to their erasure. Whether words or deeds are at stake here, by being denied and not explicitly mentioned, they are, as it were, expunged from the poet's record. In this context, the oath serves as a test of sincerity rather than one of veracity. Finally, in a broader sense, such a misdeed against the king could be construed as a sign of weakness or lack of authority on his part and therefore to mention it would be at odds with the purpose both of the ceremony and of the poetic praise (*madīḥ*).

The following three lines (41–43) constitute the poet's self-abasement and declaration of allegiance to the king. In line 41 the poet voices his recognition of the king's displeasure in a phrase that we shall later recognize as a ritual formula: "I have been informed that [the king, etc.] has threatened me" (*unbiʾtu anna Abā Qābūsa awʿadanī*) (see Kaʿb ibn Zuhayr's "Suʿād Has Departed," line 36, in chapter 2).[63] The poet's fear before the might and wrath of al-Nuʿmān is evoked through his comparison of the angry king to a roaring lion; the poet then begs for mercy and, through the traditional Arabic formula of pledging to redeem (or ransom) (*fidāʾ*) the king, swears his allegiance. If the poet's crime against the king was his denial or flouting of royal authority and power, then this passage constitutes his public recognition of and submission to that authority and power.

It is important to keep in mind as well the actual ceremonial presentation of such a poem at court. For such ceremonials are crucial for the ruler's display or enactment of his power and authority. The poet's self-abasement, declaration of allegiance, and plea for mercy are tangible enactments of the ruler's power and authority, which are otherwise intangible and merely conceptual, hence in constant need of demonstration and enunciation. Above all, mercy must be understood as an attribute of power. This can best be grasped with relation to the Arab concepts and institutions of recompense, retaliation, and vengeance. Central to the Arab concept of *lex talionis* is the principle that it only applies among equals. In the case of blood vengeance, for example, vengeance is not exacted from a weak or subordinate tribe, as it would be beneath the dignity of a powerful tribe to do so, and would result in a loss of status. When looked at in this light, an act of mercy—i.e., to willingly forgo retaliation—involves the humiliation of the recipient, the lowering of his status and the concomitant elevation of the status of the one bestowing mercy. In other words, the poet, through his self-abasement and plea for mercy, is setting the stage for the ruler to enact his power, authority, and superiority. By understanding mercy in this manner we can more fully grasp the significance of the preeminent epithets of Allāh in Islam—*al-raḥmān al-raḥīm* (the merciful, the most merciful)—as expressions of transcendent majesty and might. Certainly in the poem at hand the poet's pleas for mercy—"Go easy!" (line 42), that is, do not act rashly or precipitously out of anger, and "Don't fling at me / more than I can withstand" (line 43)—serve to convey the ruler's superior might. In this vein Aziz al-Azmeh writes of the Umayyad caliph: "Muᶜāwiya is said to have quoted the last Lakhmid king, an-Nuᶜmān b. al-Mundhir (d. ca. 602), in saying that acts of punishment or mercy by kings are performed purely as manifestations of power and capacity."[64]

In the final panegyric passage (lines 44–47) al-Nābighah reverts from the performative prosaic language of the ceremonial core of the poem to the heightened poetic idiom to present his renowned and much imitated passage (see chapter 3) in which he describes al-Nuᶜmān as the mighty Euphrates.[65] The rhetorical structure is a traditional one for the extended simile in pre-Islamic poetry: "Not even . . . [the Euphrates] . . . [long description]. . . . is more . . . [generous] . . . than he." The poet's Euphrates simile, though based on convention, is both powerful and subtle. In the description of the Euphrates itself he focuses on its formidable might, its destructive power, the swollen flood that sweeps bushes and boughs in its torrent and leaves terror-stricken sailors clinging to their vessel for dear life (lines 44–46). When he completes the simile (line 47), however, there is an unexpected shift: the description of the Euphrates has led us to assume that the basis for comparison is terrible might; instead, generosity is invoked as the shared principle of comparison. The shift may at first be disconcerting, but it has two effects. The first is the added rhetorical emphasis produced by the unexpected. Second, and more important, is the conceptual fullness that the simile thereby achieves. For certainly the image of the rain-swollen river in the Arabic tradition, as elsewhere, conveys fertility, abundance, and life-giving generosity at the same time that it conveys might and destruction. Through his "surprise ending" to the simile, al-Nābighah is able to express the highest praise for al-Nuᶜmān, that is, by attributing to him the twin virtues of rulership: magnanimity and might. For in the Near Eastern concept of kingship, to have one of these without the other was to be illegitimate or ineffectual. Might without magnanimity is tyranny or despotism, mere brute force; magnanimity without might is self-destructive folly leading to impoverishment and impotence. Furthermore, through this switch, the poet manages to modulate from praising the king's might to imploring his magnanimity.

In the closing couplet (lines 48–49) the poet, in a metapoetic gesture, steps outside of the poem, as it were, to offer his concluding remarks: "Well, there you have it," he seems to say. "Let's hope it does the trick!" At the same time, of course, he is throwing down the glove, issuing a challenge to the king, for the ceremonial apology, as we remarked above concerning the supplicatory ode, is also a form of entrapment. First, the poet has set the stage for the ruler to demonstrate his mercy; if he chooses not to, he will look like a brute before his subjects. Further, the (sly) poet insists (too much) that, even after the long poetic passages extolling the king's generosity (lines 27–30) and the extended Euphrates simile climax (line 47) on gift giving, he has not alluded to any gift for himself—all he wants, he claims, is forgiveness. The king must choose: he can bestow absolution and a generous gift upon the poet, and thereby be seen as confirming the veracity of the poet's praise; or he can withhold his bounty and be viewed as a miserly ruler, unable to live up to the high praise that has been lavished upon him. In other words, if the poem fails to elicit the expected reward, the ruler, too, will be "down on his luck."

We must, moreover, understand that the king's response to the poem, both in forgiving the poet and in rewarding him with gifts, constitutes an evaluation of the poem. In this respect its aesthetics are intimately tied up with its efficacy. How well does it perform the ceremony? How compellingly does it enact the ritual of the self-abasement of the supplicant and the elevation (praise) of the one supplicated? In performative poetry "the proof of the pudding is in the eating."

Within the Arabic literary tradition, as we have seen, al-Nābighah's "Are You Leaving Mayyah's People (Description of al-Mutajarridah)" figures as the reason for the poet's flight from the court of al-Nuʿmān. Nevertheless, given the improbability of the story on practical and logical grounds (unless, perhaps, we assume that the king and his companions [*nudamāʾ*] were well into their cups), and our inability to historically confirm pre-Islamic authorship and attribution, we can understand the conjoining of the two poems in the classical Arabic tradition in a narrative of transgression and redemption as, above all, a literary interpretive construct. The pairing of the poems is facilitated by the poetic texts themselves: they share the same rhyme (*-dī*), although a different meter (the al-Mutajarridah poem is in *kāmil,* whereas the apology is in *basīṭ*), and both mention the same feminine name, Mayyah, in the opening hemistich. That is, the two opening lines evoke each other. Now, we ask ourselves, would al-Nābighah have wanted to remind al-Nuʿmān of this poem at the time he presented the ode of apology (*iʿtidhāriyyah*), wherein he disclaims any speech against the king? What extravagant—and potentially lethal—impudence that would have been! Rather, keeping in mind that the tradition confers aesthetic preeminence upon the apology, we can speculate that the al-Mutajarridah poem was preserved and positioned in the literary tradition to bolster the rhetorical power and performative efficacy of the ode of apology. Whatever the actual circumstance and provenance of the two poems, "Are You Leaving Mayyah's People (The Description of al-Mutajarridah)" occurs in the traditional textual sources as conjoined but subordinated to al-Nābighah's masterpiece, "O Abode of Mayyah." The gist of this literary association, however, is that the more scandalous, i.e., sexually explicit—indeed, unforgivably outrageous—the description poem, the more powerful the poem that procured forgiveness for it. Further, let us keep in mind the power of rhetoric in both cases. It was the evocative/provocative power of "Are You Leaving Mayyah's People" that incriminated the poet—i.e., it is a tribute to his poetic genius that he could write a poem that convinced al-Nuʿmān that the poet had had sex with his wife, and likewise that he could compose a poem that would absolve him of the crime. In other words, as the tradition presents it, the transgression was poetic and the atonement was likewise poetic.

Against the backdrop of the al-Mutajarridah story and poem, the rhetorical and political effectiveness of the ode of apology, "O Abode of Mayyah," stands in heightened contrast. The qasida performs even more explicitly a ceremony of restoration and reaffirmation of royal dignity and authority. The gravity and decorum of the panegyric qasida's ceremonial idiom—in form, diction, imagery—counter the insolence (lines 22–24) and obscenity (lines 30–33) of "Are You Leaving Mayyah's People (The Description of al-Mutajarridah)"; the poet's ritual abasement, submission, and supplication constitute an act of recognition of the formidable might of the monarch in marked contrast to the impotence, political or otherwise, of the cuckolded king. "O Abode of Mayyah" is the price for the poet's redemption.

Another anecdote gives a different explanation for al-Nuʿmān's wrath against al-Nābighah. It relates that two of the poet's rivals or enemies at court, ʿAbd al-Qays ibn Khufāf al-Tamīmī and Murrah ibn Saʿd ibn Qurayʿ al-Saʿdī, composed invective against al-Nuʿmān, attributed it to al-Nābighah, and then recited it to al-Nuʿmān. One of the lines cited in the *Kitāb al-Aghānī* gives us a sufficient picture:

A king who fondles his mother and his slave(s),
His joints are flaccid, his penis the size of a kohl-needle.[66] [7]

Two points are of interest in this regard. First, in both the al-Mutajarridah version and the invective version, al-Nābighah's crime takes the form of poetry—erotic description (*tashbīb*) or invective (*hijāʾ*); thus, in effect, his apology panegyric is a poem as compensation for another poem. Second, in the al-Mutajarridah anecdotes, none of the narrators protests al-Nābighah's innocence. The traditional Arab reasoning is that to write such a poem, the poet must indeed have had illicit relations with al-Nuʿmān's wife, or perhaps, if we want to argue that classical Arab culture is a shame rather than guilt culture, the poet's having created, through his poem, the appearance of an illicit liaison was tantamount to actually having had one. Certainly, the al-Mutajarridah version of this episode is the one that the literary tradition favors. I would argue that the reason for this is that the greater outrage confers a higher value on the poem that negates it. As for the anecdote about falsely attributed invective, it is in perfect accord with the internal evidence in al-Nābighah's ode of apology, lines 39–40: "I never said those evil things / that were reported to you" and "It was nothing but the calumny of enemies." However more accurate, or consistent, it appears, the tradition seems to have preferred the version that heightens the performative value, or rhetorical efficacy, of al-Nābighah's renowned ode.

The power of poetry to redeem the poet and to reinstate him in the king's good graces comes across as well in a long anecdote recounted in the first person by none other than Ḥassān ibn Thābit, the celebrated Jāhilī panegyrist who later became poet laureate of the Prophet Muḥammad. Note how well everything goes for Ḥassān at the court of al-Nuʿmān until the king's favorite, al-Nābighah, appears on the scene:

> Ḥassān ibn Thābit said: I went to the court of al-Nuʿmān ibn al-Mundhir, after having written panegyric for him, and came upon his chamberlain ʿIṣām ibn Shahbar. I sat down by him, and he said, "I see an Arab, are you from the Ḥijāz?" "Yes," I replied. "Then you must be a Qaḥṭānī," he said. "I am Qaḥṭānī," I replied. "Then you must be a Yathribī," he said. "I am Yathribī," I replied. "Then you must be a Khazrajī." I replied, "I am Khazrajī." Then he said, "You must be Ḥassān ibn Thābit." "I am he," I replied. Then he said, "Have you come to compose panegyric for the king?" "Yes," I replied. "Then," he said, "let me give you some advice: When you appear before him, he will ask you about Jabalah ibn al-Ayham and pour curses on him. Be careful not to help him in this, but let his mention of him pass without expressing either agreement or disagreement and say, 'How should someone like me interfere, O King, between you and Jabalah, when you two are kinsmen!' And if he invites you to partake of food, decline. But if he then implores you with an oath, then fulfill his oath [and eat] lightly in the manner of one who honors an oath and is honored to eat with him—not like someone who is hungry or starved, and

don't talk with him for long, don't begin telling him about anything unless he asks you about it [first], and don't remain long in his company (*majlis*)." And I said: "May God be generous to you! I will take heed of your counsel." He entered [before the king] then came out to me and said: "Enter." So I entered and greeted [the king] as kings are greeted. Then he spoke to me concerning Jabalah exactly as ʿIṣām had said he would—as if he'd been present—and I answered as he had instructed me. Then I asked his permission to recite some poetry, and he granted me permission, so I recited to him. Then he invited me to eat, so [again] I followed ʿIṣām's instructions; and then to drink, and I did the same. Then he ordered me a magnificent stipend and I took my leave. ʿIṣām then said to me: "There's one piece of advice I didn't give you. I've heard that al-Nābighah al-Dhubyānī is coming before him, and if he does, then no one else has a chance. So it's better for you to excuse yourself and take your leave honorably than to be rudely turned out." So I remained at court for a month. Then the two Fazārīs [men of the Fazārah tribe] presented themselves to him, for there was a special bond between them, and with them was al-Nābighah who had sought their protection and asked them to intercede with al-Nuʿmān to procure his forgiveness. So [al-Nuʿmān], unaware that al-Nābighah was with them, pitched for them a domed leather tent. Then al-Nābighah contrived to have a singing slave girl sing his poem:

> O Abode of Mayyah on height and peak!

No sooner did [al-Nuʿmān] hear the poetry than he exclaimed, "I swear by God, that's the poetry of al-Nābighah!" He enquired about him and was told that he was with the two Fazārīs. They discussed the matter with him, and he guaranteed his safety.

And Abū Zayd ʿUmar ibn Shabbah said in his notice: When [al-Nābighah] came with [the two Fazārīs] to al-Nuʿmān, he sent to them perfume and gifts with a singing slave girl from among his maidservants. And the two of them ordered her to begin with al-Nābighah, before them. Then she mentioned this to al-Nuʿmān, so he knew that it was al-Nābighah. Then [al-Nābighah] entrusted her with this poem of his and asked her to sing it to [al-Nuʿmān] after his wine had begun to affect him. She did this and moved al-Nuʿmān to delight, and he said, "This is Highland [from the highlands of Najd] poetry! This is the poetry of al-Nābighah!" . . . Then al-Nuʿmān went out in the aftermath of a rainfall, and the two Fazārīs came up to him, and between them was al-Nābighah who had been dyed with henna, with a very dark dye. When al-Nuʿmān saw him, he exclaimed, "It would have been more fitting if you were dyed with blood!" But the two Fazārīs said, "May you disdain all curses![67] No reproach! We have given him our protection. Forgiveness is more becoming." So al-Nuʿmān guaranteed his safety and asked him to recite his poetry. At this Ḥassān ibn

> Thābit declared, "I begrudged him three things, and I don't know which I envied the most: al-Nuʿmān's bringing him close once more after his estrangement and sitting up at night conversing with him and listening to him, or the excellence of his poetry, or the hundred purebred royal camels[68] that he bestowed on him."[69]

This anecdote, which gives the impression of being cobbled together from several variants of the story, has much light to shed on the present discussion. First, it establishes the preeminence of al-Nābighah with regard to the other renowned poet of the period, Ḥassān ibn Thābit. The latter succeeds admirably at al-Nuʿmān's court, especially when he follows the (Persianate) courtly wisdom dispensed in this case by the chamberlain, ʿIṣām. Just as the newcomer to the court gains some confidence—a successful audience with the king, a generous stipend—his aspirations are dashed by the final piece of advice that ʿIṣām has up until then withheld: that no poet, Ḥassān included, can compete for al-Nuʿmān's favor when al-Nābighah is at court. The part of the passage attributed to Ḥassān ibn Thābit foregrounds the role of al-Nābighah's "O Abode of Mayyah" in securing his redemption.

The second part of this passage seems to be an interpolation, or series of interpolations, of variants, demonstrating the redemptive power of poetry within the context of court protocol and the institution of protection. First of all, it is the stirring and unmistakable beauty of al-Nābighah's poem "O Abode of Mayyah" that both reveals and redeems him. The episode with the henna and what amounts to the king's death threat serves to remind us of the gravity of the situation, i.e., that the poem has saved its poet from death. At the same time it constitutes a reduplication or variant of the story, foregrounding the institution of protection and the sacred obligation it involves. Structurally it echoes the first part of the anecdote: just as ʿIṣām advises Ḥassān that he should let the king's oath be fulfilled out of reverence for the sacred institution of the oath; so here, out of reverence for the sacredness of the institution of protection, al-Nuʿmān cannot disgrace his two Fazārī allies by slaying their protégé. The final remark attributed to Ḥassān ibn Thābit encapsulates the ritual of reconciliation that the prose narrative relates: through the striking beauty of his poetry, al-Nābighah has been reinstated in court and in the good graces of the king and, as Mauss's rules of gift exchange have led us to anticipate, the king has not only forgiven and reinstated the poet, but has bestowed on him as well a bountiful gift—one hundred of the royal camels.

The poems and anecdotes surrounding al-Nābighah and King al-Nuʿ mān, with their archetypal pattern of sedition and submission, transgression and redemption, constitute a paradigmatic myth of the relationship of ruler and ruled that informs Arabo-Islamic concepts of legitimacy. Indeed, the pattern of the poet with a death threat over his head coming incognito to a ruler to redeem himself through a panegyric ode is one that is repeated in the mythos of Kaʿb ibn Zuhayr and his submission to the Prophet Muḥammad, the subject of the following chapter.

Two

Transmission and Submission
Praising the Prophet
Kaᶜb ibn Zuhayr and the Islamic Ode

From the Jāhiliyyah to Islam

In the preceding chapter we established, through the examination of al-Nābighah's "Are You Leaving Mayyah's People (Description of al-Mutajarridah)" and his ode of apology, "O Abode of Mayyah," in their literary poetic and anecdotal environment, the role of the pre-Islamic Arabic ode as an element of court ceremonial and as the vehicle for a paradigmatic myth of transgression and redemption. We demonstrated that "O Abode of Mayyah" encoded an ideology of kingship and embodied a ritual of supplication. Its performance celebrated and enacted the authority and dignity of the king, the submission and allegiance of the poet, and the mutual subject-ruler bond that holds the polity together. Further, we established the function of the pre-Islamic qasida, as an orally preserved poetic form, in perpetuating and promoting the culture that informs it.

In the present chapter I would like to explore the role that the panegyric ode (*qaṣīdat al-madḥ*) played at a crucial juncture in Arab cultural and political history: the revelation of the Qur'ān to the Prophet Muḥammad and his proclamation of the religion of Islam and establishment of an Islamic state, which took as its calendrical starting point the Hijrah, the Migration of the Prophet with a small group of followers from Mecca to Medina in 622 C.E. = 1 H. This chapter will take as its focus the celebrated Mantle Ode, "Suᶜād Has Departed," that the great poet and scion of great poets Kaᶜb ibn Zuhayr[1] is said to have presented to the Prophet Muḥammad on the occasion of his conversion to Islam, traditionally dated as 9 H./630 C.E., and for which the Prophet conferred upon the poet his mantle (*burdah*). The gist of my argument will be that Kaᶜb's "Suᶜād Has Departed" mythicizes the poet's conversion so that it encodes and embodies the conversion of the pagan Arabs of the Jāhiliyyah to Islam, and, moreover, the submission to Islam, or co-option by Islam, of the pre-Islamic poetic tradition.[2] From this point on, the Arabic poetic tradition, especially the panegyric, becomes the major literary-ceremonial expression of Arabo-Islamic legitimacy and allegiance, and Kaʿb's "Suʿād Has Departed" becomes an expression of submission to Islam and devotion to the Prophet Muḥammad for pious Muslims the world over.[3]

In examining this ode, and with it the anecdotal (*akhbār*, singular *khabar*) and poetic (*ashʿār*, singular *shiʿr*) materials that accompany it in the classical Arabic literary tradition, I would like to demonstrate how the structure and themes of the tripartite pre-Islamic ode—the elegiac prelude (*nasīb*), the desert journey (*raḥīl*), and the praise section (*madīḥ*)—that served in al-Nābighah's poem (chapter 1) to convey a rite of (re)incorporation into the Lakhmid court are employed by Kaʿb ibn Zuhayr to express on the political level a transfer of allegiance from his tribe to Muḥammad and the nascent Islamic state and, on the religious level, the conversion from the beliefs and mores of the Jāhiliyyah to Islam. In doing so we will refer not only to the poetics of supplication and submission discussed in the preceding chapter, but also to several ritual and ceremonial patterns that help elucidate the structure and function of the qasida form.

The tripartite pattern of Arnold van Gennep's rite of passage—Separation, Liminality, and Aggregation—will be aligned with the three parts of the qasida to highlight the change in status and the psychological transition involved in the conversion process. Similarly, Theodor Gaster's bipartite seasonal pattern of Emptying (Mortification and Purgation) and Filling (Invigoration and Jubilation), with its emphasis on the waning of one lease on life and the beginning of another (death and rebirth), will be invoked to elucidate the movement from the moribund tribal ethos of the Jāhiliyyah to the triumphant new religion of Islam. Finally, in order to more fully understand the symbolic ramifications of the poet's offering of a qasida and the Prophet's conferring of his mantle to form a bond of allegiance between subject and ruler, we will draw on the insights of Marcel Mauss's formulations concerning ritual exchange.[4]

I would like to explore, as well, how the art of the qasida transforms an actual event or circumstance into ritual or myth, thus changing it from an ephemeral and transient occurrence to a permanent and transcendent message. As mentioned in chapter 1, recent studies in the field of orality and literacy have demonstrated that the function of poetry, and all those devices which we term "poetic," is essentially mnemonic, for in nonliterate societies the only way to preserve information is to memorize it. As Eric Havelock has shown, rhyme, meter, assonance, alliteration, antithesis, parallelism, and the like all serve to stabilize and preserve the oral "text."[5] The same holds true for simile, metaphor, and pun.[6] Furthermore, we can add to these rhetorical elements the ritual and ceremonial structure of the classical Arabic qasida and the sequence of themes that traditionally occur within its structural units. That is, Havelock's words, "Ritualization becomes the means of memorization,"[7] are applicable to the formal structure of the qasida as well to its prosodic and rhetorical features. The ritualization and mythicization of the historical event does not, however, merely endow it with mnemonic stability, but, more important, it imbues it with suprahistorical significance. It thus functions, as Havelock has shown poetry does in oral cultures, as "the instrument for the establishment of a cultural tradition."[8]

The Conversion Narrative

Let us begin with the anecdotal and poetic context of Kaᶜb's presentation of his renowned ode, "Suᶜād Has Departed," to the Prophet Muḥammad, as given in the classical literary and religious sources, such as the Baghdadi philologist al-Sukkarī's (d. 275/888) collection and commentary of Kaᶜb's poetry and the Egyptian scholar Ibn Hishām's (d. 218/833) Life of the Prophet (*Sīrah*).[9] A number of points of similarity are to be noted when we compare the materials concerning Kaᶜb (below) with those relating to al-Nābighah's "O Abode of Mayyah": the poet is in grave danger with a death sentence on his head; the qasida is presented as part of a ceremony of submission and declaration of allegiance; in both cases, the qasida plays a role in the redemption of the poet. Further, as will be discussed below, the story of the conversion to Islam of Kaᶜb ibn Zuhayr and his brother Bujayr forms a prose conversion narrative that serves in the Arabo-Islamic literary tradition to contextualize and elucidate the ritually structured conversion poem. Al-Sukkarī's version of the events surrounding Kaᶜb's presentation of his conversion ode, "Suᶜād Has Departed," runs as follows:

> Bujayr ibn Abī Sulmā al-Muzanī converted to Islam, and his people, including his full brother Kaᶜb, got angry with him. Bujayr met the Prophet during the Hijrah. Then Kaᶜb sent the following message to him:
>
> Take, you two, a message
> to Bujayr from me,
> "Did you accept what you said at al-Khayf,
> did you?[10]
>
> You drank with al-Maʾmūn
> a thirst-quenching cup,

He gave you a first draught,
then a second.

You abandoned the ways of right guidance
and followed him,
To what was it, woe to you,
that he guided you?

To a religion no father or mother of yours
ever followed,
Nor any one
of your kinsmen!" [8]

When these verses reached Bujayr he recited them to the Prophet who exclaimed, "He speaks the truth, I am al-Maʾmūn [the trustworthy one] and he is a liar; and certainly he found no father or mother of *his* following Islam." Then Bujayr replied to his brother:

Who will take Kaᶜb a message, "Will you accept
the religion for which
You falsely blame me, though it is
the more judicious course?

So to God alone,
not to al-ᶜUzzā nor al-Lāt,
Make for safety, while you can,
and submit,

Before a day when no one is safe
or escapes from the Fire,
Except the submissive Muslim,
pure of heart.

To me the religion of Zuhayr
—and it is nothing—
And the religion of Abū Sulmā
are now forbidden." [9]

When the Apostle of God returned to Medina from al-Ṭāʾif, Bujayr wrote to Kaᶜb: "The Prophet is intent upon killing all of the polytheist poets who attack him, and Ibn al-Zabaᶜrā and Hubayrah ibn Abī Wahb [two poets of the Quraysh tribe] have fled. So if you have any use for your life, then turn to the Messenger of God, for he does not kill anyone who comes to him repentant. If you won't do this, then flee to safety." When Bujayr's message reached him, Kaᶜb became greatly distressed and anxious, and those in his tribe spread alarming news about him, saying, "He is as good as dead," and the Banū Muzaynah [his clan] refused to shelter him. So he made his way to Medina and stayed with an acquaintance of his there. Then he came to the Apostle of God. The Prophet did not know him, so he sat down before him and said, "O Apostle of God, if Kaᶜb ibn Zuhayr were to come to you repentant and submitting to Islam, would you accept him if I brought him to you?" "Yes," he replied. Then he said, "I am Kaᶜb." Suddenly one of the Anṣār [Medinese Helpers of the Prophet] leapt up and cried, "Let me cut off his head!" But the Prophet restrained him, whereupon Kaᶜb recited his panegyric to the Prophet.[11]

The story of the conversion of Kaᶜb and Bujayr, the two sons of the master poet of the Jāhiliyyah and paradigm of pre- or proto-Islamic virtue, Zuhayr ibn Abī Sulmā, is one that points to the inner conflict involved in conversion. For embracing Islam involved the transfer of loyalties from the inherited ancestral ethos of the Jāhiliyyah, of which Zuhayr ibn Abī Sulmā had been the noblest embodiment, to a new religion founded by an orphaned upstart from the politically powerful Meccan tribe of Quraysh. The prose anecdotes and the poetic exchange that they contain first indicate that it is virtue, not inherent viciousness, that holds Kaᶜb back from Islam: *pietas,* piety and devotion to the ways and religion of his ancestors. A closer look at the first poem indicates that, from the pre-Islamic tribal point of view, Bujayr's conversion is nothing but opportunistic treachery. Whereas from the Islamic point of view to be given a drink by or share a cup with the Messenger of God suggests the cup of immortal life, from Kaᶜb's perspective it is the commensal cup of tribal membership. In drinking from it Bujayr has denied his own kin and the right guidance (*hudā*) of the ancestral ways (lines 3–4). Nor does Bujayr deny this in his reply: he has abandoned the goddesses of the Jāhiliyyah to worship the one God; the religion of his kinsmen is nothing to him, the religion of Abū Sulmā he considers forbidden. His reason: that only the Muslim, pure of heart, will escape perdition. That this is treachery by Jāhilī standards is clear if we compare it to the celebrated statement of that ethos by the last of the great Jāhilī Arab Knights (*fursān al-ᶜarab*), who refused to convert to Islam, Durayd ibn al-Ṣimmah:

I gave my orders
 at the twisted sand dune,
But they did not see that I was right
 till the morning of the morrow.

When they defied me,
 I went along with them,
Although I saw their error and that I
 was not well-guided.

For am I not of the Banū Ghaziyyah?
        If they err, I err with them;
If they are rightly guided,
        so am I.[12]   [10]

The prose narrative, further, constitutes a prosaic or literalist version of Kaᶜb's poem. The Messenger of God has outlawed Kaᶜb; his choice is to flee or to submit and convert. The situation becomes clear to him when his own tribesmen consider him "as good as dead" (*maqtūl*) (which is the equivalent of disowning him, since it implies that they will neither defend nor avenge him), and, finally, his own clan, the Muzaynah, refuse him shelter and protection. Kaᶜb does not betray the ancestral ways, his kinsmen do. And it is only when he sees that the "religion of Abū Sulmā," his father, is no more, that the old social order is extinct, that he heads for Medina to embrace the new one, Islam, and submit to its Prophet. Inasmuch as the anecdotes (*akhbār*) serve as a commentary on the qasida, they explain the poem as an expression of transfer of allegiance, as an oath of fealty to the Prophet of Islam. That the poem is likewise a redemption payment is also apparent from the anecdotes, in Muḥammad's outlawing the poet and his kinsmen's disowning him and declaring him "as good as dead." It is the poem that then redeems Kaᶜb, both in this world and the next. To make the point more explicit, the anecdote, again presenting a "prosaic" (in both senses of the word) version of salvation, depicts Muḥammad as saving Kaᶜb's mortal as well as immortal soul by restraining the zealous Anṣārī, who would behead him on the spot. As if to make the exchange of his life for his poem explicit, it is at precisely this point, according to the anecdotal narrative, that Kaᶜb recites his renowned ode.

The Conversion Ode

Although differing somewhat in its proportions and choice of traditional themes that are developed, Kaᶜb's ode follows the same full formal tripartite structure of the pre-Islamic panegyric ode (*qaṣīdat al-madḥ*) that we first encountered in al-Nābighah's ode of praise and apology to King al-Nuᶜmān (chapter 1). (1) The poem opens with the elegiac prelude (*nasīb*), lines 1–12, here constructed of the traditional motif of the bereft lover describing his departed mistress, Suᶜād ("Felicity"), first her beauty, then her perfidy. (2) The journey section (*raḥīl*), lines 13–32/33, is devoted to a detailed description of the fortitude of she-camel that alone can reach the distant dwelling of Suᶜād (which now must mean the "felicity" of Islam), its final passage comparing the she-camel's unrelenting gait to the violent lamentations of a bereft mother, to conclude that Kaᶜb himself is "as good as dead" and abandoned by his friends. (3) The culminating praise section (*madīḥ*), lines 33/34–55, comprises the poet's submission and declaration of allegiance to the Prophet Muḥammad and his conversion to Islam (lines 33–41); a passage of praise to the Prophet comparing him to a lion (lines 42–48); and a final passage of praise of the Emigrants (Muhājirūn), the early group of loyal Muslims who accompanied the Prophet Muḥammad on the Hijrah from Mecca to Medina (lines 49–55).

The significance of this three-part structural sequence is perhaps most easily grasped if viewed in light of the Van Gennepian formulation of the rite of passage. The elegiac prelude, desert journey, and praise (with submission and conversion) can be aligned, respectively, with the Separation from a past social state, the outcast Liminality phase outside the bonds and bounds of society, and the Incorporation phase in which the passenger (re)enters society, but with a new status, new rights and obligations. As mentioned above, my interpretation is that the rite of passage pattern inherent in this ode not only conveys the conversion of Kaᶜb from his ancestral tribal religion to the new religion proclaimed by the Prophet Muḥammad, but also serves emblematically to express the cultural transition from the Jāhiliyyah to Islam.

Kaᶜb ibn Zuhayr's "Suᶜād Has Departed" (*Bānat Suᶜād*)[13]
[meter: *basīṭ;* rhyme: *-ūlū/īlū*]

1. Suᶜād has departed and today
 my heart is sick,
A slave to her traces,
 unransomed and enchained.[14]

2. On the morning of departure
 when her tribe set out,
Suᶜād was but a bleating antelope
 with languid gaze and kohl-lined eye.

3. When she smiles she flashes
 side teeth wet
As if with a first draught of wine
 or with a second,

4. Mixed with cool water from a wadi's bend,
 in a pebbled streambed limpid
And sparkling in the noontime sun,
 chilled by the north wind,

5. Cleansed by the winds
of all dirt and dust,
And by white cumuli left overflowing
with a night cloud's rain.

6. Alas! what a mistress, had she been true
to what she promised,
Had true advice not gone
unheeded.

7. But she is a mistress
in whose blood are mixed
Calamity, mendacity,
inconstancy and perfidy,

8. She never stays the same
but is as mutable
As the *ghūl* in her garb
ever-changing.

9. Nor does she hold fast love's bond
once she has claimed it,
Except as sieves
hold water.

10. The false promises of ʿUrqūb
were her model,
Her promises were nothing except
empty prattle.

11. I hope and pray that in the end
they'll be fulfilled,
But they will remain forever
unfulfilled.

12. Don't be deceived by the desires
she aroused, the promises she made,
For hopes and dreams
are a delusion.

13. Suʿād alit at nightfall in a land
unreachable
But by the best of she-camels
of noble breed and easy pace,

14. Never to be reached but by a she-camel
huge and robust
That despite fatigue sustains
her amble and her trot,

15. Sweat gushing from the glands
behind her ears,
Eager for the nameless road,
its way markers effaced,

16. With the eyes of a lone white antelope
she pierces the unknown
When rough lands and sand dunes blaze
in high noon's sun,

17. Stout where the pendant hangs,
full where the shackle binds,
Her build, the best of all
the stallions' daughters,

18. Huge as a mountain, her sire her sibling,
by a dam blood-stallion bred,
Her uncle by sire and dam the same,
She is long-necked, brisk-paced.

19. The tick walks on her hide,
but then the smoothness
Of her breast and flank
makes it slip.

20. Sturdy as the onager,
her sides piled with meat,
Her knees set wide, clear of
the breastbone's daughters,

21. As if her muzzle and
the two sides of her jaw
Between her eyes and throat
were an oblong stone.

22. She brushes with a tail
like a stripped palm branch, tufted
Over a dry udder,
its milk ducts unimpaired,

23. Hook-nosed, in her ears the expert eye
discerns nobility of breed,
In her two cheeks,
great smoothness.

24. Overtaking others, she speeds
on legs lancelike and nimble,
Like an oath annulled they barely
touch the ground,

25. Brown their sole sinews, they scatter
pebbles in their wake,
So tough no shoes protect them
on the hilltops

26. On a day when the chameleon
is as burnt as if
His sun-scorched parts were bread
baked on heated rocks.

27. As if the repeating motion of her forelegs
when she is drenched in sweat
And when the narrow mountain peaks
are cloaked in the mirage,

28. And the camel driver, his song their goad,
says to the tribe
When ashen locusts kick up pebbles,
"Stop and rest,"

29. At high noon were the arms of a woman
tall and middle-aged,
Risen in lament, then others,
near barren and bereft, respond,

30. Wailing, arms flailing,
when the heralds announced
The death of her firstborn,
mad with grief,

31. Tearing her clothes from her breast
with her bare hands,
Her woolen shift ripped from her collarbone
in shreds.

32. My slanderers at her two sides
denounced me saying,
"You, O Son of Abū Sulmā, are
as good as dead."

33. And every trusted friend in whom
I put my hopes
Said, "I cannot help you, I am occupied
with other things."

34. So I replied, "Out of my way,
you bastards!"
For all that the All-Merciful decrees
will come to pass!

35. For every man of woman born,
though he be long secure,
Will one day be borne
on humpbacked bier.

36. I was told God's Messenger
had threatened me,
But from God's Messenger
pardon is hoped.

37. Go easy, and let Him be your guide
who gave to you
The gift of the Qur'ān in which
are warnings and discernment!

38. Don't hold me to account for what
my slanderers have said,
For, however great the lies against me,
I have not sinned!

39. I stood where I saw and heard
what would have made
The mighty pachyderm,
had it stood in my stead,

40. Quake with fear unless
the Messenger of God,
By God's leave,
granted it protection,

** I kept on across the wasteland,
my only coat of mail
The wing of darkness, beneath
the lowered veil of night,[15]

41. Until I placed my right hand,
without contending,
In the hand of an avenger,
his word the word.

42. He is more dreaded by me
when I speak to him
And I am told, "You will be questioned
and must answer,"

43. Than a lion,
snapping and rapacious,
Its lair in ʿAththar's hollow,
thicket within thicket,

44. Who in the morning feeds flesh
to two lion whelps
That live on human flesh,
flung in the dust in chunks,

45. Who when it assaults its match
is not permitted
To leave its match['s blade]
unnotched,

46. For whom the braying onager
falls silent,
In whose wadi no hunters
stalk their prey,

47. In whose wadi lies an honest man,
his weapons and torn clothes
Flung in the dust,
his flesh devoured.

48. The Messenger is surely a sword
from whose flash light is sought,
One of the swords of God,
an Indian blade unsheathed,

49. In a band of Qurashis whose spokesman
said to them in Mecca's hollow
When they submitted to Islam,
"Depart!"

50. They departed, but no weaklings
departed with them,
None who flee the battle,
none unsteady in the saddle, none unarmed.

51. Haughty high-nosed champions,
who on battle day
Don shirts
of David's weave,

52. White, ample, their rings
interlocking
As if they were the qafʿāʾ plant's
interlocking rings.

53. They walk as the white camels walk
when kept in check by blows,
While the stunted black ones
go astray.[16]

54. Neither jubilant when their spears
strike down a tribe,
Nor distraught when
they are struck,

55. The spear does not pierce them
except in the throat,
Nor do they shrink from
death's water troughs. [11]

The Elegiac Prelude (Nasīb): *Lines 1–12.* Kaᶜb's elegiac prelude is constructed of the traditional motif of the bereft lover describing his departed mistress, Suᶜād. If we note the derivation of the name Suᶜād (which Husain aptly translates as "Beatrice") from the root *s-ᶜ-d,* whence *saᶜādah,* prosperity, good fortune, happiness, felicity (Lane, *s-ᶜ-d*), it is possible to read this passage allegorically as an elegy to a bygone golden age, an elegy to the Jāhiliyyah. Suᶜād and all her etymological baggage—prosperity, happiness, good fortune—have departed. The forlorn poet is left behind, raving over the traces of the now-empty encampment. In the context of our argument, this must be read as a metaphor for the poet's political situation: the ethos of the Jāhiliyyah is obsolete, the poet has been abandoned and betrayed by his kinsmen. He is "unransomed, unredeemed" (*lam yufda*), or, as al-Sukkarī's recension has it, "unrequited" (*lam yujza*).[17] On the surface this diction refers metaphorically to Suᶜād's failure to return the poet's affections in kind; on a deeper level the literal usage suggests the treachery of kinsmen who have failed in their reciprocal obligations to him, which are, above all, to protect, to ransom, and to avenge.

In the description of the lost "felicity" that ensues, two aspects of the beloved are emphasized—first, in lines 2–5, her beauty, fertility, and purity, her glance like the antelope's, her flashing teeth that taste of the finest wine mixed with the cool limpid waters of rain-fed mountain streams. In lines 6–12, however, purity gives way to perfidy: beautiful as the promise of "felicity" may have been, it was ultimately a broken one. As in al-Nābighah's "O Abode of Mayyah" (chapter 1) with the introduction of Sulaymān, Lubad, and Zarqāʾ al-Yamāmah, here, too, the poem draws upon folkloric materials, a process that anchors the poem in deeper and broader layers of culture, even as it serves as vehicle and vessel to convey and preserve that culture. In line 8, Suᶜād's inconstancy is likened to that of the protean *ghūl.* In his *Lisān al-ᶜArab* (The Arab Tongue), the lexicographer Ibn Manẓūr (d. 711/1311–12) writes that "*ghūl,* pl. *ghīlān,* is a species of *shayṭān* or *jinn.* The Arabs claim that the *ghūl* appears to people in the desert and then transforms itself, that is, it changes into all sorts of different shapes; then it takes them away, that is, leads them astray and kills them."[18] In the classical Arabic literary lore, the *ghūl* appears most characteristically in the anecdotes of the pre-Islamic *ṣuʿlūk* (brigand) poet, Taʾabbaṭa Sharran, in which the Siren-like (female) *ghūl* assumes the form of a hideous and deformed Sphinx-like hybrid.[19]

Line 10 describes Suʿād's faithlessness with the proverbial phrase "the [false] promises of ʿUrqūb" (*mawāʿīdu ʿUrqūbin*). This proverb encapsulates the story of ʿUrqūb, which the philologist al-Maydānī (d. 518/1124) relates in his renowned collection of Arab proverbs (*Majmaʿ al-Amthāl*) as follows:

> According to Abū ʿUbayd, ʿUrqūb was one of the Amalikites (ʿAmālīq). One day, one of his brothers came to him importuning him, and ʿUrqūb replied, "When this date palm puts forth shoots, you can have them." When it put forth shoots and his brother came to claim what was promised him, ʿUrqūb said, "Leave them until they become green dates." When the dates were green, he said, "Wait till they are colored." When they were colored, he said, "Wait till they are ripe." When they were ripe, he said, "Wait till they are dry." When they dried, ʿUrqūb went out at night and gathered them and didn't give his brother anything. Thus ʿUrqūb became proverbial for breaking promises.[20]

Betrayed hopes and desires, deception and delusion complete the *nasīb*.

Given the Islamic context in which this qasida has come down to us, the closing lines of its *nasīb* are striking for two elements of diction that have an eminently Qurʾānic resonance. These are *abāṭīlū* ("empty prattle," rhyme word, line 10, from the root *b-ṭ-l* meaning false, vain, null, void), which occurs in the Qurʾān principally in the form *bāṭil* (false, falsehood, vanity, lie) in association with *kufr* (disbelief) and in opposition to *ḥaqq* (truth) and *niʿmat Allāh* (God's blessing) (Qurʾān 31:30; 22:62, etc.); and *taḍlīlū* ("delusion," rhyme word, line 12, from form II *ḍallala,* to lead astray, into error), which occurs most often in form I *ḍalla/yaḍillu* (to stray, err) and in association with *kufr* (unbelief), *shirk* (polytheism), and *ẓulm* (oppression, injustice) and in opposition to *hudā* (right guidance) (Qurʾān 41:1; 13:14; 34:24; 4:116; 19:38; 53:30, etc.). The effect of employing Qurʾānic diction is to point out the analogy between Qurʾānic and poetic discourse, to alert the audience to the poet's true intent. For in the poet's mind his kinsmen's failure to fulfill the obligations of Jāhilī *virtus* or manliness (*murūʾah*) reveals the bankruptcy, the ultimate falsehood and error, of the ancestral ways, and can be equated with the Qurʾānic *kufr* and *shirk* (unbelief and polytheism). Here we can invoke Gaster's seasonal pattern and consider that this elegiac prelude (*nasīb*) constitutes an expression of the Mortification phase, that is, when the seasonal breakup of the transhumant tribes marks the end of one "lease on life," and the "new lease" is not yet assured; at the same time the broken vow and unfulfilled promise mark the dissolution of the Jāhilī "social contract."

Most curious in this qasida, and yet what most confirms our reading, are the transitional lines from the elegiac prelude (*nasīb*) to the journey section (*raḥīl*) (lines 13–14). Whereas we normally find the poet eschewing the distant and unattainable mistress and declaring his intention to seek his fortune elsewhere, line 13 of Kaᶜb's poem states quite precisely that it is to regain "Suᶜād" that he undertakes the desert journey. This only makes sense, both poetically and politically, if we take this to mean a "a new Suᶜād," the "prosperity, good fortune, and felicity" of Islam.

The Journey Section (Raḥīl): *Lines 13–31.* The entire journey section of Kaᶜb's ode is devoted, not to the recounting of any particular journey, but to the description of that certain she-camel of line 13 that alone can reach the distant dwelling of Suᶜād. In the context of our reading, this ostensibly realistic and visual depiction of the physical and instinctual attributes of the poet's mount must be understood as ultimately referring to the poet's own resolve, his inner moral fortitude. For the poet's passage, the transition from the pagan *pietas* of the Jāhiliyyah to Islam, is primarily a spiritual, not a physical, journey. His camel mare is thus described as being "the best," "of noble breed and easy pace" (line 13), huge, indefatigable (line 14). The sense of aspiration (*himmah*), usually attributed to the poet himself at the end of the elegiac prelude or at the beginning of the journey section, appears in line 15 as an attribute of his mount. For *ᶜurḍah* (suited to, fit for) is taken by the commentators to mean *himmah* (ambition, aspiration, zeal).[21] "Fit" or "eager" for the unknown road whose way markers are obliterated then indicates an instinctive sense of direction or, as we would say, a "moral compass." Undaunted by the midday heat, her glance pierces the unknown (line 16).

Line 17 describes the she-camel in terms that define her domestication, for if she combines the attributes of wild animals—the gazelle's piercing glance (line 16), the onager's sturdiness (line 19)—these have been tamed to serve mankind: her neck is thus termed *muqallad* (form II passive participle as noun of place), the place-where-the-halter-goes (halter, *qilādah;* more precisely, what is hung about the neck of beasts being brought to Mecca for sacrifice, Lane, *q-l-d*); her pastern *muqayyad,* the place-where-the-shackle (*qayd*)-goes. The best qualities of the natural world have been harnessed to serve the cultural, or even sacrificial, one. The same idea is given voice in line 18, where the natural law of survival of the fittest is displaced by the cultural laws of animal husbandry. This camel mare is "in and inbred twice" (Sells's translation), so inbred that she was sired on her dam by her brother, and her maternal uncle is her paternal uncle too (line 18). Line 22 seems likewise to allude to nature serving culture: her tail is likened to a stripped palm branch, that is, a plant domesticated; her dry udder indicates perhaps first of all that she is barren, and such she-camels make sturdier mounts, but further that she serves to transport humans: she is not a milch camel, nor has she perpetuated her own species. By contrast it is her animal strength that is emphasized in line 25: her pads are so tough that even on the roughest ground they need no shoes (a preeminent symbol of "culture"). Most curious here is line 24. As a simple simile it is quite appropriate: so nimble is the she-camel's pace that her feet look as though they are about to touch the ground, but are raised again so quickly that it seems they never do—like an oath about to be fulfilled, then suddenly annulled. Read in the context of lines 6–12, however, it seems that what speeds the poet on his "journey" is the annulment or abrogation of the obsolete ethos of the Jāhiliyyah.

In all, the mixture of natural and cultural attributes amounts to an apt characterization of the she-camel as "betwixt and between" categories and classes: the most domesticated of the beasts, she is yet the most beastlike of the domesticated animals in physical power and strength of instincts. She thus embodies the "liminal" qualities of the poet/passenger himself who must make the transition from the law of the Banū Muzaynah to the law of Allāh's Messenger. Line 26 alludes, in the Lévi-Straussian language of "the raw and the cooked," to the purifying, purgative aspect of the liminal journey through a transubstantiation from living flesh to baked bread, from nature to culture. The effect of heat and hardship is to weed out the weak and unfit; the strong survive, but transformed and reborn. The raw (= nature) chameleon scorched by the sun is metaphorically metamorphosed into the cooked (= culture) (*mamlūl* refers to bread or meat baked in embers or on heated rocks).

The final passage of the journey section (lines 27–31) consists of an unusual simile which likens the relentless motion of the she-camel's forelegs in the hottest part of the day—when camel caravans normally stop to rest, when locusts, lest they burn their feet, kick aside the scorching pebbles to find cooler ground—to that of the bereaved mother's arms as she frantically tears at her clothes. The more common simile in the journey section of the qasida is, as for example in a pre-Islamic ode such as the *Muʿallaqah* (Suspended Ode) of Labīd,[22] the likening of the she-camel to the oryx doe whose calf the wolves have killed. The pathos of Labīd's simile is here replaced by an image of grief and loss that is at once instinctual and ritual: the mythic dementia of the Middle Eastern female lamentation. This culturally conditioned hysteria triggered by loss and despair endows the female mourners with the strength to shred their clothes with their bare hands, to tear their hair and scratch their faces. It is precisely the "unnatural" strength that the ritual dementia of female mourning unleashes that is likened to the unflagging energy of the she-camel. It is ultimately the poet's own relentless drive, spurred on by the bereavement of the elegiac prelude, that is implicit in this simile and explicitly expressed in the coming lines (32–33). As is evident from the diction of line 29, what is being mourned is, above all, the failure of fertility, here of the human rather than cereal reproductive cycle. The bereft woman is "middle-aged" (*naṣaf*), which implies that she is no longer of (prime) childbearing age—the smaller cycle failed—and (line 30) her firstborn is dead—the larger cycle failed, too. Her sister mourners are likewise "near barren" (*nukd*) and "bereft" (*mathākīl*).

Then, too, given the anecdotal context and the poetic text itself, the implied "death and rebirth" pattern that is expressed in the perilous liminal journey of the rite-of-passage pattern, as well as the Mortification-Invigoration movement of Gaster's seasonal pattern, this description suggests the poet's vision of his own mother and womenfolk mourning his death.[23] In this respect it adds to the sense that the poet is in mortal danger and risks his life in approaching the Prophet of Islam.

The ritual wail or lament for the dead youth is well known in the ancient Near East. Gaster relates the practice of howling and lamenting at seasonal ceremonies of Mortification. Among the many instances attested among ancient civilizations he mentions the Egyptian laments for Isis at the first harvesting of grain, the lamentations for Osiris, the ritual dirges of Demeter and Kore among the Greeks, those for Attis in Asia Minor and Adonis in Syria; and likewise the mention in *Gilgamesh* of the annual weeping for Tammuz, the lord of fertility. Gaster argues, however, that the ritual weeping is a homeopathic method of producing rain, and may not originally have been an expression of mourning at all.[24] He concludes:

> If these arguments are correct, the practices of howling and wailing at seasonal ceremonies need not be interpreted as acts of mourning, but rather as mere expressions of excitement or as functional procedures designed to promote fertility through the magical properties of tears. In the

> latter case, they would fall into the category of rites of Invigoration rather than of Mortification. This is not to deny that a certain element of mourning must always have been present.[25]

The point with regard to the poem at hand is that, coming as it does at the end of the journey section, the lamentation simile has the effect of simultaneously mourning what has been lost and reviving it, as though through that very mourning—for it is essentially, as it operates here, an image both of loss (Mortification) and, inasmuch as it describes the vigor of the she-camel, of Invigoration. In the same way, it expresses the symbolic "death" of the poet as the necessary precursor to his salvation and "rebirth." At line 32 there occurs a sudden break in subject and style. The poet abruptly shifts from the lexically rich and metaphorically dense poetic metalanguage that has characterized the elegiac prelude and the journey section to a stripped-down, univocal, apparently "prosaic" narrative discourse, as he describes his calumniators on either side of his she-camel who declare that he is "as good as dead" (*maqtūl*). This sudden change of tone also signals a transition to the third structural section of the ode.

The Praise Section (Madīḥ): *Lines 33/34–55.* This abrupt change in style that began in line 32 is the same as that we observed in our discussion of lines 37–43 of al-Nābighah's "O Abode of Mayyah" in chapter 1. In Kaᶜb's ode, this "prosaic" style dominates the entire midsection of the qasida, from lines 32–42, until, at line 43, the poet re-immerses himself in the poetic metalanguage of allusion and metaphor. It is the apparent "simplicity" of this section that gives it its power; its striking effect is due precisely to its contrast to the "poeticity"—the richness of specifically poetic diction, the allusiveness, the multivalence—of the traditional elegiac prelude and journey section that precede it. But its very simplicity is, of course, nothing but a poetic conceit. It is not really "prosaic" at all, but a subtle rhetorical construct. If we keep in mind that the anecdotes that accompany this poem have no provable factual or historical basis, it does not seem unlikely in this case that they are derived from the qasida itself. Kaᶜb ibn Zuhayr's conversion is, most probably, his own literary construct—a poetic construct so convincingly realistic that it generated the "historical" construct. In other words, the anecdotes cited above that traditionally accompany the poem in the literary sources are not the record of actual events, but most likely a narrative fleshing-out of the semantic crux of the poem, which has then been prefaced to the qasida by way of commentary.

My argument, then, is that this passage (lines 32–41) is not necessarily any more factual or historical than any other passage in the poem, but, rather, that it is a meticulously crafted literary construct whose historicity may well be a conceit. Kaᶜb ibn Zuhayr's conversion may well be his own creation. It is, in fact, precisely structured according to the ritual paradigm of sacrifice and redemption, and is as rigidly ritually controlled as the elegiac prelude and the journey section. Furthermore, this passage is far more rhetorically and semantically complex than a first "prosaic" reading suggests. The first part (lines 32–36) forms the structural and semantic core of the entire qasida and is therefore the key to reading the entire poem. This section is set off not only by the abrupt change in style (diction, etc.) that occurs between lines 31 and 32, but also by the maintenance of the form I passive participial form (*mafᶜūl*) as the rhyme word throughout the five lines. The effect of this morphological repetition is especially emphatic because the penultimate rhyming vowel is interchangeably *ī* or *ū* and is apparently randomly varied throughout the poem, except in this passage. Here the rhyme functions semantically as well as acoustically, for it brackets the conversion that generated the entire qasida from *maqtūl* (slain) in line 32 to *maʾmūl* (hoped for) in line 36; from death to hope. The transition from lost hope (line 33, cf. also lines 11–12) to hope renewed, from death—as portrayed in the bereft-woman simile and the denunciation of Kaᶜb's calumniators (lines 29–32)—to rebirth, points once again in the direction of the ritual form and antecedents of Kaᶜb's qasida, and also to its ultimate intent. Referring to two formulations of ritual patterns, the rite of passage, or initiation, and the seasonal pattern, Gaster remarks:

> The connection between Initiation and Invigoration is brought out especially by the fact that the former is frequently identified with *rebirth*. The most obvious illustration of this lies, of course, in the very word "neophyte" (lit., "newly implanted") by which initiants are commonly known, as well as ideas of regeneration (and even immortality) which are invariably associated with admission to the mysteries in ancient cults. Thus, in the mysteries of Attis, the candidate was looked upon as "one about to die"; when he had performed the required rites, he emerged to a new life.[26]

The poet begins by claiming that he was falsely accused; it is his calumniators that would see him dead (line 32). He then presents himself before the Prophet as a helpless supplicant, betrayed by friends in whom he had put his hope and trust (line 33). In both lines the poet is portrayed as passive victim: he hopes—"in whom I put my hope" (*āmuluhū*) (active)—but is rebuffed. This is in contrast to lines 34–35, in which the forceful active voice of line 34, "So I replied (*fa-qultu*), 'Out of my way . . . !'" makes it clear that the poet has some hand in his own salvation—i.e., that he is in some sense worthy. But—and this is the essence of "Islam"—the poet's forceful act is to submit to God's will, to admit his own mortality. Moreover, he must be willing to sacrifice his own life, and this is precisely the intention of line 34: that he will face possible death and leave the outcome in God's hands. It is this "sacrifice" that is the necessary requirement for the poet's redemption. To put it more clearly, the "drama" of Kaᶜb's "submission" (*islām*/Islam), and its moral value as well, requires that he face the risk of death to do it. This, as pointed out above, is made abundantly, if prosaically, clear in the anecdotal passage cited above by the attack of the Anṣārī zealot. Without this element of risk, of putting his life in God's hands, Kaᶜb's conversion would have been mere opportunism. The poet does make some attempt to positively dispose the Almighty when, in line 34, he chooses of the ninety-nine names of God "al-Raḥmān" (the Merciful).

The poet's act of submission (*islām*) is expressed with masterful concision in line 36: *unbiʾtu anna rasūla Llāhi awᶜadanī / wa-l-ᶜafwu ᶜinda rasūli Llāhi maʾmūlū* (I was told God's Messenger / had threatened me / But from God's Messenger / pardon is hoped). The first hemistich expresses Muḥammad's power; the second Kaᶜb's submission to it. Line 36 thus functions, as did lines 41–43 in al-Nābighah's qasida, as a statement of supplication, self-abasement, and declaration of allegiance. It also shares its stylistic characteristics: simplicity of diction combined with rhetorical complexity. In Kaᶜb's line this takes the form of antithesis imbedded in chiastic (*abba*) structuring. The chiasmus proceeds from a passive configuration of soft consonants *n, b, n,* then "Rasūl Allāh" (Messenger of God), to climax with the harsher and active *w, ᶜ, d* of the threat; its antithesis, pardon, also in *ᶜ, w, d,* begins the countermovement, followed by another "Rasūl Allāh," and the chiasmus then concludes as it opened with the passive in the soft liquids *m* and *l.* "Islam" as willing self-effacement is conveyed through the use of the passive voice. Whereas in line 33 the poet says, "I hope" (*āmulu*) in the first-person active, in line 36, when confronting the Messenger of God, the poet hardly dares to hope, but employs instead the passive participle *maʾmūl* (to be hoped for). "I was informed that the Messenger of God had threatened me" (*unbiʾtu . . . awᶜadanī*)—the poet is passive subject (*nāʾib fāᶜil*) and direct object, but no longer actor or agent.

Through the parallel placement of Rasūl Allāh (Messenger of God) in the middle of each hemistich this line expresses both recognition and submission. The rhetorical power of this repetition is all the more striking in that no mention has been made of Muḥammad up until now. The way was perhaps prepared by the mention of the All-Merciful in line 34, but it is only with line 36 that the poet's profession of the Islamic faith (the ***shahādah,*** or creed, formulated in the expression "I testify that there is no god but God and that Muḥammad is the Messenger of God" / ***ashhadu an lā ilāha illā Llāh wa-anna Muḥammadan rasūlu Llāh***) is completed. The religious message, the essence of Islamic faith, is also stated here: God, as represented by His Messenger, threatens perdition—an expression of might—but at the same time is capable of pardon and forgiveness. It is the submission to this divine power and authority and the hope for His mercy that constitutes Islam. Line 36 is thus rhetorically, acoustically, and semantically the crux of the qasida.

Returning to the original hypothesis of this chapter, it is evident that this core passage of Kaᶜb's qasida, inasmuch as it offers a concise statement of the ritual paradigm that informs the whole work, is, like Mauss's "ritual exchange," a total social phenomenon (see chapter 6). Simultaneous expression is given to all kinds of institutions: the poet redeems himself (economic), he swears his fealty to the new order (sociopolitical), he recognizes God's Messenger and submits to Islam (religious, moral) through a qasida whose power, value, and durability are functions of its artistry (aesthetic). The mythological aspect is expressed in the mythic or ritual pattern of death and rebirth (***maqtūl → maʾmūl***); its mythogenic aspect, as will be discussed further on, in its creation of the conversion of Kaᶜb ibn Zuhayr as a mythos of the transition of Arab society from the Jāhiliyyah to Islam.

The tension of the climax of line 36 is broken in line 37 by its opening word ***mahlan*** ("Go easy") and equally by a relaxation of the rhetorical intensity and the alteration of the rhyme from the fivefold repetition of the form ***mafᶜūl*** to a ***tafᶜīl*** (***tafṣīlū***), after which an apparently random morphological variation in the rhyme word sets in. The poet exhorts the Prophet not to act rashly, but to follow the guidance of God and the Qurʾān. At this point the near identity of key phrases in lines 36–37 of Kaᶜb's poem and lines 41–42 of al-Nābighah's alert us to the fact that we are dealing not merely with poetic influence (allusion or intertextuality), but also with explicit elements of established ritual and ceremony. Thus we find the pattern or formula ***unbiʾtu anna . . . awᶜadanī . . . Mahlan . . .*** " in al-Nābighah:

> *I've been told* that Abū Qābūs *has threatened me,*
> And no one can withstand the lion when it roars.
>
> *Go easy*! May the tribes, all of them, be your ransom,
> And all my increase both of herds and progeny!

And in Kaᶜb:

I was told God's Messenger *had threatened me,*
But from God's Messenger pardon is hoped.

Go easy, and let Him be your guide who gave to you
The gift of the Qurʾān in which are warnings and discernment!

The repetition of this formula reveals two interrelated aspects of the qasida-as-ritual. On the literary side, the allusion to a renowned masterpiece creates a mythic concordance between the supplicant/supplicated pairs—al-Nābighah / King al-Nuᶜmān and Kaᶜb / the Prophet Muḥammad. The effect of this is to confer poetic authority on Kaᶜb and moral-political authority on Muḥammad (see chapter 3). On the ritual side these flagged terms signal a specific step in the ritual of supplication and submission. Thus we witness in this qasida the Islamic cooptation of Jāhilī ritual and ceremonial forms to buttress the authority of the Prophet and the nascent Islamic state by identifying them with the authoritative models of the past.

Lines 38–41 constitute a reiteration of the ritual pattern of the poet's conversion (*islām*). The message is bracketed in rhyme words from the same root (*q-w-l,* to speak), each made more emphatic by *tajnīs* (paronomasia, verbal play on words of the same or related roots) within the line: *aqwāl* and *aqāwīl* in line 38 refer to the fabrications and false accusations of the poet's calumniators; in line 41 *qīluhu l-qīlū* refers to the veracity and authority of the Prophet's speech, his power and intention to turn words into actions. The direction of the passage is thus from falsehood to truth. The terror and danger of the transition is expressed in the "fear and trembling" of the poet, or pachyderm, before God's Messenger (lines 39–40). The point here is that the *mamdūḥ* (recipient of the panegyric), Muḥammad, has power over life and death, and only by his granting Kaᶜb protection does the poet's fear abate. Line 40 reiterates in "quake with fear . . . granted [protection]" (*yurᶜadu . . . tanwīlū*), the same antithesis as line 36 between the threat of punishment and hope for forgiveness. We can draw yet another comparison between al-Nābighah's qasida and Kaᶜb's: the wrongdoer/supplicant does not confess and beg forgiveness, but rather, he claims to be the victim of calumniators and slanderers and begs for mercy (chapter 1, al-Nābighah, "O Abode of Mayyah," lines 39–40; Kaᶜb, line 38). The apparent dramatic and narrative realism of these passages in both al-Nābighah's and Kaᶜb's qasidas is revealed by such parallel constructions to be instead the reenactment of an established ritual or ceremony.

The closing line of this passage, line 41, is, like line 36, an expression of submission to (divine) authority. As for the meaning of the poet's placing his hand in that of the Prophet without contending (*waḍaᶜtu yamīnī lā unāziᶜuhū fī kaffi* . . .), al-Sukkarī explains in his commentary: "That is, 'I placed my right hand in his by way of submission, not contention.' I.e., he surrendered himself to him and acknowledged him. For the Arabs, when they swore an oath to something, would strike each other on the right hand."[27] The intent of "exacting vengeance" (*dhī naqimātin*) (*naqimah* = vengeance, penal retribution, punishment, Lane, *n-q-m*) is to indicate that Muḥammad is a man to be feared.

This entire passage (lines 32–41) must be read in light of lines 6–11 of the elegiac prelude. For in the latter the Emptying phase of Gaster's seasonal pattern is expressed as the failure or breakdown of trust, the abrogation of the Jāhilī social contract: mendacity, inconstancy, perfidy, the failure to fulfill promises. Of special interest here is the antithesis between "her promises were nothing except empty prattle" (*mā mawāᶜīduhā illā l-abāṭīlū*) of line 10 and "his word the word" (*qīluhu l-qīlū*), i.e., who keeps his word, whose word is law, of line 41; failed hope as opposed to hope fulfilled; the seduction and misguidance (*taḍlīl*) of misplaced trust in line 12 as opposed to the right guidance (*hadā*, to guide aright), exhortation, and the discernment of right from wrong (*tafṣīl*) (line 37). The section from line 32 to 41 thus constitutes a ritual kernel whose form is the key to that of the qasida as a whole and whose conclusions thus provide the fulfillment of the elegiac prelude. The movement from Emptying to Filling is expressed in a variety of ways, but especially in the movement from unfulfilled promise to fulfilled promise, and—in the most Qurʾānic of terms—from misguidance (*taḍlīl*) to right guidance (*hudā*). The effect of this is to identify the "falsehood" of Suᶜād in the elegiac prelude with the falsehood of the poet's slanderers and calumniators. At the same time, the Filling phase of this section creates a bridge to its fuller development in the final passages of the poem.

In the following passage (lines 42–47) the subject is the fear engendered by the Messenger of God, the ritual function is that of Invigoration, and the means chosen to convey this is a simile comparing the Prophet to a lion that feeds its cubs on human flesh. The fear of the temporal judgment of Muḥammad when Kaᶜb revealed himself and his identity and had to answer for his deeds (line 42) was bound to generate an "Islamic" reading, as indeed we find cited in al-Tibrīzī's commentary.[28] For both temporal and divine judgment are involved here, both the mortal and the immortal soul. The simile is introduced in an elative phrase, "He is more dreaded" (*la-dhāka ahyabu*), that serves as a pivot point for the poet to modulate from the "prosaic" style of the poem's semantic core via the simile back into the imagery and diction of the poetic world.

The description of the warrior, by metaphor or simile, as a lion is a traditional one. The effect of the elative here is rhetorically to magnify the Prophet and the fear he inspires. In terms of the present argument, this has the effect of intensifying both sides of the fear/hope equation. For the value of a man's mercy is directly commensurate with the power of his wrath: the mercy or pardon of a weakling is worthless. We might, begging the pardon of the Muʿtazilites, term this the principle of "the promise and the threat" (*al-waʿd wa-l-waʿīd*). This principle might also explain much about the Meccan suras of the Qurʾān with their horrific descriptions of the coming of the Day of Judgment. Unless Muḥammad could inspire in his fellow Arabs the dread of divine chastisement, he could not induce them to seek divine mercy. Moreover, it must be kept in mind that the dominant image of Invigoration in Kaʿb's poem—the lion that feeds flesh to its cubs—is simply a metaphorical variant of the more common expression of Invigoration in the poetry of the warrior aristocracy, that of the warrior revitalizing his kin group by slaying the enemy.[29] The diction of line 44, *ʿayshuhumā laḥmun* (literally, "their life is meat"), is to be taken on an ultraliteral level as an expression of blood sacrifice and redemption, of Invigoration.[30]

A change from the object to the subject of the simile occurs in line 45 in the change from the bestial to the martial. Line 46 appears to shift back to the lion, describing the terror, both instinctual and rational, that both beast (the onager) and man feel for the formidable lion. But the barrier between the subject and the object of the simile is becoming more and more attenuated. In the context of the qasida the ravaged corpse of line 47 suggests what the poet's own fate might have been had he contended with Muḥammad rather than converted.

The closing passage of the poem (lines 48–55) opens with a final martial metaphor that depicts the Prophet as a sword of God, an image that would later achieve great popularity in Islamic military and caliphal panegyric. Lines 48–50 constitute a semantic core of the poem much as do lines 32–36 and display the rhetorical features that we have come to associate with such sections. In line 48 we find the description of the Prophet as the sword of God structured in very simple, straightforward diction in chiastic (*abba*) form—*inna r-rasūla la-sayfun yustaḍāʾu bihī / muhannadun min suyūfi Llāhi maslūlū*—to reiterate the Islamic message of right guidance and divine might. This leads into a description of the Emigrants (Muhājirūn), Muḥammad's early Meccan supporters who emigrated with him from Mecca to Medina. This migration, the Hijrah, is presented here as a spiritual one, for these, at least in Kaᶜb's view, are the true core of Muḥammad's followers. The "passage" that they make is thus identified with "Islam" itself. Four words from lines 49–50, ***aslamū zūlū / zālū fa-mā zāla*** (whose spokesman [Muḥammad?] said when ***they submitted to Islam, "Depart!" / They departed,*** but the weaklings ***did not depart***), constitute a remarkably concise definition of Islam and, at the same time, a separation of the wheat from the chaff: those who obey the Prophet's command are Muslims and heroes; those who do not are "damned" cowards. The Hijrah, too, thus functions as a "passage" from the Jāhiliyyah to Islam, and, as in all such rites, only the morally and physically fit complete the passage.

In the ensuing description of the Emigrants that closes the poem (lines 51–55), the poet once more re-immerses himself in the diction and imagery of the classical qasida. The Emigrants form an elite of proud high-nosed warriors, clad in chain mail of David's weave (lines 51–52). In line 53 the Emigrants in their battle ranks are described as a troop of majestic white camels that are kept in line by the stick, whereas the scrawny black ones, traditionally said to refer to the Medinese Helpers (Anṣār) of the Prophet, "stray from the road" (***ᶜarrada***), i.e., flee the battlefield.[31] Despite the apparent Jāhilī imagery and diction, the image inevitably alludes to the antithesis in the opening sura (Sūrat al-Fātiḥah) of the Qurʾān (1:7) between those that God blesses and guides on "the straight path" (***al-ṣirāṭ al-mustaqīm***) and the misguided (***al-ḍāllīn***) with whom He is angry. Finally, Kaᶜb ibn Zuhayr seals his qasida with two lines of praise for the Muhājirūn that are as purely Jāhilī as those that opened it. Both closing lines combine antithesis with litotes to express, in the understated tone of the negative, the equanimity of the hero in battle, and in death. They neither gloat when they strike the enemy nor panic when they are struck (line 54); they never turn tail and flee, so they are not struck except in the throat; they wade bravely into the perils of battle (line 55). And yet, however purely Jāhilī in diction and imagery, the Islamic context has utterly transformed the meaning of the closing line. To drink from "death's water troughs" (***ḥiyāḍi l-mawti***) in pre-Islamic times expressed Devitalization or Mortification, most often of the enemy. But for the Muhājirūn, as for any Muslim, death in battle "in the way of God" (***fī sabīl Allāh***) is an act of self-sacrifice and martyrdom that guarantees salvation and life everlasting. That is, in terms of the ritual patterns herein employed, the death of a martyr constitutes Revitalization and Invigoration.

The significance of this closing passage will become clearer in comparison with later qasidas discussed in this book. At present, in light of our understanding of Kaᶜb's political position within his newly adopted religious community, we should keep in mind that one of the roles of the ritual patterns that we have discussed is the restoration or restructuring of a legitimate social structure, starting from the top down. The first goal of the panegyric then is to negotiate the relation—the relative rank and status—between the poet and the patron. This is done through the ceremony of submission and praise and the ritual exchange of qasida and prize. The prize or counter-gift is thus an expression of the patron's estimation not only of the poem, but of the poet. The poet, from his side, uses the praise section (*madīḥ*) in the first place to express the legitimacy and authority of the patron within the social hierarchy. Often, as in this poem and others we will see in subsequent chapters, the poet also attempts to promote his own vision of the political hierarchy and to negotiate his rank vis-à-vis others in the polity. Here, if we keep in mind that it was one of the Medinese Helpers (Anṣār) who attempted to kill Kaᶜb when he first identified himself to the Prophet, it becomes apparent that the poet, having established the position of the Prophet at the head of the community, is expressing his support for another political faction, that is, the Emigrants (Muhājirūn) who accompanied the Prophet from Mecca. He thus identifies them as the true core of the Islamic community, as being, like the Prophet, of the Meccan tribal aristocracy of the Banū Quraysh, and as found "tried and true" to the Prophet and Islam by the test of the Hijrah. Thus, through the comparison of the Emigrants and the Helpers, respectively, with noble-bred white camels that walk in a line and ill-bred scrawny black camels that go astray, Kaᶜb depicts the Meccan Emigrants as nobler, both genealogically and morally, than the Medinese Helpers.

Returning to the critical premises upon which our analysis was based, we can begin to draw together the various aspects of the poem. First of all, in terms of ritual exchange, we find in Kaᶜ b's poem a "total social movement" in which multiple institutions find simultaneous expression. The institution of redemption itself is an economic, legal, and sociomorphic one. Through the payment—in Kaᶜb's case, of the qasida—the outlawed poet is admitted as a legal member of society, the legally "dead" Kaᶜb is "alive" to society once more and assumes all the rights and obligations entailed in that membership. This in and of itself indicates the poem's function in a rite of passage in which the ritual passenger changes from one social status to another and, in particular, a rite of incorporation whereby, just as in the case of al-Nābighah (chapter 1), the outlaw comes as a supplicant and is integrated into society. In addition, the poet puts forth his vision of the proper political structure of the polity—the sociomorphic aspect of the qasida. In Kaᶜb's poem, with the addition of the Islamic element, the residual mythic aspects of sacred kingship already apparent in al-Nābighah's qasida are reactivated; the poem takes on a moral and religious aspect. The transfer of allegiance is not from one bedouin liege lord to another (the Ghassānids to the Lakhmids), but from the poet's natal tribal society to a radically new social order, from the Jāhiliyyah to Islam. It is not merely Kaᶜb's mortal life that is redeemed, but also his immortal soul. It is at this point that the poesis becomes mythopoesis, and—insofar as this poem appears to have generated its prose anecdotes and in doing so to have made the conversion of Kaᶜb ibn Zuhayr paradigmatic for all Muslims—mythogenesis.

At this point, too, Kaᶜb's poetic pedigree enters the picture. Kaᶜb was the scion of one of the premier poetic families of the Jāhiliyyah: his father, Zuhayr ibn Abī Sulmā, was one of the most celebrated poets of the pre-Islamic era; Zuhayr's father was a poet, as were his maternal uncle, Bashāmah; his stepfather, Aws ibn Ḥajar; and his sisters, Salmā and al-Khansāʾ.[32] Kaᶜb's redemption by means of a qasida therefore represents as well the redemption of the Jāhilī poetic tradition in Islam. His composing of an "Islamic" qasida so fully in the tradition of the Jāhiliyyah has the effect of rendering the pre-Islamic "pagan" qasida not anti-Islamic but proto-Islamic. It is thus especially appropriate that he is the son of Zuhayr, who was renowned for the celebration of the virtues of peace, and in whose *Muᶜallaqah* (Suspended Ode) is found the mention of Allāh and of the Day of Reckoning (*yawm al-ḥisāb*).[33] This certainly must be the intent of the story of the testament of Zuhayr ibn Abī Sulmā to his sons Kaᶜb and Bujayr:

> It is related that Zuhayr saw in his sleep a rope that hung down from heaven to the earth and people were holding on to it. But every time he tried to grab hold of it, it would recede from him. He interpreted this to mean that a prophet would come at the end of time and would be an mediator between God Almighty and mankind, but that his own life span would not reach the time of [the prophet's] mission. So in his dying words to his sons he bade them to believe in [this prophet] when he appeared.[34]

The ritual patterns that have informed our discussion of qasida—the rite of passage with its Separation, Liminality, and Aggregation phases and the seasonal pattern with its Emptying (Mortification and Purgation) and Filling (Invigoration and Jubilation) sequence—are expressions of the psychosocial mechanisms for personal and societal transition. In this respect, the qasida as a literary form can be viewed as a culture-specific manifestation of a universal human, individual and corporate, process. The qasida thus is able to impose form and meaning on changing human and societal relationships and, by explaining and directing change, exert control over it. The ritual structure of the qasida allows for a multivalent layering of meaning and hence enables the poem to give simultaneous expression to a variety of institutions. Thus, as embodied in the elegiac prelude-journey-praise (*nasīb-raḥīl-madīḥ*) form of the classical qasida, the ritual structure gives expression first to Kaᶜb ibn Zuhayr's political conversion from his tribe to Muḥammad, in terms analogous to al-Nābighah's reincorporation into the Lakhmid court; then to the religious conversion of Kaᶜb from the ancestral religion of the Banū Muzaynah to Islam; this in turn becomes paradigmatic of the conversion of Arab society from the Jāhiliyyah to Islam and, further, of the subjugation of the pre-Islamic poetic tradition to Islam.

If the theory of ritual exchange explains how and why the qasida was composed, the ritual pattern explains why it was preserved and repeated. Walter Burkert's remarks on ritual will provide some insight here:

> Since the work of Sir Julian Huxley and Konrad Lorenz, biology has defined *ritual* as a behavioural pattern that has lost its primary function—present in its unritualized model—but which persists in a new function, that of communication. . . . [T]his communicating function reveals the two basic characteristics of ritual behaviour, namely repetition and theatrical exaggeration. For the essentially immutable patterns do not transmit differentiated and complex material information but, rather, just one piece of information each. This single piece of information is considered so important that it is reinforced by constant repetition so as to avoid misunderstanding or misuse. The fact of understanding is thus more important than what is understood. Above all, then, ritual creates and affirms social interaction.[35]

If the primary function, or occasional purpose, of Kaᶜb's poetic supplication is to redeem the poet, to save his mortal skin and immortal soul, its new ritual function is then to convey that single most vital piece of information in the Islamic culture that preserved and ritualized it, that is, the Islamic message of spiritual redemption and salvation. Just as the ritual of royalty in al-Nābighah's poem is reenacted to ensure and reaffirm the authority and legitimacy of Arab kingship, so the recitation of Kaᶜb ibn Zuhayr's qasida serves as a reaffirmation of Islamic faith. Furthermore, Burkert's remarks on repetition in ritual, especially when coupled with the phenomenon of redundancy that is characteristic of orally transmitted poetry, go far in explaining the numerous reiterations of the ritual pattern *within* the qasida—first in the overall structure, then in the series of shorter repetitions (lines 32–36, 37–42, 44, 49–51, 53)—and through a variety of metaphors. That is, the internal repetition of the ritual pattern functions to ensure that even if parts of the text are lost, corrupted, or misunderstood, the qasida's vital message of sacrifice and redemption will not be lost.

Proceeding from poetics to mythopoesis, we should take notice of the mythogenic capabilities of the Arabic qasida, a generative power of the poem itself which Kaᶜb's "Suᶜād Has Departed" exemplifies. Given what current theory tells us about the preservation of "texts" in societies of primary orality, that is, the relatively greater stability of poetry over prose,[36] we must assume that Kaᶜb's qasida is more "authentic" than the prose anecdotes (***akhbār***) associated with it. Furthermore, internal evidence (lines 32–36) suggests that the qasida may be the source of the anecdotes about the conversion of Kaᶜb and his brother Bujayr that were discussed in the first part of this chapter. That is, the apparently discursive section (lines 32–41) that we have termed the "semantic core" of the poem generated a prose narrative, equally ritual in structure, that was prefixed to the poem to function as a sort of commentary that directs the reader/listener to interpret the poem as an Islamic one. In other words, the anecdotal narratives make explicit the message of sacrifice and redemption that is implicit in the poem (a sort of prosification of verse [*ḥall al-manẓūm*]). The anecdotes must thus be understood primarily as literary constructs, as prose narrative restatements of the poetic "message." Their function is therefore reiterative—an external redundancy to reinforce the internal redundancy of the ritual and oral qasida—and exegetical.

From Mythopoesis to Mythogenesis: The Donation of the Mantle

No discussion of Kaᶜb ibn Zuhayr's "Suᶜād Has Departed" would be complete without the mention of the anecdote about the mantle (***burdah***) of the Prophet, so closely associated with this qasida that it is commonly referred to as the Mantle Ode (*Qaṣīdat al-Burdah*). The story goes that when Kaᶜb recited this ode to the Prophet Muḥammad, he conferred upon the poet a mantle, which, it is said, was later purchased by the Umayyad caliph Muᶜāwiyah from Kaᶜb's heirs for 20,000 dirhams and worn by the caliphs on feast days.[37] Despite its popularity, the "authenticity" of this anecdote has been considered suspect, for, unlike the rest of the anecdotes concerning the poem that appear in Ibn Hishām's/Ibn Isḥāq's Life of the Prophet (***Sīrah***), this one has no such authority and pedigree.[38] This, however, is only a problem if by "authenticity" we mean "historicity" and, furthermore, our discussion thus far has discounted the historicity even of those anecdotes traditionally considered authoritative. What concerns us is rather the meaning of the story as a literary construct.

The donation of the mantle must be understood above all in the context of the conferring of a symbolic gift, that is, as part of a ritual exchange. In this light it functions in two ways. First, as Karl Brockelmann and Georg Jacob noted, the conferring of a robe of honor (*ḥullah*) upon poets as a reward for their verse was a well-established custom among the Arabs.[39] In the Arabic literary context, to have one's poetry rewarded with a royal robe of honor was, as the Umayyad poet al-Farazdaq (d. 110/728) attests in a line about the renowned pre-Islamic poet ʿAlqamah, a distinction tantamount to having one's verse immortalized in the hearts or on the tongues of the people:

The Stallion ʿAlqamah upon whom
kings' robes were bestowed
Was proverbial among the people
for his words.[40] [12]

In the context of this study, we must understand the donation of the mantle above all as an act of ritual exchange: the qasida functions as a symbolic gift in a ritual of allegiance or fealty, and the robe or mantle then functions as the symbolic countergift. In such rituals of allegiance as al-Nābighah's "O Abode of Mayyah," the supplicant offers his life or something of himself to the ruler, and the ruler, in accepting his allegiance, grants him his protection and virtually confers life, or new life, upon his vassal. The gift and counter-gift of the fealty ritual, especially when we keep in mind Mauss's remark that the gift contains something of the giver or the soul of the giver (see below), embody the essence of fealty: that each owes the other his life, that each will protect the other with his life. The mantle thus symbolizes the Prophet's protection and, inasmuch as the garment is a symbol of the soul, the gift of immortal life. The robe or mantle functions likewise as a symbol of legitimacy.[41] Rudi Paret, giving the biblical example of the miraculous mantle of the Prophet Elijah (II Kings 2:13–15), thus quite correctly explains the interest of the Umayyad—and, we might add, ʿAbbāsid—caliphs in obtaining and retaining this relic.[42]

The symbolic function of the mantle conferred upon the poet "saved" by Islam becomes all the more clear when contrasted with the function of garments in the story of the most celebrated Jāhilī poet, whom the Prophet is said to have condemned as "the leader of the poets into hellfire,"[43] Imruʾ al-Qays. Unable to find supporters among the Arabs to aid him in his quest for extravagant vengeance for his slain royal father, Imruʾ al-Qays abandons his suits of ancestral armor (hereditary legitimacy) and seeks support from the Byzantines. When a slanderer at Caesar's court informs the emperor that

Imruʾ al-Qays is having an illicit liaison with his daughter, Caesar, who had sent the Arab prince forth with an army, sends him an embroidered robe interwoven with gold, but also "laced" with poison. The overjoyed prince no sooner dons the robe than his skin breaks out in sores and sloughs off, and he dies.[44] If his ancestral armor symbolizes hereditary legitimacy, then surely the lethal foreign robe of honor symbolizes illegitimacy. Moreover, if the Byzantine Christian robe brings perdition to the renegade Arab who dons it (surely the true sense of Imruʾ al-Qays's sobriquet "the Errant/ Erring King [*al-malik al-ḍillīl*]),[45] then the mantle of the Prophet must confer salvation. If Kaʿb, as the scion of Zuhayr ibn Abī Sulmā, represents that aspect of the Jāhiliyyah that was proto-Islamic, Imruʾ al-Qays is perceived as the embodiment of all that was anti-Islamic.

For Kaʿb, then, the mantle was not, as Paret would have it, merely a sign of recognition of his poetic achievement, but a sign of the legitimacy of poetry under Islam. Thus, I would maintain, the submission (*islām*) of the poet to the prophet became paradigmatic of the submission of the poetic to the prophetic in Islamic culture. And just as the poet had to submit to be saved, so too did the poetic tradition.

Finally, our evaluation of the ritual exchange of qasida for mantle must consider the basis for equating these two symbolic and ceremonial currencies. In the case of Kaʿb ibn Zuhayr and the Prophet Muḥammad, what is exchanged are symbols of immortality, one poetic, the other prophetic. This concept was noted by Mauss in his discussion of the archaic exchange:

> We can see the nature of the bond created by the transfer of a possession. . . . [I]t is clear that . . . this bond created by things is in fact a bond between persons, since the thing is a person or pertains to a person. . . . It follows clearly from what we have seen that in this system of ideas one gives away what is in reality a part of one's own nature and substance, while to receive something is to receive part of someone's spiritual essence.[46]

I believe we will have a much better grasp of the nature of the Arabic panegyric ode and the gift or prize (*jāʾizah*) that is traditionally conferred on the poet in return if we consider them in light of Mauss's further remarks concerning "the power of objects of exchange": "Each of these precious things has, moreover, a productive capacity within it. Each, as well as being a sign and surety of life, is also a sign and surety of wealth, a magico-religious guarantee of rank and prosperity."[47]

We must finally recognize that the panegyric ode was understood to confer immortal renown on both the poet and the patron, the subject of its praise (*mamdūḥ*), and that its worth to the patron was thus commensurate with its aesthetic worth, which was the sole guarantee of its preservation and thus his immortal renown. In this respect, the idea that Kaᶜb's gift of a qasida could elicit as a counter-gift the Prophetic mantle, an emblem of the salvation and immortality conferred by Islam, reflects the Prophet's—or more precisely the Arabic literary tradition's—estimation of the ode.

As for the immortal and immortalizing aspects of the ode, we conclude our argument and our chapter with an anecdote recorded in al-Iṣbahānī's *Kitāb al-Aghānī* concerning Kaᶜb's father, the illustrious Jāhilī poet Zuhayr ibn Abī Sulmā, and his patron, Harim ibn Sinān:

> The caliph ᶜUmar [d. 23/644] said to [Kaᶜb] ibn Zuhayr, "Whatever became of the robes of honor that Harim bestowed upon your father?" "The passage of time wore them out," he replied. "But," said the caliph, "the robes [i.e., qasidas] that your father bestowed upon Harim time has not touched."[48]

Three

Celebration and Restoration
Praising the Caliph
Al-Akhṭal and the Umayyad Victory Ode

The Qasida and the Legitimizing Past

This chapter singles out the Umayyad period (41–132 H./661–750 C.E.) as the culturally decisive moment when the panegyric ode was effectively established as the vehicle for the expression of a specifically Arabo-Islamic political allegiance and legitimacy, and, conversely, the moment when the high Jāhilī panegyric ode (*qaṣīdat al-madḥ*) was canonized as the paradigm (model and measure) for the Arabo-Islamic qasida. We saw in chapter 1 the role of the qasida in the court ceremonial of pre-Islamic Arab kingship and in chapter 2 the ability of the qasida as a literary genre to extend its mythic and ritual components to express the cultural transition from the Jāhiliyyah to Islam, to recognize the prophethood of Muḥammad and to submit to it. Although the preeminence of the panegyric ode in the Arabic poetic tradition throughout the Islamic period up through the first part of the twentieth century is indisputable, the basis for its literary domination has yet to be adequately explored.

I will begin by claiming for the Arabic panegyric qasida what most recently David Quint, building on Thomas Greene's concept of "epic continuity," has claimed for the European epic: that the continuity of this literary genre encodes and transmits an ideology of empire,[1] or, more precisely for the qasida, of Arabo-Islamic rule. In other words, we will examine the qasida as genre in light of Gian Biagio Conte's definition of genre as "the organizing system that links, in stability, particular ideological and thematic contents with specific expressive structures."[2] More particularly, we will argue that a rhetoric of the caliphate, of legitimate Arabo-Islamic rule, was developed during the Umayyad period and that the form this discourse took was, above all, the panegyric ode. Within this framework, I will try to establish further that the genre-determined poetic components—such as the departed mistress, the abandoned campsite, and the desert journey—which are dismissed by both historians and literary historians as irrelevant to the qasida's political aspects are, to the contrary, in and of themselves powerful and evocative bearers of political and religious legitimacy. I will argue that the elaboration of the "vision of a legitimizing past" that Tarif Khalidi[3] has pointed to as the special domain of historians and jurists was eminently that of the poets as well, and, further, that the Umayyad poets achieved this vision through their adoption or co-option of the high Jāhilī panegyric ode.

Finally, I will propose that the function of the qasida as an encoder and transmitter of the ideology of Islamic hegemony and as one of the insignia of legitimate (Arabo-)Islamic political authority is a decisive factor in the preeminence of this poetic genre in Arabic and its prominence in the other Islamicate literary traditions (Persian, Ottoman, etc.).[4]

The great poets of the Umayyad period, chief among them al-Akhṭal, al-Nābighah al-Shaybānī, al-Rāʿī al-Numayrī, and Dhū al-Rummah, chose to follow not the model of the Islamic qasida of the period of the Prophet and the early conquests—the characteristically short, spontaneous, and often formally incomplete (*muqaṭṭaʿāt*) occasional poetry, such as the poetry of Ḥassān ibn Thābit and Kaʿb ibn Mālik found in the Life of the Prophet (*Sīrah*)—but rather the formally fully achieved, rhetorically opaque, and metaphorically dense qasida of the high Jāhilī master panegyrists, such as al-Nābighah al-Dhubyānī, al-Aʿshā, and Zuhayr.[5] I will argue that this is not merely a matter of arbitrary artistic choice, much less a poetic servility, "slavish imitation" as Wahb Rūmiyyah sees it,[6] but rather that it constitutes, in effect, a culture-defining moment. For it was at this moment, conversely, that the high Jāhilī panegyric ode was established as the authoritative poetic paragon for the Arabo-Islamic poetic tradition: it is at this moment that the Jāhilī qasida is canonized.[7]

Following Conte's claims for the epic code in Western literature, I propose for the Arabic panegyric ode that "just such a code allows a community to consolidate its historical experiences, conferring sense on them, until they become an exemplary system that is recognized as the community's new cultural text or scripture."[8] Further, I will argue that the panegyric ode, like Conte's "epic code," "is the medium through which society takes possession of its own past and gives that past the matrix value of a model."[9] We can add to this what I have established in my work on the ʿAbbāsid panegyric ode—that the panegyric ode allows Arabo-Islamic culture to interpret contemporary events and absorb them into a larger myth of cultural identity.[10]

To appreciate and evaluate the Arabic panegyric ode we must first begin to appreciate its function as a ceremony of homage and as a lingua franca for political negotiation.[11] In this light we can detect in the Umayyad period a crisis of authority for both the caliphate, whether with regard to the Umayyads or their rivals for it, and for the poets representing these various factions. At this point, the felicity—indeed genius—of the choice of the high Jāhilī qasida as the canonical paradigm can be appreciated when we realize that both the poet and the ruler/rival needed to legitimize themselves through, to use Eric Hobsbawm and Terence Ranger's term, "the invention of tradition,"[12] which in the course of our argument will be shown to be rather the reclamation and/or co-option of a tradition.

For the Umayyad poet to establish the authority of his poetic voice, his poetry had to be measured against some standard. By choosing the high Jāhilī panegyric ode as his model, he thereby established it as the canonical paradigm. The point is that the qasida as a canonical genre and as established in the Islamic—and especially Umayyad—codification of the Jāhiliyyah becomes the basis for the poet's authority. In effect, the new text is authenticated by an authoritative old one,[13] but the reverse is also true: a reciprocity is created whereby imitation confers authority on the old text, inasmuch as it is an act of homage and recognition, and in an altogether circular and symbiotic way, the new text draws authority from its recognition and submission to the established authority of the old. In a word, imitation entails the reciprocal validation and authorization of the imitated and the imitator.[14]

Concomitant to this, the Jāhilī poetic tradition becomes an essential literary canon (source of authority) for the Arabo-Islamic political legitimacy. For the poet's adoption, or co-option, of the style of the high Jāhilī panegyric ode amounts to his claim to be the rightful heir to that literary cultural legacy, to be an authentic poetic voice, and implied in this is the claim that the patron to whom the praise is addressed (***mamdūḥ***) is the lawful heir to the political authority ceremonially and ritually conferred by the presentation of the panegyric ode. In other words, through the use of the panegyric ode as literary genre, the full weight of the tradition comes to bear on the confirmation of the poet's authority and equally on the patron's authority as ruler. That is to say, borrowing Paul Connerton's term,[15] a "mythic concordance" is established between the poet and every other qasida-poet; and likewise between the patron and every other recipient of a panegyric ode (a phenomenon we have already witnessed in the relation between al-Nābighah al-Dhubyānī's qasida to the Lakhmid king al-Nuʿmān in chapter 1 and Kaʿb ibn Zuhayr's to the Prophet Muḥammad in chapter 2). Looking at this in ritual and ceremonial terms, we see it as analogous to the religious or symbolic identification between every Muslim who performs the Ḥajj, or every Christian who partakes of the Eucharist, or every Jew who celebrates Passover. As Connerton puts it, repetition creates identity.

At the same time, although ceremony and ritual claim to be repetition or reenactment of a fixed, original act, there is always an element of variation that expresses contemporary concerns. In the context of our present argument, we will focus, following Paula Sanders's work on Fāṭimid ceremony, on ceremony as an expression of current political hierarchies and as a means of negotiating and regulating rank and status.[16] I would add here an emphasis on confirming the legitimacy of the status quo. The panegyric ode does not merely repeat or reenact the past, but rather it recreates or re-forms the past to confirm the present (Khalidi's "vision of a legitimizing past"), while at the same time forcing the present to conform to a historical and teleological myth. It is essential, therefore, to keep in mind the dual function of the panegyric ode, to confirm, or claim, contemporary authority, and at the same time to preserve, promote, and project into the future the Arabo-Islamic ideology of rule, for which each panegyric ode is but a particular embodiment or exemplar.

It was important for the Islamic ruler to establish the legitimacy of his rule, particularly vis-à-vis competing claims.[17] In this respect, we need to keep in mind that the panegyric ode is almost always polemical. The choice of the high Jāhilī panegyric form for the ceremonials of homage confirms *ʿurūbah* (Arabicity, whether racial or cultural) as a key element of legitimacy. In other words the qasida form in itself creates a "mythic concordance" between the Islamic present and the pre-Islamic Arab golden or heroic age.

In the present chapter I would like to pursue this argument in light of the most renowned qasida of the poet generally recognized as one of the greatest of the Umayyad panegyrists, al-Akhṭal.[18] "The Tribe Has Departed" (*Khaffa al-Qaṭīnu*), of bipartite (elegiac prelude [*nasīb*] and praise section [*madīḥ*]) structure, is a victory ode presented to the caliph ʿAbd al-Malik ibn Marwān (r. 65–86/685–705) near the end of the Second Civil War, the Fitnah of Ibn al-Zubayr, probably around 72/691–92 (see below). Al-Akhṭal was one of the celebrated and highly competitive triumvirate of Umayyad court poets that also included his rivals Jarīr and al-Farazdaq. The issue of which of the three was the best poet remained a hotly debated topic throughout the classical Arabic literary tradition. Their *naqāʾiḍ* (flytings or poetic duels), renowned for their *hijāʾ* (invective, satire), are recorded in the collections *Naqāʾiḍ Jarīr wa-al-Farazdaq*, compiled by the Basran philologist Abū ʿUbaydah (d. ca. 210/825), and *Naqāʾiḍ Jarīr wa-al-Akhṭal*, a compilation attributed to the third/ninth century poet, Abū Tammām (d. 231/845).[19] In this chapter we shall not deal directly with this poetic rivalry, but focus rather on the relations between al-Akhṭal and the Umayyad court through an exploration of his celebrated victory ode in the context of contemporary Umayyad politics. An anecdote from al-Iṣbahānī's *Kitāb al-Aghānī* provides an indication of the authority that this Christian poet from the tribe of the Banū Taghlib wielded at the Umayyad court:

> A man once said to Abū ᶜAmr, "How amazing al-Akhṭal was! A Christian infidel who composed invective against Muslims!" "O you wretched fool! [Don't you know that] al-Akhṭal could come clad in a silken gown and a silken girdle, around his neck a golden chain from which hung a golden cross, and with wine dripping from his beard, and thus present himself, without asking permission, before [the caliph] ᶜAbd al-Malik ibn Marwān!"[20]

The history of this period is complex, and in places obscure, so a summary of main points will have to suffice here: The first dynasty of Islam, the Banū Umayyah, or Umayyads, were descendants of Umayyah ibn ᶜAbd Shams, a notable of the Meccan tribal aristocracy of Quraysh. Two branches of the Umayyads held the caliphate: The first, the Sufyānids, are descended from Abū Sufyān ibn Ḥarb, a staunch Meccan enemy of the Prophet who converted to Islam only after the conquest of Mecca. The other, the Marwānids, were of the Abū al-ᶜĀṣ branch. The era of the Orthodox Caliphs (*al-khulafāʾ al-rāshidūn*) following the death of the Prophet Muḥammad (11/632) came to an end with the First Civil War *(al-fitnah al-ūlā)*, between the followers of ᶜAlī ibn Abī Ṭālib, the nephew and son-in-law of the Prophet, and Muᶜāwiyah ibn Abī Sufyān, the Umayyad scion. The battle of Ṣiffīn (37/657) and subsequent arbitration resulted in the caliphate of Muᶜāwiyah (r. 41–60/661–670), who took Damascus as the Umayyad capital. There was little opposition to Umayyad rule under his reign, but upon the succession of his son, Yazīd (r. 60–64/680–83), there occurred the revolt of al-Ḥusayn ibn ᶜAlī, the grandson of the Prophet, which was crushed with the massacre at Karbalāʾ (61/680), and the beginning of the Second Civil War, the Fitnah of ᶜAbd Allāh ibn al-Zubayr. Ibn al-Zubayr, the descendant of the Meccan aristocracy of Quraysh and of a leading companion of the Prophet, refused to recognize the caliphate of Yazīd and established himself as a rival caliph at Mecca. Yazīd's death led to the recall of his army, which had besieged Mecca. He was succeeded by his son, Muᶜāwiyah II (r. 64/683), who was neither widely recognized nor long-lived. In effect, Yazīd's death marked a temporary collapse of Umayyad power. The reign of the Sufyānid branch of the Umayyads thus ended, and the stage was set for the Marwānid takeover. It was at this point that Marwān ibn al-Ḥakam (r. 64–65/684–85) and his son and successor, ᶜAbd al-Malik, took over the caliphate and gradually restored and consolidated Umayyad control.[21]

Recognized as caliph by Ummayad supporters after the assassination of his father, ᶜAbd al-Malik ibn Marwān faced formidable challenges. While he maintained his Umayyad capital at Damascus, rival caliph ᶜAbd Allāh ibn al-Zubayr at Mecca controlled the Ḥijāz and his brother Muṣᶜab ibn al-Zubayr had moved to Basra and was trying to consolidate power over Iraq. Another challenge to the caliphate was the revolt, centered at Kufa, of Mukhtār ibn Abī ᶜUbayd, who was backing an ᶜAlid candidate, Muḥammad ibn al-Ḥanafiyyah. There was as well a challenge from the Khārijites, those who broke with ᶜAlī after the Battle of Ṣiffīn.[22]

All of this was further complicated by the complex, unstable, and very bloody intertribal conflicts in the Syrian Umayyad heartlands and al-Jazīrah (northern Mesopotamia), primarily along the lines of the Northerners (Qays/Muḍar) and the Southerners (Yaman). Much of the hostility seems to have been the result of disputes over grazing lands. The victorious Yamanīs had inflicted a terrible slaughter on the Qaysīs at the Battle of Marj Rāhiṭ, north of Damascus, in 64/683. At the time of Marwān's accession to the caliphate, the Yamanīs supported the Umayyads, while the Qaysīs, under the leadership of Zufar ibn al-Ḥārith al-Kilābī at Qarqīsiyāʾ on the Euphrates, recognized the caliphate of ᶜAbd Allāh ibn al-Zubayr.[23] The tribe of al-Akhṭal, the Christian Banū Taghlib—although as part of Rabīᶜah ibn Nizār genealogically closer to the Qaysīs (part of Muḍar ibn Nizār)—allied themselves with the Yamanīs in support of the Umayyads at the Battle of Marj Rāhiṭ. From that time on they were involved in a range war and blood feud in their tribal grazing lands in al-Jazīrah with the pro-Zubayrid Qaysī tribe of the Banū Sulaym.[24]

As we shall see in greater detail as we discuss his poem, al-Akhṭal himself was fully involved in the political and military affairs of his day. He came to the Umayyad court as the spokesman for his tribe, the Banū Taghlib, to assure, or negotiate, their position in the hierarchy of Umayyad clients. Al-Akhṭal's ode "The Tribe Has Departed" is from the period of ᶜAbd al-Malik ibn Marwān's consolidation of Umayyad hegemony, probably, as the internal evidence of the poem seems to suggest, from around the year 72/691–692, after his siege of the pro-Zubayrid Qaysī, Zufar ibn al-Ḥārith, at Qarqīsiyāʾ and the latter's subsequent negotiated surrender (72/691), and after the defeat of Muṣᶜab ibn al-Zubayr in that year (Jumādā al-Ūlā 72/October 691), and perhaps also after ᶜAbd al-Malik sent al-Ḥajjāj ibn Yūsuf against ᶜAbd Allāh ibn al-Zubayr in the Ḥijāz (the siege of Mecca began 1 Dhū al-Qaᶜdah 72 [25 March 692], and lasted for more than six months), but, since no final victory is mentioned, probably prior to the latter's defeat (17 Jumādā al-Ūlā 73 [18 September 692]). Whatever the precise date of its composition—if indeed we can talk of a specific date—we are probably justified in discussing this ode in association with the "Year of [the Reestablishment of] the Community" (*ᶜām al-jamāᶜah*), i.e., the end of the Second Civil War (73/692).[25]

The Victory Ode

Al-Akhṭal, the Christian Taghlibī poet laureate of the Umayyads, and his most renowned qasida are dramatically presented to us in al-Iṣbahānī's *Kitāb al-Aghānī:*

> Al-Akhṭal came before ᶜAbd al-Malik ibn Marwān who asked him to recite for him. "My throat is dry," responded the poet, "Order someone to bring me a drink." "Bring him some water," ordered the caliph. "That's for donkeys," said al-Akhṭal, "and we have plenty of it." "Then give him milk." "I've long since been weaned!" "Then give him honey." "That's for the sick!" "Well, what *do* you want?" "Wine, O Commander of the Faithful!" "Have you ever known me to serve wine, you bastard?! If it weren't for the inviolable bond (*ḥurmah*) between us, O what I would do to you!" So al-Akhṭal left and came upon one of ᶜAbd al-Malik's attendants. "Damn you," he said to him, "the Commander of the Faithful ordered me to recite, but my voice was hoarse. Give me some wine!" And he did. Then al-Akhṭal said, "Match it with another!" So he did. "You have left the two of them fighting in my stomach, better give me a third!" So he did. "Now you've left me listing to one side, give me a fourth for balance." The servant gave it to him, and al-Akhṭal went before ᶜAbd al-Malik and recited:
>
> Those that dwelt with you have left in haste
> departing at evening or at dawn,
> Alarmed and driven out by fate's caprice
> they head for distant lands.
>
> When he finished, ᶜAbd al-Malik said to a servant boy, "Take him by the hand, boy, and help him out, heap robes of honor upon him, and reward him generously." Then he proclaimed, "Every people has its poet, and the poet of the Banū Umayyah is al-Akhṭal."[26]

As we have established in the preceding chapters, such anecdotes have much more to tell us about the poetic tradition than about historical facts.[27] In this case, much as we argued in chapter 2 that Kaᶜb ibn Zuhayr's "Suᶜād Has Departed" generated the myth of the donation of the mantle, here too

I would read this anecdote as one of mythic and ritual significance. Let us recall once more Gregory Nagy's remarks on the Panhellenization of Greek poetry, "the identity of the poet as composer becomes progressively stylized, . . . the poet becomes a myth; more accurately, the poet becomes part of a myth, and the myth-making structure appropriates his identity."[28] In the case of the anecdote at hand we must above all recognize that whatever the comical and dramatic effect of the drunken Christian poet reciting before the caliph, wine here retains a liturgical function and the anecdote constitutes the enactment of a ritual or ceremony of Islamic rulership.

The pattern behind the anecdote is that of transgression and redemption that we established above in chapters 1 and 2. Wine plays a complex role in the present anecdote. First, as a sacramental element in Christianity and forbidden in Islam, it is a blatant, and offensive, indicator that the poet is a Christian infidel. The Christian poet's requesting wine from ʿAbd al-Malik—not to mention stumbling in drunk to recite his panegyric—is a severe affront to caliphal dignity and to Islam. It is only the inviolable bond (*ḥurmah*) of protection of the client (as we saw in the case of al-Nābighah and King al-Nuʿmān in chapter 1) that prevents the caliph from having the poet executed on the spot. This affront then constitutes the poet's *transgression*. At the same time, the wine seems to preserve a ritual function in marking the poet's entry into the tabooed or sacerdotal—indeed oracular—state required for the recitation of the panegyric ode. Thus, having procured the wine, in abundance, the drunken poet appears once more before the caliph and recites his celebrated ode. The ode, as we have come to expect by now, proves to be the poet's *redemption*. The caliph's anger over the wine has yielded to his delight over the poem. Signaling his forgiveness, he orders the stumbling poet to be helped out and lavishly rewarded. The caliph's final pronouncement, which alerts us again to the pattern of the rite of (re)incorporation, is the declaration of a renewed and stronger bond between al-Akhṭal and the Umayyad house. In literary critical terms, what the tradition tells us in this anecdote is that however great the transgression—the affront to the caliph and to Islam—the poet's redemptive ode, with its celebration of ʿAbd al-Malik, the Umayyad caliphate, and triumphant Islam, is greater.

This literary rendition of the ritual thus constitutes a myth of Umayyad Arabo-Islamic hegemony, a myth that we cannot understand until we understand the role of the poet and the panegyric ode and, within that context, the poetic text itself. As we have demonstrated in the preceding chapters, the ceremonial exchange of poem and prize is a ritual of homage and allegiance that reaffirms the authority of the ruler and the bond between ruler and ruled. The conferring of the reward completes the ritual exchange. In effect, ʿAbd al-Malik, in the awarding of the robes of honor and the prize (*jāʾizah*), authenticates the poem and its contents and (re)affirms the bond between himself and his poet. In the Arabic political-poetic context, the qasida in a performative sense establishes the authority and legitimacy of ʿAbd al-Malik and the Umayyad caliphate and the awarding of the lavish prize itself confirms al-Akhṭal as the laureate of the Banū Umayyah. The caliph's final proclamation is technically redundant or reiterative. Its exegetical value for us is great, however, for it tells us, through its association with this particular qasida,[29] that this is the poem that defines Umayyad hegemony in particular, and, in a broader sense, part of the vast body of poetry of this period that debates and defines the bases of Arabo-Islamic political legitimacy. Inasmuch as we take it to be of literary rather than strictly historical factual value, what it tells us is not so much how ʿAbd al-Malik valued the poem as how the Arabic literary tradition evaluated it. In sum, our argument is that this poem marks the accession of al-Akhṭal to poet laureate because it marks the (poetic) accession of ʿAbd al-Malik to caliph: it confirms the Banū Umayyah in the caliphate. Clearly, the appreciation, indeed acceptance, of this proposition requires an examination of the qasida itself.

It is indicative of the traditional literary valuation of "The Tribe Has Departed" that the literary sources show little interest in the immediate political-historical circumstances of the poem, i.e., its "occasion," but rather imbed it in mythic, archetypal anecdotal material that confirms its role in a fully achieved ritual or ceremony. It is clear, especially from line 18, that the poem is essentially a victory ode. Its structure is that of the bipartite battle ode as recently and cogently formulated by Ḥasan al-Bannā ʿIzz al-Dīn for the pre-Islamic period, viz., the elegiac prelude (*nasīb*) is dominated by the departing women motif (*ẓaʿn*), there is no journey section (*raḥīl*), and the final section features the battle theme (here, among others).[30] Accordingly, in this ode, the elegiac prelude (*nasīb*) consists of a long passage describing the departing women (*ẓaʿāʾin*) (lines 1–16); a merely vestigial suggestion of the journey section (*raḥīl*) (line 17) functions as a disengagement or transition (*takhalluṣ*) from the elegiac prelude (*nasīb*) to the praise section (*madīḥ*) (lines 18–84), which opens with a declaration of victory and congratulatory benediction. This second section is not exclusively panegyric—victory celebration and battle description—but rather it exhibits a feature that is distinctive of the Umayyad and later periods: that in addition to praise (*madīḥ*) proper of the Banū Umayyah (lines 18–44), there are extensive passages containing the poet's boast (*fakhr*) of himself and his tribe (lines 45–51) and invective (*hijā'*) against his and the caliph's enemies (lines 52–84), throughout which we find reference to military and political events of the day. Although the literary critics and historians offer little or no structural explanation for this, we hope to do so in the course of this discussion.[31]

Al-Akhṭal's "The Tribe Has Departed" (*Khaffa al-Qaṭīnu*)[32]
[meter: *basīṭ;* rhyme: *-rū*]

1. Those that dwelt with you have left in haste,
departing at evening or at dawn,
Alarmed and driven out by fate's caprice,
they head for distant lands.

2. And I, on the day fate took them off,
was like one drunk
On wine from Ḥimṣ or Gadara
that sends shivers down the spine,

3. Poured generously from a brimming wine-jar
lined with pitch and dark with age,
Its clay seal broken
off its mouth,

4. A wine so strong it strikes
the vital organs of the reveler,
His heart, hungover, can barely
sober up.

5. I was like that, or like a man
whose limbs are racked with pain,
Or like a man whose heart is struck
by charms and amulets,

6. Out of longing for them and yearning
on the day I sent my glance after them
As they journeyed in small bands
on Kawkab Hill's two slopes.

7. They urged on their mounts,
turning their backs on us,
while in veiled howdahs, if you spoke softly to them,
were maidens lovely as statues.

8. They dazzle the tribesmen
until they ensnare them,
Yet they seem feeble-minded
when questioned.

9. God damn union with beautiful women
when they are sure
That you are a man on whom
old age has blossomed!

10. They turned away from me
when my bow's stringer bent it
And when my once jet-black locks
turned white.

11. They do not heed the man who calls them
to fulfill his need,
Nor do they set their sights upon
a white-haired man.

12. They headed east when summer's blast
had wrung the branches dry,
And, except where ploughshares run,
all green had withered.

13. So the eye is troubled by tears
shed for a now-distant campsite
Whose folk will find it hard to ever
meet again.

14. Clutching at them, as if at a rope,
the eye follows after them,
Between al-Shaqīq
and al-Maqsim Spring,

15. Until they descended to a land
on the side of a riverbed
Where the tribes of Shaybān and Ghubar
alight,

16. Until when they left behind
the sandy tamarisk ground
And had reached high ground, or said,
"This is the trench [that Khosroes] dug."

17. They alighted in the evening,
and we turned aside our noble-bred camels:
For the man in need, the time had come
to journey

18. To a man whose gifts do not elude us,
whom God has made victorious,
So let him in his victory
long delight!

19. He who wades into the deep of battle,
auspicious his augury,
The Caliph of God
through whom men pray for rain.

20. When his soul whispers its intention to him
he resolutely sends it forth,
His courage and his caution
like two keen blades.

21. In him the common weal resides,
and after his assurance
No peril can seduce him
from his pledge.

22. Not even the Euphrates when its tributaries
pour seething into it
And sweep the giant swallow-wort from its two banks
into the middle of its rushing stream,

23. And the summer winds churn it
until its waves
Form agitated puddles
on the prows of ships,

24. Racing in a vast and mighty torrent
from the mountains of Byzance
Whose foothills shield them from it
and divert its course,

25. Is ever more generous than he is
to the supplicant
Or more dazzling
to the beholder's eye.

26. They did not desist from their treachery and cunning
against you
Until, unknowingly, they portioned out
the maysir players' flesh.

27. Then whoever withholds his true counsel
from us
And whose hands are niggardly toward us
in this world[33]

28. Will be the ransom
of the Commander of the Faithful,
When a fierce and glowering battle day
bares its teeth.

29. Like a crouching lion, poised to pounce,
his chest low to the ground,
For a battle in which there is
prey for him,

30. [The caliph] advances with an army
two hundred thousand strong,
The likes of which no man or jinn
has ever seen.

31. He comes to bridges which he builds
and then destroys,
He brands his steeds with battle scars,
above him fly banners and battle dust,

32. Until at al-Ṭaff
they wreaked carnage,
And at al-Thawiyyah
where no bowstring twanged.

33. The tribesmen saw clearly
the error of their ways,
And he straightened out the smirk
upon their faces.

34. Single-handed he assumed the burdens
of the people of Iraq,
Among whom he had once bestowed
a store of grace and favor.

35. In the mighty nab[c] tree of Quraysh
round which they gather,
No other tree can top
its lofty crown.

36. It overtops the high hills,
and they dwell in its roots and stem;
They are the people of generosity,
and, when they boast, of glory,

37. Rallying behind the truth, recoiling from foul speech,
disdainful;
If adversity befalls them,
they bear it patiently.

38. If a darkening cloud casts its pall
over the horizons,
They have a refuge from it
and a haven.

39. God allotted to them the good fortune
that made them victorious,
And after theirs all other lots
are small, contemptible.

40. They do not exult in it
since they are its masters;
Any other tribe, were this their lot,
would be exultant, vain.

41. Ruthless toward their foe,
till they submit;
In victory,
the most merciful of men.

42. Those that harbor rancor toward them
cannot endure their battle wrath;
When their rods are tested
no flaw is found.

43. It is they who vie with the rain-bearing wind
to bring sustenance
When impoverished supplicants
find scant food.

44. O Banū Umayyah, your munificence
is like a widespread rain;
It is perfect,
unsullied by reproach.

45. O Banū Umayyah, it was I
who defended you
From the men of a tribe
that sheltered and aided [the Prophet].

46. I silenced the Banū Najjār's endless braying
against you
With poems that reached the ears
of every chieftain of Maᶜadd,

47. Until they submitted,
smarting from my words—
For words can often pierce
where sword points fail.

48. O Banū Umayyah, I offer you
sound counsel:
Don't let Zufar dwell secure
among you,

49. But take him as an enemy:
for what you see of him
And what lies hid within
is all corruption.

50. For in the end you'll meet
with ancient rancor
That, like mange, lies latent for a while
only to spread the more.

51. Through us you were victorious,
O Commander of the Faithful,
When the news reached you
within al-Ghūṭah [of Damascus],[34]

52. They identified for you the head
of Ibn al-Ḥubāb,
Its nose bridge now marked
by the sword.

53. Ears deaf, never will he
hear a voice;
Nor will he talk till stones
begin to speak.

54. His corpse now lies on the bank
of al-Ḥashshāk River;
His head on the far side
of Mount al-Yaḥmūm and the land of al-Ṣiwar.[35]

55. The al-Ṣubr clans of Ghassān, and the al-Ḥazn,
asked him when they witnessed this,
"How did you find the hospitality
of the boys who tend the far-off herds?"[36]

56. And al-Ḥārith ibn Abī ʿAwf,
there played with him by turns
The vultures
and the hawks.[37]

57. Thanks to us the men of Qays ʿAylān
came forth hastening
To render public homage to you
after long denial.

58. May God never lead Qays back
from their error;
And the Banū Dhakwān, may no one say "Take care!"
when they stumble.[38]

59. They raise a clamor over war
when it bites their withers—
It's the nature of the Qays ʿAylān
to be annoyed.

60. They lived in blessed abundance
till they were caught
In Satan's snares,
and made false claims.

61. They were mounted on a decrepit she-camel,
her seat hard,
Bald, she had neither tail hair
nor fur.

62. And the ignorant [Ibn al-Ḥubāb] kept on leading
the Banū Sulaym,
Until they had no place to go to water
or return.

63. Looking toward the Rivers of Zāb
as they picked their bitter colocynth,
We said, "How distant is the place on which
they've set their gaze!"[39]

64. They retreated to their
two stony tracts of tribal land
As camels ever return
to natal grounds,

65. Leaving behind them
rich pasturelands,
Mount Sinjār and al-Maḫlabiyyāt,
then al-Khābūr and then al-Surar.[40]

66. They will never reach the lineage
of Farrāṣ
Until the moon reaches
the Kid of the Farqadān,[41]

67. Nor even any relation to al-Ḍibāb
when they are disgraced,
Nor to al-ʿUṣayyah, except that, like them,
they are human.[42]

68. None among them strives
to reach us,
But that he falls short,
out of breath.

69. Out of our enmity
the Banū Kilāb were struck
By one of those calamities
that stirs dread anticipation.[43]

70. And the situation became grave,
irreconcilable,
For no bond of kinship held us back,
nor any excuses.

71. As for the Kulayb ibn Yarbūᶜ, when tribes vie
to reach the water hole,
They have no way to get to water
or return.

72. Left behind, other men determine
their affairs,
Left in the dark, they neither see nor sense
what's going on.

73. Whipped to the back of the line
at the water trough,
A Dārimī [al-Farazdaq] still leaves
his mark on them.

74. What wretches they are sober!
What wretched drinkers when they're drunk!
When strong wine or mellow date-brew courses
through their veins.

75. Their tribe is where
every foul deed ends up,
And each disgrace for which
the Muḍar are reviled.[44]

76. Mounted on asses, they proceed
but slowly, in small steps,
While their vile deeds reach Najrān
and are bruited in Hajar.[45]

77. The eaters of vile provender,
in solitude;
From their obscurity they ask,
"What is the news?"

78. And remember the Banū Ghudānah
like herds of young slit-eared goats,
Runty ones, for whom
corrals are built,[46]

79. That pee on their forelegs
when they're hot,
And shiver with cold
when wet with rain.

80. The Ghudānah have no station
whatsoever;
They must restrain their thirsty flocks of sheep
till only dregs remain.

81. They claim to belong to the Banū Yarbūʿ,
but their support,
When tribes join forces,
is unknown, despised.

82. Their beards are yellowed
from the kindling of braziers
When the cold turns back empty
the milking vessels and the milker's hand.

83. Then they go home to women
that are black and defiled,
Who after their crotches' itch is satisfied
do not bathe.[47]

84. Glory has truly sworn
that it will have
No covenant with them
till the hand's palm grows hair. [13]

For our present purposes the poem can thus be divided into two parts: the elegiac prelude (*nasīb*) lines 1–16; line 17 as a transitional line; and lines 18–84, what we will term a "compound praise section" (*madīḥ*). Keeping in mind that the larger context in which the poem was produced is the Second Civil War (the Fitnah of Ibn al-Zubayr), the major challenge to the legitimacy of ʿAbd al-Malik's claim to the caliphate (see above), and within the sphere of Umayyad-Marwānid hegemony, the tribal warfare between the poet's pro-Umayyad tribe, the Banū Taghlib, and the Qaysī pro-Zubayrid tribe of Banū Sulaym, we shall analyze the structure of the poem along lines of Theodor Gaster's bipartite formulation of the seasonal pattern (see chapter 2), but change his Emptying and Filling terminology to the more suitable terms Disintegration and Restoration.[48] The first part, the elegiac prelude with departing women (*ẓaʿn nasīb*), we shall interpret, above all, as expressive of the state of social disintegration occasioned by civil war (*fitnah*), within the Islamic community (*ummah*) and within the Marwānid domain.

The sense of broken societal bonds, uncertain allegiances, and lack of political direction is amply conveyed. The second part we shall read, first of all, as the restoration of political legitimacy and the concomitant restructuring of the polity, based above all on the recognition of the victorious ruler as divinely sanctioned. In this respect we can cite Garrison's remark concerning the panegyric of English Restoration: "Traditional panegyric is a ceremonial confirmation of an institution that exists rightfully, lawfully, and by divine will; it is not the instrument for the validation of personal power seized by force, no matter how heroic."[49]

The Elegiac Prelude (Nasīb): *Lines 1–16 (17)*. The poem opens declaring its own poeticity. The opening words, or opening hemistich (*miṣrāᶜ*), not only establish the rhyme (*-rū*) and meter (*basīṭ*), but, through the evocation of a tradition-honored motif, the tribal departure, signal the poet's ceremonial or ritual intention. The opening line functions as the introit. In uttering these words, the poet claims to be a poet, claims the authoritative voice that the poetic tradition confers. (We will argue below that the caliph's prize constitutes his recognition of that claim.) In the polemical atmosphere of the Fitnah of Ibn Zubayr and the rival claimants to the caliphate, the poet's claim is also a challenge, for he would like to claim his exclusive, or superior, poetic authority, just as he claims his patron's exclusive or superior political authority (this is the gist of the second anecdote about "The Tribe Has Departed," see below; see also al-Mutanabbī in chapter 5). As Conte puts it, "poetic discourse . . . reveals first itself and then that to which it refers."[50] The poet strives for an opaque discourse that draws attention to itself as artistry,[51] thereby establishing the poet's worth and authority. In composing in the traditional, high Jāhilī panegyric genre, the poet claims the authority of that tradition for himself. In the departing women (*ẓaᶜn*) motif, the poet evokes a generic cognation or identification with the poetic works of the Jāhilī past and establishes a mythic concordance between himself and ᶜAbd al-Malik, on the one hand, and the other poet-patron pairs (al-Nābighah and al-Nuᶜmān, Kaᶜb ibn Zuhayr and the Prophet Muḥammad, and so on) on the other. Further, as Ḥasan al-Bannā ᶜIzz al-Dīn's work has shown, anyone with a refined sense of poetic structure or "ceremonial idiom" will be aware that the stage has been set for a battle poem or victory ode.[52] Once this archetypal identification has been established, however, what follows is no simple reenactment of a ritual of allegiance, but a complex negotiation of rank and status through a subtle and multifaceted performative poem.

Like all ritual and ceremonial, the qasida must be traditional and original at the same time.

Our remarks on the rhetorical opacity and ritual functionality of the elegiac prelude should not delude us into thinking that what is expressed is insignificant. Nevertheless, I would stress that what the poet strives to express is not a direct, unmitigated emotion or event, but rather a loss, a departure that is symbolically and mythically resonant and polyphonic. The actual but ephemeral event that we can extract from historical sources, the bloody intertribal "range war" between the Yamanī-allied tribe of the Banū Taghlib and the Qaysī tribe of the Banū Sulaym over certain pasturages in al-Jazīrah, has been absorbed into a mythic symbolic structure of far greater significance, a process that involves sacrificing individual identity for literary-cultural longevity.

The opening image conveys, in the melancholy lyricism of the elegiac prelude, fate's forcible eviction of the poet's tribesmen, the disintegration of the community, the alarm and uncertainty they face. Like any great artist, al-Akhṭal performs the classical repertoire with sensitivity, nuance, and originality. Just as the employ of the *ẓaʿn* motif and qasida genre establishes a cognation between, or identification of, the immediate referent with autochthonous and archetypal departures embodied in the qasida tradition, so the introduction of other traditional motifs of the elegiac prelude is not an empty rhetorical exercise, but the evocation and identification of cognate sorrows. Taking the departure of the tribe's women (*ẓaʿn*) as the controlling image, the poet subordinates to it many of the "compulsory figures" (to borrow Clarissa Burt's metaphor) of the elegiac prelude. In lines 2–4 he describes the emotional and physical effects of the grief that seizes him as an inebriation that overwhelms mind and body, thereby conjuring the greatest of the Jāhilī Bacchic panegyric poets, al-Aʿshā, traditionally recognized as a major poetic influence on al-Akhṭal.[53]

The poet then sends his eye and his mind's eye on the trail of the departing women in their howdahs (lines 7–8), only to modulate to another traditional theme of the elegiac prelude, that is, the complaint against old age (*al-shakwā min al-shayb*), or lament for lost youth, (lines 9–11), which in the qasida tradition is expressed as an attack on the fairer sex for losing interest in a man whose black hair has turned to gray. Line 12 reverts to the departing tribe while shifting subtly, now by means of what we would elsewhere term pathetic fallacy, to project the failure of the polity to a description of failed fertility in desiccated drought-struck nature. Line 13 briefly evokes the flip side of the coin of the departing women motif, that is, the preeminent theme of the elegiac prelude in the Arabic ode, the abandoned campsite (*aṭlāl*), or, more precisely, the poet weeping over the abandoned campsite. The effect here is to highlight the role reversal: for in al-Akhṭal's poem the normally subordinate departing women (*ẓaʿn*) motif dominates and the preeminent ruined abode (*aṭlāl*) theme appears only reflexively.[54]

In the last four lines of the elegiac prelude (14–17) the poet regrounds and deepens the departing women motif, pursuing an evocative topography of nostalgia that is lovingly, obsessively delineated through place-names, tribal names, and intimately remembered, or imagined, terrain, until at evening, in the eye of the poet's imagination, they alight. However lyrical and melancholy the tone the poet has achieved here, we must at the same time keep in mind, as Ezz El-Din has established, that the departing women motif carries with it an association at least of forced seasonal migration to grazing lands, but particularly when it dominates the *nasīb,* intimations of impending battle, of the anxious *qawm* (fighting men of the tribe) sending the women and children away to safety, and of the prospect of tribal disintegration—that the men will be slain and/or defeated and the women and children carried off into bondage.[55]

The poet then turns away, no doubt more psychologically than physically, and through the vestigial *raḥīl* (journey section) of line 17 makes his transition to the *madīḥ* (praise section). What we thus find here is actually not structurally a *raḥīl* at all, but rather the reduction of the *raḥīl* to a motif—"we turned aside our noble-bred camels: / . . . the time had come to journey"—employed as a *takhalluṣ* (transition) from *nasīb* to *madīḥ.* Of note here, as elsewhere in Umayyad poetry, is the "group *raḥīl*" in the first-person plural, a feature unknown in Jāhilī poetry.[56]

The Praise Section (Madīḥ): *Lines (17) 18–84.* The disintegration of the polity intimated in the *ẓaʿn nasīb* is countered by the victory and restoration celebrated in the *madīḥ.* In the immediate sense, from what we can gather of the historical "occasion" of the qasida, it recognizes and celebrates the restoration of a divinely appointed Umayyad caliphate after the Fitnah of Ibn al-Zubayr. It does not appear from the text itself that the qasida was first presented after the final defeat of the "anti-caliph" ʿAbd Allāh ibn al-Zubayr, but certainly after the defeat of his brother, Muṣʿab, and indeed the tradition recorded in the *Kitāb al-Aghānī,* that al-Akhṭal claimed to have spent more than a year on the composition of this poem,[57] does not help to clarify the situation. In literary terms, however, it is clear from the tone and scope of the qasida that it is the grander concept of Umayyad/Marwānid legitimacy being celebrated here, not merely a specific victory. In addition, we should keep in mind the contemporary range of rivals for the caliphate and for legitimate Islamic rule, and realize that in that polemical context al-Akhṭal's qasida is above all a claim, a bid, for legitimacy. Part of this claim, as we argued above, is the poet's co-option of the high Jāhilī *qaṣīdat al-madḥ* as one of the insignia of legitimacy and authority for both poet and patron. It is worth noting in this respect the anecdotes in the *Kitāb al-Aghānī* that claim that if al-Akhṭal had lived even one day in the Jāhiliyyah, no poet would be considered better than he.[58] Concomitant with victory and restoration is the elaborating of a "legitimizing vision of the past" and a reordering and reintegration of the polity, indeed the cosmos, after crisis and chaos, disruption and the threat of disintegration. It is in the presentation of the sociopolitical hierarchy that the poet negotiates rank and status, particularly for himself and the Banū Taghlib. With victory comes the incorporation of former enemies into the polity, meaning the Umayyad-Marwānid domain, and with that a threat to the position of long-time allies. Here we find al-Akhṭal jockeying for position in the new political hierarchy.

Lines 17–50. Altogether in keeping with Gaster's formulation of Emptying and Filling, the "need" (*ḥājah*) expressed in line 17 is "fulfilled" in the gifts or benefits (*nawāfil*) of the patron (*mamdūḥ*) in line 18, the opening of the praise section (*madīḥ*). The second hemistich of line 18 is a masterpiece of performative concision. The first phrase, "whom God has made victorious," defines the qasida as a victory ode in terms of genre, thereby fulfilling the formal expectations that were created by the motif of the departing women (*ẓaʿn*) that dominated the elegiac prelude. Further, it affirms or confirms the divine appointment of ʿAbd al-Malik as it transforms the military into the mythic. The second phrase, the poet's felicitation to the ruler on the occasion of his victory, constitutes a declaration of loyalty and allegiance on the poet's part: the performative point of the qasida. Lines 19–21 offer the patron an encomium with a martial bent. The legitimacy of ʿAbd al-Malik's rule is conveyed through his identification both with cosmic and divine forces and with his subjects. He is the "Caliph of God" (*khalīfat Allāh*) and the one in whom "the common weal resides," i.e., he embodies the community and enacts God's will; he is, furthermore, the conduit between the two, "through whom men pray for rain" (lines 19, 21). With regard to discussions of the theory of the caliphate, particularly the Umayyad use of the term *khalīfat Allāh,* we should add that the polemic atmosphere of this body of poetry must be kept in mind: *he,* no one else—for instance, Ibn al-Zubayr—is the Caliph of God. Otherwise, the textual evidence of this qasida supports Patricia Crone and Martin Hinds's contention that Umayyad appointment to the caliphate was understood as coming directly from God, not via the Prophet Muḥammad.[59]

With lines 22–25 al-Akhṭal moves from the more immediate religious, military, and political sphere to invoke the mythic and autochthonous archetype of the formidable Euphrates. The power of this passage does not lie merely in the simile to the river in Iraq but rather in the allusion to Jāhilī precedents such as the Euphrates simile of al-Nābighah al-Dhubyānī's panegyric to the Lakhmid king al-Nuʿmān ibn Mundhir, "O Abode of Mayyah" (in chapter 1; see lines 44–47). The poet employs a high-density poeticity, including features such as simile, poetic diction, mythic/archetypal imagery, and formulaic pattern—"not even the Euphrates . . . is ever more generous than he" (*wa-mā l-furātu . . . yawman bi-ajwada minhu*)—to create a poetic text that evokes another poetic text as much as it evokes a visual image. In other words, the listener is not called upon merely to compare ʿAbd al-Malik's might and munificence to the destructive and life-giving powers of the Euphrates, but to draw an analogy between this passage and al-Nābighah's in a way that establishes a "mythic concordance" whereby the originary and autochthonous Arab (poetic) act of homage authenticates the present one.

Inherent in this allusion is the measuring of the new poem against the old. For al-Akhṭal to produce a weaker passage would undermine both his poetic authority and ʿAbd al-Malik's political authority. In this light, we can begin to grasp the high valuation accorded a great court poet. Furthermore, we can begin to appreciate why the rhetorically opaque and polyphonic poeticity of the high Jāhilī panegyric ode was a more powerful vehicle for establishing and conveying Arabo-Islamic hegemony than the more transparent univocity of much of the poetry of Life of the Prophet (*Sīrah*) (see chapter 2). The rich mythic and archetypal dimensions of the Jāhilī tradition allow the poet to anchor current claims to legitimacy in a shared authenticating past.

With regard to the history of the qasida as genre, we should recognize that the constant reference and allusion to the past masterpieces ("intertextuality") is what assures their survival, both as integral texts and through the poetic DNA, as it were, passed down in imitation and allusion. The allusion thus functions as an act of homage to the tradition that reciprocally validates the giver and the recipient.

Having thus confirmed ʿAbd al-Malik in the caliphate and in the Arabicity (*ʿurūbah*) of his authority, al-Akhṭal turns to the self-defeating situation of the caliph's enemies. Lines 26–28 are said by one commentator to refer to the anti-caliph ʿAbd Allāh ibn al-Zubayr, by another to refer to enemies of the poet's tribe, the Banū Taghlib; in al-Iṣbahānī's *Kitāb al-Aghānī* they are taken to refer to the Qaysī chieftain, Zufar ibn al-Ḥārith (see below).[60] Playing on the pre-Islamic custom of *maysir*, gambling over the parts of a sacrificial camel, the poet quips that the caliph's enemies, in trying to deceive and destroy him, deceived and destroyed only themselves, as if they were *maysir* players portioning out their own flesh. Whoever refuses to recognize the true caliph (this is how I read "withholds his true counsel") will be the caliph's "ransom" or "redemption," which here means "will pay with his life."[61] My own preference is to read this as a threat directed at ᶜAbd Allāh ibn al-Zubayr, that in withholding allegiance from ᶜAbd al-Malik, he is digging his own grave. Line 28 serves as a pivot to the confirmation of the caliph in the title of Commander of the Faithful, as victorious Muslim leader. The military campaign is conveyed for the most part in poeticized terms rather than historically specific ones; nevertheless, several place-names are mentioned. Al-Sukkarī in his commentary identifies al-Ṭaff in line 32 as referring to the place where Muṣᶜab ibn al-Zubayr was slain (Dayr Jāthalīq, Jumādā al-Ūlā 72 [October 691])[62] and al-Thawiyyah as the burial site of Ziyād ibn Abīhi.[63] The expression "where no bowstring twanged" means that it was a battle of heroic hand-to-hand combat with the sword, rather than the (less manly, less heroic) shooting of arrows at a distance.[64] The subduing of Iraq in line 34 once more suggests that the qasida celebrates ᶜAbd al-Malik's victory over Muṣᶜab ibn al-Zubayr.

The victory itself is interpreted as a confirmation of ᶜAbd al-Malik's divine election. Victory achieved, the poet proceeds with the restructuring of the polity. At the top of the hierarchy are the Quraysh (the tribe of the pre-Islamic Meccan aristocracy and of the Prophet Muḥammad) in general and, from among the Quraysh, the Banū Umayyah in particular. This is set out in lines 35–44 in the form of a traditional Jāhilī praise section (*madīḥ*). Again, in reading such poetry we must keep in mind that it is perhaps not so much a statement of legitimacy as a bid for, or claim to, legitimacy. The military victory achieved, the Umayyads now have to win over the "hearts and minds." The ode could also have played a role in convincing the Islamic community (*ummah*) that ᶜAbd al-Malik's final victory over ᶜAbd Allāh ibn al-Zubayr, though perhaps not yet achieved at the time of the presentation of the ode, was inevitable, indeed divinely decreed.

It should be recognized that by the time the Umayyads came to power through Muᶜāwiyah's wresting of the caliphate from ᶜAlī ibn Abī Ṭālib, the nephew and son-in-law of the Prophet Muḥammad, at the battle of Ṣiffīn (37/657), the proto-system for the election of the caliph that had secured the appointments of the four Orthodox Caliphs had entirely broken down. The Islamic ummah faced a "constitutional crisis."[65] As the *shūrā* (counsel) system of caliphal election progressively failed, the panegyric ode (*qaṣīdat al-madḥ*), already established as a vehicle for confirming pre-Islamic political legitimacy and hegemony, was increasingly pressed into service. Lacking Qurʾānic, Prophetic, and "constitutional" guarantees, the rulers and would-be rulers of the Umayyad period turned to the panegyric ode to certify their legitimacy and to compete for recognition. Specifically Islamic points could be added to the caliphal platform, but the underlying principles of legitimate leadership that would be ratified by the public in question—at this point the Arab tribal aristocracy and their followers above all—were those of the Jāhilī warrior aristocracy, especially might and magnanimity.[66] That is, the traditional values of the Jāhiliyyah as expressed by and in the panegyric ode may have had as great a pull on the constituency of the new Islamic empire as the new, specifically Islamic elements, or perhaps even greater. Certainly this is what the Umayyad-period co-option of the pre-Islamic panegyric tradition, as both literary genre and ceremony, by almost all the competing political parties would seem to indicate. (The exception is the Khārijites, whose poetry resembles rather more the poetry of the "Battle Days of the Arabs" [*Ayyām al-ʿArab*] or of the Life of the Prophet [*Sīrah*]).[67]

In competing for Islamic loyalties, ʿAbd al-Malik has to demonstrate that he fits the criteria for rulership (the caliphate) that the polity recognizes and, at the same time, that his rivals do not. Conversely, he must downplay, avoid, or deny criteria that his rivals fit better than he does, such as descent from or relation to the Prophet. The poet masterfully grafts uniquely Umayyad-Marwānid caliphal criteria onto the traditional Jāhilī aristocratic virtues (lines 35–44). He begins by describing the symbolic and genealogical *nabʿ* tree (a hardwood from which bows and arrows are made) of Quraysh, the mightiest and loftiest of trees. The only Islamic element in this litany of traditional virtues is the divine election in line 39, and it is only Islamic because of the date of the poem. In line 44 the poet changes from the third-person "they," somewhat ambiguously the Quraysh or the Banū Umayyah, to the second-person "you," addressing by name the Banū Umayyah in a line of purely Jāhilī *madīḥ* that subsumes the entire preceding passage. The effect of this is to narrow the caliphal field from all of Quraysh to the Banū Umayyah (descendants of the ʿAbd Shams clan) alone, thereby excluding Zubayrid (of the Banū ʿAbd al-ʿUzzah clan of Quraysh), ʿAlid/Shiite (direct descendants of the Prophet through his daughter Fāṭimah and his nephew and son-in-law ʿAlī), and other potential contenders, such as the Banū Hāshim clan, the clan of the Prophet Muḥammad, which would produce the line of the ʿAbbāsid caliphate.

The poet's feat will be the more appreciated when we examine the Islamic credentials of the contenders as compared to those of the Umayyads. Above all, of course, is the fact that Abū Sufyān, the eponymous ancestor of the Sufyānid branch of the Umayyads, was a bitter opponent of the Prophet Muḥammad and leader of the Meccan military opposition against the Prophet at Medina; he converted to Islam only upon the conquest of Mecca. ʿAlī was the Prophet's son-in-law and nephew, his father Abū Ṭālib having been an early and staunch protector of the Prophet, although he is said to have died without converting to Islam. ʿAlī's descendants, especially his sons Ḥasan and Ḥusayn, by his wife Fāṭimah, the Prophet's daughter, are thus demonstrably closer to the Prophet genealogically and have better "Islamic" credentials. Finally, the rival caliph, ʿAbd Allāh ibn al-Zubayr, was of the ʿAbd al-ʿUzzah clan of the Quraysh on his father's side, but his mother was Asmāʾ bint Abī Bakr, the daughter of the Prophet Muḥammad's closest supporter and first caliph, Abū Bakr, and the sister of the Prophet's favorite wife, ʿĀʾishah. Moreover, he is said to be the first child born to the Emigrants (Muhājirūn) upon their arrival at Medina, thus the "firstborn" of the nascent Islamic state.[68]

The poet has achieved something much subtler as well. Although we know from the historical sources that Marwān ibn al-Ḥakam usurped power from the Sufyānid branch of the Banū Umayyah, and in fact was for a time a supporter of the Zubayrid camp, no trace of shifting loyalties or internecine struggle is detectable in al-Akhṭal's ode. Rather, the *madīḥ*-section, as it "consolidates historical experience and confers meaning on it,"[69] creates a myth of Umayyad continuity and restoration quite at odds with the historical version of events (including the assassination of ʿUthmān, the third of the Orthodox Caliphs and a member of the Umayyad family; the rivalry between Sufyānids and Marwānids; Marwānid usurpation; and awkward details such as Marwān ibn al-Ḥakam's erstwhile inclination toward ʿAbd Allāh ibn al-Zubayr).[70] It presents instead a perfectly smooth and seamless progression of divinely determined Qurashī-Umayyad(-Marwānid) hegemony.

The *madīḥ* section up until this point has been precisely that, the praise of the ruler and the confirmation of his legitimate authority. This constitutes the first step in the reordering of the polity after the chaos of external challenges, claiming for ʿAbd al-Malik the titles of Caliph of God (*khalīfat Allāh*) and Commander of the Faithful (*amīr al-muʾminīn*) on the basis of his divinely appointed military victories and his Umayyad-Qurashī descent. In what ensues, the poet is concerned above all with the power structure within the Umayyad hierarchy (Gaster's restructuring or restoration), but always with a view toward negotiating his own rank and status and that of the Banū Taghlib within that structure. It is here that we find the common

Umayyad practice of introducing other *aghrāḍ* or subgenres, such as boast (*fakhr*) and invective (*hijā'*), into *madīḥ*.[71] Al-Akhṭal employs *fakhr* to establish himself and his tribe as the foremost supporters of ʿAbd al-Malik. He then exploits *hijā'* to relegate his rivals and enemies to the lowest rungs of the social ladder. The point is that these subgenres are not randomly introduced, nor do they merely perform the political function that Shawqī Ḍayf points out,[72] but rather they are systematically subordinated both formally and structurally to the *qaṣīdat al-madḥ* to perform the functions established for it: the restructuring of the polity and the negotiation for rank and status within that structure. In this respect the qasida functions as the literary equivalent of a ceremonial or ritual procession in which the order of appearance reflects rank and status.

The element of *fakhr* is subordinated to the *madīḥ* in that the poet boasts above all of his, and his tribe's, service to the Banū Umayyah. He begins with his own poetic prowess and his willingness to put it to the service of ʿAbd al-Malik's predecessor in the Umayyad caliphate, Yazīd ibn Muʿāwiyah, when no Muslim poet would dare to compose *hijā'* against the Anṣār (the Medinan Helpers of the Prophet) (lines 45–47).[73] In the context of ritual exchange and performative speech, this passage also serves to remind the caliph of his obligation toward al-Akhṭal and the Banū Taghlib.

The poet then warns ʿAbd al-Malik against the Qaysī chieftain Zufar ibn al-Ḥārith (lines 48–50), an erstwhile supporter of Muṣʿab ibn al-Zubayr who, after his negotiated truce following ʿAbd al-Malik's siege of his stronghold at Qarqīsiyā', was courted by ʿAbd al-Malik, and thus is now al-Akhṭal and the Banū Taghlib's rival for the caliph's favors.[74]

Lines 51–70. The passage between lines 51 and 70 is a remarkable combination of boast (*fakhr*), now for the military prowess of the Taghlibīs, and invective (*hijā'*) directed against the Qaysī tribe of the Banū Sulaym and their chieftain, ʿUmayr ibn al-Ḥubāb, supporters of Muṣʿab ibn al-Zubayr, whom the Taghlibīs had defeated. In a traditional tribal victory gloat, a poetic version of the ceremonial triumph, the poet recounts the beheading and mutilation of the corpse and the display of the head of the Sulamī chieftain ʿUmayr ibn al-Ḥubāb, slain at al-Ḥashshāk in the year 70/689.[75] In lines 51–54, "Through us you were victorious," the poet appears to remind the caliph that the Banū Taghlib slew Ibn al-Ḥubāb at al-Ḥashshāk River while the caliph was safely within al-Ghūṭah, the area of gardens and orchards that surrounded the Umayyad capital at Damascus. Al-Akhṭal then credits himself, or his tribe (line 57), with forcing the recalcitrant Qays ʿAylān, who had supported Muṣʿab ibn al-Zubayr, to accept and publicly render homage and allegiance to ʿAbd al-Malik. Of particular note is the use of the word *kafarū,* here in the immediate sense of "they denied" or, functioning in a rhetorical antithesis (*ṭibāq*) with "openly" (*jihāran*), "they concealed," but conveying at the same time the notion that denial of the true caliph and recognition of the Zubayrid anti-caliphate amounts to *kufr* (infidelity), whereas public allegiance to the true caliph is equated with true belief, Islam.

The poeticized account of the failed Sulamī incursion into the Taghlibī pasturelands around the Zāb tributaries of the Tigris[76] (lines 60–70) is structured as an inverted qasida or anti-qasida. It begins with "blessed abundance," then a false claim to Taghlibī lands and a deluded journey on a decrepit she-camel (representing Zubayrid allegiance), until, cut off from water themselves, they could only look enviously at the rich Zawābī grazing lands of the Banū Taghlib. Finally, they retreat to their stony tribal lands, leaving the rich pastures to the victors. Rather than moving, in Gaster's terms, from Emptying to Filling, this passage moves in the opposite direction. Inasmuch as this entire episode takes place within the context of the Umayyad-Zubayrid struggle, al-Akhṭal gives it a religious coloring: to support Muṣᶜab ibn al-Zubayr is to be caught in Satan's snares (line 60). The Banū Sulaym are left astray in a Zubayrid moral wasteland, looking enviously at the abundant pasturage of Umayyad rule (lines 63–65).

Lines 71–84. As we have seen, the *madīḥ* (praise) section opened by placing the divinely appointed caliph at the apex of the societal hierarchy and then established the Banū Taghlib as the ranking supporters of the Banū Umayyah. Now, the poet moves further down the social-political scale to a final passage devoted to *hijāʾ* (invective) against the Banū Kulayb ibn Yarbūᶜ, the clan of Tamīm to which Jarīr, al-Akhṭal's poetic and political rival, belonged (lines 71–84),[77] and directed almost exclusively, as we shall see, to establishing their lack of rank and status. Again, it is clear in the context of the present argument that this passage of *hijāʾ* is not arbitrarily inserted within what is otherwise a *madīḥ* section, but rather, it is subordinated to the *madīḥ* structure, whose function of the restitution of the social hierarchy it serves. Likewise, our reading highlights the function of ceremony emphasized by Sanders: the negotiating of rank and status.[78]

It is of interest to see that the degradation of the Banū Kulayb ibn Yarbūᶜ and of the Banū Ghadānah ibn Yarbūᶜ is achieved through the use of bedouin pastoral categories of social hierarchy. In that scheme, as I have discussed elsewhere, social position is accurately reflected through water use.[79] The fighting men (*qawm*) go to water first, when it is purest; the women, whose menstrual blood pollutes the water, go last. Furthermore, the herds and flocks of the powerful and dominant go before those of the weak and subordinate. The Banū Kulayb are thus unable to reach the metaphorical water hole of noble deeds at all (line 71), they are pushed to the back of the line, and even the lowly Dārimī—presumably al-Farazdaq, Jarīr's and al-Akhṭal's poetic rival from the Banū Dārim, another branch of Tamīm—leaves the mark of his poetic whip on them (line 73); the Banū Ghudānah restrain their thirsty flocks (mere sheep, not camels) while others drink. Also emphasized is their lack of authority. They are not "in the know" politically, but are kept in ignorance and obscurity, outside of the decision-making circle and therefore subject to the authority and decisions of others (lines 72 and 77). So ineffectual are they that their help in cooperative ventures (raids, wars) is despised. They ride slowly, mounted on lowly asses rather than camels (for travel) or steeds (for battle and the hunt), whereas the news of their foul deeds spreads with alacrity (line 76). Line 77 is one of remarkable vituperative concision: they are destitute, stingy, consuming alone their "vile provender," (*khabītha l-zādi*), which the commentarists remark refers to the meat of jerboas and lizards,[80] and starved for news of tribal affairs, in diametrical contrast to the nobles who magnanimously slaughter their finest she-camels for their guests and clients and determine tribal affairs. In the pastoral economy where the camel is the prestige livestock, the Banū Ghudānah are compared to scrawny goats or kids (lines 78–79). Line 82 describes them at the opposite end of the social scale from the tribal military aristocracy, the *sādah*. They perform, rather, the tasks of servants, kindling fires and milking livestock,[81] and huddle in misery over their fires when it is too cold to milk their herds. Finally, whereas noblewomen live in chaste confinement (it is a sign of a tribe's nobility that their women are not mentioned at all), the lowly women of these debased tribes exhibit defiled and shameless sexuality.[82] The gist of the closing line (84) then is simply that glory is wholly unnatural to them. What is apparent above all in this passage is al-Akhṭal's attempt not merely to put rival tribes in their (political) place, but also to establish the degraded status of his poetic rivals: al-Farazdaq—himself a "lowly Dārimī"—whips Jarīr's tribe into submission, presumably with his stinging invective.

In sum, in the *madīḥ* section, al-Akhṭal has employed a "compound *madīḥ*" in which segments of *fakhr* and *hijā'* have been incorporated into the traditional encomiastic section. This has not been done arbitrarily, but in such a way as to constitute a (re)structuring of the social hierarchy from the top down: beginning with the divinely appointed caliph (Qurashī/Umayyad, male, virtuous), followed by his chief supporters, the Banū Taghlib, and by the subdued and defeated (Qays ʿAylān, Banū Sulaym), and finally the lowest of all, the Banū Kulayb and Banū Ghudānah with their base men and defiled and shameless women. Al-Akhṭal's rivals, al-Farazdaq and Jarīr, are positioned in such a way as to establish a poetic as well as a political hierarchy. The point, of course, is not that this is necessarily an accurate reflection of the contemporary political situation; rather, this is the Umayyad caliphate as al-Akhṭal would like to see it. The literary tradition depicts ʿAbd al-Malik as fully in accord with al-Akhṭal's political and poetic vision, as another anecdote about the recitation of this poem confirms:

> ʿAlī ibn Ḥammād . . . said that al-Akhṭal said to ʿAbd al-Malik, "O Commander of the Faithful, Ibn al-Marāghah [i.e., Jarīr] claims that he perfected his panegyric to you in three days, whereas I spent a year on
>
> Those that dwelt with you have left in haste
> departing at evening or at dawn
>
> and still didn't achieve all that I wanted." "Let me hear it, Akhṭal," replied ʿAbd al-Malik. So he recited it to him and I began to see ʿAbd al-Malik become more and more exuberant over it and then exclaim, "O Akhṭal, do you want me to write to the horizons that you are the best poet of the Arabs?" "It is enough for me," al-Akhṭal replied, "that the Commander of the Faithful should say so." [ʿAbd al-Malik] ordered that a large bowl that was before him be filled with dirhams and given to [al-Akhṭal]. He threw robes of honor over him, and one of ʿAbd al-Malik's men took him out before the court proclaiming, "This is the poet of the Commander of the Faithful; this is the best poet of the Arabs."[83]

In al-Akhṭal's "The Tribe Has Departed" we can see the *qaṣīdat al-madḥ* in the process of transition from the literary vehicle that encoded the ethos of the pre-Islamic tribal warrior aristocracy to one that encodes an ideology of Arabo-Islamic hegemony, an ideology of empire. So smooth is the transition that the two are melded into one continuous tradition. This process, once set in motion, then projects into the future both the qasida and the culture and ideology that it bears.

Four

Supplication and Negotiation
The Client Outraged
Al-Akhṭal and the Supplicatory Ode

Poetics and Politics

The previous chapter presented al-Akhṭal's "The Tribe Has Departed" (*Khaffa al-Qaṭīnu*) as a victory ode that celebrates and commemorates ʿAbd al-Malik ibn Marwān's victory over the Zubayrid challenge to the caliphate and confirms the restoration of the Umayyad caliphate and the accession of the Marwānid branch of the Banū Umayyah. The poet there could assume a strong negotiating stance vis-à-vis the caliph inasmuch as he was the spokesman of his tribe, the Banū Taghlib, who had contributed to the Umayyad victory over Muṣʿab ibn al-Zubayr. The ode celebrated the caliph's legitimacy and potency, reaffirmed Taghlibī loyalty, and claimed for the Banū Taghlib the right to a position at the very top of the Umayyad client hierarchy.

"Wāsiṭ Lies Deserted" (*ʿAfā Wāsiṭun*) is the product of drastically different circumstances. The Banū Sulaym, a tribe of Qays and erstwhile supporters of Muṣʿab ibn al-Zubayr, have, with the defeat of the latter, been realigned into the Umayyad domain. Thus, as discussed in the previous chapter, the Banū Taghlib's former enemies have become their fellow Umayyad clients and competitors at court for political status and caliphal favor.

As clients jockey for position, the Sulamī chieftain al-Jaḥḥāf has apparently scored a dramatic victory over his Taghlibī rivals. Rising to a poetic challenge issued by al-Akhṭal himself, al-Jaḥḥāf has, somewhat invidiously and not without implicating the caliph, launched a bloody surprise attack on the Banū Taghlib in their tribal abodes, slaying the men (including the poet's father or, as some versions have it, his son), women, and children, and slitting the wombs of pregnant women—the infamous Day of al-Bishr in the year 73 H./692–3 C.E. (below). A humiliated and defeated al-Akhṭal presents "Wāsiṭ Lies Deserted" not, like the earlier poem, to the caliph himself, but to a lesser Umayyad princeling, Khālid ibn Asīd,[1] to demand that the Umayyads pay the bloodwite for those slain at al-Bishr—to claim restitution from his supposed protector and liege lord. In making his demand, the poet threatens to cut the Taghlibī-Umayyad bond, thereby challenging the legitimacy and authority as much as "The Tribe Has Departed" had affirmed it. If the poet in "The Tribe Has Departed" is in the position of a powerful ally and client of a victorious ruler, in "Wāsiṭ Lies Deserted" the poet is in the position of an outraged and humiliated client who presents himself, at least initially, as a supplicant.

A fuller presentation of the historical-anecdotal context of al-Akhṭal's "Wāsiṭ Lies Deserted" is found in the classical Arabic tradition. What is notable above all in the various classical Arabic sources is that, regardless of our contemporary disciplinary categorization of these works as "history" or "literature," the fundamental conceptual framework within which the Qays versus Taghlib and other tribal conflicts and political alliances are expressed is the Jāhilī tribal ethos as embodied in the institutions of clientage/protection and blood vengeance or bloodwite.[2] In al-Iṣbahānī's *Kitāb al-Aghānī* (Book of Songs), we find in the notice on al-Akhṭal that "Wāsiṭ Lies Deserted" tops the philologist Abū ᶜUbaydah's (d. 209/824–5) list of al-Akhṭal's ten excellent and flawless long qasidas whereby the poet was considered to have bested his two rivals, Jarīr and al-Farazdaq. It otherwise goes unmentioned, and "The Tribe Has Departed" emerges as the preeminent poem.[3] It is only when we turn to the minor notice (ten pages) on al-Jaḥḥāf and the story of the Day of al-Bishr that "Wāsiṭ Lies Deserted" makes its contextualized appearance.[4] It should be noted, too, that this poem—clearly recognized, as Abū ᶜUbaydah's assessment indicates, as a major canonical work by a preeminent canonical poet—is in this notice referred to and cited only briefly and is otherwise subordinated to the narrative of intertribal Qaysī-Taghlibī blood feud that is played out between al-Jaḥḥāf, of the Qaysī tribe of the Banū Sulaym, and al-Akhṭal. Indeed, of the two protagonists of this narrative, al-Jaḥḥāf is the major one, and although he is virtually unknown in the poetic canon, more of his poetry is cited than that of al-Akhṭal. It is tempting to see in this notice the sort of popular narrative in which key points are articulated by poetic citations, such as we find in the elaborations of the notorious pre-Islamic feud between Bakr and Taghlib, the War of al-Basūs.[5] In brief, the narrative takes preeminence over the poetry.

As we saw in the previous chapter, during the period of the Second Civil War, the Fitnah of Ibn al-Zubayr, the rival tribes were on opposite sides, the Banū Sulaym (Qays) supporting Muṣᶜab ibn al-Zubayr and the Banū Taghlib supporting the Umayyads. At al-Ḥashshāk, the Qaysī chieftain ʿUmayr ibn al-Ḥubāb was slain by the Banū Taghlib and his head severed and presented to the caliph ʿAbd al-Malik ibn Marwān. This triggered a number of Qaysī attacks against the Taghlibīs to avenge ʿUmayr, in which the Sulamī chieftain Zufar ibn al-Ḥārith played a prominent role. On this occasion al-Akhṭal's poetic and political rival Jarīr issued the following lampoon or taunt, which succinctly sums up al-Akhṭal's situation:

> Have you forgotten your day in al-Jazīrah
> That turned out to be a plague for you?
>
> The warriors of Qays bore down on you with steeds
> Ungroomed and grim-faced, [their backs] bearing heroes.
>
> You kept thinking everything after them
> Was steeds and men charging over and over.
>
> Zufar Abū al-Hudhayl, their chieftain, annihilated you[r men],
> Then captured your women and plundered your herds.[6] [14]

The *Kitāb al-Aghānī* notice continues:

> In the year 73 H., after ʿAbd Allāh ibn al-Zubayr was killed, the fitnah [civil war] was quelled and the various factions rallied to the side of ʿAbd al-Malik ibn Marwān. Qays and Taghlib desisted from raiding each other in Syria and al-Jazīrah and each of the two rival factions thought that it had the upper hand. ʿAbd al-Malik had spoken about this, but no peace settlement (*ṣulḥ*) was actually reached. This, then, was the state of affairs when al-Akhṭal recited to ʿAbd al-Malik ibn Marwān, while the chieftains of Qays were with him:
>
> > Will no one ask al-Jaḥḥāf if he's taken vengeance
> > For the slain of Sulaym and ʿĀmir?[7]
> >
> > O Jaḥḥāf, if we descend upon you till [we] flow over you
> > [Like] high and swollen seas
> >
> > You will be like tiny bubbles of foam (*al-ḥibāb*) swept along by the sea,
> > Shaken by the raging winds.[8] [15]
>
> At this al-Jaḥḥāf, overcome with anger, jumped, trailing his silken robe, then ʿAbd al-Malik said to al-Akhṭal, "I think you've gained nothing but evil for your people by this." Al-Jaḥḥāf then forged a letter from ʿAbd al-Malik appointing him to collect the alms tax (*ṣadaqāt*) from Bakr and Taghlib, and about a thousand horsemen from his tribe accompanied him. And he incited them until he reached al-Ruṣāfah . . . where he revealed his purpose to them, recited al-Akhṭal's poetry to them, and said to them:

"There's no choice but [hell]fire [if you follow me] or disgrace [if you turn back]. So let whoever is steadfast proceed; and whoever is reluctant go back." They replied, "We have no desire to leave you." So he told them what he wanted to do, and they said, "We are in this with you for better or for worse." So they departed and traveled by night to Ṣuhayn partway through the night . . . and launched a dawn attack at ʿĀjinat al-Raḥūb south of Ṣuhayn and al-Bishr, a wadi of the Banū Taghlib. They attacked the Banū Taghlib at night and slew them and slit open any women who were pregnant, and those women that were not pregnant, they slew. . . . Al-Jaḥḥāf climbed the mountain. . . . That night he killed a son of al-Akhṭal called Abū Ghiyāth. . . . And al-Akhṭal himself fell into their hands while he was clad in a dirty cloak. When they asked him who he was, he said he was one of [the Taghlibīs'] slaves. So they let him go. . . . And [al-Jaḥḥāf] began to call out, "Let whoever is pregnant come to me"; so they came up to him and he began to slit their bellies. After this deed of his, al-Jaḥḥāf, his comrades having left him and dispersed, fled until he reached the Byzantines. . . . When ʿAbd al-Malik's anger subsided and the Qaysī leaders talked to him about granting [al-Jaḥḥāf] safe conduct, he was indecisive and dilatory, until he was told "We do not feel that the Muslims will be safe from him if he remains for long with the Byzantines." So he granted him safe conduct. When he came and arrived before ʿAbd al-Malik, al-Akhṭal met him, and al-Jaḥḥāf said to him:

> Abū Mālik [al-Akhṭal], did you blame me when you incited me
> To kill, or did my blamer blame me because of you?
>
> Abū Mālik, I obeyed you, indeed, in those things you incited me to
> Just as a thirsty man resolves [to quench his thirst].
>
> And if you were to call on me to do it again, my response
> Would be the same, for I am skilled at war, a real expert. [16]

. . . . Then al-Akhṭal said: [lines 61, 62, and 66 of "Wāsiṭ Lies Deserted"]

> At al-Bishr al-Jaḥḥāf launched an attack
> From which complaints and cries for help rose to Allāh!
>
> So ask the Banū Marwān: Why are a bond of protection
> And a weak rope still connected?
>
> If Quraysh by their sovereign authority do not change this,
> There will be a withdrawal and departure from Quraysh.

When he recited this, ʿAbd al-Malik exclaimed, "And where would you go, you son of a Christian woman?" "To Hell," he replied. "Just the place for you! If you'd said anything else [I would have killed you!]"[9]

At this point, it became clear to ᶜAbd al-Malik that if he left the rivals in their present state the matter would never be settled. So he ordered his son al-Walīd ibn ᶜAbd al-Malik to pay the bloodwite for the prior hostilities between Qays and Taghlib and, as punishment, held al-Jaḥḥāf responsible for paying the bloodwite for the Taghlibīs slain at al-Bishr. Lacking funds, al-Jaḥḥāf turned to a kinsman from Hawāzin, al-Ḥajjāj ibn Yūsuf, the notorious Umayyad governor of Iraq, who eventually supplied him with the necessary bloodwite.[10]

A final anecdote about al-Jaḥḥāf involves the pious and witty ᶜAbd Allāh ibn ᶜUmar ibn al-Khaṭṭāb, son of the pious second Orthodox Caliph, and Muḥammad ibn al-Ḥanafiyyah, the son of ᶜAlī, the Prophet's nephew and son-in-law. It is said that al-Jaḥḥāf finally repented and went on the Ḥajj, where Ibn ᶜUmar saw him clinging to the curtains of the Kaᶜbah, crying, "O Allāh, forgive me—but I don't think You will!" Ibn ᶜUmar said, "Hey, you! Even if you were al-Jaḥḥāf himself, you wouldn't keep saying such things!" He replied, "But I am al-Jaḥḥāf!" Ibn ᶜUmar said nothing. But Muḥammad ibn ᶜAlī ibn Abī Ṭālib heard what al-Jaḥḥāf had said and rebuked him, saying, "O ᶜAbd Allāh, your despair in Allāh's forgiveness is a greater [sin] than your evil deeds."[11]

Supplication and Negotiation

Incidents such as the Day of al-Bishr demonstrate, above all, the seriousness of the negotiations that are carried out in the qasida. For when such social institutions as negotiation and ceremonial competition enacted through the qasida fail, the result is bloodshed, and massacres such as that at al-Bishr ensue. The relentless taunting and boasting among political rivals—between al-Akhṭal and al-Jaḥḥāf and between al-Akhṭal and Jarīr—reveals the very intimate interaction between poetic and military hostilities at the Umayyad court.

A word about the bloodwite is in order here. What al-Akhṭal demands above all is that the Banū Taghlib be reinstated in their position as the top-ranking clients of the Banū Umayyah. The disgrace of the Day of al-Bishr can be washed away in one of two ways. The more direct and drastic option is war—to wash blood with blood. Inasmuch as both contenders are Umayyad clients, this would amount to either a civil war within the Umayyad domain or, more likely, to one of the two parties withdrawing its allegiance from the Umayyads. The latter is what the caliph's advisors feared if al-Jaḥḥāf stayed too long among the Byzantines and what al-Akhṭal threatens. The Umayyad failure to punish the Sulamīs by demanding that they pay restitution would amount to an admission of approval and/or complicity in the massacre at al-Bishr and, therefore, a betrayal and rupturing of the bonds of clientage between the Umayyads and the Taghlibīs—a declaration of war on the Umayyad side. Al-Akhṭal, under these circumstances, has no way to restore Taghlibī honor other than to issue an ultimatum: either the Umayyads uphold their obligation to protect and defend their Taghlibī clients by demanding that the Sulamīs pay restitution, the bloodwite, thereby establishing Sulamī guilt and upholding Umayyad honor, or the Banū Taghlib will withdraw their allegiance from the Umayyads. In examining the qasida, we will note that elements of the blood-vengeance or bloodwite diction recur throughout the poem. Foremost among these are the derivatives of the two roots *ḥ-m-l* (to bear a burden) and *th-q-l* (to be heavy) that appear in a number of forms to refer to bearing or being burdened with the heavy responsibility of blood vengeance or bloodwite.

The negotiations carried out through the qasida are couched in ritual and ceremonial as well as rhetorical and poetic structures. Thus, examining the qasida with an eye to the poetics of supplication will immediately shed light on its political and ceremonial dimensions. The ceremonial presentation of the panegyric ode to the patron represents, in and of itself, a choice of negotiation over open warfare. The self-abasement of the supplicant, whether physical or poetic, is precisely the opposite of an act of aggression. In this respect we should keep in mind that the qasida presentation ritual is, as I have shown in previous chapters and elsewhere, a form of gift exchange and that the proffering of a gift is always understood as a peace offering, a cessation of hostilities and a willingness to negotiate.[12] It may further indicate an admission of defeat, a surrender that implores or implies that the defeated be mercifully treated. This explains both why the ruse of the Trojan horse succeeded and why husbands bring flowers to irate wives. The initial posture of submission, which the closing section of the present poem would seem to belie, is necessary precisely because submission is the opposite of aggression.

The act of self-abasement that supplication entails is also a form of entrapment: the recipient loses face or status if he does not accept the gift and repay it with interest, as we have established in chapters 1 and 2. As we shall see, in the qasida, as elsewhere, the act of supplication and its concomitant act of self-abasement are not abject, but rather form a component in a complex ceremonial challenge.

Before moving on to a reading of al-Akhṭal's "Wāsiṭ Lies Deserted," let us look briefly at how the ceremonial pattern of supplication relates to the traditional thematic structure of the panegyric qasida. Among the most interesting of the contributions that Kevin Crotty's work on supplication in Homeric epic can make to the discussion of the Arabic panegyric ode is his remark concerning the intimate connection between supplication and praise: "Supplication . . . is a form of praise, but it is praise from the distinctive and troubling perspective of the loser."[13] The pattern that he points to in the *Odyssey* (books 7 and 9) of the shipwrecked refugee coming to the court of a local king, regaling him with the tale of his fall from prosperity and subsequent hardships and then praising the fame and generosity of his host,[14] forms a striking parallel to the thematic structure of the tripartite qasida with its opening section (***nasīb, muqaddimah***) devoted to lost bliss, its central section of the desert quest and journey (***raḥīl***), and its closing section of praise for the patron (***madīḥ***). It becomes discernible as well that the ritual of supplication and praise operates at a very basic level as a rite of incorporation wherein the alien, by virtue of his being unknown, is perceived as hostile (and attacked) unless he makes a lavish exhibition of his peaceful intentions and his willingness to submit to the local authorities. In the qasida at hand, it is perhaps difficult to refer to al-Akhṭal as a refugee or alien, but clearly his status as outraged client is, like theirs, ambiguous.

A further examination of the poetics of supplication is warranted here, and at this point we can begin to draw comparisons between al-Akhṭal's "Wāsiṭ Lies Deserted" and two of its renowned antecedents in the poetry of supplication, al-Nābighah's "O Abode of Mayyah" (chapter 1), in which the poet appeals to be reinstated into King al-Nuʿmān's good graces, and Kaʿb ibn Zuhayr's "Suʿād Has Departed" (chapter 2), in which the poet repents and/or disavows his opposition to the Prophet Muḥammad, and pleads that his life be spared and that he be admitted into the Islamic fold. The comparison of these three qasidas reveals a number of common elements.

The supplicant poet in all these cases possesses a "liminal" status, to use the term from the rite of passage; that is, he is outside of the bounds of normal society, "betwixt and between the positions assigned and arrayed by law, custom, conventions and ceremonial."[15] In al-Nābighah's case he has been branded an outlaw and traitor for his alleged crimes against his lord; Kaʿb has been branded an outlaw by his own tribe, who have converted to Islam while he has tried to remain loyal to the now-defunct ancestral ways, and is outlawed by Muḥammad as well. What must be kept in mind here is that the Arab tribal concept of "outcast" (***ṭarīd***) and "outlaw" (***damuh mubāḥ***) is that such a person has committed crimes for which he has been expelled and deprived of tribal protection. Further, the idea of protection is cast in terms of blood vengeance. The phrase ***damuh mubāḥ*** means that his blood may be shed with impunity, his kinsmen will not seek vengeance for him; he is, in our parlance, fair game, a "sitting duck." His liminal status consists above all of having no one to defend him and of being denied the single strongest deterrent to violence against his person, the threat of vengeance.

This explains how al-Akhṭal's situation is comparable to that of the other two poets. Unlike the other two, al-Akhṭal does not stand accused of any outrage against his tribe or lord. However, by allowing, wittingly or unwittingly, the Banū Sulaym to slaughter the Banū Taghlib with impunity, ʿAbd al-Malik has in effect treated the Banū Taghlib as outcasts or enemies; that is, he has denied them the protection and retribution that are their due as Umayyad clients. Al-Akhṭal is thus in an outcast, liminal state, in a no-man's-land between client and enemy. In all three poetic cases, then, the poet supplicant presents himself as a defenseless refugee, a stranger and outsider of ambiguous status (ally or enemy?) whose entrance into the patron's court constitutes a potential threat. At the same time, he is himself in mortal danger, having no protection, but only the hope of mercy from the patron.

Physical rites or ceremonies of supplication involve physical acts of submission or self abasement. Crotty points out the Homeric (and still honored) act of the supplicant grasping the knees of the supplicated.[16] And, of course, the self-abasement of the supplicant constitutes his recognition of the authority and power of the one supplicated. In the supplicatory qasida we find the cognate of this physical submission in what I shall term the "supplicatory lexicon." Normally occurring at the opening of the praise section (***madīḥ***) of the qasida, just as the poet supplicant has completed his arduous journey and arrived at the court of the patron, it forms a distinctive structural element in the poetic rite of supplication and likewise functions as a clear transition point in the thematic structural sequence of the qasida form. This characteristic diction uses terms for stranger and refugee to describe the poet supplicant; haven, refuge, mercy, and generosity to describe the patron (***mamdūḥ***); and hope or trust lost and hope or trust renewed to express the poet's present predicament. At this point we can cite several examples. al-Nābighah's "O Abode of Mayyah," line 20 (chapter 1):

> Such a she-camel conveys me
> to Nuʿmān,
> Whose beneficence to mankind, both kin and foreigner,
> is unsurpassed.

ʿAlqamah ibn ʿAbadah:[17]

> Do not withhold your favor from me,
> a foreigner,

For amidst the king's domed tents
I am a stranger.

You are the man in whom
I place my trust,
For lords before have ruled me,
then I was lost. [17]

Kaᶜb ibn Zuhayr's "Suᶜād Has Departed," lines 33–36 (chapter 2):

And every trusted friend in whom
I put my hopes
Said, "I cannot help you, I am occupied
with other things."

So I replied, "Out of my way,
you bastards!"
For all that the All-Merciful decrees
will come to pass!

For every man of woman born,
though he be long secure,
Will one day be borne
on humpbacked bier.

I was told God's Messenger
had threatened me,
But from God's Messenger
pardon is hoped.

And, finally, al-Akhṭal's "Wāsiṭ Lies Deserted," lines 43–44:

To Khālid, until they knelt
before Khālid,
What a great man to hope for
and in whom to place one's hopes.

O Khālid, your shelter is ample
for whoever alights,
For the destitute your palms pour forth
abundant rain.

A second element of this ritual submission is a plea for mercy. Al-Nābighah's "O Abode of Mayyah," lines 42–43 (chapter 1):

Go easy! May the tribes, all of them,
be your ransom,
And all my increase
both of herds and progeny!

Don't fling at me more
    than I can withstand,
Even though my foes should rally
    to support you.

Kaᶜb ibn Zuhayr's "Suᶜād Has Departed," line 37 (chapter 2):

Go easy, and let Him be your guide
    who gave to you
The gift of the Qurᵓān in which
    are warnings and discernment!

This makes apparent al-Akhṭal's distinctive situation and his deviation from the supplicatory mode of the accused wrongdoer. Al-Akhṭal, regardless of the supplicatory structure of his qasida and the posture of self-abasement he adopts throughout most of the qasida, is clearly, in the closing section of the poem, the accuser and not, like his predecessors al-Nābighah and Kaᶜb ibn Zuhayr, the accused. In the end al-Akhṭal's poetic stance is that of the outraged client, reproaching his liege lord for his failure to protect his tribe, and demanding his due.

The use of the supplicatory ritual, or qasida, to negotiate and contest power becomes clear if we turn once again to Simon Goldhill's remarks about supplication "as a social ritual which articulates the boundaries of power."[18] Once we appreciate more fully the potential for the ritual or qasida of supplication to function as a challenge to or contestation of power and authority, we can better understand how al-Akhṭal is able to manipulate the supplicatory qasida to contest and challenge, even to threaten, Umayyad power and authority. As we will see, this is done through the use of the supplicatory ode to invoke obligation: the poet counters political and military authority with moral authority. For this we can adopt Crotty's term "the paradoxical authority exerted by the suppliant."[19] For in both the Homeric or Arab cases, the supplicant has the backing of powerful institutions or virtues of the warrior aristocracy. One is the law of hospitality (*al-ḍiyāfah*) that requires the noble of the warrior aristocracy to take in, feed, and shelter the guest, the refugee, and the destitute. Such magnanimity and the military might that made it possible to acquire the necessary wealth to enact such virtue figure as the major themes of the tribal or personal boast (*fakhr, iftikhār*) and of panegyric (*madīḥ*) in the Arabic poetic tradition.[20]

Closely related to this is the institution of protection (*ijārah*) of the client, refugee, or protégé (*jār,* often translated as "neighbor"). In this case, too, the concept of honor in the warrior aristocracy of the Arabs, from pre-Islamic times onward, was expressed through how well one took care of those whom one was bound by this institution to protect. This was rated more highly than protecting blood kin, which was presumably thought to have more of a basis in affective ties and self-interest than the protection of those to whom one was obligated only by a sense of honor. Like hospitality, the concept of protection had two components: one was the raw might and wealth to be able to provide and protect; the other was the moral component, the nobility of character, that required the member of the warrior aristocracy to provide for and protect the client and refugee even at the expense of himself and his kin.

At this point it becomes clear that the qasida and its associated ceremonies serve not merely to affirm but also to challenge or question the legitimacy and moral authority of the ruler. Al-Akhṭal employs his qasida "Wāsiṭ Lies Deserted" to publicly challenge Marwānid authority and question their legitimacy. Although ʿAbd al-Malik ibn Marwān has established his military might by quelling the Zubayrid *fitnah* or challenge to the caliphate, in al-Akhṭal's poem his legitimacy and moral authority are called into question by his failure to protect his Taghlibī clients. The only way that ʿAbd al-Malik can reestablish his credibility as a legitimate Arab (Islamic) ruler, his worthiness to hold the caliphate, is to accede to the poet's request to procure the bloodwite for those slain at al-Bishr. By making his son (and successor) al-Walīd responsible for Taghlibī bloodwite from the period of the *fitnah,* ʿAbd al-Malik confirms Umayyad protection for its loyal allies during the civil war; by assigning the bloodwite for the Day of al-Bishr to al-Jaḥḥāf al-Sulamī, the caliph guarantees restitution for his Taghlibī clients while at the same time absolving himself and assigning guilt to the Qaysī tribe of the Banū Sulaym.

If at this point we once more invoke Mauss's paradigm of gift exchange, it is evident that here we have another instance in which the ritual exchange of qasida for bloodwite constitutes a "total social phenomenon" in which "all sorts of institutions will find simultaneous expression,"[21] and, in Evans-Pritchard's summary, "the exchanges of archaic societies . . . are total social movements or activities. They are at the same time economic, juridical, moral, aesthetic, religious, mythological and socio-morphological phenomena."[22] Above all, the exchange of qasida and bloodwite in this case conforms to Mauss's contention that ritual exchanges functioned above all to establish, or in this case reestablish, social—and, we can add, political—bonds.

With these remarks in mind we can then trace the movement of the present qasida along the lines of the supplicatory ceremony as it is employed to negotiate the rights and obligations attendant upon the institutions of protection (*ijārah*) and blood vengeance (*thaʾr*) or bloodwite (*diyah*).

The Supplicatory Ode

"Wāsiṭ Lies Deserted" is a beautifully achieved and elegantly proportioned tripartite ode. Highly esteemed in the classical tradition, it holds pride of place in al-Sukkarī's recension of al-Akhṭal's diwan (collected works), where it figures as the opening poem,[23] just as it tops Abū ʿUbaydah's list of the ten magisterial qasidas whose excellence established al-Akhṭal's superiority over his rivals, Jarīr and al-Farazdaq. Its structure follows the full classical tripartite model: (1) the elegiac prelude (*nasīb*), lines 1–23/24, is dominated by a wine-and-drinking passage; (2) the desert journey (*raḥīl*), lines 25–43, comprises a description of the inhospitable wasteland and the camels that cross it; and (3) the praise section (*madīḥ*), lines 44–70, includes a benediction in the form of a storm scene, followed by the poet's challenge and boast.

Al-Akhṭal's "Wāsiṭ Lies Deserted" (*ʿAfā Wāsiṭun*)[24]
[meter: *ṭawīl;* rhyme: *-lū*]

1. Wāsiṭ lies deserted
 of Raḍwā's tribe, and Nabtal, too,
 And then the junction of two wadis of al-Ḥurr,
 so patience is best.[25]

2. Al-Sakrān Hill, too, is deserted,
 there no ghost of them remains,
 But for the acrid salām bush
 and the bitter ḥarmal rue.

3. My heart is healed of all sorrows
 except the women departing
 In their howdahs led past me
 by Ibn Khallās Ṭufayl and ʿAzhal.[26]

4. I [stood] on the morning they departed
 for far-off lands, [stunned],
 Like a man condemned turned over to his executioner,
 or a drunk enduring harsh rebuke,

5. Felled by a well-aged wine,
 his fellow drinkers raise his head
 In order to revive him,
 for his limbs and joints are dead.

6. We push him then pull him
 to try to make him walk;

Except for his last breath,
he's barely conscious.

7. When they raise one limb,
he pulls himself together,
While another, from all the wine he's drunk,
remains completely numb.

8. I drank, and there met me,
when my oath had been fulfilled,
A camel caravan from Palestine
laden with thirst-quenching wine,

9. Laden with goatskins
filled to bursting with wine,
Raised up upon the camels
and carefully balanced.

10. Then I said, "Give me a morning drink,
you bastards' sons!"
And they took down their loads
to do it,

11. Then made their camels kneel and dragged off them
wineskins so bloated the legs stood erect,
Till they looked like Sudanis
without any shirts.

12. They brought out a Baysānī wine, so fine
the more the saqi pours you
The more delightfully and smoothly
it goes down.

13. Hands pass it round
from right and left;
When they put it down they cry, "God give us life!"
and when they raise it.

14. From time to time the wine cups stop circling
among us, interrupted by
The song of a singer
or slices of carved meat.

15. The wine was delightful to the reveler,
delicious to the drinker,
Till mirth and vanity
vied for my [heart].

16. All too soon the wine's effects
caught up with us

From all the drinks we'd had
and all the seconds.

* [They poured into a vessel
a wine so strong
As if, when they glanced at it,
it was a burning ember.][27]

17. [You feel] the wine
crawl through your bones
Like a stream of ants crawling down
a dune of fine loose sand.

18. So I said, "Kill it[s effect] on you
by mixing it,
How delicious it is slain,
when it's been killed!"

19. [The grapevine] grew, attended by
an expert vintner,
His foot ever pushing his spade
to turn the soil.

20. If he fears the [Dog] Star['s heat]
will make it thirsty,
He digs a trench to send a stream of water
running to it.

21. O censuress, if you do not cut short
your blame of me
I'll leave you and with new resolve
resume [my drinking].

22. I'll forsake you
once and for all,
And the petulant nights of youth
will once again be ours.

23. When love's violent passion
was dispelled,
My most hoped-for need
appeared to me

24. Of a sudden apprehension,
from the tribe of Ẓamyāʾ,
Before whom at Ṣirrīn
stands a locked door.

25. [Through] many a barren waste
in whose far-flung reaches

Like untended camels
ostrich roam.

26. In it you see the glimmerings
of the mirage,
Like men now naked,
now clad in shirts.

27. Through the very belly of the desert,
where riders never shut their eyes,
Where the guide's eye, out of fear,
does not dare blink.

28. Through every vast and pathless waste
devoid of way-marks
To guide the traveler,
or any water hole,

29. Playgrounds of the jinn,
the dust so fine
When the wind whips it up
it seems it's sifted,

30. These I crossed
when the chameleon rose,
Like a man praying toward Yemen,
or a captive in irons.

31. To Khālid ibn Asīd there bore us swiftly
camels with loose shifting saddles
That journey alone through a pathless desert
where many go astray.

32. In it when you see a year-old fox cub
standing on a rise
You think it's a fine steed
covered with a horse blanket.

33. You see a she-camel, rock solid,
cheekbones jutting out,
And striking against her backside an aborted foal,
tiny as a chick.

34. The membrane of afterbirth is ripped
from the fetus
By [the wolf], the desert's brother,
spleen-colored, starving.

35. They journey on and on until
their humps are shrunken

For they're ever alighting only to be
saddled up once more.

36. We charged them with the distant journey,
remote its road marks,
Where the chameleon twitches
[from the noonday heat].

37. So emaciate are they, their sunken eyes
are like the last remaining rainwater
In hollow rocks or like
exhausted wells.

38. The white camels' eyes are hollow
and the loops of their ropes are doubled over,
So gaunt are they
after hardship and exertion.

39. None remained but each
strong and steadfast she-camel
That after journeying all day and night
is still exuberant, vital, quivering.

40. Like birds alighting on the ground,
they kneel to rest,
In a plantless waste, with no pasture but
regurgitated cud.

41. They stop but briefly and leave only
discolored spots of urine,
And shriveled, desiccated dung,
like peppercorns.

42. Laden with weighty needs
which they bear,
Swift and haggard,
to the bestower of grace.

43. To Khālid, until they knelt
before Khālid,
What a great man to hope for
and in whom to place one's hopes.

44. O Khālid, your shelter is ample
for whoever alights,
For the destitute your palms pour forth
abundant rain.

45. He is the auspicious leader,
sought to steady

His people's handmill
when, before, it had wobbled.

46. Your rod, when tested,
is always firm;
Your two palms, when a request is made,
always bestow.

47. O you who strive
to overtake Khālid,
Desist, and refrain from
what you're doing,

48. For could you, if Khālid
held out the goal to you,
Ever measure up to him,
or bear his burdens?

49. His new-won glory, that the tribe reached before you,
and his ancestral fame
Refuse to let you ever
reach his rank.

50. Umayyah and al-ᶜĀṣī,
and if Khālid calls for help,
Hishām and Nawfal, because of his deeds,
respond to him.[28]

51. They are the wellspring
round which the tribe gathers,
They are the haven and refuge
from fear.

52. May God water a land
the best of whose people is Khālid,
With a cloud whose spouts disgorge
abundant rain.

53. When the east wind
cuts through its crotches,
Its water-laden lower parts
flow like milk.

54. When the wind shakes it,
it drags its trains,
Like the ponderous gait of newly calved she-camels
tending their young.

55. Pouring incessantly, the lightning bolts on its sides
like lamps aglow in the darkness

Or the flanks of piebald steeds
in panic bolting.

56. Then, when it turned and headed
toward al-Yamāmah,
The south wind called out to it,
and it turned back, sluggishly.

57. It watered Laʿlaʿ and al-Qurnatayn
and barely bore
Its heavy loads away
from Laʿlaʿ.

58. It left al-Ḥazn's hilltops
floating above the floodwater
Like a cluster of slender steeds
kept tethered by the tents.

59. Incessantly raining it headed east
to al-Dahnā
Like a camel laden with textiles,
decked with bells, heavily burdened.

60. At al-Maʿrasāniyyāt it alighted
and from it in Grouse Meadow
The she-camels, full-uddered, newly calved,
yearn gently over their young.

61. At al-Bishr al-Jaḥḥāf
launched an attack
From which complaints and cries for help
rose to Allāh!

62. So ask the Banū Marwān:
Why are a bond of protection
And a weak rope
still connected

63. To the leap of a thief [al-Jaḥḥāf]
after Muṣʿab passed by Ashʿath,
[And was then left dead,] neither deloused,
nor washed.

64. Was it al-Jaḥḥāf who brought you [Muṣʿab's head]
so that you ordered him
Against those under your protection,
that they be massacred in the midst of their abodes?

65. Trusting in an inviolable covenant so sure
that if you invoked it to call the mountain goats

Down from the steep peaks
they would descend.

66. If Quraysh by their sovereign authority
do not change this,
There will be a withdrawal and departure
from Quraysh.

67. We will disgrace your men
in the most abhorrent way,
And we will live as men of honor,
or else, slain in battle, die.

68. If you take on the burden of the bloodwite
for them, [know that]
No bloodwite, however weighty,
can outweigh kindred blood.

69. If you give us the [bloodwite]
that is our right,
We will not be blind to right,
our right is all we ask.

70. When we dismount and stride into
the dread breach [of battle],
Our might is feared,
our day illustrious. [18]

The Elegiac Prelude (Nasīb): *Lines 1–23/24.* The elegiac prelude opens, as did al-Nābighah's qasida in chapter 1, with the tradition-honored motif of the abandoned encampment (*aṭlāl*). This has the effect of immediately situating the poem within the qasida tradition, thereby evoking the emotional and aesthetic as well as formal expectations of the genre. The opening lines (1–2) exhibit a complex interplay between the opposed acts of erasure and mapping, oblivion and memory. The woman, whom the genre tells us is the poet's erstwhile beloved, is given a name, Raḍwā, and thus the memory of her is evoked. As the poet maps out the nostalgic topography of the now deserted abodes where his beloved and her tribe had dwelt, he once again names names—Wāsiṭ, Nabtal, the confluence of the two Wādī Ḥurrs, al-Sakrān Hill. He moves, poetically, from place to place, tracing their movements as though on a pilgrimage whereby one evokes the presence of past inhabitants by retracing their steps. But finally, he only confirms the present desolation: nothing remains but acrid shrubs, salām and ḥarmal (bitter rue)—which provide neither fodder nor shade.

In line 3 the poet claims that his heart is cured of all sorrows except for the departing women in their howdahs being led by men identified in the commentary as his Taghlibī kinsmen.[29] The line is complex. The motif of the tribal women departing in their camel litters (*ẓaʿāʾin*), as has been demonstrated by Ḥasan al-Bannā ʿIzz al-Dīn, is intimately associated with the theme of war (see chapter 3).[30] Although in the present case it does not dominate the elegiac prelude, when taken together with the Arabic poetic archetype of loss in the abandoned encampment, this image of desolation and forced tribal migration becomes identified with the Taghlibī tribal lands where the poet's kin have recently been slaughtered. We begin to perceive the bivocality of the poetic tradition which is able to speak at once at the personal and political levels while never departing from the archetypal elegiac lyricism of the prelude (*nasīb*).

Line 3 serves too as the pivot point for the modulation to an elaborated and extended wine scene. This is accomplished by a verbal sleight of hand—not quite a pun—involving a key element of Arabic poetic diction of the elegiac prelude, the verb *ṣaḥā*. To understand how the poet pivots from the departing women motif to the wine scene, we must explore the meaning of *ṣaḥā*.[31] Having as its basic denotative meaning the clearing of clouds from the sky, the sense of "clearing up" is also evident in its meaning of "recover from intoxication," "sober up," "come to one's senses"; and likewise, "to wake up" from sleep; and finally "to relinquish youthful folly and amorousness" (Lane, *ṣ-ḥ-w*), that is to say, to recover from infatuation, lovesickness, to "get over" a lost, or failed, love. The standard example is the poetic hemistich *ṣaḥā l-qalbu ʿan Salmā wa-aqṣara bāṭiluh* (The heart is cured of Salmā and has desisted from vain things) (Lane, *ṣ-ḥ-w*). Al-Akhṭal modulates through several connotations of the word, and the sense of "coming to one's senses," or, in the context of the poem, the failure to do so: he cannot recover from lost love; is stunned senseless before the executioner; is too dead drunk to sober up. Line 3 begins with the poet's inability to recover from the emotionally wrenching experience of the departing women—a synecdoche for the beloved; line 4 modulates by way of simile to the criminal's stunned disbelief as he is surrendered to his executioner; and finally, to a drunk in uncomprehending stupefaction enduring a hail of abuse. This is, in fact, quite similar to the affective modulation of motifs in al-Akhṭal's earlier poem, "The Tribe Has Departed" (chapter 3), lines 1–5, where the poet also described his state of shock at the tribe's departure as intoxication (lines 2–4) or as the state of one racked by pain or struck by charms and amulets (line 5).

In "Wāsiṭ Lies Deserted," it is the description of the hapless drunk that leads us into the extended wine theme that constitutes the bulk of the elegiac prelude (lines 5–20). The drinker has been "felled" (the term *ṣarīʿ* initially denotes being felled, as a tree, then one fallen, i.e., slain, on the battlefield, one prostrated by wine [Lane, *ṣ-r-ʿ*]), as here, and is metaphorically extended to mean "love-struck" (as in the sobriquet of the ʿAbbāsid poet Muslim ibn Walīd, "Ṣarīʿ al-Ghawānī," "love-struck by beautiful women"). The wine theme, developed at length here as compared with the three-line motif in "The Tribe Has Departed" (chapter 3, lines 2–4), is presented not as a cohesive narrative or even in the pictorial or descriptive manner we would term "wine scene," which details the drinkers, the wineskins, cups, the *saqi* (cupbearer) and singing girls, as rendered most notably by al-Akhṭal's most illustrious predecessor in that theme, the pre-Islamic poet al-Aʿshā, with whom al-Akhṭal bears comparison.[32] Instead we find loosely, almost paratactically, strung together a number of the motifs that are commonly associated with the wine scene. Classical Arab critics usually describe this absence of narrative cohesion by terms such as *iltifāt* and *iʿtirāḍ*, in the sense of digression or parenthesis.[33] To my mind such terms presume a prosaic or narrative expectation that has the effect of imposing a syntactical and logical subordination (in other words, judging that a passage is a digression, or is parenthetical) that is not necessarily poetically justifiable. As we have seen in the case of the verb *ṣaḥā*, the true poetic transitions and connections are often semantic rather than syntactic. Lines 5–7 present, by way of description of the drunk, to whom by simile the poet likens himself, a lively scene of a man prostrated from drink whose companions attempt to resuscitate him. It appears that he is barely, if at all, conscious and his comrades' exertions are likened to reviving the dead.

In line 8 the poem shifts grammatical person from the third person "he" of the drunk simile back to the first person, the "lyric I." There occurs, however, a rather dramatic shift in tone from the elegiac, melancholic mood that has dominated the prelude up to this point. This is possible because the wine scene or theme in the early Arabic qasida occupies two possible positions: one is in the elegiac prelude (*nasīb*) and the other in the third section, the poet's boast of himself and his tribe (*fakhr*). The motifs in both cases are virtually identical, so that the distinction between the two is the mood coloring, the tint provided by the poetic context. Thus the prelude location places the wine scene within the elegiac mood of loss and nostalgia, whereas the *fakhr* location is a ritualized boast over personal and tribal prosperity, success, and generosity, entailing the fulfillment of the oath (usually to take blood vengeance), reaggregation, and the commensal or communal and, at least metaphorically sacrificial, drink of wine. At the same time, the two structural possibilities create the potential for ambiguity. In the present case the passage (lines 8–21/22) opens with a boastful tone. It centers around the phrase "to fulfill my oath" (*li-ḥalli aliyyatī*). In the ritual and poetics of blood vengeance, and hence in the classical Arabic literary tradition, it is well established that the avenger would swear an oath not to drink wine until his vengeance was achieved, whereupon he would drink wine in celebration and recognition of the fulfillment of his oath. The most renowned poetic example is that of the elegy (*rithāʾ*) of the pre-Islamic brigand (*ṣuʿlūk*) poet, Taʾabbaṭa Sharran, who declares after having avenged his uncle:

> Lawful is wine (*ḥallati l-khamru*) now that once was forbidden;
> By great effort it came to be lawful.
>
> So give me a drink, O Sawād ibn ʿAmr,
> For my body, after my uncle['s] death, has wasted away.[34] [19]

In the poem at hand, it is said, with the traditional historical context of the poem in mind, that al-Akhṭal "had taken an oath not to drink wine until ʿUmayr ibn al-Ḥubāb was slain."[35] Although this appears to be in part extrapolated from the poetic text itself, it nevertheless explains the tone and significance of this wine passage: within the nostalgic mood of the elegiac prelude the poet is recalling the past days of glory—when his tribe was the victorious one, the slayers, not the slain. In other words, in this reading, al-Akhṭal reiterates here in the prelude section (*nasīb*) the boast over the death of ʿUmayr ibn al-Ḥubāb that occurs in the concluding praise section (*madīḥ*) of "The Tribe Has Departed" (in chapter 3; see lines 51–54). His new reduced circumstances have turned the tone into one of nostalgia, even irony and chagrin.

It is in this section, in lines 8–11, that we first find a complex of camel imagery and the lexicon of blood vengeance and bloodwite that will recur with distinctive variations in each formal section of the poem to create a structural and semantic progression. The first occurrence is an image of plenty: of a camel caravan laden with wineskins brimming with wine to quench the poet's thirst. In this regard we should note the metaphorical (and ritual symbolic) equivalence of blood and wine in the Arabic tradition and realize that to drink wine is a metaphor for quenching one's thirst for blood vengeance. Of the recurrent diction associated with vengeance, we find in this passage the reiteration of the root *th-q-l* (to be heavy) in the rhyme word *muthqalū* (laden, weighted) (line 8) and *al-athqāla* (heavy loads) (line 10). The image of camels laden with wineskins that forms the first occurrence of this complex is one of surfeit, though now distinctly in the past: in addition to "weighted" and "heavy," we find the wineskins filled to bursting (line 9), so full the legs stick straight out (line 11). The diction of burdens occurs as well in the "raised" (***tuḥmalū***) wine cups of line 13.

There follows a delightful depiction of the revelers at the drinking party in renowned lines (12–20) reminiscent of the wine revelry scenes of al-Aʿshā, the pre-Islamic master of the genre.[36] In keeping with the essentially sacrificial nature of wine drinking in the Arabic tradition,[37] we find the reiterative insistence throughout the longer wine passage of the diction of life and death, slaying and reviving (ultimately, sacrifice and redemption): the "revival" of the "dead" drunk in lines 5–7; the revelers' toast "God give us life!" (***Allahumma ḥayyi***) in line 13; "slaying" the wine by mixing it with water in lines 18. The passage closes with two lines that describe the vintner expertly caring for the growing vine.

Lines 21–24 constitute a transitional section from the elegiac prelude, with its nostalgic mood of loss, to the journey section, the perilous but clearly motivated and directional desert crossing. The poet first employs the motif of the termagant (***ʿādhilah***) who traditionally serves as the voice of society upbraiding the poet for his excesses. As it is positioned here, we first read the cause for blame as the poet's excessive drinking, or, as the tradition dictates, squandering his wealth to supply his fellow revelers with precious wine—but we should keep in mind that immoderate passion and excessive youthful infatuation with the beloved are also tradition-honored causes for the termagant's censure. The prelude concludes with the poet's threat to the termagant that if she does not desist he will revert to his former petulant ways with more resolve than ever.

The true transition from elegiac prelude (***nasīb***) to journey section (***raḥīl***) occurs in line 23, in which the poet declares an end to the lover's youthful passion (***ṣabābati ʿāshiqin***) and the appearance, or realization, of his "most hoped-for need." We should note that this is a rather traditional transition (***takhalluṣ***) between structural sections of the qasida and that it encapsulates above all a psychological turning point or change in mood. With the first hemistich the poet declares that he has put youthful passion behind him, and with it the passivity, nostalgia, and helpless yearning for the irretrievable past of the elegiac prelude, while in the second he expresses the his newfound resolve, the forward- or future-directed and goal-oriented aspiration. Just what this "hoped-for need" may be is encoded in the poetic idiom of line 24. Much like the second Suʿād of Kaʿb ibn Zuhayr's poem (line 13; see chapter 2), the new goal is phrased as a new beloved, here the "tribe of Ẓamyāʾ / Before whom at Ṣirrīn the door is locked." In light of the traditional context of the poem, we can read this as an allusion to the Umayyad door of clientage that has been shut in the face of the Taghlibīs. Similarly, this transitional section exhibits the diction of hope and fear—"my most hoped-for need" (*min ḥājātiya l-muta'ammalū*) (line 23) and "sudden apprehension" (*hājis*)—associated with the rite of supplication, but also with the institution of blood vengeance and bloodwite that coincides with it in this qasida. This expression of resolve and expectation sets the stage for the desert journey section.

The Desert Journey (Raḥīl): *Lines 25–43.* The desert journey section in this qasida is distinctive in that it is what I term an articulated or reduplicated *raḥīl.* By this I mean that it breaks down into two parts, that it is virtually a double *raḥīl.* Lines 25–31 form the first movement, lines 32–43 the second. As we noted in chapters 1 and 2, the hardships of the desert crossing play an essential structural role with regard to a number of the ritual and psychological aspects of the qasida. If in al-Nābighah's and Kaᶜb's qasidas the desert journey seems to constitute an expiatory rite (Gaster's Purgation), in all three poems we must understand that it serves to intensify the urgency of the supplicant's need and the strength of the trust and hope he has placed in the magnanimity of the patron. Above all, as we see in the first arc of the journey, the *raḥīl* contrasts the confusion, treachery, and waylessness of the barren liminal waste through which the poet journeys to the poet's unshakable trust in and unwavering sense of direction toward the patron. Thus, here the desert imagery is characterized by disorder and deceptiveness: ostrich roam like untended camels (line 25); the mirage flickers and glimmers (line 26); guides are fearful and vigilant, afraid even to blink (line 27).

Particularly noteworthy is the diction of line 28: *ghawl* (vast desert) derives from the root *gh-w-l* (whence our word "ghoul"). The basic sense of this word is the confusing and wayless desert in which the traveler strays farther and farther from the path until he perishes. This idea becomes personified in the *ghūl,* the protean Siren of the desert who seduces and slays the unsuspecting night traveler (see chapter 2). The sense of a confusing and directionless waste is conveyed by negating the standard denotants of right guidance—both physical and moral—perception and knowledge: *lā yuhtadā* (not guided; *hudan* = right guidance); there are no perceptible waymarkers (*bi-ᶜirfāni aᶜlāmin;* from the roots *ᶜ-r-f,* to perceive; and *ᶜ-l-m,* to know). Finally, in a delightful expression of ultimate liminality, the poet peoples the void, terming it "the playgrounds of the jinn" (*malāᶜibu jinnānin*). The effect of this liminal confusion and lack of direction is to set off by contrast the climax of lines 30–31: the resolute and unerringly directed journey of the poet: "I crossed" (*ajaztu*). Grammatically the direct object of "I crossed" in line 30 is the preposed "many a barren waste" of line 25, the intervening passage figuring as an extended description. Again, although the classical Arabic critics and their modern followers have tended to label such extended descriptions as "digressions," the analysis of such passages reveals that they convey ideas or concepts that are essential to the ritual and literary progression of the poem. In the qasida tradition, surface syntactic subordination does not imply structural or semantic subordination.

The opening phrase of line 31 is bivalent: it links back to line 30—"I crossed . . . To Khālid ibn Asīd," thereby appearing to constitute the end of the journey and concluding the first part of the articulated or reduplicated journey section (*raḥīl*) with the poet's arrival at the court of the patron (*mamdūḥ*). Rather than modulating at this point into the praise section (*madīḥ*), for which the phrase would normally serve as transition, the poet reverts to the journey: "To Khālid ibn Asīd there bore us swiftly camels . . . " (line 31), thereby initiating the second leg of the *raḥīl*, which is taken up primarily by camel description. Here we should note that whereas the poet's traditional mount, the she-camel (*nāqah*), is not mentioned—though it is implied—in the first journey section, in the second we find an innovation of the Umayyad period, a journey section featuring a group of riders, or, here, of she-camels.[38] Line 32 opens the passage with an image of the confusion of the sense of perspective: a yearling fox standing on a rise is taken to be a steed. The merciless cruelty of the desert journey is portrayed in lines 33–34 in the image of a she-camel that aborts a premature fetus only to have a starving wolf rip off the fetal membrane. The failure of fertility and the metaphoric resonances generated by this very graphic image serve to contrast the privation and barrenness of the *raḥīl* section with the abundance and fertility evoked in the *madīḥ* section, especially the full-uddered newly calved she-camels of line 60.

The bulk of this section, lines 35–42, however, consists of the description of a troop or caravan of she-camels enduring the journey. Although an Umayyad-period innovation, in the poem at hand this passage has the particular function of recalling, and contrasting with, the camel caravan passage of the wine scene in the elegiac prelude (lines 8–11). Whereas there we noted an insistence on plenitude and satiety, wineskins filled to bursting, here we find a reiterative insistence upon exhaustion, deprivation, and emaciation: their humps dwindle from the relentless journey (line 35), their eyes are sunken and hollow (line 37); the loops of their ropes are doubled because they are now so thin (line 38); they have no fodder, but only endlessly regurgitated cud (line 40); their urine is discolored and their dung desiccated from the lack of water and fodder (line 41). Nevertheless, those that have survived remain exuberant and quivering with excitement (line 39).

It is with the closing line of this section (line 42) that the imagery of the *raḥīl* comes together with the poetic lexicon of supplication and blood vengeance or bloodwite to tie all the threads of the poem together. Three key elements of this diction are compressed into one hemistich to intensify the effect. "Laden with weighty needs" (*ḥawāmilu ḥājātin thiqālin*): the root *ḥ-m-l* conveys bearing a burden or obligation, particularly, in this context, to be burdened with the obligation to achieve blood vengeance or acquire the bloodwite; related to the fertility/infertility themes at play throughout this qasida is another meaning of *ḥ-m-l*, to be pregnant, to bear fruit. The word *ḥājah* (need; plural *ḥājāt*) denotes any need, but it is also part of the specific blood vengeance and bloodwite vocabulary, and the root *th-q-l*, as we have mentioned above, is applied to weighty obligations.[39] As the camel caravan laden with wine expressed the fulfillment of a vow or obligation and the resultant sense of Gaster's Revitalization and Jubilation, the bearing of unfulfilled obligations or grave unsatisfied needs sets a tone of tension at the end of the *raḥīl.*

At this point in the ritual progression of the qasida we can evoke yet another sense of the collocation of the roots *ḥ-m-l* (to bear) and *th-q-l* (to be heavy): the ***burden*** of ***sins***, as in the Qurʾānic (29:12) expression: "And they shall assuredly bear their sins and the sins of others [whom they have seduced] with their sins" (*wa-la-yaḥmilunna athqālahum wa athqālan maʿa athqālihim*) (Lane, *th-q-l*). In this respect we are given to understand that the camels are bringing before the Banū Umayyah their sins against the Banū Taghlib; the poet, al-Akhṭal is laying before them their transgression against his tribe. The dangerous desert crossing of the heavily burdened camel caravan is thus expressive of the perils and psychological burden of the outraged client coming to lay his claim before liege lords who have failed him. In other words, in the pattern of transgression and redemption here enacted, the transgression is on the part of the *mamdūḥ*, the patron and liege lord, not the poet.

The Praise Section (Madīḥ): *Lines 43–70.* The following line (43) completes the transition from the journey to the praise section, reiterating the name Khālid[40] as the camels arrive and kneel at the patron's court. A further reiterative insistence upon the diction of supplication occurs here in the synonyms, the verbal *yurjā* (is hoped for) and the participial *al-muʾammalū* (hoped for). With line 44 we are fully in the praise section, which thereby opens with the traditional supplicatory invocation of the patron as an ample haven for the refugee and bountiful provider for the destitute. If we compare these three lines (42–44) that effect the transition from the journey to the praise section with line 23, which effected the transition from the elegiac prelude to the journey section, and further, if we compare them to similar transitional lines (see above), we can begin to see that such transitional sections are characterized by a concentration of ritual diction and that they serve to delineate the underlying structure of the qasida.

The praise section is divisible into three subsections. As we saw in the previous chapter, much more transpires in al-Akhṭal's *madīḥ* sections than that term, simply meaning "praise," would suggest. Above all, we will see in the development of this section the poet's exploitation of the traditions of the panegyric ode and the pattern of supplication inherent in it for the contestation of power.

The first subsection is a passage of praise of the sort intended to confirm the authority and legitimacy of the Umayyad princeling (lines 45–51), identified as Khālid ibn ᶜAbd Allāh ibn Khālid ibn Asīd ibn Abī al-ᶜĪṣ ibn Umayyah, one of the "magnanimous Arabs" (*ajwād al-ᶜArab*) during Islamic times.[41] Khālid is presented as the mainstay of his tribe, a steadfast leader and generous benefactor, with whom none should presume to compete. Lines 50–51 complete this subsection by invoking the patron's noble Umayyad ancestry and kin[42] and closing with praise for the Umayyads altogether in terms that once again reflect the poet's supplicatory stance: "They are a haven and refuge from fear."

The next subsection (lines 52–60) is cast initially in the form of the benediction (*duᶜāʾ*) that typically occurs toward the end of the panegyric ode (*qaṣīdat al-madḥ*), indeed, often closing the poem. Here it takes the particular form of the invocation of rain (*istisqāʾ*), but in the course of the passage the tense modulates from the perfect, used in the optative sense, through several conditional (essentially tenseless) lines, to conclude (lines 56–60) in the perfect tense. This passage is striking above all for its lyric power and delicacy as it describes the storm moving across the countryside. Despite its evident charm, the passage is poetically extremely complex. It is laden with imagery of fertility and abundance, especially of animal life. Layers of meaning are created primarily by evocatively metaphoric diction and by simile. In line 52 the pouring rain clouds are given "spouts" or "mouths" (*ᶜazālī*) like those of waterskins. With line 53 the clouds letting down rain are described with the diction of the milch camel, as having heavy udders that "flow with milk" (*taḥallaba*); their slow progression is compared in line

54 to the ponderous pace of "newly foaled she-camels tending their young." Steeds make their way into the imagery in line 55, where the lightning bolts are likened to the flanks of bolting piebald steeds, and again in line 58, where the hilltops rising above the floodwaters are compared to clusters of fine steeds kept tethered by the tents. A rain-laden cloud is compared to a camel laden with textiles (line 59), an image intended to evoke the simile of the herbs and flowers that spring up after a rainfall to figured fabrics. When the passage closes, this is no longer a simile but a description: in an image we might otherwise expect to find in the elegiac prelude (*nasīb*) section, the rain clouds alight at meadows where "she-camels, full uddered, newly calved, yearn over their young" (line 60). Here we find once more a bivalent term that joins the rain clouds and she-camels in a metaphorical yoke: *ḥuffal,* which means "full-uddered" or "giving much milk" for she-camels or oryx cows, or "yielding much rain" for a cloud.[43] This closing image serves as an expression of abundance and fertility associated with the *mamdūḥ,* in stark contrast to the privation and barrenness of the *raḥīl,* especially the aborted fetus of lines 33–34. Above all, it is an allegorical image of a "peaceable kingdom." Inasmuch as the realization of the benediction is contingent upon the *mamdūḥ*'s fulfilling the poet's request, the true message here is that if the Banū Marwān pay the bloodwite, the Umayyad polity will prosper, whereas if they refuse, it will be riven with discord.

At another level we can perceive in this storm passage a reiteration of the blood vengeance or bloodwite imagery that forms so dominant a structural and thematic role in this qasida. We can begin by noting the similarities in both content and structural position between al-Akhṭal's storm scene and that of the pre-Islamic master poet Imruʾ al-Qays in his *Muʿallaqah* (Suspended Ode).[44] There, too, I have argued that in light of the predominant role of the vengeance for his royal father in the literary anecdotal material surrounding Imruʾ al-Qays, the rainstorm functions as a metaphor for the shedding of the blood of vengeance. With this in mind, we can turn to the internal imagery of al-Akhṭal's poem, and to his poetic diction. We have already noted twice the appearance of she-camels in the present qasida. First, in the elegiac prelude, were the camels of the caravan laden with bursting wineskins that allowed the poet to drink in fulfillment of an oath to vengeance (lines 8–11); second were the haggard and emaciated she-camels of the journey section that made their way through the treacherous wastes to the court of the patron (lines 31–43)—the most elaborated of the three camel sections—and finally, in the praise section, the she-camels whose presence is insistently invoked through the diction, simile, metaphor, and juxtaposition with the rain-laden clouds of the storm scene (specifically lines 53, 54, 57, 59, 60). In brief, the poet's message is that the payment of the bloodwite will ensure the fertility and prosperity of the Umayyad realm.

Let us recapitulate at this point the diction of the bearing of heavy loads that recurs in these three camel passages. The roots involved are *ḥ-m-l* (to bear) and *th-q-l* (to be heavy, weighty), which sometimes occur together with the supplication diction that centers around the word *ḥājah/āt* (need/s) and the root *ʾ-m-l* (to hope). A chart will serve to clarify these patterns of diction:

First camel scene (elegiac prelude):

line 8: laden (*muthqalū*) with thirst-quenching wine
line 10: they took down their loads (*al-athqāla*)
line 13: when they raise (*tuḥmalū*) (lit. "are raised")

Transition from elegiac prelude to journey section:

line 23: My most hoped-for need (*ḥājātiya l-mutaʾammalū*)]

Second camel scene (transition from journey to praise section):

line 42: Laden with weighty needs which they bear (*ḥawāmilu ḥājātin thiqālin*)
line 43: a great man to hope for (*turjā*) and in whom to place one's hopes (*al-mutaʾ-ammalū*)

Third camel scene (praise section):

line 54: like the ponderous (*thiqālun*) gait of newly calved she-camels
line 57: barely bore (*yataḥammalū*) its heavy load (*athqālihi*) away
line 59: like a camel laden (*muḥammalū*) with textiles . . . heavily burdened (*muthqalū*)

The three camel sections serve as signposts to the ritual and structural progression of the qasida, along the lines of the Separation, Liminality, Reaggregation pattern of the van Gennepian rite of passage, from the state of past satiety or fulfillment subsequently lost (elegiac prelude), to the liminal state of need and unfulfillment (journey section), to the final state of new fulfillment (praise section). What finally emerges is a complex interweaving of fertility imagery derived from a web of semantic and metaphorical relationships. It is not easy to untangle the threads to see how al-Akhṭal has achieved this. We can begin with the she-camel that, as milch camel, mount, and beast of burden for desert crossings and broodmare, serves as the metaphorical ground (objective correlative) for expressing abundance, difficult passages, bearing of burdens—both literal and figurative—and fertility. The semantic range of key root words such as *ḥ-m-l* (lit., to bear a burden; *ḥamūl* means "beast of burden") contributes to the multivocity of metaphorical layers. In the sense of "burden" (*ḥaml*) and "to bear" (*ḥamala*), the camels of the *nasīb* (lines 8–9) are laden with wine symbolic of the fulfillment of the obligation of blood vengeance. The sense of "pregnant" (*ḥāmil*) is among the metaphorical resonances of these passages, as well as the aborting she-camel of lines 33–34 of the *raḥīl* and the newly calved she-camels of line 60 in the *madīḥ*.[45] The burden of the bloodwite (*ḥamālah*) is then the weighty need that the she-camels bear in the journey section. In the Arabic tradition rain clouds, too, are described as *ḥāmilāt,* that is, "laden" or "pregnant" with rain (Lane, *ḥ-m-l*). In al-Akhṭal's poem this is exploited to create a metaphorical layering of (1) clouds bearing—and dropping—rain; (2) she-camels bearing and putting down loads of textiles; (3) she-camels bearing and giving birth to their young and producing milk; (4) camels bearing the metaphorical burden of the obligation to pay the bloodwite; and, as we shall see below in the closing section of the poem (line 68), (5) the caliph ʿAbd al-Malik paying, assuming the burden of, the bloodwite for the Taghlibīs slain in the massacre of the Day of al-Bishr.

At this point we can invoke as well Gaster's "seasonal pattern" of Emptying and Filling, of the end of an old lease on life and, after a period of uncertainty, the establishment of a new one, to help explain the structural poetic movement from lost abundance to desert waste to abundant life-generating rainfall. The charming lyricism of the rainfall on the meadow where newly calved she-camels yearn over their newborn thus has a darker ritual role in the symbolic cycles of blood vengeance and bloodwite. Finally, we should keep in mind the immanent sacerdotal role of the poet as he pronounces his benediction. Not unrelated to the "paradoxical power" of the supplicant, the blessing is eminently a form of performative language that is, in the qasida tradition, the poet's prerogative. Moreover, the power to pronounce benediction implies the power to pronounce malediction, to curse (see chapter 6). Therefore we can detect in the movement from the suppliant's self-abasement and praise of the patron's might and authority of lines 43–51 to the benediction of lines 52–60 a shift in the balance of power between poet and patron. And this is only the beginning.

Even with this awareness, however, the abrupt change from the delicate lyricism that concludes the rainstorm passage to the brusque political discourse of the closing section (lines 61–70) delivers a jolt to us, as it must have been intended to do to the patron when recited before him. The switch is not merely from lyrical to hortatory, but from benedictory to minatory. If the benediction is meant to convey the restoration of the Umayyad realm and reestablishment of peaceable relations between the Banū Taghlib and the Banū Marwān that will transpire when restitution (bloodwite) is paid for those slain on the Day of al-Bishr, then the following section voices the threat of dissolution of the polity and the outbreak of hostilities should the bond of clientage be broken by the Banū Marwān's failure to pay restitution.

The passage opens in a declamatory tone, as if throwing the outrage of al-Jaḥḥāf in the Marwānids' face (line 61). Lines 62–64 are phrased as a rhetorical question; the details of the expression are somewhat unclear, but following the commentaries—although they, too, differ in interpreting some of the details—we can attempt the following paraphrase to capture the gist of the lines: So ask the Banū Marwān, "Why is it that your protection and bond of clientage remains connected to this criminal, al-Jaḥḥāf? After all, when Muṣᶜab ibn al-Zubayr was slain in vengeance for Ashᶜath (al-Nābī ibn Ziyād ibn Ẓabyān) by his brother ᶜUbayd Allāh ibn Ẓabyān, and left undeloused and unwashed on the battlefield, was it al-Jaḥḥāf who brought you Muṣᶜab's head, so that you now order him to slay us, who are under your protection, in our abodes? No, rather it was ᶜUbayd Allāh who cut off Muṣᶜab's head and brought it to you, while al-Jaḥḥāf was still fighting on the Zubayrid side!"[46]

What the poet is describing, here through a rhetorical question rather than, syntactically at least, a straightforward accusation, is an act of treachery against precisely those allies and clients—the Banū Taghlib—who were responsible for the Marwānid victory over the Zubayrids. The sense of outrage and disbelief conveyed by the rhetorical question is more effective than a declarative statement would have been. This passage falls under the classical Arabic descriptive heading of *ᶜitāb* (blame, reproach), but the term hardly does justice to the complex rhetorical trajectory of the poem.[47] There is a palpably mounting momentum and tension as the poet has now moved from self-abasing supplication to sacerdotal benediction to indignant accusation to outright challenge of Marwānid authority. And as the power and authority of the poet inexorably mount throughout the *praise* section of the poem, those of the caliph proportionately diminish. In line 65 al-Akhṭal describes the Taghlibīs' trust in the Umayyads' inviolable covenant of protection (*dhimmah*) as so strong that if it were invoked, the proverbially timid mountain goats would descend tamely from their mountain peaks.

The most daring lines of the poem are 66 and 67, in which the poet issues his threat, or ultimatum. The anecdote from the *Kitāb al-Aghānī*, quoted earlier in this chapter, that depicts al-Akhṭal reciting lines 61, 62, and 66 to the caliph ʿAbd al-Malik himself is meant to convey, above all, just how audacious the poet is in making his demands. In addition, we can read in the anecdote an element of the poetic of supplication that we witnessed in both al-Nābighah's (chapter 1) and Kaʿb's (chapter 2) poems, that is, that the supplicant poet risks his life in coming before the patron. If we focus more on the internal evidence of the poetic text, however, and note the impersonal construction of the second hemistich, "there will be a withdrawal and departure from Quraysh," and the fact that the qasida is addressed to Khālid ibn Asīd and was presumably presented to him as an intermediary between the Taghlibīs and the caliph ʿAbd al-Malik, the audacity is somewhat tempered. Nevertheless, by line 64 the effect of the framing indirect discourse, "So ask the Banū Marwān, . . . " has been lost, so that the poet now seems to be directly addressing and challenging the caliph, an effect that is intensified by addressing the caliph with the singular, rather than plural, "you": "Was it al-Jaḥḥāf who brought you . . . so that you ordered him . . . " Line 67 is quite explicitly a threat of war: hostilities will break out if the poet's terms are not met; the Banū Taghlib will disgrace the Marwānids and live honorably, or else, rather than live in ignominy, die fighting. The fact that this declaration of war is syntactically the apodosis or result clause of a conditional clause tempers the effect but little. Indeed, it could be argued that it is only the law of hospitality that the qasida has invoked in its supplicatory section that prevents the poet from being killed on the spot. The rhetorical effect is to escalate the tension still further.

It is precisely at this instant of dramatically heightened tension that al-Akhṭal defuses the situation by offering his alternative (lines 68–69), that the Banū Marwān should assure that the Banū Taghlib are paid the bloodwite for those slain at al-Bishr, and that, although this does not entirely make up for the loss of life, the Taghlibīs will graciously be content with a fair blood price. A closer look at the diction of these two lines is in order. Line 68 is particularly striking for its reiterative insistence on precisely those two roots, *ḥ-m-l* (to bear) and *th-q-l* (to be heavy), that we have traced through the three camel sections of the poem. In the analysis of the previous occurrences of these roots we suggested that they were metaphorically associated with the concept of blood vengeance and bloodwite, inasmuch as these are traditionally expressed in terms of the burden of weighty obligation. Line 68 then seems to recapitulate and state with declarative explicitness all that was subtly and metaphorically suggested:

If you take on the burden of the bloodwite (*taḥmilū*)
for them, [know that]
No bloodwite (*ḥamālatin*), however weighty (*thaqulat*),
can outweigh (*athqalu*) kindred blood.

The effect is to bring the whole weight of the previous sections of the poem to bear on this one climactic line. The next line, 69, effects a final resolution that has the effect of diffusing the tension. Threats, accusations, challenges, and demands are put aside as the poet declares in a tone that, if not altogether conciliatory, is designed to mollify while at the same time force the hand of the Marwānids. The sense of a firm and inescapable solution is achieved by the threefold repetition of the word *al-ḥaqq*, a term whose range of meaning includes "truth," "right," and "one's due" (Lane, *ḥ-q-q*). By stating the Taghlibī claim in terms of "the truth," "what is right," "what is justly due," al-Akhṭal has accomplished a rhetorical feat whereby the Marwānids cannot deny the Taghlibi claim without denying truth, right, and justice.

If you give us the [bloodwite]
that is our right (*al-ḥaqq*),
We will not be blind to right (*al-ḥaqq*),
our right (*al-ḥaqq*) is all we ask.

In other words, for ʿAbd al-Malik to deny al-Akhṭal's claim would be to relinquish all moral authority to the caliphate.

As if declaring victory, al-Akhṭal closes the qasida with a line of tribal boast (*fakhr*) celebrating the military prowess of the Banū Taghlib. Of note is the expression of the fame of Taghlibī battle days through the distinctive marks by which renowned battle steeds are recognized. What is given in the translation as "our day illustrious" is more precisely something like this: our battle day is as distinctive as a noble-bred battle steed with a blaze on its forehead *(agharr)* and white legs *(muḥajjal)*. One could argue whether this line constitutes a boast, a gloat, or a threat—it could probably be read as any or all. What is clear, in any case, is that the poet has the upper hand. Having started from the position of supplicant humbling himself before the might and authority of the patron and by extension the caliphal family, the poet ends by affirming the moral authority and the military might of the Banū Taghlib.

Conclusion: Form and Function; or, Celebration versus Supplication

If we now pause to look back over the two odes by al-Akhṭal, "The Tribe Has Departed" (chapter 3) and "Wāsiṭ Lies Deserted," it is apparent that they represent the two predominant structural forms of the qasida, the bipartite (elegiac prelude–praise section/*nasīb-madīḥ*) and the tripartite (elegiac prelude–desert journey–praise section/*nasīb-raḥīl-madīḥ*), respectively. The extensive statistical sampling and structural analysis of odes that would be necessary for a definitive conclusion is beyond the scope of the present study; nevertheless, I would like to propose that the distinction between these two odes may provide a paradigm for further exploration into the structural idiom of other qasidas. Thus, we see that the bipartite structure is employed by the poet as a celebrant in the victory of the *mamdūḥ* (patron). The structural sections, much like Gaster's Emptying and Filling, set up a dialectic between the failed polity and the victorious one, between Dissolution and Restoration. There is no change of allegiance or change of status on the part of the poet vis-à-vis the *mamdūḥ;* rather there is a change of situation from defeat to victory on the part of the polity to which he belongs and of which his patron is the ruler.[48]

The tripartite structure is particularly suited, like the van Gennepian three-part rite of passage (separation-liminality-reaggregation), to conveying a change in the status of the poet vis-à-vis the patron. It is thus the most appropriate poetic vehicle for expressing a transfer of allegiance, such as when the poet comes to the court of the patron for the first time, or for the reentry into court of a poet who is estranged from his patron. In these cases, the position of the poet is that of the supplicant, rather than the celebrant. It must be recognized, however, that although this distinction may prove a useful rule of thumb in assessing the tone of a qasida, nevertheless, given the subtleties and complexities of courtly politics, the poet's roles as supplicant and celebrant are bound to shift and overlap. In historical terms, as we move beyond the Umayyad (41–132/661–750) period into the ʿAbbāsid (132–656/750–1258), the bipartite form comes to predominate, at least in numerical terms, and, on occasion, even to give way to an essentially *madīḥ*-dominated form in which the full poetic movement is subsumed within a framework consisting of the panegyric section.

As we proceed in the following chapters to the ʿAbbāsid period, when the scions of another branch of the Quraysh, the Banū Hāshim, wrested the caliphate from the Umayyads and established their new capital at Baghdad, we will witness the poets' manipulation of the qasida's structural possibilities to express a variety of political moods and postures.

Five

Political Dominion as Sexual Domination

Abū al-ᶜAtāhiyah, Abū Tammām, and the Poetics of Power

Myth, Gender, and the Manipulation of Form

Qasidas were presented not merely to the caliph, of course, but also to the men at court, generals, governors, judges, and others. At the same time that the qasida performed its political and ideological function at contemporary courts, a process of literary canonization was taking place through which the poetic tradition gradually evolved from a tribal oral tradition to part of the Arabo-Islamic *paideia,* the traditional cultural education—and the collective memory—of the cultivated and courtly classes, what is called in Arabic *adab.*[1]

In general terms, the dominant form of the panegyric in the ᶜAbbāsid period was increasingly the bipartite structure consisting of the elegiac prelude (*nasīb*) and the praise section (*madīḥ*), though even this form often includes what I have termed a "vestigial journey section (*raḥīl*)" of a line or two suggesting its derivation from the tripartite form. The dialectical relation of the two parts and the identification of the source of caliphal praise motifs in ancient Near Eastern concepts of sacerdotal and cosmic kingship has been lucidly set forth by Stefan Sperl.[2] At the same time, however, we see the development of panegyrics that seem to be structurally and thematically dominated by the praise section with neither the elegiac prelude nor the journey section occurring as structural or thematic units. Inasmuch as these structural variants—and others—may occur in the diwan of a single poet, we can suggest that the poets had a sense of form (*Formgefühl*)[3] or a grasp of the expressive language of form that allowed them to manipulate the parts and proportions of the qasida to achieve precise and varied aesthetic and semantic or political effects.

The present chapter takes as its subject two renowned, though vastly different, examples of caliphal panegyric from the early ᶜAbbāsid period, that is, from the era when the caliphate still dominated the Islamic state, before its inexorable diminution—in terms of actual politico-military might, if not in symbolic authority—from about the middle of the third/ninth century onwards. The first, "My Coy Mistress" (*A-Lā Mā li-Sayyidatī*), is by Abū al-ᶜAtāhiyah (130–210 or 211 H./748–825 or 826 C.E.). Although he achieved his greatest renown for his later ascetic poems (*zuhdiyyāt*), prior to his renunciation of worldly poetry (ca. 178/794) he was popularly celebrated for his elegiac-erotic lyric (*ghazal*), wine poems (*khamriyyāt*), and panegyrics for the caliphs al-Mahdī (r. 158–169/775–785) and al-Hādī (r. 169–170/785–786).[4] In terms of style, Abū al-ᶜAtāhiyah's poetry is characterized by its lyrical charm, simplicity of diction, and short meters.[5] The second is by the celebrated caliphal panegyrist Abū Tammām (188–231 or 232/804–845 or 846).[6] In contrast to Abū al-ᶜAtāhiyah, Abū Tammām achieved renown, indeed notoriety, for his unrestrained embrace of the *badīᶜ* (new, innovative) style of third/ninth century Arabic poetry, of which he was the major exponent. His oeuvre, of which "The Sword Is More Veracious" (*Al-Sayfu Aṣdaqu*) figures as his masterpiece, is characterized by obscure diction, rhetorical density and complexity, and an appeal that is more conceptual-intellectual than lyrical.[7] Abū al-ᶜAtāhiyah is the sort of poet the classical Arabic critics described as *maṭbūᶜ* (naturally gifted); Abū Tammām is characterized by its antonym, *maṣnūᶜ* (artificial).[8]

In this chapter we will explore how these two almost diametrically opposed poetic sensibilities nevertheless both produce panegyric that buttresses the authority of the caliphate. As we shall see below, Abū al-ᶜAtāhiyah's qasida is shaped in mood and form by the sensibility of the elegiac prelude (*nasīb*) with its motifs of *tashbīb* (amorous-erotic description of the beloved) and the closely related freestanding form, the *ghazal* (elegiac or erotic lyric), whereas Abū Tammām's martial qasida is dominated in mood, structure, and theme by the praise section (*madīḥ*).

We will place a particular emphasis on the aspects of myth and gender. With regard to myth, we will attempt to show that Abū al-ᶜAtāhiyah's poem draws on ancient Near Eastern mythic concepts of sacerdotal kingship and sacred marriage (*hieros gamos*), which he then imposes on the contemporary political situation. In Abū Tammām's case, we will show a different directionality: the poet takes as his starting point the Muslim conquest of the Byzantine city of ᶜAmmūriyah (Amorium), and through his rhetorical treatment turns the contemporary politico-military event into a perduring myth of Arabo-Islamic dominion and ᶜAbbāsid "manifest destiny." Related to this, we will explore how both poems employ concepts, or constructs, of gender, particularly a dialectic of male domination and female submission, as the metaphorical material for conveying the relation, respectively, of the caliph to his subjects and of the triumphant Arab Muslims to the defeated Byzantine Christians.

Submission and the Renunciation of Desire

Abū al-ᶜAtāhiyah's qasida is a short lyric (11 lines) in the meter *al-mutaqārib,* a light meter whose name means to walk in short steps, trippingly.[9] In terms of the poetics of form and genre in the Arabic tradition, this information by itself would suggest a *ghazal,* a short amorous lyric, often, as in the famously chaste Umayyad-period poets of the Banū ᶜUdhrah, about unrequited love. It is this mood, established by the form and meter of the poem as well as by its contents, that subsumes the entire poem. This qasida was one that won its author renown, as is reflected in an anecdote in al-Iṣbahānī's *Kitāb al-Aghānī* (Book of Songs). There we read that one day the caliph al-Mahdī held an audience for poets. Among them were Bashshār ibn Burd; Ashjaᶜ al-Sulamī, a pupil and admirer of Bashshār's; and Abū al-ᶜAtāhiyah. As Ashjaᶜ tells it:

> When Bashshār heard [Abū al-ᶜAtāhiyah] speak, he said [to me], "O Akhū Sulaym [Ashjaᶜ], is this the one nicknamed the Kufan? "Yes," I replied. "May God not reward with good him who brought us together with him!" returned Bashshār. Then al-Mahdī told Abū al-ᶜAtāhiyah, "Recite!" Whereupon Bashshār [muttered to me], "Woe to you! Is he going to begin and also be asked to recite before us!" "So it seems," said I, and Abū al-ᶜAtāhiyah recited the first five verses of "Is my lady . . . " Then . . . Bashshār said to me, "Woe to you, O Akhū Sulaym! I don't know which I am more amazed at: how weak his poetry is, or how he [dares to] recite love poetry about the caliph's slave girl for the caliph to hear with his own ears!" Until he reached "There came to him the caliphate . . . " and the five final verses, at which Bashshār, trembling with delight, said to me, "Woe to you! I can't believe the caliph isn't jumping from his throne with joy! . . . "[10]

Abū al-ᶜAtāhiyah's "My Coy Mistress" (*A-Lā Mā li-Sayyidatī*)[11]
[meter: *mutaqārib;* rhyme: *-ālahā*]

1. What ails my lady?
   Is she coy?
   And I must bear her coyness?

2. And if not, why does she accuse me?
   What crime did I commit?
   May God send rain upon her ruined abode!

3. A slave girl of the Imām—
has not love been lodged
beneath her shirt?

4. Among maidens, dark-eyed, short-stepped,
she walked, as weighty buttocks
drew her back.

5. God has tried my soul with her,
and has tired her censurers
with blame.

6. As if before my eyes,
wherever I sojourn on earth,
I see her likeness.

7. [She was] the caliphate
[and] came to him, submissive,
trailing the train of her gown.

8. She was right only for him;
he only for her.

9. Should anyone else desire her,
the very earth would quake.

10. Should the hearts' daughters fail to obey him,
God would not accept their deeds.

11. And the caliph, out of hatred for the word "no,"
hates whoever utters it. [20]

This qasida is striking for its charm—indeed, humor—brevity, and yet great panegyric power. With masterly concision Abū al-ᶜAtāhiyah evokes within an eleven-line *ghazal* form all the essential conventions of the full panegyric in its two-part ᶜAbbāsid form. He opens, quite according to custom, lamenting his lost beloved, complaining of her coquetry, invoking God to shower rains upon the ruins of her abode (lines 1–2). In line 3 the poet reveals just how illicit and forbidden this love is—she is the property of the caliph—and yet even in the caliph's presence he continues to vaunt her charms (line 4)—chief among them her buttocks so delightfully ponderous that they pull her back when she tries to walk forward—and finally to complain of the torments of the lovesick (lines 5–6). As we witnessed in chapter 1 with al-Nābighah's description of al-Mutajarridah, the composition of *tashbīb* (erotic or amorous description) on a girl or woman was considered proof positive of carnal knowledge. Thus, as Abū al-ᶜAtāhiyah's poem stands so far, the expected, indeed obligatory, response of the caliph would be to call the executioner.

At the same time, it is clear that the poet's beloved has frustrated his desires and his love is unrequited.

But suddenly, in line 7, the concubine with trailing gown led submissively to the caliph is revealed to be a metaphor for the caliphate itself. This metaphor is as powerful as it is charming, for it is now the entire *ummah* (Islamic nation) that submits to al-Mahdī in an image whose origins lie in the ancient Near Eastern *hieros gamos* (sacred marriage).[12] In terms of the classical Arabo-Islamic construct of gender (though quite at odds with our contemporary thinking on gender relations), the sexual metaphor of caliph and concubine (lines 7–8) perfectly expresses the relation of domination and submission on the one hand, and, on the other, the perfect mutuality that defines the relation of ruler to realm. If the poet's desires in the elegiac prelude (*nasīb*) of the poem are frustrated, clearly the caliph's in this praise section (*madīḥ*) are not. Further, the master-to-slave-girl model that the poet evokes here adds to the mythic and sexual dimensions of the *hieros gamos* the element of rightful ownership—the relation of the possessor to what he rightfully possesses. In this context the vehemence of sexual jealousy serves to express both the personal anger of the outraged caliph and the cosmic rage, the earthquake, that others' designs on the caliphate would occasion (line 9). The poet's use of the earthquake (verb: *zalzala;* noun: *zilzāl*) can be read as a generically mythic or archetypal expression of cosmic rage echoing the political outrage of attempting to usurp the caliphate—basically a sort of pathetic fallacy. This effect is augmented, or perhaps overshadowed, by the Qur'ānic associations of the phrase, for it occurs in the opening verse of the Sura of the Earthquake (*Sūrat al-Zilzāl*): *Idhā zulzilati l-arḍu zilzālahā* ("When the earth is shaken with a mighty earthquake," Qur'ān 99:1), a vivid account of the cosmic turmoil that ushers in the Day of Judgment.[13] In this Islamic context, Abū al-ʿAtāhiyah's very simply stated line (line 9) amounts to the claim for the divine appointment of the caliph—a claim that is strengthened in the closing lines.

In the final two lines, the poem turns from the relation of caliph to caliphate to the relation of the subjects to the caliph. First, in line 10, obedience and submission to the caliph become an article of Islamic faith, without which one's good deeds are unacceptable to God. The exclusive claim of the caliph to the political loyalty of all Muslims is central to the theory of the caliphate. Here the concept is clothed in a sexual metaphor through the depiction of Muslims' political loyalties as "the hearts' daughters" (*banātu l-qulūbi*): they are thus presented as young girls or concubines who must submit to the sexual demands of their master. Once this metaphor is thus established, it determines as well a sexual reading for the closing line (line 11). The "no" reads as a refusal of the caliph's sexual prerogatives and advances, which thus becomes equated with the withholding of political allegiance, denying the caliph the obedience which is rightfully due him. The charm and power of this poem lie above all in Abū al-ᶜAtāhiyah's establishing a metaphor through which sexual submission and domination serve to express political relations between subject and ruler.

Let us look more closely at the sexual poetics and politics of this qasida, particularly as it exploits the inherent lyricism of the elegiac prelude (*nasīb*), here in the form of sexual desire and its suppression, to express absolutist political dominion. Structurally, the poem is divisible into two parts, lines 1–6 and lines 7–11, as the anecdote cited above confirms. Ashjaᶜ al-Sulamī's story tells us as well that the tradition read the poem as a poetic surprise, in which the poet plays with the conventional expectations of his audience to produce, in the end, something quite unexpected. As the anecdote tells us, the first six lines give the impression of conventional amorous-erotic description (*tashbīb*), which becomes shocking once we are informed that the object of the poet's affections is the property of the caliph. Nevertheless, in line with conventional or generic expectations, the audience would expect that the second part of the qasida, the praise section (*madīḥ*), would present a substitution of the fulfillment through devotion to the caliph for the failed love of the elegiac prelude. Instead, something quite different occurs, something quite delightfully surprising—at least to the caliph. Rather than the dramatic shift in tone from the effeminate lyricism of the elegiac prelude to the martial masculinity of the praise section that forms the affective contrast between the two structural sections, the lyric-erotic mood of the elegiac prelude (*nasīb*) prevails through the end of the poem. The might and dominion of the caliph, conventionally expressed in the terms and tone of the martial-heroic ethos of the warrior aristocracy that characterize the praise section, is transferred through mood and metaphor to the intimate and erotic zone of the elegiac prelude and amorous-erotic lyric (*ghazal*), first to convey the exclusive and absolute right of the caliph, al-Mahdī, to the caliphate (lines 7–9) and then the submission and obedience due him from his subjects (lines 10–11).

If the poet's amorous-erotic description of the caliph's slave girl in the elegiac prelude (lines 1–6) amounts, as we saw in al-Nābighah's description of al-Mutajarridah, to an expression of sedition, we can further, in this case, interpret the poet's erotic desire as political desire. Sexual dominion operates as a metaphor for political dominion, and the caliph's authority is absolute.

This entails a strange sexual twist for the second part of the poem, which we can still term the praise section (*madīḥ*). Rather than the poet finding fulfillment to compensate for the amorous-erotic failure of the elegiac prelude (*nasīb*), lines 7–9 present the political allegiance as sexual renunciation. In what might be termed a failed Oedipal situation, the poet, rather than ultimately defying, defeating, and replacing the father figure, renounces his own (masculine, active) sexuality. Once unmanned, as it were, he is portrayed in the closing lines (10–11) as a "feminized" subject who will only be spared the displeasure of both deity and ruler through obedience and submission to the sexual demands of the latter.

We can now begin to understand the poet's employ of the *nasīb* mood throughout the poem, for the stance of the poet in the elegiac prelude (*nasīb*) is one of passivity and submission, a posture that he finds precisely suited to express the relation of the subject to the absolute monarch. The gender construct based on the model of male domination and female submission is here doubly exploited as a metaphor for the relation of the caliph to the caliphate and of the ruler to his subjects. The conventional contrast of lyric-erotic *nasīb* and martial-heroic *madīḥ* is replaced here with a different contrast, one between a daringly seditious and subversive *nasīb* and an abjectly submissive *madīḥ* that proclaims not the fulfillment, but the repression and renunciation of desire. In more poetic terms, both the charm and efficacy of this poem derive from its controlling conceit: the use of what is formally a *ghazal* to perform the function of the *qaṣīdat al-madḥ* (panegyric ode)—in other words, the use of a "light" amorous lyric form to convey the gravity of absolute monarchy.[14]

At this point we can introduce another theme from the biographical anecdotes (*akhbār*) concerning Abū al-ʿAtāhiyah, which purport to provide a true story of desire and renunciation. In the *Kitāb al-Aghānī* we read of Abū al-ʿAtāhiyah's infatuation with ʿUtbah, a slave girl belonging to a female relative of the caliph al-Mahdī, and the efforts of the renowned singer Yazīd Ḥawrāʾ to help the love-struck poet:

> Yazīd Ḥawrāʾ was a friend of Abū al-ʿAtāhiyah. So Abū al-ʿAtāhiyah composed some verses on the subject of ʿUtbah in which he asks al-Mahdī to fulfill his promise to marry ʿUtbah to him, so that when [Yazīd] found al-Mahdī in a good mood, he could sing them to him. They went:
>
> I have inhaled the winds hoping for the scent of what I long for
> And I have found it in the breeze of your two hands.
>
> I have led my soul to drink of hope in you
> That carried me trotting and galloping toward you,

And I cast my glance at the sky of your storm cloud,
Watching for lightning, looking out for the rain,

I was on the verge of despair, then I said, "No,
Surely he who guarantees success is generous."[15] [21]

So [Yazīd] composed a tune to go with them, waited for a time when he found al-Mahdī in a good mood, and sang them to him. Thereupon [al-Mahdī] called for Abū al-ᶜAtāhiyah and said, "As for ᶜUtbah, you will never attain her, for her mistress has forbidden it. But here are fifty thousand dirhams. Use them to buy [a slave girl] better than ᶜUtbah." The money was brought to him and he left.[16]

This anecdote forms part of a varied anecdotal complex that has the effect of generating a narrative romance out of the poetic conventions of Abū al-ᶜAtāhiyah's diwan, one that culminates in his failure to attain the object of his desire, his beloved ᶜUtbah, and his renunciation of the courtly world and dedication to asceticism.[17] In the tradition this transition is associated with his long ode rhymed in *-lī* that opens "I have cut off from you the ropes of hope" (*qaṭaᶜtu minki ḥabāʾila l-āmālī*).[18] As is typical of the narrative biographical impulse, the feminine singular "you" of the ***nasīb*** convention, in the poem identified as ***al-dunyā*** (this world), is in this tradition said to refer to ᶜUtbah and, in an extended sense, to the caliph, Hārūn al-Rashīd (r. 170–193/786–809).[19] In this tradition, too, we find anecdotes that identify the "slave girl of the Imām" of "My Coy Mistress" as ᶜUtbah.[20]

Our own discussion will focus not on the fruits of the narrative biographical impulse, which can both illuminate and obscure the poetic text, but on the text itself and its politico-ceremonial message. In this respect, what this anecdote provides is an example of the failure of the qasida ceremony. As we have discussed the ceremonial presentation of the panegyric ode thus far, particularly in light of rituals of exchange, the poet has every right to expect his request to be fulfilled; that is the patron's role in the ceremony, his part in the bargain. Indeed, the closing line really means something close to "the caliph is not one to break his promises"—which the caliph then proceeds to do. Although the anecdotes vary, the real point is that caliphal prerogative overrides the demands of the qasida ceremony, as in this case where the caliph will not override his kinswoman's prerogative to determine her slave girl's future. At the same time, the patron has the authority to override ceremony and ritual and the power to frustrate the poet's hopes. If "My Coy Mistress" proposes that the subject must repress his own desires to serve and obey the caliph, and that this is the price he must pay to gain eternal salvation, Abū al-ᶜAtāhiyah's ascetic poetry proposes a further renunciation: that one should forswear the worldly life of court and politics altogether and abandon the hope of earthly reward for reward in the world to come.

Islamic Destiny: Participation and the Fulfillment of Desire

Abū Tammam's masterpiece, "The Sword Is More Veracious" (*Al-Sayfu Aṣdaqu*),[21] is a victory ode presented to the caliph al-Muʿtaṣim (r. 218–227/833–842) after his conquest of the Byzantine city of Amorium (Arabic: ʿAmmūriyah) in 223/838. Our discussion will focus on the poet's transformation of an historical event into a legitimizing myth of the ʿAbbāsid caliphate and a vehicle for the promulgation of an ideology of Arabo-Islamic "manifest destiny." In terms of the poetics of gender and its relation to qasida structure that we introduced in our discussion of Abū al-ʿAtāhiyah's "My Coy Mistress" (*A-Lā Mā li-Sayyidatī*), we will argue that whereas that poem was characterized by a "feminized" subject and short lyric-elegiac (*nasīb, ghazal*) mood and form, in Abū Tammām's poem the martial-heroic "masculine" conventions of the praise section (*madīḥ*) dominate both thematically and structurally. Sexual domination, particularly in the form of the rape of the conquered city, operates as the dominant metaphor for military conquest and political dominion. Rhymed in *-bī*, the qasida is in the meter *basīṭ*, one of the time-honored and stately meters of the Jāhilī qasida. As will become clear when we compare Abū Tammām's poem with the accounts of the Arab and Byzantine chroniclers, the poet is not attempting to reconstruct a narrative sequence of events; rather, he selects those elements of the actual occurrence that can be reconfigured within the ritual and ceremonial structure of the qasida as emblems, symbols, or metaphors of ʿAbbāsid legitimacy and an Arabo-Islamic "manifest destiny." In other words, Abū Tammām's victory ode for the Islamic conquest of the Byzantine city of Amorium, ʿAmmūriyah in Arabic, subsumes that victory in a teleological myth in which it figures as a step in the inexorable march of Islamic triumph.

A review of the historical accounts concerning the conquest of ʿAmmūriyah will provide a background for understanding Abū Tammām's choice of a *madīḥ*-dominated structure and the controlling themes and descriptive motifs: the masculine sexual imagery of the conquering Muslim armies and the feminine personification of the vanquished Byzantine city.

In 223/838, Bābak, the leader of the twenty-year Khurramite rebellion against the ʿAbbāsid state, in the hope of diverting some of Caliph al-Muʿtaṣim's armies from himself encouraged the Byzantine emperor, Theophilus, to make incursions into ᶜAbbāsid territory. Theophilus proceeded with an army of 100,000, according to the Muslim chronicler al-Ṭabarī (d. 450/1058),[22] who describes the outrage perpetrated against the Islamic *ummah* (nation):

> In this year (223) Tawfīl ibn Mīkhāʾīl, the leader of the Byzantines, attacked Zibaṭrah with his men, taking its inhabitants captive and destroying their city. He then proceeded immediately to Malaṭyah and attacked its people and the inhabitants of some of the Muslim fortresses besides. He took Muslim women captive—it is said more than a thousand—and mutilated the Muslim men who came into his hands, putting out their eyes and cutting off their ears and noses.[23]

According to the Arab philologist and commentarist al-Tibrīzī (d. 502/1109), after the Byzantines had conquered Zibaṭrah, "Word reached the caliph . . . that on that day a Muslim woman who was taken captive cried out 'Help, O Muᶜtaṣim!' (*Wāmuᶜtaṣimāh*!). When he was informed of this, there was in his hand a cup of wine that he wanted to drink, but he put it down and ordered that it be kept for him to drink when he returned from the conquest of ᶜAmmūriyah."[24] The caliph's speedy and decisive response to the capture of Zibaṭrah is attested to by al-Ṭabarī as well. He writes: "When news of it came to him he made the call to arms in his palace, then mounted his steed and fastened a shackle behind him and a die or iron and a saddlebag of provisions, and he did not rise (from the saddle) to leave, until after the troops were arrayed."[25]

The army of Emperor Theophilus had been defeated and routed by al-Muᶜtaṣim's renowned Persian general, al-Afshīn, at Damizon before the battle of ᶜAmmūriyah, so that, unlike al-Muᶜtaṣim, Theophilus did not participate personally in the ᶜAmmūriyah campaign. A. A. Vasiliev writes:

> A certain eunuch had been sent to Ancyra [Anqirah, Ankara] to defend the population in case al-Muᶜtaṣim laid siege to the city, but it was already too late: the inhabitants of Ancyra had left the city and fled into the mountains. At this news, Theophilus ordered the eunuch to head to Amorium, and he himself withdrew to Dorylium (and even, according to Genesius, as far as Nicaea), where he awaited news of the fate of his native city. . . . The victory of al-Afshīn, with its disastrous consequences for the Greek army, naturally made a strong impression on Theophilus. His courage failed him. Forgetting his triumphant campaign of the previous year, the emperor sent ambassadors to al-Muᶜtaṣim charged with offering humiliating promises and explanations. Theophilus pretended that at the time of the capture of Zapetra [Zibaṭrah] his subordinates had exceeded his orders; he promised to rebuild the destroyed city at his own expense, to

> surrender to the caliph not only the inhabitants of Zapetra who were prisoners, but in addition all the Arabs presently in captivity, and even to deliver up those of his subjects who, through the fault of his generals, had conducted themselves dishonorably during the capture of the city.[26]

Of al-Muᶜtaṣim's decision to retaliate, al-Ṭabarī relates:

> Then, when al-Muᶜtaṣim had vanquished Bābak, he said, "Which city of the Byzantines is the most defended and the best fortified?" And he was told, "ᶜAmmūriyah—not one of the Muslims has embarked against it since the appearance of Islam, and it is the wellspring and root of Christianity and more honored among them than Constantinople."[27]

ᶜAmmūriyah was indeed an appropriate target for revenge, for, as Vasiliev remarks, not only was Amorium the native city of the ruling Byzantine dynasty, but it was also in the most flourishing period in its history, a powerful fortress whose walls were fortified with forty-four towers. It was perhaps Emperor Michael II who elevated his natal city to the status of an autocephalous archbishopric.[28]

After first conquering and devastating Anqirah (Ancyra, Ankara), the caliph's armies laid siege to ᶜAmmūriyah. After three days of violent combat in which thousands perished on both sides, the city was virtually delivered into the hands of the Muslims by treason. A former Muslim resident of the city informed the Muslims of a place in the wall that had been eroded and weakened by torrents and had not been properly repaired, but only hastily filled in. Al-Muᶜtaṣim directed his ballistas to this spot and made a breach in the wall. The Byzantines attempted to stop the breach with large pieces of timber, but these were broken by the rocks from the ballistas. After three more days of siege, the gap in the wall ever widening and the Byzantines having suffered many casualties, Wandū, the commander of the section where the breach was, sought aid from the other commanders. When they refused, he decided to address himself to al-Muᶜtaṣim, pleading for mercy for the children and offering to surrender ᶜAmmūriyah to him. The caliph ordered his troops to refrain from combat until his return from the negotiations, but during the parley with Wandū, the Muslims treacherously took the city.[29] Thus, despite the heroic fighting on both sides, it was really treason and treachery that determined the Muslim victory—a traitorous old man who revealed to the Muslims the weak spot in the wall, the refusal of the other commanders of ᶜAmmūriyah to send assistance to Wandū, and the breach of promise on the part of al-Muᶜtaṣim's army, as al-Ṭabarī reports, or as Michael the Syrian, the Jacobite Patriarch of Antioch from 1166 to

1199 C.E., would have it, the treachery of Wandū (Bôdîn), who withdrew his troops from the area of the breach and let the Muslim armies enter.[30] The fall of the city is most lucidly described by Michael the Syrian in his *Chronicle*:

> When the inhabitants saw that Bôdîn had let the Ṭaiyayê [Arabs] enter the city, some fled to the church, crying *Kyrie eleison,* others into houses, others into cisterns and still others into pits; the women covered their children, like mother hens, lest they be separated from them, whether by the sword or by slavery. The sword of the Ṭaiyayê began the massacre and amassed heaps of corpses; when their sword was drunk with blood, the order came not to massacre any more, but to take the population captive and conduct them outside.
>
> Then they pillaged the city. When the king [Caliph al-Muʿtaṣim] entered to see the city, he admired the beautiful structure of the temples and palaces. But when he received some news that disturbed him, he put the city to the torch and burned it. There were convents and monasteries of women so numerous that more than a thousand virgins were led into captivity, not counting those who had been massacred. They were given over to the Turkish and Moorish slaves and abandoned to their outrages: Glory to the incomprehensible decrees (of God)! They had all those who had hidden in houses or gone up to the galleries (?) of the churches burned [alive].[31]

This then is the conquest of which the poet writes, a conquest, as al-Tibrīzī states in his commentary to Abū Tammām's poem, that was accomplished in defiance of astrological predictions:

> The astrologers had determined that al-Muʿtaṣim would not conquer ʿAmmūriyah, and the Byzantines had corresponded with him saying, "We find in our charts that our city cannot be taken except at the time of the ripening of figs and grapes, and between now and that time are months in which cold and ice will prevent you from staying here." But he refused to turn back and persevered against it, then conquered it and proved their predictions false.[32]

It is this triumph of bold action and initiative on the part of the caliph in the ʿAmmūriyah campaign over the passive submission to astrological charts that Abū Tammām takes as the opening theme of his qasida. Although a product of the age in which the bipartite ***nasīb-madīḥ*** structure predominated in the Arabic panegyric ode, including Abū Tammām's own oeuvre, "The Sword Is More Veracious" is dominated structurally and thematically by the martial-heroic praise section (*madīḥ*) of the classical qasida, to the exclusion of an elegiac prelude (*nasīb*). Although the "lyric I" of the qasida tradition is conspicuously absent, the elegiac mood of the *nasīb* is evoked later in the poem for a particular rhetorical effect. Within the *madīḥ*-determined framework we can identify a number of thematic units that will serve as a guide for reading the poem and as a basis for the subsequent discussion:

1 (lines 1–10): The caliph's sword is a truer determinant of events than the astrologers' books.
2 (lines 11–14): Jubilation: celebration of the conquest of ʿAmmūriyah.
3 (lines 15–22): Feminine personification of the city of ʿAmmūriyah.
4 (lines 23–35): Battle description.
5 (lines 36–49): *Madīḥ* proper, praise of the caliph as a military hero.
6 (lines 50–58): *Hijāʾ* (invective, satire) against the Byzantine emperor Theophilus as a coward.
7 (lines 59–66): The slaying of ʿAmmūriyah's men and the rape of its women.
8 (lines 67–71): Benediction for the caliph and Islamic "manifest destiny."

Abū Tammām's "The Sword Is More Veracious" (*Al-Sayfu Aṣdaqu*)[33]
[meter: *basīṭ;* rhyme: *-bī*]

1. The sword is more veracious
    than the book,
Its cutting edge splits earnestness
    from sport.

2. The white of the blade,
    not the black on the page,
Its broadsides clarify uncertainty
    and doubt.

3. Knowledge lies in the bright spears
    gleaming between two armies,
Not in the seven
    gleaming stars.

4. Where now is their report?
    Where are the stars?
Where the elaborate contrivances
    they forged?

5. [They were but] forgeries and fabrications which,
    if you consider,

Are neither trees for bows,
nor trees for balm.[34]

6. And marvels which, they claimed,
the days would reveal
In the mighty month of Ṣafar
or in Rajab.[35]

7. They terrified the populace
predicting dark disaster
When the western star appeared
with fiery tail.

8. They let the high Houses of the Zodiac
decide
What was overturned
and what stood firm.[36]

9. They decree the affair from Houses
that are unaware
Whether they revolve in orbit
or rotate round the pole.

10. If the stars could foretell events
before their time,
The fate of idols and crosses
would not have been kept hidden.

11. Conquest of conquests that is beyond
what poets' measured verse
Could ever encompass
or orators' unbound prose!

12. A conquest for which
the sky opened its [flood]gates
And the earth appeared bedecked
in new attire.

13. O Battle Day of ʿAmmūriyyah!
Desires went forth from you
Yielding milk
abundant, honeyed.[37]

14. You left the fortune of the Banū al-Islām
ascendant
And in decline the fortune of idolaters
and their abode.

15. In her they had a mother
for whose ransom

They would have given every dam among them
and every sire.

16. So refractory that Chosroes
failed to tame her,
And the advances of Abū Karib
she blocked.[38]

17. She was a virgin whom the hand of fate
had not deflowered,
And to whom time's ambition
could not aspire.

18. From the Age of Alexander,
or before,
The forelocks of the night had turned to gray,
but she had not grown old.

19. Till when God churned the years for her,
churning like a stingy hag,
She was the cream
of the ages.

20. She brought them black grief,
rending its robes,
She whose name had once been
"Dispeller of Griefs."

21. Sinister was her omen
when Anqirah fell
Abandoned, her squares and her courtyards
laid waste.

22. When she saw her sister's ruin
the day before,
Ruin was more contagious
than the mange.

23. How many a heroic horseman
lay between her walls,
His forelocks reddened
by hot flowing blood!

24. His hair hennaed
by the way of the sword
—Blood his henna—not by the way of Religion
and Islam.

25. In her, O Commander of the Faithful,
you abandoned to the fire

A day when wood and stone
succumbed.

26. You left in her a black night
bright as forenoon,
For in her midst a dawn of flame
dispelled it,

27. Until it seemed as if the robes of night
refused their color,
As if the sun
had never set.

28. There was light from the fire
while darkness still clung
And dark from the smoke
in the pale noonday sun.

29. The sun was rising from one
when it had set,
And setting from the other
when it had not.

30. As rain clouds clear to reveal
a limpid sky,
Fate revealed to her a battle day
pure and polluted.

31. The sun did not rise that day
upon a married man,
Nor did it set
upon a celibate.

32. No spring abode of Mayyah, full of folk,
where Ghaylān roamed,
Was lovelier in its hills
than [ʿAmmūriyyah's] ruined abode.

33. Nor did any cheek,
blushing and bashful,
Stir the gazer's passion more than
her dirt-streaked cheek,

34. Its ugliness cured our eyes
of any need
For a beautiful vision or
wondrous spectacle,

35. The reversal of our fortunes
brought forth

From their unfortunate reversal
auspicious issue.

36. If only Infidelity had known
how many ages
This outcome lay in ambush
amidst the spears and swords,

37. Directed by one relying on God,
avenging for God,
Striving and yearning
toward God,

38. Nourished on victory,
his spear points never blunt
On battle day, nor hindered from
an iron-clad soul.

39. He never assaults a nation
or goes forth against a land
Without being preceded by
a vanguard of dread,

40. Had he not led forth a vast force
on battle day,
He would have gone forth that morn,
he alone a clamorous host.

41. God hurled you against [ʿAmmūriyyah's] two towers
and destroyed her;
Had any other hurled you, he would have
missed the mark.

42. After they had entangled her in spears,
putting their trust in her
—But for each entangled stronghold
God is the key!—

43. And their commander had said,
"There is no nearby pasture
For those that drive their flocks,
nor any water hole,"

44. Out of a hope whose attainment was plundered
by the edges of swords
And by the sides
of long rapacious spears,

45. Two types of death,
by white blade and dun spear,

Were two pails of life—
of water and fodder.

46. To the Zibaṭran cry you replied,
pouring out a cup of drowsiness
And the sweet saliva
of loving wives.

47. Heat from the outraged frontiers
diverted you
From their cool teeth
and sweet pebbled waters.

48. You replied baring the sword,
penetrating
—To reply without the sword would have been
no reply—

49. Till, undistracted by tent pegs and ropes,
you left
The tent pole of Polytheism
fallen in the dust.

50. When Theophilus beheld war (*ḥarb*)
with his own eyes—
And the word "war" is taken
from plunder (*ḥarab*)—

51. He tried to turn the course of war
with money,
But the sea, its currents and billowing waves,
overwhelmed him.

52. Oh how the steady earth shook
beneath his feet,
From the attack of a reckoner,
not a seeker of gain,

53. Who had not dissipated gold
that numbered more than pebbles
So that he was in need
of gold.

54. For the lions,
the lions of the thicket,
Aspire to the plundered on the day of battle,
not to plunder.

55. Theophilus turned his back,
his tongue bridled by the Khaṭṭī spear,

While below his innards
were in uproar.

56. To his intimate companions
he issued death
And spurred on flight, the fleetest
of his steeds.

57. Safeguarding himself in the heights,
he surveyed the field,
Nimble from fear,
not spry from joy.

58. If he fled the heat of war
like an ostrich fleeing fire,
It was because you fed its flames
with fuel aplenty.

59. The lives of ninety thousand [warriors]
[fierce] as Mount Sharā's lions
Were ripe for plucking before the ripening
of figs and grapes.[39]

60. How many a bitter soul was sweetened when
their souls were plucked from them;
Had it been drenched in musk it would not
smell so sweet!

61. How many an angry warrior
did the blades bring back,
His contentment quickened by their perishing,
his anger dead!

62. War stood firm
in a tight predicament
Where standing armies, in ignominy,
sank to their knees.

63. How many a beaming moon they took
beneath war's lightning beam!
How many a white-toothed maid
beneath war's cloud!

64. How many corridors were opened
to secluded maids
By severing in war
the cords of necks!

65. How many a reed
trembling on a sand dune,

Did the drawn and trembling Indian swords
obtain!

66. The white blades, once drawn
from their sheaths,
Became worthier companions to the white-skinned damsels
than their veils.

67. O Caliph of God,
for your striving
For the root of religion, honor, and Islam,
God reward you!

68. You have beheld the greater ease
and have perceived
That it is not attained but by
the bridge of toil.

69. If among fate's vagaries
there is
Any tie of kinship or
unsevered bond,

70. Then the closest lineage
connects
The days of Badr to your
victorious days.

71. They have left the Banū al-Aṣfar
Their faces jaundiced,
The Arabs' faces burnished
with triumph. [22]

Part 1: Lines 1–10. The poem opens with the sword, thematically an element of the martial-heroic *madīḥ* (praise section) and symbolically an emblem of military and sexual conquest. In Arabic, the use of the term *fataḥa* (literally "to open") to mean both to conquer a city and to deflower a virgin serves as a sociolinguistic grounding for the metaphorical developments of the poetic metalanguage. The first contest of the sword, however, is against the books of the astrologers. The sword—decisive action—determines events more accurately than astrologers' charts; it is the cutting edge that separates jest from serious endeavor (line 1). Certainly so bold and aggressive an opening produces a jolt to the audience's formal expectation of a lyric-elegiac *nasīb,* and one could further suggest a subliminal link between the poet's triumphant claim after an Islamic victory over the Byzantine Infidel, *al-sayfu aṣdaqu* (the sword is truer), and the morphologically identical Islamic battle cry, *Allāhu akbar!* (God is the greatest). Already in the opening line the condensed and insistent employ of rhetorical devices that characterizes the *badīʿ* (new, innovative) style in general, and Abū Tammām's style in particular, is evident. The poem opens with a double antithesis (*ṭibāq*): the sword (action) versus the book (passivity) and earnestness versus sport. Implicit in this contrastive rhetorical play is a larger antithesis that dominates the entire qasida: the association of the sword (of the caliph) with the truth of Islam and divine will, and the books of the astrologers with Byzantine Christian falsehood.

In lines 2–3 the rhetorical intensity continues in the use of root play (*jinās*, paronomasia, the playing or punning on words with shared or similar root letters) and antithesis (*ṭibāq*) to contrast the flashing white blades (*bīḍu ṣ-ṣafāʾiḥi*) that illuminate and clarify what is uncertain to the black obscurity of the ink on the pages (*sūdu ṣ-ṣaḥāʾifi*) of the astrologers' books—thus the epithet *al-bīḍ* (the white ones) for swords is metaphorically extended to suggest light, clarity, and truth, while *al-sūd* (the black ones) for ink or letters is similarly semantically extended to represent darkness, obscurity, and falsehood. The poet then binds the antithesis with a pun on *matn* (plural *mutūn*): the broadside of a sword or the text of a book. Knowledge is best based on forceful action—spears gleaming on the battlefield, not on the impassive and impersonal shining of the seven planets (line 3). Ultimately the forged fables and lies of the astrologers are useless, fit for making neither bows like the wood of the nabʿ tree nor balm like the willow. That is to say, they neither incite to action nor comfort the wounded or distressed (lines 4, 5). Such calamities do the astrologers predict that time itself panics and the very days flee for refuge to the pre-Islamic sacred months of Ṣafar and Rajab, during which fighting was taboo (line 6). The appearance of a blazing comet in that year was taken as a sign of impending disaster with which the astrologers terrorized the populace. The appearance is attested by Michael the Syrian: "In the year 1149 [Seleucid era: 223 H./838 C.E.] in the month of Teshrīn [November] a star with a tail appeared in the region of the southeast, its rays directed toward the West. For fifteen days it rose before the sun appeared in the East, and was visible until sunrise."[40] The inappropriateness of their interpretation is suggested by the antithesis between the darkening (*muẓlimah*) disaster and the brightness of the blazing tail of the comet (line 7).[41] Unlike the man of action, the astrologers are characterized by passivity. They surrender the power to determine earthly events to the Houses of the Zodiac, which are as totally unaware of terrestrial events as they are of their own celestial revolutions (lines 8, 9). In the end, events have proved the astrologers wrong, for if the stars could reveal the future, surely they would have foretold the fate of ʿAmmūriyah's idols and crosses.

Part 2: Lines 11–14. The declaration and celebration of the Islamic victory in this passage sets the tone and imagery for the remainder of the poem. The cry of conquest is rhetorically amplified by the reiteration and root play on the root *f-t-ḥ* (open, conquer): *fatḥu l-futūḥi* ("Conquest of conquests," line 11) and, creating an anaphora, *fatḥun tafattaḥu* ("A conquest for which the sky opened its [flood]gates," line 12). The poet concludes his harangue against the astrologers and in line 12 turns to describe the conquest, which he declares is greater than poetry or prose can encompass, in terms of the fertility imagery of Jāhilī poetry—the rain that falls on the abandoned abode and causes fresh herbage to spring up in the ruins. The underlying sexual metaphor of conquest (*fatḥ* = opening, deflowering) by the sword (phallus) is thus expressed in vegetable terms; the death and destruction of the Infidel city is seen as reviving and renewing the Islamic *ummah*. In line 13 the poet addresses the day of ʿAmmūriyah and expresses the fulfillment of Muslim hopes in an ancient Near Eastern image of fertility and abundance, milk and honey. The effect of this conjuncture of conquest with fertility imagery is to evoke the ancient Near Eastern concept of the *hieros gamos,* the sacred marriage or ritual coitus that renews and ensures the fertility and prosperity of the realm. This subtly sets the stage for the feminine personification of the vanquished city in the following section. In line 14 the poet once more invokes the terminology of the astrologers in an antithesis (*ṣaʿad* = ascendant; *ṣabab* = descendant) to declare, with an irony not devoid of malice, the good fortune of the Muslims and the concomitant ill-fortune of the idolaters (Byzantine Christians)—clearly a matter of divine will, not blind fate.

Part 3: Lines 15–22. Whereas the conquering Muslim army is described in masculine terms, the city subsumes all the female attributes as the poet undertakes the "feminization" of the vanquished city and hence of the Byzantine foe in general. Thus, in line 15, ʿAmmūriyah is described as a mother to the Byzantines—no doubt a reference to its being the native city of the ruling dynasty—and in lines 16 and 17 as a virgin. (It is perhaps not without malice and forethought that Abū Tammām, himself apparently a Christian convert to Islam, should arrive at a description of ʿAmmūriyah as a "Virgin Mother"). The term for a female camel refusing a camel stallion (*ṣadd*) is used to describe the city's repulse of the attack of Abū Karib[42] as the refusal of sexual overtures. The poet further enforces the metaphor of sexual for military conquest by describing the undespoiled city as an ageless and undefiled virgin, and failed military ventures as unsuccessful attempts at her virtue. Michael the Syrian corroborates these verses when he states that "Amorium was a fortified city, and no one had ever had been able to capture it before Abū Isḥāq [al-Muᶜtaṣim], who in twelve days took it by force and found assembled there the population and wealth of several cities."[43] As for the established history of the city in Arab times, up until our poem, M. Canard summarizes:

> Amorium, fortified by Zenon (474–91)—al-Masᶜūdī, *Murūdj,* ii, 331, says it was built by Anastasius (491–518)—was on several occasions threatened, besieged or captured by the Arabs. Muᶜāwiya reached it in 25/646; ᶜAbd al-Raḥmān b. Khālid b. al-Walīd forced it to capitulate in 46/666; it was occupied in 49/669 in the course of Yazīd's expedition against Constantinople, it was besieged by one of his lieutenants, and relieved by the future emperor Leo the Isaurian. Leo subsequently made it a formidable stronghold, which successfully resisted al-Ḥasan b. Ḳaḥtaba in 162/779, in the reign of al-Mahdī, then in 181/797, in the reign of Hārūn al-Rashīd. It only fell in 223/838 to the powerful forces of al-Muᶜtaṣim, whose Turkish troops besieged it for twelve days, and who finally took it only by treachery.[44]

In the poet's hands, the lyric nostalgia and the sense of loss and ruin inherent in the classical *nasīb,* with its motifs of the departed mistress and the ruined abode, become associated with the devastated city. The maturing of a teleological time is then expressed by a feminine image of another sort, as God brings destiny to fruition with the slow and painstaking surety of a stingy hag churning butter (line 19).

The outstanding feature of the poet's description of the city is his ability to combine the diverse motifs of the classical *nasīb* into a unified image. ᶜAmmūriyah is at once the *maḥbūbah* (beloved) and the ruined abodes (*aṭlāl*). Thus in line 20 the ruined ᶜAmmūriyah partakes of the quintessential poeticity that both the beloved and the ruined abodes share: once the bearer or scene of joy and happiness, with the departure of the tribe, the phantomlike memory of the beloved and the traces of the encampment become bearers or scenes of grief and sorrow. So, too, ᶜAmmūriyah's sister city Anqirah is personified and described precisely in the terms of the ruined abode (lines 21, 22). In line 21 the idea of predicting the future is played on once more in the term *faʾl* (omen, augury derived from birds). Again, the true prediction is based on Islamic military action, not on stars or birds.

Part 4: Lines 23–35. Although for the sake of convenience we can term this passage a "battle description," it is immediately evident that the poet has no intention of providing a realistic depiction of the conquest. Instead, he transforms the event into a legitimizing myth of Arabo-Islamic (specifically ʿAbbāsid) dominion. Up until this point the poet has first presented masculine imagery to advocate action and initiative in the martial motifs of the *madīḥ*—white swords and flashing spears as opposed to passive submission to astrological cycles. He has then juxtaposed with this a description of the history of the city of ʿAmmūriyah using the feminine and lyrical motifs of the *nasīb:* the beloved and the ruined campsite. In lines 23 and 24 the tension between the (masculine) conquering sword and the (feminine) virgin city is resolved by the image of blood—a symbol simultaneously embodying deflowering (rape) and killing. Moreover, both forms of bloodshed have the same sacrificial value: both serve to revitalize the *ummah*. In one sense the two are identical—the killing of ʿAmmūriyah's men by the Muslim armies is equated with the metaphorical rape of the city. On the other hand, as we shall see below, the metaphorical rape of the personified city is derived from the literal abduction and rape of the female inhabitants.

It becomes evident as well that Abū Tammām's style cannot be reduced to the mere enumeration of rhetorical devices, or even to a sorting out of tropes. The relation of rape to conquest is at once semantic (*fatḥ* as conquest and deflowering), hence based on *jinās* (root play, paronomasia); analogical, thus based on *istiʿārah* (metaphor); and synecdochic, that is, rape is a part of war, so that the basis of the relation is metonymy. There is thus a breakdown of the usual distinction between metaphor and metonymy and we find complex and fluid relationships among the various levels of the literal and the figurative. So, in line 23 the forelocks of ʿAmmūriyah's men drip with blood. In a subtle layering of metaphor the poet describes the men of ʿAmmūriyah as hennaed by the way of the sword—that is, bloodied by their belligerent nature, by their hostility to the truth of Islam, and hence dead. The Muslim armies, by contrast, are hennaed in the way of Islam—that is, first, bleeding and dying *fī sabīl Allāh* (in the way of God) out of religious zeal, not lust for battle, and hence guaranteed immortal life; and second, literally dyeing their hair with henna in accordance with the *sunnah* (tradition) of the Prophet Muḥammad, likewise a symbol of renewed life or life everlasting (line 24). These two lines also suggest the deflowering of the city, since blood and henna are symbolically associated with deflowering, as expressed in the custom of hennaing the bride on her wedding day.

The complex dialectic of blood/henna and death/revitalization is an expression of the sacrificial principle according to which the polity is revived and restored by the blood of the victim. This reminds us that in Muslim eyes, as the commentaries and chronicles tell us, the Muslim conquest of ʿAmmūriyah was conceived of as avenging the Byzantine conquest of Zibaṭrah in the previous year.

In lines 25 to 31 the caliph's destruction of the city is presented. What we witness here is not poetic description as much as it is mythopoesis: the recreation of the historical event as a myth of Islamic "manifest destiny" in which the caliph assumes, at least rhetorically, cosmic powers and serves as the instrument of a divine and preordained plan. The poet begins lines 25 and 26 with *tarakta* (you left) and *ghadarta* (you abandoned)—diction that evokes the departure of the tribe in the *nasīb* and the abandonment of the abode of the beloved to ruin and desolation. Only here the caliph plays a dual role: first he is the abandoner, and second, he assumes the destructive aspect of nature and *dahr* (fate or time)—that is, he effects through military conquest, burning, and pillage what the passage of time, or fate, effects through the winds, rains, and seasonal cycles. Thus in this Islamic qasida the sword of the caliph inspired by God takes the place of the Jāhilī hand of fate.

In lines 26 through 29 the series of antitheses between day and night, light and dark, adds to the illusion that the caliph, empowered by God, has overturned the natural cycle of night and day. Here the natural progression seems to have stopped; the blackness of night has paled as though the sun had ceased its diurnal circuit and were fixed forever in the sky (line 27). In line 28 night and day are overturned by smoke and fire. Abū Tammām thus takes the poetic commonplaces of the dust, smoke, and fire of war and endows them with cosmic significance. Line 29 captures at once the terror and confusion of the people of ʿAmmūriyah and the awe of the conquering Muslims. This overthrow of the Infidel city is described as the throwing into confusion of the diurnal cycle of the sun. The caliph does not submit to the celestial cycles of the spheres, as the astrologers would have him do, but endowed with seemingly cosmic power overthrows them and establishes his own. In this passage then, the declaration of the opening line of the poem is given affirmation: the sword—serious and determined, and divinely appointed, military action—determines the future, not predictions based on the stars and the rotations of the spheres because, metaphorically at least, the divinely guided caliph can overturn these celestial cycles.

The intimate association between rape and bloodshed mentioned above is set out in explicit terms in lines 30 and 31. The poet relies on antithesis (*ṭibāq*) to contrast the two, so that the Muslim soldiers return from the battlefield pure, having performed the religious duty of *jihād* (holy war) against the Infidel, and at the same time polluted from sexual intercourse.[45] In line 31 the poet employs a double antithesis in stating that the sun did not rise on a married man of ʿAmmūriyah, that is, all the male inhabitants had been slain; nor did the sun set on a celibate (Muslim)—in other words, all the conquering soldiers had satisfied their lust. The metaphor (line 30) of the clear sky appearing after the storm connects the pollution-purification process of conquest with that of natural fertility.

The bloody and violent conquest and destruction of the city once accomplished, Abū Tammām shifts from the military-heroic tone of the *madīḥ* to that of the lyrical *nasīb*. The abandoned and devastated city now acquires the still and melancholy beauty of the beloved's ruined abodes, or more. The abode of Mayyah while she still dwelt there was not as lovely to her impassioned poet-lover Ghaylān ibn ʿUqbah (the renowned Umayyad lyricist better known by his sobriquet, Dhū al-Rummah) as ruined ʿAmmūriyah is to the conquering Muslims.

At this point we should mention that the name ʿAmmūriyah in Arabic has as its root *ʿ-m-r* (to live a long life, dwell in an abode; to be inhabited). Its position for the Byzantines is thus etymologically suggestive of the seat of Islām, *al-bayt al-maʿmūr*, "the (perpetually) inhabited abode," the epithet of the Kaʿbah (or its heavenly counterpart) (Lane, *ʿ-m-r*), but, more to the point, it suggests that it is the very heart or soul or seat of life for the Byzantines, their quintessential and ancestral abode whose destruction is thus spiritually as well as militarily devastating. All this the poet captures through a rhetorical complex of puns and antithesis in line 32 to gloat over the "ruination" of the "perpetual abode." *Maʿmūr* (inhabited, prospering) at once puns (using *jinās* or root play) on ʿAmmūriyah and forms an antithesis (*ṭibāq*) with *kharib* (ruined).

Indeed, the sight of Infidelity devastated, of the enemy defeated, is more alluring to the victors than the blushing cheek of the beloved (line 33). Line 34 involves a certain ambiguity or counterpoint of motifs, or rather resolves the ambiguity of the two preceding lines: as the poet-lover finds signs and reminders of past happiness in the desolate ruins of the encampment of his beloved, so in the ugliness and waste of the ruined city, victorious Muslim eyes find beautiful and wondrous signs of the glory of God and the victory of Islam; or, as the poet states in line 35, again employing astrological terms to ironic effect (*inqilāb*—solstice, in this case the overthrowing of darkness by light), the upturn in the fortune of Islam involves the concomitant reversal of Infidel fortune. Having thus transformed the destruction of the city into a myth of caliphal cosmic power and Islamic manifest destiny, the poet then turns at line 36 to what can be considered the *madīḥ*, or praise section proper, of this qasida.

Part 5: Lines 36–49. Abū Tammām begins the formal praise section (*madīḥ*) by declaring, as he did in line 19, that the defeat of the Infidel was foreordained, inevitable, as though it had been lying in ambush waiting for the right moment to strike (line 36). Thus, once again, time is personified not as the fickle and impersonal fate of Jāhiliyyah poetry, but as a military force fighting on the side of Islam. In line 37 the caliph's name appears, and the poet, employing *ḥusn al-taqsīm* (morphological parallelism), plays on the *ishtiqāq* (etymology) of the name and reinforces it with parallel constructions of epithets of the same morphological pattern, in this case the form VIII active participle: so the caliph is *Muʿtaṣimin bi-Llāhi* (Relying on God), *muntaqimin li Llāhi* (avenging for God), *murtaqibin* (striving [toward God]), and *fī Llāhi murtaghibī* (longing for God). The nature of the relationship between the caliph and the deity is succinctly stated: for victory, the caliph depends on God, on divine sanction and inspiration; he does not conquer in his own name, but in order to avenge God and Islam; his noble actions bring him closer to God and will lead him to heaven; his striving and longing are not for earthly and material gains but for God. A poetic concept of *nomen est omen* is here extended to a sort of morphological determinism. The caliph has been nourished on victory until the terror that he strikes in the hearts of his enemies precedes him like a clamorous army (lines 38, 39). Indeed, his soul alone has the fortitude of an entire army (line 40).

Yet ultimately the caliph's power is conferred on him by God (line 41). God is the actor, the caliph his weapon. The syntax of the rest of line 41 reinforces this: "God hurled you against [ʿAmmūriyyah's] two towers and destroyed her"—a line that evokes Qurʾān 8:17: "Then you did not kill them but God did, and you did not throw, when you threw, but God did" *(fa-lam taqtulūhum wa-lakinna Llāha qatalahum wa-mā ramayta idh ramayta wa-lakinna Llāha ramā).* Furthermore, inasmuch as this Qurʾānic verse refers to the Battle of Badr, line 41 subtly paves the way for Abū Tammām's explicit comparison in line 70 of al-Muʿtaṣim's conquest of ʿAmmūriyah with that astounding victory of the Prophet Muḥammad and his small band of vastly outnumbered followers over the Meccan armies (see below). However good the arrow, it is the archer who hits or misses; and, declares the poet, had the archer been anyone other than God, he would have missed the mark. Similarly, however much the enemy might try to fortify their city, entangling it in a thicket of spears, still God is the key to every fortified place (line 42). In line 43 the Byzantine commander expresses his confidence that there is no water or pasturage nearby to enable the Muslim army to sustain a siege. In the ensuing two lines, 44 and 45, this water and fodder is metaphorically transformed into an expression of the blood-vengeance dialectic. The lack of life-sustaining natural elements is compensated for by manmade weapons: two forms of death, by the sword and the spear, are equated with the two necessities of life, water and fodder. This image thus reinforces the theme of the destruction of the Infidel enemy as a source of rebirth and revival for Islam, as was suggested by the imagery of fertility and abundance of line 12 and the astrological imagery of lines 14 and 35.

The poet concludes the praise section (*madīḥ*) proper by addressing the caliph in the second person and epitomizing the campaign in four lines, from Theophilus's ravishment of Zibaṭrah (line 46) to the caliph's destruction of ᶜAmmūriyah (line 49). The effect of this passage is to cast the exchange of military incursions between the Muslims and the Byzantines in terms of honor and vengeance. The two major forms of violence, killing men and raping female captives, are very closely identified. In this poem, the gender-patterned violence of rape, of male domination and honor versus female victimization and degradation, is employed as the controlling metaphor for turning military victory and defeat into an ideology of Islamic dominion. Thus the previous Muslim defeat at the hands of the Byzantines is expressed as the humiliation and dishonor occasioned by the Byzantines' rape of the Muslim women captives of Zibaṭrah and it is the voice of violated Muslim womanhood that clamors for al-Muᶜtaṣim to avenge its honor. The Zibaṭran woman's cry to al-Muᶜtaṣim for help as she was carried off by her Infidel captors calls the caliph away from the women and wine of the harem to avenge the honor of Islam (line 46). Al-Muᶜtaṣim's abstention from wine and women is nothing other than the well-known ritual vow of abstention (from wine, women, washing, ointment, meat) that marks the entry into the sacrificial state (as in the Ḥajj pilgrimage) and, more pertinent here, the taking of blood vengeance (see chapter 4). The poet again plays on feminine sexual imagery in contrasting the protected ladies of the harem to the ravished womanhood of Zibaṭrah. In lines 47 and 48 there is the suggestion of both similarity and contrast in the pun (*jinās*) of *thughūr* (mouths and frontiers): the sexual connotation of the heat and violence of battle or rape (literal or figurative) is contrasted with the cool and leisurely dalliance at court.

In line 49 Abū Tammām concludes the passage of praise for al-Muᶜtaṣim by combining the image of the city of ʿAmmūriyah as the tent pole, the main support, of the Byzantines, the towns and villages its tent ropes and pegs, with one of the dominant metaphors that runs throughout the qasida —that of ʿAmmūriyah as the ruined abode (*aṭlāl*) of the classical elegiac prelude (*nasīb*). Unlike the poet-lover who turns aside and tarries at every wasted ruin, the caliph is not distracted by every little Byzantine town or village, but goes straight to the heart of the Infidel lands, leaving it dust-covered, as the implacable forces of nature—the wind, the rain, the passage of time—leave the once lively and populated (*maʿmūr)* encampment of the beloved in ruins.

Part 6: Lines 50–58. At this point Abū Tammām presents a passage of invective or satire (*hijāʾ*) against the Byzantine emperor, Theophilus, in contrast to the preceding praise section (*madīḥ*) for the caliph al-Muʿtaṣim. This passage of invective should be understood as subordinated and contributive to the overall *madīḥ*-dominated structure of this qasida and its celebration of Islam triumphant. In this respect it resembles the subordinated invective (*hijāʾ*) and boast (*fakhr*) passages in al-Akhṭal's victory panegyric to ʿAbd al-Malik ibn Marwān (chapter 3). We should begin by noting that whereas al-Muʿtaṣim participated in the ʿAmmūriyah campaign, his Byzantine counterpart did not (see historical review, above). The primary contrasts that the poet creates in this passage is between the base material motives of Theophilus and the religiously inspired desire for vengeance or justice on the part of al-Muʿtaṣim—between the cowardly passivity of Theophilus and the heroic militarism of al-Muʿtaṣim.

Theophilus's first response, when he sees the vast sea of the Muslim armies advancing, is, as the poet has it, to perceive the etymological connection between *ḥarb* (war) and *ḥarab* (plunder), and fear for his wealth (line 50). Hoping to cut his losses, he attempts to stem the tide of war with money, that is, to buy off al-Muʿtaṣim by offering reparations for Zibaṭrah (see above), but the Muslim armies, like the vast ocean flood, an unstemmable tide, overwhelm him (line 51). The metaphor changes from the mighty ocean's flood to another overwhelming natural calamity, the earthquake—a Qurʾānic commonplace for the execution of divine judgment. The expression *zuʿziʿati l-arḍu* ("the [steady] earth shook," line 52) is synonymous with Abū al-ʿAtāhiyah's phrase *zulzilati l-arḍu* ("the [very] earth would quake," "My Coy Mistress," line 9). In Abū Tammām's hands, however, the expression takes on an ironical psychological twist, for it is the emperor's own moral failure, that is, his cowardice, that causes the earth (to seem) to shake beneath his feet.

The concept of judgment is echoed in terming the caliph a *muḥtasib* (one who reckons his accounts for the Hereafter by performing pious deeds), here alluding more precisely to reckoning the accounts of Islam (or executing a divine reckoning) by avenging the fallen Muslim city of Zibaṭrah and, especially in conjunction with the earth's quaking, conjuring up a vision of *yawm al-ḥisāb,* the Day of Reckoning (see above). The *muḥtasib* is then contrasted to the *muktasib* (the seeker of material gain), Theophilus (line 52). Unlike the greedy Theophilus, declares the poet in line 54, the true lions of war lust for the plundered—i.e., killing and raping (along with the ritualistic revitalization and fertility that these entail), defending and avenging Islam against the Infidel—not for the plunder, the mere material gain. Thus we find Theophilus in line 55 struck dumb, his bowels churning from fear. Unlike al-Muᶜtaṣim who advanced, baring his sword (line 48), the Infidel turns his back and flees. Theophilus's greed for gold is balanced by his "generosity" in disbursing death to his intimates on the field of battle rather than risking his own life (line 56). Taking flight itself as his mount (a *badīᶜ* formulation characteristic of Abū Tammām's style), he heads to the safety of high ground, whence, sprightly from fear, he surveys the field of battle (line 57). In line 58 Abū Tammām concludes his invective against Theophilus with the Jāhilī image of the ostrich—renowned for its fear of fire and for its speed in running—and the fires of war: al-Muᶜtaṣim has kindled and stoked the fire, and Theophilus, ostrich-like, has fled.

Part 7: Lines 59–66. This section returns once more to the slaughter of the enemy men and the rape of their women to produce the thematic and rhetorical climax of the qasida. The poet opens the passage with yet another ironic retort to the vain predictions of the Byzantine astrologers, this time their claim that ᶜAmmūriyah could not be taken before the ripening of the figs and grapes. Thus he describes the ninety thousand slain Byzantine warriors as fruits of conquest whose lives were "ripe for plucking before the ripening of figs and grapes." The metaphorical association of the enemy dead with fruit has a further significance: that their death/plucking nourishes the Muslims (see also line 45). In keeping with the concept that the achievement of vengeance renews the prosperity of the realm, the following two lines (60 and 61) likewise employ characteristic blood-vengeance imagery to describe the dialectic of unavenged/avenged (polluted/purified):

the bitter soul of the unquenched avenger becomes sweet when the Infidel is extirpated. In a balanced pair of antitheses—life and death, contentment and anger—the poet provides a most precise and concise expression of the ritual dialectic of blood vengeance: through the perishing of the enemy, the Muslim warrior's well-being is revitalized, his anger dies. In line 62 war stands triumphant while the enemies have been brought to their knees.

At this point there is a progression from the slaughter of the warriors to the rape of the women. In a passage of extraordinary rhetorical density, Abū Tammām creates the final synthesis of the masculine motifs of the praise section (*madīḥ*) and the feminine motifs of the elegiac prelude (*nasīb*), whose dialectic alternation has produced the dynamic progression of the poem. He begins in line 63 with meteorological fertility images: the gleaming moon, a traditional poetic metaphor for a white-faced maiden, as well as a female fertility symbol, is taken under the lightning flash of war (the same male symbol as Zeus's thunderbolt) or the sword. The rain cloud, too, is a male fertility element. Root play (*jinās,* paronomasia) appears in pairs that generate semantic opposites from identical terms: *sanā* and *sanā* (the lightning flash of war and the maiden's gleaming moon-shaped face) and *ʿāriḍ* and *ʿāriḍ* (the cloud [of dust] of war and the tooth or smile of a white-toothed maiden) to produce a layering of meaning (line 63). The juxtaposition of the killing of the men and the rape of the women is given a causal connection in line 64 and the link between the two explicitly confirmed—the way to the women is through killing the men. Between the slaughter of the enemy and the rape of their women is an element of identity as well as causality, for, as Sperl remarks: "The recreation of fertility has an equivalent among the themes of war. Many poems link the Caliph's slaughter of his enemies with the creation of new life in his realm. Their death is portrayed as an act of sacrifice which will ensure prosperity for the land."[46]

More explicit still and yet rhetorically richer are lines 65 and 66. At line 65 the anaphora produced by the repetition of *kam* (how many) here and in the previous two lines, which has produced a sense of momentum and intensity in the rape imagery, now brings it to a climax. The momentum and intensity are further amplified by an increased rhetorical density that culminates in the paired wordplays that combine root play (*jinās*) and antithesis (*ṭibāq*) to resolve opposed male and female elements into verbal identity. The word *sayf,* a straightforward denotant of "sword," is now replaced by the broader term *qaḍīb* (plural *quḍub;* literally branch, rod, reed; by extension, sword, phallus), and the sexual intent only diaphanously draped in the adjective "Indian." As in line 63, here in line 65 the poet employs complex wordplay to generate opposing meanings from identical terms. Thus the drawn Indian *swords/phalluses tremble* (with excitement) (*quḍubu . . . tahtazzu*) while the slender-waisted ample-buttocked maidens, like *reeds* on sand dunes, *tremble* (with fear) (*quḍubin tahtazzu*). The perfect balance of the double wordplay creates a total verbal and semantic synthesis, an ultimate identity of the antithetical male/female and *madīḥ/nasīb* imagery that generated the dynamic tension of the qasida. The same sort of synthesis of *nasīb* and *madīḥ*, feminine and masculine, imagery is effected in line 66 where, as in line 65, complex wordplay combines verbal identity with a semantic antithesis. The poet combines the martial-aggressive *madīḥ* image of swords drawn from their sheaths, also suggestive of the sexual act, with the most classical of *nasīb* images of maidenhood—the veiled and white-skinned maiden surrounded by her companions. Thus the *white* blades (phalluses) are drawn *from their sheaths* (*bīḍun . . . min ḥujbihā*) to rend the *veils* of the *white*-skinned virgins (*al-bīḍi . . . mina l-ḥujubī*). Lines 65 and 66 thus offer a final confirmation of the potency of the sword that the poet declared in the first two lines of the qasida.

Further comment is in order on the poet's methods. Abū Tammām has achieved the rhetorical climax at lines 65–66 by several means. First, the gendered imagery that runs throughout the qasida has steadily moved from the figurative—the sword as emblem of male potency or the phallus, the personification of the city as a ravished virgin, that leads to the passage of battle, killing, torching and rape (lines 15–31)—to the literal—a recounting, however rhetorically dense and complex, of Muslim soldiers raping Byzantine women. Second, the directional momentum of this particular section (lines 59–66) is from slaying the men to raping the women. In addition, there is a rhetorical intensification, an increased density and complexity of verbal play, through which both poetic and sexual climax are achieved, as explicated in the preceding paragraph. It is worth noting that the shock effect of the culminating rape scene is achieved not through graphic or visual realism, but through rhetorically complex verbal play.

In this rape passage (lines 63–66) Abū Tammām completes and consolidates the rhetorical extension of the dialectically paired gender construct: male/female; aggressor/victim; Muslim/Infidel. There has been a chiastic progression from the feminized Muslim victim and Byzantine male aggressor at Zibaṭrah to a final image of a male Muslim aggressor and female Byzantine Infidel victim. At this point we should recall that the image of sexually defiled womanhood, however varied in detail or powerfully achieved, is the conventional means for expressing the ultimate (male) dishonor and degradation. In terms of the sociomorphic restructuring of the polity that the panegyric ode (*qaṣīdat al-madḥ*) so often entails, the alignment of the political order of Arabo-Islamic triumph and Byzantine Christian defeat with the natural order of male sexual domination and female sexual degradation is an expression of divine will.

Before proceeding to the final benedictory section, let us conclude our argument concerning the sexual gender-based imagery that dominates the qasida and culminates in lines 65–66. The operative gender dialectic in Abū Tammām's ode is one that identifies as masculine the martial-heroic values traditionally celebrated in the praise section (*madīḥ*) of the Arabic qasida. The poet employs the sword and the implicitly phallic warrior aggression that it embodies to create a qasida dominated by the metaphor (which, as we have shown, also operates as synecdoche and metonymy) of sexual conquest for military conquest. The active-passive gender dichotomy is expanded to encompass the contrast between military action and the passivity of the astrologers in determining the course of events. This is in turn extended to establish Arab Islam as the exponent of the masculine, active, and dominant principle and Byzantine Christianity as feminine, passive, and, ultimately, submissive. A moral dimension is imposed on the religious dichotomy: Muslim military activity is depicted as divinely appointed *jihād* (holy war) undertaken for the sake of eternal spiritual reward in the world to come, whereas the Byzantine Christian emperor is portrayed as fighting merely for material gain and, if his material wealth or mortal life is threatened, ignominiously fleeing the field. The *madīḥ*-related Islamic triumph dominates the qasida structurally and thematically; subordinated to it are *nasīb*-related elements of destruction, submission, and defilement of the feminized city of ʿAmmūriyah and her actual female inhabitants and elements related to invective (*hijāʾ*) in the depiction of the craven and cowardly emperor.

A comparison of Abū Tammām's employ of the gender construct of male domination and female submission with that of Abū al-ʿAtāhiyah in "My Coy Mistress" reveals striking poetic and political differences. In Abū al-ʿAtāhiyah's *ghazal*-form qasida, it is the Islamic *ummah* (community), in the form of the institution of the caliphate, that is feminized. The domination-submission relation thus becomes that of the caliph to his subjects, so that, in the end, the message—much like the "moral" of the anecdotes concerning Abū al-ʿAtāhiyah—is one of the feminization of the Muslim male subject, his submission to the (political/sexual) will of the caliph and the renunciation of his own (political/sexual) desires. By contrast, in Abū Tammām's poem, both the caliph al-Muʿtaṣim and his Muslim armies assume the male-dominant-aggressive side of the gender dichotomy, while the Byzantine Christian enemy is feminized. The caliph and his troops are thus both identified with the sword/phallus throughout the qasida and thus, by a sort of metonymic as well as metaphoric association, with each other. As the caliph is presented as the conqueror and figurative deflowerer of the virgin city, his Muslim troops are explicitly depicted, however rhetorically complex the expression, as slaughtering ʿAmmūriyah's men and raping her women. Thus the caliph and his armies participate in the fulfillment of Islamic desire and divine will. Through the conquest of ʿAmmūriyah, Islamic dominance and honor is restored and the Byzantine Infidel reduced to humiliation and submission.

Part 8: Lines 67–71. This brings us to the concluding section of the qasida and of our discussion: Abū Tammām's transformation of a contemporary military-political event into a qasida that functions as a legitimizing myth of caliphal authority and a vehicle for formulating and promoting an ideology of Arabo-Islamic dominion. It is noteworthy that after the tension created by rhetorical opacity and density of the preceding section, the style of the closing section, in terms of diction and rhetoric, is relaxed and uncomplicated. The poet addresses al-Muʿtaṣim as "Caliph of God" in a line of benediction (line 67). There is no mention here of genealogy or other bases for the claim to the caliphate; it is presented as entirely deriving from the caliph's striving in the way of Islam. Line 68 tells us further that the caliph's motives are ultimately spiritual, that he realizes that salvation in the world to come, the "greater repose" (*al-rāḥati l-kubrā*) can only be achieved through exertion and exhausting toil in this world. Thus we can discern a pattern of sacrifice and renunciation in this world leading to redemption and salvation in the next: the key moral message of the Qurʾān. The poet's benediction, "May God reward you," in line 67 is a performative speech act that amounts to a declaration of recognition and allegiance. These two lines appear to focus on striving in the path of Islam as the key legitimizing element. In the context of the qasida it suggests that successful military leadership against the Infidel is paramount in the Muslim concept of the caliphate in this period. The caliph's victory thus confirms his divine appointment. At the same time these lines reiterate and reinforce the opening theme of the qasida: that divinely inspired and appointed action—the caliph as a sword in the hand of God—is what determines the course of events. Thus, the course of events, however dependent upon human action and initiative, is ultimately teleological, inexorably marching to the ultimate triumph of Islam.

Abū Tammām closes his qasida by affirming this Islamic teleological trajectory. He does this first by establishing a "mythic concordance" between al-Muʿtaṣim's victory at ʿAmmūriyah and the Islamic foundation myth of divinely appointed and aided military victory, the Prophet Muḥammad's astounding victory over the Meccan polytheists at the battle of Badr in the year 2/624 (lines 69–70). By using the metaphor of genealogy, of biological heredity and generation, to describe the relation between the two battles, the poet creates an image of a continuous sequence of Islamic victories, each one engendering the next, uninterrupted until the Day of Resurrection. A place in the divinely ordained succession of Islamic military victories appears to have replaced biological lineage as the determinant of caliphal legitimacy. The idea that military efficacy provides a more compelling proof of legitimacy than does ancestry is a concept that regularly comes into play in the ideology of the caliphate and of Islamic rule generally, and is a sword that cuts both ways, as we shall see in chapter 6.

Abū Tammām portrays the Arab victory over the Byzantines as a biological manifest destiny. Playing on the sobriquet of the Byzantines, "Pale Faces" (literally "Sons of the Yellow Man," *Banū l-Asfar*),[47] the poet declares that defeat has left them devitalized, drained of blood, as the ill omen of their jaundiced color would suggest. There is a further association here with the Arabic poetic tradition surrounding blood vengeance, in which the slain enemy is conventionally described as "yellow-fingered" (*musfarrun anāmiluhū*),[48] whereas the bronze-faced Arabs are left with the polished and radiant complexion of victory. Here, too, there is a further association behind the glowing Arab faces, that is, the tradition that at the Battle of Badr the faces of the Muslims were imparted a divine illumination. What is important to note here is that what appears on the surface to be a mere physical comparison is ultimately a conceptual one: the preordained (as indicated by the ill omen of their epithet) defeat of the Byzantine infidel and divinely appointed victory of the Arab Muslims.

Let us not confuse this myth of Arabo-Islamic dominion with history. Given that we know from the historical sources that al-Muʿtaṣim was the first of the ʿAbbāsid caliphs to rely heavily on Turkish troops,[49] the closing line of this poem should be read as promoting a specifically *Arabo*-Islamic ideology legitimate rule rather than reflecting the increasing competition of other Muslim ethnic groups, notably Persians and Turks, for political and military power within the ʿAbbāsid empire.

The increasing reliance of the ʿAbbāsid caliphate on Turkish troops was an indicator of the waning of centralized Arab and ʿAbbāsid power. Within the coming century the ʿAbbāsid caliphate would devolve into a figurehead, its dominion dramatically diminished within the still nominally ʿAbbāsid lands by increasingly powerful local dynasties, particularly the Būyids (who controlled Baghdad, and the caliphate, from 334/945), and without by competing claimants to the caliphate, notably the Shiite Fāṭimids (297–567/909–1171) in North Africa and later Egypt, where they built their triumphant capital in Cairo, and the remnant of survivors of the former Umayyad caliphate at Damascus who fled to al-Andalus and declared the Umayyad caliphate once more at Cordova (319–422/931–1031; see chapter 7). Among the local dynasties that rose to power within the ʿAbbāsid domain in the following century are two that we will meet up with in the coming chapter, the Ḥamdānids at Mosul and then (333–359/944–969/70) Aleppo and the Ikhshīdids in Syria and Egypt (327–358/939–969).

Six

The Poetics of Political Allegiance

Praise and Blame in Three Odes by al-Mutanabbī

Politics and Poetics

In this chapter we will examine three odes by the most celebrated poet of the Islamic age, Aḥmad Abū al-Ṭayyib al-Mutanabbī (303–354 H./915–965 C.E.), to explore the ways in which the qasida is manipulated conceptually to express varying concepts of legitimacy or illegitimacy and presented performatively to establish or abrogate bonds of political allegiance, to negotiate and regulate rank and status. In doing so we will take as our starting point the role of the panegyric qasida as an object in a ritual exchange. It is of interest that at this period the ʿAbbāsid caliphal court at Baghdad is no longer the magnet for the greatest poetic talents of the day: as the caliphate's political power declined, so did its attraction for poetic talent and ambition.

In the mid fourth/tenth century we find the greatest poet of the age moving over the course of his career from one local dynastic court to another, all of them nominally under ʿAbbāsid tutelage. Chief among these are (1) the court at Aleppo of the Ḥamdānids, an Arab Taghlibī (or maybe originally Kurdish) dynasty, where al-Mutanabbī served as panegyrist for the illustrious emir Sayf al-Dawlah from 337/948 until his flight in 346/957; (2) the Turkish Ikhshīdid dynasty in Egypt and Syria with its capital at al-Fusṭāṭ, whose black eunuch slave regent, Kāfūr, was the recipient of both panegyric and invective from al-Mutanabbī; and, after his flight from Egypt in 350/962, (3) the Shiite Iranian (Daylamite) dynasty, the Būyids (Buwayhids), who ruled Iraq and Persia and were the true power behind the puppet caliphate, and whose celebrated vizier and litterateur Ibn al-ʿAmīd in Arrajān became al-Mutanabbī's patron, followed by the Būyid ruler ʿAḍud al-Dawlah, then at Fārs.[1]

The political and military instability of the period and the resultant precariousness of the local dynasts made for a poetry quite grounded in the realpolitik of the time and for a sense on the part of the poet that he, too, could be a player in the atmosphere of incessantly shifting political and military alliances. With true power in the hands of these warlords and petty dynasts, the awe and attraction of the ideologically maintained but practically impotent caliphate waned, and even the greatest panegyric of the day focused on the personal, usually military, accomplishments of individual local patrons. At the same time, the power vacuum at Baghdad opened the field for a fierce competition for authority, legitimacy, and prestige, and thus a market for the skills of a panegyrist who could frame sheer military political success in the myth and ideology of legitimate rule.

Al-Jāḥiẓ and Mauss: Rituals of Exchange

Let us begin by noting that the idea that the panegyric might compromise the poet's virtue is not merely a Western or Romantic notion. To the contrary, we read in the classical Arab critics, on the authority of such scholars as the renowned second/eighth century founder of the Basran school of grammar, Abū ʿAmr ibn al-ʿAlāʾ (d. ca. 154/770), that poetry's fall from the golden age of the Jāhiliyyah was occasioned precisely by the sycophantic blandishments of the panegyrists of the Islamic age.[2] The issue of artistic sincerity or truthfulness as it regards panegyric poetry centers around the practice of payment for poetry, which is perceived, as the title of Leslie Kurke's study of Pindar's epinikian odes, *The Traffic in Praise,* suggests, as a prostitution of art.[3] The basic perception is that the patron pays the poet to tell flattering lies about him. In truth, the situation is far more complex, as the following anecdote from *Al-Bukhalāʾ* (The Book of Misers) by the renowned third/ninth century litterateur al-Jāḥiẓ (d. 255/868–9) will illustrate:

> And then there is what Muḥammad ibn Yasīr told me about a governor in Persia—it was either Khālid Khū Mahrawayh or someone else. He said: One day this governor was in his council chamber busy with his accounts and affairs and completely engrossed in his work when suddenly a poet appeared before him and recited poetry to him in which he praised him and magnified him and glorified him. When he finished the governor said, "That was excellent!" and then turned to his secretary and said, "Give him ten thousand dirhams." The poet was overcome with joy, and when the governor saw his state he said, "I see that my words have had quite an effect on you! Make that twenty thousand dirhams!" At this the poet almost jumped out of his skin. When the governor saw that his joy had doubled he said, "Your joy doubles along with my words. Give him forty thousand!" And the joy almost killed him.

> When he was himself again, the poet said to the governor, "You, may I be made your ransom, are a magnanimous man, and I know that every time you saw my joy increase you increased my reward (*al-jāʾizah*). Accepting this from you would be the least of thanks." Then he called down blessings upon the governor and left.
>
> Then the governor's secretary turned to him and said, "God be praised! This poet used to be happy with forty dirhams and now you're ordering him forty thousand?!" "Woe to you!" replied the governor. "Do you actually want to give him something?" "Is there any way out of fulfilling your command?" said the secretary. "You idiot!" retorted the governor, "This is a man who has made us happy with words and whom we have made happy with words. When he claimed that I am more beautiful than the moon and stronger than the lion, that my tongue is more cutting than the sword and my command more effective than the spearhead, did he put in my hand anything that I could take home to my house? Don't we know that he was lying? But he made us happy when he lied to us, so we, too, say things to make him happy, and order him rewards. If it is a lie, then it is a lie for a lie and words for words. But if it were a lie for a truth or words for a deed, then this would be the 'clear loss' (*al-khusrān al-mubīn*) [Qurʾān 4:199, etc.] of which you have heard."[4]

The logic behind this anecdote is of great pertinence to understanding the relation between poet and patron, between the panegyric and the prize. For it suggests that the truth of poetry and its (monetary) value are commensurate. In other words, the reward for panegyric confirms its veracity. It is evident, too, that what is involved here is a form of regulated exchange. In this respect we can turn to Marcel Mauss's classic formulation of the characteristics and functions of ritual exchange in *The Gift* (*Essai sur le don*). Mauss gives definition of his subject as "prestations which are in theory voluntary, disinterested, spontaneous, but are in fact obligatory and interested. The form usually taken is that of the gift generously offered; but the accompanying behaviour is formal pretense and social deception, while the transaction itself is based on obligation and economic self-interest."[5]

The ritual exchange, in Mauss's formulation, subsumes three obligations: giving, receiving, and repaying.[6] "Failure to give or receive," he remarks, "like failure to make return gifts, means a loss of dignity."[7] Further, accepting a gift entails accepting the challenge to repay that it implies. Mauss states: "No less important is the role which honor plays in the transactions. . . . Nowhere else is the prestige of an individual as closely bound up with expenditure, and with the duty of returning with interest gifts received in such a way that the creditor becomes the debtor."[8] For, in Mauss's words:

> Between vassals and chiefs, between vassals and their henchmen, the hierarchy is established by means of these gifts. To give is to show one's superiority, to show that one is something more and higher, that one is *magister*. To accept without returning or repaying more is to face subordination, to become a client and subservient, to become *minister*.[9]

Applying Mauss's formulation to the relation between panegyric and prize, we can conclude that the ritual exchange involved therein amounts to the establishment and maintenance of a bond of clientage between the poet and the patron.[10]

What we are dealing with in al-Jāḥiẓ's anecdote is then an inversion or perversion of the ritual exchange between poet and patron, a renunciation of that bond. The point of the anecdote in the context of *Al-Bukhalā*ʾ is to demonstrate a degree of avarice so great that the governor would rather face ignominy, cut the bonds of clientage, and deny all the virtues the poet has attributed to him than part with his dirhams. His breach of promise confirms the poet's mendacity; the governor's false promise renders false the poet's praise.

The Arab condemnation of avarice, and the key to the whole joke, is implicit in the miserly governor's reference to the Qurʾānic *al-khusrān al-mubīn* (clear loss). For whereas the miser defends his actions on the basis that the poet has given him nothing he can put in his hand and take home, the Qurʾānic precept of "clear loss" is precisely the trading of the things of the world to come for the things of this world, that is, the choosing of the material over the spiritual, and hence damnation, as opposed to *al-fawz al-mubīn* (the clear gain)—salvation (Qurʾān 6:16; 45:29). Of the three Qurʾānic occurrences of *al-khusrān al-mubīn* (Qurʾān 4:119; 22:11; 39:15), the governor's immediate referent seems to be the first. There the clear loss is suffered by those who forsake God for Satan. Satan plants in their hearts false promises, whereby they are condemned to hellfire, whereas God's promise is true and leads to gardens with rivers flowing underfoot (Qurʾān 4:119–21).

The governor means to say that his promises of a lavish reward are not to be equated with the false promises of Satan, because his are just and fair, quid pro quo. The twist comes, however, in the governor's avarice. In his choice of the material over the spiritual, of self-serving "fairness" over selfless generosity, he reveals to the reader, though he himself remains blind to the fact, that it is he who has fallen victim to Satan's false promises; he—and not the poet—is the real loser. The miser, then, fails to grasp the essence of Islam. Implicit in the logic of this anecdote is the concept that poetry also has a more than material value, that it confers a sort of immortality, as our poet al-Mutanabbī has said: "The remembrance of a youth is his second life" (*dhikru l-fatā ʿumruhu th-thānī*).[11]

Mauss's formulation of gift exchange tells us, further, that the vice of avarice is not merely material, but that the miser in withholding his wealth, hospitality, and the like is above all withholding himself, withdrawing from or annulling the social contract. As Mauss notes of the archaic exchange: "We can see the nature of the bond created by the transfer of a possession. . . . it is clear that . . . this bond created by things is in fact a bond between persons, since the thing is a person or pertains to a person. Hence it follows that to give something is to give a part of oneself."[12]

The correlation of truth to payment promulgated in this anecdote of refusal of exchange also goes far to explain another aspect of the panegyric/prize relation: the predominance of generosity among the virtues elaborated in the praise section (*madīḥ*). This would seem to derive not merely from the shameless greed of the poet, but also from the fact that in the rewarding of the prize this virtue is immediately verifiable, thus establishing by attraction the veracity of the other virtues elaborated in the *madīḥ*.

Problematics of Poet and Patron

Of course, the opposite of al-Jāḥiẓ's anecdote, the perfectly executed ritual exchange between poet and patron in which the praise is true and the poet generously rewarded, is an ideal rather than a reality.[13] Nevertheless, it is obvious that there should be a strong positive correlation between the panegyrist and the patron for the poetic project to succeed. If the panegyrist is a bad poet, no amount of virtue and heroism on the part of the patron will enable him to produce a good poem, and as the poor or mediocre poem is consigned to oblivion, so too is the renown of the patron. Likewise, if the patron falls too short of the ideals elaborated in the *madīḥ,* the panegyric, however expertly composed, will degenerate into satire.

The ideal poet-patron match is celebrated in the Arabic poetic tradition above all in the relationship of Abū al-Ṭayyib al-Mutanabbī,[14] considered the last and the greatest of the classical poets (*khātam al-shuʿarāʾ*, "the seal of the poets"), and Sayf al-Dawlah, the Ḥamdānid prince of Aleppo, idealized as the consummate embodiment of Arabo-Islamic chivalry. Although these two have been molded into a romanticized Arab ideological construct, the prince and his mirror, the traditional sources nevertheless reveal an ultimate incompatibility between the two. A perfect balance between the poet's and the prince's valuation of the poet's work was ultimately impossible to maintain. The tradition seems to place the blame for this primarily on the poet himself, accusing him of the sin of excessive pride—consistent with his sobriquet "al-Mutanabbī" ("the would-be prophet")—and also of *bukhl* (avarice, greed).[15] But other anecdotes demonstrate Sayf al-Dawlah's failure to defend al-Mutanabbī in the viciously competitive literary and poetic circles of his court.[16]

The Qasida and the Poetics of Ceremony

The first of al-Mutanabbī's qasidas to be discussed here is his panegyric rhymed in the letter *dāl (dāliyyah),* which was presented to the Ḥamdānid emir Sayf al-Dawlah in Aleppo on ʿĪd al-Aḍḥā (the Feast of the Sacrifice), 342/953. My argument will be that the ceremonial and ritual aspects of the ode are not accidental or circumstantial, but rather constitute essential and formative elements of the poem, whose function it is to authenticate and perpetuate the renown of Sayf al-Dawlah as a legitimate Arabo-Islamic ruler and, on that basis, to render homage and allegiance to him.

The historical, ritual, and ceremonial dimensions of this qasida are given in all the major al-Mutanabbī commentaries and can also be extricated from the poetic text itself. As al-Maʿarrī tells us, al-Mutanabbī composed this poem as a panegyric and a greeting for ʿĪd al-Aḍḥā (10 Dhū al-Ḥijjah 342 /15 April 954). He recited it to Sayf al-Dawlah on his parade ground (*maydān*) in Aleppo, below his tribune (*majlis*), while both of them were mounted on horseback. Al-Maʿarrī then adds that in the poem al-Mutanabbī mentions Sayf al-Dawlah's capture of the son of the Byzantine general, and boasts of himself and his poetry.[17] For our own analytical ends we can extrapolate from these descriptive remarks that although this qasida falls under the traditional rubric of "occasional poem," this does not mean that it merely describes a specific event or incident. Instead, it is performative: the act of recitation of the poem itself to the *mamdūḥ* (patron) fulfills two obligations or performs two functions: the praise of the ruler—a topic we will come back to—and the ʿĪd greeting. As will be discussed in more detail further on, these are twin acts of political and religious homage. The first can be viewed as a declaration of political allegiance. The second is of a more explicitly religious nature, the obligatory ʿĪd greeting which amounts to a formal recognition of the legitimate Islamic rulership of the *mamdūḥ,* the withholding of which would constitute an act of sedition (*fitnah*). In both respects Paul Connerton's words concerning the performativeness of ritual verbal utterances apply to the Arabic qasida:

> Curses, blessings and oaths, together with other verbs frequently found in ritual language, as for instance, 'to ask' or 'to pray' or 'to give thanks', presuppose certain attitudes—of trust and veneration, of submission, contrition and gratitude—which come into effect at the moment when, by virtue of the enunciation of the sentence, the corresponding act takes place. Or better: that the act takes place in and through the enunciation. Such verbs do not describe or indicate the existence of attitudes: they effectively bring those attitudes into existence by virtue of the "illocutionary act."[18]

In the case of the qasida at hand, we can speak of the poet's physical attitude as well. Most striking and ultimately most revealing of the conceptual substructure of the poem is the remark that al-Mutanabbī recited it to Sayf al-Dawlah when they were both on horseback. Connerton has much to tell us about the performativeness encoded in physical postures as well. Lacking the subtlety—in Connerton's words the "ambiguity, indeterminacy and uncertainty"—of the linguistic element, the limited repertoire of ritual postures speak unequivocally and substantially:

> One kneels or does not kneel, one executes the movement necessary to perform the Nazi salute or one does not. To kneel in subordination is not to state subordination, nor is it just to communicate a message of submission. To kneel in subordination is to display it through the visible, present substance of one's body. Kneelers identify the disposition of their body with their disposition of subordination. Such performative doings are particularly effective, because unequivocal and substantial.[19]

It is well established that in classical Arabo-Islamic protocol and ceremonial the inferior dismounts to show respect for his superior.[20] The remark that al-Mutanabbī recited this ode to Sayf al-Dawlah when they were both on horseback—whether we take it as historical fact or literary semiosis—can only mean one thing: that al-Mutanabbī styles himself Sayf al-Dawlah's equal.[21]

The poet thus simultaneously offers praise and greeting and therefore—as the rules of ritual exchange and, more specifically, the Islamic prescriptions for returning the greeting require—justifiably anticipates a counter of equal or greater value. For example, of the return of greeting we read in the Qur'ān 4:87: "When someone extends a greeting to you, reply with a better greeting or return the same greeting, for indeed God takes account of everything"; so too the *ḥadīth* (tradition of the Prophet Muḥammad):

> ʿImrān ibn Ḥuṣayn reported that a man came to the Prophet and said, "Peace be upon you," to which he responded, and then when the man sat down, said, "Ten[fold peace upon you]." Another man came and said, "Peace and God's mercy be upon you," to which he responded, and then said, when the man sat down, "Twenty[fold upon you]." Another man came and said, "Peace and God's mercy and blessings be upon you," to which he responded, and then said when the man sat down, "Thirty[fold upon you]."[22]

Into this we must then integrate al-Maʿarrī's brief descriptive remark that the poet mentions Sayf al-Dawlah's capture of the Byzantine general's son and boasts of himself and his poetry. We will argue that this combination of praise and boast is the poetic structural equivalent of the patron (*mamdūḥ*) and poet both being mounted on horseback. Further, we will attempt to demonstrate how the historical event of Sayf al-Dawlah's military victory in the year 342/953 over the domesticus (Byzantine general) Bardas Phocas becomes, through the ritualizing capacity of the qasida, incorporated in the cyclical-mythical pattern of the Islamic liturgical calendar, and is thereby projected both backward and forward in time—i.e., it is monumentalized, commemorated, and, hence, immortalized.

Although the entire qasida falls thematically under the rubric of the final structural unit of the classical ode, the praise section (*madīḥ*), we can divide it for the sake of discussion and analysis into three main thematic sections. (1) Praise for Sayf al-Dawlah as a military leader who defeats the Byzantine Infidel, particularly the domesticus Bardas Phocas (lines 1–20); (2) An ʿĪd al-Aḍḥā (Festival of the Sacrifice) greeting to Sayf al-Dawlah, praising him for being as unique among men as the ʿĪd is among days, celebrating his virtue, and suggesting that his rank should be higher than that of a mere emir (lines 21–32); (3) A metapoetic closure in which the poet claims superiority over his competitors, boasts of his poetic prowess, asks Sayf al-Dawlah to favor him, and declares his allegiance to the emir (lines 33–42). In light of these remarks let us turn to the poem itself.

Al-Mutanabbī's "Each Man's Fate Is Fixed" (*Li-kulli Mriʾin min Dahrihī mā Taʿawwadā*)[23]
[meter: *ṭawīl;* rhyme: *-dā*]

1. Each man's fate is fixed
 by his own custom;
 And Sayf al-Dawlah's custom is
 to smite the foe,

2. To belie mendacious rumor
by true deed,
Thereby gaining from his foes' malevolence
greater felicity.

3. Many wished him harm
only to harm themselves;
Many guided armies against him
only to surrender them to him.

4. Many an arrogant infidel
who denied Allāh
Saw H/his sword in H/his hand,
then swore his creed.

5. He is the sea. Plunge into it for pearls
when it is calm;
But when the tempest churns its foam,
beware!

6. I have seen the true sea
throw its rider,
But when this one fells his foe,
it's by design.

7. To him the kings of the earth
submit,
Whether they flee from him and perish,
or approach him prostrate.

8. The cutting blades and spear shafts
revive his wealth,
But his smile and generosity soon slay
what they revive.

9. Acute, his wit is vanguard
to his eye;
His heart discerns today what his eye
perceives tomorrow.

10. To reaches remote and arduous
he leads his horsemen;
Were dawn's first gleam a water hole,
he'd lead them there.

11. So the son of the domesticus
called the day of his capture death,
While the domesticus called it
his birth.

12. You journeyed to the River Jayḥān from Āmid
in just three nights;
The gallop brought you near to one,
far from the other.

13. When the domesticus fled, he gave you his son
and all his armies,
But it wasn't to be praised for generosity
he gave.

14. You stood between him and his life,
obstructing his view;
In you he beheld
God's sword blade bared.

15. The blue spear tips sought
no one but him,
But his son Constantine
became his ransom.

16. So out of fear he came to wear
the monk's hair shirt,
When once he'd worn the lustrous weave
of mail.

17. Penitent he paces with crozier
the convent grounds,
He whom the sleek red roan's best pace
had failed to please.

18. He did not repent until
the battle charge had gashed his face,
And the stirred-up battle dust
inflamed his eye.

19. If monkery could save men
from ᶜAlī,
Kings would take to monasteries
singly and in pairs.

20. And every man, after the domesticus,
both east and west,
Would ready for himself
a black haircloth robe.

***

21. To you a joyous ᶜĪd whose
ᶜĪd you are!

And ʿĪd to all who invoke Allāh, sacrifice,
and celebrate the ʿĪd!

22. And may ʿĪds ever after
be your garb,
Surrendering worn garments and given
garments new!

23. For this day among the days is like
you among mankind:
As you are unique among men, it is among the days
unique.

24. It is fortune that makes one eye
sharper than its twin;
That makes one day the master
of another.

25. How amazing is the ruler
whose sword you are!
Does he not fear the two edges of
the sword he's girt?

26. He who makes the lion
his hunting falcon
Will soon find his lion
hunting him!

27. I consider you pure forbearance
in pure power;
Had you wished, your forbearance could have been
a blade of Indian steel.

28. Nothing kills noble men
like forgiveness,
But who would vouch for a noble man who's
mindful of a favor?

29. When you honor a man of honor,
you own him;
When you honor a dishonest man,
he's impudent.

30. To put generosity in the place of the sword
is as harmful to high rank
As putting the sword
in generosity's place.

31. But you surpass all men in judgment
and in wisdom

Just as you surpassed them in rank, soul,
and lineage.

32. Your deeds are too subtle
to contemplate,
So what's concealed is left and what is clear
is comprehended.

***

33. End the envy of my enviers
by humbling them,
For it was you who made them
envy me.

34. When you brace my forearm
with your high esteem
I will strike them with a sword that even sheathed
splits skulls.

35. I am nothing but a Samharī
spear you bore,
An adornment when displayed, terrible
when aimed.

36. Time itself is a reciter
of my odes;
I compose a poem,
then time recites it.

37. Recluses rush out
to bruit it abroad;
With it the tuneless raise their voice
in song.

38. Reward me for every poem
recited to you,
For what the panegyrists bring is but
my poems repeated.

39. Leave off every voice
but my voice;
Mine is the uttered cry,
the others echoes.

40. I have quit the night journey
to men of meager means,
And by your bounty I have shod my steeds
with gold.

OR

I [hereby/will] quit . . .
I [will] shoe my steeds. . . .

41. I have bound myself to your protection
out of love,
For he who finds beneficence is bound
with a firm bond.

OR

I [hereby/will] bind. . . .

42. When a man asks his days for wealth
and you are distant,
They make reaching you
his promised goal.[24] [23]

Many Happy Returns

The qasida is in the meter *ṭawīl* and rhymed in *-dā,* a rhyme which the poet exploits to the fullest. In the first place, he appropriates the by now traditional poetic wordplays (*jinās*) on the root *ᶜ-w-d* (return), whence the words *ᶜīd* (annually recurring holiday) and *ᶜādah* (habit) (Lane, *ᶜ-w-d*),[25] a custom he himself will repeat some years later, under altogether different circumstances, in his renowned invective (*hijāᵓ*) against Kāfūr (see below). In the second place, one of the most striking features of "Each Man's Fate Is Fixed" is al-Mutanabbī's extended and structurally functional development of wordplay on the metathetic permutations of this root. Indeed, we will be able to structure our analysis of the poem around this sophisticated etymological play, for the three structural-etymological sections, which we will present briefly before proceeding to a more detailed analysis, correspond to the three thematic sections of the poem.

Part 1 (lines 1–20) is constructed on the play of *ᶜādah* (habit, custom), from the root *ᶜ-w-d* (return), with *al-ᶜidā* (the foe, enemy; singular *ᶜaduww*) from the root *ᶜ-d-w,* a root whose meanings encompass "run," "cross," "transgress," "assault," and "be hostile" (Lane, *ᶜ-w-d* and *ᶜ-d-w*). This part takes as its main theme Sayf al-Dawlah's *habit* of striking the *enemy* (line 1). Here the metathetic antithesis of *ᶜ-w-d,* denoting repetition and cyclicality, as opposed to *ᶜ-d-w,* denoting crossing and transgression, is extended to establish an antithesis between the Islamic ruler, i.e., the ᶜĪd celebrant, and the Byzantine Christian enemy, *ᶜaduww,* the military transgressors and aggressors against Islam who would, therefore, cut off the repeated—that is, annual—celebration of the ᶜĪd.

Part 2 (lines 21–32) resolves the opposition of part 1 into identity. Not only does the poet extend his greeting to Sayf al-Dawlah on the ᶜĪd, but he also identifies his patron with the ᶜĪd itself (lines 21–23). In purely practical military and political terms, we can say that without Sayf al-Dawlah's successful campaigns against the Byzantine Infidel (*jihād*) the population of Aleppo would not be celebrating ᶜĪd al-Aḍḥā, because, in accordance with the *cuius regio eius religio* (the ruler determines the religion of his realm) principle then in effect, at the very least the public celebration of the ᶜĪd would have been suppressed. Thus it is the emir's *ᶜādah* (custom, habit) of part 1 that allows him to be identified with the ᶜĪd itself, thereby making him the embodiment of Islam. This, therefore, provides for a legitimization and definition of Islamic rulership in terms of military success against the Infidel. Shockingly, at least for any poet other than al-Mutanabbī, the ensuing praise section (*madīḥ*) seems to indicate that Sayf al-Dawlah should rise up against the caliph, the idea apparently being that the more victorious Islamic conqueror is the more legitimate ruler.

After part 1 has dealt with the relation of the patron (*mamdūḥ*) to the enemy and part 2 with his relation to his subjects on the one hand and his overlord, the caliph, on the other, part 3 (lines 33–42) turns to the relation between poet and patron, and to the power of poetry—specifically al-Mutanabbī's. The etymological permutation this time comes at the end (line 42), where the patron is termed the *mawᶜid* (promise, appointed time or place), from *w-ᶜ-d* (promise), of all who would seek bounty.

Thus, al-Mutanabbī virtually generates the entire structural and semantic, as well as acoustic, framework of the poem from this extended metathetic etymological play. For the poet the roots *ᶜ-w-d* (return, habit), *ᶜ-d-w* (hostility, transgression), and *w-ᶜ-d* (promise) do not bear arbitrary meanings, nor are their metathetic relations accidental; rather, in al-Mutanabbī's hands, they exemplify in a most striking manner Gian Biagio Conte's description of poetic language:

> In literary discourse . . . the poetic overrides the communicative function, so that the arbitrary nature of the linguistic sign disappears to become fully motivated by the internal system of the poetic word. The relation of signifier to signified, irreversible in prose where signification is conventional and accessible only via the signifier, is, in poetry, a reciprocal two-way movement in which even the signified can recall its signifier. In other words, the elements that make up poetic discourse (both forms of expression and forms of content) are systematically related in so far as they are all coherently *guided* by a single poetic intention. Each is distinguished by belonging to a composite organic system in which the relationship between

signifier and signified is so intimate as to be reversible. The world of contents evoked by the poem corresponds coherently to the verbal texture in which it is expressed, as if one were inherent in the other.[26]

Part 1, Praise for the Victor: Lines 1–20. The explicit theme of part 1 is military victory, but we are not dealing here with battle description. Instead the poet deploys a rhetorical strategy through which Sayf al-Dawlah's campaign of Jumādā al-Ākhirah 342/September-October 953, in which he routed the domesticus Bardas Phocas and captured his son Constantine (who died in captivity in Aleppo[27]), becomes paradigmatic of the emir's habitual and customary defeat of the Infidel and thereby proof of the Islamic legitimacy of his rule. The opening line states an aphorism (*ḥikmah*) and then exemplifies it, moving from the general and axiomatic to the specific and hypothetical. The rhetorical effect of the juxtaposition is to confirm the hypothesis by association. This is followed by a more extended repetition of the pattern as the general praise of the patron's virtue and prowess in subjugating the enemy (lines 1–10) leads to the specific exemplum of his most recent campaign (lines 11–20).

But let us tarry a bit at the two opening lines, for they introduce ideas essential to understanding the classical Arabo-Islamic concept of nobility and, therefore, of fitness to rule. "Nobility" in both senses was understood to be essentially military in character and, again in both senses, to be inherent and inherited.[28] The customs or habits (*ʿādāt*) of Sayf al-Dawlah are, to borrow Connerton's term, the "embodied experience" of noble deeds.[29] Connerton's remarks on "the force of habit" are helpful here. Building upon W. Dewey's demonstration of the power of good habits by analogy to that of bad, Connerton notes the large role that desire plays in habitual behavior, that habits compel us toward particular courses of action, that habits are affective dispositions, that "habits have power because they are so intimately a part of ourselves."[30] Further, Connerton remarks that a habit is

> an activity which is acquired in the sense that it is influenced by previous activity; which is ready for overt manifestation; and which remains operative even when it is not the obviously dominant activity. . . . The term habit conveys the sense of operativeness, of a continuously practiced activity. It conveys the fact of exercise, the reinforcing effect of repeated acts.[31]

One can only note with what striking etymological precision the Arabic term *ʿādah* conveys the concept that Connerton is trying to get across.

What the opening hemistich is really telling us, then, is that man is responsible for his own fate, that his own habit or custom, or what he has habituated or accustomed himself to, determines, or simply is, his fate. Neither the idea nor its expression is original with al-Mutanabbī; rather he takes as the gnomic or aphoristic principle with which he opens his argument a generally accepted truism hallowed by the poetic tradition. As al-ʿUkbarī notes in his commentary, the pre-Islamic poet Ḥātim al-Ṭāʾī wrote: "Each man acts as he is accustomed" (*wa-kullu mriʾin jārin ʿalā mā <u>taʿawwadā</u>*), and the Mukhaḍram (bridging the Jāhilī and Islamic periods) poet al-Ḥuṭayʾah:

> They acted according to their custom, and you acted
> according to yours,
> For, indeed, a man is his custom.
>
> *fa jāʾū ʿalā mā <u>ʿuwwidū</u> wa-ataytumū*
> *ʿalā <u>ʿādatin</u> wa-l-marʾu mimmā <u>taʿawwadā</u>*[32]

This established and authenticated by its poetic pedigree, al-Mutanabbī can state with authority that smiting the foe and defeating false rumors by true deeds are not merely "second nature" to but the true nature of Sayf al-Dawlah, and they determine his actions, the course of events, his fate. What is original, then, is not al-Mutanabbī's opening line, with its traditional gnomic premise and time-honored wordplay, but how he develops these ideas throughout the poem through the metathetic wordplay (*jinās*) that begins in the second hemistich of line 1, in the switch from *ʿ-w-d,* whence *ʿādah* (habit, custom; plural *ʿādāt*), to *ʿ-d-w,* whence *al-ʿidā* (foe, enemy; singular *ʿaduww*).

The dominant theme of the verses of general praise (lines 1–10) is the submission of the enemy to Sayf al-Dawlah and to Islam. Particularly effective in this regard is line 4, in which a double entendre is generated by the double ambiguity of the pronominal antecedent (God or Sayf al-Dawlah) and the word *sayf* (simply "sword," but also the honorary title of the emir, Sayf al-Dawlah, "the Sword of the State"): "H/his sword (*sayf*/Sayf) in H/his hand" (*sayfahū fī kaffihī*).[33] This has the effect of identifying Sayf al-Dawlah's military prowess with divine might and will; hence, submission to one constitutes submission to the other (Islam in its original meaning of *islām*/submission; see also line 7). Thus we find in al-Mutanabbī's ode the same attempt to identify or merge into one the will and actions of the Islamic conqueror, of God, and of fate that we found in Abū Tammām's "The Sword Is More Veracious" (chapter 5).

Also of note is line 8, which plays on the archetypal topos of the ancient Near Eastern king as bringer of life and bringer of death. In this verse a charming conceit and antithesis (*ṭibāq*) reveals the reciprocity between these two functions: it is only through the ruler's military might that he can acquire the wealth to be magnanimously disbursed to his subjects. Hence, war *revives* his wealth while his generosity *kills* it. The proper deployment of these two pillars of rulership is a subject the poet will take up once more, in line 30. At the same time we should be aware that this expression of the mythic power over life and death is an element not only of ancient Near Eastern concepts of sacred kingship but also of the Islamic ideology of *jihād* (holy war against the infidel). Just how mythicizing this panegyric commonplace is becomes apparent when we juxtapose it to more technical historical information. Th. Biaquis writes, summarizing Ḥamdānid rule:

> On the basis of the information given by the chroniclers as well as by the geographers, it should be possible to reconsider the balance-sheet of the Ḥamdānid dynasty. The wars between Sayf al-Dawla and the Ikhshīd had led to the destruction of the olive-groves and orchards surrounding Aleppo. The agricultural landscape was permanently altered. . . . Furthermore, this prince [Sayf al-Dawla], as well as his brother Nāṣir al-Dawla and later his nephew, al-Ghaḍanfar, princes of Mawṣil, had a policy of monopolizing fertile agricultural lands and appropriating extensive domains, with the aim of devoting them to monoculture, in particular the growing of cereals, a decidedly profitable enterprise in view of the demographic growth of Baghdād. Combining these territorial confiscations with oppressive fiscal policies, they became the wealthiest *amīrs* of the Islamic world. . . . They thus acquired lasting glory by showering with precious gifts their kinsmen and the poets who eulogized them, but they seriously destabilised agriculture and crafts, commercial exchanges and the equilibrium between towns and countryside. . . . By destroying orchards and peri-urban market gardens, enfeebling the once vibrant polyculture and depopulating the sedentarised steppe terrain of the frontiers, the Ḥamdānids contributed to the erosion of the deforested land and to the seizure by semi-nomadic tribes of the agricultural lands of these regions in the 5th/11th century.[34]

In light of this information, it becomes evident that the actual source of Sayf al-Dawlah's wealth was not so much plundering the Byzantine Infidel as confiscating lands from his own Muslim subjects. With regard to the present argument the point is that the panegyric topos of plundering the Infidel to bestow bounty upon the Islamic *ummah* is an ideologically motivated mythicization of Sayf al-Dawlah's rule.

With line 11 comes the transition from general to specific, or, more precisely, from the description of the *ʿādah* of Sayf al-Dawlah to the enactment of that "embodied experience." The basic events referred to here are corroborated in the historical sources (see above).[35] Al-Mutanabbī does not, however, give a "battle description"—the common misnomer of military passages in Arabic poetry that reflects an equally common misconception. Instead he wrests from the historical event those elements that can serve as exempla of Sayf al-Dawlah's *ʿādah.* Thus, for example, the principle established in line 7, that the kings of the earth submit to Sayf al-Dawlah, whether by fleeing or surrendering, is embodied in the flight of the domesticus and the capture of his son (who subsequently died in captivity). Hence in line 11 al-Mutanabbī employs antithesis (*ṭibāq*) to express the simultaneous retreat and capture of the domesticus and his son as the (re)birth of the former and the death of the latter; in line 15 the poet describes Constantine as his father's ransom, meaning that the domesticus redeemed himself with his son's life, gave his son's life instead of his own. The domesticus's retreat from the field of battle to the monastery, the exchange of coat of mail for haircloth robe, amounts to renouncing the active-aggressive for the passive-submissive. Al-Mutanabbī is thus quite correct in evaluating it as an act of cowardice and defeat, not of (Christian) religious devotion.

The rather fanciful hypothetical flight of cowering (Christian) kings into monasteries then serves as a rhetorically powerful transition to the triumphant celebratory Islam of the coming section. The final line (20) of part 1, while completing the apodosis of the preceding verse, provides a formal closure through the repetition in *wa-kullu mriʾin* (each, every man) of the *li-kulli mriʾin* of line 1. The antithesis of defeated Christianity and triumphant Islam is subtly restated in the Christians' preparation of black haircloth robes whose association of withdrawal, mortification of the flesh, and mourning provides the antithesis for the twofold celebratory function of garb associated with the Islamic ʿĪd al-Aḍḥā: first, the donning of new garments by the general Muslim populace, and second, for pilgrims celebrating the sacrifice as the culminating ritual of the Ḥajj, the exchange of the stark ritual garment, the *iḥrām,* for profane (and far more colorful) costume after the sacrifice on ʿĪd al-Aḍḥā. In both cases the Muslims' new garments symbolize new life, rebirth, purification (see the discussion of line 22, below).

We can now observe how al-Mutanabbī's exemplary employ of the military campaign of 342/953 allows the historical event to be subsumed into the repetitive cycle of Sayf al-Dawlah's *ʿādah.* In part 2 of the poem we will witness, through the etymological identification of Sayf al-Dawlah's *ʿādah* with the ʿĪd, the subsequent subsuming of the historical event into the Islamic liturgical calendrical cycle.

Part 2, The ʿĪd Greeting: Lines 21–32. Numerous studies of ritual and ceremonial tell us that calendrical holidays, such as the new year, celebrate above all the restoration of order after chaos[36] and that court ceremonial constitutes primarily the symbolic embodiment or recognition of the social, and indeed cosmic, hierarchy.[37] In this qasida, then, inasmuch as it comprises both panegyric (*madḥ*), which I claim is a literary form of court ceremonial, and holiday greeting or felicitation (*al-tahniʾah bi-l-ʿīd*), the liturgically obligatory greeting on the calendrically recurring holiday, both of these concepts should find expression. As I will be arguing, al-Mutanabbī in fact fuses both elements—the restoration of order after chaos and the recognition of the social/cosmic hierarchy—in this qasida. This he does quite simply by claiming that in vanquishing the Christian Byzantines, Sayf al-Dawlah has restored Islam and has thereby established his legitimate Islamic rule.

In all respects line 21 is the pivot point of the poem. Through a repetitive insistence on the word *ʿīd* itself and its verbal form II *ʿayyada* (to celebrate the ʿĪd), al-Mutanabbī anchors the poem both acoustically and semantically. What begins as a charming conceit of a personified ʿĪd conveying its felicitations to the emir concludes, through the role reversal of emir and ʿĪd, in identifying the two: the emir is an ʿĪd to every Muslim.[38] We can take this to mean that Sayf al-Dawlah's rule is recognized and his victories celebrated by all Muslims. In this way, we can say for the present ceremonial qasida what Maurice Bloch has said of the ritual of the royal bath in nineteenth-century Madagascar, that it "links the cosmic and political order and in this way legitimates the latter"[39]—a linkage that has been rhetorically achieved as well in the other qasidas that we have examined. Similarly we can say that in identifying the emir, and more precisely his habitual military victory, with the ʿĪd, al-Mutanabbī has established between the two what Connerton has termed in his analysis of Nazi commemorative ceremonies a "mythic concordance."[40] Moreover, inasmuch as the ʿĪd is personified as performing the ritual greeting to the emir, it would seem that their relationship is that of subject to ruler. The identification of the ʿĪd and the emir then forms the basis for the extended metaphor of lines 22–24.

The metaphorical complexity, even confusion, of line 22 is such that commentarists differ in their vocalization and hence their precise interpretation of it. Whichever reading we follow, the role reversal of line 21 seems to be still in effect here in the poet's benediction, itself another common category of performative speech, which basically conveys the idea of "many happy *returns* of the day." The poet styles the ʿĪds as the emir's garment. Hence, following the customary Islamic practice on ʿĪd al-Aḍḥā, each year the worn garment, here the previous ʿĪd, should be replaced with a new one, i.e., ʿĪd.

The poet's evocation of the ʿĪd custom of donning new garments in symbolic expression of spiritual renewal and rebirth serves as well as an expression of Islamic triumph, an antithesis to the Christians' garments of renunciation and mortification—in brief, defeat (see lines 16 and 20). At the same time, though in an enlarged historical and cultural arena, the association of this custom with the ruler in al-Mutanabbī's verse echoes the ancient Babylonian ritual of the annual divestiture and revestiture of the king.[41]

In what we cannot help but read as an inverted simile, line 23 explains the sociopolitical hierarchy that places the emir above his subjects by analogy to the priority of the ʿĪd among the days. In so doing it establishes the emir at the top of the social hierarchy: the emir is to the general Muslim populace as the ʿĪd is to the other (profane) days of the year.[42] Expanding on this *primus inter pares* explanation of rulership, the poet in line 24 attributes this to fortune: just as a person has two seemingly identical eyes, but one is sharper than the other. Within the ensuing political passage of this poem, this could be interpreted as a challenge to the sovereignty of the regnant ʿAbbāsid caliph, al-Muṭīʿ lil-Lāh, based on lineage at a time when military and political control of ʿAbbāsid lands was in the hands of the Būyid emirs and their rivals—not least among them the Ḥamdānids—and Sayf al-Dawlah was virtually independent.

Having established the hierarchical position of Sayf al-Dawlah vis-à-vis his subjects, al-Mutanabbī then moves up the scale in lines 25–30 to present the emir's standing with regard to his presumptive liege lord, the caliph. This section probably reflects less upon the audacity of al-Mutanabbī than on the debility of the fourth/tenth century caliphate. Playing as he did in lines 4 and 14 on the emir's name—Sayf al-Dawlah means Sword of the (ʿAbbāsid) State, an honorific title conferred on the emir by the caliph—the poet expresses his amazement that the caliph—here termed *dāʾil* (ruler, the active participle form of the noun *dawlah* [state, dynasty])—is not afraid of the sharp edges of the sword with which he's girt (line 25); like using a lion in place of a falcon for hunting, the danger is that it will turn on the hunter and make him its prey. The point of this parable, occurring as it does precisely in that part of the poem that is concerned with the sociopolitical hierarchy, is that something is out of order. Lines 27–30 then present the emir's predicament as the poet sees it. What is of interest in the course of the present argument is that it is articulated in terms of the norms of reciprocal behavior that serve to define rank and position in the hierarchical system. The two cardinal virtues, then, are forbearance (*ḥilm*) and power (*qudrah*), by which the poet means possessing power and knowing when and how to use it. Within the system of hierarchies one establishes and preserves one's position through the appropriate exercise of these virtues. What the poet suggests in the second hemistich of line 27 is that Sayf al-Dawlah's restraint toward the caliph, presumably out of respect for his exalted rank, might better have been replaced by military aggression.

Lines 28–30 serve as a definition of the rules of nobility, here understood as the reciprocal definition of ranks within a hierarchy of such ranks. Status within the hierarchy is negotiated and regulated through rituals of exchange, which in this context encompass a variety of symbolic and ceremonial forms, such as physical and verbal expressions of dominion and obeisance, dominance and submission, such as greetings and gestures, as well as material (gift) exchange. Mauss's formulation of ritual exchange, with its emphasis on the establishment of relative rank and the role of prestige and honor involved in the obligation to return a gift with interest (see above), applies equally to material and ceremonial (symbolic) exchange and is central to our understanding of the establishment and maintenance of the Arabo-Islamic court hierarchies.[43] Thus, when al-Mutanabbī states, "Nothing kills noble men like forgiveness" (line 28), he means that when you excuse a noble rather than demanding or expecting of him reciprocal noble behavior, his rank is lowered with regard to yours.

The poet then complains that the times are such that you can hardly find anyone who recognizes a favor, let alone realizes his obligation to repay it (expresses his gratitude). Line 29 states with elegance and simplicity the basic rule of nobility, that its principles of reciprocity and obligation function only among nobles, or, in other words, that adherence to these rules defines nobility: "noblesse oblige"—nobility obligates the noble to observe certain norms of reciprocal behavior; to fail to live up to these obligations is to be less than noble, to be ignoble. When you commit an act of generosity to a noble, he will acknowledge the debt incurred and his obligation to repay it; he will feel grateful and "obliged." A bond of loyalty is thereby established. Conversely, such generosity conferred upon an ignoble will elicit only insolence or contempt: he will claim he was owed it all along, or that he has cleverly outwitted you. The point, as so eloquently demonstrated by al-Jāḥiẓ at the beginning of this chapter, is that the ignoble value material gain over honor. In sum, we can say that a man's response to an act of generosity defines his position on the hierarchical scale.

Along the same lines, line 30 implies that the maintenance of high rank requires not merely the possession of the two foremost forms of power, military and economic might, but also their proper deployment. We must first remark that in Arabic poetic and political terms the latter means above all the power to give, generosity. In the poetic canon these are mythopoeically expressed as the power over life and death, the basis of the charming conceit and wordplay we witnessed in line 8.

Of particular interest is the role that lines 27–30, and especially 28–30, play within this qasida, for they perform two simultaneous functions, each one connected to a particular dimension of the poem. The first is the one already discussed: an elegant and concise definition of the courtly code on which the social structural hierarchy is founded. As such, it will remain aesthetically and morally compelling to all who subscribe to that system of values and, in turn, will serve to prop and propagate such values. In this respect they contribute to the lasting appreciation of the poem as it functions within the courtly culture of the Arabo-Islamic military aristocracy, and further as a "cultural artifact" or work of art beyond the limits of that culture.

The second function applies in a much more immediate manner to the circumstances of the poem's composition. These lines must be read in light of lines 25 and 26. Thus, in what amounts to incitement to insurrection, the poet suggests that the emir has, in the case of the caliph, confused or misplaced his greatest virtues, forbearance and might or generosity and power (lines 27–30). Thus, where we might expect to find an expression of obeisance and allegiance to the upper echelons of the Islamic political hierarchy, we find in al-Mutanabbī's qasida to Sayf al-Dawlah the presentation of a realpolitik, and an instigation to correct a hierarchy that does not reflect the true distribution of power. More to the point, the fact that al-Mutanabbī could present such a poem in itself testifies, as do the historical accounts,[44] to the debility of the ʿAbbāsid caliphate under the Būyid emirate. It is crucial to realize that al-Mutanabbī is fully backing the Arabo-Islamic courtly concept of nobility, that is, military aristocracy, as the principle for the construction and maintenance of the sociopolitical hierarchy. What he is criticizing is a malfunction that has led to "disorder" in that system. Al-Mutanabbī's call, then, is for a restitution of the proper order, an order that to him seems properly to be based on military prowess and the concomitant magnanimity that it allows for.

In both its general and its specific dimensions, al-Mutanabbī's call for restitution of a rightly ordered hierarchy can be understood in formal terms as expressing the ancient Near Eastern pattern of annually recurring rituals (new year festivals) in which what is celebrated above all is the restitution of order after chaos. Sayf al-Dawlah's identification with the ʿĪd, then, takes on two aspects. First, with regard to the Byzantine Christian enemy, his military triumph marks the restoration of the proper cosmic and political order after the "chaos" of infidel aggression. Second, with respect to the political hierarchy within the Islamic world, the poet calls for the restitution of what he sees as the proper "order" of the political hierarchy, which has been "disordered" by the subordination of Sayf al-Dawlah to a liege lord who is his inferior. In more immediate terms, perhaps what we are seeing in this qasida is an expression of the tension between the true military aristocracy and the figurehead hereditary caliphate.

Lines 31 and 32 serve as a sort of double closure of part 2. With regard to the more immediate argument, they express the poet's deference to the emir's better judgment in not rising up against the caliph, this due to Sayf al-Dawlah's superiority over all men in opinion, judgment, rank, soul, and lineage, which render many of his deeds unfathomable and unchallengeable. With regard to the broader structural lines of the qasida, these two verses provide a closure to the praise section proper (*madīḥ*), grounding allegiance to the emir and the legitimacy of his rule in his superior virtue, and establishing a principle of unquestioning obedience to him. It should be noted that my reading of these two verses is somewhat more contextual and political than that of the commentarists who remark on them as general praise for the virtues and generous deeds of Sayf al-Dawlah. The net effect, in any case, is the poet's reaffirmation on the ʿĪd of the legitimacy of the emir's rule and of the social hierarchy that his rule embodies.

The role of the poet and the ceremonial function of panegyric are such that what the poet says in his qasida is understood to be paradigmatic for the polity as a whole, for all the emir's subjects. Furthermore, as an expression of the principles upon which the Arabo-Islamic social structure is erected, the poem is paradigmatic for the relation of all Muslim subjects to their rulers. Again, it is these two aspects that explain the qasida's immediate ceremonial function—why it was presented to and accepted by Sayf al-Dawlah as a ritual ʿĪd greeting in 342/954, and why it has been preserved as part of the Arabo-Islamic cultural heritage ever since.

If, as we have argued above, the force of part 2 is to subsume the historical event or exemplum into the cyclical liturgical calendar through the identification of the *ʿādah* of Sayf al-Dawlah and the ʿĪd, then the final step remains to be taken, that is, the qasida must serve as the vehicle for the perpetuation of Sayf al-Dawlah's place in the Islamic liturgical calendar. Thus, the qasida goes far beyond its immediate ceremonial function on the particular day of its first recitation. It would have failed in its poetic and liturgical purpose if it had not been found to be so strikingly beautiful that it was itself, like the ᶜĪd, perpetually repeated. In part 3, then, we turn from the relation of the emir to his subjects and liege lord to his relation with the poet, and to the poet's, or poem's, capacity to project Sayf al-Dawlah's glory into the future.

Part 3, The Metapoetic Closure: Lines 33–42. To begin to understand the final section of the qasida, which deals, above all, with the role of poet and poetry, we must examine further the functional aspect of poetry as it relates to poetic form. First of all, we should keep in mind that the poet's presentation or recitation of a qasida to the ruler is one of the primary insignia of power in Arabo-Islamic rulership. To receive homage in this tradition-honored way is an expression of legitimate rulership. In this respect, the ritual and ceremonial aspects of the qasida—the fixed, genre-defining characteristics, which I have termed the "liturgical" characteristics—come to the fore. Thus the established monorhyme and meters, diction, tropes, themes, structure, etc., of the qasida are *necessarily* fixed, for their function is to create a trajectory back in time, reenacting the autochthonous and originary Arabic and Islamic acts of homage. In this respect the qasida functions as a commemorative ceremony of the twin authenticities or twin legitimacies of Arabo-Islamic rule. For the qasida is at once the reenactment of the panegyrics of the Jāhiliyyah, of which we might cite al-Nābighah al-Dhubyānī's "O Abode of Mayyah" (*Yā Dāra Mayyata*) (chapter 1) to the Lakhmid king al-Nuᶜmān ibn al-Mundhir as a renowned example, and thus legitimates the Arabicity, whether genetic or cultural, of the ruler who through this ritual of *imitatio* receives it. At the same time, through the Prophet Muḥammad's co-opting of the pre-Islamic qasida as a rite of homage to himself as the embodiment of Islamic rulership, the recitation of qasida to ruler likewise reenacts events of such "mythic" significance as the submission and homage of Kaᶜb ibn Zuhayr to the Prophet through the recitation of the celebrated "Suᶜād Has Departed" (*Bānat Suᶜād*) (chapter 2). Further, as we saw in the case of al-Akhṭal's "The Tribe Has Departed" (*Khaffa al-Qaṭīnu*) dedicated to the Umayyad caliph ᶜAbd al-Malik ibn Marwān, the panegyrists of the Umayyad period co-opted the high Jāhiliyyah court qasida not merely as a literary model, but as a tradition-honored insignia of legitimate Arab rule (chapter 3). Thus I would argue that the fixed or "liturgical" aspects of the qasida are necessary to establish its ritual cognation, though not so much with specific originary poetic acts of homage (although this is the explicit intention of the *muᶜāraḍah,* a poem that adopts the rhyme and meter of an earlier poem as a form of literary response; see chapter 7) as with an entire cultural poetic heritage composed of liturgically cognate qasidas. Thus, as we discussed in chapter 3, the patron (***mamdūḥ***) who participates in the qasida-presentation ceremony becomes thereby ritually or even mythically identified with every other Arabo-Islamic ruler who has been or will be the recipient of a qasida, or, in a more abstract sense, with legitimate Arabo-Islamic rulership.

But the qasida is not merely a ritual or liturgical text. For however great the formal strictures on the Arab panegyric poet, his primary mandate was to be original and beautiful. That is, in order to establish the qasida in the classical corpus and thereby immortalize the renown of the patron, the poet had to produce a poem that fell generically within the tradition—this was to achieve the backward trajectory necessary for the legitimation of both the ruler and the qasida—and at the same time a work so striking and compelling in its originality that it established its own place in that tradition, in order to achieve the forward trajectory.

This forward trajectory is of two types:. The first is what we might call "passive perpetuity": the poem is memorized, recited, written down. The second is "active perpetuity": the poem has true generative force within the tradition, a force that spawns borrowing (***sariqah,*** plagiarism) and imitation (***muʿāraḍah,*** contrafaction).[45] It is in this projection backward and forward of a unique literary work that the qasida distinguishes itself from liturgy, and in this respect too that there is no substitute for the artistic work of compelling beauty and originality. The poet is not merely invoking or intoning the sanction of time-honored rituals of homage, he is constructing a monument to a particular patron (***mamdūḥ***) that will itself stand for all time. It is with this aesthetically dependent aspect of poetry in mind that we can begin to understand part 3 of the poem.

In our opening remarks we noted that al-Mutanabbī, in reciting this qasida while he and his patron were both mounted, presented himself ceremonially as Sayf al-Dawlah's equal. In part 1 we witnessed in Sayf al-Dawlah's defeat of the Byzantine Christians the restitution of the proper cosmic order, that is, of Islam triumphant. In part 2 we observed that the poet is concerned primarily with the restitution of the proper order in what we might call the domestic sphere, that is, the relationship of the emir Sayf al-Dawlah to the caliph. In part 3 likewise, the concept of restoration of a proper order comes to the fore. Here the poet is concerned first with his rank among the other poets of the Ḥamdānid court and second with his rank vis-à-vis the emir. All of this is expressed in terms of the ritual exchange between poem and prize (*qaṣīdah* and *jāʾizah*), through which the patron expresses his valuation of a particular poem and poet, both in themselves and with regard to others, in objectively quantifiable terms.

Given the brusque imperatives that punctuate part 3 of the poem (the beginning of lines 33, 38, and 39), I think it is appropriate to speak in terms of the poet's demands, which are here phrased in a tone of what is technically termed *ʿitāb* (blame or reproach).[46] These demands should be understood as originating in the ancient Near Eastern tradition of the supplicant presenting his plea before the ruler and therefore as part of a ritual or ceremonial demonstration of the ruler's justice, mercy, and magnanimity (see chapter 1). As we know from studies of ritual exchange and from the earlier chapters of this book, this is virtually a form of entrapment, for the ruler would lose face and status if he did not respond to the plea in the most gracious and magnanimous of terms.

On the other hand, the main point in the ceremonial context is that the poet's plea, which the patron can fulfill on the spot through the simple granting (another performative act) of a prize—dirhams, dinars, horses, and slave girls are the common currency—offers the patron the opportunity to give a concrete demonstration of his justice, generosity, and other praiseworthy qualities, thereby establishing a paradigm of the relation of the Arabo-Islamic ruler to all of his subjects. Thus in a performative sense the poem incorporates and enacts the poet-patron and subject-ruler relationship. If al-Mutanabbī presents himself more as an equal than as a supplicant, it is because of his extraordinary—albeit, as the centuries have proven, correct—estimation of his poetic powers. Al-Mutanabbī's tone and posture before Sayf al-Dawlah remind us of al-Akhṭal before ʿAbd al-Malik ibn Marwān as the Umayyad poet, too, negotiated his rank and status via-à-vis his competitors—whether poetical or political—at court (see chapters 3 and 4). Whereas al-Akhṭal was concerned primarily with the political position of his tribe, the Banū Taghlib, in the Umayyad court, al-Mutanabbī is concerned rather with his rival poets. In both cases the poet's negotiation takes the form of invoking the obligations of the patron toward the poet, thereby restoring a just hierarchy at court.

Al-Mutanabbī's first demand (line 33) is for Sayf al-Dawlah to rid him of the jealousy of his rivals at the Ḥamdānid court by humbling them. This line has a certain rhetorical twist to it in that one would first expect the dispelling of jealousy to be achieved by the emir's giving as generously to al-Mutanabbī's rivals as he has to al-Mutanabbī himself. Quite the contrary, however, al-Mutanabbī means that Sayf al-Dawlah has been excessively generous with them, with the result that they now imagine that they are as deserving as al-Mutanabbī and have waxed envious. It was, the poet implies, Sayf al-Dawlah's unwarranted generosity, his raising them above their true rank, that is responsible for their envy. The situation, then, is altogether analogous to the misplaced generosity described in part 2, line 29.

Conversely (line 34), Sayf al-Dawlah's "good opinion" (*ḥusnu raʾyika*) of al-Mutanabbī, by which he means high estimation of and lavish reward for his poetry, would allow the poet to subdue his enviers. The weaponry metaphors employed in lines 34 and 35 to convey the power of the poet and of poetry establish at the same time an analogy or concordance between the poet and the prince. Just as Sayf al-Dawlah is the sword of God and sword of the state/caliph (lines 4, 25), al-Mutanabbī, or his poetry, is the sword and spear of Sayf al-Dawlah. The sword that slays even when sheathed (line 34) expresses with great force and precision the implicit or potential power of the great poet: that his rivals dare not challenge him—what we know as the principle of deterrence.

The weaponry metaphor continues in line 35, where it serves again to express with conciseness and precision the double symbolic and practical nature of the panegyric poet and his poetry. Like a Samharī spear that when displayed adorns the warrior-ruler and when aimed strikes terror in the hearts of his enemies and awe in the hearts of his followers, the mere presence of so renowned a panegyric poet adorns the court of his patron as a symbol of power and prestige (for only the heroic can attract poets and only the magnanimous can retain them), and when al-Mutanabbī's poetic powers are unleashed in panegyric to Sayf al-Dawlah they create a portrait of the patron (*mamdūḥ*) so formidable that it amazes his followers and confounds his foes. This interpretation is at variance with that of the classical commentarists, such as al-Maʿarrī, who says rather that the spear displayed refers to al-Mutanabbī's poetry at court and the aimed spear refers to his going to battle with Sayf al-Dawlah.[47] In my view this reading, though also implied, weakens the metaphor and is somewhat outside of the immediate poetic context, especially of line 34, in which the blows involved are clearly poetic ones.

Lines 36 and 37 describe the dissemination and circulation of al-Mutanabbī's poetry, and hence the patron's renown, both chronologically, in what we have termed the forward trajectory of the qasida, and geographically. The first employs a metaphysical conceit that personifies *dahr* (time, fate) itself as a reciter and transmitter of al-Mutanabbī's verse. The basis of this verse is the pre-Islamic transmission of the originally orally preserved qasida tradition through reciters or transmitters (*rāwī;* plural *ruwāt*) who memorized a poet's verse and passed it down orally generation after generation. So compelling is al-Mutanabbī's poetry that recluses rush out to bruit it abroad and, in a miracle on the order of making the blind see, the tuneless raise their voices in song. These lines thus express what I have termed above the "passive perpetuity" of poetry, that is, the power of the poem to captivate and capture an audience and thereby be incorporated permanently into the poetic canon.

In line 38 al-Mutanabbī restates the demand of line 33, now explicitly both claiming his reward and justifying it. Here the poet claims what I term the "active perpetuity," the power of the poem to generate other poetry, whether in the illicit form of plagiarism (*sariqah*) or the licit form of "rivalrous emulation" or "contrafaction" (*muʿāraḍah*) (see chapter 7). Al-Mutanabbī demands payment for all the panegyrics presented to Sayf al-Dawlah, claiming that the other court panegyrists are merely repeating, i.e., plagiarizing, his poetry. This demand is reiterated metaphorically in line 39 where al-Mutanabbī calls on Sayf al-Dawlah to reject all poetry but his, since his is the actual uttered voice, the others mere echoes.

We can thus observe in this qasida how both the poet and the patron employ the element of ritual exchange implicit in the ceremonial presentation of the qasida and conferral of the prize as a means to negotiate and regulate rank and status, much as Sanders in her study of Fāṭimid ceremony has demonstrated for ceremonial generally.[48] For the purpose of the prize in this poem is to raise al-Mutanabbī to his deserved rank. The humbling of his jealous rivals should likewise be understood in material terms. Al-Mutanabbī's plea or demand is for Sayf al-Dawlah to restore him to his proper position as the foremost of the poets of the Ḥamdānid court and to put his jealous rivals "in their place." In the poet's call for the restoration of proper poetic and courtly hierarchy after the chaotic frenzy of impudent and inferior rivals, part 3 shares with parts 1 and 2 the ancient Near Eastern new year theme of restoring order after chaos.

Al-Mutanabbī seals his qasida with three lines (40–42) that serve as closure in a more immediate sense to part 3 and in a more extended sense to the poem as a whole. The controlling image of these lines is that of the panegyrist who journeys from court to court until he finds a patron worthy of him, one who rewards him generously and to whom he therefore feels bound by ties of loyalty and obligation. It is noteworthy, however, that this closure is expressed in broad terms so as to be paradigmatically applicable to any of the liege lord's subjects or nobles. Thus al-Mutanabbī describes himself (line 40) as having given up the night journey to impecunious courts and having settled permanently with Sayf al-Dawlah, who has shod the poet's steeds with gold (referring, according to al-Maᶜarrī's commentary, to an actual incident when Sayf al-Dawlah conferred upon the poet a steed shod with golden horseshoes).[49]

But gift exchange, as Mauss has told us, involves above all the forging of bonds, and it is the bonds of love and loyalty toward his patron that al-Mutanabbī declares in line 41. It is of note here that the nature of this bond is explicitly bound up with the concept of nobility and honor propounded in line 29: he who finds beneficence a bond is, by definition, a noble. The two lines (40 and 41) taken together thus constitute a declaration of allegiance or homage, at once the *bayᶜah* (oath of allegiance) and *shukr al-niᶜmah* (gratitude for benefit, obligation).[50] As the alternative translations indicate, lines 40 and 41 can be read as constative—"I have quit . . . I have bound . . . "—or as performative (here with a contractual force), "I [hereby] quit . . . I [hereby] bind myself . . . " or even "I will quit . . . I will bind . . . "[51]

Above all, the poet, through such "illocutionary acts" as the utterance of "I have bound/bind myself to your protection," is invoking or creating bonds of reciprocal obligation. Placing "obligations" in the place of his "attitudes" and "poems" in the place of "verbs," we can restate what we quoted above from Connerton concerning curses, blessings, and oaths, as follows: the *poem* presupposes certain *obligations* which come into effect at the moment when, by virtue of the enunciation of the sentence, the corresponding act takes place. Such *poems* do not describe or indicate the existence of *obligations:* they effectively bring those *obligations* into existence by virtue of the "illocutionary act."[52] The poet, in recognizing Sayf al-Dawlah as his liege lord (what is entailed by saying "I have bound/bind myself to your protection"), invokes thereby an obligation on his part to compose panegyric virtually exclusively for him (or others at his liege's court, and not for his rivals). The obligation on the part of the lord to protect his liege men or clients we have already seen masterfully invoked by al-Akhṭal (chapter 4). The poet's payment of homage, the poem itself, in return for protection and beneficence thus ceremonially embodies the social contract upon which the Arabo-Islamic rulership was founded. Inasmuch as this poem was presented on the occasion of the ᶜĪd, its declaration of homage and allegiance functions quite precisely in accord with Gaster's formulation of the seasonal pattern whereby mutual bonds of obligation require annual renewal or reconfirmation.

The closing line (42) in one respect recapitulates the two preceding lines, but the change from the first to the third person moves the discourse from specific to the general, from the personal to the universal, particularly as "a man" (*al-insānu*) of line 42 is synonymous with the "each/every man" (*li-kulli mriʾin, wa-kullu mriʾin*) of lines 1 and 20. Finally, the closing word *mawʿid* (promise, pledge, appointed time or place), the noun of place of our final metathetic permutation, the root *w-ʿ-d* (promise), has the effect of recapitulating the entire qasida and projecting it into the future. First it recalls Sayf al-Dawlah's *ʿādah*, the habit built up through repeated exercise until it is bodily incorporated (with that habituation itself suggesting futurity), of striking the enemy/Infidel so that he has become the embodiment of Islam triumphant (part 1). Second, it recalls the calendrically repeated ʿĪd, now identified with Sayf al-Dawlah, which celebrates the cyclical restoration or restitution of Islam triumphant and of the Arabo-Islamic cosmic and social hierarchy and whereby the historical is incorporated into the mythical (part 2). Third, the reciprocal bond established by the exchange of panegyric and prize implies a reciprocal promise or pledge: it is contractual and is understood to *bind* the two parties to a *future* course of action, specifically, to continued panegyric on the part of the poet and continued prizes on the part of the patron. Thus, *mawʿid* suggests that now that the poet has delivered his panegyric, the payment has become due (part 3). Finally, if we look more closely, we perceive a subtle use of the personification of the abstract and concomitant abstraction of person in this verse, for if our usual understanding is that men make promises and the course of time fulfills them, here, then, "the days" (*al-ayyām*), synonymous with *dahr* (time, fate; see line 1), make the promises and Sayf al-Dawlah fulfills them. Thus Sayf al-Dawlah becomes not merely the fulfillment of the hopes of every supplicant, but the fulfillment of the promise, the goal, of time.

Despite the promising ending of "Each Man's Fate Is Fixed," the relationship between Sayf al-Dawlah and al-Mutanabbī was not destined to last. The next poems we will discuss come from the period following the poet's sojourn in Ḥamdānid Aleppo, when he lived at the rival court of Kāfūr, the regent of Ikhshīdid Egypt and Syria, in al-Fusṭāṭ (the capital of Egypt built by the Muslim conquerors, just southeast of present-day Cairo). The antiphrastically named Kāfūr (camphor) was the black eunuch slave of the founder of the Ikhshīdid dynasty, Muḥammad ibn Ṭughj al-Ikhshīd, who sponsored him in high political and military positions. Kāfūr enjoyed complete executive authority under his master's two successors, publicly declaring himself sole master of Egypt only after the death of the second, ʿAlī ibn al-Ikhshīd, in 355/966.[53] Our poet, his pride wounded by mistreatment at the hands of Sayf al-Dawlah, left Aleppo for Damascus in 346/957 and then proceeded to Ramlah. Meanwhile, Kāfūr had been instructing his Jewish governor in Damascus, which was in Ikhshīdid hands, to procure the celebrated panegyrist for him, and finally, after al-Mutanabbī's initial refusal ("Even if I went to Egypt, I wouldn't go intending the slave, but intending his master's son"),[54] Kāfūr was able to order the governor of Ramlah to send him to al-Fusṭāṭ.

It is of interest that the Arabic literary sources seem bent upon setting up a diametrical opposition between Sayf al-Dawlah and Kāfūr. Al-Mutanabbī is depicted as genuinely admiring the Ḥamdānid emir, their relationship as one of mutual admiration and devotion. Al-Mutanabbī fought at the emir's side in many of his military campaigns. His panegyric was true and sincere. Al-Mutanabbī's relation to Kāfūr, to the contrary, is characterized in the literary sources as one based on coercion and greed. It is said that al-Mutanabbī wrote his panegyrics to Kāfūr only in the hope or expectation of being appointed governor of Ṣayḍā or out of other purely material motivations and that in his heart he bore only contempt for the black eunuch. Furthermore, a number of lines in his panegyrics for Kāfūr are read by some critics as ambiguous, two-faced (*dhū wajhayn*) lines that could be read either as praise (*madḥ*) or as invective (*hijā*ʾ). The philologist Ibn Jinnī (d. 392/1002) is particularly zealous in defending al-Mutanabbī's unending loyalty to Sayf al-Dawlah and undying contempt for Kāfūr. In this context, then, it is not surprising that al-Mutanabbī's *hijā*ʾ for Kāfūr is credited with sincerity.

The suspicion arises, however, that this black and white contrast between the two patrons has more to do with the erection of a racial ideological construct than with the virtues or vices of the two patrons. Although evidence from the poetic texts as well as the accumulated literary materials around al-Mutanabbī certainly suggest that he was extremely attached to the Ḥamdānid prince and would have preferred to remain at his court, this in itself does not mean that he could not also have admired the Ikhshīdid ruler, whose accomplishments, as recorded in the historical, as opposed to literary, sources, are quite impressive (see below). Furthermore, it seems rather arbitrary to credit al-Mutanabbī's *madḥ* to Kāfūr with insincerity and his *ḥijā*ʾ with sincerity; likewise, his *madḥ* to Sayf al-Dawlah with sincerity and that to Kāfūr with insincerity. One begins to suspect, further, that the anecdotes about al-Mutanabbī's avarice were concocted by way of rationalization for a proud Arab poet's serving a black eunuch slave. In sum, the literary anecdotal material surrounding al-Mutanabbī appears to be largely ideologically motivated and although possessing considerable literary cultural value should not be taken as objective historical fact.

Panegyric and Political Allegiance

Having proposed in the first part of this chapter that the presentation of the panegyric and the conferring of the prize constitutes a ritual exchange along the lines formulated by Mauss, we will now attempt to explore some of its implications, particularly in light of the sincerity issue and the poet-patron relationship. In this respect E. E. Evans-Pritchard's summary of Mauss's conclusions makes a useful starting point: "The exchanges of archaic societies . . . are total social movements or activities. They are at the same time economic, juridical, moral, aesthetic, religious, mythological and socio-morphological phenomena. Their meaning can therefore only be grasped if they are viewed as a complex concrete reality."[55] It is our argument that in the qasida too, inasmuch as it is at the heart of this "total social phenomenon," "all kinds of institutions will find simultaneous expression."[56] The poem at hand, al-Mutanabbī's first panegyric ode (*qaṣīdat al-madḥ*) to Kāfūr, exhibits, both in terms of the prose materials that accompany it in the traditional sources and in explicit terms within the poetic text itself, al-Mutanabbī's transfer of allegiance from Sayf al-Dawlah to Kāfūr.

The classical sources concur that it was Kāfūr who initiated the relationship. Having learned that the renowned panegyrist had left Aleppo and was in Damascus, Ikhshīdid territory, he wrote the poet to come to Fusṭāṭ. It is related, with some variation, that Kāfūr prepared a house for him; according to some, put some agents in charge of him, showing suspicion of him; and, when al-Mutanabbī still did not eulogize him, bestowed robes of honor upon him, and brought him thousands of dirhams—whereupon, in the month of Jumādā al-Ākhirah 346/958, al-Mutanabbī recited to Kāfūr the qasida "Disease Enough!"[57] As the biographical anecdotes (*akhbār*) have it, then, it is the poet who is entrapped by Kāfūr's magnanimity, if not, indeed, by his command. The gist of the anecdotes is to overturn the usual poet-patron relationship and present Kāfūr as the virtual "supplicant." Al-Mutanabbī negotiates his rank and status by withholding his poems until the price is right. Nevertheless, the poem is in a performative sense the poet's transfer of allegiance and homage to Kāfūr, and the conceit is that the poem and the allegiance are both spontaneously proffered. Clearly, too, the qasida constitutes a prestation that expects—indeed demands—a counter-prestation.

We must take into full account, too, in pursuing the present argument, the implications of the panegyric qasida as a pledge of allegiance or oath of fealty that were discussed above. For it implies that the poet is not some itinerant peddler or wandering minstrel. Instead, on the precept that a man cannot serve more than one master, the act of delivering a panegyric entails, at least from the poet's side, an exclusive contractual obligation. In this respect we find external *akhbār* concerning the "treachery" of Sayf al-Dawlah —the *mamdūḥ* being likewise contractually bound—that become the excuse for al-Mutanabbī to leave Aleppo.[58] Likewise we find that when al-Mutanabbī meets with frustration and disappointment in al-Fusṭāṭ, he is nevertheless not free to leave his liege lord's side or to panegyrize promiscuously (see below).

The Poem of Transfer of Allegiance: Al-Mutanabbī's Panegyric to Kāfūr

In examining the poetic text, I would like to explore in particular the employ of traditional qasida motifs and structure to effect the transfer of allegiance and those elements that reflect the underlying ritual exchange pattern. Let us note first that this poem exhibits the traditional tripartite structure: the elegiac prelude (*nasīb,* lines 1–12), the desert journey (*raḥīl,* lines 13–23), and the praise section (*madīḥ,* lines 24–47). The sort of ritual patterning that has been proposed in the preceding chapters as the basis for the qasida structure—the rite of passage, the seasonal pattern—is likewise apparent here. Read in light of the tripartite van Gennepian rite of passage, the change of status of the passenger-poet comes to the fore: his Separation from his former condition reflected in the *nasīb;* the Liminal transitional stage in the *raḥīl;* and the Aggregation, reentry into society and assumption of new status, in the *madīḥ.*[59] Perceptible, too, are the elements of Gaster's seasonal pattern: the Mortification and Purgation of the Emptying phase in the *nasīb* and *raḥīl;* the Reinvigoration and Jubilation of the Filling phase in the *madīḥ.*[60] In short, I would like to demonstrate that the qasida is ritual in form as well as function. In addition, I would like to suggest that the emphasis on change of status entailed in a poem of transfer of allegiance is reflected in the poet's choice of the traditional tripartite form of the qasida, rather than the bipartite form, which was by his time more prevalent (see the remarks at the end of chapter 4).

In terms of the themes employed, the *nasīb* (lines 1–12) treats the poet's heartsickness over leaving the lover who has betrayed him; from the context that produced the poem, we can deduce that the poet's beloved but treacherous mistress is a stand-in for Sayf al-Dawlah. The *raḥīl* (lines 13–23) is directed to al-Fusṭāṭ, Kāfūr's capital in Egypt, and is undertaken by a group on horseback, rather than the lone poet on she-camel of classical convention. The *madīḥ* (lines 24–47) offers praise to Kāfūr as the fulfiller of hopes, model of all virtues, heroic warrior, appointed by God and summoned to glory by his own steadfast determination.

Al-Mutanabbī's "Disease Enough!" (*Kafā bika dā'an*)[61]
[meter: *ṭawīl;* rhyme: *-iyā*]

1. You've had enough [heart] sickness
   when death becomes your cure;
   When death becomes your hope
   then hope is dead![62]

2. You hoped for death
   when you hoped to see
   A true friend, and found none, nor even
   a dissembling foe.

3. If you are content to live
   in ignominy
   Then don't arm yourself
   with a Yemeni sword,

4. Don't choose the long spears
   for the attack,
   Nor the best bred of the full-grown
   battle steeds.

5. Timidity never helps the lions
   against hunger,
   Nor are they feared
   till they become ferocious.

6. I loved you, my heart, before you loved
   him who is now distant;
   He has been treacherous,
   so you be faithful.

7. I know that separation
   makes you complain after him,
   But you are not my heart
   if I see you complaining.

8. For the eyes' tears
   betray their master
   If they run after the trail
   of his betrayers.

9. If generosity is not bestowed
   free of reproach,

Praise is not gained,
nor wealth retained.

10. The soul has qualities that indicate
one's character:
Was it out of true munificence he gave,
or mere pretense?

11. Less passion, O heart,
for perhaps I've seen you
Give true love to one
who is untrue.

12. My nature is so loyal: if I traveled
back to youth again,
With heavy heart and weeping eye
I'd leave gray hair behind,

13. But in al-Fusṭāṭ is a sea
to which I bring
My life and loyalty, my affection
and my rhymes,

14. And sleek steeds, between whose ears
we've set our spears
So that, following the spear tops,
they raced briskly through the night.

15. They walk on hard and unshod hooves
that leave the rock
On which they tread engraved
with falcons' breasts.

16. They pierce the dark of night
with black accurate eyes
That perceive forms in the distance
as they are.

17. They prick up their ears
to the most muted sound—
To them the soul's hushed whisper seems
like a resounding cry.

18. With the dawn raid's riders
they contend with reins
Like adders writhing
on their necks.

19. We ride with a resolve
so firm it makes

The body outride the saddle,
the heart outpace the body,

20. Seeking Kāfūr,
forsaking all others,
For he who seeks the sea
despises streamlets.

21. They have brought us to the pupil
of the eye of his age
And have left behind the whites and corners
of the eye.

22. On these steeds we abandon
other benefactors
And head for him whose benefits we saw
bestowed upon them.[63]

23. We did not journey in our forefathers' loins
to his age
Except in the hope
of meeting him.

24. His noble deeds rank high
above the matronly;
He performs no deeds
but virgin ones.

25. He destroys his enviers' enmity
with kindness,
And if their enmity is not destroyed,
he destroys them.

26. O Father of Musk, this is
the longed-for face;
This is
the hoped-for day!

27. To reach it I traversed
bare deserts and high peaks;
I crossed a noon so hot it made
the water thirst!

28. Father of all Fragrances,
not Musk alone,
You who are every rain cloud,
not just the morning one!

29. When every proud man boasts
a single virtue,

The All-Merciful has joined in you
all virtues.

30. When men attain high rank
through generosity,
You among your generous gifts
confer high rank.

31. So it's not strange for a man
to come to you on foot
And return king of the two Iraqs
and governor.

32. And you may bestow an army
that came attacking
On one sole supplicant
who came entreating.

33. You treat this world with the disdain
of one who's tested it
And sees that all that's in it—except you—
will perish.[64]

34. You were not one to gain dominion
by mere desire,
But by battle days that turned
the forelocks gray.

35. Your foes see in your battles
worldly struggles,
But you see in them stairways
to the sky.

36. You donned for them the dirt
of swirling battle dust
As if you found it foul
to find fair skies.

37. You led into them each sleek steed
with swimming gallop
That took you out in fury
and brought you back content,

38. Each sharp and unsheathed blade obedient
to your command,
But defiant should you make exception
or forbid,

39. And each brown twenty-jointed spear
that quenches your thirst when it drinks,

And whose thirst you quench
when you give it horsemen to drink,

40. And squadrons that sought out
tribe upon tribe
That they had tramped through barren wastes
to reach.

41. With these you attacked
the domiciles of kings,
And the edges of their hoofs went straight
for their heads and their abodes.

42. You are the first to throw yourself
before the spearheads,
And ever disdain to be
the second.

43. If India should make
two equal battle swords,
Your sword is in a hand that
eliminates equality.

44. Had Shem seen you he would have told
his progeny:
May all my children, my soul, and wealth
be the ransom of my brother's son.

45. His Lord has made the Master reach
the highest rung,
And his own soul, which was not content
but with the utmost rank.

46. His soul summoned him to glory
and august degree,
And he took heed, while others failed to heed
the summons of their souls.

47. Thus he has surpassed
all mankind who,
Although his gracious gifts have drawn him near,
find him remote. [24]

The Elegiac Prelude (Nasīb): *Lines 1–12.* The ***nasīb*** displays the traditional lyric elegiac motifs of the betrayal of love, the cutting of bonds, and the resolve of the poet to depart. Line 1 opens expressing the severity of the poet's heartsickness through the antithesis (*ṭibāq*) of death and cure, which resolves into identity: death becomes his only cure. It follows this up in the second hemistich with his despair, the death of hope, the hope for death, which is expressed in a charming rhetorical conceit of root play (*jinās*, paronomasia), through which two antithetical words, both from the root *m-n-y* —*al-manāyā* (fates, death) and *amāniyā* (hopes)—likewise become identical. The cause for this, as line 2 explains, is the poet's failure to find a single true friend, or even a false one. He then turns to a self-admonition not to endure humiliation, but to gird the sword and mount the steed (lines 3–5). The opening five lines thus describe a trajectory from utter despair to renewed determination and aspiration that sets out the fuller pattern of the poem.

Lines 6–12 express with great psychological precision the sense of being betrayed by one's own emotions as the poet chides his heart and tears respectively for longing and for flowing over a beloved who has betrayed him (lines 6, 7, 8, 11). The beauty of these verses lies in their psychological veracity and in the ambiguity of their intended subject—former mistress or former patron. Normally such sentiments would be explicitly connected with the poet's departed mistress, although, as we saw in the fickle and perfidious Suᶜād of the *nasīb* of Kaᶜb ibn Zuhayr's "Suᶜād Has Departed" (chapter 2), they can also be implicitly political and virtually always are intended to describe more the poet's emotional state than a particular situation. Here, however, through the introduction of the issue of generosity in lines 9 and 10, the poet's former patron seems to stand in the place of the *maḥbūbah* (mistress), and indeed virtually all of the commentators take these verses to allude to Sayf al-Dawlah. Curiously, the editor of al-Maᶜarrī's commentary on the *dīwān* notes that the sole exception, among moderns and ancients, is the modern Egyptian editor Maḥmūd Shākir, who thinks rather that al-Mutanabbī was in love with Sayf al-Dawlah's sister, Khawlah.[65] Such a reading testifies at once to the pull of the tradition and to a failure to understand the metaphorical power of traditional motifs.

It is curious, too, that after all the traditional accusations of insincerity launched against the panegyrists, the poet here launches a counter-accusation aimed at the patron. Just as the poet's praise is supposed to be honest and sincere, so too the patron's gifts must be bestowed freely, out of true magnanimity, untainted by reproach or ostentation. Lines 9 and 10 reveal that the rupture between poet and patron was occasioned by the breakdown of the exchange ritual: the patron who resentfully parts with his gifts (remember Mauss's requirement of the gift appearing to be spontaneously offered) loses both the gift and the praise for magnanimity that would have been the counter-gift—another case of *al-khusrān al-mubīn*, the Qurʾānic "clear loss" of al-Jāḥiẓ's anecdote (above). Finally, in lines 11 and 12 the poet affirms that the treachery was on the part of his beloved (read: Sayf al-Dawlah), he himself being of a loyal and devoted nature.

On the poetic level, this *nasīb,* through the substitution of the former patron for the former (female) beloved, reveals in an explicit way the metaphorical possibilities or expressive potentialities of the classical *nasīb* motifs. In so doing, al-Mutanabbī's poetry serves as a commentary (*sharḥ*) for the Arabic qasida tradition. On the ritual level it expresses the van Gennepian Separation from the previous state or condition, and the Mortification or end of a lease on life of the Emptying phase of Gaster's seasonal pattern. The movement of the qasida from death to rebirth is suggested in the movement of line 12 from gray to black hair, from old age to youth, which is, of course, a metaphor for the poet's transfer from the patronage of Sayf al-Dawlah to that of Kāfūr. Above all, in the context of the present argument, the bonds that the poet cuts in this *nasīb* are his bonds of allegiance to Sayf al-Dawlah; in other words, it constitutes the poet's abrogation of his former allegiance. The blame for this is placed squarely on the shoulders of the poet's treacherous erstwhile beloved, and the worthiness and loyalty of the poet is painstakingly vindicated. Again, compare with Kaᶜb's cutting of ties to the treacherous Suᶜād (read failed or moribund Jāhilī tribal ethos) before making his way to the Prophet Muḥammad (chapter 2).

The Desert Journey (Raḥīl): *Lines 13–23.* The *raḥīl* begins with the poet already declaring his goal and his new allegiance. He brings to al-Fusṭāṭ not only his poetry, but his life, loyalty, and affection. This would seem to confirm our remarks above concerning the multidimensionality of the ritual exchange and therefore of the poet-patron relationship. Furthermore, in his choice of the word *baḥr* (sea), the standard metaphor for bounty, the poet suggests that it is above all the new patron's munificence that he seeks. The *raḥīl* then proceeds to describe the poet's steeds, already introduced in line 4, as they strive through the night toward their destination. The heroic night journey or quest depicted in the poem is at odds with the version found in the biographical anecdotes (*akhbār*) of al-Mutanabbī's reluctant compliance with Kāfūr's command. It is important to note, however, that whatever the actual or historical circumstances, the ritual form and poetic conceit, as was demonstrated in chapters 1, 2, and 4, is that of the poet enduring great hardship—indeed, risking his life—to come as a supplicant to the patron.

It is also worth noting that here the poet speaks of journeying on steeds, or more precisely, battle steeds. This is quite at odds with the Jāhilī-based convention wherein the mount for the *raḥīl* is the she-camel, and the poet's steed was celebrated in hunt and in battle in the final boast section (*fakhr*), or the patron's in the praise section (*madīḥ*). Perhaps the fact that the journey section (*raḥīl*) is often omitted or greatly contracted in the ʿAbbāsid panegyric suggests the loss of the older conventions for it; this would explain why the horse might replace the she-camel. But it is also possible that al-Mutanabbī knows precisely what he is doing as he creates a *raḥīl* in which the substitution of the heroic and military battle steed for the desert mount and pack animal produces a hybrid between the supplicant and the warrior. Thus he styles his *raḥīl* after the by-this-time-familiar military-campaign panegyrics of predecessors such as Abū Tammām, or of his own famous al-Ḥadath qasida to Sayf al-Dawlah.[66] In other words, it is not the conventional pre-Islamic bedouin transhumance but rather the military campaign that is the model here for the poet's journey. Nevertheless, in a line (19) that is as innovative (*badīʿ*) in expression as it is traditional in meaning, the poet emphasizes his sure sense of direction and resolve.

Lines 20 to 24 reiterate the poet's goal and new allegiance while repudiating his former patron. This is expressed with masterly succinctness and precision in the first hemistich of line 20 and coupled in the second by an allusion to the "sea" (of Kāfūr's bounty) versus the "streamlet" (of Sayf al-Dawlah's). Line 21 is credited by the classical critics with being a striking example of exploiting Kāfūr's blackness in *madīḥ,* the black pupil of the eye being its center, the white peripheral, marginal.[67] Likewise, line 22 is said to be a jab at Sayf al-Dawlah, who, as a recipient of funds from Kāfūr, is thus a second-tier benefactor. The *raḥīl* culminates with the declaration that Kāfūr is not merely the goal of this brief journey, but indeed the teleological goal of al-Mutanabbī's genealogical line.

The *raḥīl* thus effects both transit and transition, from Sayf al-Dawlah to Kāfūr, from the disappointment and despair of the *nasīb* to the hopeful expectations of the *madīḥ*. In the arduous night journey, which suggests that the poet fled by stealth, we can discern the liminal test of the rite of passage as well as the Purgation of noxiousness of the seasonal pattern.

The Praise Section (Madīḥ): *Lines 24–47.* The *madīḥ* completes the ritual requirements of both the rite of passage and seasonal pattern. For the former, it constitutes the poet's Aggregation or reentry into society—in this case the court of a new patron—and his performance of the obligatory rituals of homage and allegiance that his new status entails. In terms of the seasonal pattern, the Filling phase with its two parts, Reinvigoration and Jubilation, is found in the expression of the fulfillment of hope and longing (line 26) after the despair of the *nasīb* (see chapter 3); in the image of the *mamdūḥ* (patron, object of praise) as a rain cloud, or all rain clouds, the traditional metaphor for bounty and generosity, after the hot, thirsty desert crossing (lines 27–28); and in the celebration of the military victories of the *mamdūḥ,* through which the safety, prosperity, and continuance of the realm are guaranteed.

The *madīḥ* of this qasida can for the purposes of the present discussion be divided along two lines: the military valor and victory of the patron, and his great virtue, which consists above all of generosity. The interdependence of military might and magnanimity is expressed in line 25 as a sort of "carrot and stick" philosophy. He gives not from extortion or concession but, as in Mauss's economy of exchange, to establish dominance and force submission. If this fails, he has recourse to more bluntly coercive means. And of course it must be remembered that the former implies the threat of the latter. The connection is further strengthened in lines 30–33. The Maussian formulation of gift exchange is succinctly stated in the first hemistich of line 30; lines 31 and 32 add that the gifts that Kāfūr bestows are kingships, governorships, and generalships of armies he has defeated, all of which are at his disposal because of his military dominion. Lines 31 and 32 thus produce a causal relation between conquest and generosity. Line 33 seems intended to indicate that Kāfūr does not fight merely for material gain but, realizing that this world and all that is in it are ephemeral, for lasting glory and for spiritual reward, the same motif we saw in Abū Tammām's "The Sword Is More Veracious" in chapter 5 (line 52). These lines, in which the poet no doubt intends to intimate his own plea, form the basis for the celebrations of Kāfūr's military campaigns in lines 34–43.

Although much of this section consists of conventional battle *madīḥ,* there are additional elements that seem intended to evoke a sense of admiration for the extraordinary ambition and ability required for a man to rise from slavery to political and military dominion. We should keep in mind that in ceremonial symbolic terms the very act of addressing an Arabo-Islamic panegyric ode to a (eunuch slave) ruler serves as an act of recognition through which the patron (*mamdūḥ*) is inducted or incorporated into the "fraternity" of legitimate Arabo-Islamic rulers (see further chapter 7). Thus the conventional elements serve to identify, or establish a cognation or concordance, between Kāfūr and other Arabo-Islamic rulers to whom qasidas are addressed. Once this group identity is established, the poet then introduces original elements that are unique to this particular patron.

Thus line 36 seems again to play on Kāfūr's blackness to produce an inversion of the traditional Arabo-Islamic chromatic value scale, which privileged Arab olive skin over African black. The black Kāfūr heroically chooses to don the dirt of battle dust on the part of the military leader who finds fair skies (those unclouded by battle dust) foul. The Reinvigoration phase of the seasonal pattern finds expression in the battle section in which, in traditional terms, the warrior goes in fury and returns content (line 36); and the drinking of the spears (of enemy blood) quenches the thirst (for vengeance) (line 39). Like the status implied in the *mamdūḥ*'s power to appoint kings (line 31), the explicit mention of attacking the domiciles of kings should be particularly gratifying to the slave patron. Moreover, Kāfūr's victory is the result of true heroism—he is the first to take the field (line 42)—and superior strength and ability—were he and his opponent given two identical Indian swords, the one in his hand would win (line 43).

This passage culminates in a brilliantly achieved line that has the effect of overturning the Arabo-Islamic religio-political racial hierarchy while also reflecting the political reality of the day. The Arabs counted themselves among the sons of Sām (Shem), the first and favored son of Nūḥ (Noah), and considered their political hegemony to extend beyond the central Semitic lands (from the Euphrates to the Nile) to the lands of the sons of Ḥām. Now, however, Kāfūr, a black slave from among the sons of Ḥām, held sway even over Damascus. Projecting this irony backward, the poet has the eponymous ancestor of the Semites recite the traditional Arabo-Islamic oath of allegiance to this son of Ḥām. The standard oath of allegiance remains virtually the same in Arab countries today: "With our souls, with our blood, we redeem you, O so-and-so!" (*Bi-r-rūḥ, bi-d-dam, nafdīka yā fulān*!). Coming from an ethnically Arab poet who had made his reputation celebrating the Arabicity (*ʿurūbah*) of the Ḥamdānids at the court of Aleppo, the inversion of the Arabo-Islamic racial hierarchy of Arab domination / black subjugation constitutes as well the poet's own declaration of allegiance.

This declaration of allegiance leads into the closure. Two lines give expression to the idea that it is God and Kāfūr's own soul that allowed him to rise to so high a rank, and particular emphasis is given again to the credit that the patron (*mamdūḥ*) himself deserves for this. The closing line describes the *mamdūḥ* in an antithetical paradox that can only be grasped through an understanding of the workings of the political economy of the gift. For, paradoxically, it is the patron's unequaled generosity that establishes his position at the top of the politico-economic hierarchy, but it is also his gracious gifts that establish his bonds with his vassals, clients, and subjects, thereby also drawing him near. It should be clear by now that all the elements of panegyric converge upon one theme or function: the (re)affirmation of the legitimacy of the *mamdūḥ*'s rule.

From this discussion it appears that the simultaneous expression of numerous institutions that Mauss has established in the ritual gift exchange: the economic, political, religious, mythic, socio-morphological, and more are all clearly in evidence in the ritual structure and thematic content of the panegyric qasida. In the immediate context of the ritual exchange of qasida (the poet's submission and oath of allegiance) and prize (the symbol of the ruler's generosity and protection), Mauss's observation once more seems pertinent: "It follows clearly from what we have seen that in this system of ideas one gives away what is in reality a part of one's own nature and substance, while to receive something is to receive part of someone's spiritual essence."[68] In this light, too, the closing verse, inasmuch as it deals with "all mankind," or at least all of Kāfūr's subjects, indicates that the homage, allegiance, and submission of the poet are paradigmatic for all the ruler's subjects. The exchange ritual of the panegyric qasida, then, serves as a ritual of regeneration or renewal of the ruler's dominion, a reaffirmation—indeed, a bodily reenactment—of the social contract, and of the hierarchy of statuses within the polity. With the qasida and prize in mind we can entertain once more Mauss's further remarks concerning the "the power of objects of exchange": "Each of these precious things has, moreover, a productive capacity within it. Each, as well as being a sign and surety of life, is also a sign and surety of wealth, a magico-religious guarantee of rank and prosperity."[69]

Abrogation of Allegiance and the Ritual of Retraction

In our discussion of the first of our poems by al-Mutanabbī, "Each Man's Fate Is Fixed" we demonstrated how a poem of felicitation for a calendrical holiday, the ʿĪd al-Aḍḥā (Feast of the Sacrifice), functioned as a reconfirmation of the bond of allegiance and reciprocal obligation between the poet and patron—a renewal of the social contract. For the second poem "Disease Enough," we showed how the traditional tripartite qasida structure (elegiac prelude/*nasīb*; desert journey/*raḥīl;* praise section/*madīḥ*) could function to achieve the abrogation of allegiance to a former patron (Sayf al-Dawlah) and the transfer of allegiance to and establishment of new reciprocal contractual obligations between the poet and a new patron (Kāfūr). The logic of the argument then requires that we read al-Mutanabbī's renowned "ʿĪd! How Is It You Return?" (*ʿīdun bi-ayyati ḥālin ʿudta yā ʿīdū*) qasida of invective or satire (*hijāʾ*) against Kāfūr[70] as likewise operating in a performative sense to annul that contract. Further, as we shall see, just as in the context of ritual exchange of qasida and prize—the establishing of reciprocal bonds—the power of the qasida as an object of exchange could be said, in

Mauss's words, to operate as "a sign and surety of wealth, a magico-religious guarantee of rank and prosperity" (see above), in this case of abjuring of allegiance and cutting of bonds, the qasida of *hijāʾ* functions performatively as a curse and imprecation.

As al-Mutanabbī's final panegyric to Kāfūr, "I Used to Hope to Dye My Hair with White," delivered in 349/960, and its accompanying anecdotal materials (*akhbār*) indicate,[71] the contract between the poet and his Ikhshīdid patron had already met with noncompliance on both sides. Kāfūr's rewards were not up to al-Mutanabbī's expectations, and the poet's response was prolonged poetic silences in Kāfūr's direction, both preceding and following this final qasida of praise. Indeed, it is said that al-Mutanabbī did not meet again with Kāfūr after this, but merely continued to ride out in his retinue, lest he miss him, and meanwhile made secret plans to flee Egypt.[72] Further, as indicated by al-Mutanabbī's difficulty in obtaining Kāfūr's permission to compose panegyric for his erstwhile rival Abū Shujāᶜ Fātik al-Majnūn, the governor of the Fayyoum, Kāfūr had clear contractual, and largely exclusive, rights over al-Mutanabbī and his poetic production.[73] It is said that on Yawm ᶜArafah (9 Dhū al-Ḥijjah) 350 (19 January 962), i.e., on the eve of ᶜĪd al-Aḍḥā (the Feast of the Sacrifice), al-Mutanabbī composed his celebrated invective "ᶜĪd! How Is It You Return?" and on the following day, the ᶜĪd itself, he made his escape from Egypt.[74]

This invective (*hijāʾ*) qasida against Kāfūr is of great interest to us in several respects. First of all, because of the beauty of its elegiac prelude (*nasīb*) and the power of its invective, but also, in the context of the present argument, because of its contrast to the poet's two previously discussed poems, "Each Man's Fate Is Fixed," in praise of Sayf al-Dawlah, and "Disease Enough!" in praise of Kāfūr. Initially, of course, there is the difference of genres (*aghrāḍ;* singular *gharaḍ*) between praise (*madḥ*) and invective (*hijāʾ*), but perhaps of greater importance are the formal and hence, for us, ritual differences. For whereas the first two qasidas enact or perform, respectively, the reconfirmation and the transfer of allegiance (the abrogation of one allegiance and the affirmation or declaration of another), in "ᶜĪd! How Is It You Return?" we find an ode of abrogation of allegiance. These functional distinctions then govern the formal structure of the three qasidas. "Each Man's Fate Is Fixed," a victory ode and holiday felicitation to Sayf al-Dawlah, is dominated structurally by an overarching praise section (*madīḥ*) that subsumes subordinated minor movements. "Disease Enough!" a poem of transfer of allegiance from Sayf al-Dawlah to Kāfūr, follows a full ritual paradigm, so that whether viewed in terms of Gaster's seasonal pattern with its transition from Emptying to Filling, or in terms of van Gennep's rite of passage entailing the movement from Separation to Liminality to Aggregation, there is an evident progression from ritual or symbolic death to rebirth, from pollution to purification. In keeping with this, the qasida exhibits the full tripartite form, *nasīb-raḥīl-madīḥ,* and an unambiguously goal-directed momentum.

"ʿĪd! How Is It You Return?" is, by contrast, truncated and largely static in both its formal—that is, poetic—and its ritual structure, and hence, in terms of the paradigms here discussed, it is somewhat anomalous. In terms of the pattern of ritual exchange, if we are to see in the presentation of the panegyric the offering of a gift, then the invective constitutes the recantation of the praise and the retraction of the gift. As for Gaster's seasonal pattern, this poem exhibits elements of Emptying, but no Filling; in van Gennepian rite of passage terms, we find Separation and Liminality, but no Aggregation; despair, but no hope; departure, but no arrival; severing of bonds, but no retying. It is fully in keeping with the lack of goal-oriented directionality of the poem that it mixes together elements of the elegiac lyricism of the *nasīb* and the satirical invective of the *hijāʾ* (and very little from the *raḥīl*) rather than ordering motifs in accordance with the usual formal and structural progression. For the purposes of our discussion we can, however, propose dividing the poem into two sections: (1) lines 1–8, which constitute a *nasīb* centered around the theme of separation from loved ones; and (2) the remainder of the poem (lines 9–30), in which the poet attacks Kāfūr for treachery and stinginess, in brief all form of ignobility, and which we can term *hijāʾ*, but whose mood curiously combines the sense of outrage characteristic of the invective genre with the wounded and betrayed "lyric I" most associated with the *nasīb.* Rather than the triumphal tone that typifies *hijāʾ*, the poem seems to sink deeper and deeper into a *nasīb*-determined slough of despond.

Al-Mutanabbī's "ʿĪd, How Is It You Return" (*ʿĪdun bi-ayyati Ḥālin ʿUdta*)[75]
[meter: *basīṭ;* rhyme: *-īdū/ūdū*]

1. ʿĪd! How is it you return, O ʿĪd?
Bearing sorrows past,
Or bringing
tidings new?

2. Between those that I love and me
there lies a barren waste,
Oh, that wasteland after wasteland lay
between you and me.

3. But for noble rank I would not
be crossing it,
Neither borne by she-camel, high-cheeked and lean,
nor by sleek, long-necked mare,

4. And sweeter than my sword
in my embrace would be
Those, like it, radiant,
but lithe and tender.

5. But fate has left nothing
of my heart or liver,
To be enthralled by [languid] eye
or graceful neck.

6. O my two cupbearers,
is that wine in your cups?
Or do your cups bear only care
and sleeplessness?

7. Am I a rock?
What ails me
That I am moved by neither
wine nor song?[76]

8. When I want wine,
dark-hued and pure,
I find it, but still my soul's beloved
is lost.

9. What have I met in this world?!
The strangest thing
Is that what I weep over is what
I'm envied for!

10. Of wealthy men I was the most relaxed
of hand and store:
I was rich;
my wealth was promises.

11. I had alighted among liars
to whose guest
Welcome and farewell
are both denied.

12. The magnanimity of men is of the hand,
theirs of the tongue;
They are not men, then,
nor is this magnanimity.

13. Death does not snatch
one of their souls
But with a stick in hand for warding off
the putrid stench

14. Of every [eunuch],
loose-sphinctered and fat-flanked,
Counted neither among men
nor among women.

15. Every time a vile slave
slays his master
Or betrays him
has Egypt paved his way?

16. The eunuch there is now
the runaways' imam,
Till the freeman is enslaved,
the slave revered.

17. Egypt's wardens slept
unmindful of her foxes
Who glutted on her grapes that
in unfailing clusters grow.

18. The slave cannot be brother to
the free and upright man,
Even if he's born
to freeman's clothes.

19. Don't buy a slave
unless the stick comes with him;
For slaves are certainly
defiled wretches.

20. I never thought I'd live
to see the day
I'd be ill-treated by a slave
and he'd be praised!

21. Nor did I imagine that all mankind
would be lost [to me],
And one like the Father of Whiteness (Abū l-Bayḍāʾ)
be found!

22. Nor that this pierced-lipped
black slave
Would be obeyed
by these cowering lackeys.

23. Hungry, he feeds on my provisions,
and detains me
So they'll say he is of high degree,
and I intend him.

24. Any man who's managed
by a pregnant slave girl
Is degraded, disconsolate,
and has lost his mind!

25. Woeful this state
and he who's come to it!
For such as it swift and strong-necked
she-camels were made!

26. Death now tastes sweet
to him who drinks it;
To a man humiliated death tastes
like sugarcane.

27. Who ever taught the black castrate
a noble deed?
His noble kin?
His regal forebears?

28. Or his ear in the hand of the slave trader
bleeding,
Or his value when
for two more pence he'd be refused?

29. Kuwayfir is, of the vile,
the worthiest
To be excused for vileness—
though some excuse is blame—

30. For if white stallions are incapable
of magnanimity,
How then
gelded blacks? [25]

The Elegiac Prelude (Nasīb): *Lines 1–8.* The poem opens with a verse of great rhetorical power and subtle polysemy, centering, as did the opening line of "Each Man's Fate Is Fixed," on the root play (*jinās,* paronomasia) on the root *ʿ-w-d* (return):

ʿĪd! How is it you *return,* O *ʿĪd*? Bearing sorrows past
Or bringing tidings new?

ʿīdun bi-ayyati ḥālin ʿudta yā ʿīdū
bi-mā maḍā am bi-amrin fīka tajdīdū.

As mentioned in our discussion of "Each Man's Fate Is Fixed," the foremost meaning of *ʿīd* (holiday) refers in a lexically explicit way to holidays that recur, return, annually. The choice of the ʿĪd for the composition of the present poem is intriguing. We noted above that the ritual presentation of gifts or poems to rulers or liege lords on holidays (especially Nawrūz [New Year] among the Persians) served as a means of reaffirmation of the societal contract, which is perceived as lapsing, or being in danger of lapsing, with the expiration of the seasonal or ritual cycle. Al-Mutanabbī now finds himself in precisely that state of anxiety that Gaster terms Mortification—the "state of suspended animation that ensues at the end of the year, when one lease on life has drawn to a close and the next is not yet assured"[77]—only in this case the poet opts for cancellation rather than renewal. The question that the poet poses—will the new holiday or seasonal cycle merely repeat the past or will it bring something new—reveals the psychological and ontological paradox of cyclically perceived or measured time: it is both reiterative and progressive. The poet thus expresses uneasy anticipation.

But the word *ʿīd* has another, albeit related, meaning that is deeply rooted in the elegiac lyricism of the *nasīb* as mood, context, and text, that provides a further semantic dimension that is particularly appropriate to the peculiar *nasīb*-dominated nondirectional structure of this poem. For *ʿīd* also means recurrent care, sorrow, or chronic disease. Hence the unattributed verse:

> *Recurrent* sorrow over the tall maiden *returned* to my heart,
> And sleeplessness from love for her afflicted me.
>
> *ʿāda qalbī mina ṭ-ṭawīlati ʿīdū*
> *wa ʿtarānī min ḥubbihā tashīdū.*[78]

Of al-Mutanabbī's commentators, al-ʿUkbarī notes this meaning and cites an unattributed half verse from *Al-Mufaḍḍaliyyāt,* the celebrated anthology collected by the Kufan philologist al-Mufaḍḍal al-Ḍabbi (d. ca. 170/786):

> Then the heart from love of her has become
> *accustomed* to *recurrent* sorrow.
>
> *fa-l-qalbu yaʿtādu min ḥubbihā ʿīdū*[79]

Al-ʿUkbarī cites as well a couplet by the Umayyad *ghazal* poet ʿUmar ibn Abī Rabīʿah, the first verse of which is

> This heart has become aggrieved by Asmāʾ;
> When I say "Now it's sober," it becomes drunk *once more.*
>
> *amsā bi-Asmāʾa hadhā l-qalbu maʿmūdā*
> *idhā aqūlu ṣaḥā yaʿtāduhū ʿīdā*[80]

As is clear from the similarities among these three examples, this is a conventional motif involving the root play (*jinās*) of the noun *ʿīd* in the sense of recurrent sorrow or heartsickness, and the verb *ʿāda* (to recur), or the form VIII verb of the same root, *iʿtāda* (to be accustomed to). In the present poem, al-Mutanabbī has suppressed this conventional motif to the level of the subtext and, while retaining the *jinās,* introduced a new pun and new semantic level in *ʿīd* as holiday. Perhaps even more intriguing is the connection of al-Mutanabbī's opening line to that of a poem by the infamous pre-Islamic brigand-poet (*ṣuʿlūk*) Taʾabbaṭa Sharran, which shares with al-Mutanabbī's poem a nondirectional, truncated formal structure.[81]

O *ever-returning memory,*
what longing and wakefulness you bring,
And the passing phantom that, despite the terrors,
comes by night,

yā ʿīdu mā laka min shawqin wa-īrāqī
wa-marri ṭayfin ʿalā l-ahwāli ṭarrāqī[82]

The effect of this second meaning of *ʿīd* in al-Mutanabbī's poem is to suggest the unbroken circle of recurrent sorrow and care that forms its formal and semantic foundation, thereby indicating that of the two options for *ʿīd* as holiday and renewal or repetition and sorrow the etymological balance will weigh in favor of the latter. We will understand better how this verse functions as a key to the entire poem when we compare it with "Disease Enough!" in which the phrase *kafā bika* (Enough for you!) amounts to an abjuration of sorrow and despair, directing the poem and the poet to rise above them and undertake the quest implicit in the desert journey (*raḥīl*).

In line 2 the initial meaning of *ʿīd* as holiday merges into that of recurrent sorrow when, in the poet's distance from those he loves, the holiday only heightens his sense of desolation. The following lines, 3–8, describe how the poet's despair and desolation and the necessity of leaving his loved ones have been occasioned by his own nobility. The desert crossing on she-camel or mare indicates a movement from *nasīb* to *raḥīl* as the poet explains that it is his noble character or quest for glory that prevents him from tarrying in *nasīb* nostalgia but prods him instead to move on. He is too preoccupied with glory to be enthralled by the love of charming maidens, and gives up embracing them to embrace the sword. Likewise wine brings neither cheer nor forgetfulness, but only cares and wakefulness (line 6). He wonders at his own immobility, that neither wine nor song can stir his heart. Finally, he rounds off this section (line 8) in such a way as to reinforce the opening line, for just as the arrival of the ʿĪd and its festivities bring not joy but exacerbated sorrow to one far from his loved ones, so too all the accouterments of delight, though attainable, are ineffectual when his soul's beloved is not. While on one level we can read this unattainable beloved in the traditional *nasīb* sense, Ibn Jinnī's reading of *ḥabību n-nafsi* (the soul's beloved) as *majd* (glory),[83] which harks back to line 4's substitution of embracing the sword for embracing maidens, adds an important dimension: that the delights of wine, women, and song lose their appeal when taken in ignominy. Lines 4 and 8 then become synonymous with line 3 of "Disease Enough!"

The Invective (Hijāʾ): *Lines 9–30.* With lines 9–11 the tone, in typical *nasīb* fashion, modulates from one of sorrow to one of betrayal, much as we saw in Kaʿb ibn Zuhayr's "Suʿād Has Departed," with its transition from sorrow over the departed Suʿād to accusations against her of treachery and broken promises (chapter 2). Here, however, the subject is split, for the poet is ostensibly far from those he loves in lines 1–8, but they are innocent. The treachery, dashed hopes, and broken promises—in short, the mendacity—of lines 9–11 are clearly on the part of Kāfūr. What is of formal literary interest here is the employ of the traditional *nasīb* mood and emotion of betrayal to instigate the *hijāʾ* and, as it would appear from the associated anecdotal materials (*akhbār*) (see below), to describe with some precision the poet's political situation. Line 9 exhibits the conventions of the *humūm,* the motif of the poet lamenting his cares that often serves as the pivot point or transition from *nasīb* to *raḥīl.* The added twist of the poet's being envied for precisely what he weeps over or complains of reveals with precision the plight of the disappointed poet at the court of a great or powerful patron. The tone of sadness and irony persists in line 10, in which the poet quips that he suffers none of the anxieties of other rich men over keeping and storing his wealth, for it consists of nothing but (Kāfūr's false) promises.

Before examining in detail the individual elements of *hijāʾ* (invective) that constitute the bulk of this poem, it is important to add another dimension to its antithetical relation to *madīḥ* (praise). We established in our previous chapters, as well as above in the present one, that the *qaṣīdat al-madḥ* (panegyric ode) constitutes a declaration of allegiance on the part of the poet and, in introducing the present poem, that the *qaṣīdat al-hijāʾ,* by contrast, is a retraction of allegiance. Similarly, just as the panegyric takes as a major theme the legitimacy of the patron's rule and his (unique) suitability, by contrast, the invective strives to establish the illegitimacy of its target's rule and his unsuitability. Further, whereas in the Arabo-Islamic poetic scheme of things the *mamdūḥ*'s rule is the enactment of divine will, the rule of the *mahjū* (target of invective) constitutes an abomination. It is within this conceptual framework of the illegitimacy of Kāfūr's rule, his physical and moral unfitness to rule, and therefore the abomination that his rule constitutes, that the details of the *hijā*ʾ are to be read.

It is only with line 11 that gentle irony still tinged with traditional end-of-*nasīb* sorrow gives way abruptly and dramatically to the forceful invective of *kadhdhābīn* (liars) (intensive adjectival form) coupled with the quintessential vice reviled by Arabic invective, inhospitality, or avarice (*bukhl*). Their guest is both denied hospitality and forbidden to depart—i.e., he is a virtual prisoner. Although the *akhbār* claim that this accurately describes al-Mutanabbī's political situation in Egypt, it is equally, indeed initially and essentially, a fully classical conventional *hijā*ʾ formulation.[84] For whereas the traditional dictates of hospitality are to feed—preferably to slaughter a camel—and provide a riding beast, this verse presents a precise negation, as if in fulfillment of the dictum "All poetry can be summed up in three phrases: . . . When you praise you say 'you are'; when you satirize, you say 'you are not'; and when you elegize, you say, 'you were.'"[85] Line 12 then adeptly combines mendacity and avarice in the contrast of the liberal of hand and the liberal of tongue. The verse is rhetorically striking for its resolution of parallelism into antithesis—liberal of hand / liberal of tongue—and in doing so establishing the identity of the two vices of avarice and mendacity, and, further, posing and resolving the paradox or riddle of men who are not men and of liberality that is not liberality, that is, liars and false promises. Line 13 seems at first glance somewhat out of place or a non sequitur, but upon closer examination appears to have been generated by a play on *natn,* which means stench or putrefaction, but also stinginess or niggardliness. The stench of the stingy soul is thus the opposite of *ṭīb,* the sweetness, perfume, and purity of the generous soul. The stinky-stingy versus perfumed-generous inversion of values thus reiterates the antithesis of line 12.

Until this point all the lines of *hijā*ʾ (9–13), however apropos of the al-Mutanabbī-Kāfūr situation, exhibit conventional motifs and diction centering around the core Arabo-Islamic vices of avarice and mendacity. In this case, as so often, the two are virtually identical, since the lies of the *mahjū* (target of the invective) consist precisely of unfulfilled promises of generosity. The employ of conventional *hijā*ʾ elements serves above all the function of genre definition. With line 14, however, the invective focus narrows to the more precise (alleged) characteristics of the *mahjū* in question, Kāfūr, and in this regard we now can observe how line 13 serves as a transition from the moral to the physical realm, the transition pivoting on the word *natn* as the foul stench becomes identified as flatulence resulting, along with flaccidity and indeterminacy of gender, from castration.

With line 15 there is a return to moral defamation in the insinuation that Kāfūr assassinated his master, the Ikhshīd's son Anūjūr, and in so doing established himself as a paradigm for perfidy. The treachery of line 15 results in line 16 in a perversion or inversion of the religio-political hierarchy. In this we can perceive a structural inversion of one of the main themes of *madīḥ:* the restitution of the proper hierarchy, as we saw in al-Akhṭal's "The Tribe Has Departed" (chapter 3) and in al-Mutanabbī's "Each Man's Fate Is Fixed" (above). Thus the eunuch slave Kāfūr is the "*imām*" (religious leader) of runaway slaves, and through the root play (*jinās,* paronomasia) on the root *ᶜ-b-d,* whose lexical range embraces both worship and slavery, the free are enslaved and the slave worshipped. This sorry state of affairs is then blamed on the Ikhshīdids, particularly Anūjūr, to whom, as the commentators tell us, line 17 alludes in the image of the wardens who sleep unmindful of the foxes that gorge on grapes. Two lines (18–19) of aphorism (*ḥikmah*) follow, likewise said to be addressed to Anūjūr: that the slave, even if born free, is unfit to be the brother of a free man, and to the proscription of fraternizing with slaves is added the prescriptive (although negatively phrased) "Don't buy a slave unless the stick comes with him!"[86] It seems to me, however, that lines 17 and 18 could equally refer to the poet's own situation and express his self-castigation for "buying into" a relationship with Kāfūr. Such a reading flows directly into the following section of the poem.

Line 20 opens the culminating section of invective in the form of a complaint. The effect of this in formal terms is to couple a return to the *humūm* (cares) theme of the *nasīb* with *hijāʾ*. In other words, the poem is static, or, at most, circular and reiterative, rather than directional. Otherwise, it could be viewed as an inverted qasida with a negative direction, moving from the loss or absence of those that the poet loves to the presence of those that he hates (see line 21). But even if we posit such movement in topic, the *humūm* element still evokes the elegiac mood of loss and despair that is eminently the domain of the *nasīb* (see especially lines 20, 25, and 26). The poet's *humūm-hijāʾ* is constructed in antithetical terms, sometimes explicitly in the rhetorical figure of antithesis (*ṭibāq*) and sometimes on more implicit levels. It is of note that the antitheses here are not simply figures of speech in a decorative sense; rather the cumulative effect is to present the situation of the poet, and, indeed, his world, as an inversion of his expectations for himself and the "moral universe" in which he lives—much as we saw in lines 16 and 18.

Furthermore, and what seems to us perhaps ironic, the basis of al-Mutanabbī's *hijāʾ* against Kāfūr is in the end the same as that for his *madīḥ* to him: his overcoming the barriers of race and class to rise from a state of slavery to become undisputed ruler of Egypt. Thus, whereas in "Disease Enough!" this accomplishment meets with the poet's admiration, in this poem he treats it as an abomination. In lines 20–21 the poet registers his dismay: "I never thought . . . never imagined" first to be maltreated by a slave and then to be required to praise him. With this he conveys the inversion of the social and moral order (line 20) and, in the double antithesis (*ṭibāq*) (line 21), the loss of noble men and the finding of the antiphrastically phrased *Abū l-Bayḍā'* (Father of the White). In line 22 the invective takes the form of racial and class caricature. *Mishfar* means a camel lip, so that, as the commentators remark, the point is at once to ridicule the stereotypical racial features of the black African, while at the same time ridiculing his slave status by describing him as a camel whose lip is punctured to put a thong through it to lead it about. Having thus degraded his subject to a beast of burden, the poet portrays in the image of abject servitors obeying a black slave an inversion of the social order that is for al-Mutanabbī symptomatic of the depravity of the times.

Line 23 is constructed on the inversion of the poet-patron relationship. Whereas the *mamdūḥ* (recipient of panegyric) establishes his own rank and prestige by attracting and enriching his panegyrist, thereby through his munificence attracting poets and gaining the illustrious reputation of one whom poets intend and attend, the greedy *mahjū* (target of invective) tries to achieve this end by consuming the poet's supplies and retaining him against his will. The commentarists take *ya'kulu min zādī* (he feeds on my provisions) to mean Kāfūr's forcing al-Mutanabbī to use up his own supplies, but we might also take it to refer to the exhaustion of al-Mutanabbī's poetic stores. Again, to describe Kāfūr as patron with the words "hungry [greedy], he eats" amounts to an inversion of the preeminent virtue of generosity and obligation of hospitality expressed above all in Arabic poetry in the provision of the slaughter camel (*jazūr*) and feast. In brief, the *mamdūḥ* feeds the poet; the *mahjū* feeds off the poet.

In line 24 the commentators state that the poet is chastising the Ikhshīd's son Anūjūr for having allowed Kāfūr to take over his affairs.[87] But the line reads equally well—indeed, better—in the context of the poem itself, as the poet's self-castigation for attaching himself to Kāfūr. Read this way, it functions as the traditional elegiac *nasīb* motif of the disconsolate poet and leads quite conventionally to the transitional motif of the determination to mount a swift she-camel and depart, the *raḥīl* conceit of line 25. In line 24, Kāfūr, presumably owing to his blackness and to the lack of facial hair and the obesity resulting from castration, is caricatured as a pregnant slave girl. But behind this image, too, is the inversion of the traditional social (and poetic) hierarchy rooted in pre-Islamic tribal concepts of honor and purity, which are expressed in terms of sexual domination and submission that places the ruling male at the top of the scale and the female slave at the bottom.[88] Kāfūr's rule thus constitutes an abomination.

Line 25 comprises what we might term a "false transition" from *nasīb* to *raḥīl*. The line is phrased precisely in the conventional terms of the poet's *nasīb*-appropriate ***humūm*** (cares), the woeful state that the poet has come to, and *raḥīl*-directed ***himmah*** (resolution or ambition) to depart and leave the cares behind. But the following lines fail to fulfill the convention-engendered expectation. We find instead (line 26) the sort of "death wish" despair that we encountered in the opening of the *nasīb* of "Disease Enough!" In both cases this is phrased in antithetical terms: in "Disease Enough!" death is termed a "cure"; here, similarly, the taste of death is sweet, like sugarcane. It is important, however, to note the structural difference between the occurrences of this motif in the two qasidas. In "Disease Enough!" it occurs at the beginning of the poem and sets the poet off on his quest to the court of Kāfūr; in the present poem, it occurs too late for the poet to undertake, or the reader to expect, a successful quest.

The tone then turns (line 27) to one of sarcasm phrased as a rhetorical question: who could have taught the black eunuch nobility anyway? His white people? His regal forebears? Al-Maʿarrī adds that this verse is also one of self-reproach for having sought wealth from someone of such ignoble origins.[89] The poet then derides the *mahjū* for the degradations of slavery, his ear being pierced to put a ring in it, and for his ugliness—his buyer would not have paid even two pence more for him (line 28). Here it should be emphasized once more that just as the panegyric motifs of odes such as "Disease Enough!" share the common theme and function of affirming the legitimacy of the *mamdūḥ*'s rule, in this qasida the invective elements are all aimed at demonstrating the illegitimacy, the abomination—in terms of race, class, gender, morals, and the like—of the *mahjū*'s dominion.

The final couplet (lines 29–30) closes the qasida in a way that confirms our formalist expectations, particularly in light of the contrast to "Disease Enough!" The poet, now referring to Kāfūr through the diminutive of derision, Kuwayfir, concludes, through a series of antitheses, by resigning himself to the viciousness of his times. Thus in line 29, through the antitheses of worthy and base and of excuse and blame, the poet concedes that of all his base patrons, Kāfūr is most worthy of being excused—but, once again resolving antithesis into identity, some excuse is blame. This is because (line 30) the base at least have an excuse for their baseness at a time when even the noble are incapable of magnanimity. Through its powerful compound *ṭibāq* (antithesis), the closing line has the effect of reducing all the rulers of the age (especially Sayf al-Dawlah) to the level of Kāfūr, for on the one hand there is a double antithesis of white stallions and black geldings, but the antithesis is effectively neutralized by the impotence (*ʿājizah*) of the former.

The ending thus confirms the sense of despair and futility that opened the poem and completes with great rhetorical power the poem's truncated formal structure. Furthermore, it explains that despair and that structure, and solves the paradox of the poem: for if there appears to be an impulse to the *raḥīl,* to the journey and the quest (lines 3–4, 25), and at the same time an inability to escape the circle of the *nasīb*-bound *humūm* (cares), the closing verse provides an explanation. The poet knows that his noble soul requires that he flee the ignominy of the Ikhshīdid court, but he also knows that his departure will take him nowhere better.

Applying the ritual paradigms proposed above to al-Mutanabbī's *hijāʾ* qasida against Kāfūr, "ʿĪd! How Is It You Return?" we can determine that just as the employ of the full poetic structure, as in "Disease Enough!" reflected the full performance of those ritual functions, the truncated, turned-in-on-itself, or circular, structure of this poem reflects the failure or breakdown of these ritual institutions. Thus the poet here abrogates his allegiance to Kāfūr in what amounts to a ritual of retraction or recantation of his erstwhile homage and panegyric. In terms of Gaster's seasonal pattern, this poem exhibits Emptying (Mortification and Purgation), but, as the impotence of the white stallions amply conveys, no hope of finding a worthy patron elsewhere and hence no Filling (Reinvigoration and Jubilation). We find neither the renewal of the "old lease on life" nor the transfer to a new one. Viewed in light of the rite of passage paradigm, "ʿĪd! How Is It You Return?" exhibits the stages of separation and the entry into a liminal no-man's-land where the poet is without allegiance or patronage, and without any sense of direction or any final arrival and aggregation. Finally, the truncated structure of the *hijāʾ* in the context of the literary biographical anecdotes that accompany it amounts to a retraction of the ritually contracted exchange between poet and patron and therein a breaking of all the social, economic, and socio-morphological bonds that Mauss has shown that ritual exchanges entail. If we take the panegyric ode (*qaṣīdat al-madḥ*) to be the gift in a ritual exchange, then the *hijāʾ* amounts to the retraction of a gift, or, more precisely, the substitution of an act of sedition for an act of homage and submission. Above all, if, as we claimed in the beginning, the *qaṣīdat al-madḥ* constitutes an oath of allegiance and payment of homage, then the invective ode (*hijāʾ*) must constitute an act of treason and call to rebellion. If, as we have claimed earlier, the *qaṣīdat al-madḥ* entails the restructuring of the social order, al-Mutanabbī's *hijāʾ* against Kāfūr attempts the destruction of that order. In this respect, if we take the panegyric to be "payment" for the patron's generosity, we can understand al-Mutanabbī's invective as "payback" for Kāfūr's avarice.

On the more intimate level, we sense in the course of the poem the poet's sense of deep disappointment and humiliation, even "failure," giving way, in however compensatory a manner, to rage in the vituperation of his "failed" patron. The movement from the *nasīb,* in which the poet is plagued by despondency and self-doubt, to the *hijāʾ*, in which the outraged poet's wrath is vented on the patron, is a movement from passivity to aggression, and certainly al-Mutanabbī's *hijāʾ* against Kāfūr is an extraordinary example of "verbal aggression." The poet's hostility does not end with Kāfūr, however, but is extended in the closing line to a general condemnation of the rulers of his age.

The spirit of bitter pride in this qasida, together with the truncated structure and the echo of Taʾabbaṭa Sharran's outlaw ode in the opening verse, results in a poem that is both semantically and structurally akin to the poetry of the fiercely independent brigand poets (*ṣaᶜālīk;* singular *ṣuᶜlūk*) of the Jāhiliyyah,[90] who no doubt also served as models for al-Mutanabbī's own carefully constructed persona. The poet's pose is much like that of the master *ṣuᶜlūk* al-Shanfarā when he boasts in his celebrated outlaw ode, the *Lāmiyyat al-ᶜArab:* "A bitter soul does not let me remain in blame, / But prods me to move on" (*wa-lākinna nafsan murratan lā tuqīmu bī / ᶜalā dh-dhaʾmi illā raythamā ataḥawwalū*).[91]

Conclusion: Power, Political and Poetic

It will be of interest at this point to briefly compare the literary and historical accounts concerning Kāfūr. The historical accounts present Kāfūr as gifted and accomplished in the military, political, and administrative arenas, loyal to his master, al-Ikhshīd, and solely responsible for securing Ikhshīdid succession after his master's death.[92] The Mamlūk historian Ibn Taghrībirdī (d. 815/1412), for example, introduces the period of Kāfūr's rule over Egypt thus:

> Al-Ustādh (the Master) Abū al-Misk Kāfūr ibn ᶜAbd Allāh al-Ikhshīdī, the black eunuch servant, the ruler of Egypt and Shām, and the Byzantine frontier, was purchased by his master, Abū Bakr Muḥammad al-Ikhshīd, from olive-oil merchants, or from one of the headmen of Egypt, for eighteen dinars. He reared him and manumitted him, then, when he saw that he was resolute, intelligent, and an able administrator, elevated him until he made him one of the chief generals. When al-Ikhshīd died in the year 335, this Kāfūr established [al-Ikhshīd's] sons in power one after the other.

> The first one that he put in authority was Abū al-Qāsim Anūjūr ibn al-Ikhshīd. . . . And Anūjūr remained in power until his death in . . . 349. After Anūjūr's death, [Kāfūr] set up his brother Abū al-Ḥasan ʿAlī ibn al-Ikhshīd. . . . This Kāfūr was the one who administered the affairs of state for the two of them. During his own rule Kāfūr was invested by the Caliph with the safeguarding of the land, and he fulfilled this trust.[93]

Of Kāfūr's physical appearance, Ibn Taghrībirdī remarks only that he was black and glistening, of his virtues, that, in addition to being intelligent and judicious, he was known for his generosity.[94] In light of these historical sources, the power of al-Mutanabbī's *hijāʾ* and, moreover, the power of the ideological construct of race and class that both determined the elements of the invective and was in turn buttressed by it, can be seen in the literary narrative that the poetic text itself has generated. For quite at odds with the historians' accounts are the widely circulated biographical anecdotes (*akhbār*) which virtually all the poetic commentaries and literary sources attach to this poem (and to others of al-Mutanabbī's *Kāfūriyyāt,* as his poems dedicated to Kāfūr are termed) and which, when compared to the poetic text, appear to be to a large extent nothing but a *ḥall al-manẓūm* (prosification of verse), a prose rendition of the poetic text. Many of the elements appear to have their origin in the commentaries on individual verses of "ʿĪd! How Is It You Return?" but it is interesting to see that the cumulative effect has been to produce a separate, even independent, prose narrative that appears in numerous classical literary sources.[95] In the case of al-Maʿarrī's commentary, for example, we find the following passage as the introduction to the *Kāfūriyyāt,* which should suffice to establish once more the power of poetry to generate its own version of "history":

> This Kāfūr was a black eunuch Nūbian [*lābī*] slave with a pierced lower lip, fat, with misshapen feet and thick hands. There was no difference between him and a slave-girl, so that when one of the Banū Hilāl of the Ṣaʿīd [Upper Egypt] was asked about him he replied, "I saw a black slave-girl commanding and forbidding." . . . And this Kāfūr took over the affairs of the Banū Ṭughj [the Ikhshīdids] and took possession of [all] that they owned; he took control of the slaves and turned them against their masters.
>
> This black belonged to an Egyptian family known as the Banū ʿAyyāsh.[96] He would carry their purchases from the markets on his head and serve the cook. His purchase-price was eighteen dinars and Ibn ʿAyyāsh used to tie a rope around his neck when he wanted to sleep; then, when he wanted something from him, he would pull it so that he would fall, because he could not be woken up by calling. Then he entered the house of Ibn Ṭughj where people stretched out their hands to his head and described him as being of sturdy neck, and every time the slaveboys slapped him, he would

laugh! So they said, "This black is cheerful, light-hearted." Then they spoke to his master about buying him and he gave him to them and they put him in charge of ablutions and the privy. He observed Ibn Ṭughj's tricks, his frequent lies, and what his master accomplished [thereby], and from this he learned never to speak a single word of truth, but take from it and add to it, until he told lies where they did not belong and became famous for it.

Ibn Ṭughj died in Damascus while his son [Anūjūr] was still young and the black was serving him. So he received homage himself from the people at his [master's] death, and the people thought that [his master] had ordered him to do so. . . .

The black served the boy single-handedly, and his mother, since she was likewise a slave, was favorably disposed toward him, so that he gained so much influence over the boy and the woman that he brought close whomever he wished and kept away whomever he wished. The people looked at this with their small ambitions and their triviality, and they vied to get close to him and strove with one another for his favor, until no man trusted his slave or his son with his secrets, and every slave in Egypt began to think that he was better than his master and that no master's hand could reach him, deeming it not unlikely that he acquire many times what the eunuch had acquired. So it continued until [Kāfūr] held sway over the boy, and everyone that was with him was a spy for the black, and no one could talk to him or greet him. Whenever one of the slaveboys of his father or others saw him, he would flee quickly lest it be said that he had spoken to him, for the black would destroy whoever talked to him.

When the boy grew up and realized his situation, he began to divulge what was on his mind sometimes when he was drinking and everyone with him was spying on him. So the black came and poisoned his drink and killed him. Thus Egypt became [Kāfūr's] and neither [Anūjūr's] younger brother nor anyone else posed him any threat.

So when the black's letter came to al-Mutanabbī in Ramlah, he could not avoid going to him, but he thought that he would not treat him as he had treated others, taking their money, weakening their condition and preventing them from running their own affairs—for this is what the black did with every free man of stature. He would deceive him with letters and false promises until he came to him. Then, when he arrived, he would take his slaves and horses and hamper his ability to travel and prevent him from [leaving]. [Al-Mutanabbī] would remain disowned, complaining to him and weeping before him, but [Kāfūr] would neither assist him in residing in Egypt nor permit him to depart. And if he departed without his permission, he would drown him in the Nile. He would deal sincerely only with slaves, as though he sent for free men [only] out of spite.

So when Abū al-Ṭayyib [al-Mutanabbī] came to him, [Kāfūr] freed a house for him and assigned agents to him and made his suspicion of him apparent. He ordered him to panegyrize him, bestowed a robe of honor on him, and brought him thousands of dinars and other [gifts].[97]

It is only through appreciating the political and functional aspects of the court qasida, whether *madḥ* or *hijāʾ*, that we can begin to establish an aesthetics appropriate for evaluating its poeticity. ʿAbbāsid panegyric above all exhibits poetic power as it translates into political power. For the allegiance of the poet as encoded in the exchange of the *madḥ* (praise) and *jāʾizah* (prize) is above all a symbolic expression of homage in exchange for protection. It is therefore paradigmatic for all the patron's subjects and clients and, moreover, within the Arabo-Islamic courtly literary tradition, for all rulers and their subjects. The presentation of the poem and its subsequent recitation and popularity are not merely "flattering" to the ruler, but they function as pledges of allegiance whose repetition reaffirms the societal contract upon which his rule is established and thus the legitimacy of his rule. And it is precisely the power of the poem, its efficacy, that propels it and guarantees its dissemination beyond the geographical and chronological limits of the *mamdūḥ*'s dominion.

This poetic power, furthermore, is what establishes the poet's power vis-à-vis the patron. For if the ruler holds the power of life and death over his subject, so too does the poet, through the promise (of more *madḥ*) and the threat (of *hijāʾ*) implicit in the presentation of the panegyric, wield power vis-à-vis the patron—and that power is commensurate with the quality of his verse. If we then accept the paradigmatic nature of the panegyric ode (*qaṣīdat al-madḥ*) as pledge of allegiance or act of homage (*mubāyaʿah*), then it follows that the invective (*qaṣīdat al-hijāʾ*) represents an act of sedition (*fitnah*) that likewise possesses a paradigmatic validity.

Seven

The Poetics of Ceremony and the Competition for Legitimacy

Al-Muhannad al-Baghdādī, Muḥammad ibn Shukhayṣ, Ibn Darrāj al-Qasṭallī, and the Andalusian Ode

"Place, Degree, and Form"

In this chapter we will follow the trajectory of the panegyric ode west to Muslim Spain, al-Andalus.[1] In eastern Islamdom the ʿAbbāsids had wrested the caliphate from the Umayyads in 132 H./750 C.E. Shortly thereafter, a remnant of the Marwānid line of Umayyad house established itself as an emirate at Cordova (138–300/756–912). There, during a period of stunning political and cultural florescence, the emir (prince) ʿAbd al-Raḥmān III (r. 300–350/912–961) proclaimed in 319/931 the restoration of the Umayyad caliphate at Cordova and assumed the caliphal title Commander of the Faithful (*amīr al-muʾminīn*). He was succeeded in the caliphate by his son al-Ḥakam II al-Mustanṣir (r. 350–366/961–976), after whose reign the rise to power of their ʿĀmirid chamberlains (*ḥujjāb;* singular *ḥājib)* led to a period of chaos and collapse, effectively ending the Umayyad caliphate in Cordova in 422/1031.

Building on the conclusions of the previous chapters, we will argue that the Andalusian panegyric ode performed a ceremonial function as one of the insignia of authority (and culture) and, further, that this function was in no way incidental to the poem as a literary work, but essential and formative. At this point we should recall our claiming (chapter 4) for the panegyric qasida what David Quint has claimed for the European epic, that the continuity of this literary form encodes and transmits an ideology of empire, or, more precisely for the qasida, of Arabo-Islamic rule.[2] In particular, we will examine how the panegyric ode that had been established, as we have seen in the previous chapters, as one of the insignia of legitimate Arab-Islamic rule in the Islamic east is appropriated as part of the court ceremonial and cultural accouterments of the restored Umayyad caliphate in al-Andalus. Above all, we shall examine the role of the qasida in the politically charged competition for legitimacy among the contenders for the caliphate, notably the ʿAbbāsids at Baghdad, the Fāṭimids in North Africa and later Egypt, and the Umayyads at Cordova.

For the present purposes, I have chosen three qasidas presented to Umayyad caliphs in Cordova on the occasion of two Islamic religious festivals, the first two on the ʿĪd al-Fiṭr (Festival of Breaking the Fast at the end of Ramaḍān) of 363/974 and the third, under quite different politico-military circumstances, on ʿĪd al-Aḍḥā (Festival of the Sacrifice) of 403/1013.[3] By examining the explicit ritual, ceremonial, and political dimensions of these three qasidas, we shall be better able to perceive them in other poems where they may be only implied. In far broader terms, I shall propose that in the later flowering of more purely lyrical Andalusian poetry the political force of the qasida was still present implicitly or *in potentia*. Finally, in light of the numerous modern studies of the relation of ceremonial to power, the ideological formulations of the panegyrics here treated will, it is hoped, serve to decode the sometimes inarticulate symbolic language of ceremony.

The first two qasidas are particularly suited to our discussion in that they are preserved for us in the context of a description of the court ceremony of which they formed a part. In *Al-Muqtabis fī Akhbār Balad al-Andalus* (The Citation of Accounts Concerning the Land of al-Andalus), the compendium of Andalusian history compiled by the renowned historian Abū Marwān Ibn Ḥayyān (d. 469/1076), the poems occur as the first two of the poetry citations that conclude a detailed description of the ʿĪd al-Fiṭr (Festival of Breaking the Fast) ceremony in Cordova for the year 363/974, during the rule of al-Ḥakam II al-Mustanṣir.[4] The passage runs as follows:

> The first day of the month of Shawwāl [ʿĪd al-Fiṭr] fell on a Wednesday. On that day the caliph [al-Ḥakam II] al-Mustanṣir bi-Allāh held court to receive the ʿĪd greeting [*tahniʾah*], according to custom, on his throne in the east tribunal overlooking the gardens above the high extended terrace [text corrupt] in a session of the utmost magnificence, most renowned for its decorations and most elaborately arranged—this due to his consummate joy over his triumph over Ḥasan Ibn Qannūn al-Ḥasanī and his presence before him hastening in obedience, and over the harmonious extension of his dominion over hostile territory. On that day there attended him on his right the secretary-vizier, commander of the city at al-Zahrāʾ [and] Muḥammad ibn Aflaḥ, [the caliph's] client; and there joined the two rows after them the ranks of the major functionaries, consisting of the high and

middle police commanders, then the commanders of the stores, and the treasurers, and quartermasters, and others of the functionaries according to their ranks. Then the permission went out, and the first of the [caliph's] brothers arrived. After the greeting [*taslīm*], his full brother Abū al-Aṣbagh ʿAbd al-ʿAzīz sat on his right, and beneath him Abū al-Muṭarrif al-Mughīrah; and on the left sat Abū al-Qāsim al-Aṣbagh. After them, after the greeting, sat the viziers, after a gap between them, and beneath them sat Jaʿfar ibn ʿAlī al-Andalusī, while his brother Yaḥyā ibn ʿAlī stood in the row of the chamberlains, the attendants. Following them there arrived the high judge, Muḥammad ibn Isḥāq ibn al-Salīm, and a group of his magistrates who sat, after the greeting, according to their rank. And there witnessed the ceremony the two Ḥasanīs, Ḥasan and Yaḥyā the sons of Ḥ[asan ibn Q]annūn who had been forced to surrender from al-Ḥajar. They alighted before the permission [was granted] in the inner tribunals of the army quarters and arrived along with the Qurashīs of the blood. With them there arrived ʿAlī, Manṣūr, and Ḥasan, the sons of Ḥasan ibn Qannūn, and the rest of the [defeated] Ḥasanid Idrīsids, repairing to the protection of the Commander of the Faithful. At the head of their procession were Ḥasan and Yaḥyā. Right after the Qurashīs there followed to give their salutation the clients [*mawālī*], then the judges of the districts, the jurisprudents, counselors of state, and after them the notaries [*ʿudūl*], the whites of the army, Andalusians and Ṭanjīs, and from the ranks of the black/slave regiments, the Khumsīs and Ṣaydīs, and the major Khumsīs and the knights of horsemanship, and others from the ranks of the retinue. So it was the one of the most festive of customary spectacles and one of the most lavish of celebrations. During it the orators and the poets stood extemporizing and reciting, many long and excellent [orations and poems]. . . . [5]

The ʿĪd al-Fiṭr Ceremony: Cordova, 363/974

Let us begin by noting that Ibn Ḥayyān's text describing the ceremony is, as García Gómez points out, Ibn Ḥayyān's edition of ʿĪsā ibn Aḥmad al-Rāzī's (d. 364/975) text.[6] It does therefore appear that we are dealing with a contemporary eyewitness account of the ceremony.[7] Shakespeare's words are most astute in this regard: "And what have kings, that privates have not too, / Save ceremony, save general ceremony? / And what art thou, thou idol ceremony? / . . . Art thou aught else but place, degree and form, / Creating awe and fear in other men?" (*Henry V,* act 4, scene 1). "Place, degree, and form" are evident characteristics in Ibn Ḥayyān's description of al-Ḥakam II al-Mustanṣir's holding court on ʿĪd al-Fiṭr to receive the traditional felicitation and, together with the magnificence of the spectacle, were certainly intended to create "awe and fear." This alone, however, does not explain the meaning of the ceremony, nor why the historian has presented it to us in such great detail. It is our goal here to explore the meaning and function, and hence the importance, of this ceremony.

First, let us turn once more to the etymology of the Arabic word *ʿīd* (chapter 6). The classical lexicographers consider it to be from the root *ʿ-w-d* (to return) and thus to refer to holidays that recur annually. The two *ʿīds*, ʿĪd al-Fiṭr (the Festival of Breaking the Fast at the end of Ramadan) and ʿĪd al-Aḍḥā (the Festival of the Sacrifice), must first of all be understood in light of the anciently attested "new year" and "seasonal" festivals of the Near East. For the present purposes Paul Connerton's summary is the most concise:

> The celebration of recurrence is made possible, in the first instance, by *calendrically* observed repetition. Calendars make it possible to juxtapose with the structure of profane time a further structure, one qualitatively distinct from the former and irreducible to it, in which the most notable events of sacred time are assembled together and co-ordinated. Each day is thus locatable in two quite different orders of time: there is the day on which such and such events take place in the world, and there is the day on which one celebrates the memory of this or that moment of sacred or mythic history. While the co-existence of these two temporal orders runs through the course of the entire calendrical cycle, that cycle will normally contain special points at which the activity of recapitulation becomes the focus of communal attention. Throughout the Semitic world, in particular, the ceremonials of the New Year are strikingly similar. In each of these systems, we encounter the same basic idea of annual return to chaos followed by a new creation. In each, there is expressed the conception of the end and the beginning of a temporal period, based on the observation of biocosmic rhythms, and celebrated in a sequence of periodic purification—purgings, fastings, confessions of sins—in preparation for the periodic regeneration of life. And in each, the ritual enactment of combats between two groups of actors, the presence of the dead, and saturnalia, gives expression to the sense that the end of the old year and the expectation of the new year is at once an annual repetition and the repetition of a primordial moment—the mythic moment of passage from chaos to cosmos.[8]

A key element in the restoration of cosmos or order is the reaffirmation of the social order and the position of the ruler at the top of it. In this respect I believe we will find Amélie Kuhrt's remarks on the Babylonian New Year Festival quite translatable into the present context, for if, in her words, "what had been in origin merely a civic festival was transformed into an event of national significance in which not only Marduk's supreme power and world creation but also the king's position and the order for which he was responsible were confirmed and celebrated,"[9] we will observe here that the religious festival of the ʿĪd al-Fiṭr has become an event of dynastic significance in which not only God's supreme power, but also the Umayyad caliph's legitimate position and the social order of the Cordovan caliphal dominion are confirmed and celebrated.

However ancient and archetypal the origins of the Cordovan ceremony may be, it is nevertheless evident that Ibn Ḥayyān's description is concerned with contemporary religious and political matters, and it is the intersection of these two aspects—the cyclically repeated and the ephemeral contemporary, what we can otherwise term sacred and profane time—that most intrigues and concerns us here.

To begin with the cyclical repetition of the ʿĪd, we note that in the first place, it serves to identify the polity as an Islamic one and to confirm the legitimacy of al-Mustanṣir's rule. Even a quick perusal of this volume of *Al-Muqtabis* reveals a certain periodization or punctuation by passages describing the two ʿĪd celebrations of each year. I would argue that one effect of this is to create a rhythmic sense of the perpetuity or continuity of the Cordovan Umayyad dynasty. The association of the dynasty with Islamic custom has the effect of projecting it at once backward and forward in time. The ceremony purports to reenact originary Islamic practice as established by the Prophet Muḥammad, thereby creating the illusion of the original and uninterrupted Islamic legitimacy of the Umayyad house. As Connerton puts it, "All rites are repetitive, and repetition automatically implies continuity with the past."[10] At the same time, the association of the dynasty with a perpetual calendrical cycle creates the illusion that it, too, can claim perpetuity. One could go as far as to suggest, as Kuhrt does, that the emphasis on such ceremony reveals anxieties both as to the origins and future of the dynasty.[11]

In the contemporary political and religious arena, however prosperous and peaceful al-Ḥakam II al-Mustanṣir's reign, the Cordovan Umayyads' anxieties were not unfounded. Within the Islamic polity, claims to political legitimacy were largely based on some sort of (alleged) genealogical connection to the Prophet: the ʿAbbāsids claimed descent through the Prophet's uncle from the Prophet's family, the Banū Hāshim; the Umayyads from his tribe, the Quraysh of Mecca (of whom the Banū Umayyah were a powerful clan);[12] the Fāṭimids through the Prophet's daughter Fāṭimah and her husband, the Prophet's nephew, ʿAlī ibn Abī Ṭālib. These claims were backed up by political and military success which, for all practical purposes, confirmed them.

During the time in question, the Umayyad house was competing ideologically, politically, militarily, and ceremonially with the originally North African Fāṭimid house, which only a few years earlier (358/969) had captured Egypt and established its triumphant new capital Cairo (al-Qāhirah, "the triumphant") as manifest proof of its caliphal claims. Although this shift of the Fāṭimid center of gravity to the east relieved the direct North African military pressure on the Umayyads at Cordova, it was a severe blow to caliphal prestige.[13] Then, too, there was the ideologically still dominant, if otherwise debilitated, ʿAbbāsid caliphate at Baghdad. Meanwhile, beyond the Islamic pale, in Byzantium, Constantine VII Porphyrogenitus (913–59 C.E.) had just recently compiled his *De Ceremoniis* (Book of Ceremonies)[14] —not inconceivably a response to the increasing awe and threat of the Islamic east. Closer to home, in 347/958 the Fāṭimid general Jawhar had defeated the Umayyads in the Maghrib, and the Idrīsid prince Ḥasan ibn Qannūn (al-Ḥasan ibn al-Qāsim Gannūn),[15] whose dynasty claimed the imamate through its descent from ʿAlī ibn Abī Ṭālib,[16] shifted his allegiance from the Umayyads to the Fāṭimids. After al-Ḥakam II al-Mustanṣir's first attempt to redress the situation met with defeat in 362/972, he sent his renowned general Ghālib, who vanquished Ḥasan ibn Qannūn and brought him and the other Idrīsid lords and their sons as captives/hostages to Cordova, where a spectacular victory celebration was held and where the Idrīsid princes were maintained for some time in guarded luxury.[17] In this respect, the ʿĪd ceremony must also be viewed as a triumph or victory celebration, as indeed Ibn Ḥayyān states. The "ceremonial idiom"[18] is designed above all to convey "awe and fear," to give expression to the ruler's authority and might.

The result of this alignment of the Islamic calendrical Festival of Breaking the Fast with the vanquishing of the Idrīsids is to identify the religious "rebirth" and "purification" with military-political victory and restoration. In ceremonial terms, it plays the role of the cosmic ritual combat between good and evil. Thus if the breaking of the fast marks the return to the normal, "secular" diurnal order of things after Ramaḍān, the "sacred" month of fasting, so too it becomes the celebration of the reestablishment of the proper legitimate Islamic rule, here Umayyad, after a period of Idrīsid insurrection, that is, Idrīsid recognition of competing Fāṭimid claims. It is worth noting that throughout *Al-Muqtabis* Ḥasan ibn Qannūn is referred to as *al-mulḥid* (the apostate), presumably for having reneged on his Umayyad allegiance and recognized the Fāṭimids in their stead. What we see above all in the elaborate ceremonial is a ritual reestablishment or reaffirmation of the social, political, and religious hierarchy, the recreation of order after the preceding chaos.

The image of the caliph seated in majesty, flanked by his elite, ordering his (political) creation, certainly seems an *imitatio* of divine creation, and certainly it is to be understood from the meticulously orchestrated ranking, timing, and positioning that the social order mirrors the cosmic order. Here we might usefully invoke Connerton's term "the choreography of authority." He states:

> The importance of posture for communal memory is evident. Power and rank are commonly expressed through certain postures relative to others; from the way in which people group themselves and from the disposition of their bodies relative to the bodies of others, we can deduce the degree of authority which each is thought to enjoy or to which they lay claim. We know what it means when one person sits in an elevated position when everyone around them stands; when one person stands and everyone else sits; . . . There will of course be disparities between cultures in the meanings ascribed to some postures, but, in all cultures, much of the choreography of authority is expressed through the body.[19]

Not only is the caliph al-Ḥakam II al-Mustanṣir reaffirming his dominion through this ritual, but his subjects, for their part, are reaffirming their allegiance or paying homage both to the caliph and to the political and religious hierarchy of which he is the linchpin. As each awaits the permission, gives the greeting, and takes his place, he is incorporating—bodily enacting—his subordination to the hierarchy.[20] Conversely, the failure to observe the ritual and protocol of the ceremony would amount to an act of insubordination or sedition (*fitnah*). In this respect, Ibn Ḥayyān's detailed presentation serves to define the distribution of power and rank, and, with reference to the schema of other years, can provide the historian with a chart of the political rise and fall of groups and individuals.

The subduing of the forces of chaos is embodied in the ritual submission of the defeated Idrīsids to the Umayyad caliph. In such an event we see how inextricable are the social, political, military, and religious aspects of Arabo-Islamic rule. In ceremonial terms, we can observe ritualization or mythicization in the act. On 21 Jumādā al-Ākhirah 363 (19 March 974) Ḥasan ibn Qannūn's redoubt of Ḥajar al-Nasr was taken by the Umayyad forces when Ḥasan ibn Qannūn, having just lost his city of al-Baṣrah to an Umayyad column, capitulated to the Umayyad general Ghālib. His submission and surrender were officially and ritually enacted on 29 Jumādā al-Ākhirah 363 (27 March 974) when with Ghālib's assistance he delivered the Friday sermon in the name of the Umayyad caliph al-Ḥakam II al-Mustanṣir.[21] Then, on the ʿĪd al-Fiṭr, 1 Shawwāl 363 (25 June 974), that surrender or submission was ritually reenacted as one of the elements of the iconography of power. The caliph's show of mercy in accepting the submission—sparing the life—of the defeated enemy was intended to express the concept that he held power over life and death. We shall argue below that the relation between the historical event and its poeticization is cognate to that between it and its ritualization in ceremony.

Ibn Ḥayyān concludes his description of the lavish and festive celebration with the orators and poets who recited during it and finally gives us partial texts of some of the poems. I would like to discuss the first two of these with a view to substantiating and expanding upon my analysis of the ceremony itself. A few observations are in order before turning to the poetic texts.

First, I hope to elucidate the function of the qasida. In the context of ritual homage, as we have primarily defined the ceremony of the presentation of the ʿĪd greeting, we can remark that in an external sense the qasida as an object is itself one of the "royal insignia." The court poet's presentation of a qasida on the ʿĪd is an act of allegiance that is, as we discussed in chapter 6, both politically and ritually obligatory and, as a bodily performance, is part of the choreography of power. Furthermore, inasmuch as the qasida is one of the insignia of legitimate authority, it constituted a field for rivalry between rulers. As James Monroe writes of the poetry of the Cordovan caliphate:

> Concretely, what was now required was political poetry that would defend the Andalusian caliphate against the Abbasid, and later against the far more serious Fatimid challenge. . . . [I]t led to a new kind of poetry designed to express the ideal of caliphal authority and to proclaim the unifying principle of Islam against the enemies of the state, both within and without.[22]

Further, although in our analysis the ceremony creates an intersection between profane and sacred time, incorporating a historical military victory into the mythic and ritual liturgical calendar, the only way this can be perpetuated is through the vehicle of the qasida. This is the difference between ceremony and poetry: the ceremonial associated with a calendrical festival carries with it the illusion that it is repeated the same way every year. Those details that change are forgotten. Thus, for example, the defeat of Ḥasan ibn Qannūn, will not be celebrated in future ʿĪd ceremonies. The only way that particular victory can be transformed from an ephemeral event to perduring "myth"—the only way it can be permanently incorporated into the dimension of sacred time—is for it to be commemorated in a qasida. Once this happens, it becomes prototypical or paradigmatic in a broad Arabo-Islamic cultural context. Thus I would like to look at the qasida first as ritual of homage particular to a distinct historical moment and second as the vehicle or means of transforming and commemorating that event so that it becomes permanently valid and validating.

"An Imām for All Creation"

The first poem recorded as part of this ceremony is that of Ṭāhir ibn Muḥammad al-Baghdādī, al-Muhannad, who was born in Baghdād in 315/927 and migrated in 340/951 to Cordova, where he made his name as a litterateur and caliphal panegyrist. Later in his life he turned to writing ascetic poetry and epistles, continuing until his death in 390/999.[23] In terms of the traditional formal structure of the Arabic ode, his poem, "An Imām for All Creation"—or more precisely those lines of it preserved in *Al-Muqtabis*—falls fully under the thematic heading of the *madīḥ* (praise section). The qasida opens proclaiming the divine appointment of the caliph and his unique suitability for that office (lines 1–10); followed by the ʿĪd al-Fiṭr greeting (lines 11–13); this merges into the major section (lines 14–28), which is devoted to a poeticized rendition of the caliph's defeat of Ḥasan ibn Qannūn and a closing benediction. As will be discussed in detail below, this qasida is a contrafaction (*muʿāraḍah,* a poem that imitates an earlier masterpiece through adopting the same rhyme and meter) of Abū al-ʿAtāhiyah's "My Coy Mistress" (meter: *mutaqārib;* rhyme: *-ālahā*), which we discussed in chapter 5.[24]

Picking up Ibn Ḥayyān's description of the ʿĪd celebration of 363/974 where we left off:

> Among the best of what the poets recited that day was that of the foremost of them, Ṭāhir ibn Muḥammad al-Baghdādī, known as al-Muhannad, in a long poem of his, from which [we cite]:
>
> [meter: *mutaqārib;* rhyme: *-ālahā*]
>
> 1. An Imām chosen out of mercy for all creation
> Has spread wide mercy's veils.
>
> 2. The Throne's Master elected him from the elect
> Who trail their robes' trains above the sun.
>
> 3. He established Prophethood among their fathers
> And upon their progeny conferred the Caliphate.

4. So he protected his flock, seeking victory
From the Throne's Master, guarding the untended.

5. He expended his wealth on them, unsparingly,
So that their wealth would multiply.

6. His beneficence dispelled their misery;
His grace turned their penury to plenty.

7. He assumed the caliphate in its epoch,
Then by his piety perfected it.

8. His religion was its adornment;
His luminous days its very image.

9. Were any form of rule raised above it,
He would be the only ruler right for it.

10. No virtue of right guidance can be mentioned
That he has not already acquired.

11. So may God grant him joyous ʿĪds
And bring him many more like them.

12. And multiply the sweetness of his fast
And of the burdens he imposes on his soul.

13. And reveal to him the thanks for his beneficence
And his attaining for the soul its hopes.

14. And for his subduing the might of his enemies
When he shackled them with his conquest.

15. He hastened their Resurrection [Day],
For [in him] they had witnessed it and its horrors.

16. Upon them his army launched an attack
And overtook their kings and princes.

17. And his Lord gave him dominion over their land,
[All] that it bore and [all] its goods.

18. His lions slew their lions;
His thick-necked lion cubs their lion cubs.

19. And when his army marched the night march toward them,
The very earth quaked.

20. The enemy horizon seemed an infantry afoot,
Then your Lord severed their limbs.

21. He swept their puddle into their sea;
He drowned their trickling stream in the fathomless depths.

22. He brought them in submission to his abode
To dwell therein and show their veneration.

23. When he took possession of them in their error
He forgave them and God guided their errant [steps] aright.

24. His beneficence erased their evil deeds;
His acts of virtue covered up their sins.

25. His noble nature revealed its graciousness;
His hands poured forth their favors.

26. Would it have become his magnanimity
Had he requited the ignorant in kind?

27. How many a time did he forgive, though able [to punish],
Until God clothed him in [forgiveness'] shirt?

28. May he ever triumph over his enemies
And obliterate the nights and their princes.[25] [26]

The poem, or those lines of it that Ibn Ḥayyān has preserved, opens by establishing the lineage of al-Ḥakam II al-Mustanṣir bi-Allāh coupled with divine election, in keeping with the Umayyad claim that the Quraysh are the elect for both prophethood and the caliphate (lines 1–3). Line 1 evokes the imamate/caliphate of al-Ḥakam al-Mustanṣir in broad Islamic terms: he has been chosen (by God) as the ruler of "creation"—he is not merely a local emir. God is not explicitly named here; rather the word *raḥmah* (mercy) evokes him by his foremost epithets *al-raḥmān al-raḥīm* (the Merciful, the Most Merciful) in such a way that the caliph's mercy is an embodiment of divine mercy. The formulation of legitimacy proffered in line 3 is of interest in light of Crone and Hinds's discussion of the eastern Umayyads' claims to legitimacy. Arguing that Umayyad legitimacy rested on inherited authority, Crone and Hinds write:

> Ultimately, they have inherited it from ʿUthmān, a friend and helper of Muḥammad's, who was chosen by a *shūrā* and raised up by God Himself, and who was thus a legitimate caliph wrongfully killed. In raising up Umayyad caliphs, God gives His deputy something to which He [*sic;* = he?] has a hereditary right. . . . In short, the Umayyads are God's chosen lineage.[26]

The authors proceed to remark that with the enhancement of the concept of prophethood and growing prominence of Muḥammad, the Umayyad claim is weakened and the claims of direct descent from the Prophet's family by the ʿAbbāsids, ʿAlids, Fāṭimids, and others gain strength.[27] In the case at hand, al-Muhannad, no doubt as a reaction to this, offers a somewhat ambiguous formulation: "He established Prophethood among their fathers" (*aḥalla l-nubuwwata ʾābāʾahā*) (line 3) could be taken to expand the concept of the hereditary from the individual to the tribal: inasmuch as the Umayyads are Qurashite, like the Prophet Muḥammad, their claim could be understood as based on kinship to the Prophet through their common descent from ʿAbd al-Manāf; otherwise, referring to the Umayyads, it would simply mean that they were the community to whom the Prophet was sent, and thus be in accord with the widely held precept (in the form of a *ḥadīth* in the *Musnad* of Ibn Ḥanbal) that the caliphs, or imams, are from the Quraysh.[28] I believe, however, that the poet's ambiguity is intentional and that, although strictly speaking the second interpretation should apply to the Umayyads, the line is constructed to be verbally identical to the ʿAbbāsid claims.

The subsequent lines (4–10) celebrate al-Mustanṣir's personal qualifications for the caliphate: tending his flock, attending to the untended—presumably meaning the subjugation of those that do not recognize his caliphate (such as Ḥasan ibn Qannūn)—generosity, piety. He is the consummation, the adornment, the very image of the caliphate. In terms of the concepts of hierarchy discussed above, both the cosmic and social order require that al-Mustanṣir hold the caliphate. In a line that echoes Abū al-ʿAtāhiyah's original (line 8), al-Muhannad states (line 9) that if there were an office higher than the caliphate, al-Mustanṣir would be the only one to legitimately hold it. It is then by this combination of divine election and personal moral suitability that he holds this position and therefore should receive the expression of homage and allegiance of line 11.

Line 11 constitutes the ʿĪd al-Fiṭr greeting itself. Of note is the "may God bring him many more like them," which, like the expression "Many happy returns of the day," particularly suits the calendrically repeated holiday, as well as the precarious caliphal aspirations. The ensuing lines (12–14) serve to connect the concepts of religious virtue and military success, the twin pillars of legitimate rule, and to make a transition from the greeting to the recounting of the victorious military campaign. Pertinent to the present discussion are lines 14, 17, and 22–24, which present the God-given dominion of the caliph, the submission of the enemy, the caliph's leading them into the fold of Islam, and finally, the image of the caliph as redeemer. The poem closes invoking the caliph's combined might and generosity, especially forgiveness, and ends with a prayer or benediction (*duʿāʾ*) that the caliph ever triumph over his enemies and over time—be victorious and live forever.

The immediate performative function of this qasida as an act of political recognition and oath of allegiance to the legitimate Islamic ruler is clear enough. We should understand, too, from its beauty as a work of art that it is part of the lavish decoration and splendid ornament that contributed to the magnificent spectacle of the caliph's ʿĪd and victory celebration: it is part of the royal insignia and the iconography of power. The establishing of his legitimacy, the recounting of his virtues, the "ritual reenactment" of the battle in which the forces of chaos (that is, insurrection against the divinely appointed caliph) are subdued by the forces of divinely ordained order: all are in evidence. Above all, the caliph's mercy in sparing the life of his enemy so celebrated in the poem reiterates in the ceremony itself the act of submission and its acceptance. In a broader sense, we should understand that the poet's presentation of his ᶜĪd greeting and homage—the qasida—is paradigmatic for all of the caliph's subjects, and, further, that it has the effect of providing a verbal exegesis of the nature of the ceremony of which it is part.

The further function of the qasida is even more dependent on its aesthetic aspects, for it is only because of its literary quality that it was preserved at all. In large part the poem's success lies in its depiction of al-Mustanṣir in Arabo-Islamic terms of broad appeal as the consummate Muslim ruler; for long after our interest in al-Mustanṣir has waned, the model of the divinely elected merciful conqueror-redeemer remains operative. The military campaign, too, is not at all a "battle description," as such passages are traditionally called. Rather, the historical event has been recast in a very familiar poetic idiom that has the effect of absorbing the particular event into an overarching mythic agon or ritual combat (lines 18–21).[29] Just as the historical acts of defeat, submission, and mercy were ritually reenacted in the ceremony so that they assumed a mythic dimension as part of the iconography of authority, so in their poeticization they assume archetypal and mythopoetic dimensions cast in a literary-verbal form.

The purpose of poetry, however, is to confer perpetuity. Thus whereas the momentary incorporation of the historical event into the ᶜĪd ceremony produces a fleeting intersection or identity of profane and sacred time, the poeticization incorporates the historical event into the poetic-liturgical cycle. In effect, then, the qasida becomes a suitable poem to be recited by all Arabo-Islamic subjects to their rulers on any ᶜĪd al-Fiṭr; to be valued by all who ascribe to or celebrate the values embodied in it; and, ultimately, to be enjoyed by anyone who by culture or acculturation appreciates classical Arabic poetry.

In this regard we could compare the panegyric qasida in the Arabo-Islamic tradition to royal portraiture in the European tradition. Take, for example, Rubens's cycle of the life of Maria de' Medici. The painter, with precise instructions from the patroness, incorporates passing political-biographical events into a lasting artistic work by means of two transformations: first a conceptual transformation from the historical to the archetypal and mythical—Maria de' Medici as Juno, Mary, etc.—and then a material one from events that actually occurred to the conventions and materials of painting. As one of the insignia of power, the cycle of paintings provides for the enjoyment and aggrandizement of the queen herself—its immediate courtly function. In this respect we must take into account the repression of actual events and their replacement by a mythic-heroic construct. In this case the somewhat pathetic life of Maria de' Medici, who was plagued by contempt for her mercantile roots, the indifference and infidelity of her husband, Henri IV, and the perfidy of her son Louis XIII, not to mention Richelieu, is transformed into one of triumphant glory.

The cycle, moreover, functions ideologically to bolster concepts of European royalty and dominion by bonding them iconographically to the broader and deeper cultural and religious foundations. For example, "The Marriage Consummated in Lyons" presents Maria and Henri IV as Juno and Jove with their emblematic peacocks and eagle, respectively; "The Birth of Maria de' Medici" and "The Education of the Princess" further illustrate the subsuming of the biographical in the Mariological and the mythological. Thus the royal painting cycle functions as a manifesto not only of Maria de' Medici's political program, but ultimately of the Christian humanism that is one of the foundations of modern European cultural identity.[30] It will therefore be valued by all who subscribe to European cultural concepts. Furthermore, this will hold true even when these concepts have been apparently ideologically abandoned or transformed, for instance, when monarchy and church have been transformed into secular democratic European nationalism; and ultimately in a further ideologically distanced (though perhaps still ideologically conditioned) appreciation of the powerful symbolic transformations and perhaps, more exclusively, the technical mastery of a great painter.

One major aspect of al-Muhannad's qasida remains to be attended to. As we have seen, the classical Arabo-Islamic panegyric qasida as a literary genre was transferred to al-Andalus as an integral element of the courtly ceremony and the insignia of authority of the cultural hegemony of the Arab conquerors and of Arabo-Islamic rule. In this respect we can say of the qasida and the Cordovan caliphate what Paula Sanders has said of the ceremonial of the Fāṭimids:

> [T]he Fatimids challenged the hegemony of the Abbasid caliphate, and they therefore had a stake in appropriating its most visible signs of authority. Fatimid insignia of sovereignty and protocol look very much like Abbasid insignia and protocol. The protocol of both caliphates asserted their claims

> to political and religious leadership of the community of believers as well as established the relative ranks of men at court who stood beneath the caliph.[31]

This means that just as there occurred an imitation and competition in terms of claims to Arabo-Islamic legitimacy and sovereignty, there occurred a similar imitation and competition in the ceremonies, symbols, and insignia that generate the appearance of legitimacy and sovereignty.

It is in light of these remarks that we should process the information that our poet hails from Baghdad, and further, as Iḥsān ʿAbbās has noted, that our poem is a contrafaction (*muʿāraḍah,* imitation, competitive response) of a panegyric delivered by the ʿAbbāsid court poet Abū al-ʿAtāhiyah to the caliph al-Mahdī,[32] specifically of his qasida "My Coy Mistress," which we discussed in chapter 5. A brief comparison between Abū al-ʿAtāhiyah's original and al-Muhannad's *muʿāraḍah* will reveal the purpose of this "imitation."[33]

In contrast to al-Muhannad's qasida, Abū al-ʿAtāhiyah's qasida is short (eleven lines) and very lyrical, to the point of being *ghazal*-like in form and style, while at the same time packing quite a panegyric punch; moreover, it comes to us as well in a humorous anecdotal context quite at odds with Ibn Ḥayyān's formal description of the Cordovan ceremony.[34] This qasida is striking for its charm—even humor—brevity, and yet great panegyric power, as with masterly concision Abū al-ʿAtāhiyah evokes all the essential conventions of the full panegyric in its two-part ʿAbbāsid form.

When we compare Abū al-ʿAtāhiyah's original with the "imitation," what strikes us above all is how unlike they are. Al-Muhannad's poem is clearly a *muʿāraḍah:* he adopts the meter (*mutaqārib*) and rhyme (*-ālahā*) of the original and, within the twenty-eight lines of his poem that Ibn Ḥayyān has cited, twice employs the same rhyme word (*sirbālahā,* "her/its shirt," line 3 in Abū al-ʿAtāhiyah and line 27 in al-Muhannad; *adhyālahā,* "her/its trains," line 7 and line 2, respectively) and twice employs *taḍmīn,* the incorporation or quotation of an entire hemistich, from Abū al-ʿAtāhiyah's poem: first, "he was right only for her/it" *(wa-lam yaku / lamā kāna yaṣluḥu illā lahā),* line 8 and line 9, respectively; and then the Qurʾān-associated (Qurʾān 99:1) "the very earth quaked" *(la-zulzilat / tazalzalat al-arḍu zilzālahā),* line 9 and line 19, respectively. A comparison of the two hemistichs of *taḍmīn* reveals, in Abū al-ʿAtāhiyah's poem, an original metaphorical conceit of the slave girl as the caliphate to express the perfect and mutual suitability of the caliph and his office, as opposed to a literal use of the expression in al-Muhannad; similarly in the second case, the earthquake of the ᶜAbbāsid master is an expression of cosmic outrage, while his Andalusian imitator, though not entirely losing the cosmic dimension, employs the earthquake in a more quotidian fashion to describe his patron's thunderous army.

It is quite clear that al-Muhannad expects his audience, especially the caliph al-Mustanṣir, to recognize that his poem is a contrafaction of Abū al-ᶜAtāhiyah's. At the same time, his own poem is so different in style and structure and subject matter, indeed so conventional compared with Abū al-ᶜAtāhiyah's, that we do not sense that he is trying to "outdo" the master, but rather to evoke him. I would argue that this particular case of *muᶜāraḍah*, then, strives not so much to compete as to identify—qasida with qasida and caliphate with caliphate. Let us keep in mind, too, that for all its surface conceit of light *ghazal*-like lyricism, the controlling idea of Abū al-ᶜAtāhiyah's qasida was panegyric, in particular the unique suitability and legitimacy of his patron's holding the caliphate. We can thus identify the adoption of the rhyme and meter and the incorporation of rhyme words and whole hemistichs from Abū al-ᶜAtāhiyah's poem into al-Muhannad's as a form of "appropriation of the insignia of power" and of claims to legitimate Islamic rule.

"Shaᶜbān Has Completed What Rajab Had Begun"

The second qasida cited by Ibn Ḥayyān for the ᶜĪd al-Fiṭr celebration of 363/974 is a strange concoction by the Cordovan panegyrist Muḥammad ibn Shukhayṣ (d. before 400/1009).[35] As with the previous poem, we have only the lines that have been preserved in *Al-Muqtabis*. Again, the entire poem as we have it falls thematically under the heading of the *madīḥ* (praise section) of the classical qasida structure. For our discussion we can divide the poem as follows: (1) an opening section that evokes the Islamic lunar months of Shaᶜbān and Rajab to celebrate a year of abundant harvests and military victory as well as the ᶜĪd itself, and then declares the preordained defeat of Ḥasan ibn Qannūn (lines 1–17); (2) a middle section that poetically recounts the defeat and disgrace of Ḥasan and the Idrīsids (lines 18–47); and (3) a final section that celebrates the restoration of political and religious order and offers a closing benediction (lines 48–66). As will be discussed below, this poem is a contrafaction (*muᶜāraḍah*) of Abū Tammām's renowned qasida on the conquest of ᶜAmmūriyah, "The Sword Is More Veracious," which we discussed in chapter 5.

Following directly upon the quotation of al-Muhannad's poem (above), Ibn Ḥayyān continues:

> Then after him there rose his messenger Muḥammad ibn Shukhayṣ to recite a long poem of his in which he heaped [abuse] upon the Banū Ḥasan who had been humbled by the caliph's victory over them, and did this to excess. The poem begins:
> [meter: *basīṭ;* rhyme: *-bū*]

1. Shaʿbān has completed
 what Rajab had begun
 Even before hopes
 had expected it.

2. More than this the month of fasting
 met us with
 The best of two ʿĪds: the full moon
 and the [new] moon rising.

3. In a year of lush abundance,
 its ascending stars
 Surrounded us with victory and fertility,
 so perfidy and drought died.

4. God's is the deed
 through which
 Joy came to us
 before the dispatches and writs.

5. The very earth swaggered
 in wonder at him,
 But I think a swaggerer's wonder
 is no cause for wonder.

6. The horizon shone from the exuberance
 that engulfed it,
 And the earth blossomed from the delight
 that set it aquiver.

7. Then the rose mimicked the glow
 of bashful cheeks,
 And the chamomile the gleam
 of pearly teeth.

8. When the failed fool saw
 the unfolding events

Reveal to his eye harbingers
of his destruction,

9. And that the assault of God's Commander
reaches him
Whom neither steeds
nor fine-bred camels reach,

10. And that [the caliph's] resolve was an irrevocable decree,
his wrath destruction,
And that this destruction and this wrath
are on God's behalf,

11. And that even if he fled
as far as China,
It would not save him from
[the caliph's] sword

12. —For how can he whom
God is bent upon pursuing
Ever hope for a refuge
to save him?—

13. He hoped to flee,
but then his hope informed him
That ever-vigilant fate
had him surrounded.

14. Where is there a refuge
from the shadow of heaven
On a day when the tent ropes are loosed
from the horizons?

15. [Ḥasan ibn Qannūn's] surrendering authority
to our lord [the caliph]
Safeguarded his blood that I wanted to use
to cure rabies.[36]

16. He barely escaped with the last breath
of his life,
Buffeted between
life and death.

17. God hastened his misfortunes
in this world,
[Leaving him] neither life, nor kin,
nor lineage.

And he digressed to mention Ḥasan and his defeated people, saying, in an excessive and unseemly manner,

18. A motley crowd claim Hāshim
as their lineage,
But they have no true lineage
to anyone.

19. Blind in perception,
neither religion nor noble pedigree
Could bend their necks
to pious deeds.

20. Their blindness increased when the first of them
threw down his staff [= settled]
Where there was neither learning
nor civility.

21. They grew up with wild beasts
in a savage horde
Who have no thought nor aim
but slurping soup.

22. Had they claimed to be
the foremost of Quraysh,
Events and suspicions would have forced
denial of their claims.

23. All that burns
can be extinguished,
But the evil after ʿUthmān['s murder] is extinguished
only to flare up again.

24. If Ḥasan goes forth as the head
of the descendants of Ḥasan,
Then who, I wonder,
is the tail?

25. The dispatches and pens of a king
whom [the caliph] destroyed
Proved untrue when the [caliph's] spears and swords
proved true.

26. Though folly may erode the earnest resolve
of the mighty,
[The caliph's] might never lacks
for firm resolve.

27. Nor has the mill of war been turned
in his domain
Unless his decision
was its axle.

28. A decision whose Entruster
guides him to success
When opinions differ
and talk is diverse.

29. A decision that
gave the generals
More support in war
than all their clamorous host.

30. [The caliph] threw [Ḥasan] into the abyss
of the ravine
And then granted him a respite till he became the source
of his own afflictions.

31. God may be forbearing
to a people
To increase their misery,
and so He loosed their rope.

32. When [Ḥasan] came to the Peninsula
there encircled his retinue
Squadrons whose anger caused the very earth
to tremble.

33. Every time he traversed
the back of the earth
Its highlands and lowlands countered him
with cavalry and infantry.

34. Until when he drew near the precinct
of our heartlands,
His heart throbbing,
his intestines in commotion,

35. He found the armies whose march
made him imagine
The haughty hills were locusts
hopping round him.

36. They came altogether thanking God,
extolling right guidance,
One after another flowing
[over the earth].

37. The followers of him
who seeks victory from God [Mustanṣir bi-Llāh],
Their victory is the true perception
—not feigning and lies.

38. Nothing prevented them from bringing [Ḥasan]
every harm that leads to death
Except obedience
and awe [of the caliph].

39. [Ḥasan] kept crying, "There is no god but God!"
out of anguish
Like that of seafarers whose ships
are about to be wrecked.

40. Hoping for life,
fearing death,
He was in two opposite states:
elation and dejection.

41. Until there appeared
the star of good fortune
That interceded for him;
and in battle each man gets what he rode.

42. I do not think that [Ḥasan]
saw the Mahdī [caliph],
For veils of his light veiled his eyes
from his face.

43. If [the caliph] had shown [weakness] before the Shiᶜite [Ḥasan],
the veils [of his awe] would have been rent,
and [Ḥasan's] sword would have been stained
with the blood of jugular veins,[37]

44. [The caliph's might] would have perished
and passed away,
With religion crushed, the free man enslaved,
and property plundered.

45. [Ḥasan] withheld nobility,
so it was withheld from him;
This brought him the rope
by which sorrows are led.

46. And I said to the fool [Ḥasan] who kindled
with his heedlessness
A fire for which was readied
the firewood of his soul.

47. "Much discord have you sown
in the Mahdī's state;
Look at the state to which your strife
has brought you!"

And he says in it—may God be kind and gracious to him:

48. O invoker of God
in the [gallant] deed
For the year of whose date
poems and orations were composed.

49. Since the flames of war were kindled
your confidence has not flagged
In defending what divine decrees impose,
not shooting stars.

50. You took him captive after wresting his rule
from his hand;
So in your grasp he became both
plundered and plunder.

51. Your magnanimity has almost made him forget that you
gave him his soul [= life],
And that is something that
cannot be given.

52. The liege men have vowed [to you]
their constant protection,
And the Arabs have openly declared
their obedience.

53. Unflagging was the resolve
of the army
Who, when a victor among them called out your name,
were victorious.

54. The entire dominion of the west is now
devoted to you;
Its regions both far and near have given
obeisance to you.

55. So why did your victorious army
stop short of a direction [the east]
Where Egypt is oppressed
and Aleppo usurped.

56. The reversal of the deserter's fortune
informs us

That the good fortune of the renegades
has been reversed.

57. You allowed access to your domain
to followers of his call;
For unripe dates are eaten until
ripe dates mature.

58. If the tent pole of Fusṭāṭ is felled
by its stays,
Neither the tent pegs nor the ropes
will hold.

59. Nothing in the march [of prosperity]
can match your numinous face
Except
our fruitful year.

60. So may God increase you in the might
by which His blessing endures
For as long as the ages
and epochs.

61. You are a gift to Islam
from the ᶜĪd Greeter
For what He gives
and bestows.

62. May your army be inundated
with bounty;
And grades and ranks be exalted
by all of your generals.

63. And may our summers be covered with the generous rain
of your limpid grace,
Which, when a pouring stream is mentioned,
pours forth.

64. A mighty victory and a prosperous fertile year
for [this ᶜĪd] al-Fiṭr
For which your newly polished days
are named.

65. And surely the hair-parting of our lord and master
Abū al-Walīd
Should be turbaned with the crown
of dominion.

66. The [crowning] of him whose grandfather
is Marwān

And whose father is the Mahdī al-Wulāt
should not be delayed.[38] [27]

It would be difficult, indeed misleading, to discuss Ibn Shukhayṣ's poem without reference first to the issue of *muʿāraḍah* (contrafaction), for it is so strikingly an imitation of the master panegyrist of the ʿAbbāsids, Abū Tammām. In a direct and technical sense, exhibiting the same meter (*basīṭ*) and rhyme consonant (*bāʾ*, although with a different end vowel), it is a *muʿāraḍah* of "The Sword Is More Veracious" (discussed in chapter 5), that poet's renowned panegyric qasida to the ʿAbbāsid caliph al-Muʿtaṣim celebrating his conquest of the Byzantine city of ʿAmmūriyah/Amorium in the year 223/838.[39] It is also, insofar as we can determine from the lines cited by Ibn Ḥayyān, built according to the military victory ode structure that Abū Tammām employs in the ʿAmmūriyah qasida and many other well-known poems: that is, the poem begins with what we might term "archetypal" panegyric to the caliph, proceeds to a poetic presentation of the military campaign in which detailed historical referents are formulated as ritual agon between good and evil, and concludes with the reaffirmation of the "archetypal," a celebratory benediction (*duʿāʾ*) for the caliph's long life and prosperity, and, sometimes, a call for recognition or crowning of the heir apparent.[40] In addition, we find more particular themes and motifs from the ʿAmmūriyah poem—the supremacy of the sword over the book, i.e., military might over astrology; the use of astrological/astronomical terminology of rising, setting, overturning, shooting stars, the months of the year; the ripening of dates—and all of these are evoked with Abū Tammām's diction, especially through the rhyme word. We can add to this list "imitations," what the classical Arab critics would have termed *sariqah* (plagiarism) of other well-known lines by Abū Tammām. For example, compare lines 25 and 26 of Ibn Shukhayṣ's qasida with the two opening lines of Abū Tammām's ʿAmmūriyah qasida:

The sword is more veracious
than the book,
Its cutting edge splits earnestness
from sport.

The white of the blade,
not the black on the page,
Its broadsides clarify uncertainty
and doubt.

Likewise, compare line 56 above with line 35 of "The Sword Is More Veracious":

The reversal of our fortunes
brought forth
From their unfortunate reversal
auspicious issue.

Then consider line 46 above and a line from Abū Tammām's qasida to the caliph al-Muʿtaṣim on the immolation of his allegedly traitorous Persian general, al-Afshīn:

Fire's worshipper in life,
its fuel in death,
With the wicked he
shall enter it.[41] [28]

Finally, in a more general sense, we find the use of a distinctly Abū Tammāmian rhetorically ornate *badīʿ* (innovative) style[42] in lines such as line 50. In other words, to the audience then, and for that matter to any Arab audience now, what we have here is an Abū Tammāmian panegyric composed by another poet for another patron (*mamdūḥ*). In ceremonial terms, too, we can talk of its success in the translation and appropriation of insignia of sovereignty.

It should be clear from this and the preceding poem that although in a general sense the panegyric qasida was one of the insignia of power, the Cordovans were also keen to compete for the prestige conferred by the great master panegyrists of the east, Abū al-ʿAtāhiyah (who was perceived as such, although also renowned as an ascetic poet), Abū Tammām, and, as we will see below, al-Mutanabbī. In aesthetic terms, however, the problem with Ibn Shukhayṣ's poem is that the imitation is so artfully achieved that the poem lacks sufficient originality. We can interpret this as perhaps a lack of political and poetic confidence, and sense in the Cordovan caliphal culture the compensatory attitude of arrivistes. Ironically, then, although the power and beauty of this poem derive largely from its evocation of Abū Tammām's master panegyric, that is what prevents it from achieving true greatness.

Having said this, we must nevertheless admit that Ibn Shukhayṣ has composed a poem of considerable power and artistry. In archetypal and structural terms, he has successfully fused the seasonal cyclical pattern with the cycle of the military campaign to fit the Islamic lunar (and hence not meteorologically seasonal) calendar and the celebration of the ʿĪd. We can get a good grasp of this if we view the poem through the lens of Gaster's formulation of the ancient Near Eastern "seasonal cycle" of the public ceremonies that usher in years and seasons (chapter 6), wherein the rites of Emptying express the eclipse of life and vitality at the end of each lease and the rites of Filling express the revitalization that characterizes the beginning of a new lease or cycle.[43] The former he subdivides into rites of Mortification and Purgation, the latter into Invigoration and Jubilation.[44]

Opening Section: Lines 1–17. Given that the qasida was presented at the ceremony of the ʿĪd greeting, it is not surprising that its opening lines (lines 1–7) correspond to Jubilation, the final section of Gaster's formulation. The poet begins with the Islamic lunar calendrical cycle: "Shaʿbān has completed what Rajab had begun," apparently a reference to the torrential rains of the month of Rajab/April of that year,[45] is essentially equivalent to our "April showers bring May flowers." What is important in this poem, however, is the poet's alignment, or identification, of the solar seasonal (vegetable, agricultural) pattern of drought followed by rainfall and bloom with the Islamic lunar calendrical pattern, especially of the fast of Ramaḍān followed by the feast of ʿĪd al-Fiṭr, and the military political pattern of the Idrīsid sedition followed by Umayyad victory. The effect of this is to portray the victory of the caliph al-Mustanṣir over Ḥasan ibn Qannūn as part of an overarching divine and cosmic plan. This is consummated in line 3, where the seasonal-agricultural, the astrological-astronomical, and the military-political spheres are aligned: ascending stars (of good fortune) have revived victory and fertility, perfidy and drought have died. The poem then develops this "pathetic fallacy" (which might better be termed "cosmic verity") as it describes the earth swaggering in amazement at the caliph's victory and putting forth its blooms. These delightful lines (5–7) should remind us of the origin of the much-admired garden lyrics in the much-maligned panegyric genre.[46] These lines have a further Abū Tammāmian antecedent: his short lyrical panegyric to the caliph al-Muʿtaṣim that opens with the image of spring:

> The selvages of fate were delicate
> and quivering;
> The earth at morn found its ornaments
> broken [by the rain].[47] [29]

Lines 8–17 describe the futile attempt of the enemy, Ḥasan ibn Qannūn, to flee from the caliph whose will and determination are embodiments of divine decree. The effect of this is, first, to establish that his defeat is foreordained, part of the larger unfolding of a teleological Islamic history, and, second, to defame his moral character—he takes the coward's way out and flees rather than die a hero's death on the field of battle. Ultimately he saves his skin by surrendering to the inevitable, that is, the caliph al-Mustanṣir.

Middle Section: Lines 18–47. The middle section of the poem, as cited in Ibn Ḥayyān, is devoted to the defeat and disgrace of the enemy. In terms of the seasonal pattern, this corresponds to the purgation and invigoration sections, the "purgation of evil and noxiousness" and "galvanizing the moribund condition to gain a new lease on life," respectively.[48] We can understand it as well as a ritual reenactment of al-Mustanṣir's victory. Lines 18–24 present what we might in Arabic genre classification term *hijāʾ* (invective, satire), the public disgracing of the defeated enemy, much akin to the ritual humiliation of the defeated enemy that forms part of the Byzantine triumph.[49]

The previous section (lines 8–17) described Ḥasan ibn al-Qannūn's cowardice, and hence his moral incapacity for Islamic rule; this section challenges his claim to Hāshimite lineage, which in Arabo-Islamic terms constitutes a denial of the legitimacy of his hereditary claim to the imamate or caliphate. Although in an immediate sense line 18 is aimed at Idrīsid claims, within the broader political arena it constitutes a potshot at the ʿAbbāsids, the Fāṭimids, and assorted ʿAlid pretenders, for Hāshim ibn ʿAbd al-Manāf, the great-grandfather of the Prophet Muḥammad, was the common ancestor of Muḥammad, ʿAlī, and al-ʿAbbās, whereas the Umayyads claim descent from ʿAbd al-Shams ibn ʿAbd al-Manāf.[50] It should be noted that the poet does not deny the legitimizing role of heredity, but rather questions the authenticity of the Idrīsids' genealogical claims. After denying the validity of Ḥasan's Hāshimite lineage, Ibn Shukhayṣ proceeds to describe his people as likewise unsuitable for the caliphate in other respects: they are morally blind, incapable of pious deeds, barbaric, and uncouth. Their ancestors settled in a place of no learning or civility; they were savages associating with wild beasts and concerned only with "slurping soup." All these terms are perceived as dialectically opposed to the true qualifications for the (Umayyad) caliphate: true lineage to the Quraysh, piety, civility, and civilization (lines 19–22).

Of particular interest for the legitimizing of the Cordovan Umayyads is line 23, which refers to the murder in the year 35/656 of the third of the Orthodox Caliphs (*al-khulafāʾ al-rāshidūn*), ʿUthmān ibn ʿAffān, through whom the Umayyads trace their caliphal claims and Qurashī descent. The Idrīsids trace their ancestry to the Prophet's nephew and son-in-law, ʿAlī ibn

Abī Ṭālib, the fourth Orthodox Caliph, who was a staunch political opponent of ʾUthmān, in whose murder he was indirectly implicated and whose murderers he protected.[51] In the political context of this poem, then, Ibn Shukhayṣ depicts the Idrīsid sedition against the Umayyads as a reiteration of the originary ʿAlid abomination of the murder of ʿUthmān; that is, he identifies a political cycle of Umayyad defeat and restitution with the seasonal cycle.

Against the false claims of Ḥasan ibn Qannūn the poet posits the truth of the spears and swords, that is, the victory of the authentic, legitimate caliph, which culminates in line 37. Lines 38–47 then present the victorious military campaign. Of note is the appearance of the caliph as the star of good fortune (*ghurratu s-saʿdi*) who spares his enemy's life. In seasonal terms this suggests a "new lease on life" for both Ḥasan ibn Qannūn and the Umayyad *ummah*, for *ghurrah* also means the new moon that appears at the beginning of the new lunar month; here it marks the ʿĪd al-Fiṭr at the end of Ramaḍān, the first day of the month of Shawwāl. But *ghurrah* also means the radiance or numen of the caliph's face, which (line 42) by dazzling his enemy's eyes forms virtually a veil. Lines 43–44 demonstrate what would have happened had the caliph let down this veil of his might and been conciliatory toward Ḥasan: bloodshed, the oppression of religion, free men enslaved, property plundered: the overturning of the Umayyad caliphate and the decreed order of the topocosm. Lines 45–47 inform us that Ḥasan ibn Qannūn brought about his own demise: in a complex Abū Tammāmian *badīʿ* construction of combined *jinās* (root play, paronomasia) and *ṭibāq* (antithesis), the poet suggests that it was Ḥasan's own withholding of nobility—that is, his renunciation of loyalty to the Umayyads in order to render allegiance to the Fāṭimids—that brought him to this sorrowful end (line 45). Again, in a virtual case of *sariqah* (plagiarism) from Abū Tammām's renowned qasida on the immolation of the caliph al-Muʿtaṣim's general al-Afshīn (cited above), the vehemence of his insurrection renders his soul kindling for hellfire (line 46).

Final Section: Lines 48–66. The final section that Ibn Ḥayyān cites counters the chaos of insurrection with a celebration of the restoration of order, political and cosmic. It begins (line 48) by addressing the caliph in terms that define the interrelationship of Islam, military success, and the preservation of historical and cultural memory in the form of poems and orations. The following line (49), following closely in the footsteps of the theme and diction of Abū Tammām's ʿAmmūriyah qasida, stresses that the caliph's success is not the result of the astrologers' shooting stars, but of his own resolute action in effecting divine decrees. In conquering Ḥasan ibn Qannūn's domain and then taking him captive, the caliph has, as Ibn Shukhayṣ puts it—again in an Abū Tammāmian *badīʿ* formulation (see "The Sword Is More Veracious," line 54, chapter 5)—made him both plundered and plunder (line 50). In line 51 the poet reminds us that in sparing his defeated enemy, the caliph has virtually given him life: he gave him something that cannot be given—his soul.

From line 52 through 58 the poet invokes the loyalty and obedience of the al-Mustanṣir's liege-men, the bedouin (Arab) client tribes, and the devotion of the army that conquers in his name to urge the caliph, now that the entire dominion of the west is subject to him, to turn his sights toward the oppressed and unstable domains of the east, to wit, Fusṭāṭ and Aleppo. It is of interest that Ibn Shukhayṣ does not employ the name of the newly established (359/970) Fāṭimid capital in Egypt, Cairo (al-Qāhirah), but, rather than thereby acknowledge the triumph of the Umayyad's chief rival, uses the old name, al-Fusṭāṭ (line 58). García Gómez, in his discussion of this line and similar examples of poetic claims to Cordovan Umayyad rule of the Islamic heartlands, considers that "these statements concerning the Muslim states outside of Spain are not mere rhetorical pronouncements, but, on the contrary, are the announcement of plans for Umayyad expansion. According to the Cordovan poets, the Muslim lands, full of envy, look at the victorious Cordovan caliph, 'like women peeking through the slits of their veils' (Ibn Shukhayṣ)."[52]

While, indeed, nothing in poetry is simple rhetoric, and we do know that in early 363/974 the Qarmaṭī al-Ḥasan al-Aʿṣam launched an unsuccessful attack on Cairo[53] and that Aleppo was at this time subject to the Byzantines,[54] on the whole we would do best to understand these poetic claims and incitements to conquest in the Islamic heartlands not as concrete plans for Umayyad expansion, but rather as ideological statements. For all claimants to the caliphate, whether, ʿAbbāsid, Umayyad, or Fāṭimid, shared the tenet that there was only one true orthodox Islam and only one legitimate caliph. Anyone who claimed the caliphate thereby claimed to be the sole legitimate ruler of Islamdom.[55]

What is otherwise noticeable in this passage is the intense verbal imitation of Abū Tammām's "The Sword Is More Veracious" in line 56 (Abū Tammām's line 35; see above), which puns on the reversals of fortune between the two sides, and lines 57 and 58, which take their final phrases from Abū Tammām's lines 59 (ripening of figs and grapes) and 49 (tent pegs and ropes) (see chapter 5).[56] It is hard to know exactly what this unmistakable and insistent echoing, almost "parroting," of Abū Tammām's renowned ode at this point in Ibn Shukhayṣ's qasida was intended to convey to the Cordovan audience. I would suggest, however, that coming in precisely this spot its effect is to create a "mythic concordance" (as well as an acoustic and rhetorical one) whereby the Cordovan Umayyad al-Mustanṣir's defeat of the "renegade" Idrīsids and his anticipated (at least poetically) campaign against the Fāṭimids are likened to the ʿAbbasid caliph al-Muʿtaṣim's celebrated victory over the Byzantine infidel at Amorium. However awkward the current political situation between the Cordovan Umayyads and the contemporary ʿAbbasids in Baghdad, it is clear from Ibn Shukhayṣ's qasida that his predecessor Abū Tammām succeeded in mythicizing the ʿAmmūriyah campaign as a paradigmatic Islamic victory over the Infidel. With no mention whatsoever of the name of the Umayyads' rivals at Baghdad, Ibn Shukhayṣ is able through the medium of the *muʿāraḍah* (contrafaction, imitation), through the acoustic imitation of rhyme and meter and key phrases, through the stylistic imitation of Abū Tammām's "signature" *badīʿ* style, and through the near plagiarism (*sariqah*) of a few lines, to access the archetype (both mythic and poetic) of Islamic triumph and to appropriate for the Umayyads at Cordova the myth of an Islamic "manifest destiny," while assigning to their enemies within the Islamic fold the role of the enemy of Islam, played in Abū Tammām's poem by the Byzantine Christian infidel.

Lines 59–66 provide a closure for the qasida that recapitulates the celebration of military victory, vegetable fertility, and ʿĪd al-Fiṭr of the opening section (lines 1–7). Following Gaster's seasonal pattern cited above, we can identify the Emptying half with the Ḥasanid insurrection as an expression of the Mortification phase (disorder and the threat that the new lease on life—here the perpetuation of the Cordovan Umayyad dynasty—will not be obtained) and the military campaign and its attendant hardships as the Purgation phase (ridding the community of the moral contagion political and religious insurrection). The Filling half we can then identify with the military victory to mark the Invigoration phase (the galvanizing of the community to procure a new lease on life and the guarantee of the continuation of the topocosm). The military-political situation in this manner is aligned with and mythically incorporated into the agricultural (solar) seasonal cycle, so that the invigoration of the realm through military conquest is identified with agricultural or vegetable fertility. At the same time the military victory is also aligned with and mythically incorporated into the Islamic lunar calendar through its identification with the (moral) pollution → purgation → purification pattern of the fast and feast of Ramaḍān and ʿĪd al-Fiṭr.

In brief, the closure, like the opening of the qasida, we can identify with the Jubilation phase of Gaster's seasonal pattern, the celebration of the renewal of the topocosm. The dominant feature here is the mythicization of the caliph's military campaign, and through it, the perpetuation of the Umayyad house at Cordova. Thus, line 59 compares the caliph's radiant face to the fertile year, to be followed in line 60 by a *duʿāʾ* (benediction) for the caliph's enduring might. Playing on the ritual gift giving and greeting of the ʿĪd, the conceit of line 61 makes the caliph an ʿĪd gift that God "the Greeter" has bestowed upon Islam. Natural or vegetable fertility is invoked once more in line 62, in which the bounties to be bestowed on al-Mustanṣir's victorious armies are described as a flood; rather than the rank making the man, the caliph's generals have exalted their grades and ranks. In line 63, the magnanimity of the caliph is termed, according to poetic convention and fertility imagery, a "generous rain." In line 64 the entire project of the qasida—of mythicizing the military campaign in order to incorporate it into the seasonal/solar and Islamic/lunar calendrical cycles, thereby ensuring its perpetuity—is expressed with great concision: the mighty victory and prosperous fertile year which are being especially celebrated at this ʿĪd al-Fiṭr are what al-Mustanṣir's days will be named for (cf. line 48). The notion of pollution and purification is conveyed here by the word *qushubu* (new, polished, i.e., after having been rusty). In the closing couplet the poet moves from mythic and poetic perpetuity to a continuance, a "new lease on life," of a more pragmatic dynastic sort, the hereditary, in calling al-Mustanṣir to crown his son, Abū al-Walīd—to formally recognize him as heir apparent (*wālī al-ʿahd*).

Of the many functions the qasida can perform, several are noteworthy in the context of the present study. First, particularly through Ibn Shukhayṣ's identification of the cognate patterns of the military campaign, the solar agricultural calendar and the lunar Islamic liturgical calendar, the qasida mythicizes and poeticizes the event, transforming it from the ephemeral to the cyclically perpetual. Further, with respect to the ceremony that Ibn Ḥayyān describes, the qasida serves an exegetical function. Then too, the qasida itself, like the lavish decorations and extravagant spectacle, is one of the elements of the Jubilation phase. Finally, the net effect of all of these is the reaffirmation of legitimate Arabo-Islamic rule, of which al-Mustanṣir is, by virtue of the qasida, both particular exemplar and general paradigm.

"The Days Bear Witness"

The third poem in our discussion, a panegyric to the caliph Sulaymān, apparently on the occasion of ʿĪd al-Aḍḥā (the Festival of the Sacrifice) in the year 403/1013, arises out of altogether different political circumstances.

Written about forty years later than the first two poems, it is a product of the turbulent period of the disintegration of the Umayyad caliphate at Cordova. The career of the poet, Ibn Darrāj al-Qasṭallī (347–421/958–1030), spans precisely this period.[57]

In the most immediate sense, the calamitous downfall of the Umayyad house at Cordova was precipitated by al-Ḥakam II al-Mustanṣir's son and heir, Hishām II. Long the puppet of his ʿĀmirid *ḥujjāb* (chamberlains), he named the last of these, ʿAbd al-Raḥmān Sanchuelo, heir apparent in Rabīʿ al-Awwal 399/November 1008—much to the displeasure of other descendants of the Marwānid (Cordovan Umayyad) line. This sparked the *fitnah* (civil war) that brought down the Umayyad house, led to the establishment of the Petty Kingdoms *(mulūk al-ṭawāʾif),* and paved the way for the Reconquista.

Hishām II's ill-advised act was followed by a coup d'état that resulted in the caliphate of another Marwānid, Muḥammad ibn Hishām al-Mahdī (399/1009), and the capture and execution of Sanchuelo. Next, Sulaymān ibn al-Ḥakam ibn Sulaymān (the *mamdūḥ* [patron] of the present qasida), a great-grandson of ʿAbd al-Raḥmān III, with the backing of the Berbers and of Sancho García, Count of Castille, rose in rebellion. Sulaymān's forces arrived at Guadamellato on 11 Rabīʿ al-Awwal 400/3 November 1009, and two days later encountered and defeated al-Mahdī's Cordovan forces at Qantīsh. After briefly resuscitating Hishām II as caliph, Sulaymān had himself proclaimed caliph with the honorific al-Mustaʿīn (17 Rabīʿ al-Awwal 400/9 November 1009). This led to a civil war between Sulaymān with his Berber faction on one side, and his fellow Marwānid al-Mahdī on the other. Only the southern provinces ratified the accession of Sulaymān, and meanwhile, the Cordovan populace had become disaffected with the Berbers. Al-Mahdī went to Toledo, where he continued to be recognized as the sole legitimate sovereign. Having secured the support of two Frankish counts, Raymond Borrell III of Barcelona and his brother Ermengaud (Armengol) of Urgel, he headed for Cordova. He was met by Sulaymān and his Berbers at ʿAqabat al-Baqar, northwest of Cordova, where a fierce battle ensued on 5 Shawwāl 400/22 May 1010. Ermengaud was killed, Sulaymān fled, and the next day al-Mahdī and the Frankish troops took Cordova. Pressed by his Catalan auxiliaries, whom he could not pay, al-Mahdī pursued the Berbers, only to be defeated and abandoned by the Catalans. Soon we find Hishām II reinstated in Cordova, and al-Mahdī assassinated by Slavs of ʿĀmirid loyalties. The Berbers and Sulaymān refused, however, to recognize Hishām II. This led to a prolonged and debilitating siege of Cordova followed by especially brutal pillaging and rapine when the city ultimately capitulated, followed by Sulaymān's victorious reentry on 27 Shawwāl 403/10 May 1013.[58] Putting these historical facts together with the remarks of Ibn Ḥayyān that accompany the text in Ibn Bassām's *Al-Dhakhīrah* (see below) and the ᶜĪd topos of the opening and closing of the poem, Maḥmūd ᶜAlī Makkī dates the poem to the time of ᶜĪd al-Aḍḥā, 10 Dhū al-Ḥijjah 403/June 1013, after Sulaymān's restoration to the caliphate in Shawwāl of that year.[59]

Like the two previous qasidas, this poem, or rather the sections of it cited in the *Al-Dhakhīrah* version, falls thematically fully within the confines of the *madīḥ* (praise section) of the classical ode. The poem opens (lines 1–4) celebrating the caliph Sulaymān's restoration in terms of the ᶜĪd; it then turns to the subject of Sulaymān as heir to Umayyad legitimacy and the loyalty of his supporters, particularly the Berber tribes (lines 5–9). The main body of the poem consists of the mythic-poetic recounting of Sulaymān's defeat of the Christian infidel (lines 10–31), followed by a brief closure and benediction (lines 32–34).

The Andalusian poet and anthologist Ibn Bassām al-Shantarīnī (d. 543/1147) in his literary anthology *Al-Dhakhīrah fī Maḥāsin Ahl al-Jazīrah* (The Treasury of the Merits of the People of the [Iberian] Peninsula) presents the poem, citing Ibn Ḥayyān's comments:

> Abū Marwān Ibn Ḥayyān related: When Sulaymān was able to establish himself in Cordova, as we have described, those that remained of the ᶜĀmirid poets that were still residing in Cordova at that time began to compose panegyric for him in the hope of tapping the stores of his generosity. So they composed in his praise good poems in which they appealed to religion and manly virtue, and most of them recited them openly in his public audience. He listened with manifest delight, but then defrauded them in accepting the panegyric, for he neither rained down generous rewards upon them nor even sprinkled. Because of this the dispersal of the group [of poets] from Cordova was completed and most of them abandoned his protection. Thus every trace of culture [*adab*] there was erased and vanquished by barbarism, [Cordova's] people reverted from their customary humanism to blatant vulgarity, and nobility was abandoned.
>
> Among those of this elevated class whose panegyric for the caliph Sulaymān was renowned in those days and whose words were preserved was the best of them, Abū ᶜUmar Aḥmad ibn Muḥammad ibn Darrāj al-Qasṭallī. He was at that time residing in Cordova and thought that Sulaymān would grant him refuge from fate, but his luck was not that good. He went before him at his first audience at the palace and recited to him the qasida that begins:

[meter: *kāmil;* rhyme: *-īduhā/ūduhā*]

1. The days bear witness to you
that you are their ʿĪd:
For you the desolate one yearned,
to you the faraway returned;

2. The gloomy day was illumined,
the one of terror dispelled,
The disobedient submitted,
the harsh relented.

3. By you the world was purified:
the aged regained their youth once more,
When before even the newborn had turned
gray with age.

4. How solid froze the sea
before your tempest,
But now its ice is broken by
your generous dew.

. . .

5. Your house found repose
in Mecca's broad valley
Until the return of days
whose promised time drew near.

6. For processions of cavalry
whose steeds whinny for you,
And battalions whose banners
flutter over you.

7. Stirred to passion
by your call,
By which their lowlands and their highlands
had long prospered.

. . .

8. Until you rose to that station
among ranks
That makes the noble and the princely
mighty

9. In the domed tent of dominion
whose ropes and pole
Are the [Berber] tribes of Ṣanhājah
and Zanātah.

. . .

10. On battle days their swords strike
true to their promise;
When men contend for noble rank,
their pledge holds true.

11. O hour when blood kinship's bonds
were cut,
And no pious man was witness to it
or was witnessed.

12. A day when the noble were humbled
to the base
And free lords were assaulted
by their slaves—

13. Their heroes forsook them
in a terror
That crippled the chieftains
and their braves.

14. Their guide, perplexed, did not lead them
on the road to escape
Nor did their shots
hit the target.

. . .

15. Until you brought to them
a most auspicious new moon
Whose good fortune rose above them
in the sky.

And from it [are the lines]:

16. On the two sides of the River Sharanbah [Rio Jarama]
they pitched a battle
Whose thunder made
the steady mountains shake.

17. They advanced to Shahbāʾ
whose harvest-time had come;
The necks of ironclad warriors
were the crop.

18. And to the ravines of Qantīsh
where the oppressor nations
Had gathered against them
in unstoppable numbers.

19. They left there a hill
that just that morning
Had been a hollow—
the hill was of enemy corpses.

20. And when the Frankish battalions
schemed against you
With their followers, God [in turn]
schemed against them,

21. With [steeds], swimmers
in the depths of the sea,
Trailing ample mail, spreading out to flood
the empty plain.

22. They made the eagle and the crow
their guests that day,
And their seducer and leader
feasted them.

23. A remnant of Ermengaud's army rallied round him
to advance,
And then their masses marched
to hell.

24. They approached them at the Wadi Ār [Guadiaro]
beneath cutting blades
In whose steel the Muslims' might
struck sparks.

25. After they had broken the spears
and drawn white blades
As sharp
as they were Muslim.

26. Then it seemed as if their crucifixes had been raised
in the shadow of the battle dust,
And the time had come
for their prostrations.

27. On the left side so disheveled
did their troops advance
That whoever saw them gave glad tidings
of victory.

28. They dealt such blows
to its defenders' skulls
That their skulls shed tears that crossed their cheeks
like bridges.

29. In a battle that would confirm
the excuse of the swords
If their steel had melted from
the battle heat.

30. And in which the brown Khaṭṭī spear
had but a feeble excuse
For its shaft not sprouting leaves
while in your hand.

31. In it you saw might
wherever you liked,
And, wherever you liked,
ample robes of grace.

. . .

32. Accept [this poem], for her dowry
has been led to you
By matched praises,
their object not blameworthy,

33. [She is] a novelty
of exquisite order,
Her gems, both jewels and center stone,
precisely matched.

34. Let her enjoy days of glory,
all of them ᶜĪds,
And you for those who obey you
the ᶜĪd among those ᶜĪds!

. . .[60] [30]

Ibn Ḥayyān's remarks are of particular interest to us for what they reveal about the relation of panegyric to courtly values and culture in general. First, the role of panegyric qasida in a ritual exchange of poem and prize is portrayed as a sacred trust upon which courtly culture is founded. The patron's failure to reward the poets according to custom and expectation leads to their dispersal and ultimately to the demise of culture in Cordova and the rise of barbarity. These remarks inform us that this poem was Ibn Darrāj's first panegyric to the caliph Sulaymān. As we have discussed in the previous chapters (see especially chapters 2 and 6), the Arabic panegyric qasida can perform the function of declaration of allegiance (*bayᶜah, mubāyaᶜah*) to the new patron, and the exchange of poem and prize will thus be a ritual, a contractual one that establishes a bond of fidelity and clientage between the two. The sense of a declaration of a new allegiance, indeed of submission or surrender, should be particularly acute here, inasmuch as Ibn

Darrāj had been a court panegyrist of the ʿĀmirids. In light of the contemporary political situation, we can expect as well in the poem at hand an emphasis on the restoration and legitimacy of the Umayyad Marwānid house.[61] The mythic and ritual patterns thus far introduced are all applicable to or extricable from this qasida, too.

The qasida opens proclaiming the restored Umayyad caliph Sulaymān to be like the ʿĪd among the days, thereby setting the stage for the mythicization and incorporation of the historical present—in this case the restoration of Sulaymān to the caliphate—into the lunar liturgical Islamic calendrical cycle, a process with which we are by now familiar.[62] Familiar, too, is the apparent source of this controlling metaphor, which is "Each Man's Fate Is Fixed," by the master panegyrist of the east, al-Mutanabbī to the Ḥamdānid emir Sayf al-Dawlah for ʿĪd al-Aḍḥā 342/953, which we discussed in chapter 6.[63] Not only does Ibn Darrāj, whose position in al-Andalus is likened to that of al-Mutanabbī in Syria,[64] adopt al-Mutanabbī's extensive rootplay (*jinās,* paranomasia) on the word *ʿīd,* but his structuring the poem around a mythicized agon between Islam and Christianity seems also to derive from this model.[65] Ibn Darrāj proceeds in lines 1 through 4 to describe Sulaymān's reign in mythic terms of return, renewal, and rebirth. Nor is the political dimension left out, as in line 2 the submission of the rebellious is listed among the forms of purification after pollution.

The next five lines (5–10) turn to the subject of the legitimacy of the Umayyad house. Especially effective here is line 5, in which the Meccan Qurashī origins of the Banū Umayyah are invoked and described as incubating until the promised time arrived. The line is lent rhetorical force by its recalling through the phrase *miʿādi ayyāmin* (return of days) the words *al-ayyām* (days) and *ʿīd* (from the same root, *ʿ-w-d,* as *miʿād*) of line 1 and then adding *jinās* (root play) within the line in the word *mawʿūd* (promised) from the root *w-ʿ-d,* again precisely the metathetic root play we saw in al-Mutanabbī's source poem. Thus the calendrical cycle is presented as not merely repeating but fulfilling the promise of time, that is, the divinely decreed Umayyad rule. The loyalty of the military and their devotion to the call—*daʿwah* (from another metathesis of *ʿa-w-d,* that is, *d-ʿ-w,* to call) actually carries the sense of a religious claim or call—is then tied to the mythic association of the legitimate ruler and the prosperity of the land (lines 6–7). This section culminates in a reaffirmation of loyalty to the hierarchy: the elevation of the patron to the caliphate, his proper position in the ordered ranks that form society (line 8); the familiar metaphor of dominion as a tent, now with loyal Berber tribes forming the tent ropes and pole (line 9); and finally the loyalty of those tribes in battle and in politics (line 10). In short, the two foundations of the Islamic (or, for that matter, any) proper polity: a system of ranks appropriately filled by members true to their bonds of loyalty and obligation.

This evocation of the ordered and prosperous Islamic polity is countered in lines 11–14 with a picture of the chaos that reigned before Sulaymān acceded to the caliphate, referring to the events of 400/1009. The internecine nature of the struggle is expressed in a double entendre of failed fertility in line 11, where "blood kinship's bonds were cut" (*maqṭūʿatan arḥāmuhā*) can be read equally as "slit-open wombs." Line 12 depicts social and especially military disorder resulting from the abomination of unsanctioned rule: the noble humbled to the base, slaves attacking free and noble kings (cf. al-Mutanabbī's invective of Kāfūr, "ʿĪd! How Is It You Return?" lines 5–16, in chapter 6); heroes fleeing in terror, guides losing their way, shots missing their mark (lines 12–14). Sulaymān's restitution of order and prosperity is presented in line 15 in terms of the rising new moon of good fortune. The word *ghurrah* (whiteness of complexion, new moon, gleam of dawn) conveys at once the image of the caliph's radiant countenance and the renewal symbolized by the rising of the new moon. In the Islamic lunar calendar this signals the new month, and in particular is associated with the new moon of the month of Shawwāl, which signals the end of the month of fasting, Ramaḍān, and the feast of ʿĪd al-Fiṭr.

Lines 16–31 refer to the hostilities between Sulaymān and al-Mahdī that we recounted above. When viewed in light of the historical accounts of the internecine struggle between these two scions of the Marwānid line, this passage reveals a process of mythicization through which the *fitnah* (civil war) between Muslim kinsmen has been transformed into a *jihād* (holy war) between the legitimate Muslim ruler and the Christian infidel. This is accomplished above all by simply omitting any mention of al-Mahdī and his 30,000 Muslim troops, and concentrating instead on the Frankish counts with their 10,000.[66] The historical battle of Sulaymān against al-Mahdī is rendered a ritual cosmic agon between good and evil, the roles played here by Islam and Christianity, respectively. Although names and places are specified, such specificity should not gull us into accepting the text as historically accurate, for the images are archetypal, mythical, and poetic, and the aims of the qasida are highly political. Thus, for example, in line 17 the prosperity achieved by military victory is likened to agricultural fertility: harvest-time has come and the crop is enemy heads. Line 20 plays on Qurʾan 86:15–16, where God says of the enemies of Islam: "Indeed they are plotting a scheme, [but] I [too] am plotting a scheme" (*innahum yakīdūna kaydan wa akīdu kaydan*). The description of the army in line 21 is purely poetic convention in both image and diction. The victorious blades are Muslim as well as sharp (line 25); the Christian general marches his troops straight into hellfire (line 23). Finally, the regeneration of life through military victory is again expressed in terms of vegetable fertility as the poet asks why the shaft of the Khaṭṭī spear did not sprout in the caliph's hand (line 30).

What is particularly noteworthy and curious here is not merely the poet's recasting of *fitnah* as *jihād,* but that in describing the events leading to Sulaymān's restoration to the caliphate at Cordova, his loss is turned into a victory, and, no doubt with great sensitivity to the prevailing political climate, the brutal siege and reconquest of Cordova is not mentioned at all.

The closing lines (32–34) contain a charming but complex conceit through which the poet seems to style his qasida a bride and the lines of praise in it her dowry. This leads to some ambiguity, perhaps intentional, between the bride and the dowry, and then a further metaphor of the qasida-dowry-bride as an exquisitely set necklace. The qasida as bride is a conventional conceit that implies the qasida's virginity—that is, its originality—as does the opening word of line 33, *bidʿan* (a novelty). Additionally, of course, the marriage metaphor suggests that just as a bride will produce progeny to perpetuate the husband's lineage, the panegyric ode will perpetuate name of its *mamdūḥ.* The necklace metaphor is also a conventional one employed to convey not only the idea of rhyme and meter—the ordering (*naẓm*) of the qasida like the careful matching of precious stones on a necklace, but also its artistry, its uniqueness, and its lasting value and beauty. The final line begins with an ʿĪd-greeting for the qasida itself, but it must be understood that the days of glory for the poem mean the perpetual glory of the *mamdūḥ* (patron). Ibn Darrāj closes his qasida by at the same time recapitulating the opening line and declaring his submission and obedience: the caliph is, for those who obey him, the ʿĪd among ʿĪds.

Ibn Darrāj's qasida thus functions as a declaration of submission and allegiance to the Cordovan Umayyad house (with no hint that there might be other Marwānids to choose from), a confirmation of legitimacy of its rule in terms of lineage and military success, and the caliph's position vis-à-vis the Islamic topocosm. Once again, the incorporation of the ephemeral contemporary event into the recurrent Islamic liturgical cycle through the processes of mythicization and poeticization, nowhere more succinctly exemplified than in the metaphor of the opening (and closing) lines: "The days bear witness to you / that you are their ʿĪd."

Although Ibn Darraj's qasida is pleasantly, though unmistakably, Mutanabbian in style, we nevertheless perceive a comfortable sense of self-sufficiency in Ibn Darrāj's poem that distinguishes it from the anxious insecurity of the first two poems considered in this chapter. We sense now that Andalusian poetry is standing on its own two feet. Nevertheless, we must recognize that throughout the period of the Cordovan caliphate and for some time thereafter, a key element in the appropriation of the insignia of power and authority from the Arabo-Islamic east was the appropriation specifically of the poetic voices of the great master panegyrists of the east, chief among them Abū Tammām and al-Mutanabbī.

Returning once more to Ibn Ḥayyān's introductory remarks to Ibn Darrāj's poem, perhaps we can deduce from the failure of the panegyric exchange ritual more about its power and function. The ritual exchange of panegyric qasida and prize is presented as paradigmatic of the social contract and the archetypal act of allegiance upon which the entire social and cultural enterprise of the Arabo-Islamic polity is founded. Following Ibn Ḥayyān's line of reasoning we can say that the failure to properly complete this contractual ritual, as when the caliph Sulaymān fails to produce the prize to which the presentation of the panegyric obligates him, signals the collapse of Arabo-Islamic culture. If nothing else, it signals the imminent demise of the Cordovan caliphate of al-Andalus.

Conclusion

If we now review the nearly five-century trajectory of the seven chapters of this study, we can see how the classical Arabic panegyric ode appropriated pre-Islamic concepts of sacral kingship and ritual patterns, such as Transgression and Redemption, to create a literary genre capable of formulating and promulgating a specifically Arabo-Islamic ideology of legitimate rule. Divine appointment is coupled with the pre-Islamic virtues of might and magnanimity and the idea of nobility that they embody to generate the myth of an Islamic "manifest destiny," that is, a teleological history of Islam triumphant. Grounding this ideology in the panegyric ode, the conventions of the genre—its distinctive form, diction, and imagery—guarantee the stability and preservation of core Arabo-Islamic values, while at the same time the plasticity of the qasida form enables the poet to employ it for the subtle negotiation of the relative rank and status of ruler and ruled. Time-honored Arabo-Islamic values are preserved not as empty lip service, but as principles actively engaged in contemporary persuasive discourse and brought performatively to bear upon current political events. The genre stability of the Arabic qasida allows, too, for the "mythic concordance" between poets and patrons, and even poems themselves, as each poet in the ceremonial presentation of his panegyric before the patron reenacts the ritual exchange that embodies the relation of the ruler to his subjects. From pre-Islamic times down through the first third of the twentieth century, the qasida tradition enabled Arabo-Islamic culture to remember the past, to shape the present, and to envision the future.

In a broader humanistic sense we can locate the perennial aesthetic appeal of the qasida in the range of emotions and experiences, from the intimate to the imperial, that it expresses with extraordinary subtlety and precision. These range from the delicacy and refinement of the nuanced lyricism of loss, nostalgia, and despair in the elegiac prelude (*nasīb*), to the relentless determination of man testing his inner self against the outer world in the desert crossing (*raḥīl*), and, finally, to the tension and exuberance, as well as the celebratory triumphalism, of the political engagement of the praise section (*madīḥ*). Almost paradoxically, what we discover beneath the culture-specific elements of the highly conventional classical Arabic panegyric ode (*qaṣīdat al-madḥ*) are emotions and experiences that are essentially our own.

Appendix of Arabic Texts

[1] قال النّابِغة الذُّبْيانِيّ

١- أَمِنْ آلِ مَيَّةَ رائحٌ أو مُغْتَدِ　　عَجْلانَ ذا زادٍ وغيرَ مُزَوَّدِ
٢- أَفِدَ التَّرَحُّلُ غيرَ أنّ رِكابَنا　　لما تَزُلْ برحالِنا وكَأَنْ قَدِ
٣- زَعَمَ الغُرابُ بأنّ رحلتَنا غَداً　　وبذاكَ خَبَّرَنا الغُدافُ الأسودُ
٤- لا مرحباً بِغَدٍ ولا أهلاً به　　إن كان تَفْرِيقُ الأَحِبَّةِ فى غَدِ
٥- حان الرَّحِيلُ ولم تُوَدِّعْ مَهْدَداً　　والصُّبحُ والإمساءُ منها مَوْعِدِى
٦- فى إِثْرِ غانيةٍ رَمَتْكَ بسَهْمِهَا　　فأصاب قلبَك غيرَ أنْ لم تُقْصِدِ
٧- غَنِيَتْ بذلك إِذْ هُمُ لكَ جِيرَةٌ　　منها بعَطْفِ رِسالةٍ وتَوَدُّدِ
٨- ولقد أصابَ فؤادَه مِن حُبِّها　　عن ظَهْرِ مِرنانٍ بسَهْمٍ مُصْرِدِ
٩- نَظَرَبْ بمُقْلَةِ شادنٍ مُتَرَبِّبٍ　　أَحْوَى أَحَمِّ المُقْلَتَيْن مُقَلَّدِ
١٠- والنَّظْمُ فى سِلْكٍ يُزَيِّنُ نَحْرَها　　ذَهَبٌ تَوَقَّدُ كالشِّهابِ المُوقَدِ
١١- صفراءُ كالسِّيَراءِ أُكْمِلَ خَلْقُها　　كالغُصْنِ فى غُلَوائِه المُتَأَوِّدِ
١٢- والبَطْنُ ذو عُكَنٍ لطيفٌ طَيُّه　　والنَّحْرُ تَنْفُجُه بِثَدْىٍ مُقْعَدِ
١٣- مَخْطُوطةُ المَتْنَين غير مُفاضةٍ　　رَيَّا الرَّوادفِ بَضَّةُ المُتَجرِّدِ
١٤- قامت تَراءَى بين سِجْفَىْ كَلَّةٍ　　كالشَّمس يومَ طُلُوعِها بالأَسْعُدِ

١٥- أو دُرَّةٍ صَدَفِيَّةٍ غَوّاصُها بَهِجٌ متى يَرَها يُهِلَّ ويَسْجُدِ

١٦- أو دُمْيَةٍ مِن مَرْمَرٍ مرفوعةٍ بُنِيَتْ بآجُرٍّ يُشادُ وقِرْمَدِ

١٧- سَقَطَ النَّصِيفُ ولم تُرِدْ إسقاطَه فتناوَلَتْه واتَّقَتْنا باليَدِ

١٨- بمُخَضَّبٍ رَخْصٍ كأنّ بنانَه عَنَمٌ يكاد من اللَّطافةِ يُعْقَدُ

١٩- نظرتْ إليكَ بحاجةٍ لم تقْضِها نَظَرَ السَّقِيم إلى وُجُوهِ العُوَّدِ

٢٠- تَجْلُو بقادِمَتَيْ حَمامةِ أَيْكَةٍ بَرَداً أُسِفَّ لِثاتُه بالإثْمِدِ

٢١- كالأُقْحوانِ غَداةَ غِبٍّ سمائِه جَفَّتْ أعاليه وأسفلُه نَدِي

٢٢- زَعَمَ الهُمامُ بأنّ فاها باردٌ عَذْبٌ مُقَبَّلُه شَهِيُّ المَوْرِدِ

٢٣- زَعَمَ الهُمامُ - ولم أَذُقْه - أنَّه عَذْبٌ إذا ما ذُقْتَه قلتَ : ازْدَدِ

٢٤- زَعَمَ الهُمامُ - ولم أذقْه - أنّه يُشْفَى بريّا رِيقِها العَطِشُ الصَّدِي

٢٥- أَخَذَ العَذارى عِقْدَه فنَظَمْنَه مِن لُؤْلُؤٍ مُتتابِعٍ مُتَسَرِّدِ

٢٦- لو أنَّها عَرَضَتْ لِأَشْمَطَ راهبٍ عَبَدَ الإلٰهَ صَرُورَةٍ مُتَعَبِّدِ

٢٧- لَرَنَا لِرُؤْيَتِها وحُسْنِ حَدِيثِها ولَخالَه رَشَداً وإن لم يَرْشُدِ

٢٨- بتكلُّمٍ لو تستطيع كلامَه لَدَنَتْ له أَرْوَى الهِضابِ الصُّخَّدِ

٢٩- وبفاحِمٍ رَجْلٍ أَثِيثٍ نَبْتُه كالكَرْمِ مال على الدِّعامِ المُسْنَدِ

٣٠- وإذا لَمَسْتَ لمستَ أَجْثَمَ جاثماً مُتَحَيِّزًا بمكانِه مِلْءَ اليَدِ

٣١- وإذا طَعَنْتَ طعنتَ في مُسْتَهدِفٍ رابِي المَجَسَّةِ بالعَبِيرِ مُقَرْمَدِ

٣٢- وإذا نزعتَ نزعتَ عن مُستحصِفٍ   نَزْعَ الحَزَوَّرِ بالرِّشاءِ المُحْصَدِ

٣٣- وإذا يَعَضُّ تَشُدُّه أعضاؤُه   عَضَّ الكبَيرِ من الرِّجالِ الأَدْرَدِ

٣٤- لا وارِدٌ منها يَحُورُ لِمَصْدَرٍ   عنها ولا صَدِرٌ يَحُورُ لِمَوْرِدِ

[2] قال امْرُؤُ الْقَيْس

مُهَفْهَفَةٌ بيضاءُ غَيْرُ مُفَاضةٍ   تَرائِبُها مَصْقُولةٌ كالسَّجَنْجَلِ

تَصُدُّ وتُبْدِي عَنْ أَسِيلٍ وتَتَّقِي   بناظرةٍ مِنْ وَحْشِ وَجْرَةَ مُطْفِلِ

وجِيدٍ كجِيدِ الرِّيم لَيْس بِفاحشٍ   إذا هِيَ نَصَّتْهُ ولا بِمُعَطَّلِ

وفَرْعٍ يَزِينُ المَتْنَ أَسْوَدَ فَاحمٍ   أَثِيثٍ كقِنْوِ النَّخْلةِ المُتَعَثْكِلِ

[3] قال امْرُؤُ الْقَيْس

إلى مِثْلِها يَرنُو الحلِيمُ صَبَابَةً   إذَا مَا اسْبَكَرَّتْ بَيْنَ دِرْعٍ ومِجْوَلِ

[4] قال امْرُؤُ الْقَيْس

تَجَاوَزْتُ أَحراساً إليها ومَعْشَرًا   عَليَّ حِراصاً لَوْ يُسِرُّونَ مَقْتَلي

[5] قال النّابِغة الذُّبْيانيّ

١- يا دارَ مَيَّةَ بالعَلْياءِ فالسَّنَدِ   أَقْوَتْ، وطالَ عَلَيْها سالِفُ الأَبَدِ

٢- وقفتُ فيها أُصَيْلاناً أُسائِلُها   عَيَّتْ جَواباً، وما بالرَّبْعِ مِن أَحَدِ

٣- إلا الأَوَارِيَّ لأْياً ما أُبَيِّنُها   والنُّؤْيُ كالحوضِ بالمَظْلُومةِ الجَلَدِ

٤- رَدَّتْ عليه أَقاصِيه ولَبَّدَه   ضَرْبُ الوَلِيدةِ بالمِسحاةِ في الثَّأَدِ

٥- خَلَّتْ سَبِيلَ أَتِيٍّ كان يَحبِسُه   ورَفَّعَتْه إلى السِّجْفَيْنِ فالنَّضَدِ

٦- أَمسَتْ خَلاءً وأمسى أهلُها احتملوا   أَخْنَى عليها الذى أَخْنَى على لُبَدِ

٧- فعَدِّ عمّا تَرَى إذْ لا ارتجاعَ له   وانْمِ القُتُودَ على عَيْرانةٍ أُجُدِ

٨- مَقْذُوفةٍ بِدَخِيسِ النَّحْضِ بازلُها   له صَرِيفٌ صَرِيفُ القَعْوِ بالمَسَدِ

٩- كأنَّ رَحْلى، وقد زال النَّهارُ بنا   يومَ الجَلِيلِ على مُستأْنِسٍ وَحَدِ

١٠- مِن وَحْشِ وَجْرَةَ موشِيٍّ أَكارِعُه   طاوِى المصيرِ، كسَيْفِ الصَّيْقَلِ الفَرِدِ

١١- أَسْرَتْ عليه مِن الجَوْزاءِ ساريةٌ   تُزْجِى الشَّمالُ عليه جامدَ البَرَدِ

١٢- فارتاعَ مِن صوتِ كَلاَّبٍ فبات له   طَوْعَ الشَّوامِتِ من خوفٍ ومن صَرَدِ

١٣- فَبَثَّهنَّ عليه واستَمَرَّ به   صُمْعَ الكُعُوبِ بَرِيئاتٍ مِن الحَرَدِ

١٤- وكان ضُمْرانُ منه حيث يُوزِعُه   طَعْنَ المُعارِكِ عند المُحْجَرِ النَّجُدِ

١٥- شَكَّ الفَرِيصَةَ بالمِدْرَى فأَنْفذَها   طَعْنَ المُبَيْطِرِ إذْ يَشْفِى مِن العَضَدِ

١٦- كأنّه خارجاً مِن جَنْبِ صَفْحَتِه   سَفُّودُ شَرْبٍ نَسُوه عند مُفْتَأَدِ

١٧- فَظَلَّ يَعْجُمُ أَعْلَى الرَّوْقِ مُنقَبِضاً   فى حالِكِ اللَّونِ صَدْقٍ غيرِ ذِى أَوَدِ

١٨- لمّا رأى واشِقٌ إقعاص صاحبِه   ولا سبيلَ إلى عَقْلٍ ولا قَوَدِ

١٩- قالت له النَّفسُ: إنِّي لا أَرَى طَمَعاً   وإنّ مولاكَ لم يَسْلَم ولم يَصِدِ

٢٠- فتلك تُبْلِغُنِى النُّعمانَ، إنّ له   فَضْلاً على الناس فى الأَدْنَى وفى البَعَدِ

٢١- ولا أَرَى فاعِلاً فى الناس يُشْبِهُه   ولا أُحاشِى مِن الأقوامِ مِن أَحَدِ

٢٢- إلاّ سُلَيمانَ إذْ قال الإلٰهُ له   قُمْ فى البَرِيَّةِ فاحْدُدْها عن الفَنَدِ

٢٣- وخَيِّسِ الجنَّ ؛ إنِّى قد أذِنْتُ لهم   يَبْنُونَ تَدْمُرَ بالصُّفّاحِ والعَمَدِ

٢٤- فمَن أطاعكَ فانْفَعْه بطاعتهِ   كما أطاعك، وادْلُله على الرَّشَدِ

٢٥- ومَنْ عَصاكَ فعاقِبْهُ مُعاقَبَةً   تَنْهَى الظَّلُومَ ولا تَقْعُدْ على ضَمَدِ

٢٦- إلاّ لمِثلكَ أو مَن أنت سابقُه   سَبْقَ الجَوادِ إذا استولَى على الأَمَدِ

٢٧- أَعْطَى لفارِهَةٍ حُلْوٍ تَوابِعُها   مِن المواهِبِ لا تُعْطَى على نَكَدِ

٢٨- الواهِبُ المائةَ المِعْكاءَ زَيَّنَها   سَعْدانُ تُوضِحَ فى أوْبارِها اللِّبَدِ

٢٩- والأُدْمَ قد خُيِّسَتْ فُتْلاً مَرافقُها   مَشْدُودةً برِحالِ الحِيرَةِ الجُدُدِ

٣٠- والرّاكضاتِ ذُيولَ الرَّيْطِ فانَقَها   بَرْدُ الهَواجِرِ كالغِزلان بالجَرَدِ

٣١- والخَيْلَ تَمْزَعُ غَرْباً فى أعِنَّتِها   كالطَّيرِ تنجُو مِن الشُّؤْبوب ذى البَرَدِ

٣٢- احكُمْ كحكمِ فتاةِ الحَىِّ إذْ نَظَرتْ   إلى حَمامٍ شِراعٍ واردِ الثَّمَدِ

٣٣- يَحُفُّه جانِبَا نِيقٍ وتُتْبِعُهُ   مثلَ الزُّجاجَةِ لم تُكْحَلْ مِن الرَّمَدِ

٣٤- قالت : ألاَ لَيْتَما هذا الحمامُ لنا   إلى حَمامَتِنا ونصفُه فَقَدِ

٣٥- فَحسَّبُوه فَأَلْفَوْه كما حَسَبَتْ   تِسعاً وتِسعِينَ لم تَنْقُصْ ولم تَزِدِ

٣٦- فكَمَّلَتْ مائةً فيها حَمامَتُها   وأسرعتْ حِسْبَةً فى ذلك العَدَدِ

٣٧- فلا لَعَمْرُ الذى مَسَّحتُ كَعْبَتَه   وما هُرِيقَ على الأنصابِ من جَسَدِ

٣٨- والمؤمنِ العائذاتِ الطَّيرَ يَمْسَحُها   رُكْبانُ مكةَ بين الغَيْلِ والسَّعَدِ

٣٩- ما قلتُ مِن سَيِّيءٍ ممّا أُتِيتَ به　　إذاً فلا رَفَعَتْ سَوْطِي إليَّ يَدِي
٤٠- إلاّ مقالةَ أقوامٍ شَقِيتُ بها　　كانتْ مقالتُهم قَرْعاً على الكَبِدِ
٤١- أُنْبِئتُ أَنَّ أبا قابُوسَ أَوْعَدَنِى　　ولا قَرارَ على زَأْرٍ مِن الأَسَدِ
٤٢- مَهْلاً فِداءً لكَ الأقوامُ كلُّهُمُ　　وما أُثَمِّرُ مِن مالٍ ومِن وَلَدِ
٤٣- لا تَقْذِفَنِّى بِرُكْنٍ لا كِفاءَ له　　وإنْ تَأثَّفَكَ الأعداءُ بالرِّفَدِ
٤٤- فما الفُراتُ إذا هَبَّ الرِّياحُ له　　تَرْمِى غَوارِبُه العِبْرَيْنِ بالزَّبَدِ
٤٥- يَمُدُّه كلُّ وادٍ مُتْرَعٍ لَجِبٍ　　فيه رُكامٌ مِن اليَنْبُوتِ والخَضَدِ
٤٦- يَظَلُّ مِن خَوْفِه المَلاّحُ مُعْتَصِماً　　بالخَيْزُرانَةِ بعدَ الأَيْنِ والنَّجَدِ
٤٧- يوماً بأجودَ منه سَيْبَ نافِلَةٍ　　ولا يَحُولُ عَطاءُ اليومِ دُونَ غَدِ
٤٨- هذا الثَّناءُ فإنْ تَسمعْ به حَسَناً　　فلم أُعَرِّضْ - أَبَيْتَ اللَّعْنَ - بالصَّفَدِ
٤٩- ها إنّ ذِى عِذْرَةٌ إلاّ تكنْ نَفَعَتْ　　فإنّ صاحبَها مُشارِكُ النَّكَدِ

[6] قالت زَرْقاءُ اليَمامة

أُقسِمُ باللهِ لقد دبَّ الشَّجَرْ　　أو حمير قد أخذتْ شيئاً تجر

[7] قال عَبْدُ القَيْس بْنُ جُفَاف التَّمِيمِىّ ومُرّةُ بْنُ سَعْد بن قُرَيْع السَّعْدِىّ

مَلِكٌ يُلاعِبُ أُمَّه وقَطِينَه　　رِخْوُ المَفاصِلِ أيْرُه كالمِرْوَدِ

[8] قال كَعْبُ بْنُ زُهَيْر

أَلاَ أَبْلِغَا عنِّى بُجَيرًا رِسالةً فهَلْ لكَ فيما قلتُ بالخَيْفِ هَلْ لَكَا
شربتَ مع المأمون كأسًا رَوِيَّةً فأنْهَلكَ المأمونُ منها وعَلَّكَا
وخالفتَ أسبابَ الهُدَى وتَبِعْتَه على أيِّ شيءٍ وَيْبَ غَيْرِك دَلَّكَا
على خُلُقٍ لم تُلْفِ أُمًّا ولا أَبًا عليه ولم تُدْرِكْ عليه أخًا لَكَا

[9] قال بُجَيرُ بْنُ زُهَيْر

مِنْ مُبْلِغٌ كَعْبًا فَهَلْ لَكَ فى التى تَلُومُ عليها باطلاً وهى أَحْزَمُ
إلى اللّهِ لا العُزَّى ولا اللّاتِ وَحْدَه فتَنْجُو إذا كان النَّجَاءُ وتَسْلَم
لَدَى يَوْمِ لا يَنْجُو وليس بمُفْلِتٍ من النارِ إلا طاهرُ القلب مُسْلِم
فِدينُ زُهَيْرٍ وهو لا شيءَ دِينُه ودِينُ أَبِى سُلْمَى علىَّ محرَّم

[10] قال دُرَيْد بن الصِّمَّة

أمرتُهمُ أمرى بمُنْعَرَج اللِّوَى فلم يَسْتبينوا الرُّشْدَ إلاّ ضُحَى الغدِ
فلما عَصَوْنى كنتُ منهم وقد أَرَى غَوايتَهم وأنّنى غيرُ مهتد
وهل أنا إلاّ من غَزِيّةَ إن غَوَتْ غَوَيْتُ، وإن تَرْشُدْ غَزِيّةُ أرشُد

[11] قال كَعْبُ بْنُ زُهَيْر

١- بانتْ سُعادُ فقَلْبِى اليومَ مَتْبولُ مُتيَّمٌ إثْرها لم يُجْزَ مَكْبُولُ
٢- وما سُعادُ غَداةَ البَيْنِ إذ رحَلوا إلاّ أَغَنُّ غَضيضُ الطَّرْفِ مكحولُ

٣- تَجْلُو عوارِضَ ذى ظَلْمٍ إذا ابتسَمتْ ... كأنَّه مُنْهَلٌ بالرَّاحِ مَعْلُولُ
٤- شُجَّتْ بِذِى شَبَمٍ من ماءِ مَحْنِيَةٍ ... صافٍ بِأَبْطَحَ أضْحَى وهو مشمولُ
٥- تَجْلُو الرياحُ القَذَى عنه وأَفْرَطَه ... من صَوْبِ سارِيةٍ بِيضٌ يَعَالِيلُ
٦- يا وَيْحَها خُلَّةً لو أنَّها صدَقتْ ... ما وعَدتْ أو لَوَ آنَّ النُّصْحَ مقبولُ
٧- لكنَّها خُلَّةٌ قد سِيطَ من دَمِها ... فَجْعٌ وَوَلْعٌ وإِخْلَافٌ وتَبْدِيلُ
٨- فما تَدُومُ على حالٍ تَكونُ بها ... كما تَلَوَّنُ فى أثوابِها الغُولُ
٩- وما تَمَسَّكُ بالَوصْلِ الذى زعَمتْ ... إلا كما تُمْسِكُ الماءَ الغَرَابِيلُ
١٠- كانت مواعيدُ عُرْقُوبٍ لها مَثَلاً ... وما مَوَاعِيدُها إلاّ الأباطِيلُ
١١- أرجُو وآمُلُ أن يَعْجَلْنَ فى أَبَدٍ ... وما لهنَّ طَوالَ الدَّهْرِ تَعْجيلُ
١٢- فلا يَغُرَّنْكَ ما مَنَّتْ وما وعَدتْ ... إن الأَمَانِيَّ والأحلامَ تضليلُ
١٣- أمستْ سُعادُ بأرضٍ لا يبلِّغها ... إلا العِتاقُ النَّجِيباتُ المَراسيلُ
١٤- ولن يُبَلِّغَها إلا عُذَافِرةٌ ... فيها على الأَيْنِ إرقالٌ وتَبْغِيلُ
١٥- من كلِّ نَضَّاخَةِ الذِّفْرَى إذا عَرِقتْ ... عُرْضَتُها طامِسُ الأعلامِ مَجْهُولُ
١٦- تَرْمِى الغُيُوبَ بعَيْنَىْ مُفْرَدٍ لَهَقٍ ... إذا توقَّدَتِ الحُزَّانُ والمِيلُ
١٧- ضَخْمٌ مُقَلَّدُها فَعْمٌ مُقَيَّدُها ... فى خَلْقِها عن بَنَاتِ الفَحْلِ تَفْضِيلُ
١٨- حَرْفٌ أخوها أبوها من مهجَّنةٍ ... وعمُّها خالُها قَوْداءُ شِمْلِيلُ
١٩- يَمْشى القُرَادُ عليها ثم يُزْلِقُه ... منها لَبَانٌ وأَقْرابٌ زَهَالِيلُ

٢٠- عَيْرانةٌ قُذفتْ فى اللَّحْمِ عن عُرُضٍ مِرْفَقُها عن بناتِ الزَّوْرِ مَفْتولُ
٢١- كأنّ ما فات عَيْنيْها ومَذْبَحَها من خَطْمِها ومن اللَّحْيَيْنِ بِرْطِيلُ
٢٢- تُمِرُّ مِثْلَ عَسيبِ النَّخْلِ ذا خُصَلٍ فى غارزٍ لم تَخَوَّنْه الأَحَالِيلُ
٢٣- قَنْواءُ فِى حُرَّتَيْها للبَصِير بها عِتْقٌ مُبِينٌ وفى الخَدَّيْنِ تَسْهيلُ
٢٤- تَخْدِى على يَسَراتٍ وهى لاحقةٌ ذَوَابلٍ وَقْعُهنَّ الأرضَ تَحْليلُ
٢٥- سُمْرُ العُجَاياتِ يَتْرُكْنَ الحَصَى زِيَمًا لم يَقِهِنَّ رُءوسَ الأُكْمِ تَنْعِيلُ
٢٦- يومًا يَظَلُّ به الحِرْباءُ مُصْطَخِمًا كأنّ ضاحِيَه بالنارِ مملولُ
٢٧- كأن أوْبَ ذراعيْها وقد عَرِقتْ وقد تلفَّعَ بالقُورِ العَساقِيلُ
٢٨- وقال لِلقَوْمِ حادِيهم وقد جَعَلتْ وُرْقُ الجَنَادِبِ يَرْكُضْنَ الحَصَى قِيلُوا
٢٩- شَدَّ النهارِ ذِراعَا عَيْطَلٍ نَصَفٍ قامت فجاوبَها نُكْدٌ مَثَاكِيلُ
٣٠- نَوَّاحةٌ رِخوةُ الضَّبْعيْنِ ليس لها لما نعَى بِكْرَها الناعون معقولُ
٣١- تَفْرِى اللَّبَانَ بكَفَّيْها ومِدْرَعُها مشقَّقٌ عن تَرَاقِيها رَعَابِيلُ
٣٢- يَسْعَى الوُشاةُ بجَنْبيْها وقولهُمُ إنكَ يآبنَ أبى سُلْمَى لمقتولُ
٣٣- وقال كلُّ خليلٍ كنتُ آمُلُه لا أُلْفِينَّكَ إنِّى عنك مشغولُ
٣٤- فقلتُ خَلُّوا طَرِيقِى لا أَبَا لكمُ فكلُّ ما قَدَّر الرحمنُ مفعولُ
٣٥- كلُّ آبنِ أُنْثَى وإن طالت سَلاَمَتُه يومًا على آلةٍ حَدْباءَ محمولُ
٣٦- أُنبِئتُ أن رَسُولَ اللّهِ أَوْعَدنِى والعفوُ عند رسولِ الله مأمولُ

٣٧- مَهْلاً هَدَاكَ الذى أعطاكَ نافِلَةَ الـ   ـقرآنِ فيها مواعِيظٌ وتفصِيلُ

٣٨- لا تأخُذَنِّى بأقوالِ الوُشَاةِ ولم   أُذْنبْ ولم كثُرتْ عنِّى الأقاويلُ

٣٩- لقد أقُومُ مَقَامًا لو يَقُومُ به   أرَى وأسمَعُ ما لو يَسْمَعُ الفِيلُ

٤٠- لظَلَّ يُرْعَدُ إلا أن يكون له   من الرسولِ بإذنِ اللهِ تنويلُ

*- مَا زِلْتُ أَقْتَطِعُ الْبَيْدَاءَ مُدَّرِعاً   جُنْحَ الظَّلاَمِ وَثَوْبُ اللَّيْلِ مَسْدُولُ

٤١- حتى وضعتُ يَمِينى لا أُنَازِعُهُ   فى كفٍّ ذِى نَقِماتٍ قِيلُه القِيلُ

٤٢- لَذاكَ أَهْيَبُ عندى إذ أُكلِّمُه   وقيل إنكَ مسبورٌ ومسئولُ

٤٣- من ضَيْغَمٍ من ضِراءِ الأُسْدِ مُخْدَرُه   ببَطْنِ عَثَّرَ غِيلٌ دونَه غِيلُ

٤٤- يَغْدُو فَيَلْحَمُ ضِرغَامَيْنِ عَيْشُهما   لحمٌ من القومِ مَعْفُورٌ خَرَاذِيلُ

٤٥- إذا يُسَاوِرُ قِرْنًا لا يَحِلُّ له   أن يترك القِرْنَ إلا وهو مفلولُ

٤٦- منه تَظَلُّ حَمِيرُ الوَحْشِ ضامزةً   ولا تُمَشِّى بِوادِيه الأَرَاجِيلُ

٤٧- ولا يَزالُ بِوادِيه أخو ثِقَةٍ   مُطَرَّحُ البَزِّ والدِّرْسانِ مأكولُ

٤٨- إنَّ الرسولَ لسَيْفٌ يُستضاءُ به   مهنَّدٌ من سُيُوفِ اللهِ مسلولُ

٤٩- فى عُصْبةٍ من قُرَيشٍ قال قائلُهم   ببَطْنِ مَكَّةَ لما أَسْلَموا زُولُوا

٥٠- زالُوا فما زال أنكاسٌ ولا كُشُفٌ   عند اللِّقاءِ ولا مِيلٌ مَعَازِيلُ

٥١- شُمُّ العَرَانِينِ أبطالٌ لَبُوسُهُمُ   من نَسْجِ داودَ فى الهَيْجا سَرَابِيلُ

٥٢- بِيضٌ سَوَابغُ قد شُكَّتْ لها حَلَقٌ   كأنّها حَلَقُ القَفْعاءِ مَجْدُولُ

٥٣- يَمْشُونَ مَشْيَ الجِمالِ الزُّهْرِ يَعْصِمُهم ضَرْبٌ إِذا عَرَّدَ السُّودُ التَّنابِيلُ
٥٤- لا يفرَحون إِذا نالت رِماحُهمُ قومًا ولَيْسُوا مَجازِيعًا إِذا نِيلُوا
٥٥- لا يَقَعُ الطَّعْنُ إِلاّ في نُحُورِهِمُ ما إِنْ لهم عن حِياضِ الموتِ تَهْلِيلُ

[12] قال الفَرَزْدَق

وَالْفَحْلُ عَلْقَمَةُ الَّذي كَانَتْ لَهُ حُلَلُ الْمُلُوكِ كَلامُهُ يُتَمَثَّلُ

[13] قال الأَخْطَل التَّغْلِبي

١- خَفَّ القَطِينُ، فَراحُوا منكَ، أو بَكَرُوا وأَزْعَجَتْهُمْ نَوًى، في صَرْفِها غِيَرُ
٢- كأنَّنِي شارِبٌ، يومَ استُبِدَّ بِهِمْ مِن قَرْقَفٍ، ضُمِّنَتْها حِمصُ، أو جَدَرُ
٣- جادَتْ بِها، مِن ذَواتِ القارِ، مُتْرَعةٌ كَلْفاءُ، يَنْحَتُّ عن خُرْطُومِها المَدَرُ
٤- لَذٌّ، أَصابَتْ حُمَيّاها مَقاتِلَهُ فلم تَكَدْ تَنْجَلِي عن قَلْبِهِ الخُمَرُ
٥- كأنَّنِيَ ذاكَ، أو ذُو لَوْعَةٍ، خَبَلَتْ أَوصالَهُ، أو أَصابَتْ قَلْبَهُ النُّشَرُ
٦- شَوْقًا إِليهم، ووَجْدًا، يومَ أُتْبِعُهُم طَرْفِيْ، ومِنهمُ، بِجَنْبَيْ كوكبٍ، زُمَرُ
٧- حَثُّوا المَطِيَّ، فَوَلَّتْنا مَناكِبَها وفي الخُدُورِ، إِذا باغَمْتَها، الصُّوَرُ
٨- يُبْرِقْنَ لِلقَوْمِ، حَتّى يَخْتَبِلْنَهُمُ ورأيُهُنَّ ضَعِيفٌ، حِينَ يُخْتَبَرُ
٩- يا قاتَلَ اللّهُ وَصْلَ الغانياتِ، إِذا أَيْقَنَّ أَنَّكَ مِمَّن قد زَها الكِبَرُ
١٠- أَعْرَضْنَ لَمّا حَنَى قَوْسِي مُوَتِّرُها وابيَضَّ، بعدَ سوادِ اللِّمَّةِ، الشَّعَرُ
١١- ما يَرْعَوِينَ إِلى داعٍ لِحاجَتِهِ ولا لَهُنَّ، إِلى ذي شَيْبَةٍ، وَطَرُ

١٢- شَرَّقْنَ، إذ عَصَرَ العِيْدانَ بارِحُها وأَيْبَسَتْ، غيرَ مَجْرى السِّنَّةِ، الخُضَرُ
١٣- فالعَيْنُ عانِيةٌ بالماءِ، تَسْفَحُهُ مِن نِيَّةٍ، في تَلاقي أَهلِها ضَرَرُ
١٤- مُنْقَضِبِيْنَ انقضابَ الحَبْلِ، يَتْبَعُهُمْ بَيْنَ الشَّقِيقِ، وعَيْنِ المَقْسِمِ، البَصَرُ
١٥- حَتّى هَبَطْنَ مِنَ الوادي، لِغَضْبَتِهِ، أَرضاً، تَحُلُّ بِها شَيْبانُ، أو غُبَرُ
١٦- حَتّى إذا هُنَّ وَرَّكْنَ القَصِيمَ، وقد أَشْرَفْنَ، أو قُلْنَ: هذا الخَنْدَقُ الحَفَرُ
١٧- وَقَعْنَ أُصْلاً، وعُجْنا من نَجائِبِنا وقد تُحُيِّنَ، مِن ذِي حاجةٍ، سَفَرُ
١٨- إلى امرئٍ، لا تُعَرِّينا نَوافِلُهُ أَظْفَرَهُ اللهُ، فَلْيَهْنِىءْ لَهُ الظَّفَرُ
١٩- الخائضِ الغَمْرَ، والمَيْمُونِ طائِرُهُ خَلِيفةِ اللهِ، يُسْتَسْقَى بهِ المَطَرُ
٢٠- والهَمُّ، بعدَ نَجِيِّ النَّفْسِ، يَبْعَثُهُ بالحَزْمِ، والأَصمعانِ: القلبُ والحَذَرُ
٢١- والمُسْتَمِرُّ بهِ أَمْرُ الجَميعِ، فَما يَغْتَرُّهُ، بَعدَ تَوكيدٍ لهُ، غَرَرُ
٢٢- وما الفُراتُ - إذا جاشَتْ حَوالبُهُ في حافَتَيْهِ، وفي أَوساطِهِ العُشَرُ
٢٣- وذَعْذَعَتْهُ رياحُ الصَّيْفِ، واضطَرَبَتْ فَوقَ الجَآجِىءِ، مِن آذِيِّهِ، غُدُرُ
٢٤- مُسْحَنْفِراً، مِن جِبالِ الرُّومِ، تَسْتُرُهُ مِنها أَكافِيفُ، فيها دُونَهُ زَوَرُ
٢٥- يوماً بأَجْوَدَ مِنهُ، حِينَ تَسأَلُهُ ولا بأَجْهَرَ مِنهُ، حينَ يُجْتَهَرُ
٢٦- ولم يَزَلْ بِكَ واشِيهِمْ، مَكْرُهُمُ حتَّى أَشاطُوا، بِغَيْبٍ، لَحْمَ مَنْ يَسَرُوا
٢٧- فمَنْ يَكُنْ طاوِياً عَنّا نَصِيحَتَهُ وفي يدَيْهِ، بِدُنْيا غَيْرِنا، حَصَرُ
٢٨- فَهْوَ فِداءُ أَمِيرِ المُؤْمِنينَ، إذا أَبْدَى النَّواجذَ يومٌ، باسِلٌ، ذَكَرُ

٢٩- مُفْتَرِشٌ كافتِراشِ اللَّيْثِ كَلْكَلَهُ   لِوَقْعَةٍ، كائِنٍ فِيها لَهُ جَزَرُ

٣٠- مُقَدِّمٌ مائَتَيْ أَلفٍ، لِمَنْزِلَةٍ   ما إنْ رَأى مِثْلَهُمْ جِنٌّ، ولا بَشَرُ

٣١- يَغْشَى القَناطِرَ، يَبْنِيها، ويَهْدِمُها   مُسَوِّمٌ، فَوقَهُ الرّاياتُ، والقَتَرُ

٣٢- حَتّى تَكونَ لَهُمْ بالطَّفِّ مَلْحَمَةٌ   وبالثَّوِيَّةِ، لم يُنْبَضْ بِها وَتَرُ

٣٣- وتَسْتَبِيْنَ لأَقوامٍ ضَلالَتُهُمْ   ويَسْتَقيْمَ الذي في خَدِّهِ صَعَرُ

٣٤- والمُسْتَقِلُّ بأَثقالِ العِراقِ، وقد   كانَتْ لهُ نِعْمَةٌ فِيهم، ومُدَّخَرُ

٣٥- في نَبْعَةٍ، مِن قُرَيشٍ، يَعْصِبُونَ بها   ما إنْ يُوازَى بأَعْلى نَبْتِها الشَّجَرُ

٣٦- تَعْلُو الهِضابَ، وحَلُّوا في أَرُومَتِها   أَهلُ الرِّباءِ، وأهلُ الفَخْرِ، إن فَخَروا

٣٧- حُشْدٌ على الحَقِّ، عَيّافُو الخَنا، أُنُفٌ   إذا أَلَمَّتْ بهم مَكْرُوهَةٌ صَبَرُوا

٣٨- وإنْ تَدَجَّتْ على الآفاقِ مُظْلِمَةٌ   كانَ لَهُمْ مَخْرَجٌ مِنها، ومُعْتَصَرُ

٣٩- أَعطاهُمُ اللهُ جَدّاً، يُنصَرُونَ بهِ   لا جَدَّ إلاّ صَغيرٌ، بَعْدُ، مُحْتَقَرُ

٤٠- لم يَأْشَرُوا فيهِ، إذْ كانُوا مَوالِيَهُ   ولو يَكونُ لِقَومٍ، غَيْرِهِمْ، أَشِرُوا

٤١- شُمْسُ العَداوَةِ، حَتّى يُستَقادَ لَهُمْ   وَأَعظَمُ النّاسِ أَحلاماً، إذا قَدَرُوا

٤٢- لا يَستَقِلُّ ذَوُو الأَضغانِ حَرْبَهُمُ   ولا يُبَيِّنُ في عِيْدانِهِمْ خَوَرُ

٤٣- هُمُ الذينَ يُبارُوْنَ الرِّياحَ، إذا   قَلَّ الطَّعامُ على العافِيْنَ، أو قَتَرُوا

٤٤- بَنِي أُمَيَّةَ، نُعْماكُمْ مُجَلِّلَةٌ   تَمَّتْ، فلا مِنَّةٌ فيها، ولا كَدَرُ

٤٥- بَنِي أُمَيَّةَ، قد ناضَلْتُ دُوْنَكُمُ   أَبناءَ قَومٍ، هُمُ آوَوْا، وهمْ نَصَرُوا

٤٦- أَفْحَمْتُ عَنكم بَني النَّجّارِ، قد عَلِمتْ عُلْيَا مَعَدٍّ، وكانوا طالمَا هَدَروا
٤٧- حتَّى استكانُوا، وهُمْ مِنِّي على مَضَضٍ والقَولُ يَنْفُذُ مالا تَنْفُذُ الإِبَرُ
٤٨- بَنِي أُمَيَّهَ، إِنِّيْ ناصِحٌ لَكُمُ فلا يَبِيْتَنَّ، فيكم، آمِناً زُفَرُ
٤٩- واتَّخِذُوْهُ عَدُوّاً، إِنَّ شاهِدَهُ وما تَغَيَّبَ، مِن أَخلاقِهِ، دَعَرُ
٥٠- إِنَّ الضَّغِيْنَةَ تَلقاها، وإِن قَدُمَتْ، كالعَرِّ، يَكْمُنُ حِيناً، ثُمَّ يَنْتَشِرُ
٥١- وقد نُصِرْتَ، أَميرَ المُؤمنينَ، بِنا لَمّا أَتاكَ، بِبَطْنِ الغُوطَةِ، الخَبَرُ
٥٢- يُعَرِّفُونَكَ رَأْسَ ابنِ الحُبابِ، وقد أَضْحَى، وللسَّيْفِ في خَيْشُومِهِ أَثَرُ
٥٣- لا يَسْمَعُ الصَّوْتَ، مُسْتَكّاً مَسامِعُهُ وليسَ يَنْطِقُ، حتَّى يَنْطِقَ الحَجَرُ
٥٤- أَمْسَتْ إِلى جانِبِ الحَشَّاكِ جِيفَتُهُ ورأسُهُ دُونَهُ اليَحْمُوْمُ، والصِّوَرُ
٥٥- يَسْأَلُهُ الصُّبْرُ مِن غسّانَ، إِذ حَضَرُوا والحَزْنُ: كيف قَراكَ الغِلْمَةُ، الجَشَرُ؟
٥٦- والحارثَ بنَ أبي عَوفٍ، لَعِبْنَ بِهِ حَتّى تَعاوَرَهُ العِقْبانُ، والسُّبَرُ
٥٧- وقَيْسَ عَيلانَ، حتَّى أَقْبَلُوا رَقَصاً فَبايَعُوكَ جِهاراً، بعدَ ما كَفَرُوا
٥٨- فلا هَدَى اللهُ قَيْساً، مِن ضَلالَتِهِمْ ولا لَعاً لِبَنِيْ ذَكْوانَ، إِذ عَثَرُوا
٥٩- ضَجُّوا، مِنَ الحَرْبِ، إِذ عَضَّتْ غَوارِبَهُمْ وقَيْسُ عَيلانَ، مِن أَخلاقِها الضَّجَرُ
٦٠- كانوا ذَوِي إِمَّةٍ، حتّى إذا عَلِقَتْ بِهِمْ حَبائلُ للشَّيطانِ، وابْتَهَرُوا
٦١- صُكُّوا على شارِفٍ، صَعْبٍ مَراكِبُها حَصَّاءَ، ليسَ لَها هُلْبٌ، ولا وَبَرُ
٦٢- ولَم يَزَلْ بِسُلَيْمٍ أَمْرُ جاهِلِها حتَّى تَعَيَّا بها الإِيرادُ، والصَّدَرُ

٦٣- إذ يَنْظُرُونَ، وهُمْ يَجْنُونَ حَنْظَلَهُمْ،   إلى الزَّوابي، فَقُلنا : بُعْدَ ما نَظَرُوا

٦٤- كرُّوا إلى حَرَّتَيْهِمْ، يَعْمُرُونَهما   كما تَكُرُّ إلى أوطانِها البَقَرُ

٦٥- فأَصْبَحَتْ، مِنْهُمُ، سِنْجارُ خالِيةً   فالمَحْلَبِيَّاتُ، فالخابُورُ، فالسُّرَرُ

٦٦- وما يُلاقُونَ فَرَّاصاً إلى نَسَبٍ   حَتّى يُلاقِيَ جدْيَ الفَرْقَدِ القَمَرُ

٦٧- ولا الضِّبابَ، إذا اخضرَّتْ عُيونُهُمُ   ولا عُصَيَّةَ، إلاَّ أنَّهُمْ بَشَرُ

٦٨- وما سَعَى منْهُمُ ساعٍ، ليُدْرِكَنا   إلاّ تَقاصرَ عَنّا، وهْوَ مُنْبهِرُ

٦٩- وقد أَصابَتْ كِلاباً، مِن عَداوَتِنا،   إحدَى الدَّواهي التي تُخْشَى، وتُنْتَظَرُ

٧٠- وقد تَفاقمَ أمْرٌ، غيرُ مُلتئِمٍ   ما بَيْنَنا فيهِ أَرحامٌ، ولا عِذَرُ

٧١- أمّا كُلَيْبُ بنُ يَرْبُوعٍ فليسَ لَهُمْ   عندَ المَكارِمِ لا وِرْدٌ، ولا صَدَرُ

٧٢- مُخَلَّفُونَ، ويَقْضِي النّاسُ أَمْرَهُمُ   وهُمْ بِغَيْبٍ، وفي عَمياءَ، مَا شَعَرُوا

٧٣- مُلَطَّمُونَ بأَعْقارِ الحِياضِ، فَما   يَنْفَكُّ، مِن دارِميٍّ، فيهِمِ، أَثَرُ

٧٤- بِئسَ الصُّحاةُ، وبِئسَ الشَّرْبُ شَرْبُهُمُ   إذا جَرَى فيهِمِ المُزَّاءُ، والسَّكَرُ

٧٥- قومٌ تَناهَتْ إليهِمْ كُلُّ فاحِشَةٍ   وكُلُّ مُخْزِيَةٍ، سُبَّتْ بِها مُضَرُ

٧٦- علَى العِيارات هَدّاجُونَ، قد بَلَغَتْ   نَجْرانَ، أوحُدِّثَتْ سَوءاتِهِم هَجَرُ

٧٧- الآكِلُونَ خَبيثَ الزّادِ، وَحْدَهُمُ   والسّائلُونَ بِظَهرِ الغَيْبِ : ما الخَبَرُ؟

٧٨- واذكُرْ غُدانَةَ عِدّاناً، مُزَنَّمَةً   مِنَ الحَبَلَّقِ، تُبْنَى حَوْلَها الصِّيَرُ

٧٩- تَمْذِي، إذا سَخُنَتْ في قُبْلِ أَدْرُعِها   وتَزْرَئِمُّ، إذا ما بَلَّها المَطَرُ

٨٠- وما غُدانَةُ في شَيْءٍ، مَكانَهُمُ، أَلحابِسُو الشَّاءِ، حَتّى تَفْضُلَ السُّؤَرُ
٨١- يَتَّصِلُونَ بِيَرْبُوعٍ، وَرِفْدُهُمُ عندَ التَّرافُدِ مَغْمُورٌ، ومُحْتَقَرُ
٨٢- صُفْرُ اللِّحَى مِن وَقُودِ الأَدْخِناتِ، إذا رَدَّ الرِّفادَ، وكَفَّ الحالِبِ، القِرَرُ
٨٣- ثم الإِيابُ إِلى سُودٍ، مُدَنَّسَةٍ ما تَسْتَحِمُّ إذا ما احْتَكَّتِ النُّقَرُ
٨٤- قد أَقْسَمَ المَجْدُ حَقّاً لا يُحالِفُهُمْ حتّى يُحالِفَ بَطْنَ الرّاحةِ الشَّعَرُ

[14] قال جَرِير

أنَسيتَ يومَكَ بالجزيرة بعدما كانت عواقِبُه عليك وبالا!
حملتْ عليك حُماةُ قيسٍ خيلَها شُعْثاً عوابسَ تحمِلِ الأبطالا
مازلتَ تحسِبُ كلّ شيء بعدهم خيلا تَكُرُّ عليكمُ ورجالا
زفرُ الرئيسُ أبو الهذيل أبادكم فسَبَى النساءَ وأحرز الأَموالا

[15] قال الأَخْطَل

ألا سائِلِ الجحّافَ هل هو ثائرٌ بِقَتْلَى أصيبتْ مِنْ سُلَيْم وعامرِ!
أجحافُ إِنْ نهبِطْ عليك فتلتقي عليك بحورٌ طامِياتُ الزواخِرِ
تكن مثل أبداءِ الحباب الذى جرى به البحرُ تزهاهُ رياحُ الصراصِرِ

[16] قال الجَحّاف السُلَمي

أبا مالكٍ هل لمتنى إذ حضضتَنى على القتل أمْ هل لامنى لك لائمى
أبا مالكٍ إنى أطعتُكَ فى الّتى حضضتَ عليها فعلَ حَرّانَ حازمِ

فإن تدعُنى أخرى أُجبْك بمثلها   وإنى لَطَبٌّ بالوغَى جِدٌّ عالِم

[17] قال عَلْقَمَة بن عَبَدَة

فَلاَ تَحْرِمَنِّي نَائِلاً عَنْ جَنَابَةٍ   فَإِنِّي آمْرُؤٌ وَسْطَ الْقِبَابِ غَرِيبُ

وَأَنْتَ آمْرُؤٌ أَفْضَتْ إِلَيْكَ أَمَانَتِي   وَقَبْلَكَ رَبَّتْنِي فَضِعْتُ رُبُوبُ

[18] قال الأَخْطَل التَّغْلِبي

١- عفا واسِطٌ من آلِ رَضْوَى، فَنَبْتَلُ   فَمُجْتَمَعُ الحُرَّيْنِ، فالصَّبْرُ أجمَلُ

٢- فَرابِيَةُ السَّكرانِ قَفْرٌ، فما بِها   لَهُمْ شَبَحٌ، إلاّ سَلامٌ، وَحَرْمَلُ

٣- صحا القلبُ إلاّ مِن ظَعائنَ، فاتَني   بِهِنَّ ابنُ خَلاّسٍ طُفيلٌ، وَعزْهَلُ

٤- كأنّي، غداةَ انصَعْنَ لِلبَيْنِ، مُسْلَمٌ   بِضَرْبَةِ عُنْقٍ، أو غَوِيٌّ مُعذَّلُ

٥- صَرِيْعُ مُدامٍ، يَرفَعُ الشَّرْبُ رأسَهُ   لِيَحْيا، وقد ماتَتْ عِظامٌ، ومَفْصِلُ

٦- نُهادِيْهِ أَحياناً، وحِيْناً نَجُرُّهُ   وما كادَ، إلاّ بالحُشاشَةِ، يَعْقِلُ

٧- إذا رَفعوا عَظماً تَحامَلَ صَدْرُهُ   وآخرُ، مِمّا نالَ مِنها، مُخَبَّلُ

٨- شَرِبْتُ، ولاقاني لِحِلٍّ أَلِيَّتي   قِطارٌ، تَرَوَّى مِن فِلَسْطِينَ، مُثْقَلُ

٩- عليهِ مِنَ المِعْزَى مُسوكٌ، رَوِيَّةٌ   مُمَلأَّةٌ، يُعلَى بِها، وتُعَدَّلُ

١٠- فقلت: اصبَحُوني، لا أبا لأبيكُمُ!   وما وَضَعوا الأثقالَ، إلاّ لِيَفعَلوا

١١- أناخُوا، فَجَرُّوا شاصِياتٍ، كأنَّها   رِجالٌ، مِنَ السُّودانِ، لم يَتَسَرْبَلُوا

١٢- وجاؤوا بِبَيْسانِيَّةٍ، هيَ - بَعْدَما   يَعُلُّ بها السّاقيْ - أَلَذُّ، وأَسْهَلُ

١٣- تَمُرُّ بها الأَيدي سَنِيْحاً، وبارحاً   وتُوضَعُ بـ« اللّهُمَّ حَيٍّ »، وتُحْمَلُ

١٤- فتُوقَفُ أحياناً، فيَفْصِلُ بينَنا   غِناءُ مُغَنٍّ، أو شِواءٌ مُرَعْبَلُ

١٥- فَلَذَّتْ لِمُرتاحٍ، وطابَتْ لِشاربٍ   وراجَعَني مِنها مِراحٌ، وأَخْيَلُ

١٦- فما لبَّثَتْنا نَشْوَةٌ، لَحِقَتْ بِنا   توابِعُها، مِمَّا نُعَلُّ، ونُنْهَلُ

*- فصَبُّوا عُقاراً في إناءٍ، كأنَّها   إذا لَمَحُوها -جُذْوَةٌ، تَتأَكَّلُ

١٧- تَدِبُّ دَبِيْباً في العِظام، كأنَّهُ   دَبِيْبُ نِمالٍ، في نَقاً يَتهيَّلُ

١٨- فقلتُ: اقتُلوها عنكمُ بِمِزاجِها   وأَطْيِبْ بها مَقتولةً، حِينَ تُقتَلُ

١٩- رَبَتْ، ورَبا في حَجْرِها ابنُ مَدينَةٍ   يَظَلُّ على مِسْحاتِهِ يَتَرَكَّلُ

٢٠- إذا خافَ، مِن نَجْمٍ، عليها ظَماءةً   أَدَبَّ إليها جَدوَلاً، يَتَسَلْسَلُ

٢١- أَعاذِلَ، إلاّ تُقْصِري عن مَلامَتي   أَدَعْكِ، وأَعمِدْ للذي كنتُ أفعَلُ

٢٢- وأَهجُرْكِ هِجْراناً جميلاً، ويَنْتَحي   لنا، مِن لَيالِينا العَوارِمِ، أَوَّلُ

٢٣- فلمّا انجلتْ عَنّي صَبابةُ عاشِقٍ   بَدا لِيَ مِن حاجاتِيَ المُتأَمَّلُ

٢٤- إلى هاجِسٍ، مِن آلِ ظَمياءَ، والّتي   أَتى دُونَها بابٌ، بِصِرِّيْنَ، مُقْفَلُ

٢٥- وَبَيْداءَ، مِمْحالٍ، كأنَّ نَعامَها   بأرجائها القُصْوَى، أَباعِرُ هُمَّلُ

٢٦- تَرَى لامعاتِ الآلِ فيها، كأنَّها   رِجالٌ، تَعَرَّى تارةً، وتَسَرْبَلُ

٢٧- وَجَوْزِ فَلاةٍ، ما يُغَمِّضُ رَكْبُها   ولا عَيْنُ هاديها، مِنَ الخَوفِ، تَغْفُلُ

٢٨- بِكُلِّ بَعيدِ الغَوْلِ، لا يُهتدَى لهُ   بِعِرْفانِ أَعلامٍ، وَما فيهِ مَنْهَلُ

٢٩- مَلاعِبُ جِنّانٍ، كأنَّ تُرابَها، إذا اطَّرَدَتْ فيهِ الرِّياحُ، مُغَرْبَلُ

٣٠- أَجَزْتُ، إذا الحِرباءُ أوفَى، كأنَّهُ مُصَلٍّ يَمانٍ، أو أسيْرٌ مُكَبَّلُ

٣١- إلى ابنِ أَسيْدٍ، خالدٍ، أَرقلَتْ بنا مَسانِيْفُ، تَعْرَوْري فَلاةً، تَغَوَّلُ

٣٢- تَرَى الثَّعْلَبَ الحَوْليَّ فيها، كأَنَّهُ إذا ما علا نَشْزاً، حِصانٌ مُجَلَّلُ

٣٣- تَرى العِرْمِسَ الوَجناءَ، يَضرِبُ حاذَها ضَئيلٌ، كَفَرُّوجِ الدَّجاجةِ، مُعْجَلُ

٣٤- يَشُقُّ سَماحِيقَ السَّلاَ عنَ جنيْنِها أَخوُ قَفْرةٍ، بادي السَّغابةِ، أَطْحَلُ

٣٥- فما زالَ عَنها السَّيْرُ حتّى تَواضَعتْ عَرائِكُها، ممّا تُحَلُّ، وتُرحَلُ

٣٦- وتَكْليفُناها كلَّ نازِحَةِ الصُّوَى شَطُونٍ، تَرَى حِرْباءَها يَتَمَلْمَلُ

٣٧- وقد ضَمَرتْ، حتّى كأنّ عُيُونَها بَقايا قِلاتٍ، أو رَكيٌّ مُمَكَّلُ

٣٨- وغارتْ عُيونُ العِيْسِ، والتقَتِ العُرَى فَهُنَّ، مِن الضَّرّاءِ والجَهْدِ، نُحَّلُ

٣٩- وصارتْ بَقاياها إلى كلِّ حُرَّةٍ لَها، بعدَ إسآدٍ، مِراحٌ وأَفْكَلُ

٤٠- وَقَعْنَ وُقوعَ الطَّيرِ فيها، وما بِها سِوَى جِرَّةٍ، يَرْجِعْنَها، مُتَعَلَّلُ

٤١- وإلاّ مَبالٌ، آجنٌ، في مُناخِها ومُضْطَمِراتٌ، كالفَلافِلِ، ذُبَّلُ

٤٢- حَوامِلُ حاجاتٍ، ثِقالٍ، تَرُدُّها إلى حَسَنِ النُّعمَى، سوَاهِمُ نُسَّلُ

٤٣- إلى خالدٍ، حَتّى أَنَخْنَ بخالِدٍ فنِعْمَ الفَتَى يُرجَى، ونِعْمَ المُؤَمَّلُ

٤٤- أخالدُ، مَأوَاكُمْ لِمَنْ حَلَّ واسعٌ وكفّاكَ غَيثٌ، للصَّعاليكِ، مُرْسَلُ

٤٥- هُو القائدُ المَيْمُونُ، والمُبْتَغَى بهِ ثَباتُ رَحىً، كانتْ قَديماً تَزَلْزَلُ

٤٦- أَبَى عُوْدُكَ، المَعْجُومُ، إلاّ صَلابَةً   وكفّاكَ إلاّ نائلاً، حينَ تُسْأَلُ

٤٧- ألا، أيُّها السَّاعي ليُدْرِكَ خالداً،   تَناهَ، وأَقْصِرْ بعضَ ما أنتَ تَفعَلُ

٤٨- فهل أنتَ، إنْ مَدَّ المَدَى لكَ خالدٌ،   مُوازِنُهُ، أو حاملٌ ما يُحَمَّلُ؟

٤٩- أَبَى لكَ أنْ تَسْطِيْعَهُ، أو تَنالَهُ،   حَديثٌ، شآكَ القومُ فيه، وأوَّلُ

٥٠- أُمَيَّةُ، والعاصي، وإنْ يَدْعُ خالدٌ   يُجِبْهُ هِشامٌ، لِلفَعالِ، ونَوْفَلُ

٥١- أولئك عينُ الماءِ فيهم، وعِنْدَهمُ   من الخِيْفَةِ المَنْجاةُ، والمُتَحوَّلُ

٥٢- سَقَى اللهُ أرضاً، خالدٌ خَيْرُ أهلِها،   بمُسْتَفْرِغٍ، باتَتْ عَزالِيْهِ تَسْحَلُ

٥٣- إذا طَعَنَتْ رِيحُ الصَّبا في فُرُوجِهِ   تَحَلَّبَ رَيّانُ الأَسافِلِ، أَنْجَلُ

٥٤- إذا زَعْزَعَتْهُ الرِّيحُ، جَرَّ ذُيُولَهُ   كما زَحَفَتْ عُوْذٌ، ثِقالٌ، تُطَفِّلُ

٥٥- مُلِحٌّ، كأنَّ البَرْقَ في حَجَراتِهِ   مَصابيحُ، أو أَقْرابُ بُلْقٍ، تَجَفَّلُ

٥٦- فلمّا انتحَى نحوَ اليَمامةِ، قاصِداً،   دَعَتْهُ الجَنُوبُ، فانْثَنَى، يَتَخَزَّلُ

٥٧- سَقَى لَعْلَعاً، والقُرْنَتَيْنِ، فلم يَكَدْ   بأثقالِهِ، عَن لَعْلَعٍ، يَتَحمّلُ

٥٨- وغادَرَ أُكْمَ الحَزْنِ تَطْفُو، كأنَّها   ، بما احتَفَلَتْ مِنْهُ، رَواجِنُ، قُفَّلُ

٥٩- وشَرَّقَ لِلدَّهنا، مُلِثٌّ، كأنَّه   مُحَمَّلُ بَزٍّ، ذو جَلاجِلَ، مُثْقَلُ

٦٠- وَبالمَعْرَسانِيّاتِ حَلَّ، وأَرْزَمَتْ   بِرَوْضِ القَطا، منهُ، مَطافِلُ حُفَّلُ

٦١- لقد أوقعَ الجَحّافُ بالبِشْرِ وَقْعَةً   إلى اللهِ مِنها المُشتكَى، والمُعوَّلُ

٦٢- فسائلْ بَني مَروانَ: ما بالُ ذِمَّةٍ   وحَبْلٍ، ضَعِيفٍ، لا يَزال يُوَصَّلُ؟

٦٣- بِنَزْوةِ لِصٍّ، بعدَ ما مرَّ مُصْعَبٌ　　بأشْعَثَ، لا يُفْلَى، ولا هُوَ يُغْسَلُ
٦٤- أتاكَ بهِ الجَحّافُ، ثُمَّ أَمَرْتَهُ　　بِجيْرانِكُمْ، وَسْطَ البُيوتِ تُقَتَّلُ!
٦٥- لقد كانَ للجيرانِ ما لو دَعَوْتُمُ　　به عاقِلَ الأَروَى، أتتْكُم تنزَّلُ
٦٦- فإلاّ تُغَيِّرْها قُرَيشٌ بِمُلْكِها　　يكُنْ عن قُريشٍ مُسْتَمازٌ، ومَزْحَلُ
٦٧- ونَعْرُرْ أُناساً عَرَّةً، يَكْرَهُونَها　　ونَحْيا كِراماً، أو نَموتَ، فنُقْتَلُ
٦٨- وإنْ تَحمِلُوا عنْهم، فما مِن حَمالَةٍ　　، وإنْ ثَقُلَتْ، إلاّ دَمُ القومِ أَثْقَلُ
٦٩- وإنْ تَعْرِضُوا فيها لنا الحقَّ، لا نكُنْ　　عنِ الحقِّ عُمياناً، بلِ الحقَّ نسأَلُ
٧٠- وقد نَنْزِلُ الثَّغرَ المَخُوفَ، ويُتّقَى　　بِنا البأسُ، واليومُ الأغَرُّ المُحَجَّلُ

[19] قال تَأَبَّطَ شَرّاً

حَلَّتِ الخَمْرُ وكانَتْ حَراماً　　وبِلأْيٍ ما ألَمَّتْ تَحِلُّ
فَاسْقِنِيها يا سَوادَ بنَ عَمْرٍو　　إنَّ جِسْمِي بَعْدَ خالِي لَخَلُّ

[20] قال أبو العَتاهِيَة

١- أَلا ما لِسَيِّدَتِي ما لَها　　أَدَلاًّ فأَحْمِلَ إدْلالَها
٢- وإلاَّ فَفِيمَ تَجَنَّتْ وَما　　جَنَيْتُ سَقَى اللّهُ أطْلالَها
٣- أَلاَ إنَّ جارِيَةً لِلإمَا　　مِ قَدْ أُسْكِنَ الْحُبُّ سِرْبالَها
٤- مَشَتْ بَيْنَ حُورٍ قِصارِ الْخُطا　　تُجاذِبُ في الْمَشْيِ أَكْفالَها
٥- وَقَد أتْعَبَ اللّهُ نَفسى بِها　　وَأَتْعَبَ بِاللَّوْمِ عُذّالَها

٦- كَأَنَّ بَعَيْنَيَّ فى حَيْثُما   سَلَكْتُ مِنَ الأَرْضِ تِمْثالَها
٧- أَتَتْهُ الْخِلافَةُ مُنْقادَةً   إِلَيهِ تُجَرِّرُ أذْيالَها
٨- وَلَمْ تَكُ تَصْلُحُ إلاَّ لَهُ   وَلَمْ يَكُ يَصْلُحُ إلاَّ لَها
٩- وَلَوْ رامَها أَحَدٌ غَيْرُهُ   لَزُلْزِلَتِ الأَرْضُ زِلْزالَها
١٠- وَلَوْ لَمْ تُطِعْهُ بَناتُ الْقُلوبِ   لَما قَبِلَ اللهُ أَعْمالَها
١١- وَإِنَّ الْخَلِيفَةَ مِنْ بُغْضِ: لا   إلَيْهِ لَيُبْغِضُ مَنْ قالَها

[21] قال أَبو العَتَاهِيَة

ولقد تَنَسّمتُ الرياحَ لحاجتى   فإِذا لها من راحتَيْكَ نسيمُ
أشْربتُ نفسى من رجائك ماله   عَنَقٌ يَخُبّ إِليك بى ورَسِيمُ
وَرَميتُ نحوَ سماءِ جَوْدِك ناظِرى   أرْعَى مخايلَ بَرْقِهِ وأَشيمُ
ولربّما آستيأستُ ثم أقولُ لا،   إنّ الّذى ضَمِنَ النجاحَ كريمُ

[22] قال أبو تَمَّام

١- السَّيْفُ أَصْدَقُ أَنْبَاءً مِنَ الكُتُبِ   فى حَدِّهِ الحَدُّ بَيْنَ الجِدِّ واللَّعِبِ
٢- بيضُ الصَّفَائِحِ لا سُودُ الصَّحَائِفِ فى   مُتونِهِنَّ جِلاءُ الشَّكِّ والرِّيَبِ
٣- والعِلْمُ فِى شُهُبِ الأَرْمَاحِ لامِعَةً   بَيْنَ الخَمِيسَيْنِ لا فى السَّبْعَةِ الشُّهُبِ
٤- أَيْنَ الرِّوايَةُ أَمْ أَيْنَ النُّجومُ ومَا   صَاغُوه مِنْ زُخْرُفٍ فيها ومنْ كَذِبِ
٥- تَخَرُّصاً وأَحَادِيثاً مُلَفَّقَةً   لَيْسَتْ بِنَبْعٍ إذَا عُدَّتْ ولا غَرَبِ

٦- عَجَائِباً زَعَمُوا الأَيَّامَ مُجْفِلَةً   عَنْهُنَّ فى صَفَرِ الأَصْفَارِ أَوْ رَجَبِ

٧- وخَوَّفُوا النَّاسَ مِنْ دَهْيَاءَ مُظْلِمَةٍ   إِذَا بَدَا الكَوْكَبُ الْغَرْبِيُّ ذُو الذَّنَبِ

٨- وصَيَّرُوا اْلأَبْرُجَ العُلْيَا مُرَتَّبَةً   مَا كانَ مُنْقَلِباً أَوْ غَيْرَ مُنْقَلِبِ

٩- يَقْضُونَ بِالأَمْرِ عَنْها وهِيَ غَافِلَةٌ   ما دارَ فى فَلَكٍ مِنْها وفى قُطُبِ

١٠- لَوْ بَيَّنَتْ قَطُّ أَمْرًا قَبْلَ مَوقِعِهِ   لَمْ تُخْفِ مَا حَلَّ بِالأَوْثَانِ والصُّلُبِ

١١- فَتْحَ الفُتوحِ تَعَالَى أَنْ يُحِيطَ بِهِ   نَظْمٌ مِنَ الشِّعْرِ أَوْ نَثْرٌ مِنَ الخُطَبِ

١٢- فَتْحٌ تَفَتَّحُ أَبْوَابُ السَّماءِ لَهُ   وتَبْرُزُ اْلأَرْضُ فى أَثْوابِهَا القُشُبِ

١٣- يَا يَوْمَ وَقْعَةِ عَمُّورِيَّةَ انْصَرَفَتْ   مِنْكَ المُنَى حُفَّلاً مَعْسُولَةَ الحَلَبِ

١٤- أَبقَيْتَ جَدَّ بَنِى الإِسلامِ فى صَعَدٍ   والمشركين وَدارَ الشِّرْكِ فى صَبَبِ

١٥- أُمٌّ لَهُمْ لَوْ رَجَوْا أَنْ تُفْتَدَى جَعَلُوا   فِدَاءَهَا كُلَّ أُمٍّ مِنْهُمُ وَأَبِ

١٦- وبَرْزَةُ الوَجْهِ قَدْ أَعْيَتْ رِيَاضَتُهَا   كِسْرَى وصَدَّتْ صُدُودًا عَنْ أَبِى كَرِبِ

١٧- بِكْرٌ فَمَا افْتَرَعَتْهَا كفُّ حَادِثَةٍ   ولا تَرَقَّتْ إِلَيْهَا هِمَّةُ النُّوَبِ

١٨- مِنْ عَهْدِ إِسْكَنْدَرٍ أَوْ قَبْلَ ذَلِكَ قَدْ   شَابَتْ نَوَاصِى اللَّيَالِى وهْىَ لَمْ تَشِبِ

١٩- حَتَّى إِذَا مَخَّضَ اللهُ السِّنِينَ لَهَا   مَخْضَ البَخِيلَةِ كانَتْ زُبْدَةَ الحِقَبِ

٢٠- أَتَتْهُمُ الكُرْبَةُ السَّوْدَاءُ سَادِرَةً   مِنْهَا وكَانَ اسْمُهَا فَرَّاجَةَ الكُرَبِ

٢١- جَرَى لَهَا الفَأْلُ بَرْحاً يَوْمَ أَنقِرَةٍ   إِذْ غُودِرَتْ وَحْشَةَ السَّاحَاتِ والرُّحَبِ

٢٢- لَمَّا رَأَتْ أُخْتَها بِالأَمْسِ قَدْ خَرِبَتْ   كانَ الْخَرَابُ لَهَا أَعْدَى مِنَ الجَرَبِ

٢٣- كَمْ بَيْنَ حِيطَانِهَا مِنْ فَارِسٍ بَطَلِ   قَانِى الذَّوَائِبِ مِنْ آنِى دَمٍ سَرِبِ

٢٤- بِسُنَّةِ السَّيْفِ وَالْحِنَّاءُ مِنْ دَمِهِ   لَا سُنَّةِ الدِّينِ وَالْإِسْلَامِ مُخْتَضِبِ

٢٥- لَقَدْ تَرَكْتَ أَمِيرَ الْمُؤْمِنِينَ بِهَا   لِلنَّارِ يَوْماً ذَلِيلَ الصَّخْرِ وَالْخَشَبِ

٢٦- غَادَرْتَ فِيهَا بَهِيمَ اللَّيْلِ وَهُوَ ضُحًى   يَشُلُّهُ وَسَطَهَا صُبْحٌ مِنَ اللَّهَبِ

٢٧- حَتَّى كَأَنَّ جَلَابِيبَ الدُّجَى رَغِبَتْ   عَنْ لَوْنِهَا وَكَأَنَّ الشَّمْسَ لَمْ تَغِبِ

٢٨- ضَوْءٌ مِنَ النَّارِ وَالظَّلْمَاءُ عَاكِفَةٌ   وَظُلْمَةٌ مِنْ دُخَانٍ فِى ضُحًى شَحِبِ

٢٩- فَالشَّمْسُ طَالِعَةٌ مِنْ ذَا وَقَدْ أَفَلَتْ   وَالشَّمْسُ وَاجِبَةٌ مِنْ ذَا وَلَمْ تَجِبِ

٣٠- تَصَرَّحَ الدَّهْرُ تَصْرِيحَ الْغَمَامِ لَهَا   عَنْ يَوْمِ هَيْجَاءَ مِنْهَا طَاهِرٍ جُنُبِ

٣١- لَمْ تَطْلُعِ الشَّمْسُ فِيهِ يَوْمَ ذَاكَ عَلَى   بَانٍ بِأَهْلٍ وَلَمْ تَغْرُبْ عَلَى عَزَبِ

٣٢- مَا رَبْعُ مَيَّةَ مَعْمُوراً يُطِيفُ بِهِ   غَيْلَانُ أَبْهَى رُبًى مِنْ رَبْعِهَا الْخَرِبِ

٣٣- وَلَا الْخُدُودُ وَقَدْ أُدْمِينَ مِنْ خَجَلٍ   أَشْهَى إِلَى نَاظِرٍ مِنْ خَدِّهَا التَّرِبِ

٣٤- سَمَاجَةً غَنِيَتْ مِنَّا الْعُيُونُ بِهَا   عَنْ كُلِّ حُسْنٍ بَدَا أَوْ مَنْظَرٍ عَجَبِ

٣٥- وَحُسْنُ مُنْقَلَبٍ تَنْدُو عَوَاقِبُهُ   جَاءَتْ بَشَاشَتُهُ مِنْ سُوءِ مُنْقَلَبِ

٣٦- لَوْ يَعْلَمُ الْكُفْرُ كَمْ مِنْ أَعْصُرٍ كَمَنَتْ   لَهُ الْعَوَاقِبُ بَيْنَ السُّمْرِ وَالْقُضُبِ

٣٧- تَدْبِيرُ مُعْتَصِمٍ بِاللهِ مُنْتَقِمٍ   لِلّهِ مُرْتَقِبٍ فِى اللهِ مُرْتَغِبِ

٣٨- وَمُطْعَمِ النَّصْرِ لَمْ تَكْهَمْ أَسِنَّتُهُ   يَوْماً وَلَا حُجِبَتْ عَنْ رُوحِ مُحْتَجِبِ

٣٩- لَمْ يَغْزُ قَوْماً وَلَمْ يَنْهَدْ إِلَى بَلَدِ   إِلَّا تَقَدَّمَهُ جَيْشٌ مِنَ الرُّعُبِ

٤٠- لَوْلَمْ يَقُدْ جَحْفَلاً يَوْمَ الْوَغَى لَغَدَا   مِنْ نَفْسِهِ وَحْدَهَا فى جَحْفَلٍ لَجِبِ

٤١- رَمَى بِكَ اللّٰهُ بُرْجَيْهَا فَهَدَّمَها   وَلَوْ رَمَى بِكَ غَيْرُ اللّٰهِ لَمْ يُصِبِ

٤٢- مِنْ بَعْدِ ما أَشَّبُوهَا وَاثِقِينَ بِهَا   واللّٰهُ مِفْتاحُ بَابِ المَعْقِلِ الأَشِبِ

٤٣- وقَال ذُو أَمْرِهِمْ لا مَرْتَعٌ صَدَدٌ   للسَّارِحِينَ ولَيْسَ الوِرْدُ مِنْ كَثَبِ

٤٤- أَمَانِياً سَلَبَتْهُمْ نُجْحَ هاجِسِها   ظُبَى السُّيوفِ وأَطْرافُ القَنَا السُّلُبِ

٤٥- إِنَّ الحِمَامَيْنِ مِنْ بِيضٍ ومِن سُمُرٍ   دَلْوَا الحَيَاتَيْنِ مِن مَاءٍ ومن عُشُبِ

٤٦- لَبَّيْتَ صَوْتاً زِبَطْرِياً هَرَقْتَ لَهُ   كَأْسَ الكَرَى ورُضَابَ الخُرَّدِ العُرُبِ

٤٧- عَداكَ حَرُّ الثُّغُورِ المُسْتَضَامَةِ عَنْ   بَرْدِ الثُّغُور وعَنْ سَلْسَالِها الحَصِبِ

٤٨- أَجَبْتَهُ مُعْلِناً بالسَّيْفِ مُنْصَلِتاً   وَلَوْ أَجَبْتَ بِغَيْرِ السَّيْفِ لَمْ تُجِبِ

٤٩- حَتَّى تَرَكْتَ عَمُودَ الشِّرْكِ مُنْعَفِرًا   وَلَم تُعَرِّجْ عَلَى الأَوْتَادِ وَالطُّنُبِ

٥٠- لَّما رَأَى الحَرْبَ رَأْىَ العَيْنِ تُوفَلِسٌ   والحَرْبُ مُشْتَقَّةُ المَعْنَى مِنَ الحَرَبِ

٥١- غَدَا يُصَرِّفُ بِالأَمْوال جِرْيَتَها   فَعَزَّهُ البَحْرُ ذُو التَّيارِ والحَدَبِ

٥٢- هَيْهَاتَ! زُعْزِعَتِ الأَرْضُ الوَقورُ بِهِ   عَن غَزْوِ مُحْتَسِبٍ لا غَزْوِ مُكتَسِبِ

٥٣- لَمْ يُنفِق الذهَبَ المُرْبِى بكَثْرَتِهِ   على الحَصَى وبِهِ فَقْرٌ إِلى الذَّهَبِ

٥٤- إِنَّ الأُسُودَ أُسُودَ الغِيلِ هِمَّتُها   يَوْمَ الكَرِيهَةِ فى المَسْلوبِ لا السَّلَبِ

٥٥- وَلَّى وقَدْ أَلجَمَ الخَطِّىُّ مَنْطِقَهُ   بِسَكْتَةٍ تَحْتَهَا الأَحَشَاءُ فى صَخَبِ

٥٦- أَحْذَى قَرَابِينَهُ صَرْفَ الرَّدَى ومَضَى   يَحْتَثُّ أَنْجَى مَطَايَاهُ مِنَ الهَرَبِ

٥٧- مُوَكَّلاً بِيَفَاعِ الأَرْضِ يُشْرِفُهُ   مِنْ خِفَّةِ الخَوْفِ لا مِنْ خِفَّةِ الطرَبِ

٥٨- إنْ يَعْدُ مِنْ حَرِّهَا عَدْوَ الظَّلِيمِ فَقَدْ   أَوْسَعْتَ جاحِمَهَا مِنْ كَثْرَةِ الحَطَبِ

٥٩- تِسْعُونَ أَلْفاً كَآسَادِ الشَّرَى نَضِجَتْ   أَعْمارُهُمْ قَبْلَ نُضْجِ التِّينِ والعِنَبِ

٦٠- يا رُبَّ حَوْبَاءَ لَمَّا اجْتُثَّ دابِرُهُمْ   طابَتْ ولَوْ ضُمِّخَتْ بالمِسْكِ لم تَطِبِ

٦١- ومُغْضَبٍ رَجَعَتْ بِيضُ السُّيُوفِ بِهِ   حَيَّ الرِّضَا مِنْ رَدَاهُمْ مَيِّتَ الغَضَبِ

٦٢- والحَرْبُ قائِمَةٌ فى مأْزِقٍ لَجِجٍ   تَجْثُو القِيَامُ بِهِ صُغْرًا على الرُّكَبِ

٦٣- كَمْ نِيلَ تحت سَناهَا مِن سَنا قَمَرٍ   وتَحْتَ عارِضِهَا مِنْ عَارِضٍ شَنِبِ

٦٤- كَمْ كانَ فى قَطْعِ أَسْبَابِ الرِّقَابِ بِهَا   إلى المُخَدَّرَةِ العَذْرَاءِ مِنْ سَبَبِ

٦٥- كَمْ أَحْرَزَتْ قُضُبُ الهِنْدِيِّ مُصْلَتَةً   تَهْتَزُّ مِنْ قُضُبٍ تَهْتَزُّ فى كُثُبِ

٦٦- بِيضٌ إذا انتُضِيَتْ مِنْ حُجْبِها رَجَعَتْ   أَحَقَّ بالبِيضِ أَتْرَاباً مِنَ الحُجُبِ

٦٧- خَلِيفَةَ اللهِ جَازَى اللهُ سعْيَكَ عَنْ   جُرْثُومَةِ الدِّينِ والإِسْلاَمِ والحَسَبِ

٦٨- بَصُرْتَ بالرَّاحَةِ الكُبْرَى فَلَمْ تَرَها   تُنَالُ إلاَّ على جِسْرٍ مِنَ التَّعَبِ

٦٩- إن كان بَيْنَ صُرُوفِ الدَّهْرِ مِن رَحِمٍ   مَوْصُولَةٍ أَوْ ذِمَامٍ غَيْرِ مُنْقَضِبِ

٧٠- فَبَيْنَ أَيَّامِكَ اللاَّتى نُصِرْتَ بِها   وبَيْنَ أَيَّامِ بَدْرٍ أَقْرَبُ النَّسَبِ

٧١- أَبْقَتْ بَنى الأَصْفَرِ المِمْرَاضِ كاسْمِهِمُ   صُفْرَ الوُجُوهِ وجَلَّتْ أَوْجُهَ العَرَبِ

[23] قال أبو الطَّيِّب المُتَنبِّي

١- لِكُلِّ امْرِئٍ مِن دَهْرِهِ ما تَعَوَّدَا   وعاداتُ سيفِ الدَّوْلةِ الطَّعْنُ فى العِدا

٢- وأنْ يُكْذِبَ الإرْجافَ عنهُ بضِدِّهِ   ويُمْسِي بِمَا تَنْوِي أعادِيهِ أسْعَدَا

٣- وَرُبَّ مُرِيدٍ ضَرَّهُ ضَرَّ نَفْسَهُ   وهادٍ إليهِ الجَيْشَ أهْدى وَما هدَى

٤- وَمُسْتَكْبِرٍ لَمْ يَعْرِفِ اللهَ ساعَةً   رأى سَيْفَهُ فى كَفِّهِ فتَشَهَّدَا

٥- هُوَ البحرُ غُصْ فيهِ إذا كانَ رَاكِدًا   عَلى الدُّرِّ وَاحْذَرْهُ إذا كانَ مُزْبِدا

٦- فإنّى رأيْتُ البَحْرَ يَعْثُرُ بالفَتى   وَهَذَا الَّذِى يَأْتِى الفَتى مُتَعَمِّدَا

٧- تَظَلُّ مُلُوكُ الأرْضِ خاشِعَةً لَهُ   تُفارِقُهُ هَلْكَى وَتَلْقاهُ سُجَّدَا

٨- وتُحْيِى لَهُ المَالَ الصَّوَارِمُ والقَنا   ويَقْتُلُ ما يُحْيِى التَّبَسُّمُ والجَدَا

٩- ذَكِيٌّ تَظَنِّيهِ طَلِيعَةُ عَيْنِهِ   يَرَى قَلْبُهُ فِى يَوْمِهِ ما تَرَى غَدَا

١٠- وَصُولٌ إلى المُسْتَصْعَباتِ بِخَيْلِهِ   فلوْ كانَ قَرْنُ الشَّمسِ ماءً لأَوْرَدَا

١١- لذلكَ سَمَّى ابْنُ الدُّمُسْتُقِ يَوْمَهُ   مَمَاتا وسَمَّاهُ الدُّمُسْتُقُ مَوْلِدَا

١٢- سَرَيْتُ إلى جَيْحانَ مِنْ أرْضِ آمِدٍ   ثَلاثا لقدْ أدْناكَ رَكْضٌ وأبْعَدَا

١٣- فَوَلَّى وأعْطاكَ ابْنَهُ وجُيُوشَهُ   جَمِيعا ولَمْ يُعْطِ الجَمِيعَ لِيُحْمَدَا

١٤- عَرَضْتَ لَهُ دُونَ الحَياةِ وَطَرْفِهِ   وأبْصَرَ سَيْفَ اللهِ مِنْكَ مُجَرَّدَا

١٥- وَما طَلَبَتْ زُرْقُ الأَسِنَّةِ غَيْرَهُ   ولَكِنَّ قُسْطَنْطِينَ كانَ لهُ الفِدَا

١٦- فَأصْبَحَ يَجْتابُ المُسُوحَ مَخَافَةً   وَقَدْ كانَ يجْتابُ الدّلاصَ المُسَرَّدا

١٧- وَيمْشِي بهِ العُكَّازُ فِى الدَّيْرِ تائِبا   وَما كانَ يَرْضَى مَشْىَ أشقَرَ أجْرَدَا

١٨- وَما تابَ حتى غادَرَ الكَرُّ وَجْهَهُ   جَرِيحا وَخَلَّى جَفْنَهُ النَّقْعُ أرْمَدَا

١٩- فَلَوْ كانَ يُنْجِى مِنْ عَلِيٍّ تَرَهُّبٌ   تَرَهَّبَتِ الأَمْلاكُ مَثْنَى وَمَوْحَدَا

٢٠- وكُلُّ امْرِئٍ فِى الشَّرْقِ والغَرْبِ بَعْدَها   يُعِدُّ لَهُ ثَوْبا مِنَ الشَّعْرِ أَسْوَدَا

٢١- هَنِيئًا لكَ العِيدُ الَّذى أنْتَ عِيدُهُ   وَعِيدٌ لِمَنْ سَمَّى وضَحَّى وَعَيَّدَا

٢٢- وَلا زَالَتِ الأَعْيادُ لُبْسَكَ بَعْدَهُ   تُسَلَّمُ مَخْرُوقا وتُعْطِى مُجَدَّدَا

٢٣- فَذا اليَوْمُ فِى الأَيَّامِ مِثْلُكَ فِى الوَرَى   كَما كُنْتَ فِيهِمْ أوْ حَدًا كانَ أوْ حَدَا

٢٤- هُوَ الجَدُّ حتى تَفْضُلَ العَيْنُ أُخْتَها   وحتى يَصِيرَ اليَوْمُ للْيَوْمِ سَيِّدَا

٢٥- فَيا عَجَبا مِنْ دَائِلٍ أنْتَ سَيْفُهُ   أمَا يَتَوَقَّى شَفْرَتيْ ما تَقَلَّدَا

٢٦- وَمَنْ يجْعَلِ الضِّرْغامَ بازًا لِصَيْدِهِ   يُصَيِّدُهُ الضِّرْغامُ فِيما تَصَيَّدَا

٢٧- رَأيتُكَ مَحْضَ الحِلْمِ فِى مَحْضِ قُدْرةٍ   وَلَوْ شِئْتَ كانَ الحِلْمُ مِنْكَ المُهَنَّدَا

٢٨- وَما قَتَلَ الأَحْرارَ كالعَفْوِ عَنْهُمْ   وَمَنْ لَكَ بالحُرِّ الَّذى يَحْفَظُ اليَدَا

٢٩- إذا أنْتَ أكْرَمْتَ الكَرِيمَ مَلَكْتَهُ   وَإنْ أنتَ أكْرَمْتَ اللَّئِيمَ تَمَرَّدَا

٣٠- وَوَضْعُ النَّدَى فِى مَوْضِعِ السَّيْفِ بالعُلا   مُضِرٌّ كَوَضْعِ السَّيْفِ فِى مَوْضِعِ النَّدَى

٣١- وَلَكِنْ تَفُوقُ الناسَ رَأيا وحِكْمةً   كَما فُقْتَهُمْ حالاً وَنَفْسا ومَحْتِدَا

٣٢- يَدِقُّ عَلى الأَفْكارِ ما أنْتَ فاعِلٌ   فَيُتْرَكُ ما يَخْفَى ويُؤْخَذُ ما بَدَا

٣٣- أزِلْ حَسَدَ الحُسَّادِ عَنِّى بكَبْتِهِم   فأنْتَ الَّذى صَيَّرْتَهُمْ لى حُسَّدَا

٣٤- إذا شَدَّ زَنْدى حُسْنُ رَأيِكَ فِى يَدى   ضَرَبْتُ بنَصْلٍ يقطَعُ الهَامَ مُغْمَدَا

٣٥- وَما أنا إلاَّ سَمْهَرِيّ حَمَلْتَهُ   فَزَيَّنَ مَعْرُوضاً وَرَاعَ مُسَدَّدَا

٣٦- وَما الدَّهْرُ إلاَّ مِن رُوَاةِ قَلائِدِى   إذا قُلتُ شِعْرًا أصْبحَ الدَّهرُ مُنْشِدَا

٣٧- فَسارَ بِهِ مَنْ لا يَسِيرُ مُشَمِّرًا   وَغَنَّى بِهِ مَنْ لا يُغَنِّى مُغَرِّدا

٣٨- أجِزْنِى إذَا أُنْشِدْتَ شِعْرًا فإنَّمَا   بِشِعْرِى أتاكَ المَادِحُونَ مُرَدَّدَا

٣٩- وَدَعْ كُلَّ صَوْتٍ غيرَ صَوْتِى فإنَّنِى   أنا الصَّائحُ المحْكِىُّ والآخَرُ الصَّدَى

٤٠- ترَكْتُ السُّرَى خَلْفِى لِمَنْ قَلَّ مالُهُ   وأنعَلْتُ أفْراسِى بنُعْماكَ عَسْجَدَا

٤١- وَقَيَّدْتُ نَفْسِى فِى ذَرَاكَ مَحَبَّةً   وَمَنْ وَجَدَ الإحْسانَ قَيْدًا تقَيَّدَا

٤٢- إذَا سأَلَ الإنْسانُ أيَّامَهُ الغِنَى   وكنتَ على بُعْدٍ جعَلْتُكَ مَوْعِدَا

[24] قال أبو الطَّيِّب المُتَنَبِّي

١- كَفى بكَ داءً أن ترَى الموْتَ شافيا   وحَسْبُ المَنايا أنْ يَكُنَّ أمانِيا

٢- تَمَنَّيْتَها لَمَّا تَمَنَّيْتَ أنْ تَرَى   صَدِيقا فأعْيا أوْ عَدُوّا مُداجِيا

٣- إذا كُنْتَ ترْضَى أنْ تَعِيش بذلَّةٍ   فَلا تَسْتَعِدَّنَّ الحُسامَ اليمانِيا

٤- وَلا تَسْتَطِيلَنَّ الرِّماحَ لِغارَةٍ   وَلا تَسْتَجِيدَنَّ العِتاقَ المَذَاكيا

٥- فِما يَنْفَعُ الأُسْدَ الحَياءُ من الطَّوَى   وَلا تُتَّقَى حَتى تَكُونَ ضَوَارِيا

٦- حَبَبْتُكَ قَلبى قبلَ حبكَ مَن نَأى   وَقد كانَ غَدَّارًا فكُن لِيَ وَافِيا

٧- وَأعْلَمُ أنَّ البَينَ يُشْكيك بَعْدَه   فَلَستَ فؤادى إنْ رَأيتُكَ شاكِيا

٨- فَإنَّ دُمُوعَ العينِ غُدرٌ بِرَبِّها   إذا كُنَّ إثْرَ الظَّاعِنِينَ جَوَارِيا

٩- إذا الجُودُ لم يُرْزَقْ خُلاصًا من الأذى   فَلا الحَمْدُ مكْسوبا وَلا المالُ باقيا

١٠- وَلِلنَفسِ أَخلاقٌ تَدُلُّ عَلىَ الفَتَى   أَكانَ سَخاءً ما أَتَى أَمْ تَساخِيا

١١- أَقِلَّ اشْتِياقا أَيُّها القَلْبُ رُبَّما   رَأَيْتُكَ تَصفِى الوُدَّ مَنْ ليسَ جازِيا

١٢- خُلِقتُ الوُفا وَلَو رَحَلْتُ إِلى الصِّبا   لَفارَقتُ شَيْبى موجَعَ القَلْبِ باكِيا

١٣- وَلكِنَّ بِالفُسْطاطِ بحرًا أَزَرْتُهُ   حَياتى وَنُصْحى وَالهَوَى وَالقَوافِيا

١٤- وَجُرْداً مَدَدْنا بَينَ آذَانِها القَنا   فَبِتْنَ خِفاقاً يَتَّبِعْنَ العَوالِيا

١٥- تَماشَى بِأَيْدٍ كُلَّما وَافَتِ الصَّفا   نَقَشْنَ بِهِ صَدْرَ البُزاةِ حَوافِيا

١٦- وَينظرن مِنْ سودٍ صَوادِق فى الدُّجَى   يرَيْنَ بَعِيداتِ الشُّخُوص كما هِيا

١٧- وَتنصِبُ لِلجَرْسِ الخَفِيّ سَوامِعا   يَخَلْنَ مُناجاةَ الضَّمِيرِ تَنادِيا

١٨- تُجاذِبُ فُرسانَ الصَّباحِ أَعِنَّةً   كَأَنَّ عَلى الأَعْناقِ مِنْها أَفاعِيا

١٩- بِعَزمٍ يسيرُ الجِسْمُ فى السَّرْجِ راكبا   بِهِ، وَيَسِيرُ القَلْبُ فى الجِسْمِ ماشِيا

٢٠- قَواصِدَ كافُورٍ تَوارِكَ غَيْرِهِ   وَمن قصَدَ البحرَ استَقَلَّ السَّواقِيا

٢١- فَجاءَتْ بِنا إِنْسانَ عَيْنِ زَمانِهِ   وَخَلَّتْ بَياضاً خَلْفَها وَمآقِيا

٢٢- تَجُوزُ عَلَيْها المُحْسِنِين إِلى الذى   نَرَى عِنْدَهمْ إِحَسانَهُ وَالأَيادِيا

٢٣- فَتى ما سَرَيْنا فى ظُهُورِ جُدُودِنا   إِلى عَصرِهِ إِلاَّ نُرَجِّى التَّلاقِيا

٢٤- تَرَفَّعَ عَنْ عُوْنِ المَكارِمِ قَدْرُهُ   فَما يَفْعَلُ الفَعَلاتِ إِلاَّ عَذَارِيا

٢٥- يُبِيدُ عَدَاوَاتِ البُغاةِ بِلُطْفِهِ   فإِنْ لَمْ تَبِدْ مِنْهُمْ أَباد الأَعادِيا

٢٦- أبا المِسكِ ذا الوَجهِ الذى كنتُ تائِقا   إِليهِ وَذا الوَقتُ الذى كنتُ راجِيا

٢٧- لَقِيتُ المرَوْرَى وَالشَّناخيبَ دُونَهُ   وَجُبْتُ هَجيرًا يَترُكُ الماءَ صَادِيا

٢٨- أبا كُلِّ طيبٍ لا أبا المِسْك وَحْدَهُ   وكلِّ سَحابٍ لا أخُصُّ الغَوَادِيا

٢٩- يُدِلُّ بِمَعْنى واحِدٍ كُلُّ فاخرٍ   وَقَدْ جمَعَ الرَّحْمنُ فيكَ المعانِيا

٣٠- إذا كَسَبَ النَّاسُ المَعاليَ بِالنَّدى   فَإِنَّك تُعْطى فى نَدَاكَ المَعالِيا

٣١- وَغيرُ كَثيرٍ أنْ يزُورَكَ رَاجلٌ   فيرْجِعَ مَلْكا لِلعِرَاقَينِ وَاليا

٣٢- فَقَدْ تهَبُ الجيْشَ الذى جاء غازيا   لِسائلك الفَرْدِ الذى جاءَ عافيا

٣٣- وَتحْتَقِرُ الدُّنْيا احْتِقارَ مُجَرِّبٍ   يَرَى كُلَّ ما فِيها وَحاشاكَ فانِيا

٣٤- وَما كنتَ مِمَّنْ أدْرَكَ المُلكَ بالمُنى   ولكنْ بِأيَّامٍ أشَبْنَ النَّوَاصِيا

٣٥- عِدَاكَ تَرَاها فى البِلادِ مَساعِيا   وأنْتَ تَرَاها فى السَّماءِ مَرَاقِيا

٣٦- لَبِسْتَ لها كُدْرَ العجاجِ، كأنَّما   تَرَى غيرَ صافٍ أن ترَى الجوَّ صَافيا

٣٧- وَقُدْتَ إلَيها كُلَّ أجْرَدَ سابحٍ   يُوَدِّيك غَضْبانا وَيَثْنيكَ رَاضِيا

٣٨- وَمخْترِطٍ ماضٍ يُطِيعُكَ آمِرًا   وَيَعْصِى إن اسْتَثْنيتَ أوْ كُنتَ ناهيا

٣٩- وَأسمَرَ ذى عشرِين ترْضاهُ وَارِدًا   وَيرْضاكَ فى إيرادِهِ الخيْلَ ساقِيا

٤٠- كَتائبَ ما انْفكَّتْ تجُوسُ عمائرًا   منَ الأرْض قدْ جاستْ إليها فيافيا

٤١- غزَوْتَ بها دُورَ المُلوكِ فَباشرَتْ   سَنابِكُها هاماتِهِمْ وَالمَغانِيا

٤٢- وَأنتَ الذِى تَغْشَى الأسِنَّةَ أوَّلاً   وَتأنَفُ أنْ تَغْشَى الأسنَّةَ ثانِيا

٤٣- إذَا الهِنْدُ سوَّتْ بَينَ سَيْفَى كريهة   فَسَيفُكَ فى كَفٍّ تُزيلُ التَّساوِيا

٤٤- وَمِنْ قَوْلِ سامٍ لَوْ رآكَ لِنَسْلِهِ   فِدَى ابنَ أخي نَسْلِي وَنفسِي وَمالِيا
٤٥- مَدًى بَلَّغَ الأَسْتاذَ أقْصَاهُ رَبُّهُ   وَنَفْسٌ لَهُ لَمْ تَرْضَ إلاَّ التَّناهِيا
٤٦- دَعَتْهُ فَلَبَّاها إلى المَجْدِ وَالعُلا   وَقدْ خالَفَ النَّاسُ النُّفوسَ الدَّوَاعيا
٤٧- فَأصْبَحَ فَوْقَ العالَمِينَ يَرَوْنَهُ   وَإنْ كانَ يُدْنيهِ التَّكَرُّمُ نائيا

[25] قال أَبو الطَّيِّب المُتَنبِّي

١- عِيدٌ بِأيَّةِ حالٍ عُدْتَ يا عِيدُ   بِمَا مَضَى أمْ بِأمْرٍ فِيكَ تَجْدِيدُ
٢- أمَّا الأَحِبَّةُ فالْبَيْداءُ دُونَهُمُ   فَلَيْتَ دُونَكَ بِيدًا دُونَها بِيدُ
٣- لَوْلا العُلَى لم تَجُبْ بي ما أجُوبُ بِها   وَجْناءُ حَرْفٌ وَلا جَرْداءُ قَيْدُودُ
٤- وكانَ أطْيَبَ مِنْ سَيْفِى مُضَاجَعَةً   أشْباهُ رَوْنَقِهِ الْغِيدُ الأمالِيدُ
٥- لم يترُكِ الدَّهْرُ مِن قَلْبِي وَلا كَبدِي   شَيْئًا تُتَيِّمُهُ عَيْنٌ وَلا جِيدُ
٦- يا ساقِيَيَّ أخَمْرٌ فِي كُئُوسِكُما   أمْ فِي كُئُوسِكُما هَمٌّ وتَسْهِيدُ
٧- أصَخْرَةٌ أنا؟ مالي لا تُغَيِّرُنِي   هَذي المُدامُ وَلا هَذي الأغارِيدُ!
٨- إذا أرَدْتُ كُمَيْتَ الخَمْرِ صافِيَةً   وَجَدْتُها وَحَبِيبُ النَّفْسِ مَفْقُودُ
٩- ماذَا لَقِيتُ مِنَ الدُّنْيا وأعْجَبُها   أنّي بِمَا أنا باكٍ مِنْهُ مَحْسُود!
١٠- أمْسَيْتُ أرْوَحَ مُثْرٍ خازِنا وَيَدًا   أنا الغَنِيُّ وأمْوَالي المَوَاعِيدُ
١١- إنّي نَزَلْتُ بِكَذَّابِينَ ضَيْفُهُمُ   عَنِ القِرَى وَعَنِ التَّرْحالِ مَحْدُودُ
١٢- جودُ الرِّجالِ مِنَ الأيْدِي وَجودُهُمُ   مِنَ اللِّسانِ، فَلا كانُوا وَلا الجُودُ

١٣- ما يقبِضُ المَوْتُ نَفْسا مِنْ نفوسِهِمِ   إلاَّ وفِى يَدِهِ مِنْ نَتْنِها عُودُ

١٤- مِن كلِّ رِخْوِ وِكاءِ البَطْنِ مُنْفَتِقٍ   لافِى الرِّجالِ ولا النِّسْوَانِ مَعْدُودُ

١٥- أكلَّما اغْتالَ عَبْدُ السُّوءِ سَيِّدَهُ   أوْ خانَهُ فَلَهُ فِى مِصْرَ تَمْهِيدُ

١٦- صَارَ الخَصِىُّ إمامَ الآبِقِينَ بِها   فالحُرُّ مُسْتَعْبَدٌ والعَبْدُ معْبودُ

١٧- نامَتْ نَوَاطِيرُ مِصْرٍ عَنْ ثَعالِبِها   فَقَدْ بَشِمْنَ وَما تَفْنَى العَناقِيدُ

١٨- العَبْدُ لَيْسَ لِحُرٍّ صَالِحٍ بِأخٍ   لَوْ أنَّهُ فِى ثِيابِ الحُرِّ مَوْلُودُ

١٩- لا تَشْتَرِ العَبْدَ إلاَّ والعَصَا مَعَهُ   إنَّ العَبِيدَ لأَنْجاسٌ مَناكِيدُ

٢٠- ما كُنْتُ أحْسِبُنِى أبْقَى إلِى زَمَنٍ   يُسِىءُ بِى فِيهِ كَلْبٌ وَهْوَ مَحْمُودُ

٢١- وَلا تَوَهَّمْتُ أنَّ النَّاسَ قدْ فُقِدوا   وأنَّ مِثْلَ أبى البَيْضَاءِ مَوْجُودُ

٢٢- وأنَّ ذا الأسْوَدَ المَشْقُوبَ مَشفرُهُ   تُطِيعُهُ ذِى العَضَارِيطُ الرَّعادِيدُ

٢٣- جَوْعانُ يأكلُ مِن زَادى ويُمسِكُنِى   لِكَىْ يُقالَ عَظِيمُ القَدْرِ مَقْصُودُ

٢٤- إنَّ امْرَأً أمَةٌ حُبْلَى تُدبِّرُهُ   لَمُسْتَضَامٌ سَخِينُ العَيْنِ مَفْؤُودُ

٢٥- وَيْلُمِّها خُطَّةً وَيْلُمِّ قابِلِها   لِمِثْلِها خُلِقَ المَهْرِيَّةُ القُودُ

٢٦- وَعِنْدَها لَذَّ طَعْمَ المَوْتِ شارِبُهُ   إنَّ المَنِيَّةَ عِنْدَ الذُّلِّ قِنْدِيدُ

٢٧- مَن علَّمَ الأسْوَدَ المَخْصِىَّ مَكْرُمَةً   أقَوْمُهُ البِيضُ أمْ آباؤُهُ الصِّيدُ

٢٨- أمْ أُذْنُهُ فِى يَدِ النَّخَّاسِ دَامِيةً   أمْ قَدْرُهُ وَهْوَ بالفَلْسَيْنِ مَرْدُودُ

٢٩- أوْلَى اللِّئامِ كُوَيْفِيرٌ بِمَعْذِرَةٍ   فِى كلِّ لُؤْمٍ وبعضُ العُذْرِ تَفْنِيدُ

٣٠- وَذَاكَ أنَّ الفُحولَ البِيضَ عاجزَةٌ عنِ الجَميلِ فكَيفَ الخِصْيَةُ السُّودُ

[26] قال المُهَنَّد طاهِر بن مُحَمَّد البَغْدَادي

١- إمامٌ تخيرهُ رحمةً على الخلق أَسبغ اسبالها
٢- وصفّاه ذو العرش من صفوة تجرُّ على الشمس اذيالها
٣- أحلَّ النبوة آباءها وأعطى الخلافة أنسالها
٤- فحاط الرعيةَ مستنصراً بذي العرش يُحرزُ أَهمالها
٥- وأنفق أمواله جاهداً عليها يُثَمِّرُ أموالها
٦- فأذهب إحسانُه بؤسها وأكثر نعماهُ اخلالها
٧- تولّى الخلافة في عصرها فأحسن تقواه إكمالها
٨- وكانت ديانته زَيْنَها وأيامه الزُّهرُ أشكالها
٩- فلو رُفِعَتْ خطةٌ فوقها لما كان يصلحُ إلا لها
١٠- وما صفَةٌ حَسُنَتْ في الهدى من الذكر الا وقد نالها
١١- فهنأهُ الله أعيادَه وبلغه الله أمثالها
١٢- وضاعف ما طاب من صومه وتحميله النفس أحمالها
١٣- وأوزعه شكر إنعامه وتبليغه النفس آمالها
١٤- واذلاله عزّ أعدائه وقد جعل القهر اغلالها
١٥- اقام قيامتها عاجلاً فقد عاينتها واهوالها

١٦- مضى جنده نحوها غازياً فجاز الملوكَ واقيالها
١٧- وَملكهُ ربه أرضها وما حملته وأثقالها
١٨- وقتّل آسادُهُ أُسدها وأشباله الغُلبُ أشبالها
١٩- ولما سرى جندُه نحوها تزلزلت الارضُ زلزالها
٢٠- وصار له أفقها مرجلا وقطع ربك أوصالها
٢١- واذهب في بحرها ثمدها وغرّقَ في اللجّ أوشالها
٢٢- وأوردها دارهُ خضّعاً تقرُّ وتظهر إجلالها
٢٣- ولما تملكها ضللا عفا فهدى الله ضلالها
٢٤- وعفى الاساءاتِ احسانهُ وغطت معاليه افعالها
٢٥- وابدت سجاياه إنعامها وصابت أياديه افضالها
٢٦- وهل كان يحسنُ في فضله الـ ـأعمٌّ يقارض جهالها
٢٧- وكم مرة قد عفا قادراً فألبسه الله سربالها
٢٨- فلا زال يقهر أعداءهُ ويفني الليالي واقيالها

[27] قال مُحَمَّد بن شُخَيْص

١- أتمّ شعبانُ ما أبدا به رجب من قبل ما كانت الآمال ترتقبُ
٢- وزادنا أن شهرَ الصوم قابلنا بخير عيدين منه: البدر والعِقبُ
٣- في عام غضراء لفتنا طوالعه نصراً وخصباً فمات النكثُ والجدب

٤- للّه صنعٌ تلقانا السرورُ به	من قبل ان تُتلقى البُردُ والكتب
٥- فاختالت الارض من عجب به وأرى	أنْ ليس في عُجبٍ مختال به عَجَب
٦- وأشرق الأفقُ لما عمه جَذلٌ	ونوّرَ الارضُ لما هزّه طرب
٧- فالوردُ يحكي خدوداً راقها خجلٌ	والأقحوانُ ثغوراً زانها شنب
٨- لما رأى الخائنُ المخذولُ ما كشفت	لعينه من دواعي حَينه العقب
٩- وان غَزْوَ أميرِ الله لاحقُهُ	مَنْ ليس تلحقه خيلٌ ولا نُجُبُ
١٠- وأنّ عَزْمَتهُ حَتْمٌ وغضبته	حَتْفٌ، وفي الله منه الحتفُ والغضب
١١- وأنه لو رماه الجِدُّ في هربٍ	بالصين لم يُنْجِهِ من سيفه الهرب
١٢- وكيف يطمعُ في منجى يُفوّته	مَنْ جَدّ لله في آثارهِ الطلب
١٣- رجا الفرارَ فأنباه الرجاءُ له	أنَّ القضاءَ له من حَوْله رِقَب
١٤- وأين يوجد عن ظلٍّ السماءِ حمىً	من يوم رَوّقَ من آفاقها الطنب
١٥- إعطاؤه الحكمَ مولانا وقى دمه	وكنت أطمعُ ان يشفى به الكَلَب
١٦- نجا بامكانه من نفسه رَمَقٌ	بين الحياة والموت مضطرب
١٧- تعجل الله في الدنيا فواقره	فلا حياةٌ ولا اهل ولا نسب

. . .

١٨- أُشابة تدعي في هاشم نسباً	وما يصح لها في معشرٍ نَسبُ
١٩- عُميُ البصائر لم يُسلِسْ معاطِفها	الى مساعي التقى دين ولا حسب

٢٠- وزادها في عماها أن اولها	ألقى العصا حيثُ لا علمٌ ولا أدب
٢١- نَشَتْ مع الوحشِ في دهماءليس لها	في غير حَسْو الحُسَى رأيٌ ولا أرب
٢٢- ولو غدَتْ من قريش في ذوائبها	لأوْجَبَتْ نَفْيها الأحداثُ والريب
٢٣- وكل ملتهب يُطْفَا وَشَرُّهمُ	مِنْ بعدِ عثمانَ يُطْفَا ثم يَلْتَهِبُ
٢٤- اذا غدا حَسَنٌ في الآلِ من حَسَنٍ	رأساً فيا ليت شعري أيّما الذّنب
٢٥- ما صحّت البرد والاقلام من ملك	أرداه مُذ صحّت الأرماحُ والقُضب
٢٦- ولا خلتْ من معاني الجِدّ قدرته	وربما شاب جدّ القادرِ اللعب
٢٧- ولا أُديرت رحى حربٍ بساحته	حتى يكون لها من رأيه قطب
٢٨- رأيٌ هداه الى التوفيق مودعهُ	والرأيُ مختلفٌ والقول منشعب
٢٩- رأي اذا ورد القوادُ قام لهم	في الحرب ما لا يقوم الجحفلُ اللجب
٣٠- ألقاه في نفنف المهوى وأمهله	حتى اتيحت له من نفسه النكب
٣١- واللهُ يملي لقوم كي يزيدهم	من بأسه ولهذا أُرخيَ اللّبب
٣٢- وافى الجزيرةَ فالتفت بموكبه	كتائبٌ تقشعرُّ الارض ان غضبوا
٣٣- وكلما جاب ظهر الارض قابله	بالخيل والرجل منها الوهد والحدب
٣٤- حتى اذا ما دنا من حَوز بيضتنا	والنفسُ تخفق والاحشاء تضطرب
٣٥- لاقى الجموع التي خيلت بوطأتها	شُمَّ الربى كالدبا من حوله تثب
٣٦- جاءت بأجمعها لله شاكرة	وللهدى نخوةً تترى وتنسرب

٣٧- أشياعُ مستنصر بالله نصرتها　　صِدْقُ البصائر لا التمويه والكذب
٣٨- ما صدَّها عن تلقيه بكلِّ أذىً　　يوفي على الحتف إلا الطوعُ والرهب
٣٩- مضى يُذكرُ بالتهليل من جزع　　رُكاب بحر دنا من سُفْنها العطب
٤٠- يرجو الحياة ويخشى الموتَ فهو على　　حالين ضدين : مسرورٌ ومكتئبُ
٤١- حتى اجتلى غرة السعد التي شفعت　　له وللكل في اللقاء ما ركبوا
٤٢- وما أراهُ رأى المهديَّ اذ حَجبتْ　　عينيه عن وجهه من نورهِ الحجُب
٤٣- ولو حناها على الشيعيّ لانكشفت　　وسيفهُ من دم الأوداج منتضب
٤٤- ولانقضت ومضت والدين مهتضم　　والحُر مُسْتعبدٌ والمال منتهب
٤٥- إخلاؤه الكرم المخليه من كرمٍ　　أهدى له كرباً تُهْدى به الكُرب
٤٦- قد قلت للحائن المذكي بنزوته　　ناراً أُعِدَّ لها من روحه حطب
٤٧- اكثرتَ في دولة المهدي من شغب　　فانظر الى أيّ حال ساقك الشغب

. . .

٤٨- يا داعيَ اللهِ في الصنع الذي صنعتْ　　في عام تاريخه الاشعارُ والخطبُ
٤٩- ما زلت مُذْ أوقدَ الهيجا على ثقة　　بِدَفع ما تُوجِبُ الاقدارُ لا الشهب
٥٠- أسرته بعد سلب الملك من يده　　فصار في قبضك المسلوب والسّلبُ
٥١- لكاد فضلك ينسي ما وهبت له　　من روحه وهو مما ليس يُتَّهب
٥٢- والتْ رجالُ الموالي في حمايتها　　وأعربت عن صريح الطاعة العرب

٥٣- وما ونتْ عزمة الجند الذين اذا ما صاح باسمك فيهم غالبٌ غلبوا
٥٤- وقد صفا لك ملْكُ الغرْبِ أجمعهُ ودان منتزحٌ منه ومقتربُ
٥٥- فما توقُّفُ جُنْدِ النصر عن جهة ضِيمت بها مصر واجتثت بها حلب
٥٦- تقلبُ الحال بالمخذول يخبرنا أن الزمان بأهل الرفض منقلب
٥٧- وقد أبحتَ الحمى من أهل دعوته ويؤكلُ البسرُ حتى ينضج الرطب
٥٨- اذا العمود من الفسطاط صرعه الـ ـاعضاد لم تثبت الأوتاد والطنب
٥٩- لا شيء في مذهب الإقبال مقترن بوجهك الطلق الا عامنا الخصبُ
٦٠- فزادك الله عزاً تستديم به نعماه ما دامت الاعمار والحقب
٦١- فانما انت للاسلام موهبة من المهنى لما يعطي وما يهب
٦٢- فاضت على جندك الأرزاق وارتفعت بكلٍّ قوادك الاقدار والرتب
٦٣- وعمّ من نيلك الصافي صوائفنا غيثٌ اذا قيل سكبُ السيب ينسكب
٦٤- نصرٌ عزيزٌ وعامٌ مخصبٌ رغدٌ للفطر تدعى به أيامك القشب
٦٥- وان مفرق مولانا وسيدنا أبي الوليد بتاج الملك معتصب
٦٦- وما يؤخر عنها من يكون له مروان جد ومهديّ الولاة أب

[28] قال أَبو تَمَّام

صَلَّى لها حَياً وكانَ وَقُودَها مَيْتاً ويَدخُلُها معَ الفُجَّارِ

[29] قال أَبو تَمَّام

رَقَّتْ حَوَاشِى الدَّهْرِ فَهْىَ تَمَرْمَرُ   وغَدَا الثَّرَى فى حَلْيِهِ يَتَكسَّرُ

[30] قال ابن دَرَّاج القَسْطَلِّي

١- شَهِدَتْ لك الأَيّامُ أنك عيدها   لك حَنَّ موحِشُها وآبَ بعيدها

٢- وأضاءَ مُظلِمُها، وأفْرَخ رَوْعها   وأطاعَ عاصيها، ولان شَديدها

٣- وَصَفتْ بك الدنيا فشبَّ كبيرُها   في إثْرِ ما قد كان شابَ وليدها

٤- ما كان أجْمدَ قبل نَوْئِكَ بحرَها   فالآن فُجّرَ بالنَّدى جُلْمُودها

٥- فارتاحَ بَيْتُكَ في أباطحِ مكةٍ   لِمَعادِ أيّامٍ دنا مَوْعودهـا

٦- لِمَوَاكِبٍ صَهَلتْ إليك خُيولُها   وكتائبٍ خَفَقتْ عليك بنُودها

٧- شَغَفاً بدعوتكَ التي قد طالَما   عَمَرتْ تهائِمُها بها ونُجُودها

٨- حتّى ارتقيتَ من المنارلِ رُتْبَةً   عَزَّتْ بها غُرُّ الرِّجالِ وصِيدها

٩- في قُبّةِ المُلْكِ الّتى صِنْهاجَة   وَزَنَـاتَة أطْنـابُها وَعَمُـودها

١٠- صَدَقتكَ أيامَ النزالِ سيوفها   ضَرْباً وفي يومِ النِّفَارِ عُهُودها

١١- يا ساعةً مقطوعةً أرحامُها   لا البِرُّ شاهِدُها ولا مَشْهُودها

١٢- يـومـاً أُذِلَّ كِـرامُـهُ لِـلِـئـامِـهِ   وسَطَتْ بأحرارِ الملوكِ عبيدها

١٣- وتَوَاكلتْ أبْطالُهَا في كُرْبةٍ   عَيّتْ بها ساداتُها ومَسُودها

١٤- لا يهتدي سَمْتَ النّجاةِ دليلُها   دَهَشاً ولا وَجْةَ السَّدادِ سديدها

١٥- حتى طَلَعْتَ لهم بأسْعدِ غُرَّةٍ   طَلَعتْ عليهم في السماءِ سُعُودها

. . .

١٦- واستوْدعوا جنبيْ شُرُنْبَةَ وقْعةً   هَزَّ الجِبالَ الراسياتِ رعودها

١٧- دَلَفُوا إلى شَهْباءَ حانَ حَصادُها   وطُلَى رُؤوسِ الدَّارِعِين حصيدها

١٨- وشِعابِ قنتيشٍ وقد حشرتْ لهم   أُمَم بُغاة لا يُكَفُّ عديدُها

١٩- تَرَكُوا بها ظَهْرَ الصَّعيدِ وقد غدا   بَطْناً، وأجسادُ العِدَاةِ صعيدها

٢٠- وكتائبُ الإفْرَنْجِ إذ كَادَتْكَ في   أشياعِها واللّهُ عنك يكيدها

٢١- بسوابحٍ في لُجّ بحرِ سوابغٍ   فاضَتْ على الأرْضِ الفضاءِ مُدُودها

٢٢- ولقد أضافُوا نَسْرَها وغُرَابَها   وقراهما طاغُوتُها وعميدها

٢٣- شِلْوٌ لأرْمنقُودِهَا حشدَتْ به   للزَّحْفِ ثُمَّ إلى الجحيم حشودها

٢٤- ودَنَوْا لها في آرَ تحت صوارمٍ   وَرِيَتْ بعِزّ المسلمين زُنُودها

٢٥- من بعدما قَصَفوا الرِّماحَ وأصْلَتُوا   بيضاً يُشايعُ حَدَّها توحِيدُها

٢٦- فَكأنّما رُفِعَتْ لها صُلْبَانُها   في ظِلّ هبْوَتِهَا فحانَ سحودها

٢٧- وبجانب الغربيّ إذ قَدَّمَتها   شُعْثاً يُبشّرُ بالفتوحِ شهيدها

٢٨- ضَرَبوا على الأخْدُودِ هامَ حُماته   حتّى عَبرْنَ وَجسْرُهُنَّ خدودها

٢٩- في وقعةٍ قامَتْ بِعُذْرِ سُيُوفِهِم   لو ذابَ من حَرّ الجلادِ حديدها

٣٠- ويَضيقُ فيها العُذْرُ عن خَطّيّةٍ   سَمْراءَ لم يُورِقْ بكفّكَ عودها

٣١- فيها رأيتَ العزَّ حيثُ تريدُه وسوابغَ النّعماءِ حيثُ تُرِيدها

٣٢- فاقْبَلْ فقد ساقتْ إليك مُهورَها أكْفَاءُ حَمْدٍ لا يُذَمُّ حميدها

٣٣- بِدْعاً من النظم النّفيسِ تشابَهَت فيها الجواهرُ دُرُّها وفريدُها

٣٤- وَلْيَهْنِها أيّامُ عِزٍ كُلها عيد وأنت لمن أطاعَكَ عيدها

Notes

1. Transgression and Redemption

Earlier versions of parts of this chapter were presented at the Graduate/Faculty Seminar of the Department of Arabic at the University of Jordan, Amman, March 1977; the Seventh Conference on Literary Criticism at Yarmouk University, Irbid, Jordan, July 1998; the annual meetings of the Middle East Studies Association, Chicago, Illinois, November, 1998 and Orlando, Florida, November, 2000; and the American Oriental Society Meeting, Portland, Oregon, March 2000.

1. The present study in no way attempts to offer a survey of Arabic literature. For the English reader a thorough introduction and survey is provided by Roger Allen, *The Arabic Literary Heritage: The Development of Its Genres and Criticism* (Cambridge: Cambridge University Press, 1998). See especially ch. 2, "The Contexts of the Literary Tradition," pp. 11–81; and ch. 4, "Poetry," pp. 103–217.

2. A detailed discussion of the complex process of transmission, collection, edition, and recension of the pre-Islamic poetic corpus, along with the modern scholarly controversies involved, is beyond the scope of this study. I offer here merely the broadest general description. For more on this subject see Régis Blachère, *Histoire de la littérature arabe des origines à la fin du XVe siècle de J.-C.*, 3 vols. (Paris: Maisonneuve, 1952, 1964, 1966), esp. vol. 1, passim; Nāṣir al-Dīn al-Asad, *Maṣādir al-Shiʿr al-Jāhilī wa-Qīmatuhā al-Tārīkhiyyah* (Cairo: Dār al-Maʿārif, 1962); James T. Monroe, "Oral Composition in Pre-Islamic Poetry," *Journal of Arabic Literature* 3 (1972): 1–53; Michael Zwettler, *The Oral Tradition of Classical Arabic Poetry: Its Character and Implications* (Columbus: Ohio State University Press, 1972), esp. ch. 4, "Variation and Attribution in the Tradition of Classical Arabic Poetry." See my own treatments of this subject in Suzanne Pinckney Stetkevych, *Abū Tammām and the Poetics of the ʿAbbāsid Age* (Leiden: E. J. Brill, 1991), chs. 10 and 11; and Suzanne Pinckney Stetkevych, *The Mute Immortals Speak: Pre-Islamic Poetry and the Poetics of Ritual* (Ithaca, N.Y.: Cornell University Press, 1993), ch. 4.

3. See S. Stetkevych, *The Mute Immortals Speak,* passim.

4. Gregory Nagy, *Pindar's Homer: The Lyric Possession of an Epic Past* (Baltimore: Johns Hopkins University Press, 1991), p. 433.

5. For an extensive study of the tribal-based poetry of the Jāhiliyyah, including genres such as the tribal boast (*fakhr*), men's and women's elegy (*rithāʾ*), and brigand (*suʿlūk*) poetry, see S. Stetkevych, *The Mute Immortals Speak,* passim.

6. See Irfan Shahid, "Ghassān" and "Lakhmids," in *Encyclopaedia of Islam,* new ed. (Leiden: E. J. Brill, 1954–).

7. Al-Nābighah al-Dhubyānī, Ziyād ibn Muʿāwiyah ibn Ḍabāb ibn Jābir ibn Yarbūʿ ibn Salamah of the Banū Murrah (Ghaṭafān). See Albert Arazi, "Al-Nābigha al-Dhubyānī," in *Encyclopaedia of Islam,* new ed. (Leiden: E. J. Brill, 1954–). Arazi offers a concise summary of al-Nābighah's career and extensive bibliography, so I confine my remarks here to the qasida at hand. See also Fuat Sezgin, *Geschichte des*

Arabischen Schrifttums, Band II: Poesie bis ca. 430 H. (Leiden: E. J. Brill, 1973), pp. 110–13 [hereafter Sezgin, *Poesie*].

8. Arazi, "Al-Nābigha al-Dhubyānī," and Sezgin, *Poesie,* pp. 110–13.

9. Abū al-Faraj al-Iṣbahānī, *Kitāb al-Aghānī,* ed. Ibrāhīm al-Abyārī, 32 vols. (Cairo: Dār al-Shaᶜb, 1969–79), 11: 3794–801. I have dealt extensively with these *akhbār* in an unpublished paper presented at the Seventh Arabic Literary Criticism Conference at Yarmouk University, Irbid, Jordan, July 1998, "Naẓariyyat al-Talaqqī wa Akhbār al-Shuᶜarāʾ: *Dāliyyat* al-Nābighah al-Dhubyānī wa Tarjamatuh fī *Kitāb al-Aghānī.*"

10. These figure as nos. 1, 8, and 75 in Ibn al-Sikkīt's recension of the diwan. See Muḥammad Abū al-Faḍl Ibrāhīm, ed., *Dīwān al-Nābighah al-Dhubyānī,* 3rd ed. (Cairo: Dār al-Maᶜārif, 1990); and Shukrī Fayṣal, ed., *Dīwān al-Nābighah al-Dhubyānī,* recension of Ibn al-Sikkīt (Beirut: Dār al-Fikr, 1968).

11. Arazi, "Al-Nābigha al-Dhubyānī." See, for example, al-Tibrīzī's recension of ten *Muᶜallaqāt,* in al-Khaṭīb Abū Zakariyyā Yaḥyā ibn ᶜAlī al-Tibrīzī, *Sharḥ al-Qaṣāʾid al-ᶜAshr,* ed. ᶜAbd al-Salām al-Ḥūfī (Beirut: Dār al-Kutub al-ᶜIlmiyyah, 1985), pp. 349–75.

12. Al-Iṣbahānī, *Kitāb al-Aghānī,* 11: 3794, 3798. All translations are my own except where otherwise noted.

13. Al-Iṣbahānī, *Kitāb al-Aghānī,* 11: 3799–800.

14. Al-Iṣbahānī, *Kitāb al-Aghānī,* 11: 3800–801. It is of note that the celebrated philologist al-Tibrīzī (d. 502/1109), in his commentary on a poem by al-Munakhkhal al-Yashkurī in the *Ḥamāsah* of Abū Tammām, cites the following anecdote:

> Al-Munakhkhal was suspected of having an affair with al-Mutajarridah, the wife of al-Nuᶜmān, renowned for her looseness and debauchery, and the mother of two sons who were reputed to be by al-Munakhkhal. Some of the reports say that al-Nuᶜmān had a certain day when he would go for a long ride and was known to return at a certain hour. Al-Munakhkhal would come to al-Mutajarridah and stay with her until al-Nuᶜman's return, when he would leave. One day he came to her when al-Nuᶜmān was out riding and she was playing with him with a shackle that she had put around his leg and hers. Such was their state when al-Nuᶜmān returned unexpectedly and found them. He took al-Munakhkhal and turned him over to his jailor, ᶜAkabb, to torture. . . . ᶜAkabb shackled him and began to drag him around by the shackles. It was in this condition that al-Munakhkhal recited for his two sons:
>
> Who will report to the two gallant youths about me
> That the tribe has killed a haughty man?
>
> Mounted on a swift camel, ᶜAkabb drags me around the Arab tribes
> And jabs a stick into the nape of my neck.
>
> *a-lā man mublighu l-ḥurrayni ᶜaniyyā*
> *bi-anna l-qawma qad qatalū abiyyā*
>
> *yudawwiru bī ᶜAkabbun fī Maᶜaddin*
> *wa-yaṭᶜanu bi-ṣ-ṣamlati fī qafiyyā*

See Yaḥyā ibn ʿAlī al-Tibrīzī, *Sharḥ Dīwān Ashʿār al-Ḥamāsah,* 2 vols. (Cairo: Būlāq, 1296/1879) 2: 48–49. For a translation and discussion of the poem and anecdote, see S. Stetkevych, *Abū Tammām,* pp. 307–11.

15. Al-Iṣbahānī, *Kitāb al-Aghānī,* 11: 3801–802.

16. For the text and translation I have followed al-Aṣmaʿī's recension of the text and al-Shantamarī's commentary as edited by Muḥammad Abū al-Faḍl Ibrāhīm in Ibrāhīm, *Dīwān al-Nābighah,* pp. 89–97 (34 lines). I have also consulted the text and commentary of Shukrī Fayṣal's edition of Ibn al-Sikkīt's recension (35 lines). The two recensions exhibit occasional differences in diction and considerable differences in the order of the lines, although the general shape of the poem is the same. Lines 5 and 33 of the Ibrāhīm text are not found in Fayṣal, and lines 22 and 23 of the former are conflated into one line (24) in the latter. Conversely, lines 14, 27, 31, and 34 of the Fayṣal text are not found in Ibrāhīm. I have occasionally altered the vocalization of Ibrāhīm's text.

17. Ibrāhīm, *Dīwān al-Nābighah,* p. 89.

18. Lines 3 and 18 of this qasida exhibit the rhyme defect termed *iqwāʾ,* that is, the alternation of the final rhyme vowel, in this case from *-dī* to *-dū*. See Ibrāhīm, *Dīwān al-Nābighah,* p. 89, commentary on line 3.

19. Ibrāhīm, *Dīwān al-Nābighah,* p. 90.

20. S. Stetkevych, *The Mute Immortals Speak,* pp. 252–53, lines 31–34. For a full translation and discussion of the *Muʿallaqah* of Imruʾ al-Qays, see pp. 241–85. For the Arabic text, see Abū Bakr Muḥammad ibn al-Qāsim al-Anbārī [= Ibn al-Anbārī], *Sharḥ al-Qaṣāʾid al-Sabʿ al-Ṭiwāl al-Jāhiliyyāt,* ed. ʿAbd al-Salām Muḥammad Hārūn (Cairo: Dār al-Maʿārif, 1969), pp. 58–62.

21. Root *j-r-d* in Edward William Lane, *Arabic-English Lexicon,* 8 vols. (New York: Frederick Ungar, 1958) [London, 1863]. Henceforth cited as Lane.

22. For a discussion of the concept of the "free woman" or *ḥurrah* of the tribal aristocracy as opposed to the captive or slave, see S. Stetkevych, *The Mute Immortals Speak,* ch. 5, "The Obligations and Poetics of Gender," pp. 165 and 161–205, passim. With reference to Imruʾ al-Qays's illicit exploits, see pp. 267–72.

23. See S. Stetkevych, *The Mute Immortals Speak,* p. 253, line 40, and p. 269; [Ibn] al-Anbārī, *Sharḥ al-Qaṣāʾid al-Sabʿ,* p. 68.

24. S. Stetkevych, *The Mute Immortals Speak,* pp. 252, line 24; [Ibn] al-Anbārī, *Sharḥ al-Qaṣāʾid al-Sabʿ,* p. 49.

25. Line 33 seems to me rather gratuitous, not really strengthening the overall effect and creating a break in the "subliminal" imagery of lines 31, 32, and 34.

26. Ibrāhīm, *Dīwān al-Nābighah,* p. 98.

27. I would like to clarify my critical stance as regards the relation of the ode of apology to the panegyric ode. Accurately enough called "*iʿtidhāriyyah*" (*iʿtidhār* = "apology" or "excuse"), this term to my mind denotes what should best be understood as a subgenre of the panegyric ode (*qaṣīdat al-madḥ*). As I discuss in detail (below and in chs. 2 and 4), supplication (in this case, the apology or appeal for forgiveness) and panegyric are not two distinct genres, but rather, following the work of Kevin Crotty, supplication and praise are intimately conjoined (Kevin Crotty, *The Poetics of Supplication: Homer's* Iliad *and* Odyssey [Ithaca, N.Y.: Cornell University Press, 1994], p. 90). That is, in the light of my own work on the qasida,

the ritual exchange that is embodied in the qasida is the poet's proffering praise and requesting or demanding something in return. The object of supplication can vary greatly, from granting a simple favor, political or material, to granting the poet's life, or may merely be the explicit or implied expectation of a prize/*jāʾizah* in return for the poem. I thus reject, on the one hand, Arazi's description of al-Nābighah's apology poems (*iʿtidhāriyyāt*) as "hybrid pieces containing a combination of excuses and panegyric" (Arazi, "Al-Nābigha al-Dhubyānī") and, on the other, Wahb Rūmiyyah's contention that the *iʿtidhāriyyah* constitutes a separate generic category distinct from the panegyric ode (*qaṣīdat al-madḥ*) (Wahb Rūmiyyah, *Qaṣīdat al-Madḥ ḥattā Nihāyat al-ʿAṣr al-Umawī: Bayn al-Uṣūl wa-al-Iḥyāʾ wa-al-Tajdīd* [Damascus: Manshūrāt Wizārat al-Thaqāfah wa-al-Irshād al-Qawmī, 1981], pp. 19–21, 49, 168–69). While at pains to distinguish between *madḥ* and *iʿtidhār,* and careful to point out thematic characteristics of the latter (see pp. 168–69), Rūmiyyah nevertheless recognizes that *iʿtidhār* is a branch of *madḥ* (p. 21). My formulation of supplication as an inseparable element of *madḥ,* and *iʿtidhār* as merely a particular form of supplication, is intended to bring such poems to the center of any discussion of the *qaṣīdat al-madḥ.* Of note in this regard is Rūmiyyah's remark that the pre-Islamic *qaṣīdat al-iʿtidhār* is closer to Ibn Qutaybah's classical formulation of the qasida than is the pre-Islamic *qaṣīdat al-madḥ* (p. 44). Ibn Qutaybah's (d. 276/889) oft-cited formulation runs as follows:

> I have heard from a man of learning that the composer of Odes began by mentioning the deserted dwelling-places and relics and places of habitation. Then he wept and complained and addressed the desolate encampment, and begged his companion to make a halt, in order that he might have occasion to speak of those who had once lived there and afterwards departed; for the dwellers in tents were different from townsmen or villagers in respect of coming and going, because they moved from one water-spring to another, seeking pasture and searching out the places where rain had fallen. Then to this he linked the erotic prelude (*nasīb*), and bewailed the violence of his love and the anguish of separation from his mistress and the extremity of his passion and desire, so as to win the hearts of his hearers and divert their eyes towards him and invite their ears to listen to him, since the song of love touches men's souls and takes hold of their hearts, God having put it in the constitution of His creatures to love dalliance and the society of women, in such wise that we find very few but are attached thereto by some tie or have some share therein, whether lawful or unpermitted. Now, when the poet had assured himself of an attentive hearing, he followed up his advantage and set forth his claim: thus he went on to complain of fatigue and want of sleep and travelling by night and of the noonday heat, and how his camel had been reduced to leanness. And when, after representing all the discomfort and danger of his journey, he knew that he had fully justified his hope and expectation of receiving his due meed from the person to whom the poem was addressed, he entered upon the panegyric (*madīḥ*), and incited him to reward, and kindled his generosity by exalting him above his peers and pronouncing the greatest dignity, in comparison to his, to be little. (Trans. Reynold A. Nicholson; Abū

Muḥammad ʿAbd Allāh ibn Muslim Ibn Qutaybah, *Kitāb al-Shiʿr wa-al-Shuʿarāʾ*, ed. M. J. de Goeje [Leiden: E. J. Brill, 1904], pp. 14–15)

This suggests to me that the *qaṣīdat al-iʿtidhār* is centrally formative to the qasida tradition and that, however astute Rūmiyyah's distinction of its formal and thematic particularities, it should be discussed centrally, not peripherally, in assessing the *qaṣīdat al-madḥ*. This is not to say that the term is not useful and accurate to denote poems in which the supplication side of the exchange ritual embodied in the *qaṣīdat al-madḥ* takes the form of an apology or excuse that is thematically prominent in the poem, but rather that it should be understood to constitute a variant of a dominant form in which the give-and-take of ritual exchange embraces structurally and integrally both the supplication (here, the excuse and plea for forgiveness) and the panegyric. This approach has the advantage of conferring coherence upon the poetic structure and of explaining why certain *iʿtidhāriyyāt* (notably the one at hand and Kaʿb ibn Zuhayr's "Suʿad Has Departed" to the Prophet Muhammad, in ch. 2) have had so profound an influence formally and thematically on the mainstream *qaṣīdat al-madḥ* tradition.

28. Marcel Mauss, *The Gift: Forms and Functions of Exchange in Archaic Societies*, trans. Ian Cunnison (New York: Norton and Co., 1967) [*Essai sur le don, form archaïque de l'échange*, 1925]. I have proposed and explored the application of Mauss's theories of ritual exchange as they apply to the exchange of the Arabic panegyric ode for the patron's prize in Suzanne Pinckney Stetkevych, "Pre-Islamic Poetry and the Poetics of Redemption: *Mufaḍḍalīyah 119* of ʿAlqamah and *Bānat Suʿād* of Kaʿb ibn Zuhayr," in Suzanne Pinckney Stetkevych, ed., *Reorientations: Arabic and Persian Poetry* (Bloomington and Indianapolis: Indiana University Press, 1994), pp. 1–57. See further discussion and references in ch. 6.

29. Of the structural variants of the classical Arabic qasida, scholars of the present generation have debated the issue of whether the qasida is essentially bipartite, composed of the amatory prelude (*nasīb*) and the praise section (*madīḥ*) or tripartite, composed of the amatory prelude (*nasīb*), the desert journey section (*raḥīl*), and the praise section (*madīḥ*). Although a chronological transition from predominant tripartite in the Jāhiliyyah to bipartite in the ʿAbbāsid period is generally recognized, recent studies by Ḥasan al-Bannā ʿIzz al-Dīn and myself suggest further that whereas the battle or victory ode tends to be bipartite, even in the Jāhiliyyah, the ode involving the transfer of political allegiance or of incorporation tends to adopt the tripartite structure (see ch. 4).

30. For the text and translation I have relied on the recension of al-Aṣmaʿī and the commentary of al-Shantamarī as edited by Muḥammad Abū al-Faḍl Ibrāhīm, in Ibrāhīm, *Dīwān al-Nābighah*, pp. 14–28 (49 lines). I have also consulted the text and commentary in Shukrī Fayṣal's edition of the recension of Ibn al-Sikkīt, in Fayṣal, *Dīwān al-Nābighah*, pp. 2–26 (50 lines), and al-Tibrīzī's *Muʿallaqāt* recension and commentary, al-Tibrīzī, *Sharḥ al-Qaṣāʾid al-ʿAshr*, pp. 347–75 (50 lines). The recensions of Ibn al-Sikkīt (in Fayṣal) and al-Tibrīzī are quite close to each other, whereas the differences between those two on the one hand and al-Aṣmaʿī's recension (in Ibrāhīm) on the other are more pronounced. There are a number of minor variations in diction and phrasing; of greater interest are differences in the order of lines

(see discussion below) that affect the reading of the poem. Line 40 in both the al-Tibrīzī and Ibn al-Sikkīt recensions is lacking in al-Aṣmaʿī. For other recensions, commentaries, and editions see Ibrāhīm, *Dīwān al-Nābighah,* intro., pp. 6–7; Arazi, "Al-Nābigha al-Dhubyānī"; and Sezgin, *Poesie,* 112–13. A recent translation, with which mine is at variance in a few places, is that of Renate Jacobi, "Al-Nābigha al-Dhubyānī (Sixth Century) in Praise of al-Nuʿmān III Abū Qābūs," in Stefan Sperl and Christopher Shackle, eds., *Qasida Poetry in Islamic Asia and Africa,* vol. 1: *Classical Traditions and Modern Meanings;* vol. 2: *Eulogy's Bounty, Meaning's Abundance: An Anthology* (Leiden: E. J. Brill, 1996), 2: 72–79.

31. Gian Biagio Conte, *The Rhetoric of Imitation: Genre and Poetic Memory in Virgil and Other Latin Poets,* trans. Charles Segal (Ithaca, N.Y.: Cornell University Press, 1986), pp. 35 n. 5, 70, 76–77.

32. See Jaroslav Stetkevych, "Toward an Arabic Elegiac Lexicon: The Seven Words of the *Nasīb,*" in S. Stetkevych, *Reorientations,* pp. 105–19; and John Seybold, "The Earliest Demon Lover: The *Ṭayf al-Khayāl* in *al-Mufaḍḍalīyāt,*" in ibid., pp. 180–89.

33. See Walter J. Ong, *Orality and Literacy: The Technologizing of the Word* (London: Methuen, 1982), passim; and Eric A. Havelock, *The Muse Learns to Write: Reflections on Orality and Literacy from Antiquity to the Present* (New Haven, Conn.: Yale University Press, 1986), passim.

34. The phrase is Conte's; see Conte, *Rhetoric of Imitation,* p. 44.

35. Jaroslav Stetkevych, *The Zephyrs of Najd: The Poetics of Nostalgia in the Classical Arabic* Nasīb (Chicago: University of Chicago Press, 1993), pp. 16–26, where the mood sequence of the *nasīb* and of the qasida generally is discussed in terms of the sonata form.

36. In his discussion of the etymological, intertextual, and mythpoeic aspects of conventional Arabic elegiac diction, J. Stetkevych gives particular attention to the *nasīb* of this poem. See his discussion of *dār* (abode) (line 1), pp. 61–65; *rabʿ* (spring camp) (line 2), pp. 66–68; *nuʾy* (trench) (line 3), pp. 68–74; and *suʾāl* (question) (line 2), in J. Stetkevych, "Toward an Arabic Elegiac Lexicon," pp. 105–19.

37. For the translation and discussion of a number of *nasībs* that contain the description of the beloved, see Michael A. Sells, "Guises of the *Ghūl:* Dissembling Simile and Semantic Overflow in the Classical Arabic *Nasīb,*" in S. Stetkevych, ed., *Reorientations,* pp. 130–64.

38. See B. Heller and N. A. Stillman, "Luḳmān," in *Encyclopaedia of Islam,* new ed. (Leiden: E. J. Brill, 1954–), and Abū al-Faḍl Aḥmad ibn Muḥammad al-Maydānī, *Majmaʿ al-Amthāl,* ed. Muḥammad Muḥyī al-Dīn ʿAbd al-Ḥamīd, 2nd ed., 2 vols. (Cairo: Al-Maktabah al-Tijāriyyah al-Kubrā, 1959), 1: 429–30. Heller and Stillman note that Luqmān is a composite legendary figure: *muʿammar* (granted long life), hero, sage, maker of proverbs, and author of fables, to whom various legends and materials were attracted at different periods. Cf. Sūrat Luqmān in the Qurʾān. I limit myself here to the legend at hand. See Heller and Stillman for an overview of this figure and references.

39. Al-Maydānī, *Majmaʿ al-Amthāl,* 1: 429, no. 2265.

40. Al-Maydānī, *Majmaʿ al-Amthāl,* 1: 430, no. 2265.

41. On the Arabic linguistic phenomenon of identity/polarity and the generation of antithetical meanings see Jaroslav Stetkevych, "Arabic Hermeneutical Ter-

minology: Paradox and the Production of Meaning," *Journal of Near Eastern Studies* 48, no. 2 (April 1989): 81–95.

42. See Mary Carruthers, *The Book of Memory: A Study of Memory in Medieval Culture* (Cambridge: Cambridge University Press, 1990), pp. 136–64, 216.

43. See, for example, the discussion in G. J. H. van Gelder, *Beyond the Line: Classical Arabic Literary Critics on the Coherence and Unity of the Poem* (Leiden: E. J. Brill, 1982), pp. 32–34.

44. The root *ᶜ-d-w,* of which *ᶜaddi* is the Form II imperative, means simply "to run" but also indicates transition and transgression (Lane, *ᶜ-d-w*); The root *w-d-ᶜ*, whence the imperative form *daᶜ*, conveys the meaning "to leave off, stop, cease, . . . desist" only in the imperfect and imperative, and of those two forms is found predominantly in the latter (Hans Wehr, *A Dictionary of Modern Written Arabic,* ed. J. Milton Cowan, 3rd ed. [Ithaca, N.Y.: Spoken Language Services, 1971], see under *w-d-ᶜ* [hereafter Wehr]). This suggests that its true etymological root may lie elsewhere—perhaps even as a lightened (*mukhaffaf*) metathesis (*qalb*) of *ᶜaddi*?

45. Jaroslav Stetkevych, "The Hunt in the Arabic *Qaṣīdah:* Antecedents of the *Ṭardiyyah,*" in J. R. Smart, ed., *Tradition and Modernity in Arabic Language and Literature* (Sussex: Curzon Press, 1996), pp. 102–18, passim; Abū ᶜUthmān ᶜAmr ibn Baḥr al-Jāḥiẓ, *Al-Ḥayawān,* ed. ᶜAbd al-Salām Muḥammad Hārūn, 8 vols. (Cairo: Muṣṭafā al-Bābī al-Ḥalabī, 1965–69), 2: 20.

46. See S. Stetkevych, *The Mute Immortals Speak,* pp. 26–33.

47. Crotty, *Poetics of Supplication,* p. 90. Crotty's study brings up points and references throughout that are applicable to the aspect of supplication in the qasida tradition and its relation to praise, negotiation, the authority of the poet, and the function of poetry.

48. Crotty, *Poetics of Supplication,* p. 9.

49. Crotty, *Poetics of Supplicaiton,* pp. 12–13.

50. Crotty, *Poetics of Supplication,* p. 91.

51. Simon Goldhill, *The Poet's Voice: Essays on Poetics and Greek Literature* (Cambridge: Cambridge University Press, 1991), pp. 73–75.

52. The major discussions of *kleos* (immortal fame) are those of James Redfield, *Nature and Culture in the Iliad: The Tragedy of Hector* (Chicago: University of Chicago Press, 1975), and Gregory Nagy, *The Best of the Achaeans: Concepts of the Hero in Archaic Greek Poetry* (Baltimore: Johns Hopkins University Press, 1979). See also Goldhill, *The Poet's Voice,* ch. 2, "Intimations of Immortality: Fame and Tradition from Homer to Pindar." The ethos of what Redfield terms the "warrior aristocracy" of Homeric epic and within it the concept of *kleos,* as discussed especially by Redfield and Nagy, and its relation to poetry as discussed by Goldhill, are broadly applicable to the ethos of pre-Islamic Arabia with its formative influence on Arabo-Islamic culture. On praise and poetry as conferring immortal renown in the Arabic tradition, see al-Ḥādirah's line: "Praise us then, you sons of bastards, for our deeds, / For surely praise is immortality" (*fa-athnū ᶜalaynā lā abā li abīkumū / bi-afᶜālinā inna th-thanāʾa huwa l-khuldū*). Cited in ᶜAbd al-Qādir ibn ᶜUmar al-Baghdādī, *Khizānat al-Adab wa Lubb Lubāb Lisān al-ᶜArab,* ed. ᶜAbd al-Salām Hārūn, 13 vols., 2nd ed. (Cairo: Maktabat al-Khānjī, 1984), 5: 46. See further, S. Stetkevych, *The Mute Immortals Speak,* pp. 170–71, 175, 188.

53. I am extending the use of Connerton's term, which he applies to the iden-

tification between two events in commemorative ceremonies, to include the identification of two figures, in this case, Sulaymān and al-Nuʿmān. See Paul Connerton, *How Societies Remember* (Cambridge: Cambridge University Press, 1989), p. 43; and also ch. 6 of the present work.

54. See Leslie Kurke, *The Traffic in Praise: Pindar and the Poetics of Social Economy* (Ithaca, N.Y.: Cornell University Press, 1991), pp. 94–95, 105–106, 155–59.

55. It is worth noting that in both the Ibn al-Sikkīt (Fayṣal, *Dīwān al-Nābighah,* pp. 14–16) and al-Tibrīzī's *Muʿallaqāt* (al-Tibrīzī, *Sharḥ al-Qaṣāʾid al-ʿAshr,* pp. 357–58) versions, the section that opens with *wa-ḥkum* (and judge!) (lines 32–36 of the version used here) occurs directly after our line 26 as lines 27–31 and thus forms a part of God's address to Sulaymān, rather than the poet's direct address to the king.

56. Arazi, "Al-Nābigha al-Dhubyānī."

57. Narrative is not, however, the only form: the elements of the Sulaymānic model and myth, though, I would argue, essentially part of a vast ancient Near Eastern folkloric bedrock, are for us today primarily textually traceable—but I hasten to add that this does not make Sulaymān primarily a textual entity. From the Hebrew Bible, the Midrash, pre-Islamic poetry—notably this qasida—the Qurʾān, Qurʾānic commentary, *qiṣaṣ al-anbiyāʾ* (stories of the prophets), *Thousand and One Nights,* to *ḥadīth* concerning the rule of the *imām* and caliphal rule, elements of the prototypical magician-monarch myth take a variety of forms. As a rule of thumb, we might say that that form depends on the overall rhetorical strategy of the text in which they appear (see J. Stetkevych, *Zephyrs of Najd,* pp. 168–71). For example, in the Qurʾān, where the rhetorical imperative of the message of submission and salvation/rebellion and damnation subordinates other goals, the mythic material of the pre-Islamic period appears in primarily non-narrative form, much as it does in the qasida, whose rhetorical imperative is determined by its performative function. Once the seal of overarching rhetorical imperatives is broken, the narrative jinni is released, and a full narrative form is (re)generated. Like Arazi, I see no reason to doubt, as some recent scholars have, the authenticity of the Sulaymān passage in al-Nābighah's poem (see Arazi, "Al-Nābigha al-Dhubyānī"). These avenues of enquiry are explored at length in my unpublished paper, "Solomon and Mythic Kingship in the Arabo-Islamic Tradition," presented as the Solomon Katz Distinguished Lecture at the University of Washington, Seattle, May 1999.

58. According to the commentary on line 32, the Basran philologist al-Aṣmaʿī (d. 213/828), on bedouin authority, took these lines to refer to Bint al-Khuss, whereas his contemporary and rival Abū ʿUbaydah (d. 209/824–25) took them to refer to Zarqāʾ al-Yamāmah, who was credited with being able to see three days into the future. To my mind the diction of line 33, "clear as glass, not inflamed and lined with kohl," is more suggestive of Zarqāʾ al-Yamāmah, but both figures are largely legendary and share, through contamination or otherwise, a number of the same elements. Fayṣal, *Dīwān al-Nābighah,* pp. 23–24.

59. On Bint al-Khuss, Zarqāʾ al-Yamāmah, and this passage from al-Nābighah's ode, see Maḥmūd Shukrī al-Ālūsī al-Baghdādī, *Bulūgh al-Arab fī Maʿrifat Aḥwāl al-ʿArab,* ed. Muḥammad Bahjat al-Atharī, 3 vols. (Beirut: Dār al-Kutub al-ʿIlmiyyah, n.d.) 1: 339–42.

60. Al-Ālūsī, *Bulūgh al-Arab,* 2: 341–42.

61. See S. Stetkevych, "Pre-Islamic Poetry and the Poetics of Redemption," pp. 12–13 (ᶜAlqamah) and pp. 34–36 (Kaᶜb).

62. In the Ibn al-Sikkīt and al-Tibrīzī versions, line 39 does not specify the nature of the offense as verbal: "I have not done anything to offend you. . . . " (*mā in nadaytu/ataytu bi-shayʾin anta takrahuhū*). See Fayṣal, *Dīwān al-Nābighah,* p. 20; and al-Tibrīzī, *Sharḥ al-Qaṣāʾid al-ᶜAshr,* p. 360.

63. In the Ibn al-Sikkīt and al-Tibrīzī versions, line 41 of our version occurs, respectively, as line 48 and line 49, where it plays a similar role to its placement here, that is, as recognition of and submission to the king's might and wrath before making a final plea for mercy. See Fayṣal, *Dīwān al-Nābighah,* p. 25; and al-Tibrīzī, *Sharḥ al-Qaṣāʾid al-ᶜAshr,* p. 362.

64. Aziz al-Azmeh, *Muslim Kingship: Power and the Sacred in Muslim, Christian, and Pagan Polities* (London: I. B. Tauris Publishers, 1997), p. 77 (and passim on the enunciation and representation of royal power, though with very little attention to poetry).

65. For a late-antique instance of this archetype involving the Nile, see Peter Brown, *Power and Persuasion in Late Antiquity: Towards a Christian Empire* (Madison: University of Wisconsin Press, 1992), p. 83. On Claudian's river simile (the Nile) in his *Panegyricus Dictus Manlio Theodoro Consuli* and its translation/imitation by the English poet Samuel Daniel in his panegyric to King James I, see James D. Garrison, *Dryden and the Tradition of Panegyric* (Berkeley: University of California Press, 1975), pp. 93–94. As the river in these cases is the Nile, the gist of the simile is *tranquilla potestas,* as Daniel puts it, "calme power."

66. Al-Iṣbahānī, *Kitāb al-Aghānī,* 11: 3799.

67. *Abayta l-laᶜna,* approximately "May you disdain to utter curses," was the traditional greeting for the Lakhmid kings. Lane gives the meaning "May thou refuse, or dislike, to do a thing that would occasion thy being cursed." This would give the meaning "May you repel all curses" or "May you never be cursed." But I would suggest that my translation better conveys the sense of the verb *ʾabā,* to disdain, forbear, etc. (Lane, *ʾ-b-y*). I take the verbal noun *laᶜn* in an active, not passive, sense: the supplicants greet the king with a prayer that he forbear from exercising his (mythic) powers of curse and imprecation against them.

68. This refers to the fine Lakhmid royal camels, known as *ᶜaṣāfīr al-Mundhir,* "al-Mundhir's sparrows," and *ᶜaṣāfīr al-Nuᶜmān,* "al-Nuᶜmān [ibn al-Mundhir]'s sparrows." See Lane, *ᶜ-ṣ-f-r.*

69. Al-Iṣbahānī, *Kitāb al-Aghānī,* 11: 3813–14.

2. Transmission and Submission

An earlier version of this chapter appeared as part 2 of Suzanne Pinckney Setkevych, "Pre-Islamic Poetry and the Poetics of Redemption: *Mufaḍḍalīyah 119* of ᶜAlqamah and *Bānat Suᶜād* of Kaᶜb ibn Zuhayr," in Suzanne Pinckney Stetkevych, ed., *Reorientations: Arabic and Persian Poetry* (Bloomington and Indianapolis: Indiana University Press, 1994), pp. 21–57.

1. Sezgin, *Poesie,* pp. 229–35.

2. This is not, by any means, to say that Kaᶜb was the first or only poet to serve the Prophet. Pride of place in that respect goes to the Prophet's main panegyrist,

formerly an acclaimed pre-Islamic panegyrist, Ḥassān ibn Thābit. It is of note, however, that the classical Arabic critics concur that Ḥassān's pre-Islamic oeuvre was artistically superior to that written for the Prophet. There are in addition the minor poets of Ibn Hishām's edition of Ibn Isḥāq's Life of the Prophet (*Sīrah*) (see below, n. 9), such as Kaᶜb ibn Malik, who were always at hand to compose praise (*madīḥ*), incitement (*taḥrīḍ*), or invective (*hijāʾ*) as needed, on the whole not of outstanding quality. Panegyric (*madḥ*) in this period tends to be short, extemporaneous and spontaneous, rather direct in style, and often without a preceding elegiac prelude (*nasīb*) or journey section (*raḥīl*). See Rūmiyyah, *Qaṣīdat al-Madḥ*, pp. 274–76; and James T. Monroe, "The Poetry of the *Sīrah* Literature," ch. 18 of A. F. L. Beeston, T. M. Johnstone, R. B. Serjeant, and G. R. Smith, eds., *The Cambridge History of Arabic Literature*, vol. 1: *Arabic Literature to the End of the Umayyad Period* (Cambridge: Cambridge University Press, 1983), pp. 368–73. Kaᶜb ibn Zuhayr, by contrast, was something of a latecomer to the Islamic fold (see below). His "Suᶜād Has Departed," which bears the sobriquet "The Mantle Ode," is the most celebrated qasida of its period and, throughout the centuries, one of the most revered and influential poems of the Arabic and Islamic traditions.

3. To be supplanted or supplemented from the seventh/thirteenth century onward by the immensely popular "Mantle Ode" of al-Būṣīrī. I will address the relation and history of *al-Burdatān* (The Two Mantles) of Kaᶜb and al-Būṣīrī in a separate project.

4. Arnold van Gennep, *The Rites of Passage*, trans. Monika Vizedom and Gabrielle L. Caffee (Chicago: University of Chicago Press, 1960) [*Les rites de passage*, 1908]; Theodor Gaster, *Thespis: Ritual, Myth, and Drama in the Ancient Middle East* (New York: Norton and Co., 1977); and Mauss, *The Gift*. See the fuller description and discussion of the theoretical formulations of van Gennep, Gaster, and Mauss in ch. 6.

5. Eric A. Havelock, *The Literate Revolution in Greece and Its Cultural Consequences* (Princeton, N.J.: Princeton University Press, 1982), pp. 116–17; and S. Stetkevych, *The Mute Immortals Speak*, chs. 5, 6.

6. See S. Stetkevych, *The Mute Immortals Speak*, p. 81.

7. Havelock, *The Muse Learns to Write*, p. 70.

8. Havelock, *The Muse Learns to Write*, p. 71.

9. Of the many recensions of and commentaries on "Suᶜād Has Departed," I have relied primarily on Abū Saᶜīd al-Ḥasan ibn al-Ḥusayn al-Sukkarī, *Sharḥ Dīwān Kaᶜb ibn Zuhayr* (Cairo: Al-Dār al-Qawmiyyah, 1965), pp. 3–25; Yaḥyā ibn ᶜAlī al-Tibrīzī, in Fritz Krenkow, "Tabrīzīs Kommentar zur Burda des Kaᶜb ibn Zuhair," *Zeitschrift der Deutschen Morganländischen Gesellschaft* 65 (1911): 241–79; and Abū Muḥammad ᶜAbd al-Malik ibn Hishām, *Al-Sīrah al-Nabawiyyah*, 4 vols. (Cairo: Dār al-Fikr, n.d.), 3: 1353–66. Ibn Hishām's work is actually an edition of the older *Sīrah* by Ibn Isḥāq (d. 150/767), which has been reconstructed by Guillaume in his translation, below. English versions of the qasida and its *akhbār* are found in M. Hidayat Husain, "Banat Suᶜad of Kaᶜb bin Zuhair," *Islamic Culture* 1 (1927): 67–84; and A. Guillaume, trans., *The Life of Muhammad: A Translation of Ibn Isḥāq's Sīrat Rasūl Allāh* (Lahore and Karachi: Oxford University Press, 1974), pp. 597–601 (which quotes Nicholson's translation). A translation by Michael A. Sells has appeared as "*Bānat Suᶜād:* Translation and Interpretative Introduction," *Journal of*

Arabic Literature 21, no. 2 (1990): 140–54. For further sources, see Sezgin, *Poesie,* pp. 230–35.

10. Reading *qulta* for *qultu.*

11. Al-Sukkarī, *Sharḥ Dīwān Kaᶜb ibn Zuhayr,* pp. 3–5. This story occurs with a number of minor variations. See the sources cited above, n. 8. The *Sīrah* version dates these events quite explicitly as occurring after the capture of al-Ṭāʾif (8 H.), with Kaᶜb's conversion thus taking place in the year 9/630. See Ibn Hishām, *Al-Sīrah al-Nabawiyyah,* 3: 1353; Guillaume, *The Life of Muhammad,* p. 597; Sezgin, *Poesie,* p. 229.

12. Al-Iṣbahānī, *Kitāb al-Aghānī,* 10: 3472.

13. I have followed al-Sukkarī's recension, except where otherwise noted: al-Sukkarī, *Sharḥ Dīwān Kaᶜb ibn Zuhayr,* pp. 6–25.

14. Reading *lam yufda.* See al-Sukkarī, *Sharḥ Dīwān Kaᶜb ibn Zuhayr,* p. 6.

15. Ibn Hishām, *Al-Sīrah al-Nabawiyyah,* 3: 1363.

16. As the commentarists read it, this line would translate:

They walk as the white camels walk,
and their sword's blow
Protects them when
the black runts flee the field.

See al-Sukkarī, *Sharḥ Dīwān Kaᶜb ibn Zuhayr,* pp. 24–25; and Krenkow, "Tabrīzīs Kommentar," p. 278. See discussion below.

17. Al-Sukkarī, *Sharḥ Dīwān Kaᶜb ibn Zuhayr,* p. 6.

18. Root *gh-w-l* in Muḥammad ibn Mukarram ibn Manẓūr, *Lisān al-ᶜArab,* 15 vols. (Beirut: Dār Ṣādir, 1955–56). Henceforth cited as *Lisān.*

19. On the *ghūl* as a simile for fickleness and mutability in this poem, see the discussion of the *nasīb* in Sells, "Guises of the *Ghūl,*" pp. 137–41. For a comparative study of Taʾabbaṭa Sharran and the *ghūl* with Oedipus and the Sphinx, see ch. 3, "Taʾabbaṭa Sharran and Oedipus: A Paradigm of Passage Manqué," in S. Stetkevych, *The Mute Immortals Speak,* pp. 87–118.

20. Al-Maydānī, *Majmaᶜ al-Amthāl,* 2: 311, no. 4071.

21. Al-Sukkarī, *Sharḥ Dīwān Kaᶜb ibn Zuhayr,* p. 10; Ibn Hishām, *Al-Sīrah al-Nabawiyyah,* 3: 1358.

22. Lines 36–46; see [Ibn] al-Anbārī, *Sharḥ al-Qaṣāʾid al-Sabᶜ,* pp. 553–65. See the translation and discussion in S. Stetkevych, *The Mute Immortals Speak,* pp. 13–14, 31–32.

23. On this reading of the image, see Annemarie Schimmel, *And Muhammad Is His Messenger: The Veneration of the Prophet in Islamic Piety* (Chapel Hill and London: University of North Carolina Press, 1985), pp. 179–80.

24. Gaster, *Thespis,* pp. 30–34.

25. Gaster, *Thespis,* p. 34.

26. Gaster, *Thespis,* p. 43.

27. Al-Sukkarī, *Sharḥ Dīwān Kaᶜb ibn Zuhayr,* p. 21, n. 2.

28. Krenkow, "Tabrīzīs Kommentar," p. 273.

29. See S. Stetkevych, "Pre-Islamic Poetry and the Poetics of Redemption," in *Reorientations,* pp. 13–15.

30. Just as we see a shift in the seasonal pattern from the agrarian to the bedouin

warrior ethos, so too we see a semantic shift in the meaning of the root *l-ḥ-m*. In the Hebrew agrarian context *leḥem* means bread; whereas in the Arabic bedouin warrior/hunt society *laḥm* denotes meat.

31. See al-Sukkarī, *Sharḥ Dīwān Kaʿb ibn Zuhayr,* pp. 24–25.

32. Al-Iṣbahānī, *Kitāb al-Aghānī,* 10: 3778; A. J. Arberry, *The Seven Odes: The First Chapter in Arabic Literature* (London: George Allen and Unwin, 1957), p. 98.

33. Zuhayr's *Muʿallaqah,* lines 26–27; see [Ibn] al-Anbārī, *Sharḥ al-Qaṣāʾid al-Sabʿ*, p. 266.

34. Al-Ālūsī, *Bulūgh al-Arab,* 3: 101.

35. Walter Burkert, *Homo Necans: The Anthropology of Ancient Greek Ritual and Myth,* trans. Peter Bing (Berkeley: University of California Press, 1983), p. 23. See also S. Stetkevych, *The Mute Immortals Speak,* pp. 82–83.

36. See Havelock, *The Muse Learns to Write,* pp. 63–78.

37. Versions of this anecdote are found in Ibn Qutaybah, *Kitāb al-Shiʿr wa al-Shuʿarāʾ,* p. 60; Muḥammad ibn Sallām al-Jumaḥī, *Ṭabaqāt Fuḥūl al-Shuʿarāʾ,* 2 vols., ed. Maḥmūd Muḥammad Shākir (Cairo: Maṭbaʿat al-Madanī, 1974) 1: 103; and 1: 23–24, etc. See Rudi Paret, "Die Legende der Verleihung des Prophetenmantels (*burda*) an Kaʿb ibn Zuhair," *Der Islam* 17 (1928): 9–14; and Sezgin, *Poesie,* pp. 229–30. The most extensive study of the sources, variants, and politico-historical significance of the *burdah* anecdote is that of Zwettler, which serves as an update and corrective of Paret. See Michael Zwettler, "The Poet and the Prophet: Towards an Understanding of the Evolution of a Narrative," *Jerusalem Studies in Arabic and Islam* 5 (1984): 313–87. Of particular interest is his tracing its development into a "Prophetic *Ḥadīth*" in the early third century H., pp. 334–72.

38. See Paret, "Die Legende," pp. 9–14; and Sezgin, *Poesie,* p. 230.

39. Cited in Paret, "Die Legende," p. 13.

40. Cited by al-Anbārī in Charles James Lyall, ed. and trans., *The Mufaḍḍalīyāt: An Anthology of Ancient Arabian Odes Compiled by Al-Mufaḍḍal Son of Muḥammad, According to the Recension and with the Commentary of Abū Muḥammad al-Qāsim ibn Muḥammad al-Anbārī,* vol. I: *Arabic Text;* vol. II: *Translation and Notes* (Oxford: Clarendon Press, 1918), 1: 764.

41. On the "witness value of symbolic objects," see Ong, *Orality and Literacy,* p. 97.

42. Paret, "Die Legende," pp. 12–13. Moreover, by expanding Paret's citation back to II Kings 2:8, it is clear that the "mantle" of Elijah that Elisha takes up is identified with the "spirit" of Elijah.

43. Ibn Qutaybah, *Al-Shiʿr wa-al-Shuʿarāʾ,* p. 51.

44. Al-Iṣbahānī, *Kitāb al-Aghānī,* 9: 3219–21.

45. See the preceding discussion of *ḍ-l-l* in this chapter.

46. Mauss, *The Gift,* p. 10.

47. Mauss, *The Gift,* p. 43.

48. Al-Iṣbahānī, *Kitāb al-Aghānī,* 10: 3769.

3. Celebration and Restoration

An earlier version of this chapter was presented at the annual meeting of the Middle East Studies Association in Providence, R.I., November 1996, and appeared as

Suzanne Pinckney Stetkevych, "Umayyad Panegyric and the Poetics of Islamic Hegemony: al-Akhṭal's *Khaffa al-Qaṭīnu*" ('Those That Dwelt with You Have Left in Haste')," *Journal of Arabic Literature* 28, no. 2 (1997): 89–122.

1. David Quint, *Epic and Empire: Politics and Generic Form from Virgil to Milton* (Princeton, N.J.: Princeton University Press, 1993), p. 8 and passim.

2. Conte, *The Rhetoric of Imitation,* p. 147.

3. Tarif Khalidi, *Arabic Historical Thought in the Classical Period* (Cambridge: Cambridge University Press, 1994), p. 29.

4. On the scope of the qasida tradition, see Sperl and Shackle, *Qasida Poetry,* passim.

5. This follows in part the argument presented in Rūmiyyah, *Qaṣīdat al-Madḥ,* on the poetry of *ṣadr al-Islām,* p. 276 and pp. 261–96 passim; on the "revivalists" of the Jāhilī *qaṣīdat al-madḥ,* pp. 304–305 and pp. 299–502 passim. I take exception to some of Rūmiyyah's conclusions; see below. See also al-Nuʿmān al-Qāḍī, *Shiʿr al-Futūḥ al-Islāmiyyah fī Ṣadr al-Islām* (Cairo: Al-Dār al-Qawmiyyah lil-Ṭibāʿah wa al-Nashr, 1965), pp. 217, 276, 304ff. [as cited in Rūmiyyah]. On the concept of rhetorical opacity and metaphorical density, the "thickness" of poetic discourse as opposed to transparency and literalness of non-poetic discourse, see Conte, *Rhetoric of Imitation,* pp. 46, 55, 68–69.

6. Although I am indebted to Rūmiyyah for his detailed and extensive study and analysis of this literary historical phenomenon, I am at odds with him in interpretation. For him, the massive comeback of the high Jāhilī *qaṣīdat al-madḥ,* which he attributes to the mistaken notion that the preservation of the pure Arabic language of the Jāhiliyyah required the retention of its forms of expression, i.e., the Jāhilī qasida, constitutes a "form of artistic suicide" (Rūmiyyah, *Qaṣīdat al-Madḥ,* pp. 304–5), that it was nothing but slavish imitation (p. 329) and an obsession with the ancient/s (p. 316); that it was the greatest crime that these poets could have perpetrated against themselves and against poetry; that they virtually slit the throat of poetry; that they were enslaved by the old poetry (p. 502).

7. In this respect, Henri Lammens's assessment of the poetry of the Umayyad period as a Renaissance/renaissance is most provocative. See Henri Lammens, *Études sur le siècle des Omayyades* (Beirut: Imprimerie Catholique, 1930), pp. 220–21. This proposition is one that deserves serious comparative consideration beyond the scope of the present study.

8. Conte, *Rhetoric of Imitation,* p. 142.

9. Conte, *Rhetoric of Imitation,* p. 142.

10. See S. Stetkevych, *Abū Tammām,* pp. 185–86, 107–235 passim.

11. On the ceremonial aspects of poetry, see below. On ceremony as negotiation of rank and status, see Paula Sanders, *Ritual, Politics, and the City in Fatimid Cairo* (Albany: State University of New York Press, 1994), ch. 2, "The Ceremonial Idiom," pp. 13–38. A valuable introduction to Umayyad ceremony and its source materials with a useful bibliography is O. Grabar, "Notes sur les cérémonies umayyades," in Myriam Rosen-Ayalon, ed., *Studies in Memory of Gaston Wiet* (Jerusalem: Institute of Asian and African Studies, the Hebrew University of Jerusalem, 1997), pp. 51–60. I would amend Grabar's assessment of Umayyad ceremonial, however, by suggesting that he has overlooked the centrality of the presentation of the *qaṣīdat al-madḥ* to Umayyad ceremonial (p. 53) and the function of the qasida and its at-

tendant ceremony as a concrete symbol of caliphal authority. In all fairness, it must nevertheless be pointed out that the literary anecdotes that we possess cannot be accepted prima facie as authentic descriptions of actual ceremonial.

12. Eric Hobsbawm and Terence Ranger, eds., *The Invention of Tradition* (Cambridge: Cambridge University Press, 1983). The concepts presented in Hobsbawm's introduction could profitably be applied to the qasida in the early Islamic and Umayyad period.

13. See Conte, *Rhetoric of Imitation,* p. 59.

14. For a discussion of many aspects of imitation and influence in the Arabic and Persian, see Paul E. Losensky, "'The Allusive Fields of Drunkenness': Three Safavid Mogul Responses to a Lyric by Bābā Fighānī," in S. Stetkevych, ed., *Reorientations,* pp. 227–62; and Losensky's monograph *Welcoming Fighānī: Imitation and Poetic Individuality in the Safavid-Mughal* Ghazal (Costa Mesa, Calif.: Mazda Publishers, 1998).

15. See Connerton, *How Societies Remember,* p. 43. I deal more precisely with Connerton's use of this term in my discussions of aligning qasidas with calendrical holidays in chs. 6 and 7; and Suzanne Pinckney Stetkevych, "The Politics and Poetics of Genre: A *Qaṣīdah* for ʿĀshūrāʾ by al-Sharīf al-Raḍī," unpublished paper presented at Aspects of Arabic Literature Conference, University of California, Berkeley (April 1996).

16. See Connerton, *How Societies Remember,* ch. 2, "Commemorative Practices," pp. 41–71, and Sanders, *Ritual, Politics, and the City,* p. 37 and pp. 13–37 passim. In the treatment of the Arabic qasida, and the Umayyad in particular, the awareness of its function as political negotiation is most foregrounded in Shawqī Ḍayf, *Al-Taṭawwur wa-al-Tajdīd fī al-Shiʿr al-Umawī,* 2nd ed. (Cairo: Dār al-Maʿārif, 1959), e.g., pp. 136, 172.

17. On the Umayyad qasida, esp. *madīḥ* and *hijāʾ,* as a vehicle for political claims, again see Ḍayf, *Al-Taṭawwur wa-al-Tajdīd,* pp. 131–218 passim.

18. Ghiyāth ibn Ghawth ibn al-Ṣalt, Abū Mālik. On al-Akhṭal and his standing among the Umayyad poetic triumvirate with Jarīr and al-Farazdaq, see, e.g., Ibn Qutaybah, *Al-Shiʿr wa-al-Shuʿarāʾ,* p. 301; al-Iṣbahānī, *Kitāb al-Aghānī,* 8: 3028–38; and al-Jumaḥī, *Ṭabaqāt Fuḥūl al-Shuʿarāʾ,* 1: 297–99. Although al-Akhṭal has many prominent supporters, there was no consensus over which of the three was the best (*Kitāb al-Aghānī,* 8: 3028). A major western-language study of al-Akhṭal is Henri Lammens, "Le chantre des Omaides: Notes biographiques et littéraires sur le poète arabe chrétien Aḫṭal," *Journale Asiatique* ser. 9, no. 4 (1894): 94–176, 193–241, 381–459. For the classical sources and modern bibliography on al-Akhṭal, see Sezgin, *Poesie,* pp. 318–21.

19. A. A. Bevan, ed., *Kitāb al-Naqāʾiḍ: Naqāʾiḍ Jarīr wa-al-Farazdaq,* 3 vols. (Leiden: E. J. Brill, 1905–12) [Photo-offset, Baghdad: Maktabat al-Muthannā, n.d.]; and Anṭūn Ṣāliḥānī, ed., *Naqāʾiḍ Jarīr wa-al-Akhṭal taʾlīf al-Imām al-Shāʿir al-Adīb al-Māhir Abī Tammām* (Beirut: Al-Maṭbaʿah al-Kāthūlīkiyyah, 1922; reprint, Beirut: Dār al-Mashriq, 1986), pp. 148–65.

20. Al-Iṣbahānī, *Kitāb al-Aghānī,* 8: 3045.

21. I have followed G. R. Hawting's thorough and concise article "Umayyads," in *Encyclopaedia of Islam,* new ed. (Leiden: E. J. Brill, 1954–); see also ʿAbd al-Ameer Dixon, *The Umayyad Caliphate, 65–86/684–705: A Political Study* (London: Luzac

and Co., 1971), for a detailed study and exposition of the reign of ʿAbd al-Malik ibn Marwān based closely on the original sources. The major classical historical source for the events covered here is Aḥmad ibn Yaḥyā ibn Jābir al-Balādhurī, *Ansāb al-Ashrāf*, part 5, ed. S. D. F. Goitein (Jerusalem: School of Oriental Studies, Hebrew University, 1936), pp. 188–379.

22. Following Hugh Kennedy, *The Prophet and the Age of the Caliphs: The Islamic Near East from the Fifth to the Eleventh Century* (London and New York: Longman, 1986), pp. 93–94, and 78–99 passim.

23. Kennedy, *The Prophet and the Age of the Caliphs*, pp. 92, 94. See also Dixon, *The Umayyad Caliphate*, pp. 98–102.

24. Dixon, *The Umayyad Caliphate*, pp. 98–103.

25. See H. A. R. Gibb, "ʿAbd Allāh ibn al-Zubayr," in *Encyclopaedia of Islam*, new ed. (Leiden: E. J. Brill, 1954–); and H. Lammens [and Charles Pellat], "Muṣʿab ibn al-Zubayr," in *Encyclopaedia of Islam*, new ed. (Leiden: E. J. Brill, 1954–); see also Gernot Rotter, *Die Umayyaden und der zweite Bürgerkrieg (680–692)*, Abhandlungen für die Kunde des Morgenlandes, 45, part 3 (Wiesbaden: Franz Steiner, 1982), pp. 208–51, and chronology, p. 252; and Dixon, *The Umayyad Caliphate*, pp. 131–42. For the historical details as they relate to the poetic text, see below.

26. Al-Iṣbahānī, *Kitāb al-Aghānī*, 8: 3040.

27. See S. Stetkevych, *The Mute Immortals Speak*, passim; and the discussions in chs. 1 and 2.

28. Nagy, *Pindar's Homer*, p. 433; and ch. 1.

29. ʿAbd al-Malik's pronouncement appears as well in another anecdote associated with the same qasida, now cast in terms of a poetic competition between Jarīr and al-Akhṭal. See al-Iṣbahānī, *Kitāb al-Aghānī*, 8: 3052–53.

30. See Ḥasan al-Bannā ʿIzz al-Dīn, *Shiʿriyyat al-Ḥarb ʿind al-ʿArab qabl al-Islām: Qaṣīdat al-Ẓaʿāʾin Namūdhajan*, 2nd ed. (Riyadh: Dār al-Mufradāt lil-Nashr wa-al-Tawzīʿ, 1998); and Hassan el-Banna Ezz El-Din, "'No Solace for the Heart': The Motif of the Departing Women in the Pre-Islamic Battle Ode," in S. Stetkevych, ed., *Reorientations*, pp. 165–79.

31. See Rūmiyyah, *Qaṣīdat al-Madḥ*, p. 470; and Ḍayf, *Al-Taṭawwur wa-al-Tajdīd*, p. 136.

32. For the text I have followed the recension in Fakhr al-Dīn Qabāwah, ed., *Shiʿr al-Akhṭal, Abī Mālik Ghiyāth ibn Ghawth al-Taghlibī, Ṣanʿat al-Sukkarī, Riwāyah ʿan Abī Jaʿfar Muḥammad ibn Ḥabīb*, 2nd ed., 2 vols. (Beirut: Dār al-Āfāq al-Jadīdah, 1979), 1: 192–211. Also consulted were Īliyyā Salīm al-Ḥāwī, ed., *Sharḥ Dīwān al-Akhṭal al-Taghlibī* (Beirut: Dār al-Thaqāfah, n.d.), pp. 160–79; Anṭūn Ṣāliḥānī, ed., *Shiʿr al-Akhṭal, Riwāyat Abī ʿAbd Allāh Muḥammad ibn al-ʿAbbās al-Yazīdī ʿan Abī Saʿīd al-Sukkarī ʿan Muḥammad ibn Ḥabīb ʿan Ibn al-Aʿrābī* (Beirut: Dār al-Maṭbaʿah al-Kāthūlīkiyyah, n.d.; reprint, Beirut: Dār al-Mashriq, 1969), pp. 98–112; and Ṣāliḥānī, *Naqāʾiḍ Jarīr wa-al-Akhṭal*, pp. 148–65. The recensions exhibit a number of variants (including, in the *Naqāʾiḍ* version, a divergent ordering of lines), some of which affect the identification of referents as well as the meaning.

33. This line has a couple of variants and the commentarists seem unsure of its meaning. I have tried to give a reading that gives some coherence to the poetic passage.

34. The Ghūṭah of Damascus "is the area of gardens and orchards which sur-

round the former Umayyad capital below the gorges of Rabwa" irrigated by the Baradā River. N. Elisséeff, "Ghūṭa," in *Encyclopaedia of Islam,* new ed. (Leiden: E. J. Brill, 1954–).

35. On the place-names, see Ṣāliḥānī, *Naqā᾽iḍ Jarīr wa-al-Akhṭal,* p. 162 note a (line 69); and Rotter, *Die Umayyaden,* pp. 203–205 and map, p. 194.

36. It is related that ᶜUmayr ibn al-Ḥubāb used to say, "The Taghlib are nothing to me but *jashar* (approximately "boys that tend the far-off camel herds"), I can take from them whatever I want." So when these Yamanī (Ghassān are Yamanī) tribes were shown ᶜUmayr's head, they mocked him saying, "How do you like the herdboys' hospitality?!" Qabāwah, *Shiᶜr al-Akhṭal,* p. 204.

37. Al-Ḥārith ibn Abī ᶜAwf is identified as a man from the Banū ᶜĀmir ibn Ṣaᶜṣaᶜah (of Qays ᶜAylān). Qabāwah, *Shiᶜr al-Akhṭal,* p. 204.

38. The Banū Dhakwān are the clan of ᶜUmayr ibn al-Ḥubāb.

39. The Greater and Lesser Zāb are two tributaries of the Tigris. See map in Rotter, *Die Umayyaden,* p. 194.

40. Places in al-Jazīrah, see Qabāwah, *Shiᶜr al-Akhṭal,* p. 206 n. 4; and Rotter, *Die Umayyaden,* p. 206 and map, p. 194.

41. The "Kid of the Farqadān" is the last star of Ursa Minor and therefore always in the northern sky, whereas the moon rises and sets in the southern sky. See Ṣāliḥānī, *Naqā᾽iḍ Jarīr wa-al-Akhṭal,* p. 160.

42. Line 67 is somewhat ambiguous. Following the commentaries' identification of the proper names, Farrāṣ of line 66 is a Taghlibī; al-Ḍibāb of line 67 is of the ᶜĀmir ibn Ṣaᶜṣaᶜah, and therefore, like the Banū Sulaym, of Qays ᶜAylān; and al-ᶜUṣayyah is of the Banū Sulaym (Ṣāliḥānī has the variant Suwā᾽ah, identified as ibn ᶜĀmir ibn Ṣaᶜṣaᶜah, p. 161). The meaning is then that Ibn al-Ḥubāb's band of the Banū Sulaym cannot match the noble lineage of the Banū Taghlib, nor even the other lineages of Qays ᶜAylān. Al-Ḥāwī takes it to mean rather that these Qaysīs cannot measure up to the noble lineage of Farrāṣ either. See Qabāwah, *Shiᶜr al-Akhṭal,* p. 207; Ṣāliḥānī, *Naqā᾽iḍ Jarīr wa-al-Akhṭal,* p. 161; and al-Ḥāwī, *Sharḥ Dīwān al-Akhṭal,* p. 177. I take *ikhḍarrat ᶜuyūnuhumū* to mean something like *iswadda wajhuhu.*

43. The Kilāb ibn Rabīᶜah are one of the tribes of the ᶜĀmir ibn Ṣaᶜṣaᶜah [of Qays ᶜAylān]. See W. M. Watt, "Kilāb b. Rabīᶜa," in *Encyclopaedia of Islam,* new ed. (Leiden: E. J. Brill, 1954–). In the *Naqā᾽iḍ* recension, this line reads "Sulaym" instead of Kulayb and appears as line 57, near the beginning of the section on the Sulamī excursion into Taghlibī territory. See Ṣāliḥānī, *Naqā᾽iḍ Jarīr wa-al-Akhṭal,* p.159.

44. Muḍar is the common ancestor of most of the north Arabian tribes. See H. Kindermann, "Rabīᶜa and Muḍar," in *Encyclopaedia of Islam,* new ed. (Leiden: E. J. Brill, 1954–).

45. Najrān is in the Yemen; Hajar in Baḥrayn. See Qabāwah, *Shiᶜr al-Akhṭal,* p. 209.

46. Ghudānah is identified as Ghudānah ibn Yarbūᶜ ibn Ḥanẓalah. See Ṣāliḥānī, *Naqā᾽iḍ Jarīr wa-al-Akhṭal,* p. 164.

47. A variant is *lā yastaḥīna* (feel no shame) for *lā tastaḥimma* (do not bathe). See Ṣāliḥānī, *Naqā᾽iḍ Jarīr wa-al-Akhṭal,* p. 165; and al-Ḥāwī, *Sharḥ Dīwān al-Akhṭal,* p. 179.

48. Garrison gives prominence to the theme of restoration in panegyric—not surprisingly, as he is dealing with the poetry of Restoration England. See Garrison, *Dryden,* ch. 2, pp. 81–140 passim.

49. Garrison, *Dryden,* p. 115.

50. Conte, *Rhetoric of Imitation,* p. 45.

51. See Conte, *Rhetoric of Imitation,* pp. 45–47.

52. Again see ʿIzz al-Dīn, *Shiʿriyyat al-Ḥarb;* and Ezz El-Din, "'No Solace for the Heart.'"

53. See ch. 4, n. 32.

54. See, for example, the *nasīb* of the *Muʿallaqah* of Labīd, where the ratio is reversed, i.e., the *ẓaʿn* motif is subordinated to the *aṭlāl* theme. See S. Stetkevych, *Mute Immortals,* ch. 1; [Ibn] al-Anbārī, *Sharḥ al-Qaṣāʾid al-Sabʿ,* pp. 505–98.

55. ʿIzz al-Dīn, *Shiʿriyyat al-Ḥarb;* and Ezz El-Din, "'No Solace for the Heart.'"

56. Rūmiyyah, *Qaṣīdat al-Madḥ,* p. 411.

57. Al-Iṣbahānī, *Kitāb al-Aghānī,* 8: 3033–34, and see below.

58. Al-Iṣbahānī, *Kitāb al-Aghānī,* 8: 3031–32.

59. On this issue, see Patricia Crone and Martin Hinds, *God's Caliph: Religious Authority in the First Centuries of Islam* (Cambridge: Cambridge University Press, 1986), pp. 4–42; and Ḍayf, *Al-Taṭawwur wa-al-Tajdīd,* pp. 97–101 and 150–51.

60. See, respectively, Ṣāliḥānī, *Naqāʾiḍ Jarīr wa-al-Akhṭal,* p. 153; al-Ḥāwī, *Sharḥ Dīwān al-Akhṭal,* p. 169; and al-Iṣbahānī, *Kitāb al-Aghānī,* 8: 3041. Dixon mentions that ʿAbd al-Malik had said of ʿAbd Allāh ibn al-Zubayr that "he has every qualification for a caliph were it not for his miserliness." Dixon, *The Umayyad Caliphate,* p. 16. Perhaps line 27 reflects this?

61. It is worth noting that in an anecdote in the *Kitāb al-Aghānī* featuring this line (here 28), it is given in the form *nafsī fidāʾu amīri l-muʾminīna. . . .* ([Let] my soul be the ransom of the Commander of the Faithful. . . .), thereby rendering the line as the poet's traditionally phrased declaration of allegiance to the caliph. See al-Iṣbahānī, *Kitāb al-Aghānī,* 8: 3043.

62. See Lammens, "Muṣʿab ibn al-Zubayr."

63. Qabāwah, *Shiʿr al-Akhṭal,* p. 200.

64. Qabāwah, *Shiʿr al-Akhṭal,* p. 200.

65. The issue of political authority in the Islamic world and the place of ceremony, *adab,* and the qasida in political culture bears comparison, mutatis mutandis, to Brown's description of culture and politics in late antiquity in terms of "*paideia* and power," which has shaped my discussion here. See Brown, *Power and Persuasion,* pp. 3–70.

66. On the primacy of these two virtues in *madīḥ,* see Rūmiyyah, *Qaṣīdat al-Madḥ,* p. 162.

67. See Ḍayf, *Al-Taṭawwur wa-al-Tajdīd,* esp. pp. 85–101; and al-Nuʿmān al-Qāḍī, *Al-Firaq al-Islāmiyyah fī al-Shiʿr al-Umawī* (Cairo: Dār al-Maʿārif, 1970).

68. See Gibb, "ʿAbd Allāh b. al-Zubayr"; and W. Montgomery Watt, "Ḳuraysh" and "Abū Sufyān," in *Encyclopaedia of Islam,* new ed. (Leiden: E. J. Brill, 1954–).

69. Conte, *Rhetoric of Imitation,* p. 142.

70. See C. E. Bosworth, "Marwān I," in *Encyclopaedia of Islam,* new ed. (Leiden: E. J. Brill, 1954–).

71. See Rūmiyyah, *Qaṣīdat al-Madḥ,* p. 470; and Ḍayf, *Al-Taṭawwur wa-al-Tajdīd,* p. 136.

72. Ḍayf, *Al-Taṭawwur wa-al-Tajdīd,* p. 136.

73. For this anecdote, see Ibn Qutaybah, *Al-Shiʿr wa-al-Shuʿarāʾ,* p. 302. It is perhaps worth noting in the political context of this qasida that the Anṣār were known to have given their allegiance to ʿAlī. See Rotter, *Die Umayyaden,* p. 19.

74. See Dixon, *The Umayyad Caliphate,* p. 94; and Rotter, *Die Umayyaden,* p. 201. For more on al-Akhṭal's antipathy to this former enemy turned rival for ʿAbd al-Malik's favor, see al-Iṣbahānī, *Kitāb al-Aghānī,* 8: 3042–43.

75. On the tribal war between Qays and Taghlib at this period, including political and economic factors, see Dixon, *The Umayyad Caliphate,* pp. 88–104; and Rotter, *Die Umayyaden,* 193–207. In general, it should be noted that the Banū Taghlib had sided with the Kalbīs/Yamanīs in supporting the Umayyads at the battle of Marj Rāhiṭ (64/683), whereas the Qaysīs were supporters of ʿAbd Allāh ibn al-Zubayr (Dixon, p. 88). See also al-Iṣbahānī, *Kitāb al-Aghānī,* 12: 4364–65; and al-Balādhurī, *Ansāb al-Ashrāf,* 5: 308–31. See also ch. 4.

76. For the tribal lands of Taghlib and Sulaym, see the map in Rotter, *Die Umayyaden,* p. 194.

77. See Sezgin, *Poesie,* pp. 356–59.

78. See Sanders, *Ritual, Politics, and the City,* pp. 13–38.

79. See S. Stetkevych, *Abū Tammām,* pp. 300–303; and S. Stetkevych, *The Mute Immortals Speak,* pp. 193–96.

80. See Qabāwah, *Shiʿr al-Akhṭal,* p. 209; Ṣāliḥānī, *Naqāʾiḍ Jarīr wa-al-Akhṭal,* p. 164.

81. See al-Ḥāwī, *Sharḥ Dīwān al-Akhṭal,* p. 179.

82. See S. Stetkevych, *The Mute Immortals Speak,* pp. 165–66, 197–99.

83. Al-Iṣbahānī, *Kitāb al-Aghānī,* 8: 3033–34.

4. Supplication and Negotiation

Parts of this chapter were presented in earlier versions (in Arabic) Graduate/Faculty Seminar, Department of Arabic Literature, University of Jordan, May 1997; Literary Criticism at the Turn of the Century Conference, Cairo, Egypt, October 1997; (in English) the First Ahatanhel Krimsky Memorial Conference, Kiev and Zvenyhorodka, Ukraine, May 1997; Middle East Studies Association, San Francisco, November 1997. Parts have appeared in Suzanne Pinckney Stetkevych, "Qaṣīdat al-Madḥ wa-Marāsim al-Ibtihāl: Fāʿiliyyat al-Naṣṣ al-Adabī ʿabr al-Tārīkh" (The Panegyric Ode and the Ritual of Supplication: The Efficacy of the Poetic Text throughout History), in ʿIzz al-Dīn Ismāʿīl, ed. *Al-Naqd al-Adabī fī Munʿaṭaf al-Qarn 3: Madākhil li-Taḥlīl al-Naṣṣ al-Adabī,* etc./ *Literary Criticism at the Turn of the Century, Papers Presented to the First International Conference on Literary Criticism (Cairo, October 1997),* 3 vols., 3: 175–96.

1. See the Umayyad genealogical tables in Rotter, *Die Umayyaden,* following p. 251, no. 4.

2. The two major classical sources concerned with this episode are al-Iṣbahānī's *Kitāb al-Aghānī* (see below) and al-Balādhurī, *Ansāb al-Ashrāf,* 5: 313–31. For additional materials, see the "Survey of Sources" in Dixon, *The Umayyad Caliphate,*

pp. 1–13. On blood vengeance and bloodwite in pre-Islamic poetry and lore, see S. Stetkevych, *The Mute Immortals Speak,* pp. 55–83 and index.

3. See al-Iṣbahānī, *Kitāb al-Aghānī,* 8: 3026–66; Abū ʿUbaydah's list appears at 8: 3038.

4. See al-Iṣbahānī, *Kitāb al-Aghānī,* 12: 4364–74.

5. See S. Stetkevych, *The Mute Immortals Speak,* ch. 6: "Memory Inflamed: Muhalhil ibn Rabīʿah and the War of al-Basūs," pp. 206–38.

6. Al-Iṣbahānī, *Kitāb al-Aghānī,* 12: 4366.

7. The Qaysī tribes of the Banū Sulaym and the Banū ʿĀmir had been massacred in raids by al-Ḥumayd ibn Ḥurayth ibn Baḥdal, an episode in the tribal warfare between Qays and Kalb (Yaman). See Dixon, *The Umayyad Caliphate,* p. 95.

8. Note in lines 2 and 3 the play on names: al-Jaḥḥāf suggests *juḥāf* (torrent, sweeping away) (line 2) and *al-ḥibāb* (bubbles of sea foam) (line 3) suggests the slain ʿUmayr ibn al-Ḥubāb. In other words, if we attack you, you will die just as ʿUmayr ibn al-Ḥubāb died.

9. Al-Iṣbahānī, *Kitāb al-Aghānī,* 12: 4366–69.

10. Al-Iṣbahānī, *Kitāb al-Aghānī,* 12: 4369–70.

11. Al-Iṣbahānī, *Kitāb al-Aghānī,* 12: 4369–70. See also al-Balādhurī, *Ansāb al-Ashrāf,* 5: 328–31. For a composite narrative of these events based on a number of sources, see Dixon, *The Umayyad Caliphate,* pp. 100–104.

12. See S. Stetkevych, "Pre-Islamic Poetry and the Poetics of Redemption," pp. 7, 17.

13. Crotty, *Poetics of Supplication,* p. 90.

14. Crotty, *Poetics of Supplication,* ch. 8, "Supplication and Narrative," pp. 160–80.

15. Victor Turner, *The Ritual Process: Structure and Anti-Structure* (Ithaca, N.Y.: Cornell University Press, 1977), p. 95. See ch. 6 of the present work. For further discussion of the tripartite qasida in terms of the van Gennepian rite of passage, see S. Stetkevych, *The Mute Immortals Speak,* ch. 1, pp. 3–54 and passim; also, J. Stetkevych, *The Zephyrs of Najd,* pp. 40–43.

16. Crotty, *Poetics of Supplication,* p. 18. On the choreography of authority as expressed through bodily posture, see Connerton, *How Societies Remember,* ch. 3, "Bodily Practices," pp. 72–104.

17. Lyall, *Al-Mufaḍḍalīyāt,* 1: 779–86, poem 119, lines 21–22. For a translation and discussion of the full poem, see S. Stetkevych, "Pre-Islamic Poetry and the Poetics of Redemption," pp. 2–20.

18. Goldhill, *The Poet's Voice,* p. 73; and ch. 1 of the present work.

19. Crotty, *Poetics of Supplication,* p. 129; and ch. 1.

20. See S. Stetkevych, *The Mute Immortals Speak,* pp. 33–42, on the *fakhr* section of the Muʿallaqah of Labīd; see Rūmiyyah, *Qaṣīdat al-Madḥ,* pp. 162–63, on might and generosity (*al-quwwah wa-al-karam*).

21. Mauss, *The Gift,* p. 1.

22. Mauss, *The Gift,* p. vii.

23. See the editions of al-Sukkarī's recension, Qabāwah, *Shiʿr al-Akhṭal,* pp. 13–34; and al-Ṣāliḥānī, *Shiʿr al-Akhṭal,* pp. 1–11.

24. I have followed the recension of the text and consulted the commentary of Qabāwah, *Shiʿr al-Akhṭal,* pp. 13–34 (followed by a composite narrative on the Day

of al-Bishr based on the classical sources, pp. 35–38). Also consulted were the texts and commentaries in al-Ḥāwī, *Sharḥ Dīwān al-Akhṭal,* pp. 259–73; Ṣāliḥānī, *Shiʿr al-Akhṭal,* pp. 1–11; and Ṣāliḥānī, *Naqāʾiḍ Jarīr wa-al-Akhṭal,* pp. 48–63. The recensions exhibit a number of variants, including, in the *Naqāʾiḍ,* substantial variation in the order of the lines.

25. For the identification of proper names, Ṣāliḥānī, *Shiʿr al-Akhṭal,* both the commentary and the editor's notes, is the most complete, although many of these are not definitively identified and are often extrapolated from this poem or others (often citing Yāqūt's *Muʿjam al-Buldān*). I have noted only those needed to clarify the meaning and only those not identified in the discussion of the poem. The reader should refer to the above source for the others. Wāsiṭ is a village on al-Khābūr River (a tributary of the Euphrates) near Qarqīsiyāʾ, hence part of the Taghlibī tribal lands in al-Jazīrah. Raḍwā is a woman's name (Ṣāliḥānī, *Shiʿr al-Akhṭal,* p. 2).

26. Ibn Khallās Ṭufayl and ʿAzhal are two cousins (*abnā ʿamm*) of Taghlib. Ṣāliḥānī, *Shiʿr al-Akhṭal,* p. 2. Here they presumably refer to clans departing before that of the women he mentions.

27. This verse does not occur in al-Sukkarī's recension. See Qabāwah, *Shiʿr al-Akhṭal,* p. 19, and n. 32 below.

28. There is disagreement concerning the meaning of the last two names, Hishām and Nawfal; see Qabāwah, *Shiʿr al-Akhṭal,* p. 28, commentary and notes. Otherwise Umayyah (ibn ʿAbd al-Shams) is the eponymous ancestor of the Umayyad dynasty and al-ʿĀṣ is one of his sons; Khālid ibn Asīd, however, is a direct descendant of Abū al-ʿĪṣ ibn Umayyah. See Rotter, *Die Umayyaden,* genealogical tables following p. 251.

29. Ṣāliḥānī, *Shiʿr al-Akhṭal,* p. 2.

30. See Ezz el-Din, "'No Solace for the Heart,'" pp. 165–79; and ʿIzz al-Dīn, *Shiʿriyyat al-Ḥarb,* passim.

31. Related to this, see Sells's formulation and discussion of the movement from *dhikr* (memory) to *ṣaḥw* (waking) in the *nasīb* in his "Guises of the *Ghūl,*" p. 134 and passim; this, however, deals with only one sense of the word.

32. As suggested, for example, in the anecdotes recounted in Qabāwah, *Shiʿr al-Akhṭal,* p. 13; and al-Iṣbahānī, *Kitāb al-Aghānī,* 8: 3039. See also Rūmiyyah, *Qaṣīdat al-Madḥ,* p. 369. On the poetics and symbolism of wine in Arabic poetry and the Qurʾān, see Suzanne Stetkevych, "Intoxication and Immortality: Wine and Associated Images in al-Maʿarrī's Garden," in J. W. Wright, Jr., and Everett K. Rowson, eds., *Homoeroticism in Classical Arabic Literature* (New York: Columbia University Press, 1997), pp. 210–32, which translates and discusses some citations of al-Aʿshā's wine descriptions in the *Risālat al-Ghufrān* (Epistle of Forgiveness) of the blind poet and prose writer of the late ʿAbbāsid period, Abū al-ʿAlāʾ al-Maʿarrī (d. 449/1058). Al-Maʿarrī also quotes twelve lines from the present poem by al-Akhṭal (lines 10–20 with some variation in the order, plus the unnumbered line included here between lines 16 and 17). See Abū al-ʿAlāʾ al-Maʿarrī, *Risālat al-Ghufrān (wa-maʿah Naṣṣ Muḥaqqaq min Risālat Ibn al-Qāriḥ),* ed. ʿĀʾishah ʿAbd al-Raḥmān (Bint al-Shāṭiʾ) (Cairo: Dār al-Maʿārif, n.d.), pp. 345–46.

33. See van Gelder, *Beyond the Line,* p. 87 and index.

34. Al-Tibrīzī, *Sharḥ Dīwān Ashʿār al-Ḥamāsah,* 2: 163; see also S. Stetkevych, *The Mute Immortals Speak,* p. 60; on ritual and poetics of blood vengeance, see ch.

2, "Eating the Dead / The Dead Eating: Blood Vengeance as Sacrifice," pp. 55–83. Another celebrated case is that of Imruʾ al-Qays, who, it is said, upon hearing news of his father's death, went on a seven-day drinking binge and, when he sobered up, swore an oath not to eat meat, drink wine, anoint himself with oil, touch a woman, or wash his head of impurity until he had achieved his vengeance. See al-Iṣbahānī, *Kitāb al-Aghānī,* 9: 3207–8; S. Stetkevych, *The Mute Immortals Speak,* p. 245.

35. See Ṣāliḥānī, *Naqāʾiḍ Jarīr wa-al-Akhṭal,* p. 49; and Qabāwah, *Shiʿr al-Akhṭal,* p. 16, n. 1.

36. See n. 32 above.

37. See S. Stetkevych, "Intoxication and Immortality," passim.

38. See Rūmiyyah, *Qaṣīdat al-Madḥ,* pp. 398, 411. Part of this section (lines 33–34) describes a single she-camel, but the main part is plural; due to the ambiguous use of the third-person feminine singular for both the singular and plural at times, the number in some lines is not entirely clear.

39. The same idea of assuming a weighty burden of the obligation of blood vengeance is conveyed in the renowned *rithāʾ* (elegy) of Taʾabbaṭa Sharran. There the diction varies, but it includes synonyms of the terms found here; cf. line 2, describing the poet's being burdened with the obligation to avenge his uncle:

He *left the burden* to me and departed, *entrusting* [it to me]
I have *assumed* that *burden* for him.

khallafa l-ʿibʾa ʿalayya wa-wallā
anā bi-l-ʿibʾi lahū mustaqillū

See S. Stetkevych, *The Mute Immortals Speak,* pp. 58, 61; for a translation and discussion of the full poem, pp. 57–73. For the text of the poem, see al-Tibrīzī, *Sharḥ Dīwān Ashʿār al-Ḥāmasah,* 2: 160–64.

40. In some recensions the second time reads *makhlad,* which is basically also reiterative, as it is from the same root and has the same meaning as *khālid,* "immortalized, ageless." See Ṣāliḥānī, *Shiʿr al-Akhṭal,* p. 8.

41. See Qabāwah, *Shiʿr al-Akhṭal,* p. 13; Rotter, *Die Umayyaden,* genealogical table 4, following p. 251.

42. See n. 28 above.

43. See Qabāwah, *Shiʿr al-Akhṭal,* p. 31.

44. This passage bears comparison with the renowned storm scene of the Muʿallaqah of Imruʾ al-Qays, which is similarly situated in the concluding section of the poem. See [Ibn] al-Anbārī, *Sharḥ al-Qaṣāʾ id al-Sabʿ,* pp. 99–112; lines 71–82. For a translation and discussion, see S. Stetkevych, *The Mute Immortals Speak,* pp. 256–57, 278–83. It can also be compared to the storm scenes which occur in the *nasīb* section of al-Akhṭal's other qasidas. See Rūmiyyah, *Qaṣīdat al-Madḥ,* pp. 333–34.

45. I am grateful to Clarissa Burt for her suggestion that the female reproductive aspect of the she-camel warrants emphasis here.

46. See Qabāwah, *Shiʿr al-Akhṭal,* pp. 32–33; Ṣāliḥānī, *Shiʿr al-Akhṭal,* pp. 10–11; Ṣāliḥānī, *Naqāʾiḍ Jarīr wa-al-Akhṭal,* pp. 62–63.

47. Ibn Rashīq in his discussion of *ʿitāb* (blame, reproach) is quite aware that this rhetorical term covers a range of attitudes from conciliation to protest to outright hostility. See Ibn Rashīq al-Qayrawānī, Abū ʿAlī al-Ḥasan, *Al-ʿUmdah fī Ma-*

ḥāsin al-Shiʿr wa-Ādābih wa-Naqdih, 2 vols., ed. Muḥammad Muḥyī al-Dīn ʿAbd al-Ḥamīd (Beirut: Dār al-Jīl, 1972), 2: 160–67.

48. This observation is in keeping with Ezz el-Din's conclusion that the battle ode is normally bipartite, consisting of the *nasīb* and *fakhr* (boast)—the latter in the place of the *madīḥ* section of the poems discussed here—to the exclusion of the *raḥīl.* See Ezz el-Din, "'No Solace for the Heart,'" passim, and ʿIzz al-Dīn, *Shiʿriyyat al-Ḥarb,* pp. 53–90.

5. *Political Dominion as Sexual Domination*

An earlier version of the Abū al-ʿAtāhiyah section of this chapter was part of a paper presented at a conference on Languages of Power in Islamic Spain, Cornell University, Ithaca, N.Y., November 1994, and appeared in Suzanne Pinckney Stetkevych, "The *Qaṣīdah* and the Poetics of Ceremony: Three ʿĪd Panegyrics to the Cordoban Caliphate," in Ross Brann, ed. *Languages of Power in Islamic Spain,* Occasional Papers of the Department of Near Eastern Studies and Program of Jewish Studies, Cornell University, no. 3 (Bethesda, Md.: CDI Press, 1997), pp. 29–32. An earlier version of the Abū Tammām section appeared in S. Stetkevych, *Abū Tammām,* ch. 8, pp. 187–211.

1. I am indebted here to Peter Brown's formulation and discussion of Greek *paideia* in Brown, *Power and Persuasion,* pp. 3–4, 70, and 3–70 passim. A study of classical Arabo-Islamic courtly culture in light of Brown's discussion, though beyond the bounds of the present study, would prove extremely fruitful. On the process of collection in historical terms, see Blachère, *Histoire de la littérature arabe,* 1: 93–166. On the collection process and canon formation, see S. Stetkevych, *Abū Tammām,* pp. 241–81, and refs. p. 241. On *adab,* see F. Gabrieli, "Adab," in *Encyclopaedia of Islam,* new ed. (Leiden: E. J. Brill, 1954–).

2. See Stefan Sperl, "Islamic Kingship and Arabic Panegyric Poetry in the Early Ninth Century," *Journal of Arabic Literature* 8 (1977): 20–35. Some scholars have mistakenly concluded that Sperl has proven that all qasidas are essentially bipartite. This is an unfortunate distortion of an important piece of scholarship. Sperl examines the bipartite qasida, the form that increasingly dominates in the ʿAbbāsid period, and provides a cogent analysis of the structural relations and themes that are typical of it. He offers as well translations of a selected corpus of examples. In terms of the ritual patterns discussed in the present study, Sperl's formulation is entirely consonant with Gaster's "seasonal pattern" of Emptying and Filling (see ch. 6 of the present work). As should be evident, Sperl's discussion does not deal with or explain other formal structures and variants of the panegyric ode, viz., the tripartite (*nasīb-raḥīl-madīḥ*) or the *madīḥ*-dominated essentially monopartite qasida that becomes increasingly common in the ʿAbbāsid era, as we will see in this and subsequent chapters. It also does not take into account or deal with those bipartite odes in which there is an extended development within what we would normally term the *madīḥ* section of the ode—such as those that represent a military expedition. See, for example, the qasidas discussed in S. Stetkevych, *Abū Tammām,* part 2, pp. 109–235.

3. The use of the term *"Formgefühl"* with regard to the Arabic qasida is Jaroslav Stetkevych's.

4. For another of Abū al-ʿAtāhiyah's renowned panegyrics that is, like the

one studied in this chapter, strikingly short and lyrical, see Shukrī Fayṣal, ed., *Abū al-ʿAtāhiyah: Ashʿāruh wa-Akhbāruh* (Damascus: Maktabat Dār al-Mallāḥ, 1964), pp. 544–46 (*lahfī ʿalā z-zamani l-qaṣīri / bayna l-khawarnaqi wa-s-sadīri*). The poem, which is addressed to the caliph al-Hādī, is translated and discussed in J. Stetkevych, *The Zephyrs of Najd,* pp. 66–78 and Michael Zwettler, "The Poetics of Allusion in Abu l-ʿAtāhiya's Ode in Praise of al-Hādī," *Edebiyât,* n.s. 3, no. 1 (1989): 1–29.

5. Abū al-ʿAtāhiyah ("Father of Craziness") is the sobriquet of Abū Isḥāq Ismāʿīl ibn al-Qāsim ibn Suwayd ibn Kaysān. For brief biographical notices and classical sources, see Sezgin, *Poesie,* 534–35; and A. Guillaume, "Abu 'l-ʿAtāhiya," in *Encyclopaedia of Islam,* new ed. (Leiden: E. J. Brill, 1954–).

6. The poet's full name is Abū Tammām Ḥabīb ibn Aws al-Ṭāʾī. For brief biographical notices and classical sources, see Sezgin, *Poesie,* pp. 551–58; H. Ritter, "Abū Tammām," in *Encyclopaedia of Islam,* new ed. (Leiden: E. J. Brill, 1954–). For a monograph-length study in English, see S. Stetkevych, *Abū Tammām.*

7. On the classical Arab critics' reception of the *badīʿ* style and of Abū Tammām's innovative poetry in particular, see S. Stetkevych, *Abū Tammām,* part 1, pp. 5–106; for the translation and analysis of five of Abū Tammām's major panegyric qasidas, see part 2, pp. 109–235.

8. See S. Stetkevych, *Abū Tammām,* pp. 10, 49–50, 94–95.

9. See W. Wright, *A Grammar of the Arabic Language,* 3rd ed., 2 vols. (Beirut: Librairie du Liban, 1971) 2: 363–64.

10. Al-Iṣbahānī, *Kitāb al-Aghānī,* 4: 1247–48.

11. Fayṣal, *Abū al-ʿAtāhiyah,* poem no. 197, pp. 609–13.

12. To the best of my knowledge, the first to point out the topos of the "sacred marriage" in Arabic panegyric is Stefan Sperl: "In some poems this newly found fertility is expressed by an image reminiscent of the pagan '*hieros gamos*' (the sacred marriage of the ruler): *al-khilāfa* or *al-imāma* appear as female linked to the caliph to stay with him faithfully." See Sperl, "Islamic Kingship," p. 30. On the fertility imagery of the *madīḥ* expressed symbolically in terms of a sacred marriage (*hieros gamos*) between the caliph and the *ummah* (Islamic nation; from the same root as *umm,* "mother"), see S. Stetkevych, *Abū Tammām,* p. 133; and S. Stetkevych, "The *Qaṣīdah* and the Poetics of Ceremony," p. 31. Beatrice Gruendler deals with some examples of marriage imagery and sacred marriage in later ʿAbbāsid panegyric and provides a discussion of and sources for the ancient Near Eastern parallel in "The Motif of Marriage in Select Abbasid Panegyrics," in Angelika Neuwirth, Birgit Embaló, Sebastian Günther, and Maher Jarrar, *Myths, Historical Archetypes, and Symbolic Figures in Arabic Literature: Towards a New Hermeneutic Approach—Proceedings of the International Symposium in Beirut, June 25th–June 30th, 1996* (Beirut [Stuttgart]: Franz Steiner Verlag, 1999), pp. 109–22.

13. See also Qurʾān 2:214, 22:1, 33:11.

14. There are other aspects of this poem that can add more dimensions to our reading. As Clarissa Burt has pointed out to me, Abū al-ʿAtāhiyah's poem also constitutes a contrafaction (*muʿāraḍah,* imitation), in the technical sense of the term, of a highly regarded 31-line elegy (*marthiyah*) by the renowned Mukhaḍramah (spanning the pre-Islamic and Islamic eras) poet al-Khansāʾ, in that the poems have the same rhyme and meter. Al-Khansāʾ's elegy strikes me, as does most of her poetry,

as quite conventional women's *rithā᾿* in terms of imagery and diction, although its meter, *al-mutaqārib,* is far less common in her diwan that the more stately Jāhilī meters such as *al-basīt* and *al-ṭawīl,* the two most common, and *al-wāfir* and *al-kāmil.* In this light, I believe that my argument, above, for the generally light lyrical effect of *al-mutaqārib* remains valid. Particularly effective is Abū al-ᶜAtāhiyah's echoing the opening, rather conventional, lament of the elegy: for al-Khansā᾿'s "Oh, what ails your eye, what ails it?" (*a-lā mā li-ᶜayniki am mā lahā*), he voices the lament of the lover ill-treated by his mistress (translated literally): "Oh, what's wrong with my lady, what's wrong with her?" (*a-lā mā li-sayyidatī mā lahā*). We also find the same phrase (al-Khansā᾿, line 19; Abū al-ᶜAtāhiyah, line 9), "the very earth quaked/ would quake" (*wa/la zulzilati l-arḍu zilzālahā*); and three rhyme words in common: *sirbālahā* (line 3 / line 3), *akfālahā* (line 25 / line 4) and *adhyālahā* (lines 24 and 26 / line 7). See al-Khansā᾿, *Sharḥ Dīwān al-Khansā᾿ bi-al-Iḍāfah ilā Marāthī Sittīn Shāᶜirah min Shawāᶜir al-ᶜArab* (Beirut: Dār al-Turāth, 1968), pp. 72–76. Further discussion is beyond the scope of this study and, additionally, complicated by the extremely formulaic and liturgical nature of Arabic women's elegy. (On this issue, see S. Stetkevych, *The Mute Immortals Speak,* ch. 5, "The Obligations and Poetics of Gender," pp. 161–205.)

15. The translation of the poetry lines is loose.

16. Al-Iṣbahānī, *Kitāb al-Aghānī,* 3: 1097–98.

17. For examples garnered from a number of classical sources, see the notes in Fayṣal, *Abū al-ᶜAtāhiyah,* pp. 547–49; 609–10.

18. Fayṣal, *Abū al-ᶜAtāhiyah,* pp. 280–84.

19. See the anecdote in Fayṣal, *Abū al-ᶜAtāhiyah,* p. 632.

20. See the anecdote in Fayṣal, *Abū al-ᶜAtāhiyah,* p. 610.

21. The semantic and structural function of rhetoric in this qasida has been the subject of several earlier studies. See Andras Hamori, "Notes on Paronomasia in Abū Tammām's Style," *Journal of Semitic Studies* 12 (1967): 83–90, and Andras Hamori, *On the Art of Medieval Arabic Literature* (Princeton, N.J.: Princeton University Press, 1974), pp. 125–34, also primarily on paronomasia (*jinās*); M. M. Badawi, "The Function of Rhetoric in Medieval Arabic Poetry: Abū Tammām's Ode on Amorium," *Journal of Arabic Literature* 9 (1978): 43–56, adds as well a discussion of *ṭibāq* (antithesis). The poem is also treated in Suzanne Stetkevych, "The ᶜAbbāsid Poet Interprets History: Three Qaṣīdahs by Abū Tammām," *Journal of Arabic Literature* 10 (1979): 60–64, and S. Stetkevych, *Abū Tammām,* pp. 185–211. The last article forms part of the basis for a recent article, Heiko Wimmen's "ᶜAmmūriyyah as a Female Archetype: Deconstruction of a Mythical Subtext from Abū Tammām to Jabrā Ibrāhīm Jabrā / ᶜAbd al-Raḥmān Munīf," in Neuwirth et al., eds., *Myths, Historical Archetypes, and Symbolic Figures,* pp. 573–82.

22. The fullest account of the campaign against ᶜAmmūriyah is that of al-Ṭabarī; see Abū Djafar Mohammed ibn Djarir at-Tabari, *Annales,* ed. M. J. de Goeje (Leiden: E. J. Brill, 1964–65), photo ed., ser. 3, 2: 1234–55 (= Abū Jaᶜfar Muḥammad ibn Jarīr al-Ṭabarī, *Kitāb al-Rusul wa-al-Mulūk*). For an English translation with excellent annotation, see al-Ṭabarī, *The History of al-Ṭabarī* (Ta᾿rīkh al-rusul wa'l mulūk), vol. 33: *Storm and Stress along the Northern Frontiers of the ᶜAbbāsid Caliphate,* trans. and annot. C. E. Bosworth (Albany: State University of New York Press, 1991). A

thorough treatment of the campaign from Greek as well as Arabic sources is provided by A. A. Vasiliev, *Byzance et les Arabes: Tome I: La dynastie d'Amorium,* ed. H. Grégoire and M. Canard (Brussels: Editions de l'Institut de Philologie et d'Histoire Orientales, 1935), pp. 137–77.

23. At-Tabari, *Annales,* ser. 3, 2: 1234.

24. Abū Tammām, *Dīwān Abī Tammām bi-Sharḥ al-Khaṭīb al-Tibrīzī,* ed. Muḥammad ʿAbduh ʿAzzām, 4 vols. (Cairo: Dār al-Maʿārif, 1951) 1: 61–62.

25. At-Tabari, *Annales,* ser. 3, 2: 1235.

26. Vasiliev, *Byzance et les Arabes,* pp. 158, 160. Translation mine.

27. At-Tabari, *Annales,* ser. 3, 2: 1236.

28. Vasiliev, *Byzance et les Arabes,* pp. 143, 160–61.

29. At-Tabari, *Annales,* ser. 3, 2: 1245–52, and Vasiliev, *Byzance et les Arabes,* pp. 161–68.

30. Michael I, Jacobite Patriarch of Antioch, *Chronique de Michel le Syrien, Patriarche Jacobite d'Antioche (1166–1199),* ed. and trans. Jean-Baptiste Chabot, 4 vols. (Paris: Ernest Leroux, 1905), 3: 98–99.

31. Michael I, *Chronique de Michel le Syrien,* 3: 99–100. Translation mine (from French).

32. Commentary of al-Tibrīzī, in Abū Tammām, *Dīwān,* 1: 40.

33. Abū Tammām, *Dīwān,* 1: 40–74. For another translation, see A. J. Arberry, *Arabic Poetry: A Primer for Students* (Cambridge: Cambridge University Press, 1965), pp. 51–62.

34. I have taken *gharab* (a willow tree whose sap is used as an ointment for camels) and *nabʿ* (a hardwood used for making bows) to refer to their functions, but the meaning could also be merely "neither soft nor hard." Also, *gharab* could be used here for *gharb*—"the edge of a sword"—hence, they are "neither bows nor swords," i.e., useless. In any of these the intention is the same: that these fancies of the astrologers are, as al-Tibrīzī puts it, "neither wine nor vinegar" (Abū Tammām, *Dīwān,* 1: 43)—or, as we would say, "neither fish nor fowl."

35. I have followed Abū al-ʿAlāʾ al-Maʿarrī's suggestion that *ajfala* here means reveal, so that the verse means "they declare that matters will appear in Ṣafar or Rajab and the days are hastening to reveal them." See Abū Tammām, *Dīwān,* 1: 44.

36. I have taken "*mā kāna* . . . " to be the direct object of the active participle *murattibatan* (ordering), so that *munqaliban* (literally "overturned"), although clearly alluding to the astrological terminology for unfixed and fixed constellations, here is extended to mean the effect of these constellations on earthly events. This is, however, a minority opinion. For variant readings and interpretations, see Abū Tammām, *Dīwān,* 1: 44–45 and Arberry, *Arabic Poetry,* p. 52.

37. The usual spelling is ʿAmmūriyah, but Abū Tammām has lengthened the penult to fit the meter (ʿAmmūriyyah). Yāqūt, *Muʿjam al-Buldān,* 6: 226, as cited in Arberry, *Arabic Poetry,* p. 53.

38. Arberry misses the basic metaphor upon which this line is built: the comparison of the city, or maiden, to an untamed horse or unbroken mount. Thus, *barzatu l-wahji* means perhaps "brazen-faced," but refers in particular here to the way a recalcitrant mount pulls its head away from the rein or bridle. This interpretation is in keeping with *riyāḍah* (the breaking or training of a horse) and *ṣaddat*

(for a she-camel or mare to refuse a stallion). According to Arberry, Abū Karib was one of the Tubbaʿs of Yemen, d. ca. 420 C.E.; he was said to have conquered Persia (Arberry, *Arabic Poetry,* p. 53).

39. The "ninety thousand" of line 59 appears to refer to fallen Byzantines. The "bitter soul" and "angry warrior" of lines 60 and 61 are then Muslims; "their" refers again to the Byzantines. See Arberry, *Arabic Poetry,* p. 60.

40. Michael I, *Chronique de Michel le Syrien,* 3: 97. Translation mine (from French).

41. Concerning this, al-Tibrīzī remarks, "They had judged that the appearance of the comet described here meant great civil discord (*fitnah*) and a change of affairs in the provinces." See Abū Tammām, *Dīwān,* 1: 44.

42. See n. 38, above.

43. Michael I, *Chronique de Michel le Syrien,* 3: 99. Translation mine (from French).

44. M. Canard, "ʿAmmūriya," in *Encyclopaedia of Islam,* new ed. (Leiden: E. J. Brill, 1954–).

45. See al-Tibrīzī's commentary, in Abū Tammām, *Dīwān,* 1: 55.

46. Sperl, "Islamic Kingship," p. 30

47. See al-Tibrīzī's commentary, in Abū Tammām, *Dīwān,* 1: 73–74.

48. See S. Stetkevych, *The Mute Immortals Speak,* pp. 177, 186–87.

49. B. Lewis, "ʿAbbāsids," in *Encyclopaedia of Islam,* new ed. (Leiden: E. J. Brill, 1954–).

6. The Poetics of Political Allegiance

Earlier versions of parts of this chapter were (1) (on Sayf al-Dawlah) presented at the Second Shaban Memorial Conference, Exeter University, Exeter, United Kingdom, in September 1994 and appeared as Suzanne Pinckney Stetkevych, "ʿAbbāsid Panegyric: The Politics and Poetics of Ceremony: Al-Mutanabbī's ʿĪd-poem to Sayf al-Dawlah," in J. R. Smart, ed., *Tradition and Modernity in Arabic Language and Literature* (Surrey, England: Curzon, 1996), pp. 119–143; and (2) (on Kāfūr) presented at the Conference on the Qasida, School of Oriental and African Studies, University of London, July 1993 and appeared as Suzanne Pinckney Stetkevych, "Abbasid Panegyric and the Poetics of Political Allegiance: Two Poems of al-Mutanabbī on Kāfūr," in Sperl and Shackle, *Qasida Poetry,* 1: 35–53; 2: 92–105.

1. It is beyond the scope of the present study to even begin to go into the complex political and military history of this period, when the three dynasties mentioned were in constant competition, both military and political, with each other and with other forces internal and external to the ʿAbbāsid lands. Summaries and ample references are available in Cl. Cahen, "Buwayhids"; M. Canard, "Ḥamdānids"; Th. Biaquis, "Sayf al-Dawla"; J. L. Bacharach, "Muḥammad b. Tughdj al-Ikhshīd"; and A. S. Ehrenkreutz, "Kāfūr Abu 'l-Misk" in *Encyclopaedia of Islam,* new ed. (Leiden: E. J. Brill, 1954–).

2. See [Abū ʿUthmān ʿAmr ibn Baḥr] al-Jāḥiẓ, *Al-Bayān wa-al-Tabyīn,* 4 vols., 5th ed., ed. ʿAbd al-Salām Muḥammad Hārūn (Cairo: Maktabat al-Khānjī, 1985) 1: 241; and Ibn Rashīq, *Al-ʿUmdah,* 1: 82–83.

3. Kurke, *The Traffic in Praise.* Kurke analyzes Pindar's epinikian odes as objects

in a ritual exchange. Parts 1 and 2 contain much that is, mutatis mutandis, applicable to the study of Arabic panegyric well. Chief among Kurke's points of interest with regard to the present argument are the recognition of poetry as conferring immortality (part 1, passim); praise as part of a gift-exchange system (part 2, passim); and the reckoning of the poem as among the *agalmata* (precious objects used in gift exchange). See pp. 94–95, 105–106, and 155–59.

4. [Abū ʿUthmān ʿAmr ibn Baḥr] al-Jāḥiẓ, *Al-Bukhalāʾ*, ed. Ṭāhā al-Ḥājirī (Cairo: Dār al-Maʿārif, 1958), pp. 26–27.

5. Mauss, *The Gift*, p. 1

6. Mauss, *The Gift*, p. 37.

7. Mauss, *The Gift*, p. 40.

8. Mauss, *The Gift*, p. 35.

9. Mauss, *The Gift*, p. 72.

10. For a discussion of the exchange of poem and prize with reference to both classical Arabic and modern critical work on gift exchange and to modern poetic dedications, see Muhsin J. al-Musawi, "Dedications as Poetic Intersections," *Journal of Arabic Literature* 31, no. 1 (2000): 1–37.

11. Al-ʿUkbarī (see full reference in n. 14 below), 3: 288 (rhyme: *-ālū*).

12. Mauss, *The Gift*, p. 10.

13. The relation between poet and patron involving an earlier ʿAbbāsid poet is treated in Beatrice Gruendler, "Ibn al-Rūmī's Ethics of Patronage," *Harvard Middle Eastern and Islamic Review* 3 (1996): 104–60.

14. Abū al-Ṭayyib ibn al-Ḥusayn ibn al-Ḥasan (ca. 303–354/915–965), known by his sobriquet, "al-Mutanabbī," "the would-be prophet." The bibliography on al-Mutanabbī, both classical and modern, is extensive. See Sezgin, *Poesie*, 484–97; Régis Blachère [and Charles Pellat], "Al-Mutanabbī," in *Encyclopaedia of Islam*, new ed. (Leiden: E. J. Brill, 1954–); Régis Blachère, *Un poète arabe du IVᵉ siècle de l'Hégire (Xᵉ siècle de J.-C.): Abou ṭ-Ṭayyib al-Motanabbî*. (Paris: Adrien-Maisonneuve, 1935), pp. xv–xix. See pp. 23–262 for an extensive biography compiled from the classical sources. For the purposes of the present study I have relied mainly on the section on al-Mutanabbī in Abū Manṣūr ʿAbd al-Malik al-Thaʿālibī al-Naysabūrī, *Yatīmat al-Dahr fī Maḥāsin Ahl al-ʿAṣr*, ed. Mufīd Muḥammad Qamīḥah, 5 vols. (Beirut: Dār al-Kutub al-ʿIlmiyyah, 1983) 1: 139–277; Yūsuf al-Badīʿī, *Al-Ṣubḥ al-Munbī ʿan Ḥaythiyyat al-Mutanabbī*, ed. Muṣṭafā al-Saqqā, Muḥammad Shattā, and ʿAbduh Ziyādah ʿAbduh (Cairo: Dār al-Maʿārif, 1963); and the following commentaries on al-Mutanabbī's diwan: ʿAbd al-Raḥmān al-Barqūqī, *Sharḥ Dīwān al-Mutanabbī*, 4 vols. (Beirut: Dār al-Kitāb al-ʿArabī, 1986) [hereafter al-Barqūqī]; Abū al-ʿAlāʾ al-Maʿarrī, *Sharḥ Dīwān Abī al-Ṭayyib al-Mutanabbī, "Muʿjiz Aḥmad,"* 4 vols., ed. ʿAbd al-Majīd Diyāb (Cairo: Dār al-Maʿārif, 1986) [hereafter al-Maʿarrī] [Some questions have been raised as to whether this is in fact al-Maʿarrī's commentary, *Muʿjiz Aḥmad*, but on the whole I find Diyāb's presentation of the manuscript and historical materials in his introduction quite convincing (1: 5–27). For the purposes of the present chapter, what is important is that it is an authentic classical commentary, even if, given the vagaries of the manuscript tradition, al-Maʿarrī's authorship cannot be definitively established]; Abū al-Baqāʾ al-ʿUkbarī, *Dīwān Abī al-Ṭayyib al-Mutanabbī, al-Musammā bi-al-Tibyān fī Sharḥ al-Dīwān*, 4 vols., ed. Muṣṭafā al-Saqqā, Ibrāhīm al-Abyārī, and ʿAbd al-Ḥafīẓ Shalabī (Beirut: Dār al-Maʿrifah, 1936) [hereafter al-

ᶜUkbarī]; Abū al-Ḥasan ᶜAlī ibn Aḥmad al-Wāḥidī, *Dīwān Abī al-Ṭayyib al-Mutanabbī wa-fī Athnāʾ Matnih Sharḥ al-Imām al-ᶜAllāmah al-Wāḥidī,* ed. Friedrich Dieterici (Cairo: Dār al-Kitāb al-Islāmī, n.d.) [hereafter al-Wāḥidī]; and Nāṣīf al-Yāzijī, *Al-ᶜArf al-Ṭayyib fī Sharḥ Dīwān Abī al-Ṭayyib,* 2 vols. (Beirut: Dār Ṣādir / Dār Bayrūt, 1964) [hereafter al-Yāzijī].

15. See al-Thaᶜālibī, *Yatīmat al-Dahr,* 1: 149; and al-Badīᶜī, *Al-Ṣubḥ al-Munbī,* pp. 92–95.

16. Al-Badīᶜī, *Al-Ṣubḥ al-Munbī,* pp. 87–100 passim.

17. Al-Maᶜarrī, 3: 372; see also the commentaries of al-Barqūqī 2: 3; al-ᶜUkbarī, 1: 281; al-Wāḥidī, p. 529; and al-Yāzijī, 2: 179.

18. Connerton, *How Societies Remember,* p. 58. The basic work on performative theory is J. L. Austin, *How to Do Things with Words* (Cambridge: Harvard University Press, 1962); see especially pp. 98–100 and passim.

19. Connerton, *How Societies Remember,* p. 59.

20. Sanders, *Ritual, Politics, and the City,* p. 22. For a concise overview of classical Arabic ceremonial and protocol, as well as a bibliography of primary and secondary sources, see Paula Sanders, "Marāsim," in *Encyclopaedia of Islam,* new ed. (Leiden: E. J. Brill, 1954–).

21. This is in keeping with another anecdote about al-Mutanabbī, that he negotiated with Sayf al-Dawlah to be permitted to deliver his odes to the emir at court while sitting rather than standing before the emir, as was the usual posture for panegyric poets. See al-Badīᶜī, *Al-Ṣubḥ al-Munbī,* p. 71. This was discussed by Majd Yasser al-Mallah, "Panegyric Poetry and Court Ceremonial: al-Mutanabbī's Victory Ode," unpublished paper presented at the annual meeting of the American Oriental Society, March 1999.

22. A. J. Wensinck et al., *Concordance et indices de la tradition musulmane* (Leiden: E. J. Brill, 1936–62), 4: 215 [Abū Dāwūd *adab:* 132].

23. For the text and commentary I have followed primarily al-ᶜUkbarī, 1: 281–92; I have also consulted the commentaries of: al-Barqūqī, 2: 3–16; al-Maᶜarrī, 3: 372–86; al-Wāḥidī, pp. 529–35; and al-Yāzijī, 2: 179–85.

24. Reading *jaᶜalnaka* for *jaᶜaltuka;* see al-ᶜUkbarī, 1: 292, n. 1.

25. Al-Barqūqī, 2: 3, 8. But see also Arthur Jeffery, *The Foreign Vocabulary of the Qurʾān* (Baroda: Oriental Institute, 1938), p. 218.

26. Conte, *The Rhetoric of Imitation,* pp. 75–76.

27. For historical sources see Blachère, *Un poète arabe,* p. 169; Marius Canard, *Extraits des sources arabes,* part 2 of A. A. Vasiliev, *Byzance et les Arabes: II, La dynastie macédonienne (867–959),* ed. Henri Grégoire and Marius Canard (Brussels: Éditions de l'Institut de Philologie et d'Histoire Orientales et Slaves, 1950).

28. Connerton, *How Societies Remember,* p. 85.

29. Connerton, *How Societies Remember,* p. 93.

30. Connerton, *How Societies Remember,* p. 94.

31. Connerton, *How Societies Remember,* p. 94.

32. Al-ᶜUkbarī, 1: 281. I have cited the line as it appears in al-Ḥuṭayʾah, *Dīwān, Sharḥ Abī Saᶜīd al-Sukkarī* (Beirut: Dār Ṣādir, 1967), p. 245.

33. See al-Yāzijī, 1: 179.

34. Th. Biaquis, "Sayf al-Dawla."

35. See Blachère, *Un poète arabe,* p. 169; Marius Canard, *Extraits des sources arabes;* a useful summary can be found in Biaquis, "Sayf al-Dawla," p. 107.

36. See, e.g., A. J. Wensinck, "The Semitic New Year and the Origin of Eschatology," *Acta Orientalia* 1 (1923): 158–99; Connerton, *How Societies Remember,* p. 65; Maurice Bloch, "The Ritual of the Royal Bath in Madagascar: The Dissolution of Death, Birth, and Fertility into Authority," in David Cannadine and Simon Price, eds., *Rituals of Royalty: Power and Ceremony in Traditional Societies* (Cambridge: Cambridge University Press, 1987), pp. 276–80.

37. See, e.g., Cannadine and Price, *Rituals of Royalty,* pp. 1–5; Amélie Kuhrt, "Usurpation, Conquest, and Ceremonial: From Babylon to Persia," in Cannadine and Price, *Rituals of Royalty,* p. 44; Bloch, "The Ritual of the Royal Bath," p. 278. See also ch. 7.

38. Al-Barqūqī, 2: 7–8.

39. Bloch, "The Ritual of the Royal Bath," p. 284.

40. Connerton, *How Societies Remember,* p. 43.

41. Kuhrt, "Usurpation, Conquest, and Ceremonial," p. 33.

42. Al-Barqūqī, 2: 8–9.

43. It is within this conceptual framework that Roy Mottahedeh's important discussion of the bonds of obligation entailed by *niʿmah* (benefit), dealing precisely with this period, should be read; certainly, the addition of poetic materials to his argument would both strengthen and refine it. See Roy P. Mottahedeh, *Loyalty and Leadership in an Early Islamic Society* (Princeton, N.J.: Princeton University Press, 1980), pp. 72–78.

44. See Cahen, "Buwayhids," and Canard, "Ḥamdānids."

45. For a discussion of various types of *imitatio,* ranging from plagiarism to rivalrous emulation, in the Arabic and Persian traditions, see Losensky, "'The Allusive Fields of Drunkenness'"; and Losensky, *Welcoming Fighānī,* passim.

46. See the discussion of the rhetorical category of *ʿitāb* (blame, reproach) in classical Arabic poetry, see Ibn Rashīq, *ʿUmdah,* 2: 160–67; on al-Mutanabbī in particular, see 2: 164–65.

47. Al-Maʿarrī, 3: 384.

48. Sanders, *Ritual, Politics, and the City,* p. 37.

49. Al-Maʿarrī, 3: 385.

50. See Mottahedeh, *Loyalty and Leadership,* pp. 50–54, 72–78.

51. See Austin, *How to Do Things with Words,* passim; Wright, *A Grammar of the Arabic Language,* 2: 1–3.

52. See the original quotation from Connerton, above.

53. Ehrenkreutz, "Kāfūr Abu 'l-Misk."

54. Al-Badīʿī, *Al-Ṣubḥ al-Munbī,* p. 110.

55. Mauss, *The Gift,* p. vii.

56. Mauss, *The Gift,* p. 1.

57. Al-Badīʿī, *Al-Ṣubḥ al-Munbī,* pp. 110–11, and *Dīwān* commentaries; see n. 23.

58. Al-Badīʿī, *Al-Ṣubḥ al-Munbī,* p. 87, etc.

59. See van Gennep, *The Rites of Passage,* passim. A concise restatement is Victor Turner's:

> Van Gennep has shown that all rites of passage or "transition" are marked by three phases: separation, margin (or *limen*, signifying "threshold" in Latin), and aggregation. The first phase (of separation) comprises symbolic behavior signifying the detachment of the individual or group either from an earlier fixed point in the social structure, from a set of cultural conditions (a "state"), or from both. During the intervening "liminal" period, the characteristics of the ritual subject (the "passenger") are ambiguous; he passes through a cultural realm that has few or none of the attributes of the past or coming state. In the third phase (reaggregation or reincorporation), the passage is consummated. The ritual subject, individual or corporate, is in a relatively stable state once more and, by virtue of this, has rights and obligations vis-à-vis others of a clearly defined and "structural" type; he is expected to behave in accordance with certain customary norms and ethical standards binding on incumbents of social position in a system of such positions. (Turner, *The Ritual Process*, pp. 94–95)

For the analysis of the pre-Islamic Arabic qasida in light of this pattern, see S. Stetkevych, *The Mute Immortals Speak*, passim.

60. Gaster formulates the "seasonal pattern" thus:

> The activities fall into two main divisions which we may call, respectively, rites of Kenosis, or Emptying, and rites of Plerosis, or Filling. The former portray and symbolize the eclipse of life and vitality at the end of each lease, and are exemplified by lenten periods, fasts, austerities, and other expressions of mortification or suspended animation. The latter, on the other hand, portray and symbolize the revitalization that ensues at the beginning of the new lease, and are exemplified by rites of mass mating, ceremonial purgations of evil and noxiousness (both physical and "moral"), and magical procedures designed to promote fertility, produce rain, relume the sun, and so forth. (Gaster, *Thespis*, p. 23)

These two sections are subdivided to produce four major elements:

> First come rites of ***mortification***, symbolizing the state of suspended animation that ensues at the end of the year, when one lease on life has drawn to a close and the next is not yet assured. Second come rites of ***purgation***, whereby the community seeks to rid itself of all noxiousness and contagion, both physical and moral, and of all evil influences which might impair the prosperity of the coming year and thereby threaten the desired renewal of vitality. Third come rites of ***invigoration***, whereby the community attempts, by its own concerted and regimented effort, to galvanize its moribund condition and to procure that new lease on life which is imperative for the continuance of the topocosm. Last come the rites of ***jubilation***, which bespeak men's sense of relief when the new year has indeed begun and the continuance of their own lives and that of the topocosm is thereby assured. (Gaster, *Thespis*, p. 26)

I have discussed the structure and function of the qasida in light of Gaster's seasonal pattern in S. Stetkevych, *The Mute Immortals Speak*, pp. 258–85.

61. For the text and commentary I have followed primarily al-ʿUkbarī, 4: 281–

94; I have also consulted al-Barqūqī, 4: 417–32; al-Maʿarrī, 4: 18–32; al-Wāḥidī, 623–29; and al-Yāzijī, 2: 293–302.

62. I've taken some liberty with the translation to achieve a convincing English line.

63. Reading *najūzu* for *tajūzu;* see al-Maʿarrī, 4: 24.

64. The editors' note in Sperl and Shackle, *Qasida Poetry,* 2: 421, n. 4, takes this line as an (irreverent) allusion to the Qurʾānic verses: *"kullu man ʿalayhā fānin wa-yabqā wajhu rabbika"* (All who are on the earth will perish and only the face of your Lord will remain) (Qurʾān 55:26–27).

65. Al-Maʿarrī, 4: 20, n. 3.

66. Al-ʿUkbarī, 3: 378–92 (rhyme *-mū*). For an English translation, see Arberry, *Arabic Poetry,* pp. 84–91.

67. Al-Thaʿālibī, *Yatīmat al-Dahr,* 1: 236; al-Badīʿī, *Al-Ṣubḥ al-Munbī,* p. 116.

68. Mauss, *The Gift,* p. 10.

69. Mauss, *The Gift,* p. 43.

70. See references below, n. 75.

71. Al-ʿUkbarī, 1: 188–201 (*munan kunna lī anna l-bayāḍa khiḍābū*).

72. Al-Badīʿī, *Al-Ṣubḥ al-Munbī,* p. 124; al-Yāzijī, 2: 396.

73. Ibn Khallikān, as quoted in al-Yāzijī, 2: 365.

74. Al-ʿUkbarī, 2: 39, etc.

75. For the text and commentary I have followed primarily al-ʿUkbarī, 2: 39–46; I have also consulted al-Barqūqī, 2: 139–48; al-Maʿarrī, 4: 167–76; al-Wāḥidī, pp. 691–95; and al-Yāzijī, 2: 396–400.

76. Reading *tuḥarrikunī* for *tughayyirunī;* see al-ʿUkbarī, 2: 40, n. 1.

77. Gaster, *Thespis,* p. 26.

78. Lyall, *The Mufaḍḍalīyāt,* 1: 2.

79. Al-ʿUkbarī, 2: 39.

80. Al-ʿUkbarī, 2: 39.

81. For a discussion and full translation of the poem, see S. Stetkevych, *The Mute Immortals Speak,* pp. 104–18.

82. Lyall, *The Mufaḍḍalīyāt,* 1: 2.

83. Al-ʿUkbarī, 2: 41; etc.

84. Ibn Rashīq, *Al-ʿUmdah,* 2: 175.

85. Ibn Rashīq, *Al-ʿUmdah,* 1: 123.

86. Al-Maʿarrī, 4: 172; etc.

87. Al-Maʿarrī, 4: 174; al-Wāḥidī, p. 695.

88. See S. Stetkevych, *The Mute Immortals Speak,* pp. 161–205.

89. Al-Maʿarrī, 4: 175.

90. See S. Stetkevych, *The Mute Immortals Speak,* chs. 3 and 4.

91. Muḥammad ibn ʿUmar al-Zamakhsharī, *Aʿjab al-ʿAjab fī Sharḥ Lāmiyyat al-ʿArab* in al-Shanfarā, *Qaṣīdat Lāmiyyat al-ʿArab wa-yalīhā. . . .* (Istanbul: Maṭbaʿat al-Jawāʾib, 1300 H.), pp. 10–70; line 24.

92. Ehrenkreutz, "Kāfūr Abu 'l-Misk."

93. Jamāl al-Dīn Abū al-Maḥāsin Yūsuf Ibn Taghrībirdī, *Al-Nujūm al-Zāhirah fī Mulūk Miṣr wa-al-Qāhirah,* 14 vols. (Cairo: Al-Muʾassasah Al-Miṣriyyah al-ʿĀmmah lil-Taʾlīf wa-al-Tarjamah wa-al-Nashr, 1968 [photo-offset of Dār al-Kutub ed.]), 4: 1, see also 4: 2; and Abū al-ʿAbbās Shams al-Dīn Aḥmad ibn Muḥammad Ibn Khal-

likān, *Wafāyāt al-Aʿyān wa-Anbāʾ Abnāʾ al-Zamān,* 7 vols., ed. Iḥsān ʿAbbās (Beirut: Dār al-Thaqāfah, 1968), 4: 99–105.

94. Ibn Taghrībirdī, *Al-Nujūm al-Zāhirah,* 4: 2–3.

95. See, for example, al-Badīʿī, *Al-Ṣubḥ al-Munbī,* pp. 110–11.

96. On "ʿAbbās," see Blachère, *Un Poète arabe,* p. 191, n. 5.

97. Al-Maʿarrī, 4: 14–17.

7. The Poetics of Ceremony and the Competition for Legitimacy

An earlier version of this chapter was presented at a conference on Languages of Power in Islamic Spain, Cornell University, Ithaca, New York, in November 1994 and appeared as Suzanne Pinckney Stetkevych, "The *Qaṣīdah* and the Poetics of Ceremony: Three ʿĪd Panegyrics to the Cordoban Caliphate," in Ross Brann, ed. *Languages of Power in Islamic Spain,* Occasional Papers of the Department of Near Eastern Studies and Program of Jewish Studies, Cornell University, no. 3 (Bethesda, Md.: CDI Press, 1997), pp. 1–48.

1. For an overview and examples of the richness and variety of Andalusian Arabic poetry, see James T. Monroe, *Hispano-Arabic Poetry: A Student Anthology* (Berkeley: University of California Press, 1974). For a recent literary history, see María Rosa Menocal, Raymond Scheindlin, and Michael Sells, eds., *The Literature of al-Andalus* (Cambridge: Cambridge University Press, 2000).

2. See Quint, *Epic and Empire,* esp. p. 8.

3. Among the qasidas composed as holiday felicitation (*al-tahniʾah bi-al-ʿĪd*) with particular emphasis on ceremonial and the insignia of caliphal authority in the "Abbāsid period is al-Buḥturī's (d. 284/897) poem addressed to the caliph al-Mutawakkil on the occasion of ʿĪd al-Fiṭr, to which I hope to turn in a subsequent study of the mantle (*burdah*) of the Prophet. See [Abū ʿUbādah al-Walīd ibn ʿUbayd Allāh] al-Buḥturī, *Dīwān al-Buḥturī,* ed. Ḥasan Kāmil al-Ṣīrafī, 3rd ed., 4 vols. (Cairo: Dār al-Maʿārif, 1977) 2: 1070–73, poem no. 421.

4. For a detailed description and analysis of this volume of *Al-Muqtabis* (which does not, however, deal with the poetry texts), see Gabriel Martinez-Gros, *L'idéologie omeyyade: La construction de la légitimité du Califat de Cordoue (Xe–XIe siècles)* (Madrid: Casa de Velázquez, 1992), ch. 5. "Le califat immobile: Les *Annales* de ʿĪsā al-Rāzī," pp. 129–55. On the ceremonials described in *Al-Muqtabis* in the years 971–974 C.E., with some reference to the earlier published version of this chapter, see Janina M. Safran, "Ceremony and Submission: The Symbolic Representation of Recognition of Legitimacy in Tenth-Century al-Andalus," *Journal of Near Eastern Studies* 58, no. 3 (1999): 191–201; and Janina M. Safran, "The Command of the Faithful in al-Andalus: A Study in the Articulation of Caliphal Legitimacy," *International Journal of Middle East Studies* 30 (1998): 183–98.

5. Abū Marwān Ibn Ḥayyān al-Qurṭubī, *Al-Muqtabis fī Akhbār Balad al-Andalus,* ed. ʿAbd al-Raḥmān ʿAlī al-Ḥajjī (Beirut: Dār al-Thaqāfah, 1965), p. 155. See also the Spanish translation, Emilio García Gómez, trans., *Anales palatinos del califa de Córdoba al-Hakam II, por ʿĪsā Ibn Ahmad al-Rāzī (360–364 H. = 971–975 J.C.) [El califato de Córdoba en el "Muqtabis" de Ibn Hayyān]* (Madrid: Sociedad de Estudios y Publicationes, 1967), p. 196. Both the Arabic edition and the Spanish translation are based on a single extant nineteenth-century manuscript (see the introduc-

tions), and both are obscure in places. I have tried to produce a coherent English rendering.

6. García Gómez, *Anales palatinos,* p. 13.

7. David Cannadine has insightfully chosen this passage for the epigraph of his introduction. See Cannadine and Price, *Rituals of Royalty,* p. 1.

8. Connerton, *How Societies Remember,* p. 65. He notes, too, that in Christianity "emphasis shifts in this schema from the prototype of creation to that of salvation," p. 65. See also Wensinck, "The Semitic New Year and the Origin of Eschatology" and Gaster's formulation of the "seasonal pattern" in Gaster, *Thespis* (see chs. 1 and 6).

9. Kuhrt, "Usurpation, Conquest, and Ceremonial," p. 31.

10. Connerton, *How Societies Remember,* p. 45.

11. Kuhrt, "Usurpation, Conquest, and Ceremonial," p. 40.

12. On the precept that the imamate is from the Quraysh, see W. Montgomery Watt, "Ḳuraysh," in *Encyclopaedia of Islam,* new ed. (Leiden: E. J. Brill, 1954–).

13. See É. Lévi-Provençal, *Histoire de l'Espagne musulmane, Tome II: Le califat umaiyade de Cordoue (921–1031),* new ed. (Paris: Maisonneuve/Leiden: E. J. Brill, 1950), pp. 184–96 passim, and esp. pp. 186–87.

14. Much work has been done on Byzantine ceremonial and the similarities with the Arabo-Islamic ceremonial are often striking. See Averil Cameron, "The Construction of Court Ritual: The Byzantine *Book of Ceremonies,*" in Cannadine and Price, *Rituals of Royalty,* pp. 106–36; also Michael McCormick, *Eternal Victory* (Cambridge: Cambridge University Press, 1987), esp. chs. 4 and 5 on the Byzantine triumph. The classic in this field is Sabine G. MacCormack, *Art and Ceremony in Late Antiquity* (Berkeley: University of California Press, 1981).

15. I will be giving the name as Ḥasan ibn Qannūn, as it appears in *Al-Muqtabis* of Ibn Ḥayyān and according to the standard Arabic transliteration. The name is normally transliterated as Gannūn.

16. See D. Eustache, "Idrīs I" and "Idrīsids," in *Encyclopaedia of Islam,* new ed. (Leiden: E. J. Brill, 1954–).

17. Eustache, "Idrīsids"; Lévi-Provençal, *Histoire de l'Espagne musulmane,* 2: 190–95; Ibn Ḥayyān, *Al-Muqtabis,* pp. 96–155, passim; García Gómez, *Anales palatinos,* pp.123–96, passim.

18. For this term, see Sanders, *Ritual, Politics, and the City,* ch. 2, "The Ceremonial Idiom," pp. 13–38.

19. Connerton, *How Societies Remember,* pp. 73–74.

20. See Connerton, *How Societies Remember,* pp. 58–60.

21. Lévi-Provençal, *Histoire de l'Espagne musulmane,* 2: 190–94, and see map, 2: 192. Eustache gives the name of Ḥasan ibn Qannūn's redoubt as Ḥajar al-Naṣr (Victory Rock) instead of Ḥajar al-Nasr (Eagle's Rock) (Eustache, "Idrīsids").

22. James T. Monroe, "Hispano-Arabic Poetry during the Caliphate of Córdoba," in Gustave E. von Grunebaum, ed., *Proceedings of the Third Giorgio Lévi della Vida Memorial Conference* (Berkeley and Los Angeles: University of California Press, 1971), pp. 137–38. It should be noted that by "new," Monroe means for al-Andalus, for, as he points out in his discussion, the "Neoclassical" panegyric reigned in the Arab east in the fourth/tenth century just at the time of the Andalusian Umayyad caliphate, which was officially proclaimed in 317/929 (p. 136). See also Monroe's

examples, pp. 136–38; and Emilio García Gómez, "La poésie politique sous le califat de Cordoue," *Revue des Études Islamiques* 1 (1949): 5–11.

23. Sezgin, *Poesie,* p. 690.

24. In regard to Abū al-ᶜAtāhiyah's poem in turn being a contrafaction of an elegy of al-Khansāʾ, see n. 14, ch. 5, above.

25. Ibn Ḥayyān, *Al-Muqtabis,* pp. 156–57.

26. Crone and Hinds, *God's Caliph,* pp. 31–32.

27. Crone and Hinds, *God's Caliph,* pp. 31–32.

28. See Watt, "Ḳuraysh."

29. On this subject see S. Stetkevych, "Pre-Islamic Panegyric and the Poetics of Redemption," pp. 13–19.

30. On myth and politics in Rubens's Maria de' Medici Cycle, see Ronald Forsyth Millen and Robert Erich Wolf, *Heroic Deeds and Mystic Figures: A New Reading of Rubens'* Life of Maria de' Medici (Princeton, N.J.: Princeton University Press, 1989), esp. chs. 3, 4, and 8.

31. Sanders, *Ritual, Politics, and the City,* p. 7. See also p. 29 and ch. 2, "Ceremonial Idiom," pp. 13–37, esp. p. 37 on ritual as negotiation.

32. Iḥsān ᶜAbbās, *Tārīkh al-Adab al-Andalusī: ᶜAṣr Siyādat Qurṭubah,* 2nd ed. (Beirut: Dār al-Thaqāfah, 1975), p. 104, where, however, he states that it was presented to Hārūn al-Rashīd; the other sources give al-Mahdī. ᶜAbbās addresses the issue of *muᶜāraḍah* throughout his book. On the influence of Abū al-ᶜAtāhiyah and Abū Tammām, etc., at this period, see esp. pp. 125ff.

33. For a far-ranging and insightful discussion of *muᶜāraḍah* and the poetics of imitation generally in the Arabo-Persian poetic tradition, see Paul Losensky, "'The Allusive Field of Drunkenness,'" and, more extensively, Losensky's monograph *Welcoming Fighānī.*

34. Fayṣal, *Abū al-ᶜAtāhiyah* poem no. 197, pp. 609–13. See the translation and discussion of the poem and anecdote in ch. 5.

35. See Sezgin, *Poesie,* p. 689. Lines from several of his poems are dealt with in García Gómez, "La poésie politique," pp. 8–9.

36. It was believed that the blood of kings would cure rabies.

37. The passage from line 42–44, especially line 43, is quite obscure. García Gómez's translation is extremely opaque, bordering on the incoherent (García Gómez, *Anales palatinos,* p. 201). I have emended my own previous (and problematic) translation to achieve a modicum of clarity.

38. Ibn Ḥayyān, *Al-Muqtabis,* pp. 158–62.

39. Abū Tammām, *Dīwān,* qasida no. 3, 1: 40–74. See discussion and references in ch. 5.

40. See S. Stetkevych, *Abū Tammām,* pp. 108–235, passim.

41. Abū Tammām, *Dīwān,* 2: 203, qasida no. 72, line 24; for a translation and discussion of the full poem, see S. Stetkevych, *Abū Tammām,* pp. 212–31.

42. See S. Stetkevych, *Abū Tammām,* pp. 3–106, passim.

43. Gaster, *Thespis,* p. 23.

44. Gaster, *Thespis,* p. 26.

45. Ibn Ḥayyān, *Al-Muqtabis,* p. 154.

46. On the function of floral elements in panegyric, esp. that of Ibn Darrāj, see James T. Monroe, *Risālat at-Tawābiᶜ wa-z-Zawābiᶜ: The Treatise of Familiar Spirits*

and Demons by Abū ʿĀmir ibn Shuhaid al-Ashjaʿī al-Andalusī (Berkeley and Los Angeles: University of California Press, 1971), pp. 8–10.

47. Abū Tammām, *Dīwān,* 2: 191, qasida no. 71, line 1. For a translation of the full poem, see Julia Ashtiany, trans., "Abū Tammām (d. 845) in Praise of an Abbasid Caliph," in Sperl and Shackle, *Qasida Poetry,* 2: 80–85. On the cosmic association of the victorious caliph with spring, see Sperl, "ʿAbbāsid Kingship and Islamic Panegyric," pp. 23–24; 29–31.

48. Gaster, *Thespis,* p. 26.

49. See McCormick, *Eternal Victory,* pp. 161–63.

50. In fact, the hereditary claims of the dynasties are shrouded in obscurities and complications, and even the term "Hāshimite" appears originally to have referred to the supporters of the imamate of Abū Hāshim, the son of the ʿAlid Muḥammad ibn al-Ḥanafiyyah. See B. Lewis, "Hāshimiyya" and "ʿAbbāsids," in *Encyclopaedia of Islam,* new ed. (Leiden: E. J. Brill, 1954–); and M. Canard, "Fāṭimids" (under genealogy of the Fāṭimids), in ibid.

51. See M. Hinds, "Muʿāwiya," in *Encyclopaedia of Islam,* new ed. (Leiden: E. J. Brill, 1954–); and L. Veccia Vaglieri, "ʿAlī b. Abī Ṭālib," in ibid.

52. García Gómez, "La poésie politique," p. 8. Translation mine.

53. Canard, "Fāṭimids."

54. Canard, "Ḥamdānids."

55. On the authority of the caliphate, including references to poetry, see Crone and Hinds, *God's Caliph.*

56. Further comparisons can be noted, for example, between Ibn Shukhayṣ's lines 34, 49, and 50 and, respectively, Abū Tammām's "The Sword Is More Veracious," lines 55, 3, and 54; see ch. 5.

57. See M. ʿA. Makkī, "Ibn Darrādj al-Ḳasṭallī," in *Encyclopaedia of Islam,* new ed. (Leiden: E. J. Brill, 1954–); and Sezgin, *Poesie,* pp. 699–700.

58. This is only the sketchiest of summaries of a very complex period. For a full account, see Lévi-Provençal, *Histoire de l'Espagne musulmane,* 2: 291–326.

59. Abū al-Ḥasan ʿAlī Ibn Bassām al-Shantarīnī, *Al-Dhakhīrah fī Maḥāsin Ahl al-Jazīrah,* 4 vols. in 8, ed. Iḥsān ʿAbbās (Beirut: Dār al-Thaqāfah, 1979), vol. 1, pt. 1, pp. 67–70. See Ibn Darrāj al-Qasṭallī, *Dīwān,* ed. Maḥmūd ʿAlī Makkī, 2nd ed. (n.p.: Al-Maktab al-Islāmī, 1389/1969), p. 51. The date is given as 26 Shawwāl 403 / 9 May 1013 in Lévi-Provençal, *Histoire de l'Espagne musulmane* 2: 319.

60. Ibn Bassām, *Al-Dhakhīrah,* vol. 1, pt. 1, pp. 67–70. In the present discussion, I am using the poem as it appears in *Al-Dhakhīrah* in 34 lines, as edited by Iḥsān ʿAbbās. Ibn Darrāj's *Dīwān* contains a much longer version of 89 lines, along with some variants in the common lines. See Ibn Darrāj, *Dīwān,* poem no. 27, pp. 51–57. The ellipses in the translation indicate where additional lines occur in the *Dīwān* version.

61. Again, for an excellent study of panegyric with emphasis on the theme of restoration, see Garrison, *Dryden and the Tradition of Panegyric.*

62. On the association of *bayʿah* and the ʿĪd, see the examples from the poetry of Ibn ʿAbd Rabbih in ʿAbbās, *Tārīkh al-Adab al-Andalusī,* pp. 190–91.

63. See al-ʿUkbarī, *Dīwān Abī al-Ṭayyib al-Mutanabbī,* 1: 281–92; for the translation, discussion, and further references, see ch. 6.

64. Al-Thaʿālibī, *Yatīmat al-Dahr,* 2: 119.

65. Inasmuch as this pattern emerges more clearly in the 34-line version given by Ibn Bassām (who cites al-Thaʿālibī's remark [vol. 1, pt. 1, p. 60]) in *Al-Dhakhīrah* (vol. 1, pt. 1, pp. 67–70) than in the *Dīwān* version (pp. 51–57), we might credit Ibn Bassām's sense of *Formgefühl* for extracting from Ibn Darrāj's rather rambling imitation of al-Mutanabbī's qasida a formally tighter and closer reflection of the original. This is particularly the case with his choice of closing lines that most resemble al-Mutanabbī's closure.

66. These are the figures given by Lévi-Provençal, *Histoire de l'Espagne musulmane,* 2: 313.

Works Cited

ᶜAbbās, Iḥsān. *Tārīkh al-Adab al-Andalusī: ᶜAṣr Siyādat Qurṭubah.* 2nd ed. Beirut: Dār al-Thaqāfah, 1975.

Abū Tammām. *Dīwān Abī Tammām bi-Sharḥ al-Khaṭīb al-Tibrīzī.* Ed. Muḥammad ᶜAbduh ᶜAzzām. 4 vols. Cairo: Dār al-Maᶜārif, 1951.

Allen, Roger. *The Arabic Literary Heritage: The Development of Its Genres and Criticism.* Cambridge: Cambridge University Press, 1998.

al-Ālūsī al-Baghdādī, Maḥmūd Shukrī. *Bulūgh al-Arab fī Maᶜrifat Aḥwāl al-ᶜArab.* Ed. Muḥammad Bahjat al-Atharī. 3 vols. Beirut: Dar al-Kutub al-ᶜIlmiyyah, n.d.

al-Anbārī [= Ibn al-Anbārī], Abū Bakr Muḥammad ibn al-Qāsim. *Sharḥ al-Qaṣāʾid al-Sabᶜ al-Ṭiwāl al-Jāhiliyyāt.* Ed. ᶜAbd al-Salām Muḥammad Hārūn. Cairo: Dār al-Maᶜārif, 1969.

Arazi, Albert. "Al-Nābigha al-Dhubyānī." In *Encyclopaedia of Islam.* New Edition. Leiden: E. J. Brill, 1954–.

Arberry, A. J. *Arabic Poetry: A Primer for Students.* Cambridge: Cambridge University Press, 1965.

——. *The Seven Odes: The First Chapter in Arabic Literature.* London: George Allen and Unwin, 1957.

al-Asad, Nāṣir al-Dīn. *Maṣādir al-Shiᶜr al-Jāhilī wa-Qīmatuhā al-Tārīkhiyyah.* Cairo: Dār al-Maᶜārif, 1962.

Ashtiany, Julia, trans. "Abū Tammām (d. 845) in Praise of an Abbasid Caliph." In Sperl and Shackle, *Qasida Poetry,* 2: 80–85, 418–19.

Austin, J. L. *How to Do Things with Words.* Cambridge: Harvard University Press, 1962.

al-Azmeh, Aziz. *Muslim Kingship: Power and the Sacred in Muslim, Christian, and Pagan Polities.* London: I. B. Tauris Publishers, 1997.

Bacharach, J. L. "Muhammad b. Tughdj al-Ikhshīd." In *Encyclopaedia of Islam.* New Edition. Leiden: E. J. Brill, 1954–.

Badawi, M. M. "The Function of Rhetoric in Medieval Arabic Poetry: Abū Tammām's Ode on Amorium." *Journal of Arabic Literature* 9 (1978): 43–56.

al-Badīᶜī, Yūsuf. *Al-Ṣubḥ al-Munbī ᶜan Ḥaythiyyat al-Mutanabbī.* Ed. Muṣṭafā al-Saqqā, Muḥammad Shattā, and ᶜAbduh Ziyādah ᶜAbduh. Cairo: Dār al-Maᶜārif, 1963.

al-Baghdādī, ᶜAbd al-Qādir ibn ᶜUmar. *Khizānat al-Adab wa Lubb Lubāb Lisān al-ᶜArab.* Ed. ᶜAbd al-Salām Hārūn. 13 vols. 2nd ed. Cairo: Maktabat al-Khānjī, 1984.

al-Balādhurī, Aḥmad ibn Yaḥyā ibn Jābir. *Ansāb al-Ashrāf.* Part 5. Ed. S. D. F. Goitein. Jerusalem: School of Oriental Studies, Hebrew University, 1936.

al-Barqūqī, ᶜAbd al-Raḥmān. *Sharḥ Dīwān al-Mutanabbī.* 4 vols. Beirut: Dār al-Kitāb al-ᶜArabī, 1986.

Bevan, A. A., ed. *Kitāb al-Naqāʾiḍ: Naqāʾiḍ Jarīr wa-al-Farazdaq.* 3 vols. Leiden: E. J. Brill: 1905–12. [Photo-offset, Baghdad: Maktabat al-Muthannā, n.d.]

Biaquis, Th. "Sayf al-Dawla." In *Encyclopaedia of Islam*. New Edition. Leiden: E. J. Brill, 1954–.
Blachère, Régis. *Histoire de la littérature arabe des origines à la fin du XVe siècle du J.-C.* 3 vols. Paris: Maisonneuve, 1952, 1964, 1966.
——. *Un poète arabe du IVe siècle de l'Hégire (Xe siècle de J.-C.): Abou ṭ-Ṭayyib al-Motanabbî.* Paris: Adrien-Maisonneuve, 1935.
Blachère, Régis [and Charles Pellat]. "Al-Mutanabbī." In *Encyclopaedia of Islam*. New Edition. Leiden: E. J. Brill, 1954–.
Bloch, Maurice. "The Ritual of the Royal Bath in Madagascar: The Dissolution of Death, Birth, and Fertility into Authority." In Cannadine and Price, *Rituals of Royalty*, pp. 271–97.
Bosworth, C. E. "Marwān I." In *Encyclopaedia of Islam*. New Edition. Leiden: E. J. Brill, 1954–.
Brown, Peter. *Power and Persuasion in Late Antiquity: Towards a Christian Empire.* Madison: University of Wisconsin Press, 1992.
al-Buḥturī, [Abū ʿUbādah al-Walīd ibn ʿUbayd Allāh]. *Dīwān al-Buḥturī.* Ed. Ḥasan Kāmil al-Ṣīrafī. 3rd ed. 4 vols. Cairo: Dār al-Maʿārif, 1977.
Burkert, Walter. *Homo Necans: The Anthropology of Ancient Greek Ritual and Myth.* Trans. Peter Bing. Berkeley: University of California Press, 1983.
Cahen, Cl. "Buwayhids." In *Encyclopaedia of Islam*. New Edition. Leiden: E. J. Brill, 1954–.
Cameron, Averil. "The Construction of Court Ritual: The Byzantine *Book of Ceremonies*." In Cannadine and Price, *Rituals of Royalty*, pp. 106–36.
Canard, Marius. "ʿAmmūriya," "Fāṭimids," and "Ḥamdānids." In *Encyclopaedia of Islam*. New Edition. Leiden: E. J. Brill, 1954–.
——. *Extraits des sources arabes.* Part 2 of A. A. Vasiliev, *Byzance et les Arabes: II, La dynastie macédonienne (867–959).* Ed. Henri Grégoire and Marius Canard. Brussels: Éditions de l'Institut de Philologie et d'Histoire Orientales et Slaves, 1950.
Cannadine, David, and Simon Price, eds. *Rituals of Royalty: Power and Ceremony in Traditional Societies.* Cambridge: Cambridge University Press, 1987.
Carruthers, Mary. *The Book of Memory: A Study of Memory in Medieval Culture.* Cambridge: Cambridge University Press, 1990.
Connerton, Paul. *How Societies Remember.* Cambridge: Cambridge University Press, 1989.
Conte, Gian Biagio. *The Rhetoric of Imitation: Genre and Poetic Memory in Virgil and Other Latin Poets.* Trans. Charles Segal. Ithaca, N.Y.: Cornell University Press, 1986.
Crone, Patricia, and Martin Hinds. *God's Caliph: Religious Authority in the First Centuries of Islam.* Cambridge: Cambridge University Press, 1986.
Crotty, Kevin. *The Poetics of Supplication: Homer's* Iliad *and* Odyssey. Ithaca, N.Y.: Cornell University Press, 1994.
Ḍayf, Shawqī. *Al-Taṭawwur wa-al-Tajdīd fī al-Shiʿr al-Umawī.* 2nd ed. Cairo: Dār al-Maʿārif, 1959.
Dixon, ʿAbd al-Ameer. *The Umayyad Caliphate, 65–86/684–705: A Political Study.* London: Luzac and Co., 1971.

Ehrenkreutz, A. S. "Kāfūr Abu 'l-Misk." In *Encyclopaedia of Islam*. New Edition. Leiden: E. J. Brill, 1954–.
Elisséef, N. "Ghūṭa." In *Encyclopaedia of Islam*. New Edition. Leiden: E. J. Brill, 1954–.
Encyclopaedia of Islam. New Edition. Leiden: E. J. Brill, 1954–.
Eustache, D. "Idrīs I" and "Idrīsids." In *Encyclopaedia of Islam*. New Edition. Leiden: E. J. Brill, 1954–.
Ezz El-Din, Hassan El-Banna [also see ᶜIzz al-Dīn, Ḥasan al-Bannā]. "'No Solace for the Heart': The Motif of the Departing Women in the Pre-Islamic Battle Ode." In S. Stetkevych, ed., *Reorientations*, pp. 165–79.
Fayṣal, Shukrī, ed. *Abū al-ᶜAtāhiyah: Ashᶜāruh wa-Akhbāruh*. Damascus: Maktabat Dār al-Mallāḥ, 1964.
——, ed. *Dīwān al-Nābighah al-Dhubyānī*. Recension of Ibn al-Sikkīt. Beirut: Dār al-Fikr, 1968.
Gabrieli, F. "Adab." In *Encyclopaedia of Islam*. New Edition. Leiden: E. J. Brill, 1954–.
García Gómez, Emilio. "La poésie politique sous le califat de Cordoue." *Revue des Études Islamiques* 1 (1949): 5–11.
——, trans. *Anales palatinos del califa de Córdoba al-Hakam II, por ᶜĪsā Ibn Ahmad al-Rāzī (360–364 H. = 971–975 J.C.) [El califato de Córdoba en el "Muqtabis" de Ibn Hayyān]*. Madrid: Sociedad de Estudios y Publicationes, 1967.
Garrison, James D. *Dryden and the Tradition of Panegyric*. Berkeley: University of California Press, 1975.
Gaster, Theodor. *Thespis: Ritual, Myth, and Drama in the Ancient Middle East*. New York: Norton and Co., 1977.
Gibb, H. A. R. "ᶜAbd Allāh ibn al-Zubayr." In *Encyclopaedia of Islam*. New Edition. Leiden: E. J. Brill, 1954–.
Goldhill, Simon. *The Poet's Voice: Essays on Poetics and Greek Literature*. Cambridge: Cambridge University Press, 1991.
Grabar, O. "Notes sur les cérémonies umayyades." In Myriam Rosen-Ayalon, ed., *Studies in Memory of Gaston Wiet*, pp. 51–60. Jerusalem: Institute of Asian and African Studies, the Hebrew University of Jerusalem, 1997.
Gruendler, Beatrice. "Ibn al-Rūmī's Ethics of Patronage." *Harvard Middle Eastern and Islamic Review* 3 (1996): 104–60.
——. "The Motif of Marriage in Select Abbasid Panegyrics." In Neuwirth et al., eds., *Myths, Historical Archetypes, and Symbolic Figures*, pp. 109–22.
Guillaume, A. "Abu 'l-ᶜAtāhiya." In *Encyclopaedia of Islam*. New Edition. Leiden: E. J. Brill, 1954–.
——, trans. *The Life of Muhammad: A Translation of Isḥāq's Sīrat Rasūl Allāh*. Lahore and Karachi: Oxford University Press, 1974.
Hamori, Andras. "Notes on Paronomasia in Abū Tammām's Style." *Journal of Semitic Studies* 12 (1967): 83–90.
——. *On the Art of Medieval Arabic Literature*. Princeton, N.J.: Princeton University Press, 1982.
Havelock, Eric A. *The Literate Revolution in Greece and Its Cultural Consequences*. Princeton, N.J.: Princeton University Press, 1982.

———. *The Muse Learns to Write: Reflections on Orality and Literacy from Antiquity to the Present.* New Haven, Conn.: Yale University Press, 1986.

al-Ḥāwī, Īliyyā Salīm, ed. *Sharḥ Dīwān al-Akhṭal al-Taghlibī.* Beirut: Dār al-Thaqāfah, n.d.

Hawting, G. R. "Umayyads." In *Encyclopaedia of Islam.* New Edition. Leiden: E. J. Brill, 1954–.

Heller, B., and N. A. Stillman, "Luḳmān." In *Encyclopaedia of Islam.* New Edition. Leiden: E. J. Brill, 1954–.

Hinds, M. "Muᶜāwiya." In *Encyclopaedia of Islam.* New Edition. Leiden: E. J. Brill, 1954–.

Hobsbawm, Eric, and Terence Ranger, eds. *The Invention of Tradition.* Cambridge: Cambridge University Press, 1983.

Hubert, Henri, and Marcel Mauss. *Sacrifice: Its Nature and Function.* Trans. W. D. Halls. Chicago: University of Chicago Press, 1981.

Husain, M. Hidayat. "Banat Suᶜad of Kaᶜb bin Zuhair." *Islamic Culture* 1 (1927): 67–84.

al-Ḥuṭayʾah. *Dīwān, Sharḥ Abī Saᶜīd al-Sukkarī.* Beirut: Dār Ṣādir, 1967.

Ibn Bassām al-Shantarīnī, Abū al-Ḥasan ᶜAlī. *Al-Dhakhīrah fī Maḥāsin Ahl al-Jazīrah.* 4 vols. in 8. Ed. Iḥsān ᶜAbbās. Beirut: Dār al-Thaqāfah, 1979.

Ibn Darrāj al-Qasṭallī. *Dīwān.* Ed. Maḥmūd ᶜAlī Makkī. 2nd ed. N.p.: Al-Maktab al-Islāmī, 1389/1969.

Ibn Ḥayyān al-Qurṭubī, Abū Marwān. *Al-Muqtabis fī Akhbār Balad al-Andalus.* Ed. ᶜAbd al-Raḥmān ᶜAlī al-Ḥajjī. Beirut: Dār al-Thaqāfah, 1965.

Ibn Hishām, Abū Muḥammad ᶜAbd al-Malik. *Al-Sīrah al-Nabawiyyah.* 4 vols. Cairo: Dār al-Fikr, n.d.

Ibn Khallikān, Abū al-ᶜAbbās Shams al-Dīn Aḥmad ibn Muḥammad. *Wafāyāt al-Aᶜyān wa-Anbāʾ Abnāʾ al-Zamān.* 7 vols. Ed. Iḥsān ᶜAbbās. Beirut: Dār al-Thaqāfah, 1968.

Ibn Manẓūr, Muḥammad ibn Mukarram. *Lisān al-ᶜArab.* 15 vols. Beirut: Dār Ṣādir, 1955–56.

Ibn Qutaybah, Abū Muḥammad ᶜAbd Allāh ibn Muslim. *Kitāb al-Shiᶜr wa-al-Shuᶜarāʾ.* Ed. M. J. de Goeje. Leiden, E. J. Brill, 1904.

Ibn Rashīq al-Qayrawānī, Abū ᶜAlī al-Ḥasan. *Al-ᶜUmdah fī Maḥāsin al-Shiᶜr wa-Ādābih wa-Naqdih.* 2 vols. Ed. Muḥammad Muḥyī al-Dīn ᶜAbd al-Ḥamīd. Beirut: Dār al-Jīl, 1972.

Ibn Taghrībirdī, Jamāl al-Dīn Abū al-Maḥāsin Yūsuf. *Al-Nujūm al-Zāhirah fī Mulūk Miṣr wa-al-Qāhirah.* 14 vols. Cairo: Al-Muʾassasah al-Miṣriyyah al-ᶜĀmmah lil-Taʾlīf wa-al-Tarjamah wa-al-Nashr, 1968. [Photo-offset of Dār al-Kutub ed.]

Ibrāhīm, Muḥammad Abū al-Faḍl, ed. *Dīwān al-Nābighah al-Dhubyānī.* 3rd ed. Cairo: Dār al-Maᶜārif, 1990.

al-Iṣbahānī, Abū al-Faraj. *Kitāb al-Aghānī.* Ed. Ibrāhīm al-Abyārī. 32 vols. Cairo: Dār al-Shaᶜb, 1969–79.

ᶜIzz al-Dīn, Ḥasan al-Bannā. *Shiᶜriyyat al-Ḥarb ᶜind al-ᶜArab qabl al-Islām: Qaṣīdat al-Zaᶜāʾin Namūdhajan.* 2nd ed. Riyadh: Dār al-Mufradāt lil-Nashr wa-al-Tawzīᶜ, 1998.

Jacobi, Renate, trans. "Al-Nābigha al-Dhubyānī (Sixth Century) in Praise of al-Nuʿman III Abū Qābūs." In Sperl and Shackle, *Qasida Poetry,* 2:72–79.
al-Jāḥiẓ, [Abū ʿUthmān ʿAmr ibn Baḥr]. *Al-Bayān wa-al-Tabyīn.* 4 vols. 5th ed. Ed. ʿAbd al-Salām Muḥammad Hārūn. Cairo: Maktabat al-Khānjī, 1985.
——. *Al-Bukhalāʾ.* Ed. Ṭāhā al-Ḥājirī. Cairo: Dār al-Maʿārif, 1958.
——. *Al-Ḥayawān.* Ed. ʿAbd al-Salām Muḥammad Hārūn. 8 vols. Cairo: Muṣṭafā al-Bābī al-Ḥalabī, 1965–69.
Jeffery, Arthur. *The Foreign Vocabulary of the Qurʾān.* Baroda: Oriental Institute, 1938.
al-Jumaḥī, Muḥammad ibn Sallām. *Ṭabaqāt Fuḥūl al-Shuʿarāʾ.* 2 vols. Ed. Maḥmūd Muḥammad Shākir. Cairo: Maṭbaʿat al-Madanī, 1974.
Kennedy, Hugh. *The Prophet and the Age of the Caliphs: The Islamic Near East from the Fifth to the Eleventh Century.* London and New York: Longman, 1986.
Khalidi, Tarif. *Arabic Historical Thought in the Classical Period.* Cambridge: Cambridge University Press, 1994.
al-Khansāʾ. *Sharḥ Dīwān al-Khansāʾ bi-al-Iḍāfah ilā Marāthī Sittīn Shāʿirah min Shawāʾir al-ʿArab.* Beirut: Dār al-Turāth, 1968.
Kindermann, H. "Rabīʿa and Muḍar." In *Encyclopaedia of Islam.* New Edition. Leiden: E. J. Brill, 1954–.
Krenkow, Fritz. "Tabrīzīs Kommentar zur Burda des Kaʿb ibn Zuhair." *Zeitschrift der Deutschen Morganländischen Gesellschaft* 65 (1911): 241–79.
Kuhrt, Amélie. "Usurpation, Conquest, and Ceremonial: From Babylon to Persia." In Cannadine and Price, *Rituals of Royalty,* pp. 20–55.
Kurke, Leslie. *The Traffic in Praise: Pindar and the Poetics of Social Economy.* Ithaca, N.Y.: Cornell University Press, 1991.
Lammens, Henri. "Le chantre des Omaides: notes biographiques et littéraires sur le poète arabe chrétien Ahṭal." *Journale Asiatique,* ser. 9, no. 4 (1894): 94–176, 193–241, 381–459.
——. *Études sur le siècle des Omayyades.* Beirut: Imprimerie Catholique, 1930.
—— [and Charles Pellat]. "Muṣʿab ibn al-Zubayr." In *Encyclopaedia of Islam.* New Edition. Leiden: E. J. Brill, 1954–.
Lane, Edward William. *Arabic-English Lexicon.* 8 vols. New York: Frederick Ungar 1958 [London, 1863].
Lévi-Provençal, É. *Histoire de l'Espagne musulmane, Tome II: Le califat umaiyade de Cordoue (921–1031).* New ed. Paris: Maisonneuve/Leiden: E. J. Brill, 1950.
Lewis, B. "ʿAbbāsids" and "Hāshimiyya." In *Encyclopaedia of Islam.* New Edition. Leiden: E. J. Brill, 1954–.
Losensky, Paul E. "'The Allusive Fields of Drunkenness': Three Safavid Mogul Responses to a Lyric by Bābā Fighānī." In S. Stetkevych, ed., *Reorientations,* pp. 227–62.
——. *Welcoming Fighānī: Imitation and Poetic Individuality in the Safavid-Mughal* Ghazal. Costa Mesa, Calif.: Mazda Publishers, 1998.
Lyall, Charles James, ed. and trans. *The Mufaḍḍalīyāt: An Anthology of Ancient Arabian Odes Compiled by Al-Mufaḍḍal Son of Muḥammad, According to the Recension and with the Commentary of Abū Muḥammad al-Qāsim ibn Muḥam-*

mad al-Anbārī. Vol. I: *Arabic Text;* vol. II: *Translation and Notes*. Oxford: Clarendon Press, 1918.

al-Maᶜarrī, Abū al-ᶜAlāʾ. *Risālat al-Ghufrān (wa-maᶜahā Naṣṣ Muḥaqqaq min Risālat Ibn al-Qāriḥ)*. Ed. ᶜĀʾishah ᶜAbd al-Raḥmān (Bint al-Shāṭiʾ). Cairo: Dār al-Maᶜārif, n.d.

——. *Sharḥ Dīwān Abī al-Ṭayyib al-Mutanabbī, "Muᶜjiz Aḥmad."* 4 vols. Ed. ᶜAbd al-Majīd Diyāb. Cairo: Dār al-Maᶜārif, 1986.

MacCormack, Sabine G. *Art and Ceremony in Late Antiquity*. Berkeley: University of California Press, 1981.

Makkī, M. ᶜA. "Ibn Darrādj al-Ḳasṭallī." In *Encyclopaedia of Islam*. New Edition. Leiden: E. J. Brill, 1954–.

al-Mallah, Majd Yasser. "Panegyric Poetry and Court Ceremonial: al-Mutanabbī's Victory Ode." Unpublished paper presented at the annual meeting of the American Oriental Society, March 1999.

Martinez-Gros, Gabriel. *L'idéologie omeyyade: La construction de la légitimité du Califat de Cordoue (Xe–XIe siècles)*. Madrid: Casa de Velázquez, 1992.

Mauss, Marcel. *The Gift: Forms and Functions of Exchange in Archaic Societies*. Trans. Ian Cunnison. New York: Norton and Co., 1967. [*Essai sur le don, form archaïque de l'échange,* 1925.]

al-Maydānī, Abū al-Faḍl Aḥmad ibn Muḥammad. *Majmaᶜ al-Amthāl*. Ed. Muḥammad Muḥyī al-Dīn ᶜAbd al-Ḥamīd. 2nd ed. 2 vols. Cairo: Al-Maktabah al-Tijāriyyah al-Kubrā, 1959.

McCormick, Michael. *Eternal Victory*. Cambridge: Cambridge University Press, 1987.

Menocal, María Rosa, Raymond Scheindlin, and Michael Sells, eds. *The Literature of al-Andalus*. Cambridge: Cambridge University Press, 2000.

Michael I, Jacobite Patriarch of Antioch. *Chronique de Michel le Syrien, Patriarche Jacobite d'Antioche (1166–1199)*. Ed. and trans. Jean-Baptiste Chabot. 4 vols. Paris: Ernest Leroux, 1905.

Millen, Ronald Forsyth, and Robert Erich Wolf. *Heroic Deeds and Mystic Figures: A New Reading of Rubens'* Life of Maria de' Medici. Princeton, N.J.: Princeton University Press, 1989.

Monroe, James T. *Hispano-Arabic Poetry: A Student Anthology*. Berkeley: University of California Press, 1974.

——. "Hispano-Arabic Poetry during the Caliphate of Córdoba." In Gustave E. von Grunebaum, ed., *Proceedings of the Third Giorgio Lévi della Vida Memorial Conference,* pp. 125–54. Berkeley and Los Angeles: University of California Press, 1971.

——. "Oral Composition in Pre-Islamic Poetry." *Journal of Arabic Literature* 3 (1972): 1–53.

——. "The Poetry of the *Sīrah* Literature." Ch. 18 of A. F. L. Beeston, T. M. Johnstone, R. B. Serjeant, and G. R. Smith, eds., *The Cambridge History of Arabic Literature,* vol. 1: *Arabic Literature to the End of the Umayyad Period*. Cambridge: Cambridge University Press, 1983.

——, trans. *Risālat at-Tawābiᶜ wa-z-Zawābiᶜ: The Treatise of Familiar Spirits and Demons by Abū ᶜĀmir ibn Shuhaid al-Ashjaᶜī al-Andalusī*. Berkeley and Los Angeles: University of California Press, 1971.

Mottahedeh, Roy P. *Loyalty and Leadership in an Early Islamic Society.* Princeton, N.J.: Princeton University Press, 1980.

al-Musawi, Muhsin J. "Dedications as Poetic Intersections." *Journal of Arabic Literature* 31, no. 1 (2000): 1–37.

Nagy, Gregory. *The Best of the Achaeans: Concepts of the Hero in Archaic Greek Poetry.* Baltimore: Johns Hopkins University Press, 1979.

——. *Pindar's Homer: The Lyric Possession of an Epic Past.* Baltimore: Johns Hopkins University Press, 1991.

Neuwirth, Angelika, Birgit Embaló, Sebastian Günther, and Maher Jarrar, eds. *Myths, Historical Archetypes, and Symbolic Figures in Arabic Literature: Towards a New Hermeneutic Approach—Proceedings of the International Symposium in Beirut, June 25th–June 30th, 1996.* Beirut [Stuttgart]: Franz Steiner Verlag, 1999.

Ong, Walter J. *Orality and Literacy: The Technologizing of the Word.* London: Methuen, 1982.

Paret, Rudi. "Die Legende der Verleihung des Prophetenmantels (*burda*) an Kaᶜb ibn Zuhair." *Der Islam* 17 (1928): 9–14.

Qabāwah, Fakhr al-Dīn, ed. *Shiᶜr al-Akhṭal, Abī Mālik Ghiyāth ibn Ghawth al-Taghlibī, Ṣanᶜat al-Sukkarī, Riwāyah ᶜan Abī Jaᶜfar Muḥammad ibn Ḥabīb.* 2nd ed. 2 vols. Beirut: Dār al-Āfāq al-Jadīdah, 1979.

al-Qāḍī, al-Nuᶜmān. *Al-Firaq al-Islāmiyyah fī al-Shiᶜr al-Umawī.* Cairo: Dār al-Maᶜārif, 1970.

——. *Shiᶜr al-Futūḥ al-Islāmiyyah fī Ṣadr al-Islām.* Cairo: Al-Dār al-Qawmiyyah lil-Ṭibāᶜah wa-al-Nashr, 1965.

Quint, David. *Epic and Empire: Politics and Generic Form from Virgil to Milton.* Princeton, N.J.: Princeton University Press, 1993.

Redfield, James. *Nature and Culture in the Iliad: The Tragedy of Hector.* Chicago: University of Chicago Press, 1975.

Ritter, H. "Abū Tammām." In *Encyclopaedia of Islam.* New Edition. Leiden: E. J. Brill, 1954–.

Rotter, Gernot. *Die Umayyaden und der zweite Bürgerkrieg (680–692).* Abhandlungen für die Kunde des Morgenlandes. 45 pt. 3. Wiesbaden: Franz Steiner, 1982.

Rūmiyyah, Wahb. *Qaṣīdat al-Madḥ ḥattā Nihāyat al-ᶜAṣr al-Umawī: Bayn al-Uṣūl wa-al-Iḥyāᵓ wa-al-Tajdīd.* Damascus: Manshūrāt Wizārat al-Thaqāfah wa-al-Irshād al-Qawmī, 1981.

Safran, Janina M. "Ceremony and Submission: The Symbolic Representation of Recognition of Legitimacy in Tenth-Century al-Andalus." *Journal of Near Eastern Studies* 58, no. 3 (1999): 191–201.

——. "The Command of the Faithful in al-Andalus: A Study in the Articulation of Caliphal Legitimacy." *International Journal of Middle East Studies* 30 (1998): 183–98.

Ṣāliḥānī, Anṭūn, ed. *Naqāᵓiḍ Jarīr wa-al-Akhṭal taᵓlīf al-Imām al-Shāᶜir al-Adīb al-Māhir Abī Tammām.* Beirut: Al-Maṭbaᶜah al-Kāthūlīkiyyah, 1922. [Reprint, Beirut: Dār al-Mashriq, 1970.]

——, ed. *Shiᶜr al-Akhṭal, Riwāyat Abī ᶜAbd Allāh Muḥammad ibn al-ᶜAbbās al-Yazīdī ᶜan Abī Saᶜīd al-Sukkarī ᶜan Muḥammad ibn Ḥabīb ᶜan Ibn al-Aᶜrābī.*

Beirut: Dār al-Maṭbaᶜah al-Kāthūlīkiyyah, n.d. [Reprint, Beirut: Dār al-Mashriq, 1969.]

Sanders, Paula. "Marāsim." In *Encyclopaedia of Islam*. New Edition. Leiden: E. J. Brill, 1954–.

——. *Ritual, Politics, and the City in Fatimid Cairo*. Albany: State University of New York Press, 1994.

Schimmel, Annemarie. *And Muhammad Is His Messenger: The Veneration of the Prophet in Islamic Piety*. Chapel Hill and London: University of North Carolina Press, 1985.

Sells, Michael A. "*Bānat Suᶜād:* Translation and Interpretative Introduction." *Journal of Arabic Literature* 21, no. 2 (1990): 140–54.

——. "Guises of the *Ghūl:* Dissembling Simile and Semantic Overflow in the Classical Arabic *Nasīb*." In S. Stetkevych, ed., *Reorientations*, pp. 130–64.

Seybold, John. "The Earliest Demon Lover: The *Ṭayf al-Khayāl* in *al-Mufaḍḍalīyāt*." In S. Stetkevych, ed., *Reorientations*, pp. 180–89.

Sezgin, Fuat. *Geschichte des Arabischen Schrifttums, Band II: Poesie bis ca. 430 H.* Leiden: E. J. Brill, 1973.

Shahid, Irfan. "Ghassān" and "Lakhmids." In *Encyclopaedia of Islam*. New Edition. Leiden: E. J. Brill, 1954–.

Sperl, Stefan. "Islamic Kingship and Arabic Panegyric Poetry in the Early Ninth Century." *Journal of Arabic Literature* 8 (1977): 20–35.

Sperl, Stefan, and Christopher Shackle, eds. *Qasida Poetry in Islamic Asia and Africa*. Vol. I: *Classical Traditions and Modern Meanings;* vol. II: *Eulogy's Bounty, Meaning's Abundance: An Anthology*. Leiden: E. J. Brill, 1996.

Stetkevych, Jaroslav. "Arabic Hermeneutical Terminology: Paradox and the Production of Meaning." *Journal of Near Eastern Studies* 48, no. 2 (April 1989): 81–95.

——. "The Hunt in the Arabic *Qaṣīdah: Antecedents of the Ṭardiyyah*." In J. R. Smart, ed., *Tradition and Modernity in Arabic Language and Literature*, pp. 102–18. Sussex: Curzon Press, 1996.

——. "Toward an Arabic Elegiac Lexicon: The Seven Words of the *Nasīb*." In S. Stetkevych, ed., *Reorientations*, pp. 58–129.

——. *The Zephyrs of Najd: The Poetics of Nostalgia in the Classical Arabic* Nasīb. Chicago: University of Chicago Press, 1993.

Stetkevych, Suzanne Pinckney. "Abbasid Panegyric and the Poetics of Political Allegiance: Two Poems of al-Mutanabbī on Kāfūr." In Sperl and Shackle, *Qasida Poetry*, 1: 35–53; 2: 92–105.

——. "ᶜAbbāsid Panegyric: The Politics and Poetics of Ceremony: Al-Mutanabbī's ᶜĪd-poem to Sayf al-Dawlah." In J. R. Smart, ed. *Tradition and Modernity in Arabic Language and Literature*, pp. 119–43. Surrey, England: Curzon, 1996.

——. "The ᶜAbbasid Poet Interprets History: Three Qaṣīdahs by Abū Tammām." *Journal of Arabic Literature* 10 (1979): 49–65.

——. *Abū Tammām and the Poetics of the ᶜAbbāsid Age*. Leiden: E. J. Brill, 1991.

——. "Intoxication and Immortality: Wine and Associated Images in al-Maᶜarrī's Garden." In J. W. Wright, Jr., and Everett K. Rowson, eds., *Homo-*

eroticism in Classical Arabic Literature, pp. 210–32. New York: Columbia University Press, 1997.

——. *The Mute Immortals Speak: Pre-Islamic Poetry and the Poetics of Ritual.* Ithaca, N.Y.: Cornell University Press, 1993.

——. "Naẓariyyat al-Talaqqī wa Akhbār al-Shuʿarāʾ: *Dāliyyat* al-Nābighah al-Dhubyānī wa-Tarjamatuh fī *Kitāb al-Aghānī.*" Unpublished paper presented at the Seventh Arabic Literary Criticism Conference, Yarmouk University, Irbid, Jordan, July 1998.

——. "The Politics and Poetics of Genre: A *Qaṣīdah* for ʿĀshūrāʾ by al-Sharīf al-Raḍī." Unpublished paper presented at Aspects of Arabic Literature Conference, University of California, Berkeley, April 1996.

——. "Pre-Islamic Poetry and the Poetics of Redemption: *Mufaḍḍalīyah 119* of ʿAlqamah and *Bānat Suʿād* of Kaʿb ibn Zuhayr." In S. Stetkevych, ed., *Reorientations,* pp. 1–57.

——. "The *Qaṣīdah* and the Poetics of Ceremony: Three ʿĪd Panegyrics to the Cordoban Caliphate." In Ross Brann, ed., *Languages of Power in Islamic Spain,* pp. 1–48. Occasional Papers of the Department of Near Eastern Studies and Program of Jewish Studies, Cornell University, no. 3. Bethesda, Md.: CDI Press, 1997.

——. "Qaṣīdat al-Madḥ wa-Marāsim al-Ibtihāl: Fāʿiliyyat al-Naṣṣ al-Adabī ʿabr al-Tārīkh" (The Panegyric Ode and the Ritual of Supplication: The Efficacy of the Poetic Text throughout History). In ʿIzz al-Dīn Ismāʿīl, ed., *Al-Naqd al-Adabī fī Munʿaṭaf al-Qarn 3: Madākhil li-Taḥlīl al-Naṣṣ al-Adabī,* etc. / *Literary Criticism at the Turn of the Century, Papers Presented to the First International Conference on Literary Criticism (Cairo, October, 1997).* 3 vols. Cairo, 1999. 3: 175–96.

——. "Solomon and Mythic Kingship in the Arabo-Islamic Tradition." Unpublished paper presented as the Solomon Katz Distinguished Lecture at the University of Washington, Seattle, May 1999.

——. "Umayyad Panegyric and the Poetics of Islamic Hegemony: al-Akhṭal's *Khaffa al-Qaṭīnu* ('Those That Dwelt with You Have Left in Haste')." *Journal of Arabic Literature* 28, no. 2 (1997): 89–122.

——, ed. *Reorientations: Arabic and Persian Poetry.* Bloomington and Indianapolis: Indiana University Press, 1994.

al-Sukkarī, Abū Saʿīd al-Ḥasan ibn al-Ḥusayn. *Sharḥ Dīwān Kaʿb ibn Zuhayr.* Cairo: Al-Dār al-Qawmiyyah, 1965.

at-Tabari, Abu Djafar Mohammed ibn Djarir. *Annales.* Ed. M. J. de Goeje. Ser. 3, vol. 2. Leiden: E. J. Brill, 1964–65. Photo ed. [= Abū Jaʿfar Muḥammad ibn Jarīr al-Ṭabarī, *Kitāb al-Rusul wa-al-Mulūk*].

al-Ṭabarī, [Abū Jaʿfar Muḥammad ibn Jarīr]. *The History of al-Ṭabarī (*Taʾrīkh al-rusul wa'l-mulūk*). Vol. 33: Storm and Stress along the Northern Frontiers of the ʿAbbāsid Caliphate.* Trans. and annot. C. E. Bosworth. Albany: State University of New York Press, 1991.

al-Thaʿālibī al-Naysabūrī, Abū Manṣūr ʿAbd al-Malik. *Yatīmat al-Dahr fī Maḥāsin Ahl al-ʿAṣr.* Ed. Mufīd Muḥammad Qamīḥah. 5 vols. Beirut: Dār al-Kutub al-ʿIlmiyyah, 1983.

al-Tibrīzī, Yaḥyā ibn ʿAlī. *Sharḥ Dīwān Ashʿār al-Ḥamāsah*. 2 vols. Cairo: Būlāq, 1296/1879.

———. [= al-Khaṭīb Abū Zakariyyā Yaḥyā ibn ʿAlī al-Tibrīzī]. *Sharḥ al-Qaṣāʾid al-ʿAshr*. Ed. ʿAbd al-Salām al-Ḥūfī. Beirut: Dār al-Kutub al-ʿIlmiyyah, 1985.

Turner, Victor. *The Ritual Process: Structure and Anti-Structure*. Ithaca, N.Y.: Cornell University Press, 1977.

al-ʿUkbarī, Abū al-Baqāʾ. *Dīwān Abī al-Ṭayyib al-Mutanabbī, al-Musammā bi-al-Tibyān fī Sharḥ al-Dīwān*. 4 vols. Ed. Muṣṭafā al-Saqqā, Ibrāhīm al-Abyārī, and ʿAbd al-Ḥafīẓ Shalabī. Beirut: Dār al-Maʿrifah, 1936.

Vaglieri, L. Veccia. "ʿAlī b. Abī Ṭālib." In *Encyclopaedia of Islam*. New Edition. Leiden: E. J. Brill, 1954–.

van Gelder, G. J. H. *Beyond the Line: Classical Arabic Literary Critics on the Coherence and Unity of the Poem*. Leiden: E. J. Brill, 1982.

van Gennep, Arnold. *The Rites of Passage*. Trans. Monika Vizedom and Gabrielle L. Caffee. Chicago: University of Chicago Press, 1960 [*Les rites de passage*, 1908].

Vasiliev, A. A. *Byzance et les Arabes: Tome I: La dynastie d'Amorium*. Ed. H. Grégoire and M. Canard. Brussels: Editions de l'Institut de Philologie et d'Histoire Orientales, 1935.

al-Wāḥidī, Abū al-Ḥasan ʿAlī ibn Aḥmad. *Dīwān Abī al-Ṭayyib al-Mutanabbī wa-fī Athnāʾ Matnih Sharḥ al-Imām al-ʿAllāmah al-Wāḥidī*. Ed. Friedrich Dieterici. Cairo: Dār al-Kitāb al-Islāmī, n.d.

Watt, W. Montgomery. "Abū Sufyān," "Kilāb b. Rabīʿa," and "Ḳuraysh." In *Encyclopaedia of Islam*. New Edition. Leiden: E. J. Brill, 1954–.

Wehr, Hans. *A Dictionary of Modern Written Arabic*. Ed. J. Milton Cowan. 3rd ed. Ithaca, N.Y.: Spoken Language Services, 1971.

Wensinck, A. J. "The Semitic New Year and the Origin of Eschatology." *Acta Orientalia* 1 (1923): 158–99.

Wensinck, A. J., et al. *Concordance et indices de la tradition musulmane*. Leiden: E. J. Brill, 1936–62.

Wimmen, Heiko. "ʿAmmūriyyah as a Female Archetype: Deconstruction of a Mythical Subtext from Abū Tammām to Jabrā Ibrāhīm Jabrā / ʿAbd al-Raḥmān Munīf." In Neuwirth et al., eds., *Myths, Historical Archetypes and Symbolic Figures*, pp. 573–82.

Wright, W. *A Grammar of the Arabic Language*. 3rd ed. 2 vols. Beirut: Librairie du Liban, 1971.

al-Yāzijī, Nāṣīf. *Al-ʿArf al-Ṭayyib fī Sharḥ Dīwān Abī al-Ṭayyib*. 2 vols. Beirut: Dār Ṣādir / Dār Bayrūt, 1964.

al-Zamakhsharī, Muḥammad ibn ʿUmar. *Aʿjab al-ʿAjab fī Sharḥ Lāmiyyat al-ʿArab*. In al-Shanfarā, *Qaṣīdat Lāmiyyat al-ʿArab wa-yalīhā. . . .* Istanbul: Maṭbaʿat al-Jawāʾib, 1300 H.

Zwettler, Michael. *The Oral Tradition of Classical Arabic Poetry: Its Character and Implications*. Columbus: Ohio State University Press, 1972.

———. "The Poet and the Prophet: Towards an Understanding of the Evolution of a Narrative." *Jerusalem Studies in Arabic and Islam* 5 (1984): 313–87.

———. "The Poetics of Allusion in Abu l-ʿAtāhiya's Ode in Praise of al-Hādī." *Edebiyât*, n.s. 3, no. 1 (1989): 1–29.

Index

abandoned, ruined abode (*aṭlāl*): ʿAmmūriyah (Amorium) as, 166, 172; in "O Abode of Mayyah," 25–28; in "The Tribe Has Departed," 99–100; in "Wāsiṭ Lies Deserted," 128

ʿAbd al-Malik ibn Marwān (ruler): anecdotes about, 84, 86–89, 109; caliph, 83; compared to the Euphrates River, 102; Islamic credentials of rivals, 104–105; treating tribe of al-Akhṭal as outlaws, 117; "The Tribe Has Departed" as victory ode to, 83

ʿAbd al-Qays ibn Khufāf al-Tamīmī (poet), 43

Abū al-ʿAtāhiyah (poet): anecdotes about, 146, 150–151; author, "My Coy Mistress," 145; his "My Coy Mistress" as contrafaction (*muʿāraḍah*), 347n14; as "naturally gifted" poet, 145; types of poems of, 145

Abū al-Faraj al-Iṣbahānī (litterateur), 3

Abū al-Ṭayyib al-Mutanabbī. *See* al-Mutanabbī

Abū Tammām (poet), 83; author, "The Sword Is More Veracious," 145; Christian convert to Islam, 165; embraced *badīʿ* (new, innovative) style, 145; as "artificial" poet, 145

Abū ʿUbaydah (philologist), 83, 111

Abū Zayd ʿUmar ibn Shabbah (commentator), 45

ʿādah (custom, habit): as classical Arabo-Islamic concept of nobility, 194–195; as determining one's fate, 195; as legitimizing agency, 193

ʿAfā Wāsiṭun. *See* "Wāsiṭ Lies Deserted"

Aḥmad Abū al-Ṭayyib al-Mutanabbī. *See* al-Mutanabbī

al-Akhṭal (poet): as accuser in "Wāsiṭ Lies Deserted," 119; anecdotes about, 84, 86–89, 111–114; author, "The Tribe Has Departed," 83; author, "Wāsiṭ Lies Deserted," 110; Christianity of, 84; involvement in political, military affairs, 85; poet, 81; tribe attacked in response to poetic challenge, 110

A-Lā Mā li-Sayyidatī. *See* "My Coy Mistress"

ʿAlī ibn Ḥammād, 109

Allāh: in "O Abode of Mayyah," 36, 39, 41; in "Suʿād Has Departed," 67, 74

allegiance: abrogation of, 223, 224; Arabic poetic tradition as major expression of, 49; declaration of, 40, 277; oath of, 222, 252; pledge of, 211, 240; reconfirmation of, 223; retraction of, 231; as sexual renunciation, 149; transfer of, 223

ʿAlqamah ibn ʿAbadah (poet), 117

Amalikites (*ʿAmālīq*), 61

A-Min Āli Mayyata. *See* "Are You Leaving Mayyah's People (The Description of al-Mutajarridah)"

ʿAmmūriyah (Amorium) (city): as abandoned, ruined abode (*aṭlāl*), 166, 172; Byzantine Christian city, 145; conquest of, 145, 152–155; feminine personification of, 152, 165–166, 175–177

ʿAmr ibn al-Ḥārith (Ghassānid court), 3

al-Andalus (Muslim Spain): brief history of, 241; competition for prestige of poets, 265; downfall of Umayyad caliphate and civil war in, 272; qasida as element of ceremony and insignia of authority in, 254

Andalusian panegyric ode: ceremonial function of, 241. *See also specific subjects*

anecdotal materials (*akhbār*): about ʿAbd al-Malik ibn Marwān, 84, 86–89, 109; about Abū alʿAtāhiyah, 146, 150–151; about al-Akhṭal, 84, 86–89, 111–114; about ʿAlī ibn Ḥammād, 109; about al-Jaḥḥāf, 111–114; about al-Munakhkhal, 4; about al-Mutajarridah, 3–4; about al-Mutanabbī, 219, 224, 232; about al-Nābighah al-Dhubyānī, 3–4, 43–47; about al-Nuʿmān ibn al-Mundhir, 3–4; about "Are You Leaving Mayyah's People (The Description of al-Mutajarridah)," 3–4, 43–47; about Ashjaʿ al-Sulamī, 146; about Bashshār ibn Burd, 146; about Day of al-Bishr, 111; about "The Days Bear Witness,"

Index

of Mayyah" as, 32, 33; poetic devices as mnemonic function, 49; poetic duels (*naqāʾiḍ*), 83; pre-Islamic courtly poems, 2; tribal poems, 2; wine poems (*khamriyyāt*), 145. *See also specific poems; specific subjects*
poetry: ceremonial aspects of, 337n11; confers immortality, 184; description of poetic language, 193; as mnemonic function, 49; perpetuation as the purpose of, 253; practice of payment for, 181. *See also specific subjects*
poets: appropriation of insignia of qasida as appropriation of the voice of the poet, 281; bond of clientage between poet and patron, 183; and misers, 181–184; mythicization of, 2; obligation to compose qasida for the patron, 208; poetic power of, 240; qasida as canonical genre becomes the basis for poet's authority, 82. *See also specific poets; specific subjects*
political dominion: sexual domination as metaphor for, 152; sexual dominion as metaphor for, 149
power: poetic power of ʿAbbāsid panegyric, 240; qasida (*qaṣīdah*) as iconography of, 253; ritual or ceremony of supplication as enactment of authority and legitimacy, 34; supplication as articulation of boundaries of, 33
praise section (*madīḥ*): in "Disease Enough!" 220–223; in "O Abode of Mayyah," 32–47; in "Suʿād Has Departed," 65–76; in "The Sword Is More Veracious," 170–172; in "The Tribe Has Departed," 100–109; in "Wāsiṭ Lies Deserted," 135–142
pre-Islamic odes, 3
pre-Islamic period, 1
pre-Islamic poetic tradition, 48
prize (*jāʾizah*): as expression of patron's estimation of poem and poet, 73; gift exchange of poem and prize as contractual ritual, 277; and the power of objects of exchange, 78–79
Prophet Muḥammad: anecdotes about, 50–53; concerning greetings and the return thereof, 186; ʿĪd al-Fiṭr (Festival of Breaking the Fast at the end of Ramadan) ceremony as reenactment of originary Islamic practice established by, 245; intent on killing polytheistic poets who attack him, 51; mantle as symbol of his protection, 77; mantle conferred upon poet Kaʿb ibn Zuhayr, 48; mantle confers salvation, 78; mantle in "Suʿād Has Departed," 76–79; as Rasūl Allāh (Messenger of God) in "Suʿād Has Departed," 67
protection (institution of protection (*ijārah*)), 120
pun, punning. *See* root-play (*jinās*)

qasida (*qaṣīdah*) (poetic form): ʿAbbāsid bipartite qasida, 30; antecedents of, 1; appropriated by Umayyad caliphate in al-Andalus, 242; as canonical genre becomes the basis for poet's authority, 82; conceit of as bride implies virginity/originality of, 280; as declaration of allegiance, 277; elegiac prelude (*nasīb*) in, 4; elements of ceremony of, 34; erotic description of the beloved (*tashbīb*) in, 10; forms summarized, 143; functions of in "Each Man's Fate Is Fixed," 201–203; as genre, 80–81; as iconography of power, 253; ideology of Arabo-Islamic rule encoded in, 241; incorporation of historic event into Islamic liturgical calendar through qasida, 278; as instrument for establishment of a cultural tradition, 50; invective (*hijāʾ*) in, 14; journey section (*raḥīl*) in, 29; legitimacy reaffirmed by, 271; as mythicization of an event, 253; mythogenic capabilities of, 76; as negotiation of relation between poet and patron, 73; perennial aesthetic appeal of, 282; poetic devices, 49; poetic power of, 240; as reaffirmation of loyalty, 278; recitation of as insignia of legitimacy, 203–204, 241; as ritual exchange for bloodwite, 120; ritual exchange of qasida and prize, 18; ritual in form and function, 212; as ritual of submission, 33; ritualizing capacity of, 187; as royal insignia, 248, 253; stability of allows for mythic concordance, 281–282; as vehicle to permanently validate an event, 249. *See also specific subjects*
Quint, David, 80
Qurʾān (sacred text): concerning greet-

SUZANNE PINCKNEY STETKEVYCH is Professor of Arabic Literature at Indiana University, Bloomington. She has held the Ruth N. Halls Professorship in Near Eastern Languages and Cultures at IUB and the Solomon Katz Distinguished Professorship in the Humanities at the University of Washington in Seattle. She is the author of *Abū Tammām and the Poetics of the ʿAbbāsid Age* and *The Mute Immortals Speak: Pre-Islamic Poetry and the Poetics of Ritual.* She is the editor of *Reorientations: Arabic and Persian Poetry,* and, since 1997, of the *Journal of Arabic Literature.*